# The Captive's Quest for Freedom

The political crisis produced by the passage and enforcement of the 1850 Fugitive Slave Law is at the heart of events leading up to the Civil War. The crisis was driven by the growing number of slaves who, largely on their own initiative, defied the law in the search for freedom. Their actions had a profound effect on the politics of the areas (and states) from which they escaped, as well as those to which they ran. Every effort to enforce the law in northern communities produced levels of subversion that generated so much national debate that, on the eve of secession, many in the South, looking back on the decade, could argue with conviction, that the law had been effectively subverted by those individuals and states who came to the assistance of fleeing slaves.

R. J. M. Blackett is the Andrew Jackson Professor of History at Vanderbilt University. He is former President of the Association of Caribbean Historians, Associate Editor and Acting Editor of the *Journal of American History*, and Editor of the *Indiana Magazine of History*. Professor Blackett also taught at the University of Pittsburgh as well as Indiana University, and the University of Houston, where he was the John and Rebecca Moores Professor of History and African American Studies.

D1319598

SLAVERIES SINCE EMANCIPATION

General Editors
Randall Miller, St. Joseph's University
Zoe Trodd, University of Nottingham

Founding Editor
Robert E. Wright, Augustana College

Slaveries since Emancipation publishes scholarship that links slavery's past to its present, consciously scanning history for lessons of relevance to contemporary abolitionism and that directly engages current issues of interest to activists by contextualizing them historically.

**Also in this series:**
Anna Mae Duane, *Child Slavery before and after Emancipation: An Argument for Child-Centered Slavery Studies*

# The Captive's Quest for Freedom

*Fugitive Slaves, the 1850 Fugitive Slave Law, and the Politics of Slavery*

**R. J. M. BLACKETT**
*Vanderbilt University, Tennessee*

CAMBRIDGE
UNIVERSITY PRESS

# CAMBRIDGE
UNIVERSITY PRESS

One Liberty Plaza, 20th Floor, New York, NY 10006, USA

Cambridge University Press is part of the University of Cambridge.

It furthers the University's mission by disseminating knowledge in the pursuit of education, learning, and research at the highest international levels of excellence.

www.cambridge.org
Information on this title: www.cambridge.org/9781108407779
DOI: 10.1017/9781108275439

First published 2018

Printed in the United States of America by Sheridan Books, Inc.

A catalogue record for this publication is available from the British Library.

Library of Congress Cataloging-in-Publication Data
Names: Blackett, R. J. M., 1943– author.
Title: The captive's quest for freedom : Fugitive Slaves, the 1850 Fugitive Slave Law, and the Politics of Slavery / R. J. M. Blackett, Vanderbilt University, Tennessee.
Description: Cambridge; New York, NY: Cambridge University Press, 2018. |
Series: Slaveries since emancipation | Includes bibliographical references and index.
Identifiers: LCCN 2017043999 | ISBN 9781108418713 (hardback) |
ISBN 9781108407779 (pbk.)
Subjects: LCSH: Fugitive slaves – United States. | Fugitive slaves – Legal status, laws, etc. – United States. | United States. Fugitive slave law (1850). | Slavery – Political aspects – United States – History – 19th century. | Slavery – United States – Legal status of slaves in free states. | Antislavery movements – United States – History – 19th century.
Classification: LCC E450.B589 2017 | DDC 973.7/115–dc23
LC record available at https://lccn.loc.gov/2017043999

ISBN 978-1-108-41871-3 Hardback
ISBN 978-1-108-40777-9 Paperback

*To my grandchildren: Joseph, Lilith, Theodore, Olivia, Vivian, and Oliver*

# Contents

*List of Figures and Maps*                                    *page* x
*Preface*                                                           xi

PART I    THE SLAVE POWER ASSERTS ITS RIGHTS
  1   The Fugitive Slave Law                                        3
  2   The Law Does Its Work                                        42
  3   Compromise and Colonize                                      88

PART II    FREEDOM'S FIRES BURN
  4   Missouri and Illinois                                       137
  5   Western Kentucky and Indiana                                180
  6   Eastern Kentucky and Ohio                                   222
  7   Southeast Pennsylvania                                      269
  8   Eastern Shore of Maryland and Philadelphia                  308
  9   New York                                                    357
 10   Massachusetts                                               396
      Conclusion                                                  441

*Bibliography*                                                   461
*Index*                                                          483

# Figures and Maps

FIGURES

  1  The Christiana Tragedy     *page* 81
  2  Ripley from the Kentucky Side of the Ohio     225
  3  The Oberlin Rescuers at Cuyahoga Co. Jail, April 1859     259
  4  Samuel Green     317
  5  William Still     328
  6  Jane Johnson     330
  7  Rescue of Jane Johnson and Her Children     331
  8  Passmore Williamson     332
  9  The Fugitive Slave Law…Hamlet in Chains     377
10  Lewis Hayden     402
11  Likeness of Thomas Sims     414
12  Marshal's Posse with Burns Moving Down State Street     427

MAPS

1  Missouri and Illinois     138
2  Western Kentucky and Indiana     181
3  Eastern Kentucky and Ohio     223
4  Southeast Pennsylvania     270
5  Eastern Shore of Maryland and Philadelphia     309
6  New York     358

# Preface

There would have been no need for a fugitive slave law, either in 1793 or 1850, had slaves not escaped regularly, and in such numbers, that their activities came to be seen as a threat to the survival of the slave system. Taking as its point of departure the passage of the 1850 Fugitive Slave Law, this study focuses on the many ways the enslaved, by fleeing their enslavement, raised questions both about the law's legitimacy and the economic and political system it was meant to protect. As a Cleveland editor put it on the eve of the Civil War, in struggling for their freedom, slaves, by their actions, were responsible for starting "an 'underground railroad' system of escape" that, over the years, had amassed an impressive record of success, even if it had not totally undermined the system of slavery.[1] Their actions were sustained by informal networks and alliances in slaveholding communities, by abolitionists who opposed the law, by those who had no particular aversion to the law but who were dragged nonetheless into the political maelstrom caused by efforts to reclaim fugitives from slavery in free states, and by the concerted efforts of black communities, large and small, urban and rural, that openly defied the implementation of the law. If it is true that laws can only gain their legitimacy by being assented to by all they wish to bind, then the 1850 Fugitive Slave Law was doomed to failure from its very inception. It met with strong opposition in and out of Congress for its violations of bedrock principles of jurisprudence and for its pandering to slave interests, which had been clamoring, for some time, for a more effective law to facilitate the recapture of escaped slaves, or, as the Constitution denominated them, "fugitives from labor." Slaveholding interests unabashedly declared that on its passage and enforcement rested the future of the Union. Many observers were convinced, however, that nowhere in the Constitution was Congress expressly granted the power to enact such a law. Yet advocates thought it did

[1] Cleveland *Leader*, January 4, 1861.

and their position carried the day. The result was a law that nationalized the recapture of fugitive slaves. Consequently, every effort to retake an escapee had the potential to create deep political crises in the communities in which it occurred. To borrow a poignant phrase from Toni Morrison, the law seemed perversely designed to authorize political chaos in the "defense of order." An attorney put it starkly: the law was an "abomination."[2]

The book is divided into two parts. Part I comprises three chapters. The first is devoted to an exploration of the law's passage, the second to an analysis of its impact in the first year of operation. Exploring the workings of the law, during that first year as the authorities developed mechanisms of enforcement, provides an opportunity to trace the ways it was implemented, how it was challenged, and what impact opposition to its enforcement had on state and national politics. One of the unintended consequences of the law was a resurgence of the movement to colonize free blacks and freed slaves in Africa supported, in large part, by those who endorsed the Fugitive Slave Law and who saw it as a way to peacefully address the racial problems that had long tortured the country. Chapter 3 explores these efforts and their impact, particularly on northern black communities and, more generally, on the abolitionist movement.

The flight of slaves had the potential to become – and many times did become – politically charged with national implications. The work of recapturing slaves who escaped prior to 1850 was generally considered the responsibility of state and local authorities. All that changed after 1850. Understanding what occurred at the points of departure, for example, whether it was from the Eastern Shore of Maryland or from southeast Missouri, helps us appreciate the many and complex ways the politics of scale affected conditions in these and at other points of friction between slavery and freedom. When, for example, slaves escaped from Berlin, Worcester County, on the Eastern Shore of Maryland, or from the lead mines near Ste. Genevieve, Missouri, their actions had a local political impact that quickly rippled outward to influence state politics. Did these slaves act on their own initiative or were they assisted by internal or outside subversives of order? Border States did what they could to counter these forces. Slaveholders formed local defense organizations in an effort to curtail losses. They also pressured state legislatures to enact more draconian laws to stem the flow of escapes. Efforts to reclaim fugitives who reached the relative security of a northern community had the potential to increase political tensions between states and many times did. Although the record shows that, in the majority of cases that came under the purview of the Fugitive Slave Law, fugitives were returned, in many instances they were not, either because local authorities were pressured not to adhere to the terms of the law or because the fugitive was rescued from under the noses of authorities

---

[2]  Toni Morrison, *A Mercy* (New York: 2008), 11; Charles Rawn Diary, Rawn Collection, MG062, Dauphine County Historical Society, Harrisburg, Pennsylvania.

and sent to the safety of Canada. Tracing the contours of these cases provides a geopolitical map of the possible impact departures of slaves from Ste. Genevieve had, first, on Jefferson City, the state capital, and, ultimately, on Washington, DC. What started in Ste. Genevieve continued in the small towns of southern and central Illinois as slaveholders took advantage of the opportunities the law provided. Under the terms of the law, citizens of Free States were compelled, if requested by federal marshals, to assist in the recapture of slaves. As a result, the residents of Springfield and Quincy, or any other town in Illinois, were instantly transformed into slave catchers. As a consequence, the law alienated large numbers of Free State residents, even those who were otherwise unconcerned about slavery. It also stiffened the resolve of those in the black and abolitionist communities who opposed slavery. In order to trace these connections, most of Part II is built around the coupling of Slave States with adjoining Free States, for example, western Kentucky with Indiana and eastern Kentucky with Ohio. The exception are the last two chapters, which cover New York and Massachusetts, which do not abut Slave States but to which slaves fled in increasing numbers during the decade. They came by sea from Delaware, Virginia, North Carolina, and Georgia. Both states were major ports of call for escapees. Here were found some of the most organized arms of the Underground Railroad (UGRR), including local vigilance committees, which sheltered and protected fugitives, fed and clothed them, found them temporary employment or moved them on to more secure locations. The organizational connections went back decades. When, for example, Frederick Douglass fled Maryland in 1838, he went first to New York City, where he was welcomed by David Ruggles, head of the local vigilance committee, and where he was married by Rev. J. W. C. Pennington – himself an escaped slave from Maryland a dozen years earlier. Following their marriage, Douglass and his new bride, Anna, left for the relative security of New Bedford, Massachusetts. They would later settle in Rochester, New York, where Douglass launched a sustained assault against slavery. It is these sorts of connections that are at the heart of the movement to destroy slavery. Both states had a history of sustained abolitionist activities. They were also the home of relatively large and well-established black communities. But also pivotal to the story were the commercial, economic, and political connections that existed between these states and slaveholding states. Every case that came to trial, and many that did not, were consequently freighted with wider national significance.

In order to trace these political links, one necessarily has to start at the point of departure that is in the slave states. Recent histories of slavery and the UGRR have explored the many reasons slaves decided to leave family and the places they knew for the uncertainty of a new life among strangers. This study covers similar ground in an effort to understand what drove slaves to seek their freedom. It is built around the "stories" of those individuals who left few records on the assumption that we can best determine what motivated slaves to escape, that is, what they thought of freedom, by what they did. These stories also tell us what slaves thought of themselves, their sense of family connections, and the reasons they rejected slavery, or as one escapee put it, what prompted him "to take [his] feet feel for Canada" and "let the conscience" of his former master "feel [it in his] pocket." Their actions were informed by what E. P. Thompson has called a "general notion" of rights and a desire for freedom. Theirs, as C. L. R. James argues, was a "self-expressive presence" without which it is impossible to imagine a movement capable of such a sustained assault against slavery.[3]

It is for this reason that each chapter opens and is built around an escape and the commissioners' hearing that sometimes ensued. Unearthing these stories required careful reading of countless local newspapers on both sides of the slavery divide. It is here that one comes to appreciate what drove slaves to seek freedom; here, too, are found the many ways southern authorities tried to stymie these activities, to control all they considered a threat to the security of slave property and against those they considered subversives of good order. Definitions of "subversive" were elastic. They included slaves who helped fellow slaves to escape; northern legislators who found ways to undermine enforcement of the Fugitive Slave Law through the adoption of local ordinances known collectively as personal liberty laws; northern black communities and their white abolitionist supporters who impeded slaveholders in their efforts to reclaim lost property; southern whites who were "corrupted" by abolitionist propaganda and who chose to act on those beliefs; free blacks, who were seen as close allies of the slaves and for that reason should be watched closely or, better yet, expelled, re-enslaved or persuaded to go to Liberia or other tropical settlements; and northern whites and African Americans who went south, hidden in the general flow of commerce and expanding connections between the sections, "disguised" as traders, schoolteachers, seamen, and laborers, bent on "enticing" slaves to escape. It is here too that one finds accounts of the many ways local and state authorities marshaled the full weight of their judicial and law enforcement powers to impose their will on anyone suspected of undermining the system.

Opposition to the law took many forms, from sheltering fugitives out of sight of the authorities to rallying the black and abolitionist communities to prevent the recapture of escapees, sending to safer places those who were about to be taken, providing legal challenges to those who were brought before commissioners, ransoming those who were about to be returned and, finally, rescuing suspects. The law may have been implemented in the majority of cases that came to a hearing, but to Southerners, the sustained and sometimes dramatic defiance with which it was met became a mark of the law's ineffectiveness

---

[3] John Blassingame, *Slave Testimony: Two Centuries of Letters, Speeches, Interviews, and Autobiographies* (Baton Rouge: 1977), 114; E. P. Thompson, *Customs in Common* (New York: 1991), 212; C. L. R. James, "The Atlantic Slave Trade and Slavery," *Amistad,* vol. 1 (1970), 142; C. L. R. James, *Every Cook Can Govern. A Study of Democracy in Ancient Greece* (Detroit: 1956), 20.

and a statement of the government's – and especially the North's – inability or unwillingness to meet their constitutional obligations. The crisis caused by escaping slaves was not enough to bring on the Civil War, but there is no doubt that it was a major contributing factor. By their actions the slaves placed themselves at the center of the political debate about the future of slavery. Men who are nothing, or who allow themselves to be nothing, V. S. Naipaul has observed, have no place in the world in which they find themselves.[4] Those who put distance between themselves and slavery made a mockery of such claims. By their actions they contributed to a fundamental reordering of the world they knew and opened the possibility of joining that world as full-fledged citizens.

This book has taken a long time to complete. When I began I was a father of four; now I am the proud grandfather of six! Every time the topic of the book came up with family and friends it was greeted by one refrain: Why is it taking so long? All I could do was plead patience. I hope their patience has been rewarded. The research not only required rummaging through countless newspapers that were published in out-of-the-way places, but through many competing city dailies. Had I started the project in the last few years, at a time when the digitization of newspapers was being perfected, it is possible the book would have been written much sooner. But I doubt the new technology would have been much help, as many of the cases uncovered were found in little and sometimes obscure newspapers that are yet to be digitized. Students looking for me at any time outside of class times sometimes found me in the library, my head buried in the hole of an antique microfilm reader, slowly turning the handle of the machine. I was usually disrupted by the same question: Are these newspapers not digitized? It would have taken too long to explain. I relied on the hardworking staff of the Interlibrary Loan Office at Vanderbilt University, especially Jim Toplon and Rachel Adams, who seem to know where every microfilmed newspaper was located and who filled every request with a promptness that forced me to take up residence in the microfilm reading room. If my wife, Cheryl, needed to reach me she would call the library's front desk and I would be startled out of my research reverie by an announcement on the public-address system. Why could I not be reached by cell phone, you ask? The answer I leave to your imagination. But the research also required trips to holdings in archives from Jefferson City, Missouri, to Annapolis, Maryland, and places in between. In Ripley, Ohio, I climbed the steep hill overlooking the city to the Rankin house perched on the hilltop, visible for miles from the opposite bank of the Ohio River, in which a lantern in the window beckoned the escapee at any time of the day or night. Before starting the ascent, the fugitive was welcomed by John Parker to his home that sat along the river's edge. In Ripley's local library, Alison Gibson pointed the way to local records and the community's history. It would take pages to thank

---

[4] V. S. Naipaul, *A Bend in the River* (New York: 1980), 3.

all the many librarians and archivists who willingly offered assistance. I hope they know who they are. Some of these trips were nothing if not exciting. On one such visit, in the middle of a steamy summer, to search through the court records of a town whose name I better not divulge, my research assistant and I were handed the keys to the vault and a straw broom. When I asked the clerk of court why the broom, I was told it was to ward off spiders. I grew up in the tropics and so am unfazed by all varieties of spiders, but not so my research assistant, who took the clerk's response to heart. Not surprisingly, the search was aborted. We will never know what gems we abandoned to the spiders. Like some northern authorities, we thought it best not to go into a place inhabited by fugitive spiders. Braver souls may someday discover what we missed.

Much of what was unearthed on these summer research trips was due to three bright and hardworking students who were my research assistants: undergraduates Renee Stowitzky and Alex Cartaya and graduate Paula Gajewski, who cheerfully went along for the ride. Together we raised eyebrows wherever we went.

Many librarians and historians – too many to mention – promptly responded to my pleas for help. I have acknowledged some of them by name in footnotes; the others I hope know how much their assistance was appreciated. Friends and former colleagues did what they could to make my archival visits enjoyable. On the way to Louisville, Kentucky, I contacted Pamela Peters, who had recently published a history of the UGRR in Floyd County, Indiana. She invited us to her home in New Albany and before we could get around to a discussion of the movement, provided lunch. Pamela knew the importance of food and libations to any successful research trip. On one of my visits to Detroit, Greg Sumner took me to a Tigers baseball game, where I discovered a gem of American cuisine: the piling on of totally unrelated condiments and other foods onto hot dogs, all the while insisting they were still hot dogs!

In this business we rely on friends and colleagues to help us avoid embarrassing mistakes. Among those who took the time to read and comment on chapters are Stanley Harrold, David Blight, Eric Foner, Keith Griffler, Robert Churchill, Nicholas Guyatt, Sebastian Page, James Madison, Kate Larson, Christopher Densmore, and Leigh Fought. My old friend from undergraduate days, Martin Crawford, read every chapter as they were written. Thanks to Danielle Picard who prepared the maps. The staff of the Rothermere American Institute, Oxford University, where I spent a year as the Harmsworth Professor of American History, was unfailingly supportive. They included Jane Rawson and the staff of the library, former director Nigel Bowles, and Rhodes Professor Pekka Hamalainen. It is there that I started writing and was able to test some of my ideas on Nick Guyatt, Seb Page, Jay Sexton, and Randall Woods, who was a Fellow at the Institute for a semester. Page took me on pub crawls – a cultural high point. Guyatt and I had long conversations about the historical significance of the colonization movement and the contending merits of Arsenal and Stoke football teams over Thai food and beer. The products of the fine wine cellar at Queen's College, my college affiliation during the year, were even more helpful! The Provost, Paul Madden, his wife Alison, and staff of the College were warm and welcoming hosts. My wife, Cheryl, has been with me throughout the journey. Our children, Leila, Lavinia, Victor, and Peter, maintain a perverse pride in never having read anything I have written – a peaceful protest against history, I presume. Periodically, they would inquire about the book's progress but only as a way, I suspect, to needle the old man. But I think they know how much even these few expressions of interest matter.

PART I

THE SLAVE POWER ASSERTS ITS RIGHTS

# The Fugitive Slave Law

When twenty-three-year-old Peter Green left Newport, Giles County, Virginia, in early September 1850, his plan was to get to Richmond and from there to a Free State. He got only as far as Lynchburg, roughly one hundred miles from his home, when he was intercepted at the Franklin Hotel as he tried to buy a train ticket. When questioned, Green claimed he was a free man going on a visit to Pennsylvania. But it quickly became apparent that his free papers, which he readily produced, were forged. Those who took him into custody found that he was also carrying an atlas, pen, ink and paper – which possibly could be used to forge additional passes as needed – and on which was carefully recorded the mileage between Newport and Richmond. A few weeks earlier, a group of eight slaves from Clarke County, in the Shenandoah Valley of Virginia, had arrived in Harrisburg, Pennsylvania. Three of them, Samuel Wilson, George Brocks, and Billy, decided to try their luck in the city, unaware that their masters were hot on their heels. From Chillicothe, Ohio, came word that more than 110 slaves had passed through the town from Kentucky in the six months before October 1850. One slave catcher told a not-too-sympathetic correspondent that, over the spring and summer of 1850, Maryland and Virginia had lost more slaves than in "any former period." Among them must have been the seven who together fled Maryland in August 1850, five of whom were captured in Shrewsbury, Pennsylvania, one mile above the Maryland line, as well as the ten Virginia slaves who got lost in the Allegheny Mountains and were captured in Bedford, Pennsylvania. These were just a few examples of what, to many Southerners, was a disturbing pattern of slave escapes.

A few of these escapes were nothing if not spectacular. William and Ellen Craft had escaped from Macon, Georgia, over the 1848 Christmas holidays. Phenotypically white, Ellen dressed as a master traveling to Philadelphia for medical treatment; William accompanied her as her slave. Traveling openly by train and boat, they made it to Pennsylvania in just four days. Three months later, Henry Brown came up with the ingenious scheme to have himself crated and mailed to Philadelphia. Hours later he emerged triumphantly from his box at the offices of the American Antislavery Society, if a little worse for wear. Both the Crafts' and Brown's escapes were celebrated by abolitionists as feats of daring and a demonstration of the determination of the enslaved to be free. But even in failure, so too were Green's, Wilson's, Brock's, and Billy's and the many others who fell short of their mark. Not a day passes, one frustrated Maryland editor reported, when one or more slaves did not take a chance on reaching a Free State. The consequent losses, he despaired, were "immense."[1]

The immensity of the problem, many insisted, was in large part due to interference from outside forces, of abolitionists and their agents, black and white, who seemed to circumvent all the mechanisms slaveholders had put in place to stanch the bleeding. In Peter Green's case, it was a "scoundrel of a Yankee" who had accompanied him as far as Lynchburg only to abandon him once he was captured. The unidentified Yankee, who we can assume was white, was supposedly part of an organized band of robbers who came south under different guises. Following Green's capture, a local newspaper called on the community to be on its guard, for, it warned, nearly every area of the upper South had "one or more abolition emissaries in its midst, colporteurs, book-sellers, tract agents, school teachers, and such like characters, who omit no occasion to poison the minds of our slaves, and then steal them." The list of subversives seemed endless, reflecting a deep sense of slavery's vulnerability made worse by the inability to control the flow of people and goods on which most of the commerce and culture of these communities depended. Similar warnings came from port cities, such as Norfolk, Virginia, which many observers considered gateways to freedom points at which escaping slaves were aided by Northern free black sailors who found ways to circumvent legal restrictions

---

[1] Lynchburg *Republican* (n.d.), in *Liberator,* September 27, 1850; *Pennsylvania Freeman,* August 29, 1850; Richmond *Whig,* September 3, 1850; New York *Tribune,* September 6, 1850; Maysville *Eagle,* October 15, 1850; *The North Star,* September 5, 1850; Baltimore Sun (n.d.), in Hagerstown *Herald of Freedom,* August 14, September 4, 1850; *Sanduskian,* October 8, 1850; Lynchburg *Virginian,* October 10, 1850; William Craft, *Running a Thousand Miles for Freedom. The Escape of William and Ellen Craft* (London: 1861); Jeffrey Ruggles, *The Unboxing of Henry Brown* (Richmond: 2003). There were many others in the years leading up to 1850, including the rescue of Adam and Sarah Crosswhite, fugitives from Kentucky who had settled with their children in Marshall, Michigan, where they were retaken and soon after rescued and sent to Canada. Marty Debian, "One More River to Cross. The Crosswhites' Escapes from Slavery," in Karolyn Smordz Frost, and Veta Smith Tucker, eds., *A Fluid Frontier. Slavery, Resistance, and the Underground Railroad in the Detroit Borderland* (Detroit: 2016). There was another dramatic rescue at South Bend, Indiana, of fugitives on their way south. Charles H. Money, "The Fugitive Slave Law of 1850 in Indiana," *Indiana Magazine of History,* XVII (September 1921), and Dean Kotlowski, "'The Jordon is a Hard Road to Travel;' Hoosier Responses to Fugitive Slave Cases, 1850–1860," *International Social Science Review,* 79, Nos. 3 & 4 (2003); Scott Mingus, *The Ground Swallowed Them Up. Slavery and the Underground Railroad in York County, Pa.* (York, PA: 2016), 110–13.

placed on black crews employed on ships from the North. Some of these ships, one Norfolk newspaper reported, make "the abduction of slaves a matter of trade and a source of profit. Scarcely a week passes that we do not hear of one or more being taken off." But even more troubling was the fact that these free black sailors indoctrinated "the minds of the slaves with the notions of freedom, and afterwards afford[ed] them the means of transportation to free soil." It was common wisdom that white and black outsiders were responsible for first corrupting and then encouraging slaves to escape. Peter Green, and any other slave, simply could not have acted on their own.[2]

The losses were staggering. According to Arthur Butler, a senator from South Carolina, Kentucky alone lost $30,000 worth of slaves every year, a figure that rose to as much as $200,000 for the entire border slave states. His colleague, James Mason of Virginia, put the loss at "a hundred thousand annually." Thomas Pratt, former governor of Maryland, spoke from experience: during his administration, the state lost slaves, valued at $80,000, every year. Never one to miss an opportunity to exaggerate, David Atchison of Missouri, while he could not be more specific, was certain that "depredations to the amount of hundreds of thousands of dollars [were] committed upon property of the people of the Border States of this Union annually."[3] These were wildly imprecise figures. But they nonetheless reflected the depth of frustration and the anxiety the flight of fugitives generated as well as the inability to curtail apparent interference from outside forces. Such interference with and pilfering of private property in the South was buttressed by Free State laws, such as Pennsylvania's (1847), which barred holding suspected fugitive slaves in state prisons. The activities of abolitionists, free blacks, and fugitive slaves only compounded the problem by making it even more difficult, if not impossible, to reclaim slaves once they reached a Free State. Together, laws such as Pennsylvania's were, Mason declared, the "greatest obstacle" to reclaiming escapees. He reached for an appropriate metaphor to capture the difficulty of reclaiming fugitives: it was, he said, like searching for fish in the sea. Colleagues may have found such tropes inept, but it was the best Mason could conjure up during the heated debate over the need for a new and more effective fugitive slave law. Pratt was more practical. Maryland fugitives did not simply vanish once they

---

[2] Lynchburg *Republican* (n.d.), in *Liberator,* September 27, 1850; Norfolk *Southern Argus,* November 11, 1850; Richmond *Whig,* September 24, 1850. The daring attempt to take seventy-seven men, women and children, from Washington, DC, on the schooner, *Pearl,* in April 1848, was yet another example of the levels to which these emissaries were willing to go to subvert the system. For coverage of the incident, see Stanley Harrold, *Subversives. Antislavery Community in Washington, DC, 1828–1865* (Baton Rouge: 2003), 116–18, and by the same author, *Border Wars. Fighting Against Slavery before the Civil War* (Chapel Hill: 2010), 131–33. Mary Kay Ricks, *Escape of the Pearl. The Heroic Bid for Freedom on the Underground Railroad* (New York: 2007).

[3] *Appendix to the Congressional Globe, First Session, Thirty-First Congress* (1850), 81, 1605, 1603, 1601.

reached Pennsylvania; local mobs, made up largely of African Americans, had prevented their return.[4]

These were losses the Slave States could no longer endure. Something had to be done to find a more effective means to reclaim lost slaves as required by Article 4, Section 2 of the Constitution. The 1793 Fugitive Slave Law, Mason and his colleagues believed, had become, over the years, a dead letter. The solution was a new, expanded, and more effective fugitive slave law – a law with teeth – which Mason submitted to the Senate in January 1850. Mason may have drawn on a report of a Select Committee of the Virginia General Assembly, which, after looking into the history of the crisis, made a number of recommendations to address the problem. The report was premised on what, by mid-century, had become a generally accepted historical myth: namely, that Southern states would not have consented to join the Union had the Constitutional Convention not addressed the issue of fugitive slaves. Quoting Associate Justice of the US Supreme Court Joseph Story, in the case of *Prigg v. Pennsylvania* (1842), the authors of the report observed that the agreement to return fugitive slaves "constituted a fundamental article, without whose adoption the Union would not have been formed." The 1793 law was meant to buttress this "solemn compact." For the first two decades of the nineteenth century, this agreement was widely enforced, until it came under attack, in the wake of the 1820 Missouri Compromise, by political fanatics driven by "sectional jealousy." A series of personal liberty laws – what the report described as "disgusting and revolting exhibitions of faithless and unconstitutional" legislations – meant that slaveholders could no longer rely on the aid of Free State officers. Not only were fugitive slaves harbored and protected, but "vexatious suits and prosecutions were initiated against owners or their agents, resulting sometimes in imprisonment." Irresponsible mobs, "composed of fanatics, ruffians and fugitive slaves, who had already found asylum abroad, were permitted by local authorities to rescue recaptured slaves in the lawful custody of their masters, and imprison, beat, wound and even put to death citizens of the United States." As a consequence, the cost of recapture often exceeded the value of the slaves retrieved. These actions were buttressed by the activities of abolitionist societies, which aimed to destroy slavery by, among other means, sending emissaries into the "very heart of the slaveholding states" to induce slaves to escape. These forays had made slave property increasingly tenuous by imposing what, in effect, was a "heavy tax" on the border states. If an owner wished to reclaim his slave, he must venture into hostile territory, seize the slave himself, march him off to a judge, sometimes over great distances, all the while hounded by hostile forces. And even then, there was no guarantee his property would be returned. Something had to be done immediately if "border warfare," was to be prevented. The committee recommended

[4] Ibid., 1610, 1592.

the establishment of a federal policing system. Commissioners, clerks, marshals, postmasters, and collectors of customs would be given authority to issue certificates to claimants; marshals would have the power to make arrests and to call out a posse to ensure the return of the slave, all expenses to be covered by "the public treasury of the United States." Finally, the committee recommended increasing the penalty for obstructing renditions, making "assemblies meant to obstruct the operation of the law" a misdemeanor, and "any death resulting from resistance" a felony.[5]

Mason's recommended fugitive slave bill not only stiffened the penalties imposed by the original Fugitive Slaw Law of 1793, it also made it easier for slaveholders to reclaim slaves who had escaped to a Free State. Commissioners, traditionally minor legal administrators, were to be vested with expanded judicial authority. Hearings were to be perfunctory and a commissioner's decisions final and not subject to appeal; suspected fugitives were not allowed to testify on their own behalf or be allowed legal representation; jury trials were not permitted; whenever they suspected there would be community resistance to their decisions, commissioners were empowered to call out a posse to enforce their order, the cost to be borne by the federal treasury. If requested to do so by the authorities, citizens of Free States had to become involved in the recapture of slaves. Those who impeded the application of the law, gave aid to a fleeing fugitive, or refused to aid in the recapture of slaves, faced stiff penalties. It would serve no purpose, Mason insisted, to adopt new legislation without teeth. The new law had to be effective and tailored to meet the needs of new political realities brought on by rising levels of slave escapes and abolitionist activities, which together made slave property increasingly vulnerable.

In early February 1850, Kentucky's Henry Clay proposed a set of compromise measures that he told the Senate were meant as a balm to soothe his "distracted" and "unhappy country" which, he feared, stood on the "edge of a precipice." Clay called on both sides to give ground, "not on principle" but "of feeling of opinion" in an effort to solve the pressing problems facing the country following the end of the war with Mexico, which saw the United States acquire vast tracts of land in the west.[6] The country was mired in a potentially

---

[5] "Report of the Select Committee," Virginia General Assembly, House of Delegates. House Documents No. 50 (1848–1849), 5, 9–11, 14, 18–19. Interestingly, many of the same arguments were made by Mason's mentor, John C. Calhoun, the South Carolina senator, who a year earlier had called for the creation of a Southern party to defend Southern interests. In Calhoun's analysis of the history of what he called "acts of northern aggression and encroachment," the crisis could be traced to 1835 and the emergence of organized aggressive abolitionist activity, which included sending "incendiary publications" into the South as well as emissaries to "incite discontent among the slaves" and agitating "the subject in Congress." Clyde N. Wilson and Shirley Bright Cook, eds., *The Papers of John C. Calhoun*, 28 Vols. (Columbia, SC: 2001), Vol. 26, 225–44. See William A. Link, *Roots of Secession. Slavery and Politics in Antebellum Virginia* (Chapel Hill: 2003) for a discussion of the relationship between slavery and Virginia state politics.

[6] Quoted in Fergus M. Bordewich, *America's Great Debate. Henry Clay, Stephen A. Douglas and the Compromise that Preserved the Union* (New York: 2012), 5–7.

debilitating crisis over what to do with the lands. It was, in part, to address this problem that, in 1847, John C. Calhoun had called for the creation of a unified Southern party to promote Southern interests. He demanded that slaveholders be allowed to take their slaves into the new territories. Such insistence met with stiff resistance from those who believed that the 1820 Missouri Compromise had set the permanent limits of slavery. In 1846, David Wilmot's demand that the House accept President Polk's request for additional funds to fight the war with Mexico only on the condition that slavery be banned from any territory acquired as a result of the war became the political marker dividing the two sections. Although what became known as the Wilmot Proviso was never adopted by the Senate, it continued to win support in the House. In addition, all Northern legislatures, bar one, called on Congress to ban slavery in the territories, and to abolish the slave trade in Washington, DC. A few even demanded the total abolition of slavery.[7] Clay was right: the country was in crisis.

Clay included Mason's bill as part of his Compromise, which, he hoped, would address the outstanding concerns of both sections. Under his recommendation, California would enter as a Free State, the residents of the Utah and New Mexico territories were vested with the power to determine whether they entered the Union as a Free or Slave State; the contested lands between Texas and New Mexico were to be finally adjudicated, with Texas giving up much of the land it now claimed; and the slave trade but not slavery was to be abolished in Washington, DC. Clay's plan applied five plasters to five seeping sores. Over the next nine months, the attention and energy of both houses of Congress would be focused, almost exclusively, on the final terms of the Compromise. Try as they might, the fugitive slave wound continued to seep. In fact, for many in the North, especially those opposed to the extension of slave territory, the law became the one element of the Compromise that was totally unacceptable. In the South, its adoption and enforcement was seen as the ultimate measure of the North's commitment to a resolution of the crisis. Opponents of the law cried foul: the powers vested in commissioners were unprecedented and unconstitutional, and the differential payments they were to receive – $10 if their decision favored the claimant, and $5 if it did not – struck many as grossly unfair and an incentive, the equivalent of a bribe, to commissioners to rule in favor of the slaveholder. Two pillars of the judicial system, the right to a trial by a jury of one's peers and the right to habeas corpus, seemed to be eviscerated by the proposed law. Without these rights, free blacks could fall victim to false claims by slaveholders. As it stood, the law would give a free hand to kidnappers, a problem that had bedeviled the residents of black communities for decades. The steep penalties imposed on those who aided accused fugitives to elude their captors violated the biblical

---

[7] John C. Waugh, *On the Brink of Civil War. The Compromise of 1850 and How it Changed the Course of American History* (Wilmington, DE: 2003), 4–5.

command to aid the poor, the hungry and weary traveler. In effect, it turned the average citizen into a slave catcher. The fact that the cost of rendition was to be borne by the national treasury imposed a hidden tax on all citizens. And the authority to call out a posse created a national police enforcement mechanism. The law, moreover, did not provide a statute of limitation. A fugitive who for years had been living as a free person, had started a family, had been gainfully employed and was a productive member of his community, could be snatched from his family and community and returned to slavery at any time. Salmon Chase of Ohio spoke for many opponents. The law, he argued, was illegal if for no other reason than the Constitution did not grant Congress the power to legislate for the return of fugitive slaves. "The power to provide by law for the extradition of fugitives is not conferred by an express grant," he told his colleagues. "We have it, if we have it at all, as an implied power; and the implication which gives it to us, is, to say the least, remote and doubtful. We are not bound to exercise it. We are bound, indeed, not to exercise it, unless with great caution, and with careful regard, not merely to the alleged right sought to be secured, but to every right which may be affected by it." Prior to the decision in *Prigg v. Pennsylvania*, Chase observed, each state had developed "its own legislation to address the issue." The new law would destroy that tradition and shift enforcement to the federal government.[8]

Those who argued the need for a new law considered the old law a dead letter. The 1793 law relied too heavily on state officials to enforce its provisions, mandated penalties were distressingly minor, abolitionists and their black supporters either ignored or defied rulings, and Northern states had set in place laws that undermined its effectiveness. Mason demanded one thing of the new law: it had to impose more draconian enforcement mechanisms. Without them, the citizen's claims would not be adequately addressed. It is the duty of government, he argued, to protect its citizens, "not merely to give them a remedy; but if one form of remedy will not accomplish the end, then to enlarge it in every possible respect till it becomes effectual." If that could not be done then the government was obligated to indemnify the claimant for any loss that resulted from inefficiency or inaction. Maryland's Thomas Pratt offered a supportive amendment to Mason's bill, which called on the federal government to indemnify slaveholders for any loss they may incur as a result of negligence or inactivity on the part of federal officials. A vote in support of his suggestion by Northern senators, Pratt almost pleaded, would give the South "substantial

---

[8] *Appendix to the Congressional Globe, First Session, Thirty-First Congress* (1850), 47; *Appendix to the Congressional Globe, Second Session, Thirty-First Congress* (1851), 309. Chase had employed these arguments in earlier defenses of fugitive slaves in Ohio. See Paul Finkelman, *An Imperfect Union. Slavery, Federalism, and Comity* (Chapel Hill: 1981), 157. For this argument's wider appeal see Daniel Feller, "A Brother in Arms: Benjamin Tappan and the Antislavery Democracy," *Journal of American History*, Vol. 88, No. 1 (June 2001), 48–74. As Rumpole of the Old Bailey is fond of saying, trial by jury is "the lamp that shows that freedom lives." John Mortimer, *Forever Rumpole. The Best of Rumpole Stories* (London: 2011).

evidence" of the North's commitment to do justice to those who lost their property. Without indemnification, Mason threatened, slaveholders, and by extension the South, would be forced to take "their own protection into their own hands."[9] Pratt's amendment failed to win support, but, in the end, the law did mandate that the federal treasury cover the cost of returning captives.

Henry Clay insisted that the right and most effective way to address Northern concerns about the denial of trials by jury was first to return captives to the states from which they escaped and there to allow a hearing before a jury. This, he suggested, was one practical way to address the many petitions Congress had received calling for trials at the point of capture. The place from which the alleged fugitive had escaped was, Clay countered, the only location where, under the Constitution, a trial was even permissible. His proposed solution had one additional merit: it would cause "very little inconvenience." William H. Seward, of New York, and other Northern senators, countered that jury trials had to occur at the place where the accused was seized. Anything else would not guarantee a fair and impartial hearing. William Dayton of New Jersey went a step further: in all hearings before commissioners, depositions had to be authenticated and proof provided that the person claimed was a fugitive. Proof must also be provided that slavery existed in the state from which the accused had escaped. Dayton's proposal was meant to address what many saw as a lax and total reliance on Southern courts for verification and certification. All a slaveholder had to do was apply to a local court for a certificate confirming that his slave had escaped. Only after these conditions were met would the commissioner be able to issue a warrant for the fugitive's return. But if the accused denied he was a fugitive, a jury of twelve had to be empaneled to try the case. This was clearly a blocking mechanism aimed at delaying, if not impeding, hearings. Mason rejected these proposals out of hand: jury trials, he knew, could cause interminable delays and were nothing more than devises meant to disrupt enforcement. George Badger of North Carolina agreed; trials by jury at the place of capture were meant to prevent extradition through interminable delays and appeals. Such proposals, he responded, supposed "us so stupid as not to be able to see through the most shallow artifice, or detect the most clumsy device of concealment." All talk of jury trials, whether in the North or the South, was nothing more than a "miserable expedient" meant to deny slaveholders the right to reclaim "our property." Mississippi's Jefferson Davis, who expressed little interest in the law, convinced it would not "be executed to any beneficial extent," nonetheless condemned the calls for jury trials in the places where fugitive slaves were apprehended as a violation of state rights. Clay's fellow Kentuckian, Joseph Underwood, thought the offer of a trial in the South, once the slave was returned, merited serious consideration, as it provided a way out of a sticky political impasse. It had the additional

---

[9] *Appendix to the Congressional Globe, First Session, Thirty-First Congress* (1850), 1591–92, 1603–04.

advantage of mollifying Northern opinion without conceding the constitutional need for a speedy return of captives.[10] But Underwood's amendment generated little support.

There would be no jury trial at either the point of capture or escape, although throughout the 1850s those who applied the law would continue to insist, in the face of all evidence to the contrary, that accused fugitives could go to court in the South to challenge their status. But the issue did not die and reappeared frequently in subsequent congressional debates. During his maiden speech on the subject of the Fugitive Slave Law in 1852, for example, Charles Sumner of Massachusetts raised the issue in his call for the law's repeal. Lewis Cass, Democrat of Michigan, and James Cooper, a Pennsylvania Whig, both of whom had voted for the law, now recalled that, at the time, they had raised the question with Southern senators and were assured that there was no need for such a provision, as trials were available to those who requested them in the South. In the face of Sumner's criticism, Cass now seemed to back away from his original endorsement, wondering if the provision for such trials already existed, why it was not explicitly articulated in the law. By not doing so, he lamented, supporters of the law had paid a political price. "If that provision had been inserted in the bill as it was finally passed," he now admitted, "it would have taken away a great many of the objections to the law." Those outside of Congress who supported the law also found themselves at a disadvantage. A correspondent of John Floyd, governor of Virginia, wondered if there was a provision in state law allowing for jury trials for returned slaves who claimed they were free. The existence of such a provision, he believed, would go a long way to silence critics, especially abolitionists, "whose infernal system of falsehood and misinterpretation is pursued with all the zeal of blind and traitorous fanaticism."[11]

Mason also gave no ground on the issue of habeas corpus. Robert Winthrop of Massachusetts argued that a commissioner's certificate should never invalidate a habeas corpus ruling by a state judge. Mason countered that commissioners were not empowered to try the question of "freedom or slavery"; their sole role was to determine if the person brought before them was a slave and whether he had escaped from the claimant. Neither Congress nor state legislatures, he reminded Winthrop, were permitted to address the question of habeas corpus except in cases of invasion or rebellion. Furthermore, a commissioner's certificate of rendition was "conclusive evidence" that the fugitive was held "in custody under the provisions of the law" and so trumped any writ issued by a state judge. These concerns about the rights of fugitives Mason dismissed as misplaced. The constitutional mandate was clear and to the point: fugitives

---

[10] Ibid., 572, 386–87, 526, 1583–88; Bordewich, *America's Great Debate*, 225.
[11] *Appendix to Congressional Globe, First Session, Thirty-Second Congress* (1852), 1125; George W(illegible), to Floyd, Dayton, Ohio, January 10, 1851, Executive Papers, January–February 1851, Governor Floyd, Virginia State Library and Archives, Richmond, VA.

from labor "shall be delivered up." Following delivery, he conceded, "the title will unquestionably be tried," but it would be "utterly unaffected by any adjudication as to the right of custody upon the mere question of surrender." Underwood again tried to bridge the divide with an amendment that once again raised the issue of a trial: if a fugitive should claim to be free upon return, the claimant would post a bond of $1,000 so the claim could be heard by a local court. Mason objected to the bond requirement, admitting something that most Southerners knew from experience; in most cases, owners found it necessary, as he delicately put it, to "dispose" of returned slave.[12]

Throughout the debate, which lasted nine months, Mason did not give an inch. His rejection of the guarantees of habeas corpus and trial by jury were freighted with political and judicial significance, so much so that, before President Millard Fillmore approved the law, he asked his attorney general, John J. Crittenden, for his opinion on whether the last sentence of Section 6 of the law in effect suspended habeas corpus in cases involving fugitive slaves, as most opponents claimed. The section was unambiguous. It declared that fugitives did not have a right to testify at their hearings, that the certificates granted by commissioners were final and empowered claimants to return fugitives to the state or territory from which they escaped, and, most tellingly, that certificates of rendition were immune from "all molestation of such persons by any process issued by any court, judge, magistrate, or other person whomsoever." How else to interpret the molestation clause but as a suspension of habeas corpus? Crittenden submitted his opinion the very day the president put his signature to the law, which suggests that the issue had been under review by the administration for some time. Crittenden's conclusion was that it did not. But his reasoning seems strangely circuitous: it did not, because the law said nothing about habeas corpus; that under the Constitution, Congress could only suspend the writ in times of war; that, clearly, Congress had no intention to suspend it; and, finally, there was no conflict between the law and habeas corpus in "its utmost constitutional latitude." Crittenden pointed out that the ruling of the Supreme Court was clear: once a person charged is under "the sentence of a competent jurisdiction," the judgment is conclusive. There was simply no appeal to the decisions of a "tribunal of exclusive jurisdiction." All the law did was provide a more effective mechanism for the securing of fugitive slaves who have "no cause for complaint," because it did not provide any additional coercion to that "which his owner himself might, at his own will, rightfully exercise." Rather, its aim was to impose an "orderly, judicial authority" between fugitive slaves and owners and, as such, offered a form of protection to both parties. Its intention, he concluded, was the same as that of the 1793 law. A certificate of rendition was nothing more than a "sufficient warrant" for the return of a fugitive and, he concluded, did "not mean a suspension of the

---

[12] *Appendix to the Congressional Globe, First Session, Thirty-First Congress* (1850) 1589–90, 1610–11.

habeas corpus."[13] There was little difference between Crittenden's and Mason's positions. Both skirted the question, for while the law did not technically suspend the writ of habeas corpus, it clearly gave writs little effect. All that was needed was a certificate from a commissioner based on largely ex parte evidence from a distant jurisdiction, one that was largely impossible to verify, to preclude an appeal for a writ. Over the next decade, hearings before commissioners would test the law's mandate on habeas corpus. Supporters of the law in Congress and the White House had spoken with one voice.

The law passed the Senate on August 23rd by a vote of 29–12 and, subsequently, the House, by a margin of 109–76. Many Northerners from both parties abstained or found it politically convenient to be absent at the times the votes were taken.[14] Acceptance of the Compromise had only been made possible by Illinois senator Stephen A. Douglas' deft political decision to separate Henry Clay's Omnibus bill, as it was called, into its constituent parts and then marshaling sufficient support for each to assure passage. But there were deep divisions in Congress. For some Southern senators, such as Jefferson Davis, the Compromise was nothing more than a "great medicatory measure." To Thomas Benton of Missouri, its elements were a "patchwork of statutory legislation...dignified with the name of compromise." Hopkins Turney of Tennessee employed an interesting measure: how many Southerners, he asked rhetorically, voted for the bill to abolish the slave trade in Washington, DC, and for the admission of California as a Free State; and how many Northerners voted in support of the Fugitive Slave Law. By this measure, both parties had acted in bad faith. The different elements of the Compromise were nothing more than "force bills" pushed through Congress against the will of the minority. As far as William Seward was concerned, the Fugitive Slave Law was nothing more than an attempt to impose on "the free States...the domestic and social economy of the slave States."[15]

Like Turney and others in Congress, historians have questioned if what was finally agreed to was in fact a compromise, one in which both sides conceded important ground in the interest of a broader resolution. It was what

---

[13] *Congressional Globe, First Session, Thirty-First Congress* (1850), 463–64. Crittenden's opinion is reprinted in Chapman Coleman, *The Life of John J. Crittenden with Selections from his Correspondence and Speeches*, 2 Vols (Philadelphia: 1871), I, 376–81; *National Era*, October 10, 1850. The opinion was widely circulated and reprinted in newspapers. See, for example, Cleveland *Herald*, October 24, 1850, and Detroit *Free Press*, October 25, 1850. In arguing for the constitutionality of the law, Allen Johnson agrees with Crittenden that the law did not suspend habeas corpus. Left unanswered is whether a writ from a state judge is a form of "molestation." See Allen Johnson, "The Constitutionality of the Fugitive Slave Acts," *Yale Law Journal*, Vol. 31 (1921), 173–74.

[14] Michael F. Holt, *The Rise and Fall of the American Whig Party. Jacksonian Politics and the Onset of the Civil War* (New York: 1999), 72, 81–82.

[15] *Appendix to the Congressional Globe, Second Session, Thirty-First Congress* (1850), 325, 307; *Appendix to the Congressional Globe, First Session, Thirty-First Congress* (1850), 446–50; *Congressional Globe, Second Session, Thirty-First Congress* (1850), 575.

Henry Clay had hoped to achieve with his original proposal. David Potter has called it an "armistice, certainly a settlement, but not a true compromise," a conclusion with which William Freehling agrees, although he calls it a "sell-out" to Southern demands that did little to "defuse explosive questions." Paul Finkleman dismisses it out of hand as the "Appeasement of 1850," an "utterly one-sided" concession to Southern demands. Allan Nevins was more sanguine: the Compromise, he writes, overrode and rebuked "the extremists" and so held the center together.[16] But Turney's questions to his colleagues went largely unanswered. As he lay on his dying bed, John Calhoun, in one of those rare prescient moments, told James Mason: "Even were the questions which now agitate Congress settled to the satisfaction and with the concurrence of the Southern States, it would not avert, or materially delay, the catastrophe. I fix its probable occurrence within twelve years or three Presidential terms....The mode by which it is done is not so clear; it may be brought about in a manner that none now foresee. But the probability is, it will explode in a Presidential election."[17] Unlike the Missouri Compromise of 1820, which resisted efforts to derail it for thirty-four years, until the passage of the Kansas-Nebraska Act, the 1850 agreement did little to quiet the roiling political waters. Every instance involving the recapture of an escaped slave in the North had the potential to make those waters more turgid and a danger to the future of the compact.

Robert Barnwell Rhett, Calhoun's fellow South Carolinian, who had nothing good to say about the Compromise because he believed it violated state rights, wondered how the new law was to be effectuated when it was not in harmony with the "opinions and feelings of the community" in which it was to operate.[18] His concerns were soon to be confirmed; over the next two months and deep into 1851, scores of meetings were held throughout the North to condemn and declare open defiance of the law. Some of these meetings were called in the wake of particular fugitive slave cases, but the great majority was community-based responses to the law and a declaration of support for endangered fugitive slaves who had taken up residence in these communities. African Americans, those who were most vulnerable to the law, called the earliest meetings. All of these, not surprisingly, took place in cities – Boston; New York City; Syracuse; Rochester; Buffalo; Chicago; Philadelphia; Pittsburgh; Cleveland; Columbus, Ohio; Portland, Maine; and elsewhere – where blacks had a large enough presence. These meetings were followed, in a matter of days, in many of these same cities, by interracial assemblies, which drew on the long traditions of abolitionist activity. Meetings were also organized in small towns and

---

[16] David Potter, *The Impending Crisis, 1848–1861* (New York: 1976), 113; William W. Freehling, *The Road to Disunion. Secessionists at Bay, 1776–1854* (New York: 1990), 509–10; Allan Nevins, *Ordeal of the Union. Fruits of Manifest Destiny, 1847–1852* (New York: 1947), 347; Paul Finkelman, *Millard Fillmore* (New York: 2011), 81, 88.

[17] Quoted in Bordewich, *America's Great Debate*, 203.

[18] *Appendix to the Congressional Globe, Second Session, Thirty-First Congress* (1851), 318.

villages in areas noted for strong abolitionist traditions, areas that, over the years, had become magnets for fugitive slaves who had settled and started new lives there. Fugitive slaves actively participated in these meetings. At the conclusion, associations were organized to resist enforcement of the law and resolutions passed condemning the law as inhumane and unconstitutional and calling for its repeal or amendment. A number of church associations, either through public meetings or in their annual synods, also condemned the law. Defiance of the law, Benjamin Quarles has written, became a "new commandment." By the end of October, the editor of the *Daily Union* despaired that abolitionists, Free-Soilers, "higher law prophets and negroes"– a "motley gang" of every "color, caste and character" – had held "mongrel gatherings" in "every city, and nearly every village of the North," which made "nights hideous by their turbulences and folly in negro churches, at cross-roads, in barns and market houses." This plague had to be stayed, by the good people of the Free States, he pleaded.[19] The anti-law element seemed to be everywhere threatening implementation of the law as well as the country's future.

Aware that Fillmore was about to put his signature to the bill, African Americans called a meeting in Springfield, Massachusetts, under the leadership of James Mars, a Methodist clergyman. The law, the meeting declared, was not only disastrous for those who were now enjoying "a state of normal freedom," but also for "every free colored person" who at any moment was liable to be "claimed and forced into bondage." The meeting welcomed all fugitives and pledged to defend them with arms if necessary. Days later they formed a vigilance committee.[20] Fourteen months later, after a meeting with John Brown, who would, in 1859, lead an attack on the federal arsenal at Harpers Ferry, Virginia, the committee reorganized as the United League of the Gileadites. Forty-four blacks signed the pledge to defend the community against any attempt to retake fugitives. Twelve have been identified. Five were laborers; the others included a barber, a cook, a soap seller and a whitewasher. The occupations of two are not stated and one, Anna Johnson, aged twenty-four, was married to Henry Johnson, aged twenty-five and a laborer. Six of the members were born in Slave States, including William Green, the whitewasher, and a fugitive slave who had escaped from the Eastern Shore of Maryland around 1840. The League, which pledged to give "notice to all members in case of an attack upon any of our people," and to make plans to ensure that no fugitives were removed from the city, took its name from the biblical story of the allies of Gideon who, as Tony Horwitz has written, "guarded fords across the Jordon River and slew wicked Midianites fleeing across it."[21]

[19] Benjamin Quarles, *Black Abolitionists* (New York: 1969), 204; Washington, *Daily Union*, March 25, 1851. I have accounted for at least 168 such meetings.
[20] Springfield *Republican*, October 10, 15, 1850; *Impartial Citizen*, September 28, 1850; Boston *Herald*, September 30, 1850.
[21] Louis Ruchames, ed., *A John Brown Reader* (New York: 1959), 74–78; F. B. Sanborn, ed., *The Life and Letters of John Brown* (Boston: 1885), 125–26; Tony Horwitz, *Midnight Rising*.

UNNUMBERED MAP 1. [Thanks to Erica Hayden for preparing the map. Note: I was unable to locate the site of a handful of meetings on a modern road map.]

*John Brown and the Raid that Sparked the Civil War* (New York: 2011), 37; William Green, *Narrative of Events in the Life of William Green* (Springfield, MA: 1883), 21. My thanks to Leigh Fought for providing me with the information on members of the League. Roy Finkenbine, "A Community Militant and Organized. The Colored Vigilance Committee of Detroit," in Frost and Tucker, *A Fluid Frontier*, 154–64.

UNNUMBERED MAP I (*continued*)

Earlier, Brown had been instrumental in the formation of a similar organi-zation in Chardon, northern Ohio. The Chardon Fugitive Guards, an armed company of fifty of the town's "most respectable, influential, and wealthy citi-zens," pledged to resist the new law and "the officers of the government with the force of arms, and if necessary, sacrifice their fortunes and their lives in resisting them." Nothing is known about the operation of either league or even if they remained active, but the fact that no fugitives were returned from either place suggests that slave catchers gave these areas a wide berth.[22] There were other vigilance committees scattered throughout the North – in Philadelphia, New York City, Boston, and Pittsburgh to mention a few. Richard Hinton, a John Brown biographer, recalls the existence of similar organizations all along the shore of Lake Erie between Syracuse and Detroit. Some, such as the one in Kenosha, Wisconsin, were formed in the wake of the law's passage. Others, such as the Philanthropic Society in Pittsburgh, had a long and distinguished history reaching back to 1834, and yet others, as in the case of Detroit's, would be called on at a moment's notice to address specific incidences.[23]

The Springfield gathering was the first of a number of meetings organized by African Americans in the weeks after the law came into effect. In Lockport, New York, north of Buffalo, they pledged to resist "even to death" any effort to retake fugitives living in or passing through the town. African Americans in Portland, Maine, formed a vigilance committee, convinced there was no alternative remedy left them but "to solemnly warn our fellow-citizens that, being left without legal and governmental protection for [their] liberties," they were obliged to protect their rights and freedom "at whatever cost or risk." A Chicago meeting, in late September, condemned the law's tendency to enslave "all colored men," as it contained no provisions to defend blacks against false claims. The meeting formed a liberty association with an initiation fee of 25 cents and weekly dues of 10 cents, the money to be used to provide "mutual protection" against the law. Weeks later, the association was reorganized as a "Colored Police Organization" made up of seven divisions, each of six people, to defend the city at night.[24] Blacks in the little town of Elmira, New York, also formed a vigilance committee and pledged, if they discovered any person "aiding or making themselves a tool of the slave-catcher," to "meet them as enemies." Their counterparts in Columbus, Ohio, seemed not as committed to absolute resistance to the law. While the meeting – presided over by John

---

[22] Cleveland *Herald*, November 2, 1850; Chicago *Democrat*, November 8, 1850. The Scioto *Gazette*, November 7, 1850, poking fun at the Chardon group, wondered why such an organization was necessary to protect the eight blacks and two mulattoes who lived in the town.

[23] Richard Hinton, *John Brown and His Men* (1894, rpr., New York: 1968), in Katherine DuPre Lumpkin, "'The General Plan Was Freedom': A Negro Secret Order of the Underground Railroad," *Phylon*, Vol. 28 (Spring 1967), 73; *Pennsylvania Freeman*, October 31, 1850; *Frederick Douglass' Paper*, October 23, 1851; *Voice of the Fugitive*, December 3, 1851; Boston *Herald*, October 8, 1850. Later, Joshua McCarter Simpson, the Oberlin graduate, reported on the existence of a "Company of Israel," a secret society with twenty members in Zanesville, Ohio, and the "American Mysteries Secret Underground Railroad Society" of Sandusky, Ohio, with thirty-one members. *Minutes of the Second Underground Railroad Convention for the State of Ohio. Held in the City of Zanesville on the 6th, 7th and 8th of January, 1858* (n.p., n.d.), 9–10.

[24] Lockport *Courier* (n.d.), in *Liberator*, November 15, 1850; *Liberator*, September 20, 1850; *Impartial Citizen*, October 26, 1850; Chicago *Democrat*, October 9, 1850; Encyclopedia of Chicago, www.encyclopedia.chicagohistory.org/pages/1430.html; Chicago *Independent* (n.d.), in New Albany *Ledger*, November 8, 1850; *Western Citizen*, October 8, 1850; Cleveland *Herald*, November 6, 1850.

Mercer Langston, an Oberlin graduate – called for the formation of a vigilance committee, it pledged that no fugitive would be taken in the city until they had done all in their power "to secure his or her release," a rather uncharacteristic qualifier for a black meeting. The meeting also called on any fugitive living in the town to go to Canada.[25]

A meeting of blacks in Syracuse implicitly rejected such options when they formed a vigilance committee. They instead pledged to protect themselves, and families, to "wear daggers in [their] belts" and to "take the scalp of any government hound, that dares to follow on our track," as they were resolved to be free. They rejected the idea of flight, first, because they had committed no crime "against the law of the land, second that resistance to tyrants is obedience to God, and third that liberty which is not worth defending here is not worth enjoying elsewhere."[26] One of the participants in this meeting, Rev. Jermain Loguen, may not have thought he had committed a crime against the country, but he was a fugitive from slavery in Tennessee. So was William Craft, who participated in the first meeting in Boston at the end of September. Since their escape he and his wife had become fixtures in the city's black community. The meeting was chaired by Lewis Hayden, an escapee from Kentucky, a few years earlier. Hayden called for "united and persevering resistance" to the "ungodly anti-republican law." The "god-defying and inhuman law," the meeting declared, was a violation of human rights. The meeting called for the formation of a "League of Freedom" and insisted that blacks remain in the city and resist any attempts to enforce the law. The gathering issued "The Fugitive Slave Appeal," which called on citizens of good faith to "exert a moral influence towards breaking the rod of oppression." A second black meeting days later repeated the pledge of resistance and argued in part that, as South Carolina imprisoned black seamen for fear they may foment rebellion among the slave population, Massachusetts, and especially Boston, should imprison slave hunters on similar grounds.[27]

Two meetings were held the same day in western Pennsylvania, one in Pittsburgh and the other across the river in Allegheny City. Speakers such as Rev. Charles Avery – a supporter of black causes, and the person for whom

---

[25] *North Star*, October 24, 1850; *Ohio State Journal*, October 16, 1850; *Ohio Statesman*, October 15, 1850.

[26] Syracuse *Standard*, September 24, 27, 1850; Angela Murphy, "'It Outlaws Me, and I Outlaw it,' Resistance to the Fugitive Slave Law in Syracuse, New York," *Afro Americans in New York Life and History*, 28, No. 1 (January, 2004), 44. My thanks to Angela Murphy for sharing her notes on this and other meetings in Syracuse.

[27] *Liberator*, October 4, 1850; Wilber Siebert, *The Underground Railroad in Massachusetts* (Worcester, MA: 1936), 39–40; Harold Schwartz, "Fugitive Slave Days in Boston," *New England Quarterly*, vol. XXVII (1984), 192. On Lewis Hayden see Stephen Kantrowitz, *More Than Freedom. Fighting for Black Citizenship in a White Republic, 1829–1889* (New York: 2012), 93–99. For the meetings of African Americans in Buffalo, New York, see the Buffalo *Express*, October 8, 1850, and Tim Boyd, "Resistance in the Queen City; the Fugitive Slave Law in Buffalo," (Paper prepared for a seminar at Vanderbilt University, 2002), 12.

the Avery Institute, which educated a generation of African Americans, was named – questioned the constitutionality of the law for its denial of trial by jury and its suspension of habeas corpus for the accused. He called on Congress to repeal the law and on communities to treat as lepers anyone who accepted a commission. Avery laid down the political markers, which other speakers eagerly followed. To raise questions about the constitutionality of the law and to defy its application was to reject the apparent legislative "compromise" crafted by the majority of Whigs and Democrats in Congress. In fact, the first meeting condemned those in the state's congressional delegation who voted for the law. They also adopted a series of resolutions that, among other things, condemned the law for encroaching on the rights of citizens of Free States; for converting men into chattel instead of securing liberty for the oppressed; for bribing commissioners to rule in favor of masters; for violating the principle of trial by jury; and for making it easy for masters to call for the aid of city sheriffs and federal marshals on the mere suspicion of community opposition to the return of a fugitive. The meeting called on state newspapers to publish a "black list" of all those who accepted commissions.[28]

In announcing their determination to stay put and resist the law, African Americans asserted their sense of belonging to what they considered free spaces, which they had built over decades. In these spaces they provided the requisite institutional structures, including churches, schools, and benevolent societies. Whites in these cities, many of whom had no known abolitionist background, also joined the protest against the law in the days after blacks had rallied. Two weeks after the first meeting in Syracuse, for example, an interracial meeting, presided over by the city's mayor, agreed to form a new vigilance committee made up of both blacks and whites. Jermain Loguen predicted open resistance to the law. The people of Syracuse and of the entire North, he implored, had to decide to meet tyranny with force or be subdued by it. He made it clear he had refused all efforts by friends to buy his freedom. To do so would be to "countenance the claims of a vulgar despot of my soul and body." Loguen spoke for many throughout the North: "I don't respect the law – I don't fear it – I won't obey it! It outlaws me, and I outlaw it, and the men who attempt to enforce it on me." As if to confirm that the city and its black community was free soil and protected space, the meeting declared Syracuse an "open city" from which no fugitive would be taken.[29]

Ten days after Boston's first meeting, 3,500 gathered at Faneuil Hall to oppose the law. Speakers included Frederick Douglass, Wendell Phillips, Theodore Parker, and Charles Lennox Remond – leading lights in the struggle

[28] Pittsburgh *Gazette*, September 30, 1850; Pittsburgh *Post*, September 30, 1850.

[29] Syracuse *Standard*, October 3, 1850; Murphy, "'It Outlaws Me," 47; Jermain Loguen, *The Rev. J. W. Loguen As A Slave and As a Freeman. A Narrative of Real Life* (1859, rpr., New York: 1968), 392–95; Carol M. Hunter, *To Set the Captives Free. Reverend Jermain Wesley Loguen and the Struggle for Freedom in Central New York, 1835–1872* (New York: 1993), 113.

against slavery. Constitution or no Constitution, law or no law, one speaker promised, no slave would be taken from Massachusetts. The meeting agreed to form a new vigilance committee. A subcommittee comprised of some of the best legal minds in the state was dedicated to challenging the law in court. The group of lawyers would come to the aid of the Crafts a few weeks later when two agents attempted to return them to Georgia. It is not clear how funds to finance the committee's operations were raised, but some of the lawyers undoubtedly contributed their services pro bono. In other areas, such as New York City, blacks held a series of benefit concerts to raise money for their efforts. During the last two months of 1850, the Boston Vigilance Committee helped forty-six fugitives to places of safety in other parts of the state and, in the case of John Thomas and his wife, to Canada. The Crafts were sent to England. It is not clear from the records that all of these fugitives were living in Boston at the time; some may simply have been passing through the city on their way elsewhere. The pace of assistance continued in 1851; the committee aided eighty-four on their way, the majority to Canada. In the month of November 1850, the committee also posted three hundred handbills throughout the city warning of the presence of slave catchers. It also paid for the lodging, boarding, and transportation of fugitives. Many of them found temporary refuge at the Haydens' until it was safe to move on.[30]

As can be seen from the map, many meetings were also held in small towns and villages – some of them within relatively easy reach of large cities. There were thirty-one meetings, for example, in and around Cleveland, Ohio, between October and November 1850. The same pattern held around Ashtabula on Lake Erie and east of Cleveland. Many of the places can no longer be located on a modern map. This was an area strongly represented in Congress by some of the most strident opponents of the law, including Joshua Giddings and Ben Wade. It was an area settled largely by migrants from New England and, over the years, had developed a reputation for protecting fugitive slaves who had made the town and villages their home. Elisha Whittlesey, the comptroller of the Treasury in the Fillmore administration, and a resident of the Western Reserve of Ohio, recalled that many of his neighbors "including clergymen [had] been engaged for years in harboring, rescuing and running negroes."[31]

---

[30] *Liberator,* October 11, 18, 1850; "List of Fugitive Slaves Aided by the Vigilance Committee Since the Passage of the Fugitive Slave Law, 1850," Massachusetts Anti-Slavery Collection, New York Historical Society in Black Abolitionists Papers (BAP), Reel 6: 10367; New York *Tribune,* February 4, 1851. There was a similar pattern to the meetings in Albany, New York: first a black meeting followed by a gathering of whites and blacks. See Albany *Evening Journal,* October 4, 9, 1850. An exception to this pattern of meetings in major cities occurred in Rochester, New York, where the first meeting drew a large interracial crowd. The same was true in Pittsburgh. See Rochester *Democrat,* October 10, 1850, November 9, 1850; Rochester *American,* October 11, 1850; Pittsburgh *Gazette,* September 30, 1850.

[31] Elisha Whittlesey to Mr. E. M. Whittlesey, Washington, DC, October 12, 1850, Container 50, Elisha Whittlesey Papers, Western Reserve Historical Society, Cleveland, Ohio.

Reports of these meetings made it a point to emphasize that those who participated were of all political persuasions. Giddings spoke at one Painesville meeting where he reiterated his position that Congress had no power to legislate on
fugitives. Like Salmon Chase, he insisted that the so-called fugitive slave clause
of the Constitution was solely a compact between the states. At a series of
meetings in Windsor, Ohio, resolutions condemned the law as a violation of the
Constitution, criticized those who voted for it, and promised protection to any
slave who came among them. The entire county, a local historian has observed,
was a "no-man's land insofar as slave catchers and owners were concerned,"
made so by organizations of militant abolitionists who were "not averse to
using violence to protect charges."[32] There was a similar pattern of meetings
in and around Richmond in eastern Indiana, an area heavily influenced by the
Society of Friends and with a long history of Underground Railroad activities.
Thirteen meetings were held there in an eight-month period between October
1850 and June 1851.[33]

But it was not all clear sailing for those opposed to the law. Supporters
of the law and, by extension, the Compromise, managed to mount a number of challenges. A meeting in Dayton, Ohio, in mid-October 1850, recommended a series of typical resolutions opposing the law ending with a call for
its repeal. These were opposed by Clement L. Vallandigham, a leader of the
state's Democrats, who declared his support for the Compromise and criticized efforts to whip up public opposition to the law. It was the duty of all
"good citizens," he declared, to obey the law. Not to do so was to encourage
further agitation that only endangered the Union. In response, organizers tried
unsuccessfully to adjourn the meeting. Vallandigham moved quickly to organize a counter demonstration in support of the Compromise measures. They
were, he maintained, the best way to quiet the vexed question of slavery, which
had long agitated the country. Vallandigham invited Judge Joseph H. Crane,
a former congressman, to preside, but Crane declined because of frail health.
In a letter read to the meeting, Crane made it clear that what mattered most
was enforcement of the Fugitive Slave Law. He drew on Attorney General
Crittenden's arguments to justify the law's existence. The meeting declared the
nation in "imminent peril" from years of ceaseless abolitionist agitation. The

---

[32] Ashtabula *Sentinel*, November 11, 1850, January 18, May 17, 1851; Painesville *Telegraph*,
October 23, 1850; R. H. Fuller, *Underground to Freedom. An Account of the Anti-Slavery
Activities in Ashtabula County Prior to the Civil War* (Jefferson, OH: 1977), 17. There was
a vibrant "Relief Society" in Lake and other adjoining counties that collected donations to
support fugitive slaves who had reached Canada. See Ashtabula *Sentinel*, December 14, 1850,
March 11, 22, 1851, and Painesville *Telegraph*, March 26, 1851.
[33] See the Indiana *True Democrat*, October 18, November 8, 15, 22, 29, 1850, December 5, 12,
19, 1850, February 27, June 5, 1851. For meetings in northern Illinois see the *Western Citizen*,
for the months between November 1850 and March 1851.

Union as it is, therefore, had to be defended at all costs and that included the law, which the meeting endorsed as a "necessary enactment."[34]

From Chicago came the first open defiance of the law by a municipal corporation – the majority of whose members were Democrats who, at least on the national level, were ardent supporters of the Compromise. The law, the city council declared on October 21, was "cruel and unjust." The following day, a public meeting endorsed the council's position. During one of the speeches, a copy of the law was trampled underfoot. Stephen Douglas, the engineer of the Compromise's successful passage through the Senate, hurried back to Chicago to repair the damage. Three days later, in an address lasting three and a half hours, Douglas condemned the actions of the council and defended the Compromise, by which, he maintained, no side had gained an advantage. Aware of what mattered most to the four thousand who gathered to hear him, Douglas, who must have known better, nonetheless assured his listeners that the Fugitive Slave Law did not violate the right of either a trial by jury or habeas corpus. The next evening, the Council reversed itself in spite of the views of a large public meeting, which had met earlier in the day, at which Douglas' interpretations of the law's effects were roundly condemned. A contentious pro-Douglas meeting on October 26th broke up without passing any resolutions. There the matter rested until the council revisited the issue at a meeting on November 29th. Although its original resolutions were softened slightly, the council stuck to its guns: the law, it reaffirmed, was "an outrage," and, as such, state officers did not have to comply with its requirements. While the council's original vote was almost unanimous, this time its criticism of the law was carried by a narrower margin of 9–3.[35]

Criticism from the Chicago City Council and the many public meetings that were held during the last three months of 1850, while galling to supporters of the Compromise, was nothing compared to the vitriol that greeted foreigners, especially those from Britain who condemned the law. American nationalists, and especially Southern slaveholders, had always been sensitive to British criticism, especially so in the years since West Indian emancipation in 1834. Such criticism was like salt poured into the raw wound of slavery. When, for

---

[34] *Ohio State Journal*, October 24, 30, 1850. There were similar divisions in Toledo, Ohio, which threatened the political future of one of its federal senators, who it was suspected had skipped the final vote on the law so as not to alienate voters back home. See Toledo *Blade*, October 19, 22, 23, 25, 26, 28, 29, November 21, 22, December 2, 3, 1850. Because there are no extant copies of the city's other newspaper, the *Commercial Republican*, these reports may have been partial to the senator.

[35] *Missouri Republican*, October 27, 29, 1850; Chicago *Journal* (n.d.), in *Missouri Republican*, October 31, 1850; Springfield *Register*, October 29, 1850; Scioto *Gazette*, October 29, 1850; Charles W. Mann, *The Chicago Common Council and the Fugitive Slave Law of 1850* (Chicago: 1903), 85–86; James L. Hudson, *Stephen L. Douglas and the Dilemma of Democratic Equality,* (New York: 2007), 70–83.

example, a meeting in Cork, Ireland, chaired by the city's mayor, condemned the law and declared its solidarity with the slaves, one editor dismissed such sentiments as the product of an "ignorant and holy zeal" on the subject of slavery. What, he wondered, could be said of men who allowed twenty thousand "starving persons to howl with hunger, and hundreds of them to perish?" No slave in America, he continued, had "to eat the pairings of potatoes, picked from the...gutter of a public street."[36] The editor spoke for many worried by the potential impact of such criticism from abroad at a time when the country was wracked by political uncertainty. The presence of scores of fugitive slaves in London, including the recently arrived Crafts and Henry Box Brown, and their public condemnation of the law, only heightened American sensitivity to British criticism. Henry Highland Garnet, who as a child had escaped slavery with his family, and who in 1850 was on a lecture tour of Britain, exploited the presence of Lajos Kossuth in the United States to raise an unfavorable parallel between the Hungarian's struggle against Austrian oppression and the slave's fight against American slavery. How, he asked, could Americans rally to the support of Hungarian independence while they continued to oppress their black population? In Britain, he wrote home, Henry Clay, James Mason, and other supporters of the law, were spoken of in the "same scornful breath" as the Austrian general who crushed the Hungarian uprising.[37]

The arrival of George Thompson, the British abolitionist and Member of Parliament, in Boston, in the fall of 1850, as the city was engulfed in the debate over the law, confirmed for many Americans Britain's continued interference in their domestic affairs. It was Thompson's second visit to the United States. His first, in the mid-1830s, had so stirred up anti-abolitionist sentiment that he was forced to flee ahead of an angry mob. Initially, his second tour went off smoothly, until the welcome meeting organized by his Boston friends in mid-November. An estimated three thousand packed the hall. Blacks and women occupied the galleries, but those in the main hall were unfriendly and prevented the speakers, including William Lloyd Garrison, Wendell Phillips, Frederick Douglass, and Thompson himself, from speaking. They cheered for Daniel Webster, Henry Clay, and the Union, whistled Yankee Doodle, swayed "to and fro like big waves," one unfriendly newspaper reported, "while all manner of noises filled the air." The same newspaper dismissed Douglass as "that black scab on the face of humanity." The breakup of the meeting also provided an opportunity for anti-abolitionists and supporters of the law to unleash a

---

[36] New York *Herald*, June 24, July 27, 1851; Lynchburg *Virginian*, July 10, 1851. A meeting of blacks in Bridgetown, Barbados, two months earlier, expressed sympathy for black Americans following passage of the law, abhorred the "spirit of the act, the principles on which it was passed," and planned to collect funds to help fugitives "effecting their escape from such injustice, tyranny and oppression." *Pennsylvania Freeman*, April 10, 1851.

[37] *Impartial Citizen*, October 26, 1850. William P. Powell of New York City, who moved his family to Britain in the wake of the law's passage, reported that he had met "several thousand dollars' worth of slave property," in the weeks since his arrival. *Liberator*, February 7, 1851.

torrent of abuse against foreign interference in the country's affairs. Thompson was described variously, and always unfavorably, as the "British meddler," the "mad Englishman," a member of the British Parliament for "the lowest and vilest part of Cockneydom," a "paid spy of a hostile government," imported by "abolitionist agitators" to "stir up the negro race to revolt and bloodshed" at a time when the country was deeply divided.[38] Henry Clay wondered aloud in the Senate if the British would allow an American member of Congress to peddle such daring, impudent, and insolent drivel in London and not drive him out on a rail. Thompson was, Lewis Cass of Michigan agreed, a "vile disturber of the public peace."[39] A couple of days later, Boston blacks softened the blow of the failed meeting by providing a warm welcome for Thompson at the Belknap Street Church. Much of the rest of his visit went smoothly until his visit to Springfield, Massachusetts, in April 1851, when a mob hung him in effigy.[40]

By the time of Thompson's return home in mid-1851, the level of public agitation over the law had eased somewhat, although it never abated entirely. Anti–Fugitive Slave Law meetings continued to trouble supporters of the law if only because of their geographical reach and concentration. They were more than a New England and, especially, a Massachusetts phenomenon, as Allan Nevins has argued.[41] Every instance involving the recapture of a runaway would rekindle the agitation. Overall, the frequency of these public expressions of opposition deeply concerned those who saw the Compromise as the most hopeful resolution to a crisis that had dogged the country for decades and which, since the end of the war with Mexico, had grown in intensity. One editor put it bluntly: if the Fugitive Slave Law was the most critical component in what he called "the great scheme of adjustment and pacification" then something had to be done to dissuade its critics. When, he worried, "meetings are openly held in northern cities by the men of color and abolitionists, and resolutions are adopted to resist the law of the land, at the risk of shedding blood, does it not become the friends of law and order, and of the constitution itself, to meet in overwhelming force and counteract open rebellion by the moral force of public opinion?"[42]

[38] Boston *Herald*, November 16, 18, 26, December 10, 28, 1850; New York *Mercury* (n.d.), in Boston *Herald*, November 22, 1850; Detroit *Free Press*, December 4, 12, 1850; *Kentucky Statesman*, November 16, 1850; Gary Collison, *Shadrach Milkins. From Fugitive Slave to Citizen* (Cambridge, MA: 1997), 100–01. The Washington, DC, *Union*, April 3, 1851, dismissed Thompson as the "finger of a foreign hand." I am not sure what that means!

[39] *Appendix to the Congressional Globe, Second Session, Thirty-First Congress* (1851), 294, 297.

[40] Boston *Herald*, November 19, 1850. On the Springfield incident see Springfield *Republican*, February 17, 18, 19, 21, 1850; Theresa A. Harrison, "George Thompson and the 1851 'Anti-Abolition' Riot," *Historical Journal of Western Massachusetts*, Vol. 5, No. 1 (1976), 38–41; Ronald M. Gifford II, "George Thompson and Atlantic Anti-Slavery, 1831–1865" (PhD, Indiana University, 1999), 275–87.

[41] Nevins, *Ordeal of the Union*, 383.

[42] Washington, DC, *Union*, October 11, 1850.

There were meetings in support of the law, but their results, much to the disappointment of the editor, were not always easy to measure. I have identified twenty-five meetings in the weeks between late October 1850 and early 1851. Twenty-one of these took place in the North; four in the South. Of the Northern meetings the majority, not surprisingly, occurred in major cities, such as New York, Philadelphia, and Boston, with strong commercial ties to the South. The exception was Cincinnati, which had strong links to the South, but hosted only one relatively minor gathering. There were a few meetings in small cities and towns in the East, such as Geneva; Utica; and Tarrytown, New York; Bath, Maine; and Manchester, New Hampshire. Only four meetings took place in the Old Northwest – in Belleville, Illinois; Massillon, Ohio; Dubuque, Iowa; and Newcastle, Indiana. The Southern meetings were held in St. Louis and Benton, Missouri; New Market, Virginia; and Mobile, Alabama. These do not include the many meetings in the South that were called to express opposition to the entire Compromise as something that offered little by way of guaranteeing the future of slavery in the newly acquired territories.

Sixty years ago, Allan Nevins described these meetings as "largely spontaneous"; they were anything but. They were, in fact, carefully orchestrated and led by prominent local merchants, bankers, manufacturers, professionals, and politicians. In defending the law and the Compromise, they aimed to reaffirm close commercial and political links between North and South. These commercial links were, for example, what made New York City what it was. Two-thirds of the South's imports and exports, estimated to be worth $250 million, passed through the city. It was reported that, in 1849 alone, the South bought over $76 million worth of merchandise in the city. If neither Whigs nor Democrats could protect these vital connections, organizers proposed the formation of a new national political party that would isolate both the abolitionist and pro-slavery extremists, the better to ensure the survival of the Union as they knew it. One editor saw these meetings as having long-lasting political consequences, as they promised to influence future elections and so silence the demagogues.[43]

The first of these "cotton meetings," as an opponent dismissed them, took place at Castle Garden, New York City, in late October 1850. Nearly three thousand of the city's "bone, sinew, wealth, enterprise, intelligence and moral worth," one friendly editor pointed out, had signed the call for the meeting. They were all devoted to the "Union and the constitution," and hated "demagogueism, anti-slavery, anti-rent and socialist agitation." It was time, he declared, for the "conservative portion of society to arouse and avert the

---

[43] Nevins, *Ordeal of the Union,* II, 347–48; New York *Herald,* November 12, 1850, March 25, 1851. See Philip S. Foner, *Business and Slavery. The New York Merchants and the Irresistible Conflict* (Chapel Hill: 1941), especially chapters 1 and 2, for a discussion of these connections. George Thompson agreed: these pro-Union meetings were nothing more than a "grand combination...to put down abolition, [and] to secure Southern support to some particular Northern political project." *Liberator,* January 3, 1851.

danger" that threatened "to sweep into the gulf of destruction all that is good, to corrupt the youthful mind, pervert the nature of men, and overturn all the social, religious, and political landmarks, which distinguish civilization from barbarism, and Christianity from paganism." Other supporters were more circumspect, yet saw the meeting as the last best chance to show a deeply suspicious South that the North favored the Compromise at a time when its opponents threatened to carry state and local elections.[44] Although the majority of those in attendance at Castle Garden were merchants, the main speakers were all lawyers. Much of what they had to say involved the merits of the Fugitive Slave Law. Neither trial by jury nor the denial of habeas corpus, they declared, was threatened by the law. James W. Gerard departed from the message, if only briefly, to declare that he was a lifelong Whig, but one who was willing to abandon his affiliation if the party did not purge its ranks of abolitionists. "My country first and party last," he thundered. The meeting affirmed its commitment to see that the law was enforced and declared the Compromise a fair resolution of the difficulties facing the country. A "Union Safety Committee" was formed, made up of Whigs and Democrats, dedicated to ensuring that all aspects of the Compromise were permanent. The committee declared itself in favor of the formation of a Union party made up of Whigs and Democrats committed to the election of supporters of the Compromise.[45]

Robert West, editor of the *Journal of Commerce,* had earlier proposed a new slate of candidates to contest the upcoming New York state elections even before the meeting had convened. One of the potential leaders of the new party was Daniel Webster, the former Whig senator from Massachusetts and now the secretary of state in the Fillmore administration, a man with ambitions to become president, but whose chances were damaged, apparently beyond repair, when he came out in favor of Henry Clay's compromise motion in March 1850. Webster's March speech in the Senate surprised and angered many in the North. After all, he had often stated his opposition to the expansion of slavery. Now, he insisted, the South had a "well-founded ground of complaint" against those who harbored and encouraged slaves to escape, and that Southerners had a right to a law that ensured the return of their runaway slaves. Meetings of irate constituents and former supporters were called in the weeks after the speech to condemn the turncoat. Rev. Samuel Ringgold Ward, a former slave, now the pastor of an all-white congregation in upstate New York, condemned Northern doughfaces such as Webster, who supported the new fugitive slave law and who pledged themselves "to lick up the spittle of the slaveocrats and swear it is delicious."[46] Some of Ward's listeners may have winced at such

---

44 New York *Tribune,* October 25, 1850; New York *Herald,* October 10, 29, 1850; *Journal of Commerce,* October 30, 1850.

45 New York *Herald,* October 31, 1850; Holt, *The Rise and Fall of the American Whig Party,* 591–92.

46 Charles M. Wiltse, ed., *The Papers of Daniel Webster. Speeches and Formal Writings,* 2 Vols (Hanover, NH: 1988), II, 541; *Liberator,* April 5, 1850. In May, Webster wrote supporters in

imagery, but it was one that captured their deep sense of betrayal. African Americans meeting in New York City and Boston in the days after Webster's speech denounced him for his "recreancy to Freedom." The man who had once been in the "advanced guard of liberty and humanity," Rev. Samuel J. May, the abolitionist, lamented that he had gone over to the enemy. It would have been "better for him and the country," May suggested, had Webster died twenty years earlier and so saved his good name.[47]

Over the next few weeks, many of the potential leaders of the new party – senators such as Solomon Downs of Louisiana, Henry Foote of Mississippi, Lewis Cass of Michigan, Daniel Dickinson of New York and Howell Cobb, the Speaker of the House from Georgia – were feted by the Union Safety Committee. At a reception for Cass, Dickerson, and Cobb in late November, Cobb pointed out that Whigs who supported the Compromise had recently carried the elections in Georgia, a demonstration, he believed, of Southern commitment to the Union. Now, white Southerners were all looking to the North to carry out its obligations to the Compromise, especially the enforcement of the Fugitive Slave Law. Such expressions of solidarity, they hoped, would allay deep Southern suspicions of the North's commitment to the Compromise. The maintenance and execution of the law, he insisted, was "necessary to the perpetuity of this great and glorious Union."[48]

By the end of November, James Gordon Bennett, editor of the New York *Herald,* came out in support of the proposed new national party because, he argued, the two established parties had conceded too much ground to abolitionists and had monopolized elections in Northern states. A new party, pledged to the Union as it is, he speculated, would be seen as a form of "reparations" for past wrongs towards the South. Webster had sent a letter to the Castle Green meeting praising those who were not slaves to the party and pledging to support the proposed new party "whose principles and practice" were best calculated "to uphold the Constitution and to perpetuate the glorious Union." He reiterated his position at a reception in his honor organized by the Union Safety Committee.[49] But recent election results in Ohio, New Hampshire, and New York disappointed supporters of the proposed party. By the end of

Newburyport, MA, that, under both the 1793 and 1850 laws, the accused has to be removed to "the State from which he fled, that his liabilities and rights may all be there regularly tried and adjudicated, by the tribunals of that State, according to its laws." Such arguments did nothing to improve Webster's image among opponents of slavery. Boston *Atlas,* May 30, 1850.

[47] *Liberator,* April 5, 1850; *North Star,* April 5, 1850; Samuel J. May, *Some Recollections of Our Antislavery Conflict* (1869, rpr., New York: 1968), 348; Donald Yacavone, *Samuel Joseph May and the Dilemma of the Liberal Persuasion, 1797–1871* (Philadelphia: 1991), 137.

[48] New York *Herald,* November 29, 1850. The other visits are given extensive coverage by the *Herald,* November 29, December 10, 25, 1850. At the reception in his honor on Christmas Eve, Webster expressed optimism that the "acrimony of sectional disputes was dying away." New York *Tribune,* December 25, 1850; New York *Herald,* December 25, 1850.

[49] New York *Herald,* November 28, December 9, 25, 1850. Webster is quoted in Holt, *The Rise and Fall of the American Whig Party,* 592. Elisha Whittlesey supported the formation of the

January 1851, the *Herald* announced the new party stillborn. The established parties, especially the Democrats, had gotten cold feet, the editor lamented. But as Michael Holt points out, Webster was still trying to pull together a Union party as late as summer 1851 as a base for his presidential ambitions. By June, however, even these plans had evaporated.[50]

Plans for the new party may not have gone as hoped, but the Union Safety Committee continued its activities. It raised money to encourage ministers to preach in support of the Compromise, and especially the law, and to have these published and circulated widely. It is likely the committee turned to ministers as the best way to counter criticism of the law by church synods and conventions. City merchants contributed $25,000 to print and have copies of the sermons distributed. Copies were also sent to members of Congress. December 12, 1850, was set aside as a special day on which sermons supporting the "Peace Measures" were to be delivered. Several were given in New York City by "eminent divines" on the need to obey the law. Rev. Dr. Springs's was typical. They were friends of the law, he declared, and did not wish to interfere in the domestic affairs of the South. While they welcomed "free colored men" to their "doors and charity," they were obliged to turn their backs on fugitive slaves. Springs was happy to see that one effect of the law was the rapid disappearance of fugitive slaves from cities such as New York. They were all required to recognize the relationship between master and slave as it was guaranteed by the Constitution. Anyone who thought slavery was a sin and felt compelled to resist it was "a perjured man." Springs announced he was neither a supporter of slavery nor emancipation, but he had no doubt that freeing the slaves would be dangerous to the peace and stability of the country and ruinous to the economy. The destruction of the island economies of the West Indies in the wake of emancipation was clear for all to see. The lesson to be drawn from places such as Jamaica was that emancipation should be neither sudden nor immediate. What slaveholders should do instead was make every effort to ameliorate the condition of their charges. Keep your slaves, he told slaveholders, but "treat them well and when you think you could do better for them let them go." The permanence, "the honor, and the integrity" of the country, he concluded, should never be sacrificed for the protection of fugitive slaves.[51]

In Boston, where a hundred-gun salute greeted word that the Compromise had been passed, the city's mercantile and manufacturing interests gathered for what was described as a "constitutional meeting" a few days after the assembly at Castle Garden. George T. Curtis, a close political ally of Daniel Webster, organized it as the city was recovering from the excitement over the

---

new party as the best way to "arrest the progress of disunionists." Whittlesey to Richard Rush, Washington, DC, November 18, 1850, Container 50, Elisha Whittlesey Papers.

[50] New York *Herald*, January 20, 1851; Holt, *The Rise and Fall of the American Whig Party*, 643–44.

[51] Philip S. Foner, *Business and Slavery*, 57–58; New York *Herald*, December 13, 1850.

attempted recapture the Crafts. All of the speakers were drawn from the ranks
of Webster's supporters. The main speaker was Benjamin R. Curtis, the brother
of the organizer, and a prominent lawyer soon to be elevated to the federal
Supreme Court. Curtis condemned recent meetings that vowed to resist the
law as well as threaten the lives of those who tried to enforce it. With George
Thompson in mind, Curtis wondered if it was "fit and proper" for foreigners
to intrude into the country's affairs. Nationals such as Theodore Parker, the
prominent Massachusetts divine who had been active in the defense of the
Crafts, and who had dismissed the law as unconstitutional and "the warrant
of misery," were also openly defying the law and ought to be punished. Such
breaches of the law were acts of revolution that must be confronted by the
patriotic. Drawing on rising nativist sentiments, Curtis insisted that states had
every right to pass laws to protect themselves. They had a right, for example,
to limit the entry of immigrants, such as the Irish, who were "ground down by
the oppression of England." By the same token, states had endorsed the fugitive
slave clause in the Constitution because it guaranteed "incalculable benefits."
This was an act of "self-preservation." Runaways had "no right to be *here*. Our
peace and safety they have no right to invade....Whatever natural rights they
have, and I admit those natural rights to their fullest extent, *this* is not the *soil*
on which to vindicate them. This is *our* soil – sacred to *our* peace – on which
we intend to perform *our* promises." Such arguments, as we will see in a later
chapter, were the foundation on which Indiana and Illinois would build their
policies of black exclusion. David Henshaw of Leicester, who could not attend
the meeting but sent the customary letter of apology, expressed serious doubts
about the capacity of blacks for civilization. After all, they had not progressed
in three thousand years in Africa and had shown only limited improvement
in the years of contacts with whites in the United States. He even wondered
if God, in his inscrutability, meant slavery to be a state of "probation and
preparation for the black race for higher political and social condition." The
meeting denounced disobedience to the law, and called for a cessation of agitation because it endangered the "peace and harmony of the Union." Webster
was delighted with the outcome of the meeting and suggested that organizers
print fifty thousand copies of the speeches and resolutions for distribution in
Washington, DC, and the South.[52]

[52] *Proceedings of the Constitutional Meeting at Faneuil Hall, November 26th, 1850*
(Boston: 1850), 8–18; Holt, *The Rise and Fall of the American Whig Party,* 606; Boston *Post,*
November 27, 28, 1850; Edward L. Pierce, *Memoir and Letters of Charles Sumner,* 3 Vols.
(1894, rpr., New York: 1969), III, 204–08; Collison, *Shadrach Milkins,* 102–03; David D. Van
Tassel, "'Gentlemen of Property and Standing': Compromise Sentiment in Boston in 1850,"
*New England Quarterly,* Vol. 23 (September 1950), 307–19. For Parker's views on the law see
John Weiss, *Life and Correspondence of Theodore Parker,* 2 Vols. (London: 1863), II, 94–95;
Benjamin R. Curtis, ed., *A Memoir of Benjamin Robbins Curtis LL.D,* 2 Vols. (Boston: 1879),
I, 136.

A few days earlier, a similar meeting was held in Philadelphia organized by Josiah Randall, a "conservative Whig," at which the main speaker was George Mifflin Dallas, a Democrat and former vice president of the United States. Dallas followed a line typical of speakers at other Union meetings. He emphasized the need to obey the Fugitive Slave Law and to stifle the "alarming movement," and the "lawless and criminal violence" of its opponents, who were bent on disrupting the government. They aimed to trample on the rights of "the whole people." As such, they were guilty of what he guardedly called "moral treason." Dallas seemed reluctant to go as far as Webster and others who considered any form of organized opposition to the law treasonous. Another speaker, Col. Page, was less circumspect: the fanaticism that drove opposition to the law was nothing more than a "black tide of treason." Dallas believed, however, that the law was in "perfect harmony with the Constitution" and necessary for its maintenance. It was also just to fugitive slaves because it provided "protection of legal forms and hearing...and responsible officers to direct the arrest, to adjudicate upon the identity, and ultimately to supervise and authorize" their removal. Such protections would have come as a surprise to accused fugitives. But Dallas' position was in keeping with those articulated by James Mason in the Senate and John Crittenden in his report to the president. Josiah Randall rounded out the cast of speakers by calling for the repeal of the state's 1847 law, which banned the use of state prisons to hold runaway slaves, as the "most odious and unconstitutional measure," and a form of nullification.[53]

Almost simultaneously, an estimated two thousand attended a Union meeting in Manchester, New Hampshire, where speakers called on participants to stand by the "constitution as it is, and by [the] country as it is, one, united, and entire." The country had just been brought through a dark period by wise men who had relied on compromise, one of its founding political principles, to effect an agreement. While they recognized the right of citizens to lobby for modifications of laws, no one had the right to resist their enforcement once enacted. The resolution supporting the law ran into some opposition from the floor but, in the end, was adopted. When a Rev. Ross, a Free Will Baptist minister, asked to be heard, he was denied; the meeting, he was told in no uncertain terms, was restricted to "citizens who were in favor of supporting the constitution and laws." Over the succeeding months, meetings were held away from the East Coast and the mid-Atlantic, in places such as Belleville, in southwest Illinois, and in the small town of Elliottsville in northwest New York, close to the Pennsylvania state line. They addressed many of the same issues, but were less concerned to adopt Webster's larger political agenda. There were also a scattering of smaller meetings in the Border South, in places such as St. Louis and Cape Girardeau, Missouri, whose agendas had less to do with the

---

[53] *Proceedings of the Great Union Meeting held in the Large Saloon of the Chinese Museum, Philadelphia on the 21st of November 1850* (Philadelphia: 1850), 9–16, 32; Washington, DC, *Union*, November 24, 1850; Holt, *The Rise and Fall of the American Whig Party*, 606.

Fugitive Slave Law and more with the need to ensure the political survival of the Compromise as a whole.[54]

If these Union meetings were meant to overwhelm opponents of the law and, simultaneously, reassure the South that those in the North who mattered were squarely behind all the measures of the Compromise, and none more so than the Fugitive Slave Law, then the organizers were to be disappointed. Supporters of the law were ridiculed, especially in black communities, which felt the full brunt of the law's mandates. Jermain Loguen spoke for many in these communities when he dismissed supporters and operatives of the law as "pimps of power." Opposition meetings, especially those organized by African Americans, pledged to resist violently any effort to enforce the law. As early as April 1850, Samuel Ringgold Ward set the standard of defiance when he called on his listeners in Boston to make enforcement the "last act in the drama of a slave-catcher's life." It was better for the slave catcher if he made peace with his God before he came into Ward's home. At the second opposition meeting in Pittsburgh, Martin Delany spoke for many: "My house is my castle; in that castle are none but my wife and my children, as free as angels of heaven, and whose liberty is as sacred as the pillars of God. If any man approaches that house in search of a slave... if he crosses the threshold of my door, and I do not lay him a lifeless corpse at my feet, I hope the grave may refuse my body a resting place, and righteous Heaven my spirit. O, no! He cannot enter that house and we both live." This commitment of defiance struck a responsive chord with many in Northern communities. Henry Bibb, who had escaped slavery in Kentucky, employed more lofty reasoning, but to the same effect, in a speech in Boston: Death was preferable to a return to slavery. The act of escape, he argued, restored a "portion of lost rights," particularly the right to self-defense, which slavery had usurped. The law and the declarations of African American defiance also pushed some white abolitionists to abandon their principled commitment to nonviolence. Henry C. Wright, a Garrisonian abolitionist, and long a leading proponent of peaceful resistance to slavery, for instance, told a Cleveland, Ohio, meeting that, if he were a fugitive slave he would not hesitate "to plunge a knife into the heart of his pursuer" before he would allow himself to be taken back. An individual known only as "Seth" of Syracuse, New York, captured the promise of violence in verse:

[54] Boston *Post*, November 22, 1850. For some of the other Union meetings see Belleville *Weekly Advertiser*, November 28, 1850, *Illinois Republican*, November 27, 1850, Boston *Herald*, February 1, 5, 1851, Washington, DC, *Union*, December 13, 22, 1850, *Missouri Republican*, September 25, 1850, Cape Girardeau, *Western Eagle*, March 7, 1851, and Detroit *Free Press*, November 1, 1850. The meeting held in the small town of Elliotsville, Cattaraugua County, New York, attended by five hundred, an impressive figure for such a small town, was contested. Attempts were made to break it up but organizers retreated only to return to finish their discussions and to adopt resolutions in favor of the Compromise. See Rochester *Democrat*, November 28, 1850; Albany *Evening Journal*, November 18, 1850; Albany, *Argus*, December 23, 1850.

"Colored friends fear not the *knaves*
Stick by your sons and daughters
We'll protect you with our *arms*
Up to our necks in slaughter.[55]

There were abolitionists who worried over what they saw as an unmistakable drift to violence. The movement's chances of success, they believed, were predicated on an unwavering commitment to nonviolent resistance. Gamaliel Bailey, editor of the *National Era,* who had experienced the anger of anti-abolitionists mobs in both Cincinnati and Washington, DC, spoke for many worried about calls to resist the law violently. If good men, he wrote in the wake of the rescue of the Crafts, "undertake to nullify bad laws by force, bad men will be encouraged to nullify good laws by force. It will never do to recognize the principle of Lynch law in a law-abiding community." If one chose to disobey any law, one must be prepared to accept the consequences. That may be so, many responded, but what Congress had done was enact a law that was morally indefensible, one which flew in the face of traditional legal rights and traditions. William Jay, a New York abolitionist, was even more explicit than Bailey. While he was not opposed to violence in principle, the death of a slave catcher, he wrote a group of black New Yorkers, would be considered murder, not civil disobedience. Violent responses to "kidnappers" were both unnecessary and "morally wrong" and, he predicted, would "prove to be the source of great evil" to the black community. Resistance of this sort would lead inevitably to counterviolence by "Southern ruffians and their Northern mercenaries." Jay had no doubt that the law would result ultimately in bloodshed, but when it did, he pleaded, "let it be the blood of the innocent, not of the guilty." If anything could rouse "the torpid conscience of the north," it would be "our streets stained with human blood, shed by slave-catchers." Jay's pleas fell on deaf ears; as Ward and the others promised, the blood in the streets would not be theirs. But Bailey's and Jay's worries were largely misplaced. In the heat of the dispute over the law, black communities were practical, if not always rational, when it came to dealing with slave catchers. Henry E. Peck spoke for many: the type of resistance employed had to be tailored to what Peck, writing from Rochester, New York, called the "character of the wrong" and the circumstances in which it occurred. In some instances, passive resistance was appropriate, in others,

---

[55] Loguen, *The Rev. J. W. Loguen as a Slave and a Freeman,* 397; *Impartial Citizen,* April 10, 1850; *Liberator,* April 12, 1850; Cleveland *Herald,* September 2, 1850. For Delany's speech see Victor Ullman, *Martin R. Delany. The Beginnings of Black Nationalism* (Boston: 1971), 112. Carleton Mabee calculates that there were forty-seven declarations of defiance in the first six months after the passage of the law. Of these, eleven called for violent disobedience, eight for nonviolent opposition, and twenty-eight did "not make a clear decision." See Carleton Mabee, *Black Freedom. The Nonviolent Abolitionists from 1839 through the Civil War* (New York: 1970), 416–17. The entire poem is published in the Syracuse *Standard,* October 9, 1850. My thanks to Angie Murphy for a copy of the newspaper.

noncompliance, and in yet others, violence.[56] This approach gained some traction as the forms of resistance to the law evolved over the course of the decade.

These early and frequently repeated declarations of resistance, violent or otherwise, set the background to a widespread and often heated debate in the North over the meaning and significance of the law. Not surprisingly, local newspapers drove as well as reported on the debate. As a rule, the partisan affiliation of a newspaper largely determined the position it took. But the Compromise, and especially the Fugitive Slave Law, did complicate these responses. Those with Whig proclivities divided depending on whether they supported the Fillmore administration or the president's opponents in the party, such as William Seward. Democratic newspapers were also divided over the issue. Those who supported Ben Wade, Salmon Chase, and Joshua Giddings and the Free Democrats in Ohio and elsewhere, staunch opponents of slavery, took positions diametrically opposed to those who toed the conventional Democrat line.

The editor of the New York *Herald* was fond of claiming that his newspaper was an independent force free from normal political shackles. Yet his position on the law was in unison with that of the Democratic Party. The Compromise, which he fondly considered an "adjustment," rather than a full-blown compromise, was, he maintained, the work of a handful of farsighted senators, including Cass, Webster, Clay, Foote, and Dickinson, as well as the "independent press," led by the *Herald,* that appealed to the country's patriotism against "fanaticism and ultraism" to resolve the dispute over slavery in a way that looked to the interests of both sections. This group had risen above sectional interests in search of a "generous, liberal, and comprehensive adjustment of the whole territorial question," one that could win the approval of the "moderate, sensible and patriotic masses of the people." When the "adjustment" ran into opposition, the editor retreated into his customary vitriol in defense of what he thought was his and the country's best interests.

In Detroit, the *Free Press,* which long saw itself as the region's leading Democratic bulwark against forces that threatened the country's political stability, ran almost daily editorials, each progressively more intemperate than the other, against opponents of the law. It insisted there was no difference between the 1793 and 1850 laws except that the latter multiplied the "facilities for the recapture of slaves." Claims that the law imposed penalties on those who refused to assist in the recapture of runaways were baseless. In their customary fashion, abolitionists had whipped themselves into a lather, their

---

[56] *National Era,* September 12, November 21, 1850; *Anti Slavery Standard,* October 17, 1850; Rochester *American,* October 15, 1850. For a position similar to Bailey's see John Smith's letter in Cleveland *True Democrat,* November 29, 1851 and "Address of the Pennsylvania Abolition Society to the People of Color in Relation to the Fugitive Slave Bill Passed by the Congress of the United States in 1850," in Pennsylvania Anti-Slavery Society Papers, Pennsylvania Historical Society, Philadelphia, Pennsylvania.

"insolent schemes" designed to push the South to leave the Union. But before this could happen, the editor predicted, they and "their fugitive slaves shall be driven from the country." Concerned citizens must rally to put a stop to any further agitation in support of uneducated, "half-civilized" slaves who lived either upon the sympathy of the community or by "plunder." Agitation threatened to involve "millions of the Anglo-Saxon race in a worse bondage." One Springfield, Illinois, newspaper spoke for many Democrats in the state: those who opposed the law, it declared flatly, were "enemies of the Union."[57]

Some Democratic newspapers tried to turn a blind eye to what was happening. The Buffalo *Courier* announced, almost hopefully, that the Compromise measures had ended all bitterness and strife once and for all. It had forced extremists in both sections into isolation. Its Whig counterpart was not so certain. While it distrusted abolitionists, it worried that, by its action, Congress had provided abolitionists with fodder to continue their attacks on slavery. There was simply no need for the new law; with some tweaking, the old law could have served its constitutional purpose adequately. As it stood, the new law was a dead letter, unenforceable where, as in Buffalo, it did not meet with public approval. But like most Whig newspapers, the editor insisted that, because the law had been legally enacted by the representatives of the people, it had to be obeyed until it could be successfully challenged in court or repealed by an act of Congress. How this was to be achieved without agitation, and why anyone would take a case to a Supreme Court, a majority of whose members were slaveholders, the editor did not say. Nonetheless, he suspected that public reaction to fugitive slave cases in the city and elsewhere in the North would keep the political kettle on the boil. His colleague in Rochester doubted the law would be repealed or even modified, but he was convinced that the South would soon come to the realization that it did violence to every notion of rights held dear in the North. That, and the fact that runaways showed no interest in returning, he predicted, would compel a new approach to this vexing problem. But he did not see fit to offer an alternative that would address the demands of the slaveholders, the needs of the fugitives and, as he saw it, the reluctance of Northerners to become active agents in the recapture of runaways.[58]

While Northern editors debated the meaning and significance of the law and agonized over how or if it could be implemented, there were signs from other quarters that if the federal law could not be immediately repealed, some state authorities would make it next to impossible for it to function as intended. In states such as Pennsylvania, which, given its location adjoining three Slave States, was critical to the implementation of the law, there was a law that

---

[57] New York *Herald*, September 9, 1850; Detroit *Free Press*, October 8, 9, 10, 15, 1850; Springfield *Register*, September 14, 26, October 4, 1850.

[58] Buffalo *Courier*, September 21, 1850; Buffalo *Express*, September 17, 20, October 18, 1850; Rochester *Democrat*, December 19, 1850; Rochester *American*, October 9, 1850. See also Albany *Argus*, November 30, 1850, and Albany *Evening Journal*, November 21, 1850, for similar exchanges.

barred state and local prisons from holding suspected fugitive slaves while their cases were being adjudicated. The 1847 law would impede the work of commissioners and marshals in the months after the passage of the Fugitive Slave Law. Yet efforts to repeal what some Democrats considered an act of "nullification" were resisted by Governor William Johnson, a Whig. It was not until Johnson's defeat in the wake of the death of a slaveholder at the hands of slaves he was attempting to recapture in Christiana in September 1851 that the offending section of the law was finally repealed.[59]

Within weeks of the passage of the federal law, a joint resolution of the House and Senate of Vermont expressed its disapproval of the law for its violation of the "first principles of civil liberty and of the Constitution" for, among other reasons, its transferring of judicial authority to commissioners, and its denial of habeas corpus and trial by jury for the accused. As such, the law placed "the liberty of the citizens at the mercy of cupidity and fraud." In mid-November 1850, the legislators adopted a competing state law to guarantee to all those claimed as fugitive slaves the right to a trial by jury and habeas corpus. There were few fugitive slaves living in Vermont at the time, but the state had a long and cherished history of opposition to slavery. In the new law the state reconfirmed that opposition and at the same time thumbed its nose at the South by sending copies to Southern legislatures. In his annual message, the governor insisted that the law was designed to give the accused fugitive slave "the way and means of having his claim to freedom established by a judicial tribunal and proffering the professional aid of the State's Attorney to defend him from any unlawful seizure not warranted by the law and the Constitution." The habeas corpus provision, he observed, "protects the citizen from all unlawful imprisonment, and it matters not how obscure the person illegally detained, or how high the pretended authority who claim to detain." It was a stunning statement for its declaration that the state considered a fugitive slave a "citizen." The act and governor's message angered Southern legislators, who threatened retaliation. Vermont's actions generated widespread condemnation, accusations of nullification and a coupling of the state with South Carolina as the twin evils of extremism that endangered the future of the nation.[60]

---

59 *Pennsylvania Freeman*, January 30, 1852; Philadelphia *Evening Bulletin*, February 5, 1852; Washington, DC, *Union*, January 16, March 23, June 27, July 24, October 11, 1851; Harrisburg *Whig State Journal*, August 12, 1851; *National Era*, July 3, 1851; W. W. Griest, ed., *Pennsylvania Archives*, Vol. 7, *Papers of the Governors* (Harrisburg: 1902), 491–96, 520.

60 *Journal of the House of Representatives of the State of Vermont, October Session, 1850* (Burlington, VT: 1851), 30–31, 59–60, 183, 169, 265, 302; *Journal of the Senate of the State of Vermont, October Session, 1850* (Burlington, VT: 1850), 262–63, 266; Burlington *Watchman and State Journal*, November 28, 1850; *Liberator*, December 19, 26, 1850, January 17, 1851; New York *Tribune*, October 23, 1851. A similar bill was submitted to the New York legislature, but as one newspaper opposed to the measure reported, it was sent to the judiciary committee to "take a nap." Albany *Argus*, January 11, 23, April 25, 1851; Rochester *American*, January 14, 1851; Buffalo *Express*, January 15, 1851. See also Springfield *Republican*, March 31, 1851,

Although the Virginia legislature received resolutions from New Hampshire, Maryland, Indiana, and Illinois condemning both the Vermont law and the growing call for repeal of the Fugitive Slave Law, both the Virginia governor and the legislature saw Vermont's position as the entering wedge of a broader Northern movement to defy federal law and deny Virginia's citizens their constitutional rights. In his annual message, Gov. John B. Floyd called for the levying of a 10 percent tax on all produce from non-slaveholding states as retaliation for "gratuitous intermeddling with our slaves." The way the federal law was received in the North was "nothing short of open rebellion and utter defiance." Floyd condemned the many impediments put in the way of recapturing fugitive slaves. "It is a thing of constant occurrence," he observed, "to see the master, in pursuit of his slave, openly insulted and outraged, treated with more contumely and contempt than if he were himself a fugitive from justice, fleeing the crime of murder." The law had been received in the North as if it were the "proclamation of an invading foe." These reactions, he concluded, were "eminently calculated to embitter still more the feeling of enmity between the free and slave states."[61]

Floyd was an active member of his state's Southern Rights Association, which held its organizational meeting in early December 1850. The first association of its kind had been organized in South Carolina in 1848 and spread to Virginia, Mississippi, North Carolina, Alabama, and Florida, following the adoption of the Compromise. The Virginia association brought together those opposed to "Northern aggression upon Southern Rights," to promote the interests of merchants and manufacturers, to resist the stranglehold of and reliance on non-slaveholding states and, as Dan H. Landon, a wholesale dry goods dealer and importer, who presided at its founding meeting said, to demand the enforcement of the Fugitive Slave Law "at every hazard." The organization planned to pressure state government to boycott Northern goods, especially those from Massachusetts and Vermont, the two states it considered leaders in opposition to the Compromise and the new federal law. Its auxiliary in Prince George County went a step further, calling not only for a boycott of Northern goods, but also for not hiring Northern school teachers, terminating any association with Northern preachers not connected to a Southern church, banning the distribution of Northern newspapers that did not promote Southern interests, refusing to ship goods in Northern vessels and refusing to take pleasure

for a similar measure submitted to the Massachusetts legislature. In 1840, Vermont had adopted a law guaranteeing trial by jury, the right to counsel, and the benefit of habeas corpus to those claimed as fugitive slaves. Three years later, it passed a law banning state judges, magistrates, and justices of the peace from recognizing or granting certificates to anyone claiming a fugitive slave under the 1793 federal law. Wilbur H. Siebert, *Vermont's Anti-Slavery and Underground Railroad* (Columbus, OH: 1937), 52–55.

[61] *Journal of the Senate of the Commonwealth of Virginia Begun and Held in the Capitol, in the City of Richmond on Monday the Second day of December in the Year One Thousand Eight Hundred and Fifty* (Richmond: 1850), 31–34.

trips to the North. Clearly, the years of frustrations with Northern handling of fugitive slave cases, and the apparent increase of abolitionist activities, had come to a head in the weeks since the passage of the federal law. Dr. Thomas E. Peter said it best: "We are sick and tired of our dependence upon a people who have no fraternal feelings for us farther than their interests." Nathaniel F. Bowe thought he saw a wider conspiracy. As he told the association, he was prepared to die before "the people of New England and Old England should take his negroes."[62]

The association reflected the sentiments of many other similar organizations in the South. The test of Northern commitment to the Union, they all asserted, was its willingness to enforce the Fugitive Slave Law. A meeting in Edenton, North Carolina, for instance, called on state legislatures to impose a tax on Northern goods and warned that, if resistance to the federal law and agitation over slavery continued, the Union would be destroyed. Why were there calls for a boycott, one editor wanted to know, when the federal law had done more to protect Southern property than any similar enactment? But his was a largely lonely voice. There were other voices, however, which called for going further than the Virginia association, and doing so immediately, for the Fugitive Slave Law, they argued, was not worth the paper on which it was printed because the North had shown little interest in its enforcement. Like Aaron's rod, resistance had come to dominate Northern politics. The law was a "poor boon" received by the South in exchange for "the surrender of its rights in the vast territories acquired by the war" with Mexico. A couple of fugitives might on occasion be returned in the first few weeks after the passage of the law, another editor predicted, but once Northern public opinion swung into action the law would be unenforceable.[63]

Under such circumstances, it was best if the South left the Union immediately. Those proposing secession had convened in Nashville, Tennessee, in June 1850 as the congressional debate over the compromise proposals dragged on interminably. The 176 delegates were roused to action by Nathaniel Beverley Tucker, a leading constitutional expert and professor at the College of William and Mary, who condemned the proposed compromise as a delusion and a plot to rob the South of its liberties. Cass, Clay, Webster, and the others who were its principal promoters were all charlatans. If South Carolina, Georgia, Alabama, Florida, and Mississippi were to leave, Tucker predicted, others would follow immediately. Together they could withhold cotton and bring the economies of the North and England to their knees. To postpone secession, Robert Barnwell

[62] Minute Book, Central Southern Rights Association of Virginia, 1850–1860, Virginia Historical Society, Richmond, Virginia. See minutes for December 7, 11, 1850; Richmond *Whig*, December 13, 1850; Norfolk *Southern Argus*, December 14, 1850; Eric H. Walther, *William Lowndes Yancey and the Coming of the Civil War* (Chapel Hill, NC: 2006), 128.

[63] Jefferson City *Enquirer*, September 14, 1850; Norfolk *Southern Argus*, October 8, 1850; Nashville *American*, June 27, 1851; *Georgia Telegraph*, October 22, 1850.

Rhett of South Carolina counseled, was to give the false impression that the South cherished the Union more than it did slavery. But to the disappointment of Tucker, Rhett, and the other promoters of secession, the meeting decided to be cautious and wait on the conclusion of the congressional debate before deciding on what action to take and to meet again in Nashville in November. The disunionists continued to push their cause in the intervening months. In September, William Lowndes Yancey called for the convening of a "Congress of Southern States." But none of these efforts bore fruit and when the delegates left Nashville in November they had little to show for their efforts. As Fergus Bordewich and others have shown, fulfilling Calhoun's dream of creating a bloc of Southern states willing to work for independence had fizzled.[64]

Southern opponents of secession dismissed both the June and November meetings as a "festering ulcer upon the body politic." In response, anti-secessionists organized a series of pro-union meetings in Nashville, Tennessee, Jackson, Mississippi, and elsewhere. Dominated by Southern Whigs, such as Andrew Jackson Donelson, Felix Zollicoffer, and Andrew Ewing, the Nashville meeting declared that Southerners were, by and large, a "Union-loving, law-abiding people" who recognized the Constitution as the only legitimate law provider. While the meeting condemned what it called the Northern "riots" against the Fugitive Slave Law, it also denied that states had a constitutional right to secede. While the Jackson meeting covered similar ground, it was equally critical of leading politicians in the state, especially the governor and the legislature that had endorsed the resolutions of the June Nashville meeting.[65]

The editor of the Baltimore *Sun* spoke for many of those who occupied the middle ground between the secessionists and those in the North unalterably opposed to the law, between what another editor described as "Abolitionist Fury" and "Southern Brimstone." The *Sun* had no doubt that the new law was necessary given that individual Northern states had failed to meet their constitutional obligation and had made the situation worse by passing laws that impeded the restoration of fugitive slaves. But sounding surprisingly like Salmon Chase, the editor lamented that it would have been far more "honorable, and vastly more in conformity with the federative relations, for each State to have made provisions for the delivery of fugitive slaves, upon the established claims of the owner" rather than force the federal government to take on that responsibility. The editor was even concerned about the aims of the upcoming Union meeting in New York City. What was most needed at this juncture were cool heads and measured discussions of the merits of the law.

[64] Eric H. Walther, *The Fire-Eaters* (Baton Rouge: 1992), 47, 61; Walther, *William Lowndes Yancey*, 122–23; Bordewich, *America's Great Debate*, 256–58; Freehling, *The Road to Disunion*, 181–86; *National Era*, October 24, 1850.

[65] Nashville *True Whig*, November 21, 26, 1850; Baltimore *Sun*, October 4, 1850; Nashville *Union*, October 7, 1850. For the Union meeting in Mobile, Alabama, see the Mobile *Advertiser*, October 12, 1850 in Washington, DC, *Union*, October 19, 1850.

But he had no doubt that, in the end, the law would have the effect all reasonable people desired. He predicted that, if Northern states enforced the law, it would improve the condition of the slaves to a "merely nominal condition," as masters would feel secure in their property and so allow greater freedoms to the slaves.[66]

The results of the law's effectiveness in the first few months after its passage were distinctly mixed, in spite of widespread efforts by slaveholders to reclaim those who had absconded. Some fugitives were successfully returned, but these successes were punctuated by a few spectacular failures and, in a handful of instances, dramatic rescues of suspected fugitives by blacks and their white supporters. When measured by how effective it was in returning runaways, the law left a great deal to be desired. And more alarming, renditions generally produced a firestorm of protest in the cities and towns where they occurred. Beyond their potential for violence, such disputes fueled continued debate over the merits, constitutionality, and fairness of the law and, as far as Southern observers were concerned, produced a toxic alliance of "colored fugitives," "full-blooded abolitionists," and free blacks who were working to destroy the Union by first undermining the law. The active participation of "runaway negroes" in many Northern public meetings and, in some cases, their involvement in rescues, was, according to one Southern editor, a "gross insult to the nation." One way to address, if not totally quiet, continued agitation was to declare a moratorium on any future discussions of the law among politicians and to pledge, as both major parties did, not to vote for anyone who did not support the Compromise in its entirety. The prescription to end the agitation turned on a number of approaches working simultaneously: enforce the law and pledge not to repeal or amend it; repeal all personal liberty laws, such as those adopted by Massachusetts, Vermont, and Pennsylvania; silence abolitionists and Southern extremists; and declare that the Compromise was final and could not be modified or repealed. Pennsylvania Whigs took this approach. In a meeting in Philadelphia in late February 1851, the majority committed to support all aspects of the Compromise and called for the repeal of the "obnoxious features" of the state's 1847 law. They also acknowledged the right of "a citizen of another State to secure his property, which he may find within our borders," and pledged to furnish a slaveholder with "such facilities he may in such case require." Both national parties' platforms also declared the dispute over slavery "finally settled" by the Compromise. By the end of January 1851, 44 of Congress's 290 members had signed a pledge not to vote for anyone who did not support all the Compromise's measures. Others would later add their name to the roster.[67]

---

[66] Baltimore *Sun*, October 29, 31, November 2, 1850.

[67] Washington, DC, *Union*, October 20, 1850; Baltimore *Republican* (n.d.), in Norfolk *Southern Argus*, October 8, 1850; *Pennsylvania Freeman*, March 6, 1851; Baltimore *American*, September 5, 1851; New York *Tribune* (n.d.), in Ripley *Bee*, February 8, 1851.

Yet as far as moderates were concerned, extremists in both sections continued to threaten the effectiveness of this tenuous approach. In the North, a single slave rescue could and usually did upset the political calm, and in the South, disunionists, such as the leaders of Southern Rights Associations, continued to call for immediate secession. The Boston rescue of the fugitive slave Shadrach Minkins in February 1851, for example, generated heated discussions in Congress. The rescue angered Henry Clay, who spoke for many supporters of the law when he asked if the country was to be ruled by a black mob. He also demanded immediate action from President Fillmore. Concerned about the potential for civil strife, a Boston editor tried to quiet the rising fury. Reverence for the Union, he pleaded, required that all allow the law to be peaceably executed. Instead of using force to free suspected fugitives, those opposed to the return of fugitive slaves should purchase their freedom while simultaneously working to repeal the law. The outcome might not be predictable, the editor conceded, but the actions of opponents should always be guided by the biblical precept that time works its wonders: "Truth and purity, ever gentle though powerful in their repose, should calm the judgments, enlighten the understandings, and elevate the moral character of mankind." Only time would destroy the "parasitic evil" of slavery. To act otherwise, he concluded, was to commit treason.[68] The editor's call for cooler heads did not prevail, even when the law was enforced. The economic calculus of renditions rarely favored the slaveholder, as the cost of recapture and return was usually greater than the market value of the runaway. Given how long and hard they had fought for a law that catered to their needs, successful renditions gave slaveholders little comfort and did even less to appease those committed to secession. Simultaneously, tension over recaptures and renditions continued to divide Northern communities.

[68] Boston *Herald*, April 7, 1851. For the call for Southern secession by the South Carolina Southern Rights Association, see the *Liberator*, May 30, 1851.

# 2

# The Law Does Its Work

Long before the passage of the Fugitive Slave Law, the enslaved chose to leave the places and the people they knew, in numbers that could only be guessed at, in search of the unknowns of freedom among strangers in black communities scattered throughout the North and in Canada. They created new lives for themselves among free blacks and other fugitive slaves in cities, towns, and rural hamlets. Those from the Shenandoah Valley of Virginia, for instance, found refuge in black rural settlements in Washington County, and another south of Meadville, Pennsylvania, as well as jobs in the booming economy of Pittsburgh. Those from the northern counties of Maryland headed for the relative safety and anonymity of Philadelphia, Harrisburg, and York. From the eastern districts of Maryland, Virginia, and North Carolina, they headed to such cities as New York, Boston, and New Bedford, Massachusetts, and places in between. They decamped from northern Kentucky to Cincinnati, and Columbus, Ohio, and further north to the small towns and cities that lined the Great Lakes from Chicago and Detroit in the west to Buffalo, Rochester, and Syracuse in the east. Others chose to stay closer to the places they knew in the relative safety of a black rural settlement with a strong Underground Railroad network near Ripley, Brown County, Ohio, just across the river from Kentucky. In 1850, there were reputed to be forty black settlements in the state. Settlements, some established by Quakers in eastern Indiana, drew slaves both from Kentucky and North Carolina. One historian has estimated that there were roughly sixty black settlements in the state by the outbreak of the Civil War. Some of these would disband after the passage of the law, only to be reestablished further north in the state and even further afield in Michigan, Wisconsin, and Canada. Slaves from Missouri headed for black rural settlements in western Illinois, such as the one at Rocky Fork near Alton and to Chicago further north. One distraught delegate to the Illinois State Constitutional Convention that passed a series of draconian laws banning blacks from entering the state pointed to a number of "little settlements" of blacks in the Egypt district of southern Illinois, an area notorious for its unwillingness to tolerate the presence of blacks, but in which, he remarked, fugitive slaves from Missouri found comfort and protection.[1]

The mystery surrounding the lives of those who settled in the North is compounded by the fact that, in 1850, no one knew with any certainty how many fugitives slaves had managed to create new lives for themselves away from slavery. Weeks after the passage of the law, one New York newspaper, partial to the law, boldly asserted that fugitives from slavery were scattered "all over the North, especially in the cities and large towns, and who, for some years past, have resided here as securely as if the Compact between the States…had contained no provisions for their surrender." Its competitor, the New York *Herald*, eager to downplay the size of their presence in the city, thought they numbered just one hundred. In Boston, the large number of fugitives, estimated to number about 1,200 by one calculation, had been in the city for years. One observer put the number in New Bedford, Massachusetts, at seven hundred. As blacks fled the city at the end of 1850, a Pittsburgh editor was genuinely surprised to discover that "so many of the colored people…were runaway slaves." In an effort to gauge the scope of the crisis that the law tried to address, a Charleston, South Carolina, newspaper claimed there were somewhere in the region of thirty thousand fugitives living and working in the North. The New York *Herald* put the figure at half that number, while its crosstown rival, the New York *Tribune,* set the figure at fifty thousand. Over the course of the next few months, as the debate over the law held the attention of legislators in Washington, the *Herald's* figure became the standard measurement of the size of the problem.[2]

---

[1] Howard Wallace, *Historical Sketches of the Underground Railroad from Uniontown to Pittsburgh* (n.p., n.d.), 5. My thanks to Larry Glasco for bringing this pamphlet to my attention; Ellen Eslinger, "Freedom Without Independence: The Story of a Former Slave and Her Family," *Virginia Magazine of History and Biography*, 114 (2006), 264–66; Charles D. Spitts, *The Pilgrim's Pathway. The Underground Railroad in Lancaster Country* (Lancaster, PA.: 1966), 26; Scott Mingus, *The Ground Swallowed Them Up. Slavery and the Underground Railroad in York County, Pa.* (York, PA.: 2016); Ann Hagedorn, *Beyond the River: The Untold Story of the Heroes of the Underground Railroad* (New York: 2002); Keith P. Griffler, *Front Line of Freedom: African Americans and the Forging of the Underground Railroad in the Ohio River Valley* (Lexington, KY: 2004); Stephen A. Vincent, *Southern Seed, Northern Soil: African American Farm Communities in the Midwest, 1765–1900* (Bloomington, IN: 1999); Xenia E. Cord, "Rural Black Settlements in Indiana Before 1860," in Wilma L. Gibbs, ed., *Indiana's African-American Heritage: Essays from Black History News & Notes* (Indianapolis: 1993); Cheryl Janifer LaRoche, *The Geography of Resistance. Free Black Communities and the Underground Railroad* (Urbana, IL: 2014); New York *Tribune*, October 23, 1850; Arthur Charles Cole, ed., *The Constitutional Delegates of 1847* (Springfield, IL: 1919), 202–03.

[2] New York *Journal of Commerce*, October 3, 1850; *North Star*, March 30, 1851; Kathryn Grover, *The Fugitive's Gibraltar: Escaping Slaves and Abolitionism in New Bedford, Massachusetts* (Amherst, MA: 2001), 221; Boston *Herald*, October 3, 1850; Pittsburgh *Journal*, n.d., in *Pennsylvania Freeman*, October 3, 1850; Charleston *Mercury* (n.d.), published in the *New Era*,

Although blacks and their abolitionist supporters had kept abreast of the heated and long, drawn-out debate over the law in Congress, and had prepared themselves for its eventual passage, its adoption, nevertheless, was a firebrand thrown into every black community. Immediately, there were widespread and credible rumors that slave masters and their agents were ready to descend on black communities to reclaim their lost property. Although slaveholders were generally skeptical of the law's efficacy, they were prepared to test it by going after fugitives wherever they lived. It was rumored, for example, that Maryland slaveholders had established a fund "to press the matter with the best talent to be procured at the bar." A number of owners of slaves living in Philadelphia, New York City, Boston, and Springfield, Massachusetts, were the first to test the law's reach by procuring warrants, as the law required in their local communities, and hiring agents to travel north to retake their lost property.[3]

Leaders of black communities, with the aid of their abolitionist supporters, immediately issued warnings alerting fugitives to the presence of slave catchers. Meetings of blacks called on fugitives to arm themselves and pledged to protect those in danger. The warnings, issued by Philadelphia opponents of the law, were fairly representative. Posters plastered throughout the city announced the presence of slave catchers, and, in some instances, provided detailed descriptions. "In person," one such poster announced, "he is nearly 6 feet high, slender, with sandy whiskers, light hair, blue eyes, full moustache, and wears a drab overcoat lined with red."[4] No one could miss him. But these efforts did little to ease the deep fear that gripped black communities. Harriet Jacobs, the North Carolina fugitive, recalled she spent the winter of 1851 in New York City in dread of being recognized by the "snakes and slaveholders" who frequented the city in search of former slaves. Scores fled in the wake of the law. In Boston, Theodore Parker observed movingly: they left like "doves, with plaintive cry, flee from a farmer's barn when summer lighting [sic] stabs the roof." Such poetic imagery was meant to move his audiences – and it did – but Parker knew firsthand that while the exodus was deeply destructive of the lives men, women, and their extended families had created since settling in the city, nothing about their departure was dovelike. Frederick Douglass employed more appropriate imagery: they left, he told an audience, like "a dark train going out of the land, as if fleeing from death." What Parker and Douglass chose to ignore was the fact that those fleeing usually left well-armed, determined not to be retaken.[5]

November 21, 1850; New York *Herald*, September 9, October 10, 1850; New York *Tribune*, November 28, 1850.

3 New York *Tribune*, September, 18, 1850; Baltimore *Clipper* (n.d.), in New York *Tribune*, November 2, 1850; Boston *Herald*, September 30, 1850; Albany *Argus*, October 3, 1850.

4 *Pennsylvania Freeman*, December 26, 1850, February 6, April 4, 1851. Vigilance committees in Boston, New York City, and elsewhere produced similar posters.

5 Harriet A. Jacobs, *Incidents in the Life of a Slave Girl* (Boston: 1861), 150; Henry Steele Commager, *Theodore Parker Yankee Crusader* (Boston: 1960), 229; John Blassingame, ed., *Frederick Douglass Papers*, Series 1, Vol. 2, 1847–54 (New Haven: 1982), 245.

The tragedy is that many of the most vulnerable had integrated themselves fully into the lives of these communities. They joined existing churches and sometimes founded their own, as they did in Boston. They married and started families, found jobs in field and factory, and purchased homes – all the traditional hallmarks of success and independence symbolic assertion of a claim to citizenship. Not long after the law came into effect, a Georgia slaveholder turned up in Saratoga, New York, in search of a former slave who had been brought to the spa in 1846 but who had chosen not to return. Within a year of abandoning her owner, she married a local barber. When her former owner discovered she had left for Canada, he tried unsuccessfully to force her husband to pay, as it were, a ransom of $600. It was a desperate attempt to gain some measure of recompense based on an undisclosed calculation of the former slave's worth. Henry Thomas, who had escaped from Nashville, Tennessee, in 1834 with the support of his mother, Sally, established a relatively prosperous life, as a barber, in Buffalo, New York. Soon after his arrival, he married a free woman and started a family. The success of his business provided him with the means to invest in real estate in and around the city. He also became involved in the state's Negro Conventions and in local meetings that condemned the Fugitive Slave Law. Thomas did not leave immediately, but all the evidence suggests he was deeply troubled by efforts to recapture fugitives in the city. Within a year, he would close his barbershop, sell his property, and move his family to the black settlement in Buxton, Canada. In the wake of reports that warrants had been issued for the arrest of several fugitives in Boston, Jake Latimer, owner of a dance hall and a fugitive from Virginia, fled the city when his former master turned up at his place of business. Particularly vulnerable were those fugitives who, in freedom, had become strident critics of slavery and the recently passed law. Rumors were rife in Syracuse, New York, that slave catchers were searching for Jermain Loguen, the prominent Methodist minister, who had escape slavery in Tennessee many years earlier. In spite of the protection his prominence afforded, Loguen, a militant critic of the law, continually worried about his vulnerability. "I feel myself to be in constant danger," he wrote a colleague, so much so that he did not stray far from the relative safety the city afforded him.[6]

There were some heartrending stories of flight. Three times since his escape, Rev. Bulah had bought property in upstate New York and each time, one local observer reported, he was forced to sell his home and move ahead of slave

[6] *Pennsylvania Freeman*, September 18, 1851; the Thomas incidents are covered in John Hope Franklin and Loren Schweninger, *In Search of the Promised Land. A Slave Family in the Old South* (New York: 2006), 95–99; for the Latimer case see the Boston *Herald*, October 25, 1850. See also Chicago *Democrat*, November 5, 6, 1850, for a similar case; on Loguen see Syracuse *Standard*, October 11, 1850. My thanks to Angela Murphy for a copy of the article. See also Carol M. Hunter, *To Set the Captive Free. Reverend Jermain Loguen and the Struggle for Freedom in Central New York, 1835–1872* (New York: 1993), 114.

catchers. Local supporters in the aptly named village of Jordon, Onondaga County, pledged to protect him but, in the end, had to admit they could not ensure his safety. Bulah finally decided to cross over into Canada. It was a story retold many times in the weeks and months following passage of the law. Quite a number of families, one New Bedford newspaper reported, "where either the father or mother are fugitives have been broken up, and the furniture sold off with a view to leaving for safer quarters, in either Nova Scotia or Canada." After a visit to a small village in the interior of New York, one observer sent word that fugitives settled there were forced to sell property they had acquired. Some of them agonized between leaving all they had built up over the years and the families they had started, or staying put in the hope the community would defend them. But in the end, many, like those in this village, opted for the safety and security of Canada, leaving their "comfortable homes, provided with all the necessities of life," as one editor lamented, to take refuge among strangers in Canada just as winter was setting in. There were reports of fugitives who abandoned their families in a desperate attempt to evade recapture, hoping that they could be reunited later in Canada. One such incident involved a fugitive who had been a slave in Virginia for thirty years, and a resident in Ohio for seventeen, who left his family in the spring of 1851, just ahead of slave catchers. As proponents of the law had asserted, there was to be no statute of limitation.[7]

Fugitives and their families fled in droves in the days and weeks after the law's adoption. The promise of protection by free blacks and white abolitionists fell largely on deaf ears. Forty left Boston in three days. Some of these may have headed north through Vermont, where one historian has estimated fugitive "parties of two or three" arrived almost daily. As word of the law's provisions spread, small groups began to abandon Pittsburgh, Pennsylvania, for places further north. Two hundred left the area before the bill was signed by President Fillmore on September 18th. Six days later, thirty-five more took their leave, followed, three days later, by another one hundred and fifty. Even the gods seemed to be against them. On the evening of the 27th, a hail storm raked the city with stones, one observer reported, as "large as hickory nuts." People were injured, horses ran off, and glass windows throughout the city were shattered. By the end of the month, it was reported, there was a "shortage of waiters at the hotels and of hands on the waterfront." In early October, an Erie, Pennsylvania, newspaper reported that, in one day, forty-five "fugitive slaves" from Pittsburgh passed through the city on their way to Canada. They

[7] *Pennsylvania Freeman*, November 6, 1851; the New Bedford incident is quoted in Grover, *The Fugitives Gibraltar*, 222. The report on New York can be found in the New York *Tribune*, November 11, 1850. See also *Voice of the Fugitive*, January 20, 1851; *Western Citizen*, November 5, 1850; Cleveland *True Democrat*, April 23, 1851. The *Anti-Slavery Standard* ran a regular feature called the "Chronicle of Slave-Hunting," which featured accounts of disruption in the face of attempted recaptures. See, for instance, October 17, 1850.

left in groups, sometimes as large as twenty to fifty, "armed and organized for mutual defense," with "rifles, revolvers and bowie knives." There were rumors of slaveholders in the city searching for runaways. One newspaper, concerned about the potential for violence, breathed a sigh of relief: "It is well that they have gone, since there would almost assuredly have been bloodshed had the masters endeavored to recapture them. The escaped slaves have all armed themselves and declare that they were resolved to die rather than be again carried into bondage." All told, an estimated eight hundred left the area in the last few months of 1850.[8]

By early October, more than three hundred, from unknown locations, had passed through Cleveland on their way to Canada. Roughly forty-three left Detroit in one night following an attempt to retake a fugitive there. One observer may have overestimated the size of the exodus when he reported that 130 members of the Baptist church, and a "considerable number" of Methodists had abandoned Buffalo. George Weir, a member of the Baptist church, dismissed these numbers as sheer fabrication. The church, he insisted, had lost but two or three members. The Baptist church in Rochester was hit hard when 112 of its members left. It is estimated that between two hundred and six hundred blacks left Syracuse in the fall of 1850. Although one Detroit newspaper dismissed these numbers as highly inflated, and a device to undermine the law in the eyes of the public, it was clear that a large number – some estimates placed it as high as two thousand – passed through the city on their way to Canada by the end of the year. By some estimates, another one thousand made their way by different routes to Montreal. The sheer size of the exodus overwhelmed facilities for their reception in lower Ontario.[9]

The scramble to evade recapture was a mix of bravery, determination, and desperation. Many may have chosen to leave their worldly goods behind, but they were equally determined to preserve their freedom in another, and hopefully safer, location. In an effort to ensure their safety, many, such as those who

---

[8] Victor Ullman, *Martin R. Delany. The Beginning of Black Nationalism* (Boston: 1971), 12; Dorothy Sterling, *The Making of an Afro-American. Martin Robison Delany, 1812–1885* (New York: 1971), 119; Pittsburgh *Gazette*, September 24, 25, 1850; Pittsburgh *Post*, September 26, 1850; *Liberator*, October 4, 1850; Gettysburg *Republican Compiler*, October 21, 1850; New York *Tribune*, October 1, 1850.

[9] Gary Collision, "The Boston Vigilance Committee. A Reconsideration," *History Journal of Massachusetts*, 12 (June 1994), 111; *Liberator*, October 18, 1850; John Weiss, *Life and Correspondence of Theodore Parker*, Vol. II (London: 1883), 92; Wilbur H. Siebert, *Vermont Anti-Slavery and the Underground Railroad* (Columbus, OH: 1937), 82–83, 101; Detroit *True Democrat*, October 5, 1850; Chicago *Democrat*, October 21, 1850, March 8, 1851; Buffalo *Express*, October 8, 1850; *North Star*, March 30, 1851; *Pennsylvania Freeman*, March 6, 1851; Fergus M. Bordewich, *America's Great Debate. Henry Clay, Stephen A. Douglas and the Compromise that Preserved the Union* (New York: 2012), 362; Detroit *Free Press*, October 25, 1850. One historian has estimated that three thousand entered Canada by the end of 1850. Fred Landon, "The Negro Migration to Canada After the Passage of the Fugitive Slave Act," *Journal of Negro History*, V. (January 1920), 26–27.

left Pittsburgh in September and October, went well armed. Even more surprising, there were few recorded incidences of recapture during this exodus. Flight, nonetheless, took a terrible toll. The case of the Harris family was atypical, but it shines a light on the price some were willing to pay to reach freedom and avoid recapture. William Harris, his wife Catherine, and their young child had escaped from South Carolina and made their way to Philadelphia, where they were received by members of the local Underground Railroad and sent on to Albany, New York. From there they were sent, via the Erie Canal, to Rochester a few days later. Suspecting they were fugitives, the white crew thought they would play a trick on the family by claiming that their master was hot on their heels. The result was disastrous. In an act of desperation, Catherine jumped into the canal with the child. She was pulled to safety but the baby was not found. William then tried unsuccessfully to slit his throat when he was told by the captain that he had sent for the authorities.[10]

The public pledge by black leaders and their abolitionist supporters to resist the law and to protect fugitives persuaded many to stand their ground. There were also individual acts of defiance in the face of imminent danger. When, for instance, a slave catcher approached a black woman on the streets of Buffalo, the hometown of President Fillmore, she drew a revolver and dared him to take her into custody. He thought better of it. She was not alone; there were reports that many fugitives in the city were well armed and determined to protect themselves. That may help to explain why, in spite of reports to the contrary, the local Baptist church lost so few members. George Weir spoke for many: it would "require more force than any of the Fillmore Clique could summon," he wrote Frederick Douglass, "to drive us from the homes of our adoption, at least in such numbers spoken of." Such acts of defiance were widespread. When slave catchers caught up with Bishop, a blacksmith and fugitive from Kentucky, at his forge near Ripley, Ohio, he shot them and made his escape. In Chicago, Mitchell was persuaded by a slave catcher to return with him to Missouri. A group of blacks had other ideas; they followed the pair, finally catching up with them near Vincennes, Indiana. Mitchell was retaken and sent off to Canada. Cornered at his home near Centerville, Washington County, Pennsylvania, Renols Parker was prepared to defend himself when what was called a "regiment" of blacks came to his assistance and Parker made his escape. Such acts of resistance sometimes ended in disaster, as was the case with the group of ten from Virginia who got lost in the Allegheny Mountains in late September 1850 and were caught by a group of locals following a shootout near Bedford, Pennsylvania. In spite of the odds, fugitives were determined to defend themselves.[11]

---

[10] Syracuse *Standard*, October 24, 28, 1850; Syracuse *Journal*, October 24, 1850. My thanks to Angela Murphy for both references. Troy *Whig*, October 26, 1850; Baltimore *Sun*, October 28, 1850.

[11] Buffalo *Express*, October 8, 1850; *North Star*, March 30, 1851; *Pennsylvania Freeman*, December 5, 1850; New York *Tribune*, November 15, 1850; Chicago *Democrat*, November 1,

This determination to stand their ground may have persuaded some of the less vulnerable, and those with deep roots in their community, to stay a while longer, hopeful that the crisis would blow over. Martha is a case in point. Sometime in 1841, she crossed the Ohio River to New Albany, Indiana, where she later married Charles Rouse. The couple subsequently moved to the black settlement of New Philadelphia in Washington County, convinced they would be more secure there. In the fall of 1851, while Charles was in the fields, five armed slave catchers dragged Martha from their home and headed for Louisville. Although a group of local whites followed and caught up with the slave catchers near Jeffersonville, they failed to win Martha's release. Decisions such as Martha's to see out the law, not surprisingly, tended to fade under the constant danger of recapture. Following the capture of Daniel Davis in August 1851, for example, Henry Thomas, the Buffalo barber, decided that leaving was the better part of valor. It was a pattern replicated in other areas. In the days after the fugitive Rose was taken in Detroit, in October 1850, an estimated three hundred blacks left for Canada, forty-three in one night. Following the capture and rendition of Daniel Franklin and his wife in Columbia, Pennsylvania, in April 1851, scores left the city. Some estimates put the loss at a staggering 40 percent of the resident black population in this small Lancaster County city.[12]

For many in the South, deeply skeptical as they were of the law's efficacy, the dislocation caused by the law, showed, as one Nashville, Tennessee, newspaper gloated, that the medicine was working. Expanding the metaphor, he chortled, "all free-negrodom," finds itself in a deep "fever of anxiety." Not to be outdone, one of his competitors looked to the developments' political impact: the law, he declared, had fallen on "fugitive slaves, free negroes, abolitionists and free soilers in the Northern states, like a bomb-shell amongst a nest of Pirates."[13] These

25, 1850; Wallace, *Historical Sketches of the Underground Railroad*, 6–7. See also Maysville *Eagle*, October 24, 26, November 2, 1850, and the *Anti-Slavery Bugle*, March 8, 1851, for other incidents that occurred when northern Kentucky slave catchers attempted to intercept fugitives in southern Ohio; *Sanduskian*, October 8, 1850; Ashtabula *Sentinel*, October 12, 1850; Lynchburg *Virginian*, October 10, 1850.

[12] Coy D. Robbins, *Reclaiming African Heritage at Salem, Indiana* (Bowie, MD: 1995), 103; Charles H. Money, "The Fugitive Slave Law in Indiana," *Indiana Magazine of History*, Vol. XVII (September 1921), 272–73; Buffalo *Express*, October 8, 1850; *North Star*, March 30, 1851; Franklin and Schweninger, *In Search of the Promised Land*, 98–99; New York *Tribune*, October 15, 1850; Baltimore *Sun*, October 21, 1850; Roy Finkenbine, "A Community Militant and Organized: the Colored Vigilant Committee of Detroit," in Karolyn Smardz Frost and Veta Smith Tucker, *A Fluid Frontier. Slavery, Resistance, and the Underground Railroad in the Detroit River Borderland* (Detroit: 2016), 160; Fergus Bordewich, *America's Great Debate*, 362, sets the 40 percent figure. Benjamin Quarles, on the other hand, states that the loss of 487 of the city's 943 black inhabitants occurred over a five-year period. See Quarles, *Black Abolitionists* (New York: 1969), 200; Mingus, *The Ground Swallowed Them Up*, 118; Charles Garlick, who had escaped from Virginia in 1843 and settled in Ashtabula, Ohio, decided to leave for Canada only after the death of his benefactor in 1852. See Charles A. Garlick, *Life Including His Escape and Struggle for Liberty* (n.p., 1902), 8.

[13] Nashville *Republican Banner*, October 2, 1850; Nashville *True Whig*, October 3, 5, 1850; Nashville *Union*, October 15, 1850.

Nashville editors echoed the views of those in the South who viewed the law as the cornerstone on which the political edifice of the Compromise, and by extension, the future of the Union, rested. Many in the North agreed; were this "adjustment'" to the Constitution to fail, the Union would be imperiled. They spoke with one voice: the law had to be enforced at all costs by the federal government. If the exodus in the fall of 1850 was an appropriate measure of the law's impact then the enemies of the Union in the North, particularly abolitionists, free blacks and their political allies, as well as those in the South who doubted its usefulness, had been vanquished. But such gleeful political calculations rested uneasily with those familiar with what was actually happening.

Even as many blacks were moving to safer locations in Canada and other areas of the North, they were being replaced by what some believed was an even larger number of new escapees from the South. While it is not easy to predict the destination of those fleeing in the weeks and months following passage of the law, advertisements published in newspapers from Norfolk, Virginia, in the east to St. Louis, Missouri, in the west, and places in between, point to a steady flow of fugitives. Some slaveholders went beyond the usual physical descriptions – color of skin and hair, facial features, visible scars, gait, disposition, etc. – contained in published and printed advertisement to speculate on the likely destination of fugitives. They were not being overly sensational; they knew, with some degree of certainty, where escapees were heading, especially if they had family or friends in the North, and whether they had acquired passes to aid their escape. When, in September 1851, the Maryland slaveholder Edward Gorsuch finally decided to go after his slaves, he knew they were with family and friends in Christiana, Pennsylvania. When Henry Banks fled Front Royal, Virginia, in early 1853, his master was certain the slave was planning to join his brother in western Pennsylvania.[14] For the rest of the decade, a local newspaper in the upper South reported on the regular stream of fugitives. J. Blaine Hudson's "Kentucky Fugitive Slave Data Base," which covers the years 1788 to 1861, shows that fully 42 percent of all advertised escapes occurred between 1850 and 1859. Even more significant were the numbers of females, children, and older women found in the ads covering the decade. Group escapes, or what slaveholders took to calling stampedes, Hudson shows, increased substantially, accounting for fully 36 percent of the escapes in the 1850s. It is not always easy to determine how many made it to a Free State, but if one were a slave in Jefferson County, Kentucky, just across the Ohio River from Indiana, it is very likely Indiana, or places further north, were probable destinations. Others, the records show, made their way through

---

[14] For an account of the conflict that followed Gorsuch's arrival in Christiana see Thomas P. Slaughter, *Bloody Dawn. The Christiana Riot and Racial Violence in the Antebellum North* (New York: 1991) and for the correspondence following Banks's escape see Kenneth Stampp, ed., "Records of the Ante-Bellum Southern Plantations from the Revolution through the Civil War" (microfilm), series E, reel 9.

Madison, Indiana, and from there by boat to Cincinnati, Ohio, or by train to Indianapolis. In mid-1851, it was reported that three slaves from Louisville made it safely to Canada, although they were pursued all the way to Lake Erie. A cursory look at ads published in a couple of Lexington, Kentucky, newspapers shows there were thirteen escapes from the area between August and December 1850, a pattern that continued throughout 1851. A similar pattern held true for other parts of the upper South. In November 1850, a family of seven, including five children, escaped from Miles River Neck, near Easton on the Eastern Shore of Maryland. Weeks earlier, a mother and her five children made it safely out of Middletown, west of Frederick, Maryland. Two others had left the same town days earlier. Local newspapers recorded the escape of a family of five, two owned by Thomas Ashcon, two by William Stevens, and the fifth by John Bryan. This was the kind of escape that obviously required careful planning on the part of the slaves. In early December, a mother and her five children left Chestertown, Maryland. As far as one Kentucky editor was concerned, these group escapes may not have achieved the levels of a plague, but they were, nonetheless, a "leave-taking fever" that seemed to defy all cures.[15]

The solution to this malady, many insisted (or, more appropriately, hoped) was the unflinching enforcement of the law. Senator James Mason of Virginia, its principal architect, suggested the legal apparatus essential not only to the recovery of "fugitives from labor," but, equally as important, to the curtailment of the activities of those who had long supported and facilitated the escape and protection of slaves in Northern communities: the appointment of commissioners in every city and county in the North. Mason's plan would, in effect, create a massive legal bureaucracy backed by an enforcement mechanism of marshals and deputy marshals with the potential to reach into all areas of the North. In fact, the law envisaged as many as three commissioners assigned to every county, a recommendation scoffed at by Salmon Chase and other opponents. Why, Chase declared in disbelief, his home state of Ohio would require 261 – 3 commissioners in each of its 87 counties – to enforce a law he considered palpably unconstitutional, especially when these were men who Chase's colleague William Dayton of New Jersey dismissed as men of little "judicial acquirements...persons having but a limited legal or judicial experience."[16]

---

[15] *Liberator,* August 6, 1852; J. Blaine Hudson, *Fugitive Slaves and the Underground Railroad in Kentucky Borderland* (Jefferson, NC: 2002), 31–48. See the Lexington *Observer and Reporter* and the *Kentucky Statesman* for the period between July 1850 and December 1851; Louisville *Courier,* June 12, 1851; Easton *Democrat* (n.d.), in Baltimore *Sun,* November 12, 1850; Baltimore *Sun,* October 7, 1850; Gettysburg *Republican Compiler,* October 14, 1850; Chestertown *News* (n.d.), in Baltimore *Sun,* December 3, 1850; Maysville *Post Boy* (n.d.), in Louisville *Journal,* May 5, 7, 1851; Maysville *Eagle* (n.d.), in Ripley *Bee,* May 17, 1851.

[16] *Appendix to the Congressional Globe, First Session, Thirty-First Congress* (Washington, DC: 1850), 477, 1590. Two years later Charles Sumner, himself a former commissioner in Boston, dismissed the commissioners as a "mere mushroom of courts" in his maiden speech

Chase, Dayton, and others refused to concede that the original Fugitive Slave Law of 1793 was, as Mason insisted, a dead letter. Something had to be done, a new mechanism found, Mason declared, to ensure enforcement of the constitutional requirement to return those who had escaped slavery. The office of commissioner, in use since the early decades of the century, had been created as a way to get around the refusal of states to enforce some federal laws. They were vested with responsibilities that resembled those of state magistrates and justices of the peace. They were nothing more, Samuel Nelson, former associate justice of the Supreme Court argued, than a "substitution" for state magistrates who were prevented by state law from enforcing the 1793 federal law.[17]

Under the new law, the remit of commissioners was vastly expanded. Whereas in the past they served a largely ministerial function, now they were expected to act in a quasi-judicial role. Not surprisingly, much of the controversy over the law came to rest squarely on the office: How were they to be appointed and by whom? How were they to be remunerated? What were their powers? If these were courts with traditional judicial powers, could Congress grant them the power to adjudicate cases? Could their decisions be appealed? What was to be their remit? What was to be the length of their appointment? And was it constitutionally permissible for Congress to vest the power of selection to justices of circuit and territorial courts? George Badger, senator from North Carolina, thought that, by putting their appointment in the hands of circuit court justices, Congress hoped to minimize the chance that political consideration would influence the selection process. Selected by judges who were, he believed, "separated from all the ordinary influences which may pervert the judgment of men; and because selected by, and amenable to, such judges, the commissioners themselves will be removed from such influences." William Jay, the New York abolitionist, had little truck with Badger's reasoning. A person whose usual function was taking affidavits, he declared, was now to be "elevated to the office and dignity of a JUDGE." They were not to be elected, as Jay argued they should be, but were to be appointed by federal judges. "Among the wonders of the times," he scoffed, "is the discovery of judicial generation" by which "judges procreate judges...for the convenience of the slaveholders." Supporters of the law countered that these were largely administrative positions, their responsibilities limited to conducting hearings, not trials, to determine if certificates of return should be granted to someone who claimed a slave. Under the law, a slaveholder who had lost a slave would

to Congress. See *Appendix to the Congressional Globe, First Session, Thirty-Second Congress* (Washington, DC: 1852), 1112.

[17] See Charles Lindquist, "The Origins and Development of the United States Commissioner System," *American Journal of Legal History*, 14 (1970), 1–7. For a more dated history of the system see Allen Johnson, "The Constitutionality of the Fugitive Slave Acts," *Yale Law Journal*, 31 (1921–22), 170–71, which argues that commissioners merely had "concurrent jurisdiction with the judges of the District and Circuit Courts." Albany *Argus*, June 6, 1851.

go before a local magistrate and show that the person he owned had escaped. If convinced, the magistrate would issue a warrant for the slave's recapture, embossed with an official seal. The certificates would then be presented by the slaveholder or his agent to a commissioner who would determine if a warrant of arrest should be issued. Although hearings before the commissioners were meant to be summary, with no testimony permitted, commissioners found themselves under constant pressure from lawyers for the accused to permit testimony. Contrary to the law, hearings were invariably transformed into full-blown trials. Finally, commissioners were paid a fee for their services, the size of remuneration depending on the outcome: if the accused slave were returned, the commissioner received $10; if the decision went against the claimant, the payment was halved to $5. Not surprisingly, many considered the fee structure a bribe – an incentive, as it were, for commissioners to rule in favor of slave owners. The "ten dollar judges...spawned into existence by the law," as Senator John Hale of New Hampshire dismissed them, would be in the eye of the storm over the law for the rest of the decade.[18]

There were areas where new commissioners were never appointed because no one could be found who would agree to serve. The authorities compensated by simply appointing current commissioners to adjudicate fugitive slave cases. Of the six sitting commissioners in Boston, for example, only two would hear cases under the law. In spite of Senator George Badger's reasoning, appointments were generally based on political considerations – those who judges knew would enforce the law. The Harrisburg, Pennsylvania, commissioner, Richard McAllister, was fairly representative. Like many others, his was the result of political connections; his father had lobbied US Supreme Court Justice Robert Grier to have his son named commissioner of Dauphin County. The McAllister family were among the last slaveholders in the state, and Richard had been trained in a law office in Savannah, Georgia. At his first hearing, on the day of his appointment, McAllister returned two slaves – Samuel Wilson and George Brocks – to their Virginia owners. Over the next fifteen months, he heard seven additional cases, each time ruling in favor of the claimant. In each case, he refused to allow attorneys, who had volunteered to represent the fugitives, to cross-examine witnesses for the claimant. All hearings were held in McAllister's cramped offices, where there were no facilities for lawyers and whose size had the added advantage of limiting the number of potential supporters who could attend to disrupt or influence the proceedings. If he did not allow representation, McAllister was not shy about asking the accused the

[18] Albany *Evening Journal*, October 18, 1850; *Anti-Slavery Standard*, October 17, 1850; *The Fugitive Slave Bill; its History and Unconstitutionality With an Account of the Seizure and Enslavement of James Hamlet* (New York: 1850), 18–19; *Liberator*, September 27, November 1, 1850; *Appendix to the Congressional Globe, First Session, Thirty-First Congress* (Washington, DC: 1850), 388; *Congressional Globe, Second Session, Thirty-Second Congress* (Washington, DC: 1852), 991.

sorts of questions that would have been impermissible in any court of law. He would frequently asked suspected fugitives if they wished to return to their masters. When lawyers tried to raise objections, he ridiculed them, insisting it was within his mandate as a magistrate to determine the views of the slave. Slaveholders in search of warrants for the arrest of fugitives anywhere in middle Pennsylvania beat a path to McAllister's door, assured of a friendly reception. Although it is clear that he was appointed a commissioner for the city and county, he was not averse to issuing warrants for the arrest of fugitives outside his jurisdiction. As McAllister's actions demonstrate, commissioners could – and frequently did – reach beyond their remit. The law was, it appears, what commissioners such as McAllister said it was. Within a year of his appointment, McAllister could boast with some justification that more fugitives had "been remanded by me than any other U.S. Com." The precautions he had taken – holding speedy hearings, appointing large police forces to remand fugitives, and keeping the black community and their supporters from interfering with his decisions – meant that, in Harrisburg, the law was not subverted as it was elsewhere. "It is much better for the peace and interest of the country," he rationalized in a letter to a superior, "that proper force should be employed than by a niggardly parsimony that Fugitives should escape and their claimants and the U.S officers killed." His was the sort of success story that proponents of the law had hoped for. But in his enthusiasm, McAllister inevitably overreached. It was widely rumored that, at times, he had benefitted financially by actively colluding with slaveholders in the recapture of their slaves. In the end, the community, which he had vowed to protect from being overrun by escaping slaves, turned against him, repulsed by the accusations leveled against him and wary of the zeal he brought to the job. McAllister resigned his commission in March 1853 and headed for a new life, first in Iowa where he practiced law, and later in the Kansas Territory, where he became deputy secretary to the governor with responsibility for ending John Brown's guerilla activities in the territory.[19]

McAllister's colleague in Philadelphia, Edward D. Ingraham, was equally as uncompromising in his enforcement of the law. Unlike the Harrisburg commissioner, however, he was forced by the sheer weight of public opinion, and unremitting pressure from the black community, to, on occasion, concede to the demands from defense lawyers to permit the cross-examination of witness for slaveholders and to present witnesses for defendants. Even when he permitted black witnesses to testify, as he did in the case of Adam Gibson in late 1850, Ingraham made it clear he would not be influenced by their testimony. Like McAllister, Ingraham also had a passionate dislike of black people – something

[19] For the history of McAllister's activities see R. J. M. Blackett, *Making Freedom. The Underground Railroad and the Politics of Slavery* (Chapel Hill, NC: 2013), 36–51; See also the pathbreaking essay by George G. Eggert, "The Impact of the Fugitive Slave Law on Harrisburg: A Case Study," *Pennsylvania Magazine of History and Biography*, 109 (October 1985).

he found impossible to conceal. During Gibson's hearing, David Paul Brown, attorney for the accused, and a man proud to be a member of the venerable Abolition Society, confronted Ingraham directly: "I have known you, Sir, for twenty five years," he said at one point during the hearing, "and while there is no man in whose judgment I have more confidence, there is none in whose prejudice I have more fear. I have known you, Sir, to be engaged in many cases as this, and never known you to be engaged on the side of liberty and the colored man." Although Brown took every opportunity to make it clear he was not there to "interfere with the right of property in a slave," only to ensure suspected fugitives had a fair hearing, Ingraham was unmoved. His inflexibility and prejudice clouded his judgment. Refusing to give credence to the evidence of black witnesses who testified for Gibson, and denying delay motions so more witnesses could be called, Ingraham ruled in favor of the slaveholder. Suspecting all was not right, the Philadelphia marshal who returned Gibson to Maryland was not surprised when the slaveholder informed him that Gibson was not his slave nor would he accept someone else's property. Gibson was promptly returned to Philadelphia where he was greeted by a large crowd at a public meeting at the Philadelphia Institute. As opponents of the law had predicted, such results were to be expected if the accused were not permitted a fair trial before a jury. In situations that involved issues of freedom or slavery, the law, they argued unsuccessfully, should err on the side of freedom. Proponents of the law consistently rejected such suggestions as efforts designed to delay the adjudication of cases so as to give opponents an opportunity to spirit the accused to safety.[20]

The case created a minor political storm. A few editors, diehard supporters of the law, came to Ingraham's defense even though they knew Gibson had been arrested at his market stall by George Alberti, a man with a long history of kidnapping blacks and selling them into slavery. Ingraham's supporters also chose to ignore other important bits of evidence. David Paul Brown had produced and read at the hearing the will of Gibson's former master, which showed that Gibson and his wife had been freed on condition they migrate to Liberia. In spite of such evidence, one New York editor suspected Gibson was trying to martyr himself, but to what end the editor did not say. Another was a little more circumspect. While he believed the law should be dutifully obeyed, he nonetheless thought it should be administered with "humanity, with equality,

[20] *Pennsylvania Freeman*, December 23, 26, 1850. The case received widespread local, state, and national coverage. Philadelphia *Public Ledger*, December 23, 1850; *Pennsylvanian*, December 23, 27, 30, 1850; West Chester *Village Record*, December 31, 1850; New York *Tribune*, January 1, 1851; Washington, DC, *Union*, January 10, 1851; Lancaster *Examiner & Herald*, January 11, 1851; *Seventeenth Annual Report of the Philadelphia Female Anti-Slavery Society* (Philadelphia: 1851), 8–9. For Brown's views see Philadelphia *Evening Bulletin*, November 6, 1852. Brown had a long history of working to protect fugitives in Philadelphia. In 1841, the black community recognized his services with a set of silver plates. See Benjamin Quarles, *Black Abolitionists* (New York: 1969), 166.

with justice, and that where a man's liberty is concerned, a merciful humane interpretation." In Congress, Senator James Cooper of Pennsylvania, a Whig who had voted in favor of the law, although with some reservations, insisted the decision did not reflect negatively on the law; it was instead the result of haste, a misunderstanding of the law's mandate and the unfortunate rejection of legitimate evidence. The commissioner, he concluded, had created the sort of error that could have been easily avoided. His colleague, Senator James Pearce, a former governor of Maryland, admitted that an error had occurred, but insisted that Ingraham was a "man of honor and a lawyer of ability." What impressed Pearce even more, and the point he wished to drive home, was "the promptitude with which the error was corrected" by one of his constituents, which, he insisted, gave the lie to the criticism of opponents that the "law would be deliberately converted into an instrument of fraud and oppression." Pearce, Cooper, and other supporters of the law could look the world in the eye convinced that here was ample proof for anyone who wanted to see it that the law worked and was even humane. As the Gibson case demonstrated, the law had worked as it should, for ultimately decisions about the slave's future resided, as it always had, with the slaveholder.[21]

On Ingraham's death, at age sixty, in late 1854, one editor remembered him fondly as a widely read man, a "virtuoso and belles-lettres" scholar whose role as a commissioner, he had to concede, may have "given offence to some persons." No one in the black community was willing to grant Ingraham even that limited a recognition. To African Americans, Octavius V. Catto, the black educator wrote, word of Ingraham's death brought "glad tidings of great joy." His death was a form of "Providential deliverance." Not one to mince words, Catto dismissed Ingraham as "a bad man," coarse and vulgar, and "utterly devoid of all moral sensibility." No fugitive brought before him, he recalled, "ever found a ray of hope." They were all returned, he reminded his readers, even Adam Gibson. In his estimation, Ingraham had issued more warrants, and was "the means of more arrests, than any other slave-commissioner in the United States."[22]

Catto and other opponents of the law were not able to persuade politicians that the law was deeply flawed, nor could they muster the power to remove commissioners such as Ingraham. But they did all they could to influence potential appointees to reject advancements by the government. Their actions may have been largely responsible for the fact that the law never met its expected quota of commissioners as envisaged by James Mason. Public meetings, especially those

[21] For the view of the New York *Herald*, see a printed extract in the New York *Tribune*, January 1, 1851; New York *Commercial Advertiser* (n.d.), in Burlington *Free Press*, December 30, 1850; *Congressional Globe, Thirty-First Congress, Second Session* (Washington, DC: 1851), 578.

[22] *Evening Bulletin*, November 6, 1854; *National Anti-Slavery Standard*, November 11, 1854. For a biography of Catto see Daniel R. Biddle and Murray Dubin, *Testing Freedom. Octavius Catto and the Battle for Equality in Civil War America* (Philadelphia: 2010).

in the northernmost areas of the Free States, promised to ostracize anyone who accepted a commission. A meeting in Sardinia, Ohio, for instance, pledged to neither "buy, sell, lend [nor] borrow with anyone" who agreed to serve. Anyone, be they commissioner, marshal, or deputy marshal, who involved himself with the law, an Ashtabula, Ohio, meeting declared, will be considered "moral nuisances, contaminating the air of freedom." Resolutions from nearby Williamsfield and Vermillion condemned them as "monsters in human form," who were a "putrid, moral pestilence." Describing what they would do to those who were base enough to accept appointments and then try to enforce the law's mandate, a meeting in Wilmington, Ohio, attended by Frederick Douglass and Abby Kelly, reached back for a well-worn abolitionist description of slaveholders, promising to do all it could to make the public "rank them among the man-stealers, woman-whippers, and cradle-plunderers."[23]

The pressure had the desired effect in some areas where, try as they may, the authorities found it difficult to either fill the position or to replace a commissioner who had resigned. The absence of a commissioner mattered. For the rest of the decade, following Richard McAllister's resignation, there were two recorded incidents in Harrisburg and the warrant for that arrest had to be issued in Philadelphia. In other areas of the North, especially those through which escaping slaves regularly passed, and so badly needed the services of a commissioner, there were few to be found. Confronted by the need to adjudicate the case of Jerry Daniel, a Missouri fugitive, Joseph Sabine, the Syracuse commissioner, balked. He clearly had grave doubts about the law. In fact, he had only consented to continue as commissioner under pressure from his family and friends who thought he was exactly the sort of person who could bring a certain dispassion and balance to the office. Sabine resigned within weeks of Jerry's rescue.[24]

The paucity of commissioners in many areas, as well as the ostracism of those who accepted the post, became evident in the effort of local opponents of the law to remove John Moore from his position in Vincennes, Indiana. The town, located on the Wabash River, was an important route for slaves escaping from western Kentucky, Alabama, and Tennessee. A commissioner, one editor pleaded, was "much needed to enable masters speedily to recover their slaves." Moore, a Democrat, reluctantly accepted the appointment when no one else would. In the first case to come before him, in June 1854, Moore remanded George Givens, who had escaped from Union County, Kentucky, six years earlier. The decision produced a political firestorm – one that ultimately required the intervention of the federal government. Moore was accused of

---

[23] Ripley *Bee*, November 23, 1850; Ashtabula *Sentinel*, November 9, December 28, 1850; Sandusky *Weekly Mirror*, November 12, 1850; Washington, DC, *Union*, November 24, 1850; *Western Citizen*, October 8, 1850.

[24] Angela F. Murphy, *The Jerry Rescue: The Fugitive Slave Law, Northern Rights, and the American Sectional Crisis* (New York: 2016), 27–28.

kidnapping by Andrew L. Robinson, a Free-Soil Democrat, and former state assemblyman. His party's 1852 platform had denounced the Fugitive Slave Law as a "derogation of the genius of our free institutions," and dismissed both Whigs and Democrats as little more than political factions beholden to the Slave Power. Moore was indicted by a grand jury, with bail set at $1,000. John Law, a friend of Moore's, and other major figures in the state's Democratic Party, came to Moore's defense, with appeals to the attorney general and the president. Something had to be done, Law told anyone who would listen, to ensure that Moore had adequate legal counsel, for, if nothing else, the charges leveled against him were an indictment of the federal government. It was the first time, Law pointed out, that a federal commissioner, officiating at a fugitive slave case, had been indicted in state court for kidnapping. If found guilty, he predicted, Moore would be sentenced to a lengthy stay in a state prison. The indictment, not surprisingly, put considerable strain on the elderly Moore's limited finances. Law pleaded with the federal government to cover the cost of Moore's defense. Should the charge stick, Law anticipated that critics of the law would be buoyed by the precedent set in Vincennes. In his plea to the president, attorney general, and Jessie Bright, the state's senior senator, Law made it clear that Moore had only accepted the appointment reluctantly and only under pressure from friends "at a time when it was very difficult to procure anyone to take it." If he was not supported now that he was under attack for doing his job, and was found guilty, Law had no doubt it would be impossible to find a replacement, especially because in "some parts of our State it is now very difficult to get one to do so." The case against Moore languished in the courts until September 1855, when it was finally dropped.[25] The resolution of the case against Moore occurred almost simultaneously with the public outcry against the decision of Edward G. Loring, the Boston commissioner, to remand Anthony Burns, a decision that initially was challenged unsuccessfully by prominent Boston abolitionists but would ultimately lead to his removal from office in 1858.

As Law's intervention made abundantly clear, not only were opponents willing to confront commissioners, legally and politically, for the decisions they made, the authorities also had difficulty finding candidates willing to take on what many thought were onerous and unpalatable responsibilities. There were numerous reports, in the weeks and months after the law's adoption, that some sitting commissioners had resigned or prospective candidates declined

[25] Vincennes *Gazette,* June 21, 1850, April 3, 1851; Louisville *Journal,* June 26, 1854; *National Era,* July 1, 1852; John Law to the President, Vincennes, March 14, 1855, Law to Caleb Cushing, Vincennes, March 16, 1855, Law to Jesse Bright, Vincennes, April 30, 1855; B. M. Thomas to Sir, Indianapolis, February 9, 1855. "Letters Received by the Attorney General, 1809–1870, Northern Law and Order," Reel 5; Rebecca A. Shepherd et al., compilers, *A Biographical Directory of the Indiana General Assembly, Vol. I, 1816–1899* (Indianapolis: 1980); Knox County Circuit Court, Order Book L, Historical Collection, Knox County Public Library. My thanks to Brian Spangle for information on the resolution of the case.

to accept appointments either because they thought the law unconstitutional or because of community disapprobation. Five Pennsylvania sitting commissioners were rumored to have resigned in the first month after the law was passed. One was Reade Washington of Pittsburgh, rumored to be a descendant of the first president of the United States. In Cleveland, Commissioner Charles Stetson announced that he would resign if he were ever asked to enforce the law. He did in July 1851, prompting one local newspaper to call on fugitives to leave the city in case Stetson was replaced by someone more amenable to the law. The fact that there were no recorded cases of rendition from the city until 1860 suggests that Stetson's resignation may have affected enforcement. Samuel E. Johnson, the county court judge in Kings County, New York, publicly declined to be appointed commissioner because he thought the law unconstitutional. More significantly, he reasoned, to accept such a position would conflict with his duties as a judge should he be applied to for a writ of habeas corpus. Although Orlando Hastings accepted an appointment in Rochester, New York, one local newspaper was convinced that there was no one who would scrutinize the claims of slaveholders more closely, or with "a more humane desire to shield the colored man" than he. The fact that Rochester was the home of Frederick Douglass, and a city with a long abolitionist tradition, may have had more to do with the fact that the law's tentacles never reached into the community, but a commissioner sympathetic to the fugitive's plight undoubtedly helped.[26]

In an effort to understand the reach of the law, and to craft an interpretation of its meaning in the midst of such contentious political disputes, commissioners sought advice from superiors about the extent of their powers, and struggled to interpret the law's mandate, all the while facing hostile black communities and lawyers who challenged their rulings every step of the way. In the first few months after the law took effect, many flew by the seats of their pants. Few were as convinced of their untrammeled powers as was Richard McAllister in Harrisburg. When approached by a slave catcher sent from Georgia to retake William and Ellen Craft in October 1850, George T. Curtis, one of Boston's six commissioners, refused to act, unsure of his authority to issue arrest warrants. But he was also sensitive to the political significance of a case like this in the cradle of abolitionism. It was, he observed, of "public importance that the first hearing under the new law should be so conducted here, as to prevent the dangers of a rescue." He had grounds to be concerned. Three months later, a suspected fugitive slave, Shadrach Minkins, would be rescued from

---

[26] Pittsburgh *Gazette*, November 4, 1850; Boston *Chronotype* (n.d.), in *Liberator*, November 1, 1850; *Pennsylvania Freeman*, October 31, 1850; *The Fugitive Slave Bill: Its History and Unconstitutionality*, 4, 30; Cleveland *True Democrat*, October 14, 1850, July 23, 1851; Rochester *Democrat*, September 30, 1850. Stanley W. Campbell, *The Slave Catchers. Enforcement of the Fugitive Slave Law, 1850–1860* (New York: 1968), 204 mentions a case of rendition from Cleveland in 1857, but I have not been able to confirm it.

his courthouse. The rescue may have stiffened Curtis' resolve. Weeks later, he ordered the return of Thomas Sims to Georgia, justifying his decision in a lengthy opinion, which also tentatively broached the question of the law's constitutionality. The duties of the commissioner were, he conceded, a mix of the ministerial and the judicial. Such an arrangement had a long and honored tradition in both the legal systems of England and the United States, one in which certain officers are given the power to act judicially without being judges. Not so, reasoned Sam S. Carpenter, a Cincinnati commissioner, who insisted, in 1854, that the powers granted commissioners were unconstitutional. The decisions of commissioners were not ministerial, as Curtis and other supporters of the law claimed, but had "all the forms of judicial acts"; commissioners, in fact, acted as judges in all but name. More troubling to Carpenter was the acknowledgement that such decisions were arrived at without due process, were final, and not subject to appeal. The commissioner, he observed, "holds a court, issues process, hears and determines the matter in question." Carpenter resigned, insisting he could not, in good conscience, perform the duties of the office.[27]

While Curtis initially agonized over the safest approach to take, other commissioners found ways to put their stamp on the law, to interpret its clauses in ways they thought best guaranteed its enforcement. Few other elements of the law created more concern for commissioners than the constant challenges to the legality and legitimacy of the affidavits issued in Southern jurisdictions. What constituted a bona fide affidavit was always in dispute. Under the law, all slaveholders needed was an official document from their district stating that their slave had escaped. To the affidavit containing a description of the slave, the district in which she lived, and the date of her escape, was to be affixed an official seal, which all seemed clear enough. Lawyers for fugitives, however, consistently challenged the validity of the descriptions contained in affidavits, as well as their seals, in an effort to undermine the claimant's case. At the August 1851 hearing for Daniel Davis in Buffalo, for instance, Commissioner Henry K. Smith, the Democratic former mayor of Buffalo, came up with what the fugitive's lawyer thought a rather loose interpretation of what constituted

---

[27] Boston *Herald*, April 7, 9, 1851; Washington, DC, *Union*, April 15, 1851. For Curtis' role as commissioner see Gary Collison, *Shadrach Minkins. From Fugitive Slave to Citizen* (Cambridge, MA: 1997) and Stephen Kantrowitz, *More than Freedom. Fighting for Black Citizenship in a White Republic, 1829–1889* (New York: 2012); Cincinnati *Gazette*, June 20, 1854; Cincinnati *Atlas* (n.d.), in Chicago *Tribune*, June 27, 1854; Stephen Middleton, "The Fugitive Slave Cases in Cincinnati, 1850–1860: Resistance, Enforcement and Black Refugees," *Journal of Negro History*, Vol. 72 (Winter, Spring 1987), 26. There were other prominent resignations, including that of Thomas Kane, the second son of Judge John K. Kane, Philadelphia's district court judge, who had been instrumental in his son's appointment as a commissioner. The young Kane drove his father, a strong advocate for the law, to distraction by his involvement in the UGRR. See Nat Brandt & Yanna Kroyt Brandt, *In the Shadow of the Civil War. Passmore Williamson and the Rescue of Jane Johnson* (Columbia, SC: 2007), 67–68.

an appropriate affidavit's seal. Davis's lawyer objected to the affidavit because it did not contain the official seal of any court. The law, he insisted, required the seal be impressed on wax, wafer, and "other adhesive substances," not paper, as was the one issued in Louisville, Kentucky. While conceding that there was a potential problem, Smith nonetheless accepted the affidavit because each state, he ruled, had the power to determine what constituted an official seal. Smith would make a similar ruling two months later in the case of Harrison Williams. Again conceding that the warrant of arrest was not as comprehensive as it should be, he ruled it was enough under the terms of the Fugitive Slave Law and could be supplemented by oral testimony.[28] Smith did not bother to tell the lawyers, or their clients, where in the law such an interpretation was permissible. But such actions were possible, Smith knew, only because there could be no appeals of a commissioner's ruling.

Lawyers for the accused continued to challenge the law, coming up with inventive ways to undermine the claims of slaveholders. Nothing did so more effectively than questioning the descriptions of fugitives contained in affidavits from Southern courts. In the simplicity of the question lay the challenge's effectiveness: Was the person before the commissioner the same person described in the affidavit? The issue proved particularly difficult for the claimant of Euphemia Williams, a mother of six who, it was asserted, had escaped from her Maryland owner in 1829 when she was eighteen. Defense counsel called for a dismissal on the grounds that both the warrant's description of Williams and the testimony of witnesses for T. J. Purnell of Worcester, the son of Williams' deceased owner, were much too vague and contradictory. Four black witnesses, one of them Sarah Gayley, testified that they had known Williams prior to 1829. When one of the witnesses for the owner was asked how he could be so positive that the person before him was the person he claimed to have known in 1829, he responded: "I never saw a great deal of change in a nigger, from 16 to 35 or 40 – sometimes they grow fatter and sometimes leaner." On the other hand, Sarah Gayley was an especially convincing witness. When challenged by Purnell's lawyer to prove how she could be so positive about the time she first met Williams, Gayley drew on the memory of an important event in the history of the city, the visit of General Lafayette. That, she said, was how she remembered when she first met Williams. But even more critical to the case was the fact that, unknown to Purnell's lawyer, both Williams and Gayley, who were of similar build and complexion, had similar scars on their foreheads. Aware of the significance identity could play, Williams and Gayley hid the scars under turbans when they came to court. When witnesses for the claimant admitted they knew of no visible identifying marks on Williams, she and Gayley were asked to stand together, at which point the turbans were removed. The judge, who had taken over the hearing because of a successful habeas corpus

---

[28] Buffalo *Courier*, January 9, 1851; Buffalo *Express*, October 3, 1851.

application, ruled in favor of Williams on the grounds that it was next to impossible to identify someone after twenty-four years and because the black witnesses, especially Gayley, were credible.[29]

Similar issues were influential in the decision by the Chicago commissioner to free the Missouri slave Moses Johnson in the summer of 1851. The affidavit contained no description of Johnson, only saying that he had escaped from his owner Crawford Smith of Lafayette. Johnson was represented by four of the city's most prominent lawyers, including George Manierre and E. C. Lerned. When asked, a witness for Smith described the fugitive as "copper colored" when it was clear, a newspaper reporter observer, Johnson was "jet black." Johnson was also visibly shorter than the affidavit claimed. The hearing then turned to a wide-ranging discussion of the nature and different shades of blackness. One witness observed that Johnson was not black but fell instead in a range between "copper colored" and "jet black." At this point, a person in the room described as black was asked to stand next to Johnson. There was no visible difference. Ten white witness followed. All were either born or had lived in the South and so, it was presumed, were experts on the complex nature of color gradations among black people. All came to the same conclusion: Johnson was black. Smith's case collapsed not on any of the other objections raised by Johnson's attorneys, but on the singularly nebulous grounds of color variations.[30]

In the case of John Bolding – a fugitive slave from South Carolina, who had settled in Poughkeepsie, New York, and who was described in one report as "somewhat darker than the average white man" – lawyers for both sides called on phrenologists, physiologists, and even some who had lived among Indians, to question whether Bolding was even black. Dr. Alfred C. Post gave as his scientific opinion, after a careful physiological examination of Bolding, that, at the very least, he was a "half-blood Indian." Another who claimed to have made "physiology a study" concluded that Bolding was a mix of European and Indian with "no portion of negro blood in him." Were Bolding a "fair mulatto," this witness asserted, his hair would have been "crooked." More to the point, he pointed out, his "skeleton (or bones)...is purely Indian." A Mr. Fowler, who described himself as a phrenologist and physiologist in practice for more than twenty years, concluded, after stroking Bolding's head, that there was no "African blood in him." During his testimony, Fowler held the skulls of an Indian and an African in each hand – symbols, one can only assume, of his scientific expertise. If there were any African blood in Bolding, he nonetheless conceded, it would be no more than "two-twentieths." The weight of such scientific expertise did little to forestall Bolding's return to slavery. One suspects

[29] *Pennsylvania Freeman*, February 13, 1851; Philadelphia *Evening Bulletin*, February 6, 8, 1851; New York *Tribune*, February 11, 1851.
[30] Chicago *Democrat*, June 4, 5, 6, 7, 1851; *Western Citizen*, June 10, 17, 1851; *Pennsylvania Freeman*, June 19, 1851.

that the attempt to prove him an Indian was beyond the ken of most at the hearing, including the commissioner. Discussions of racial origin, it appears, were more easily comprehensible when limited to shades of black and white.[31]

Lawyers for fugitives generally insisted on a burden of proof so rigorous in its requirement that, if implemented, few fugitives would have been remanded. The case of Harrison Williams was fairly typical. Williams, nineteen years of age, had escaped with a number of others from Hardy County, Virginia, to Busti, a small western New York village, in early January 1851. The hearing, lawyers for Williams insisted, was unwarranted because it violated Article 4, Section 2 of the Constitution, which mandated that, before a slave could be brought before a commissioner, a claimant had first to show that the accused owed service or labor in the slaveholder's state and, secondly, had escaped from his owner to another state. Where the provision of the Constitution and the law of Congress are in "derogation of the common law," and restrain human liberty "which God has confirmed" on all men, black and white, both the Constitution and the law, they argued, should be construed in favor of liberty. Proof that Williams was a slave and had escaped, therefore, had to be irrefutable. The slave owner had provided no proof that Williams had left home without his consent. In fact, they contended, no evidence had been provided to contradict the assumption that Williams was a free man. But Williams' lawyers were swimming against a stiff current for, in this instance, the slave owner had arrived equipped with a record of the proceedings before the court in Hardy County, showing that Williams was his slave and that he had absconded.[32]

Other commissioners looked for ways to bring some semblance of control – they would say efficiency – to the conduct of hearings. Following a string of hearings in Philadelphia that were raucous and contentious, Edward Ingraham adopted an approach he hoped would limit the ways lawyers for fugitives could challenge the law. He sent out a series of letters to Southern governors, especially those in the upper South, requesting copies of their statutes. As he told the governors, he was frequently called on "to hear the claims of citizens of the southern and western states, whose servants escape from their masters." Under the challenge of lawyers for the defense, he was forced frequently to refer to laws copies of which he did not have. As a result, he had been "much embarrassed and claimants much delayed" by lawyers' objections and his ignorance of specific Southern laws. He was certain these challenges could be deflected if he had easy access to the relevant statutes. In requesting copies of Missouri's

---

[31] *Evening Post* (n.d.), in New York *Tribune*, August 27, 1851, September 1, 2, 1851; Poughkeepsie *American* (n.d.), in Albany *Journal*, August 28, 1851; Poughkeepsie *Eagle*, September 6, 1851; New York *Commercial Advertiser*, August 30, September 1, 1851; *Liberator*, September 12, 1851.

[32] Hardy *Whig* (n.d.), in Richmond *Whig*, October 28, 1851; New York *Tribune*, October 2, 1851; Buffalo *Courier*, October 2, 4, 1851; Buffalo *Express*, October 2, 3, 1851; *Ohio Star* (n.d.), in *Frederick Douglass' Paper*, November 6, 1851.

statutes, Ingraham informed the governor he had already received those of other states.[33]

But whatever stumbling blocks were thrown in their way, commissioners were men with powers that could only be curtailed by constant public protests and pressure from the black community and their abolitionist allies. Even in cases where rulings favored the fugitive, it was glaringly apparent that, had decisions gone against them, there was nothing they could do but attempt to rescue the fugitive. The power of commissioners, a Chicago editor observed, was unrivaled: "[F]rom him there is no appeal. He holds the scepter of life or death, of liberty or slavery. What an awful responsibility rests upon him! How dangerous such a power in the hands of any man!!"[34] Additionally, nothing in the law denied a claimant a second – or even third – opportunity at a new trial. That may help explain why in almost every instance where a ruling went in favor of the fugitive, he was sent immediately to the safety of Canada. When decisions ran into opposition from the black community, commissioners had the power, under Section 9 of the law, to call out large police forces, not only to prevent possible rescue, but also to ensure the safe return of fugitives. Usually, they did not even wait for slaveholders or their representatives to request such protection. Richard McAllister's record in Harrisburg is illustrative. The police forces he marshaled cost the federal government hundreds of dollars in the months between October 1850 and June 1852. The posse of almost twenty he gathered to return Samuel Wilson and George Brocks, in September 1850, may have been unusually large, but he thought it was what was needed if an abduction was to be prevented, either in Harrisburg or anywhere along the journey to Virginia. The 191-mile round-trip to Clarke County, Virginia, cost the federal treasury $262.91.[35]

All indications are that implementation of the law had gotten ahead of the federal treasury's ability to determine methods of payment. McAllister's officers had to wait months before they were reimbursed, and when they were they regularly complained of being shortchanged. No one seemed to know how payments were to be calculated. Who, for instance, determined the size of per diem expenses? Would payments cover the cost of boarding and lodging for members of the posse as well as the fugitive? No one in the auditor's office seemed to have a clue. There was even a suggestion from Washington that local

---

[33] Edward Ingraham to Sterling Price, Philadelphia, November 8, 1853. Records of Governor Sterling Price, 1853–1857, RG 3: 11, Office of Governor, Missouri State Archives, Jefferson City, Missouri.

[34] Chicago *Democrat*, June 6, 1851.

[35] Richard McAllister to John Kane, Harrisburg (n.d.), RG 217, Settled Miscellaneous Treasury Accounts, September 6, 1790–September 29, 1894, National Archives, Washington, DC. The *Pennsylvania Freeman*, November 13, 1850, dismissed McAllister's first posse as "kidnappers' pimps" and wondered if it was legal to use a constabulary force for such a purpose. See also the Charles Rawn Diary, Rawn Collection, MG 062, Diaries, Dauphin County Historical Society, Harrisburg, Pennsylvania.

authorities should cover the cost of renditions, a clear violation of Section 9 of the law. Even when payments were approved, the auditors regularly questioned the size and type of expenses claimed. Elisha Whittlesey, first comptroller of the Treasury, even suspected that the system was being abused and the "judiciary fund" plundered. Federal marshals, it seems, were expected to cover the cost of returning remanded slaves out of their own pockets, expenses they could later reclaim. Because of the interminable delays in receiving reimbursements from Washington, some marshals requested advances to cover the anticipated cost of renditions. Marshal Bush of the Northern District of New York, for instance, requested an advance of $2,500 – some of it to defray anticipated expenses. At the time, Bush claimed, he was owed almost $20,000.[36]

Such inefficiencies, when coupled with organized resistance from the black community, deeply troubled the authorities. In Philadelphia, Robert C. Grier, an associate justice of the US Supreme Court, tried to lay down a political marker by assuming responsibility for the first case that came to a hearing. It involved Henry Garnett, who it was claimed had escaped Thomas Price Jones of Cecil County, Maryland, nine years earlier. Grier met secretly with the slaveholder and warned him not to proceed until he had all the requisite documents. He also recommended that Jones hire a competent lawyer. Unfortunately, the slaveholder failed to heed the judge's advice. When his affidavit was challenged by the defense, Jones pleaded for a postponement. Visibly frustrated, Grier refused and freed the fugitive.[37] The judge had taken the political temperature of the black community and was troubled by the reading. There were unmistakable signs of open resistance to the law in Philadelphia and elsewhere. Days earlier a group of blacks had stormed the courtroom in Harrisburg after a preliminary hearing, and freed Billy, one of three Clarke County, Virginia, fugitives, provided him with a pistol and sent him on his way to Canada. Not long after, the authorities in Detroit called out three volunteer companies and one company of US soldiers to prevent the rescue of Rose, a fugitive from Tennessee. The jail where Rose was being held was also heavily guarded. Evidently, when a posse was called out as further reinforcement, they refused to come and pledged to

---

[36] See the series of letters between Harrisburg, Philadelphia, and Washington in the period January 1851 and July 1852 for the problems over repayment. Settled Miscellaneous Treasury Accounts; Elisha Whittlesey to Editors of the Baltimore *Patriot*, December 12, 1851, Container 51, Whittlesey Papers, Western Reserve Historical Society, Cleveland, Ohio. In the wake of the Margaret Garner case in Cincinnati, the Treasury Department sent out a team to investigate suspected abuses, which were rumored to include the discounting of payment scripts by members of the posse. See Steven Weisenburger, *Modern Medea. A Family Story of Slavery and Child-Murder from the Old South* (New York: 1998).

[37] *Pennsylvania Freeman*, October 24, 1850; Gettysburg *Republican Compiler*, November 4, 1850; West Chester *Village Record*, October 22, 1850; Leon Friedman and Fred L. Israel, eds., *The Justices of the United States Supreme Court, 1789–1978. Their Lives and Major Opinions*, Vol. II (New York: 1980), 873–74.

resist all slave catchers. Even the mayor endorsed resistance, pledging not to hand over fugitives who took refuge at his home.[38]

Grier may even have been reacting to the large crowd of blacks who kept a daily vigil outside his courtroom and were there to greet Henry Garnett once he was released. It was a pattern that would be replicated in other parts of the North throughout the decade. These demonstrations of community opposition to the law were always raucous and were meant to intimidate local authorities as well as slaveholders and their agents. They threatened to become violent and frequently did. The authorities' responses, in turn, were rarely measured. Overreaction only exacerbated political tensions. These crises may not have been of the protesters' doing, but it was clear to Grier and anyone with eyes to see that blacks and their abolitionist allies were eager and ready to exploit every opportunity to push the country toward a political reckoning with slavery. All of this played out in the streets of Boston in October 1850, when two slave catchers from Georgia came in search of William and Ellen Craft. While the vigilance committee's legal team brought a series of suits against the slave catchers for violating local ordinances, members of the black community kept a close watch on them wherever they went, making it impossible for them to get close to the Crafts. It took the slave catchers eight days to secure an arrest warrant, by which time all of black Boston was aware of their presence. Five suits were brought against them, all, as one of the slaveholders lamented, for "the purpose of harassing me and driving me away." The continuous presence of large and rowdy black crowds finally persuaded the two to give up the chase and leave town empty handed.[39]

The black community and their white allies understandably rejoiced at turning away the slave catchers. Boston, the cradle of abolitionism, would, as their meetings against the law promised, always be a safe city for fugitives and dangerous ground for slave catchers. Frederick Douglass spoke for many at a crowded Faneuil Hall meeting: "We must be prepared," he pleaded with his listeners, "should the law be put into operation here, to see the streets of Boston running with blood." Under pressure from the owners of the Crafts, President Fillmore promised to do all he could to ensure that the law was enforced, even if that included calling out the military. There were also calls for the removal of those federal officers who had failed to act. Others were a little more forgiving: the city, they reasoned, had not yet put in place the requisite mechanisms to enforce the law. But to those who believed federal and state authorities should have anticipated that the law would have an early test in the home of

---

[38] Harrisburg *Telegraph,* August 28, 1850; Lancaster *Examiner & Herald,* August 28, 1850; Detroit *Herald,* October 10, 1850, in New York *Tribune,* October 14, 1850; New York *Tribune,* October 15, 21, 1850; Detroit *Free Press,* October 9, 11, November 1, 1850; Baltimore *Sun,* October 21, 1850; Chicago *Democrat,* October 12, 1850.

[39] See the slave catcher's letter in the *Georgia Telegraph,* November 26, 1850, reprinted in the Washington, DC, *Union,* of November 28, 1850, and elsewhere.

abolitionism, and so should have been prepared, it appeared that the law was already a dead letter. Opposition was the work of "disorganizers," "disturbers of the peace," "rebels and traitors," "incendiaries and truly dangerous men" who were bent on "reopening the wounds inflicted by them on the body politic, after they were healed" by the patriotism of those who had put together the Compromise. As one editor put it, opposition to the law was treason and treason stalked the city. Such reactions gave the impression that the political skies were falling. These cries of treason and anarchy would soon become a feature of the vocabulary of those committed to the enforcement of the law, and would lead to legal and political overreach, months later, following the shoot-out at Christiana, Pennsylvania, during which a slaveholder was killed.[40]

In spite of their success in getting the Crafts to England, opponents of the law who lived in what slave hunters believed was a sinkhole of freedom, knew they faced formidable odds. Some worried they may have woken a sleeping giant. George Thompson, the British abolitionist and a Member of Parliament, on a visit to the United States in 1850, gave an appropriate accounting of the forces arrayed against them: there were commissioners, marshals, federal judges, the militia, and US troops, lawyers for the government, a secretary of state "in the person of the 'godlike' Daniel Webster," and President Fillmore, the "grand huntsman, to cheer on and direct the pack." In spite of the instruments of power at their disposal, the city and federal government could do nothing to stop the rescue of Shadrach Minkins in February 1851. Minkins, a fugitive from Norfolk, Virginia, was captured at the coffeehouse where he worked on a warrant issued by George Curtis, who, months earlier, had been reluctant to act when the slave catchers seeking the Crafts had requested an arrest warrant. Within thirty minutes of Minkins's arrest, and even before lawyers from the vigilance committee could make it to the hearing, a crowd of blacks estimated to be in excess of 150 milled about outside the courthouse. Twenty of them forced their way into the courtroom, seized Minkins, and took him off to a safe house in the black community before shipping him off to Canada.[41]

This is exactly what the editor of the New York *Herald* had predicted would happen if federal authorities failed to protect slaveholders in their efforts to retake their property. Others believed Fillmore should have sent a clear message of purpose during the crisis surrounding the Crafts by issuing a "warning proclamation," dismissing the marshal and showing he was determined to use the military to support the law. Had he done so, the "infuriated mob of colored people, who knocked down the officers, and carried the fugitive

---

40 Boston *Herald*, October 15, 1850; Salem *Freeman* (n.d.), in *Anti-Slavery Bugle*, December 7, 1850; *Anti-Slavery Standard*, February 13, 1851; Washington, DC, *Union*, November 16, 1850; New York *Herald*, November 5, 1850.

41 Boston *Herald*, February 15, 1851; see Collison, *Shadrach Minkins*, for a detailed account of the Minkins's case; *Liberator*, January 3, 1851; Henry Steele Commager, *Theodore Parker. Yankee Crusader* (Boston: 1947), 218.

away in triumph" may have thought twice before acting. This second blight
on the city's good name, in less than six months, had to be punished, even if
it involved the shedding of blood. It was the only way for Boston to reclaim
its good name.[42] Henry Clay feared that the Compromise, which he had done
so much to fashion, was under assault from a people, as he put it, "who possess no part…in our political system." Clay spoke for many: the poor, deluded
blacks who had carried out the rescue, he believed, could not have acted on
their own initiative. They were the tools – the "catspaws" – of abolitionists
who had long been advocating for the overthrow of the slave system. This
insane crusade had to be brought to an end by a government dedicated to and
prepared for the enforcement of the law.[43]

The authorities' state of preparedness would soon be tested and this time
not found wanting. Thomas Sims was arrested in early April under warrant
from James Potter, a wealthy rice planter from Chatham County, Georgia. Sims
was held on the third floor of the courthouse. Later, bars were placed on the
window of the room when it was rumored that an attempt would be made
to rescue him. In an act of great political symbolism, chains were also placed
around the courthouse. The vigilance committee brought a number of suits in
state courts seeking Sims' release: they petitioned for writs of habeas corpus
and drew up criminal complaints against Sims for stabbing a policeman during
his arrest in an effort to have him brought before a state court. They also questioned the constitutionality of the federal law and petitioned the state senate
to pass a special law requiring that Sims be granted a writ of habeas corpus,
none of which passed muster. Once the decision was made that Sims should be
extradited, a large military force was mustered to prevent any possible rescue.
Sims was escorted under heavy guard to the harbor where he was put on a ship
for Savannah.[44]

Supporters of the law had finally won a victory in the very heart of abolitionism, but at what price? The city, some observers lamented, had been put
under the sort of military occupation it had not witnessed since the retreat of
British forces during the Revolution. The large military presence, as well as
the hearing and return of Sims, had cost at least $10,000. Some put the cost at

[42] Washington, DC, *Union*, February 23, 1851; Boston *Herald*, February 15, 17, 1851.
[43] Springfield *Republican*, February 24, 1851; Baltimore *Sun*, February 24, 1851; Washington,
    DC, *Union*, February 22, 1851; *Appendix to the Congressional Globe, Second Session, Thirty-
    First Congress* (Washington: 1851), 292–93, 299–301, 351; *Liberator*, February 21, March 28,
    1851; Boston *Herald*, March 3, 1851; Collison, *Shadrach Minkins*, 141–47, 194–95; Boston
    *Post*, February 18, 1851.
[44] The fullest coverage of the case can be found in Leonard W. Levy, "Sims' Case: the Fugitive
    Slave Law in Boston in 1851," *Journal of Negro History*, 35 (1950), 39–74; Boston *Post*, April
    7, 1851; Boston *Herald*, April 4, 5, 8, 12, 1851; Savannah *News*, April 7, 14, 17, 22, 1851;
    Philadelphia *Evening Bulletin*, April 7, 1851; *National Era*, July 31, 1851; Gary Collison, "The
    Boston Vigilance Committee. A Reconsideration," *Historical Journal of Massachusetts*, 12
    (1984), 105; Commager, *Theodore Parker*, 222.

$20,000. A victory, supporters of the law seemed to be saying, was one worth having regardless of the cost. Daniel Webster, the secretary of state, and the state's main advocate for the law, was delighted. Boston had made amends for its past errors. The return of Sims, he told a public meeting attended by a crowd estimated at ten thousand, would both ease sectional asperities as well as quiet the storm of abuse disunionists had heaped upon him. The rendition also seemed to settle the issue of whether Boston would continue to defy the law. In the eyes of many, the city had finally redeemed itself. For proponents of the law in Congress, there was a general consensus (and optimism) that Boston had taken a step back from the brink of disunion. To Henry Clay, it was another sign of reconciliation. James Mason, however, was a little more cautious. The law may have been enforced in this instance, but he saw no signs that the mood of the city had changed in any appreciable way. The hallmark of an effective fugitive slave law, he reminded his colleagues, was the speed, diligence, zeal, and good faith with which it was enforced. Sims may have been returned, but there were few signs that the sentiment of the Northern people had shifted in favor of the law. Masters still had to endure delays, annoyances, unnecessary expenses, and even personal dangers.[45]

If the jury was still out on the law's effectiveness in April 1851, the record of enforcement since September 1850 helps to substantiate whether Clay's optimist or Mason's skepticism was closer to the mark. Historians have tried, not always successfully, to determine the exact number of incidences involving fugitive slaves in the fifteen months following passage of the law. In his pathbreaking book on the law and the efforts to enforce it, Stanley Campbell estimates that there were 110 cases; James McPherson accounts for only 85. Both conclude that most of these resulted in the return of the suspected fugitives. Of Campbell's 110 cases, 45 were returned "without due process," that is, without a hearing; 52 were remanded following a hearing before a commissioner or judge; 8 were rescued; and 5 released after a hearing.[46] While it is impossible to be exhaustive, the numbers I have found are slightly larger than Campbell's. While following his lead I have expanded on the disposition of cases. Of the 147 I have identified, I agree with Campbell that 45 were returned "without due process"; 53 were returned following a hearing; 16, among them the Crafts, escaped; 17 were rescued by the black community, including Billy in Harrisburg and Shadrach Minkins in Boston; 7, including Bolding, were returned and subsequently ransomed; 7 were freed following a

<hr>

45  Boston *Herald*, April 4, 15, 16, 18, 22, 1851; Savannah *Republican*, April 14, 22, 1851; Savannah *News*, April 17, 1851; New York *Herald*, April 13, 1851; *Appendix to the Congressional Globe, Second Session, Thirty-First Congress* (Washington, DC: 1851), 293–94, 297–98, 306–07.

46  Campbell, *The Slave Catchers*, 199–200; James M. McPherson, *Ordeal By Fire. The Civil War and Reconstruction* (New York: 1982), 77. Gary Collison estimates that by February 1851 there were reports of "more than 60 separate legal and extralegal attempts to recapture fugitives on Northern soil," involving 105 escapees, *Shadrach Minkins*, 107.

hearing, including Euphemia Williams in Philadelphia and Moses Johnson in Chicago; and 2 were purchased prior to their return. Typical of the group that was returned "without due process," were the eighteen from Lewis County, Kentucky, who, in July 1851, managed to reach as far as Adams County, Ohio, before they were betrayed by locals pretending to be friends. Under the terms of the law, locals, such as those in Adams County, were perfectly within their rights to capture, hold, and return fugitives without recourse to a hearing.[47]

Among those who were returned following a hearing were Samuel Wilson and George Brocks from Harrisburg, Pennsylvania, in September 1850, and Harrison Williams from Buffalo, New York, one year later. But the case that became the standard by which all subsequent cases would be judged, involved claims against thirty-year-old Henry Long, who escaped to New York City from Richmond, Virginia. Long was picked up just before Christmas 1850 and rushed before a commissioner. As always, the black community turned up in large numbers at the commissioner's office and gave warning that they intended to do all they could to prevent Long's rendition. Long was also represented by a group of lawyers with impeccable abolitionist credentials who tested the limits of the law by suing successfully for a writ of habeas corpus. On the sixth day of the hearing, the Union Safety Committee threw its considerable "weight of purse," as one newspaper put it, behind the claimant, raising money to hire George Wood, a prominent city attorney. The champions of the law were successful and Long was returned to Richmond under guard. Henry Clay rejoiced at what he termed the "beautiful exhibition of the moral power of the law, and...the disposition of the population...to see the law executed." It had silenced the naysayers. But James Mason had his doubts. Speed and execution were the only legitimate measures of success; two weeks struck him as dangerously long, allowing time for opponents to rally public and legal opinion against the law.[48]

The sense of accomplishment following Long's return was tempered by his owner's decision to sell him further south. Few questioned his owner's right to do so. But it would have been far better, leading lights in the Union Safety Committee believed, had they been given the opportunity to ransom Long as they had done in the case of James Hamlet two months earlier. The purchasing

---

[47] *Free Presbyterian* (n.d.), in *Anti-Slavery Standard*, July 31, 1851. See also St. Louis *Times* (n.d.), in New York *Tribune*, July 21, 1851, for the recapture of a Missouri slave in southern Illinois. For another such case in Lebanon, Pennsylvania, this one leading to the prosecution for kidnapping, see Lebanon *Advertiser*, April 23, 1851; *Pennsylvania Freeman*, January 23, March 20, 1851; Harrisburg *American*, April 21, 1851; Lancaster *Examiner & Herald*, April 23, 1851; Harrisburg *Whig State Journal*, April 30, 1851.

[48] New York *Tribune*, December 24, 1850, January 31, 1851; New York *Herald*, December 27, 31, 1850; *Liberator*, January 31, 1851; *National Anti-Slavery Standard*, January 31, 1851; Richmond *Whig*, January 14, 1851; Boston *Herald*, January 22, 1851; Richmond *Enquirer* (n.d.), in *Liberator*, January 24, 1851; *Appendix to the Congressional Globe, Second Session, Thirty-First Congress* (Washington, DC: 1851), 298, 595.

of fugitives who, through their own devices and genius, had made it to freedom was always contentious. Why, many asked, should a slaveholder be compensated for the morally indefensible practice of holding humans in bondage, especially after a fugitive had made it to freedom under his own initiative? Allowing someone who had experienced freedom, if only for a brief period, to be returned to slavery, was equally unacceptable. What, in practice, was the difference between ransoming someone like Long, and the daily purchase of the produce of slave labor? For members of the Union Safety Committee, however, such purchases had two positive outcomes: they recognized the slaveholder's right to his property while at the same time promoting the gradual and legal emancipation of slaves. In the context of the politics of slavery, it mollified Southerners while acknowledging Northern desires to encourage manumissions. The security of the Union was best assured when slavery and freedom were permitted to coexist.

James Hamlet was the first to be returned and subsequently ransomed. Since his escape in 1848 from Mary Brown of Baltimore he had started a family and was gainfully employed in New York City. Buying Hamlet's freedom, many had to admit, was also one way of breaking the master's control. Frederick Douglass, William Wells Brown, and J. W. C. Pennington, former slaves and now prominent figures in the abolitionist movement, had all consented to allow supporters in Britain to buy their freedom. In doing so, their freedom was assured and legally unassailable. Others, such as Jermain Loguen, however, defiantly rejected this option. As he put it, "I will not, nor will I consent, that any body else shall countenance the claims of a vulgar despot of my soul and body." But his principled stand, Loguen knew, put him in constant danger of being retaken. Following Jerry's rescue in October 1851, Loguen was forced to take temporary refuge in Canada, concerned he may be sent back to slavery. Purchases were also seen by some slaveholders as a way to recover the value, if not the body, of a slave, even while they agonized over the wisdom of reintroducing an intransigent slave into their household. But agreeing to a purchase was sometimes the only option available to slaveholders if they ever hoped to recoup their losses. That was what prompted Aaron Mihardo of Norfolk, Virginia, to suggest to Cornelius Sparrow, a free black of Boston, that he pay $450 to ransom his wife, Martha Ann Whitehead, who, Mihardo claimed, was his slave. Sparrow declined and he and Whitehead left for the safety of Canada with the aid of the vigilance committee. A slaveholder's acceptance of a ransom offer was sometimes the result of intimidation and not infrequently a way to avoid anticipated violence. When it was rumored, for instance, that two fugitive slaves had been captured in Uniontown, Pennsylvania, in early 1851, an armed group of blacks was organized to retake them. Anticipating a violent confrontation, the mayor called out a local volunteer unit. The standoff was broken when the owner agreed to accept a ransom offer. But over all of these possible options hung the real possibility of extortion; prices could be, and sometimes were, increased during negotiations. Following John Bolding's return to South

Carolina in late summer 1851, those claiming him raised their asking price 100 percent, from $1,000 to $2,000. The increase delayed Bolding's return as friends in Poughkeepsie, New York, scrambled to raise the additional funds. Such large sums, one editor predicted ominously, would "first stimulate slave catchers to renewed diligence, and then raise the price of Fugitives."[49]

Black New Yorkers may not have liked the method used to free Hamlet, but in the end rejoiced at the return of the man to his family. What was of more immediate concern, however, was the fact that few were aware initially of his speedy arrest and trial; they were caught off guard and unprepared. They pledged never to allow it to happen again. Slave catchers who came into the community did so, they warned, at their own risk and peril. The two meetings held to welcome Hamlet's return to the city expressed that new commitment. They opposed the law as unconstitutional, committed themselves to protect the "Panting Slave" by force, if necessary, and ensured that "Freemen" would never be made slaves. They also called on fugitives to arm themselves, formed a committee to protect the community and planned to establish a register of all fugitives, along with the names of their masters. George Downing, the black caterer, spoke for many: his home, he declared, was his "castle" and anyone who crossed its threshold should be prepared to be sent to hell.[50] As we have seen, similar organizations were established in black communities throughout the North. Some, such as the ones in Detroit and Pittsburgh, had been in existence long before 1850. Others flowered for brief periods to address specific challenges, disbanded once the danger had passed, only to spring into life again as the situation warranted.[51]

But even in places where there were no formal organizations, the black community made their opposition known by preventing the recapture of

---

[49] For a general discussion of slave redemptions see Margaret M. R. Kellow, "Conflicting Imperative: Black and White American Abolitionists Debate Slave Redemption," in Kwame Anthony Appiah and Martin Bunzl, eds., *Buying Freedom: The Ethics and Economics of Slave Redemption* (Princeton, NJ: 2007), 200–10; New York *Tribune*, October 1, 1850; Boston *Post*, December 3, 1850; Norfolk *Herald* (n.d.), in Boston *Herald*, December 13, 1850; *The Rev. J. W. Loguen As a Slave and As a Freeman. A Narrative of Real Life* (1859, rpr., New York: 1968), 392–93; *North Star*, April 3, 1851; for comment on the Rose ransom see Cleveland *Democrat*, October 18, 1850; for ransoming as a result of intimidation see Stephen Kantrowitz, *More Than Freedom*; for the Bolding ransom see Albany *Evening Journal*, September 4, 5, 1851; *Liberator*, September 5, 12, 1851; New York *Tribune*, September 3, 6, 13, 1851, February 18, 1853; Harrisburg *Pennsylvania Telegraph*, March 2, 1853; the names of the Poughkeepsie contributors to Bolding's ransom can be found in "The Year Book, Dutchess County Historical Society," Volume 20, 1935, 53–55, a copy of which was kindly supplied by Lynn K. Lucas, Local History Librarian, Adriance Memorial Library, Poughkeepsie.

[50] *Anti-Slavery Standard*, October 10, 1850; *Impartial Citizen*, October 26, 1850; New York *Herald*, October, 2, 1850.

[51] See Finkenbine, "A Community Militant and Organized," and Katherine DuPre Lumkin, "'The General Plan Was Freedom': A Negro Secret Order on the Underground Railroad," *Phylon*, 28 (Spring 1967) for a history of the Detroit organization. See Chapter 1 for a discussion of these organizations.

fugitives, making their presence felt at commissioners' hearings, and, wherever possible, frustrating efforts to return fugitives. At the heart of the resistance were the ubiquitous black crowds that materialized with a speed that surprised local observers. They were sometimes few in number, other times their size overwhelmed the authorities' capacity to control them. And always, at least as far as local reporters were concerned, there was the troubling presence of black women, who in many situations took the leading role. These black crowds were the foot soldiers without whom resistance would have been muted if not impossible. When Stephen Bennett, a fugitive from Baltimore, Maryland, was taken at Columbia, Pennsylvania, "Tow Hill," the black section of the city, marched "en masse" on the jail in an unsuccessful attempt to rescue him. Bennett had lived in the city nearly four years, married, and started a family. He was, as far as the crowd was concerned, a free man and a full-fledged member of the community. An onlooker was struck by the many women in the crowd and how excitable and "intractable" they were – much more so than the men, he reported. This observer called on all the conventional descriptions of female political agitation with one significant twist: their actions, he was convinced, were the result of "their ignorance of the law."[52]

Courthouses, commissioners' rooms and the surrounding streets were turned into theaters of political resistance. Sometimes these crowds were reinforced by white abolitionist women who attended hearings to bear witness and to lend their support. The response to the arrest of Euphemia Williams in Philadelphia and her hearing on an "intensely cold day," in February 1851, was fairly typical. A black crowd filled the streets outside the court as well as the front and rear of the "State House." Inside, one side of the courtroom was occupied by white women, mainly Quakers, including Lucretia Mott, a leading figure in the local and national abolitionist movement. Williams sat "surrounded by her colored female friends," opposite the judge, her infant daughter in her arms. Her other children – "too young to comprehend the danger which threatened them" – sat on the floor by her feet. The judge's decision in her favor was cause for immediate celebration. Williams was taken to an impromptu meeting at the Philadelphia Institute, at the end of which the family was placed in carriages, the horses untied and replaced by many of "her colored friends," who pulled them home. Her female friends marched behind, keeping up with the "dog-trot of those who were dragging" them. In the final scene of defiance, the parade route took the crowd past the home of the attorneys for the defense, where they were serenaded with "hearty cheers," then to the hotel where Williams' claimant had met with his lawyers to plan

[52] Lancaster *Examiner & Herald*, January 29, 1851; Columbia *Spy*, January 15, 1851; Philadelphia *Evening Bulletin*, January 24, 25, 1851; *Pennsylvanian*, January 15, 1851; *Pennsylvania Freeman*, January 30, 1851.

her capture, and finally past the home of the slaveholder's attorney, who was "saluted with hideous groans."[53]

When coupled with such open defiance of the law as occurred in the case of Shadrach Minkins, victories such as Williams', even if they were few, worried supporters of the law. It mattered little that in the majority of cases that came to a hearing fugitives were remanded. There were disturbingly too many instances where reclamation had either been delayed or failed. More significantly, there was ample evidence that the law had no appreciable effect on the number of slaves who continued to escape. Frequent articles on the movement of former slaves in the North and almost daily advertisements for runaways in border state newspapers, gave the lie to the law's ability to stem the tide of escapes. For every runaway taken and returned, scores were reported on their way to a new life in Canada or in less secure areas of the North.

A law that denied some of the fundamental principles of jurisprudence to the accused on the grounds that to do so would undermine its very purpose and yet failed to stem the tide of escapes was ineffective, to say nothing of its constitutionality. Commissioners, the sole arbiters of an accused fugitive's future and over whose decision there could be no appeal, quickly became the focus of community resentment. They were not constrained by the usual safeguards of civil or criminal law; they were, one historian has written, "a kind of chartered tyrant." Frequently compared unfavorably to the judges who wielded unrestrained power and tyrannized England during the reigns of Charles II and James II, these "ten-dollar, pettifogging, unconstitutional judges," elevated to power by the "kidnapping act of 1850," were, one editor observed, transformed from the humble duties of "taking affidavits and acknowledgement of bail" to exercising "jurisdiction" and rendering judgments that were "absolute, and without appeal." It was for this reason that, whenever the opportunity presented itself, opponents constantly looked for ways to challenge their authority. The cumulative effects of such pressure led, in part, to Richard McAllister's decision to leave his post in Harrisburg before his term had expired. When the son of David Paul Brown, who for years had been the lead defender of fugitives in Philadelphia, accepted a position as commissioner following the death of Edward Ingraham, the black community's disappointment was palpable; they felt deeply betrayed.[54] Every decision to remand a fugitive raised the level of agitation and in so doing increased political tensions on both sides

---

[53] *Pennsylvania Freeman*, February 13, 1851; Philadelphia *Telegraphic Evening Bulletin*, February 5, 1851; New York *Tribune*, February 11, 1851. Whenever slaveholders' claims were rejected, the black community celebrated, as they did in Chicago following the release of Moses Johnson in June 1851. A meeting at the local AME Church started a fund to buy engraved cups for Johnson's lawyers. A second meeting issued an address of thanks to the entire defense team. Their work, the address concluded, had resulted in the "triumph of liberty." Chicago *Democrat*, June 20, 1851; *Western Citizen*, June 24, 1851; *Liberator*, July 11, 1851.

[54] Von Frank, *The Trials of Anthony Burns*, 140; New York *Tribune*, March 1, 1856; *National Anti-Slavery Standard*, February 14, 1857.

of the slavery divide. It quickly became apparent to all those who viewed the Compromise – and especially the law – as the last best chance to keep the country together that something had to be done to stop the agitation.

Those who put their faith in the law to ease the growing rift between the sections must have known better. Northern opponents had made it abundantly clear that their voices would not be silenced. Salmon Chase spoke for many: the law, he had predicted, would "produce more agitation than any other which has ever been adopted by Congress." Ignoring such warnings, supporters insisted it was the best (and possibly only) way to address a problem that had driven a political wedge between the sections. Moreover, once it was enacted, there seemed to be no earthly reason why it should not be enforced. To not do so was to challenge the legitimacy and majesty of all laws. The result would be anarchy. If there was such a thing as a morally indefensible law, opponents countered, then the Fugitive Slave Law was one. As such, it should not be obeyed. "Things have come to a sad pass indeed," an Indiana Free-Soil editor observed, "if our reverence for law is so unbounded that an act of Congress which tramples upon the Constitution and outrages humanity is to stifle the utterances of our cherished convictions and thus preclude the possibility of its own repeal, lest the people should become 'excited with angry controversy.' " Every refusal to assist in the recapture of a fugitive when commanded to do so by the authorities was, consequently, a legitimate act of resistance. He saw no other peaceful option than the law's repeal.[55]

Chase was right; the meaning and reach of the law would come to dominate the political life of communities, large and small, in the weeks and months after its passage. Debate over its merits dominated the editorial pages of newspapers. One such editorial in Lawrenceburg, a small town on the Ohio River near where Indiana, Kentucky, and Ohio intersect, provides a glimpse into just how far the debate over the merits of the law reached. Like other southern Indiana towns, Lawrenceburg was established by settlers with deep roots in Virginia and Kentucky. They were later joined by former residents of the Northeast and England. There was also, by 1850, a small black community, which was at the heart of a surprisingly vibrant arm of the Underground Railroad led by Elijah Anderson. An editorial in the local newspaper calling for support of the law produced a blistering response from state senator James P. Milliken, a member of the Free-Soil Party, who denounced the law as "tyrannical," a violation of human rights and a disgrace in the "eyes of the whole civilized and Christian world." It might be reasonable, he was willing to concede, for a law to ask that fugitives not be assisted, but it could never compel people to join a master in the pursuit of his slave. On this matter, he was a proponent of nonintervention: let the slaveholder take care of his own slaves and catch them if he

---

[55] For the Chase quote see Frederick J. Blue, *Salmon P. Chase. A Life in Politics* (Kent, OH: 1987), 82; *Indiana True Democrat*, November 15, 29, 1850.

can, but he "would have nothing to do with it." The law, Milliken concluded, should be repealed. The editor responded with all the standard defenses of the law: it gave the slaveholder no new powers, it protected habeas corpus, and trials were not necessary, although the accused could introduce testimony. More importantly, it was the responsibility of communities such as Lawrenceburg to "act in justice to the South, and leave the redemption of the slave from bondage where he must be left, or harm to the whole Union be done." Laws may not always be fair but the philanthropic must be patient, "hoping for the coming of a better day when the spirit of reform shall be felt by all the people." The editor thought he saw unmistakable signs that a better day was at hand. What these signs were he did not say. But until that dawn broke, Lawrenceburg should continue to cling to its ties with its sister states across the river.[56]

The dispute over the law and its enforcement in Lawrenceburg echoed throughout the North. Many Whigs worried that continued agitation would be their political undoing. One Rochester editor put it bluntly: agitation endangered the Party. For others, it was diverting the country's attention from more important matters, such as reform of the tariff regime – an issue which, if addressed, could ease tensions and spur a faltering economy. Yet the Party seemed to wring its hands over every fugitive rendition. Others worried about the effects of agitation on the economy. Should it continue, one editor cautioned, the South would be pushed to find alternative markets and take steps to develop its own industries based on slave labor. The result would be damaging to Northern manufacturers, merchants and laborers. Both capital and labor, therefore, had a stake in seeking an end to the agitation. Every "capitalist and every laboring man at the North," one editor declared, has "a direct interest in allaying this slavery agitation, from which no possible good can come." The greatest harm would befall white laboring men if the agitation were allowed to continue unchecked, for the South would retaliate by expelling its free black population. That "dark cloud" of one and a half million "idle and desolate" and "generally thriftless" free blacks would descend on the North with dire consequences for white laboring men. Worried by the prospect of an influx of Southern free blacks, a few Northern legislatures, including Indiana, enacted laws to exclude them. In his first message to Congress, President Fillmore attempted to throw the full weight of his office behind the calls for patience and a cessation of agitation. The recent "adjustment" as he delicately called the Compromise, was a just and "final settlement" of a set of "dangerous and

---

[56] Lawrenceburg *Independent Press*, November 1, 8, 22, 1850, March 30, 1865. Milliken left the Senate in 1852 to return to his farm. By the end of the decade, he and his brother, Elias, took the inexplicable decision to move to Kirksville, Missouri, where they promptly ran afoul of proslavery forces and were forced to move once again, this time to Drakesville, Iowa. At the outbreak of the war, James enlisted in the Union army at the advanced age of sixty and died during the siege of Vicksburg in May 1863. Shepherd, *A Biographical Directory of the Indiana General Assembly*, 274. My thanks to Chris McHenry and the staff of the Lawrenceburg public library for copies of the local newspaper.

exciting subjects," that, he hoped, would allay growing "asperities and animosities" between the sections. The majority of the country, he declared, ignoring all the signs to the contrary around him, approved of the agreement and was willing to sustain all its features because they cherished the Union and had an abiding distrust of those who violated the law. The adjustment had rescued the country from a "wide and boundless agitation" and was guaranteed to restore "peace and quiet to the country and maintain inviolate the integrity of the Union." The law, therefore, had to be given a "fair trial." Fillmore's message, and his declared intention following the escape of the Crafts to use whatever authority he possessed to enforce the law, prompted one Detroit editor to predict the imminent end to antislavery agitation; its flame, he had no doubt, had been finally extinguished.[57]

Yet the calls for repeal or modification did not abate. Both houses of Ohio's legislature passed motions in support of repeal. In Michigan a similar resolution was defeated and in New York the legislature debated a resolution to nullify the law in the wake of the Henry Long case. Abolitionists flooded state and federal legislatures with petitions calling for repeal. The Boston Vigilance Committee circulated a number of petition blanks throughout the state comprising two columns, one for voters and another for nonvoters demanding that state legislators reaffirm the ban on the use of state jails to hold fugitives and calling for repeal on the grounds that the law was "immoral, inhuman and unconstitutional." In Pennsylvania, Governor William Johnson, a Whig, pocket vetoed a bill calling for repeal of the state's 1847 law, which refused the use of state prisons to hold suspected fugitives. Petitions to Congress brought to mind the damaging debate over the effort, twenty-five years earlier, to silence antislavery protest by banning petitions. It was a politically damaging decision no one wanted to revisit. When Senator David Atchison of Missouri moved to table a minor petition from Maine containing only three signatures, William Seward, his New York counterpart, took the opportunity to remind his colleagues of the earlier disastrous effort to table automatically all petitions and prevent any discussions of abolition, a decision that had exposed anti-abolitionists to the charge of wishing to curtail free speech. The right to petition, Seward insisted, had to be "respected and held sacred." Atchison got the message and retreated, proposing instead that the Maine petition be sent to the Judiciary Committee where, he hoped, it would languish. But in doing so, he provided opponents with another opening to continue the debate over the merits of the law. Andrew Butler of South Carolina threw up his hands in despair. It was impossible to silence agitation over the law; the Senate, he

---

[57] Troy *Daily Whig*, December 9, 28, 1850; Rochester *Daily American*, October 8, December 16, 1850; Albany *Argus*, November 21, 29, 1850; James D. Richardson, ed., *A Compilation of the Messages and Papers of the Presidents*, 11 Vols. (Washington, DC: 1912) IV, 2929; Detroit *Free Press*, March 15, 1851.

declared in obvious frustration, "might as well attempt to put a maniac asleep by lullabies as to restrain agitation on this subject."[58]

Butler's analogy notwithstanding, that was precisely what proponents of the law, in and out of Congress, were attempting to do. By late 1850 there were calls in Congress and in the press for a moratorium on any further discussions of the law. It had been legally enacted, declared constitutional by some of the most eminent legal minds, including members of the Supreme Court, and, as Henry Clay pointed out, with a few minor glitches, had been implemented. The country should now turn its attention to more pressing matters. David Yulee, senator of Florida, announced that he had been instructed by his state legislature not to vote on any "question touching on the Fugitive Slave Law" and he intended to follow those instructions to the letter. Over in the House, many signed on to a pledge calling on members to refuse any further discussion of slavery and to not elect or vote for anyone who was not committed to all aspects of the Compromise. Were it up to Senator James Cooper of Pennsylvania, all forms of agitation would cease so that "harmony and good feeling between the different sections of the Union" could, in his words, be cultivated, and obedience to the "constitution and laws...be inculcated and acted upon." Cooper spoke for many, but his choice of words was telling: on this score, the Union was still very much a work in progress and its future by no means assured. If the agitation did not cease, and the law was not enforced, it could lead, Associate Justice Samuel Nelson predicted, to anarchy and the destruction of the compact between the states. "If anyone supposes that this Union can be preserved," he warned, "after a material provision of the fundamental law upon which it rests is broken and thrown to the wind by one section of it...he is laboring under a delusion which the sooner he gets rid of the better."[59]

The problem for those calling for a cessation of agitation was how best to plug the political volcano of resistance that had erupted around the North. Pledges and pleadings were unavailing. The attempt to silence agitation, moreover, flew in the face of the history of the nation's founding, Senator John Hale of New Hampshire reminded his colleagues. Without it there would have been no Revolution and no Constitution, and were it to cease "everything worth having in our existence will die." Where there is no agitation, he warned, there is "stagnation, fetid corruption, and death." It is the means by which errors are addressed. Only those "hugging delusion and errors" have anything to fear

[58] *Congressional Globe, Second Session, Thirty-First Congress* (Washington, DC, 1851) 576; New York *Tribune,* March 29, 1851; Detroit *Free Press,* April 23, 1851; *Liberator,* November 1, 1850, January 3, 1851; *National Era,* April 3, 1851; New York *Herald,* January 14, 1851; Washington, DC, *Union,* January 18, 1851.

[59] *National Era,* January 23, 1851; *Congressional Globe, Second Session, Thirty-First Congress* (Washington, DC: 1851), 166, 578; Albany *Argus,* June 6, 1851; Albany *Evening Journal,* January 29, 1851.

from "the life-giving elements which will impart its healing as did the waters of the pool at the Beautiful Gate of the Temple." Even if Hale's historical claims could be dismissed as sheer hyperbole, Cooper was well aware of elements in the South who remained deeply suspicious of the government's ability, or its willingness, to enforce the law. Even more telling was the continued and widespread opposition to the law in the Free States. The editor of the New York *Herald* put his finger on the problem: "[E]very case of recapture, successful or unsuccessful," he pointed out, "affords material for agitation." Given such conditions, calls for repeal or modification of the law, Henry Clay insisted, had to be rejected. In the midst of such political turmoil, Congress could not entertain calls for changes. Let the "authority of the law be maintained; let it be executed," he declared, "let its defects, if there are any defects, be developed during the progress of its execution, and when there is a spirit of obedience pervading...the whole country, then and not till then will" it be time for a reassessment.[60]

In spite of the efforts of supporters to throw a blanket of silence over the law, opponents continued openly to defy federal and state authorities. They continued to shelter fugitives, pay for their passage to safety, temporarily house them, sometimes found them employment, and generally made life difficult for those who tried to enforce the law. Defiance of the law was unmistakable and may have been troubling, but it was, many claimed, quintessentially American. The threats faced by those who came North to claim slaves grew, it seemed, with every case. Opponents did not simply throw up barriers to enforcement, they vowed that the law had to be made a dead letter. The best way to do so, Frederick Douglass told a Syracuse meeting of the American Anti-Slavery Society, was to kill "two or three...slaveholders." Although he declared himself a peace advocate, someone opposed to the shedding of blood, slaveholders, nonetheless, had to be convinced they were in "danger of bodily harm." The South knew how to keep abolitionists away; it was time to do the same to slave catchers who came North. How else to "test the fidelity of men and women who hitherto have professed to believe in Human Brotherhood," especially when confronted by a president who had pledged openly the support of "the whole power of the army and navy" to ensure the law was enforced.[61]

Taken together, the calls for open defiance of the law, aiding slaves to escape, preventing the recapture of fugitives, and creating organizations the sole purpose of which was to prevent the smooth functioning of the law, struck some

---

[60] New York *Herald*, February 28, 1851; *Congressional Globe, Second Session, Thirty-First Congress* (Washington, DC: 1851), 577, 597.

[61] Syracuse *Standard*, January 10, 1851; New York *Tribune*, January 9, 11, 1851; Blassingame, ed., *The Frederick Douglass Papers*, Vol. 2, 272–76; Donald Yacavone, *Samuel Joseph May and the Dilemmas of the Liberal Persuasion, 1797–1871* (Philadelphia: 1991), 141. Jermain Loguen claimed he was doing just that in northwest New York and in Pennsylvania, but that more needed to be done if they ever hoped to make the law a dead letter. *Frederick Douglass Paper*, August 21, 1851.

proponents of the law as nothing short of treason. Those who cautioned against such intemperate language were brushed aside. What was a person to do who considered it a "bad law"? Were they simply to fold their tents or were they morally obligated to work against its enforcement by using long-established tools, that is, by agitation? History proved such activities worked; they were largely responsible for the repeal of First National Bank in the 1830s; in more recent times, those who opposed the Mexican War had adopted a similar approach. In neither case, one observer wrote, were they considered traitors.[62] But in the highly charged political atmosphere surrounding the law and its enforcement, those who organized to oppose it were labeled exactly that. The idea may have had its fullest articulation in a speech given by Daniel Webster in Syracuse, a place he and the president saw as a hotbed of resistance and one that, therefore, had to be cowed. "I am a lawyer and I value my reputation as a lawyer more than anything else," he told his audiences, "and I tell you, if men get together and declare a law of Congress shall not be executed in any case, and assemble in numbers to prevent the execution of such a law, they are traitors, and are guilty of treason, and bring upon themselves the penalties of the law." The law will be enforced, he pledged, "in all the great cities, here in Syracuse; in the midst of the next Anti-Slavery Convention, if the occasion shall arise; then we shall see what becomes of their lives and sacred honor."[63]

Webster would get his chance following events that took place on a farm near the small Pennsylvania town of Christiana in September 1851. Tensions had been on the rise in the area for some time as slaveholders stepped up their efforts to reclaim former slaves who had found refuge among black settlers, many of them fugitives, just north of the Maryland state line. Free black residents were also under constant threat from kidnappers. In response, blacks created an organization to resist these incursions. It was led by William Parker, who, in 1839 at the age of seventeen, escaped slavery in Anne Arundel County, Maryland. Parker spoke for the organization: "I thought of my fellow-servants left behind, bound in the chains of slavery – and I was free! I thought that, if I had the power, they should soon be free as I was; and I formed a resolution that I would assist in liberating every one within my reach at the risk of my life, and that I would devise some plan for their entire liberation."[64] Parker and the others would get their chance in early fall 1851. A few months earlier, Edward

[62] See the exchange between an anonymous letter writer and the editor in the Springfield *Republican*, April 24, 1851.

[63] Daniel Webster, *The Writings and Speeches of Daniel Webster*, 18 Vols. (Boston: 1903), XIII, 419–20.

[64] *Liberator*, January 17, 1851; Parker quoted in Thomas P. Slaughter, *Bloody Dawn: The Christiana Riot and Racial Violence in the Antebellum North* (New York: 1991), 49; Baltimore *Sun*, September 18, 1851; Washington, DC, *Union*, September 17, 1851; Roderick W. Nash, "William Parker and the Christiana Riot," *Journal of Negro History*, 46 (January 1961), 24; Jonathan Katz, *Resistance at Christiana. The Fugitive Slave Rebellion, Christiana, Pennsylvania, September 11, 1851* (New York: 1974), 23, 28, 76; W. H. Hensel, *The Christiana Riot and the Treason Trials of 1851. An Historical Sketch* (Lancaster, PA: 1911), 15–17.

THE CHRISTIANA TRAGEDY

FIGURE 1. The Christiana Tragedy. (William Still, *Underground Railroad*)

Gorsuch of Baltimore County had gotten word from an informant that three of his former slaves, who had escaped in late 1849, were living and working on a farm in Christiana. Gorsuch, along with five others, including members of his family, went first to Philadelphia, where they obtained an arrest warrant from Edward Ingraham and procured the services of Henry H. Kline, the deputy marshal, and two local policemen. The Philadelphia black community soon got wind of their plans and dispatched Samuel Williams, a local tavern keeper and a member of the "Special Secret Committee," formed sometime before 1850, to tail the Gorsuch party and to alert Parker and the others to the danger. Soon after Gorsuch's arrival, the alarm was sounded, bringing 150 blacks from adjacent farms. Gorsuch was surprised by the speed with which the opposition was summoned and the fact that the fugitives and Parker were prepared and well armed. The standoff also attracted a few white onlookers to the scene. In spite of warnings from Parker that they were determined to defend those in the farm house, Gorsuch decided to attack. The result was a disaster. Gorsuch was killed and one of his sons seriously injured. Parker and two others left immediately for Canada, going through Rochester, New York, where they were housed temporarily by Frederick Douglass. A $1,000 reward, later raised to $2,000, was posted for Parker's arrest.[65]

---

[65] William Parker, "The Freedmen's Story," *The Atlantic Monthly*, XVII (February 1866), [http://docsouth.unc.edu/parker/parker.html] 159–62; Slaughter, *Bloody Dawn*, 53, 66, 77.

A force of one hundred, including marines and Philadelphia policemen, was immediately dispatched to the area. The initial sweep by the military netted twenty-five suspects, twenty-three of them black. Days later an additional thirteen were arrested. Newspapers throughout the North gave extensive coverage to what many considered an open act of treason. "Here is treason," one trumpeted, and "war levied against the United States." The area, another observed, had been the focal point of opposition to the Fugitive Slave Law, a place where passions had been "inflamed by abolitionist harangues and incendiary speeches," and where fanatics called on blacks to resist its enforcement, suggesting the "commission of various high crimes, even including murder." Others hoped cooler heads would prevail. While resistance to law is always an offense against the peace of society, inherent in the foundation of all laws, one editor cautioned, was the concept of a "higher law." Abolitionists, therefore, should not be condemned for their conscientious opposition to the law, but those who took the life of the slaveholder should be brought to trial. But none of this, the editors of the New York *Times* concluded, rose to the level of treason.[66]

Webster's Syracuse speech, and the threats he leveled against opponents of the law, were echoed in the general responses to the shoot-out. In early October, thirty-six blacks and five whites, including Castner Hanway, a local farmer who had only been an onlooker, were indicted by a grand jury for the crime of levying war against the country, with being armed and with having "prepared, composed, published, and dispersed divers books, pamphlets, letters, declarations, resolutions, addresses, papers and writings [containing] incitement, encouragement, and exhortations, to move, induce, and persuade" runaway slaves to resist the law.[67] As if to make it unmistakably clear that these were indictments driven exclusively by political considerations, Gorsuch's death was conspicuously absent from the indictment. E. Louis Lowe, governor of Maryland, reminded the president that his state had always stood resolutely against those calling for secession. But harmony between the two states, he seemed to threaten, could only be guaranteed if the judges and jury in Pennsylvania completely vindicated the law. Fillmore needed little persuasion. As he told Lowe, he had already ordered the arrest of all those remotely associated with what had occurred, and that the district attorney was looking into whether the crime rose to the level of treason. Lowe, in turn, had come under pressure from public meetings in Baltimore that called on him to act in defense of the state's interests. The composition of the team of prosecutors also reflected the political nature of the trial. It was made up, in part, of Robert

---

[66] Washington, DC, *Union*, September 10, 1850; Lancaster *Examiner & Herald*, September 17, 1851; Philadelphia *Evening Bulletin*, October 4, 1851; Harrisburg *State Journal*, September 23, 1851; New York *Times*, September 19, 1851.

[67] Slaughter, *Bloody Dawn*, 115; Steven Lubet, *Fugitive Justice. Runaways, Rescuers, and Slavery on Trial* (Cambridge, MA: 2010), 75.

J. Brent, Maryland's attorney general, Z. Collins Lee, US district attorney for Baltimore, and the Pennsylvania senator, James Cooper, who had supported the passage of the law.[68]

Like fugitive slave hearings, the treason trial in the district court, located in Philadelphia's iconic Independence Hall, attracted large crowds of both women and men, black and white, who packed the court bearing, as Slaughter has written, "silent witness to the proceedings." As was done at Euphemia Williams' hearing, the black defenders wore similar clothes and scarfs, making it difficult for policemen to identify them. In his remarks to the jury, Robert Brent argued that the entire neighborhood around Christiana was infested with a hatred of the law and that whites such as Hanway went to the farm by "pre-arrangement"; blacks knew they were reliable. Hanway should not be convicted because he refused to assist in the recapture when requested, as the law required; it was his actual "*conniving, inciting, aiding and abetting,*" that was at the heart of the indictment, for he had connected himself to an "organized band, which had been formed there for treason." The armed blacks were simply "his instruments of war," an "ignorant and infuriated horde" who depended on him for advice. Hanway, Brent concluded, could have incited them by either "word, speech or gesture." Samuel Williams, the spy, sent by the "foul treachery going on in Philadelphia" to warn of the coming of the slave catchers, gave them ample opportunity to arm themselves and to be prepared. That, in itself, was an act of treason. "Any combination...of white and black persons to prevent the execution of the Fugitive Slave Law," he concluded expansively, "is treason."[69]

In his charge to the grand jury, Judge John Kane echoed what had become, for supporters in the months since the passage of the law, a mainstay of their political vocabulary. Even before his speeches in Syracuse, Webster had written, "[i]f any law of the land be resisted by force of arms or force of numbers with a declared intent to resist the application of that law in all cases, this is levying war against the government within the meaning of the Constitution." The rescue of Shadrach Minkins had confirmed that interpretation. It was, one editor argued, a "virtual insurrection against the government." Treason, Kane now told the jury, was committed whenever officers of justice are "impeded and repelled by menaces and violence," when there exists a combination to "forcibly resist" the law, and when gatherings pledged to defy execution of the law. He concluded with a simple formula: "To instigate treason, is to commit it."[70]

---

[68] Baltimore *Sun*, September 19, 1851; Hensel, *The Christiana Riot*, 38–39; Paul Finkelman, "The Treason Trial of Castner Hanway," in Michael R. Belknap, ed., *American Political Trials* (Westport, CT: 1994), 84–86.

[69] *Speech of the Hon. Robert J. Brent, Attorney-General of Maryland, in the Case of the United States v. Castner Hanway, for Treason* (Philadelphia: n.d.), 7–24.

[70] Boston *Herald*, February 1, 1851; New York *Herald*, April 5, 1851; Collison, *Shadrach Minkins*, 139; Lubet, *Fugitive Justice*, 74–75; William Still, *The Underground Railroad* (1872, rpr., Chicago: 1970), 371–73.

But the efforts of Kane and the prosecutors were unavailing; all of the accused were found innocent. Treason in this case required that the prosecution prove that Hanway and the others meant to nullify the law. Being on the scene, as Hanway's defense counsels readily admitted he was, was not, in itself, an act of conspiracy. Nor was provoking resistance to the law. Samuel Williams, cleared of treason, would face a subsequent misdemeanor charge under Section 7 of the Fugitive Slave Law. Someone, it seemed, had to be punished for what had happened at Christiana. Henry Kline and one of Gorsuch's nephews testified that Williams had followed them to Christiana to alert the fugitives and so frustrate the application of the law. He did no such thing, Williams told the court; he had gone to the area only to inform free blacks of another planned kidnapping. Williams was cleared of all charges. In the end, the federal government had spent an estimated $50,000 to bring a case to trial that only a relatively small circle of politicians and newspaper editors thought stood much chance of success.[71]

The editor of the New York *Times* was right: if the issue was the murder of the slaveholder then the accused should have been brought to trial in state court. Clearly it was not. "Never before – and, indeed, never since," Slaughter writes, "were so many Americans charged in court with a treasonous crime." The decision to charge the defendants with 117 counts of treason was driven solely by political considerations. It is even unlikely that those who decided what charges to levy could have taken comfort in the fact that Hanway was financially ruined as a result of the case, and that the others found themselves deep in debt. Recognizing the significance of the case, black communities throughout the North rallied to the support of the black defendants. Meetings in large and small cities raised funds to cover their debt. The women of the Chicago Mutual Protection Society, for example, raised $20 following a large meeting. The Sadsbury Monthly Meeting of Friends agreed to cover the costs of the white defenders, including Hanway, who was not a Quaker.[72]

The actions of William Parker and the other defenders at Christiana, the promptness with which the organized black community in Philadelphia moved to subvert Gorsuch's plans to recapture his lost slaves, and the fact that a small number of witnesses gathered outside the farm to bear witness to the assault on the fugitives and their protectors, pushed the government to overreact in an effort to save political face. It was an overreaction based on a conviction

---

[71] Lubet, *Fugitive Justice*, 107; Philadelphia *Evening Bulletin*, October 1, 3, 1850, January 13, 1852; *Federal Cases, United States v. Williams*, Book 28, No. 16, 704, 634.

[72] *Frederick Douglass' Paper*, October 16, 1851, January 8, 1852; Slaughter, *Bloody Dawn*, 109, 134. An Ohio editor denounced the black residents of Zanesville for holding a meeting and passing resolutions in support of those who took their stand against Gorsuch. Such activities, he warned, could result in them being driven from the state. *Ohio State Journal*, November 3, 1851.

that blacks, as Henry Clay had argued earlier, were not citizens, not members of the political family, and so were not covered by any guarantees of the Constitution. Moreover, they and their abolitionist masters were largely responsible for the crisis that had engulfed the country following adoption of the law. "Modern abolitionists," as one Pennsylvania editor put it, were a danger to the country. The political question continued to linger throughout the first year of the law's operation; who shall prevail, the editor wanted to know, the majority who supported the law or the minority who did not, the "old Saxon blood, which, at vast sacrifice, founded the republics; or these African fugitives, whom…Pennsylvanians neither wish, nor will have?" The editor even ventured to think the impossible: while secession would undoubtedly be bad, he conceded, the result, should modern abolitionism prevail, would, he predicted, be "infinitely worse."[73]

The Philadelphia editor's worst fears would be confirmed within days of the close of the Christiana treason trial with news that William Henry, commonly known as Jerry, another wanted fugitive slave, had been rescued, this time in Syracuse, New York, the city where Daniel Webster had issued his dire warnings to abolitionists and all those who chose to resist the law. As if to drive home the political nature of the rescue, it occurred at a time when the radical abolitionist Liberty Party was holding its annual meeting in the city. Church bells sounded the warning that a fugitive had been taken, bringing a large group of blacks and whites into the streets and to the commissioner's room where the hearings were to be held. Before the hearings could begin, Jerry was whisked away. But he made it only as far as the street before he was retaken and lodged in the police office. A crowd of about three hundred responded, battering down the door of the office and removing the fugitive, who was rushed off in a carriage to a safe home in the city, after which he was taken to Canada. Critics of the rescue immediately circulated a petition, signed by nearly seven hundred, calling for a "Law and Order" meeting later that month. Supporters countered with a meeting of "Friends of Human Freedom," which met two weeks after the rescue. The rescue, Samuel J. May, the Unitarian minister and prominent abolitionist, told the meeting, did not "violate the law," it simply "trampled on tyranny."[74] The rescue seemed to confirm the views held

---

[73] Philadelphia *Evening Bulletin*, September 12, 1851.

[74] Angela Murphy, "'It Outlaws Me, and I Outlaw It,' Resistance to the Fugitive Slave Law in Syracuse, New York," *Afro Americans in New York Life and History*, 28 (January 2004), 56–58; Jayme A. Sokolow, "The Jerry McHenry Rescue and the Growth of Northern Anti-Slavery Sentiment During the 1850s," *Journal of American Studies*, 16 (1982), 433; Hunter, *To Set the Captives Free*, 128; Monique Palernaude Roach, "The Rescue of William "Jerry" Henry: Antislavery and Racism in the Burned-over District," *New York History*, 82 (April 2001), 138–42. For an early history of the rescue see Earl E. Sperry, *The Jerry Rescue October 1, 1851* (Syracuse, NY: 1924); Murphy, *The Jerry Rescue*.

by many Southerners – that the law could not be enforced in communities where opposition to slavery was strong.

With the memory of Christiana still painfully fresh, John J. Crittenden, the attorney general, eschewing any talk of treason, called instead on the US attorney for Syracuse to bring charges against the rescuers for violating the law. Thirteen were charged for participating in the rescue. The trials, which lasted two years at an estimated cost of $50,000, resulted in the conviction of only one of the accused – Enoch Reed, an African American, who died while awaiting the appeal of his conviction. In a final act of symbolic defiance, supporters of the rescue sent President Fillmore the shackles used to hold Jerry.[75]

By the end of the first year of the law's operation it was clear to all dispassionate observers that, rather than quieting agitation over slavery as so many of its proponents had hoped, it had stirred passionate opposition and defiance. Blacks and their white supporters, who packed hearings and courthouses, who insisted on representation for all accused of being fugitives, who publicly pledged to defy the law and prevent the return of fugitives, may not have had it all their own way, but they could claim some stunning successes. Those in Congress who called for a cessation of agitation and who vowed no longer to discuss the law or, for that matter, slavery, looked on in disbelief as each fugitive slave case was transformed into a rallying cry against the law and the institution itself. Those who pleaded for political calm and the cessation of agitation looked longingly for signs of hope. As 1851 drew to a close, the editor of the New York *Herald,* a staunch supporter of the law, concluded rather optimistically that, on the whole, the law was being enforced satisfactorily. More importantly, the South could see that the North was acting in good faith. Yet he worried that the "danger was not yet over," for there were, he had to admit, still a few irritating spots of contention that seemed to defy the best efforts of the authorities. Abolitionist agitation, which another observer decried as the "wet nurse of treason," had not been silenced; the "snake" may have been "scotched," but, another had to admit, it had not been killed. Bluster and threats from leading politicians such as Daniel Webster also had little effect; agitation continued and showed no sign of abating. Following the shoot-out at Christiana and the rescue of Jerry, a meeting of blacks in Cleveland decided to raise money to offset the cost of the trials. Their acts of solidarity with the fugitives, they declared, were a vital part of a wider international struggle against oppression, which included their support for struggles in Germany and

---

[75] Syracuse *Standard,* January 31, September 27, 1852, February 2, 1853. My thanks to Angela Murphy for providing me with copies of the reports. New York *Tribune,* January 28, 1853; Murphy, "'It Outlaws Me, and I Outlaw It,'" 58–61; Samuel Ringgold Ward, *Autobiography of a Fugitive Slave* (London: 1855).

Hungary. Theirs, they maintained, was a fight for freedom and the rights of the oppressed everywhere.[76] Their sustained actions pushed the authorities to over-react. In doing so, they helped to keep alive the political debate over the future of slavery and the rights of African Americans, a debate that many had hoped the law would have silenced.

[76] New York *Herald*, October 20, November 13, 14, 1851; Rochester *American*, April 15, 1851; Cleveland *Herald*, November 22, 1851.

# 3

## Compromise and Colonize

When, at the end of almost three months of agitation over the Fugitive Slave Law, it appeared that the country was no closer to reconciliation, Elisha Whittlesey, the first comptroller of the Treasury in the Fillmore administration and the person responsible for covering the cost of the rendition of fugitive slaves, suggested a possible solution to what seemed like an increasingly intractable problem. He knew of what he spoke. His was a conservative Whig solution. It included a declaration of opposition to slavery; a condemnation of abolitionist agitation; recognition that, in the end, slavery's future depended entirely on those who owned slaves; and, finally, the removal of free blacks and freed slaves from the country. Although he was opposed to slavery, it answered no "good purpose," as he quaintly put it to a friend, to interfere in "the domestic relations" of slaveholders. There were thousands, if not "tens of thousands" of slave owners, he estimated, who would "liberate their slaves" if people in the Free States would cease "interfering with the institution of slavery." The fact that abolitionists did little to help escaping slaves to settle permanently among them struck Whittlesey as utterly perverse. Under the circumstances, the only option available, the one that would ensure the ultimate emancipation of the slaves and the peace of the country, was to cease agitation, allow slaveholders the time and freedom to do with their slaves as they saw fit and, when they did decide on a policy of manumission, provide them with a place where they could send the emancipated. The obvious location was Africa and the colony of Liberia, now thirty years old, a place where, because of its climate, whites could not live, a place set aside by nature and Providence for the black man. The void created by the removal of former slaves would be filled, he predicted, by the starving "lower classes" of Europe who would be invited to come to America as laborers. In that way, over time, Whittlesey reasoned, America would rid itself of slavery and become both prosperous and wholly white.[1]

---

[1] Elisha Whittlesey to S. S. Southworth, Washington, DC, January 13, 1851, container 51, Elisha Whittlesey Papers, Western Reserve Historical Society, Cleveland, Ohio; David Brion Davis,

At the time, Whittlesey was riding a wave of resurgent colonization-ism, which peaked in the years after Liberian independence in 1847 and the Compromise of 1850, with its promise of sectional reconciliation. In the weeks following adoption of the Compromise, newspapers throughout the North ran frequent articles on the history of Liberia, highlighting its accomplishments as well as its potential for expanding trade and missionary work, curtailing the slave trade, and bringing civilization to the backward. A sense of optimism that the tide had turned in favor of the colonizationists' plans for Liberia was captured in a letter by "J" to his local newspaper. Colonizationist societies in the East were reenergized in the wake of Liberian independence, he observed, trade was improving, native tribes were no longer restless, $10,000 had been donated for the establishment of a college in Monrovia – Liberia's capital – and Virginia was leading the way with an allocation of $30,000 to its local colonization society to aid in the relocation of black Virginians to Liberia, a lead, he predicted, other states would soon follow. The Virginia Colonization Society, like so many others, was reconstituted in 1849 after years of inactivity with the governor at its head, a clear sign of the state's commitment to the cause. Not only was the new interest in Liberia spurred on by its independence, Governor John B. Floyd told the new leadership of the Virginia Colonization Society, but it was also driven by what he described as the "excited state of the public mind" over slavery. What lay hidden behind Floyd's rather cryptic phrasing was the push by many in the western part of the state to break the stranglehold of eastern slaveholders whose political supremacy rested on counting slaves for purposes of representation. The westerners looked to a new constitution to subvert, as Tyler-McGraw argues, old politics. Support for African colonization was part of the agenda to "weaken the power of eastern Virginia." The removal of the free black population, a later annual meeting declared, was the best way to respond to the "demands of Southern patriotism and benevolence" and the only way to counter "the mischievous and reckless enterprise of Abolitionists." Removal, in other words, was both a "political and social necessity." But removal also had wider national political resonance for, as one Washington, DC, newspaper put it, free blacks continued to be a "source of excitement between the states of the Union." They were the great evil, the "extraneous substance that irritated the social system of America." Admittedly, the many fugitive slave cases that had occurred in the weeks since

*The Problem of Slavery in the Age of Emancipation* (New York: 2014), 146–17 explores this solution in more detail as does Nicholas Guyatt in *Bind Us Apart. How Enlightenment Americans Invented Racial Separation* (New York: 2016). Over the next few years, Whittlesey's views would be echoed almost literally by newspaper editors. See the *Southern Illinoisan*, July 29, 1853, which considered slavery "morally wrong and utterly opposed to reason," but which condemned abolitionists. The editor saw signs of growing support for emancipation in the South but warned that slaveholders should be left to themselves to sort through the best way to achieve it. But he had no doubt emancipation had to be coupled with colonization.

the passage of the law had "excited for them a temporary sympathy," nonetheless everything should be done, another editorial advised, to remove what it called this "bone of contention."[2]

But how best to resolve this problem and heal a divided nation continued to exercise the minds of advocates of colonization. In a series of expansive editorials, one Pennsylvania newspaper offered a solution that Elisha Whittlesey would have endorsed. How was America to resolve the continuing crisis between the races when neither social nor political equality was possible and when blacks demonstrated a frustrating reluctance to work for their own advancement, the editor asked? He had no doubt that the destiny of the "colored race" must be resolved if the country was ever to attain peace. Were they to be kept in their present condition or be allowed to rise to a status of equality with whites were questions that carried as much significance as how best to address the issue of slavery. The answer, the editor declared, was to be found in the separation of the races. Unlike the Saxons, Negroes were not "fond of labor," were not producers and were quite content with their present lot. The race lacked industry and energy. Whites who endured similar treatment would have done something to ameliorate their condition long ago. Because of this lack of initiative, blacks had become a burden on society. They inhabited jails and almshouses in disproportionate numbers, and epidemics were rampant in "black suburbs." Lifting them up would not only be enormously expensive, it would, he anticipated, have little impact. Moreover, the climate of America was not one where blacks could prosper. As a tropical plant cannot thrive "side by side with a temperate plant in the latter's environment," the Negro, he observed, may live in this nonnative soil but could never prosper, even if he were granted full social and political equality, something no one thought possible. The "rough Saxon and the gentle African" could never "thrive in common," for social equality meant racial amalgamation, an idea he dismissed as a "horrible monstrosity" and a "violation of the laws of Nature." Where two races cannot intermarry there could be no social equality, he pontificated. Furthermore, medical science had shown that "the progeny of a black and white perish invariably in the fourth generation unless a return is made to one of the original stocks and the stamina of the degraded breed thus kept up." All of this was governed by what he called the "law of race," under which amalgamation led simultaneously to

---

[2] For the "J" letter see *Missouri Republican*, September 12, 1850. For a sample of pro-colonization editorials see Quincy *Herald*, August 28, September 29, 1851, Detroit *Free Press*, February 25, 26, 1851, and Springfield *Republican*, January 28, 1851; "Minutes of the Virginia Branch of the American Colonization Society, November 4, 1823–February 5, 1859," Virginia Historical Society, Richmond, Virginia; "Appropriation by the State of Virginia with an Appeal for Additional Funds," Mss. 1 L5684, Folder 32, John Letcher Papers, Virginia Historical Society; Marie Tyler-McGraw, *An African Republic. Black and White Virginians in the Making of Liberia* (Chapel Hill, NC: 2007), 54–55; for the Washington *Republican* article see *National Era*, November 28, 1850; *Southern Illinoisan*, July 29, 1853.

the deterioration of Saxon stock and the disappearance of the colored race. Granting blacks political rights would be equally futile, for it would only lead to further alienation between the races by heightening jealousies that would "convulse the country" and eventually either destroy the republic or lead to "the expulsion or enslavement of the blacks." The editor could not imagine a time when blacks would serve in Congress or share in the operation of government. Such an eventuality would lead to a racial civil war resulting in the devastation of the land and the ruin of blacks. It was simply impossible for the lion to lie down with the lamb. What galled even more was the "blind tenacity" with which blacks clung to the idea that America was as much their country as it was the whites'. What was to be gained, he wondered, by blacks such as Frederick Douglass insisting on social equality, on the right to travel unmolested, to a seat at "the public table, the most luxurious state-room, and room on the promenade deck to walk with white females on his arm"? The white race shrank instinctively from such social mixing, a revulsion that could not be dismissed as idle prejudice, for it was an "instinct of race," which ensured the "health and vigor of all the races." The only way to avoid such calamitous results was the separation of the races and the colonization of blacks in Africa. There was no nobler mission open to blacks than "colonizing, civilizing and Christianizing" their "native continent." For the last thirty years "the angel" had been hovering over the heads of Negroes, offering them the "golden crown" of colonization in Africa, but they were so busy "raking among the muck and slothfulness and ease" that they had failed to recognize this "heavenly visitant." The editor ended with a rallying cry: "Men of Africa awake, gird your loins, go forth and do the work before you!"[3]

The editorials produced a flurry of supportive letters, some calling for the removal of this "social pest" by forced emigration, each one prompting the editor to revisit the subject and expand his views on the causes of the problem as well as to offer further suggestions on the best way to address them. Insisting he was a "friend of the African," whom he regarded as a brother deserving of his aid, the editor saw no other alternative but to be bluntly honest: the African's place, he insisted, was in Africa, not America. Expatriation, moreover, was an act of self-preservation. Every country, he declared, had a right to "expatriate, for good and sufficient reasons, any portion of its population." It was done in the case of criminals. But even when no crime was committed, the right to do so could never be abridged. The proof was to be found in the nation's removal of the Indians. If the people willed it, the government had the power and responsibility to colonize "negroes, if necessary, by *force*." He, however, did not anticipate such an eventuality because there were unmistakable signs that public opinion was moving in the direction of accepting colonization as inevitable. The Negro, it appeared, would have no choice but to leave. The

[3] Philadelphia *Evening Bulletin*, January 21, 25, February 1, 11, 1851.

fact that they continued to reject this proffered hand of friendship was ample proof of their "positive inferiority."[4]

Other supporters of colonization had less to say about the political power of the majority to impose its will, choosing instead to emphasize the philanthropic benefits to be gained from expanded missionary activity in Africa. Providence, one editor observed, seemed to be calling black Americans to "the great and noble work of civilizing and Christianizing the benighted millions in the land of their forefathers." Africans, it seemed to another editor, had been placed in America with that specific end in mind. Without the slave trade and slavery, none of this would have been possible. "In these things," he concluded, "we see how Providence is ever ruling human slavery for good, how, through its instrumentalities, perhaps all of Africa is to be redeemed, Christianized and civilized." There was a purpose to slavery, he repeated: through it the African was exposed to the mysteries of Christianity so that he could return to spread the word in the land of his forefathers. The victims of American slavery were to be the benefactors of African civilization, called by Providence, David Brion Davis writes, to "lift Africa out of darkness."[5]

If, prior to 1840, the call for removal was seen as an opportunity for blacks to create "their own America" somewhere else, as Nicholas Guyatt has convincingly argued, in the wake of the political crisis created by the Fugitive Slave Law colonization came increasingly to be seen as a need to get rid of a troublesome group. While some proponents pleaded with their colleagues to avoid the sort of harsh language employed by the editor of the Philadelphia Evening Bulletin if they wished to attract blacks to the cause, they were clearly in the minority. The call for expulsion would grow increasingly strident during the 1850s.[6] Elisha Whittlesey may have wished for a calm and dispassionate discussion of the merits of colonization, but when, in mid-January 1851, his mentor, Henry Clay, rose in the Senate to renew the call for the removal of free blacks "with their own consent," and the establishment of a line of steamers to Africa, financed by the federal government, the debate over colonization became part and parcel of the wider political struggle over the best ways to reconcile differences between North and South. Like Whittlesey, Clay insisted that the continued agitation over the recapture of fugitive slaves, which had

[4] Philadelphia Evening Bulletin, January 25, March 22, August 28, 1851. For similar, if less developed, views on the subject see the Rochester American, April 14, 1851.
[5] Rochester American, September 25, 1851; Detroit Free Press, November 15, 1851; Davis, The Problem of Slavery in the Age of Emancipation, 155; David Brion Davis, "Reconsidering the Colonization Movement: Leonard Bacon and the Problem of Evil," Intellectual Historical Newsletter, Vol. 14 (1992), 10.
[6] Nicholas Guyatt, "'Outskirts of Our Happiness': Race and the Lure of Colonization in the Early Republic," Journal of American History, Vol. 95, No. 4 (March 2009), 1000. There was an explicit call to tone down the harsh language at the annual meeting of the Missouri Colonization Society and among some supporters of the movement in Maryland; Penelope Campbell, Maryland in Africa. The Maryland Colonization Society 1831–1857 (Urbana, IL: 1971), 184.

"distracted our country too long, and so greatly," had now to cease and the South be allowed "to manage their own domestic affairs in their own way." Continued agitation endangered the Union. Clay submitted two memorials, one from Indiana calling for the removal of free blacks, the "greatest cause of discord," and recommending Congress pass a bill "providing means to remove from our country all that portion of the African race who are both willing and ready to emigrate to Africa." The second was signed by the governor, all the members of the House and Senate, college presidents and what were described as the literati of Rhode Island, calling for more effective means to suppress the slave trade, the strengthening of Liberia, which, by its presence, had done more to curtail the slave trade along its coast, and the establishment of a line of steamers to transport emigrants to Liberia so as to encourage and promote trade in the area. Clay insisted that, should Congress adopt the call of the two memorials, commerce, civilization, and religion would be promoted by "the transfer of the free people of color with their own consent from the United States to Africa."[7]

The line of steamers, derisively labeled the "Ebony Line" by opponents, was proposed by Joseph Bryan of Alabama. The steamers would facilitate the removal of free blacks to Africa, increase US trade to the area and further afield in the Mediterranean, aid in the suppression of the slave trade and eliminate the need to maintain the expensive and ineffective African squadron. Removal was critical to the political and social stability of the country; it was also a cure for the "evil" besetting the country. The presence of blacks was "neither agreeable to the whites," nor was their condition "advantageous to themselves." The proposal conveniently linked the benefits of expanded trade and military security with expulsion. A couple of powerful political figures in the Senate, however, had their doubts about the political objectives behind the proposal, to say nothing of its constitutionality. As he did earlier, Jefferson Davis of Mississippi linked Clay's recommendation to the earlier debate over the politics of slave renditions. He thought he saw a connection between the call for colonization and opposition to the Fugitive Slave Law. He had no doubt it was meant to relieve "non-slaveholding States from the best check we have upon the popular feeling in favor of runaway slaves, their willingness to have negroes among them, and charge the whole country with the expense of removing this practical and wholesome restraint upon the growing disposition to violate our property rights, in disregard of the constitutional obligation which we are now, by other means, endeavoring to enforce." There was no clearer expression of the connection between colonization and the needs to recapture and return fugitive slaves. Although James Mason of Virginia doubted Congress had the authority to spend public money "directly or indirectly, for the deportation of free negroes," the "Ebony Line" won the endorsement of the governors

---

[7] *Congressional Globe, Second Session, Thirty-First Congress* (Washington, DC: 1851), 246–47.

and legislators of Virginia, Delaware, Rhode Island, New York, New Jersey, Indiana, and Pennsylvania. Newspapers in these and other states also gave their support.[8]

One week after endorsing the establishment of the line of steamers, Henry Clay was the principal speaker at the annual meeting of the American Colonization Society. It was a role he had filled on many occasions, going back to the founding of the society in December 1816. Colonization, he reiterated, would benefit the North and South, free blacks and slaves as well as boost the cause of African civilization. Frederick Stanton of Tennessee, the main proponent of the "Ebony Line" in the House, was opposed to Davis's position. He saw a direct connection between the removal of free blacks and the restoration of harmony between the states; in the South, free blacks encourage slaves to escape, while in the North, they were the leading violators of the Fugitive Slave Law, impeding recaptures and threatening violence. Also in attendance at the meeting were President Fillmore and many members of his cabinet, a gathering suggesting a return to a time when the national government was, to the dismay of many opponents of the movement, an active supporter and sometime financier of colonization.[9]

Even more troubling was the fact that, in spite of recently adopted Senate rules that banned those submitting memorials from immediately speaking in their favor – adopted, in part, to gag any discussion of antislavery petitions following passage of the Fugitive Slave Law – Clay was allowed to make an extended speech endorsing colonization and the establishment of the line of steamers. When John Hale attempted to test the gag by speaking in favor of a petition calling for the repeal of the Fugitive Slave Law, he was promptly silenced by the chair.[10] For opponents of colonization and the Fugitive Slave Law these were indeed ominous times. The resurgence of the movement in the years since the independence of Liberia, in 1847, was unmistakable. State colonization societies were up and running once again, financed by appropriations from state governments and increased donations from supporters. A proposal in Indiana coupled a ban on blacks entering

[8] Ibid., 491; *Appendix to the Congressional Globe, First Session, Thirty-First Congress* (Washington, DC: 1850), 1614; *Congressional Globe, Second Session, Thirty-First Congress* (Washington, DC: 1851), 491; House Committee on Naval Affairs, "John Bryan: Report to Accompany Bill, H.R. No. 367," Thirty-First Congress, First Session, August 1, 1850. House Report, No. 438, pp. 3–4; see Miscellaneous No. 95, Documents of the Senate of the United States, Thirty-Second Congress, First Session (Washington, DC: 1852) for the Indiana memorial. A copy of the Virginia memorial can be found in the John Letcher Papers, Virginia Historical Society. John Blassingame, ed., *Papers of Frederick Douglass, Vol. 2: 1847–54* (New Haven: 1982), 301. For newspaper support for the proposal see Rochester *Democrat*, January 21, 1851, Hagerstown *Herald of Freedom*, February 19, 1851; *Pennsylvanian*, February 3, 1851.
[9] *National Era*, January 30, 1851.
[10] *Congressional Globe, Second Session, Thirty-First Congress* (Washington, DC: 1851), 247–48; *National Era*, January 23, 1851; New York *Tribune*, January 21, 1851.

the state with the establishment of a state colonization board led by lead-ing figures in state government. New Jersey and Pennsylvania followed soon after with appropriations for removal. Not surprisingly, African Americans were alarmed by these new developments. Almost every meeting called to oppose the Fugitive Slave Law condemned what they saw as an unmistakable link between the aims of the law and the designs of Liberian colonization. A Springfield, Massachusetts, meeting was fairly typical. Among its resolu-tions was one that pledged to oppose "any and every scheme that may be devised in Congress, or out of it, to drag or drive us from our native land, for which our fathers fought and bled, and…[to] resist with our tongue, our pen, our votes, our influence, and if need be, at the sacrifice of our lives every such attempt."[11]

These meetings drew on a tradition dating back to the founding of the American Colonization Society (ACS) in 1816. Days after its formation, a meeting of three thousand blacks met at Bethel African Methodist Episcopal (AME) Church in Philadelphia and resoundingly rejected the society's objec-tives. As the "first successful cultivators of the wilds of America," they declared, their descendants were entitled "to participate in the blessing of her luxuriant soil which their blood and sweat matured." Banishment, therefore, was both cruel and a "direct violation of these principles, which have been the boast of this republic." Criticism of them by colonizationists was an "unmerited stigma" and an assault on their reputation. Such criticism ignored the wrongs inflicted on them. The meeting pledged never to abandon the country until all those enslaved were freed. A second meeting, eight months later, reaffirmed the commitment to continue the fight against slavery and oppose any form of deportation. Colonization, they concluded, was nothing more than a thinly disguised scheme to ensure the perpetuity of slavery. What was Africa to gain, Richard Allen, bishop of the AME Church, later asked, by sending "unlettered people" among them? As David Walker would later put it, men who were "resolved to keep us in eternal wretchedness" were now "bent upon sending us to Liberia." Those who argued that resettlement movements had historically been adopted by the oppressed to escape their oppressors, and to establish a new life for themselves in a new country, overlooked one salient feature: they had acted voluntarily and were not coerced into leaving. Colonizationists were fond of holding up the settlement of America as an example worth following. But what, given the history of American colonization, Rev. Peter Williams of New York City wondered, was to be gained by emulating its early settlers? "The colonies planted by white men on the shores of America," he observed, "so far as benefitting the aborigines, corrupted their morals, and caused their ruin: and yet those who say we are the most vile people in the world, would

---

[11] *Impartial Citizen*, April 10, 1850. Similar sentiments were expressed at a meeting in Portland, Maine. See the *Liberator*, September 20, 1850.

send us to Africa to improve the character and condition of those natives."
Anyone of "common intelligence" Rev. Samuel Cornish declared, who supported colonization beyond its "missionary objectives," should be treated as a
traitor.[12]

Very rarely did blacks and radical abolitionists waver in their opposition to
the policies of the ACS or in their condemnation of those blacks who endorsed
colonization. But at the dawn of the 1850s, the resurgent movement did garner a measure of support among free blacks. Earlier, a few leading figures,
including John Russwurm, the Bowdoin College graduate and coeditor, with
Samuel Cornish, of *Freedom's Journal,* the first black newspaper published in
the country, had thrown in his lot with colonizationists and gone to Liberia.
But few followed Russwurm's lead. Now, it seemed more blacks were willing to
listen to the siren calls of colonizationists. James McCune Smith, the Glasgow
University–trained medical doctor, worried that blacks were increasingly
becoming infected with the "distemper" of colonization. Not surprisingly, condemnation of this new development was immediate and strident: blacks who
supported colonization, according to the editor of the *Voice of the Fugitive,*
were traitors and "pumpkin-headed" dough faces. A meeting in Syracuse,
New York, dismissed them as "utterly lost to every sense of manhood," as
moral lepers, foes of their "best interests and those of [the] race" and traitors
to humanity.[13]

But it was Henry Clay's speech in the Senate, and his proposal for the line
of steamers, that became the focus of much of the African American opposition to the resurgent movement. Clay, after all, had been the one surviving link
with the founders of the ACS and had remained one of the movement's intellectual driving forces. It was he who had laid out the movement's agenda at
the society's first meeting. There was no nobler cause, he had argued, than that
which "whilst it proposed to rid our country of a useless and pernicious, if not
dangerous portion of its population, contemplates the spreading of the arts of
civilized life, and the possible redemption from ignorance and barbarism of a
benighted quarter of the globe."[14] Little seemed to have changed in the thirty-
five years since he had expressed those views except that, in 1851, they were
once again in the ascendency. Opponents saw the need to challenge such views;

---

[12] Reports of the two Philadelphia meetings were published in William Lloyd Garrison, *Thoughts on African Colonization* (1831, rpr., New York: 1969), 10–13; "Walker's Appeal, in Four Articles Together With a Preamble, to the Colored Citizens of the World," in Sterling Stuckey, ed., *The Ideological Origins of Black Nationalism* (Boston: 1972), 102; Richard Allen and Samuel Cornish are quoted by Walker, pp. 94–95 and 105; the Peter Williams quote can be found in Guyatt, "'The Outskirts of Our Happiness,'" 1005.

[13] *Voice of the Fugitive,* April 22, 1852; *Frederick Douglass' Paper,* December 25, 1851, for the Smith quote; *Liberator,* April 15, 1853.

[14] The Clay quotation can be found in P. J. Staudenraus, *The American Colonization Movement 1816–1865* (New York: 1980), 28. See also Davis, *The Problem of Slavery in the Age of Emancipation,* 172.

left uncontested they would cut deeply into the already limited rights of black Americans. Frederick Douglass led the charge against what he called the "cant of colonization." Scathing and dripping with sarcasm, Douglass' speeches were masterful and deeply analytical. Clay, he observed, had always been, and continued to be, a danger to black interests. "Trembling with age, and standing upon the very verge of the grave, his vanity, superciliousness, scorn and contempt towards colored freemen, are as active and sprightly now, as when he was in the pride and buoyancy of youth. If it be true that the ruling passion be strong in death, then the last words on the quivering lips of such a man may be expected to be charged with malice and detestation towards those against whom he has exerted the magic powers of his eloquence through nearly the whole length of his public career." Clay's aim was first to make colonization a "national government measure," and secondly to guarantee the protection of slavery through the enforcement of the Fugitive Slave Law, the latter "to hunt down fugitives, the former *free* colored citizens." The removal of free blacks was to be achieved "with their own consent," a phrase that had "the power of mischief." They were words that "savor of justice, of humanity, of respectful consideration for the feeling and wishes" of free blacks; they even smacked of "affection." But such consent under prevailing conditions was the equivalent of a highway robber putting a gun to a victim's head and demanding his purse. Blacks, he insisted, would never give their consent to a conspiracy so "dangerous to the interest of freedom." Douglass, like so many others, was also deeply troubled by the number of editors, among them Horace Greeley of the New York *Tribune*, long considered a friend of black causes, who had come out in support of some form of removal. While blacks knew their long-standing opposition had not silenced the movement, they, at least, had hoped they had drawn its sting. Colonizationists, Douglass was forced to admit, were successfully taking "advantage of the present anguish and distress into which the Fugitive Slave Law [had] thrown the free people of color."[15]

Others joined the fray. William P. Powell, the proprietor of a home for black seamen in New York City, and someone who had been actively involved in the local anti-Fugitive Slave Law campaign, approach the editors of the *Journal of Commerce* and the New York *Tribune* to publish his rebuttal of the former's views on the benefits of the proposed line of steamers. When both editors declined his request, Powell turned to his abolitionist friends. The estimate that the line of steamers, by taking 2,500 blacks a year to Africa, would ultimately rid the country of that population was, Powell insisted, a total fiction. Using ACS figures, he demonstrated that in the thirty-four years of its existence, the society had removed a mere 6,800 blacks, at a yearly average of two hundred. During the same period, the free black population had grown by roughly ninety thousand per year. It would, therefore, take the "Ebony Line" thirty-six

[15] Blassingame, ed., *The Frederick Douglass Papers*, 303–14

years to remove just one year's increase in the free black population.[16] It was a total demolition of colonizationists' calculations. But such rejoinders had little effect on the ACS or its supporters. Powell was studiously ignored. Numbers like those employed by Powell, and comments on the steep mortality rates in Liberia, were met with a studied silence, for, colonizationists insisted, these were not the true measure of the movement's success. That was to be measured not in the absolute numbers who emigrated, or by any other extraneous factors, but solely by whether migrants were provided, "safe and comfortable home[s] in a congenial climate."[17]

By the time his letter was published, Powell had decided to leave the United States, distraught over the passage of the Fugitive Slave Law and the rising popularity of colonization. But before he left, he decided to test whether those who supported expatriation were willing to cover the cost of removal if the decision about where to settle was left to the migrant. If it were, then the cost of expatriation would be seen by African Americans as an acceptable form of reparations for past wrongs. Powell petitioned the New York legislature in July 1851 for support to take his family to England where, as he said, "character and not color – capacity and not complexion, are the tests of merit." As he explained, his grandmother, Elizabeth Berjona, had cooked for members of the Continental Congress, keeping them fed during the most testing times of the War of Independence, providing them with the sustenance necessary to write the Declaration of Independence, whose principles neither he nor his family had ever enjoyed. Furthermore, his father, Edward Powell, had been a slave for life in New York. Although born free, William had found it impossible to provide his children with the sort of education that would equip them with the skills necessary to take advantage of the "opportunities for a livelihood and a respectable position in society," to which all "American citizens" were entitled. Powell could not have been surprised when his local representative refused to submit his petition to the state legislature. But Powell had made his point and, as he announced before leaving, he was going to "another country where my children will not, because of their color alone, be compelled to fight the battle of life at a disadvantage, which I too well know how to appreciate." No colonizationist would have disagreed with Powell; his family would never be allowed to enjoy the fruits of citizenship in America. But one could not imagine Henry Clay or Elisha Whittlesey, or any other colonizationist for that matter, endorsing either Powell's right to choose where to settle, or his insistence that he and his family be compensated for past wrongs.[18]

[16] *National Anti-Slavery Standard*, August 7, 1851.
[17] Campbell, *Maryland in Africa*, 199; Eric Burin, *Slavery and the Peculiar Solution. A History of the American Colonization Society* (Gainesville, FL: 2005), 81.
[18] *National Anti-Slavery Standard*, July 17, 1851; *Anti-Slavery Bugle*, July 26, 1851; "William P. Powell Militant Champion of Black Seamen," in Philip S. Foner, *Essays in Afro-American History* (Philadelphia: 1978), 98. Powell spent ten years in England, where his children were

Given their ascendency, colonizationists could afford to ignore the likes of Douglass and Powell. The movement might have been a "morally convenient monstrosity," as Fergus Bordewich has argued, but in the early years of the 1850s few blacks thought it was either "ineffectual" or "destined for oblivion."[19] Although dominant, the ACS did not have a monopoly on possible sites of settlement. Seeing an opportunity following the adoption of the Fugitive Slave Law, Jamaican planters, who continued to experience a shortage of labor in the years since emancipation, renewed their offer to black Americans, first made in the 1840s, to settle on the island. An 1851 meeting of government officials and planters in Kingston commissioned William Wemyss Anderson, a Scot who had settled in Jamaica just before emancipation and had become active in liberal politics, to visit the United States to encourage black migration to the island. Those displaced by the law in America were offered a new life in Jamaica. Promoters of the scheme, however, had to contend with the island's image as a place that was once prosperous but, since 1834, had been in decline, a symbol of the failed experiment in emancipation. Not long before Anderson's departure for America, John Bigelow's report on his tour of the island, *Jamaica in 1850 or, the Effects of Sixteen Years of Freedom on A Slave Colony*, a refutation of much of what had been written about the causes of the island's economic collapse, was published to much acclaim. In fact, Anderson claimed copies of the book were sold out by the time he got to New York a few months later. An editor of the New York *Post*, an antislavery Democrat and founding member of the Free-Soil Party, Bigelow did not endorse emigration but, nonetheless, gave a balanced account of the island's history since emancipation, refuting much of the proslavery explanation of its economic collapse that, by then, had become fashionable in the United States. Unlike their counterparts in the United States, all black Jamaicans, including those who were recently freed, he pointed out, enjoyed social and political equality. They also served as members of the military and police. More importantly, land was cheap and available. There were indeed problems, he admitted, but they were not the result of the freedmen's refusal to work, as so many argued. In fact, the freed people had shown considerable ingenuity in the face of daunting odds. All in all, he concluded, there had been remarkable progress since emancipation.[20]

educated, one of his sons as a medical doctor, before returning to the United States at the outbreak of the Civil War.

[19] Fergus M. Bordewich, *America's Great Debate. Henry Clay, Stephen A. Douglas, and the Compromise that Preserved the Union* (New York: 2012), 370.

[20] Gad Heuman, *Between Black and White. Race, Politics, and the Free Coloreds in Jamaica, 1792–1865* (Westport, CT: 1981), 145; John Bigelow, *Jamaica in 1850 or, the Effects of Sixteen Years of Freedom on a Slave Colony* (1851, rpr., Urbana, IL: 2006), XXV–XXVI, 20–26, 116; *Liberator*, August 8, 1851, July 16, 1852; Gale L. Kenny, "Manliness and Manifest Destiny: Jamaica and African American Emigration in the 1850s," *Journal of the Civil War Era*, Vol. 2, No. 2 (June 2012), 151–54.

Bigelow's conclusions may have been influenced by Anderson, whom he met on several occasions during his visit. Not surprisingly, while in America the *Post* became Anderson's major organ for the dissemination of his message. Articles on the mission were republished widely. Anderson also published two pamphlets that gave a history of the island since emancipation, both its problems as well as its prospects. Little effort had been made to educate the population following the end of slavery, he wrote. As a result, the freed people were less inclined to focus on things beyond the pressure to meet their immediate needs. Sugar, the major export crop, was still being produced the old-fashioned way, with only very limited attention given to technological innovations. The economy was also undermined by the British government's adoption of free trade policies in 1846, which put the island's goods at a competitive disadvantage. There had been little land redistribution following emancipation; in fact, land ownership was still the monopoly of absentee owners. Although the assumption that it was better to import necessities rather than produce them at home still dominated the thinking of the island's leaders, Anderson was optimistic that the freed people had demonstrated the capacity to produce much of what they needed. The immigration of English-speaking black Americans rather than Africans recaptured from slave ships, or labor imported from India, would give an important boost to the island's economy and set the country on a productive new course.[21]

In meetings with Rev. J. W. C. Pennington and Rev. Samuel Cornish soon after his arrival in New York City, Anderson hoped to glean the extent of black American interest in settling in Jamaica. He and John Scoble, the former secretary of the British and Foreign Anti-Slavery Society, also spoke at Rev. Henry Ward Beecher's church. But it was not until the Liberty Party convention in Buffalo, New York, in mid-September, that Anderson was exposed to black Americans' abiding ambivalence, if not open hostility, to any attempt to remove them from the country. Jamaica was not Liberia and Anderson was not a representative of the ACS, which must have raised his hopes of a positive response to his offer. In fact, four years earlier, following a visit to Jamaica, Pennington had proposed to a convention of blacks in Troy, New York, the need for establishing closer commercial ties with the Jamaican Hamic Association, an organization of black Jamaicans formed at the time of Pennington's visit. But nothing came of the plan. Anderson found it hard going in Buffalo. Even before he could address the gathering, a resolution was submitted that declared that free blacks would never leave the country while slavery existed, nor should they be forced to abandon the country of their birth. Anderson was in a quandary; it would be difficult to differentiate any plan of removal from that which was promoted by

[21] William Wemyss Anderson, *Jamaica and the Americas* (New York: 1851), 6–7; William Wemyss Anderson, *A Description of the History of the Island of Jamaica* (Kingston: 1851); *National Era*, October 25, 1850, March 13, 1851; Rochester *American*, September 12, 1851; New York *Times*, October 23, 1851; Kenny, "Manliness and Manifest Destiny," 155–56.

the ACS. Anderson's sounded disconcertingly familiar: America was steeped in discrimination and prejudice against the black man; Jamaica offered a refuge for people of color, including fugitive slaves – a place where they could enjoy social and political equality in an overwhelmingly black society. Unfortunately for Anderson, Frederick Douglass was at the meeting. Unlike his earlier reactions to Henry Clay, Douglass was gracious yet adamant that blacks should not be forced or encouraged to leave the country. Anderson, he admitted, had come to them in the "spirit of benevolence" from an island where the colored man had risen to the highest ranks of society. Yet, in the end, Anderson's offer differed little from those of African colonizationists. While there was no doubt that black Americans were hemmed in by "malignant and bitter prejudice," to accept Anderson's offer would be to stab their "cause in the vitals." To leave would be to concede that prejudice was invincible and unconquerable. The continued presence of free blacks acted as a brake on the slave system by what he called a "reflex influence upon slavery." That is why slaveholders and their supporters were so anxious to get rid of them. But blacks belonged in the United States. They had been present since its founding. Speaking over Anderson's head, Douglass then addressed white America on the two races' historical connections: "We have grown up with you, we have watered your soil with our tears, nourished it with our blood, tilled it with our hands. Why should we not stay here?" He continued: "We have been with you, are still with you, have been with you in adversity, and by the help of God will be with you in prosperity." Douglass saw signs of change for the better, especially in places such as New England where, he insisted, segregation was on the retreat. Then, as if to ease the tension caused by his rejection of the Jamaican offer, Douglass employed one of those ironic and humorous stories for which he was known. After a long and exhausting lecture tour, he recalled, he boarded a train in Massachusetts and curled his large frame into two seats so he could sleep, hoping that the memory of segregation would work to his advantage and dissuade anyone from demanding the seat next to him. Not long after he had dozed off, a white passenger shook him awake and demanded he give up the extra seat. Quick on his seat as he was on his feet, Douglass wondered why the white man would want to violate age-old traditions. But the white man insisted that he sit next to Douglass. If there was a moral to the story, Douglass suggested, it was that white people, at least those in Massachusetts, were beginning not to care who they sat next to.[22]

Anderson left Buffalo deeply disappointed. There seemed to be little appetite among blacks for migration to Jamaica or anywhere else. A convention in Toronto, a couple of weeks earlier, may have boosted his hopes for a more favorable reception in Buffalo. The convention had called for the formation of

[22] R. J. M. Blackett, *Beating Against the Barriers. Biographical Essays in Nineteenth-Century Afro-American History* (Baton Rouge: 1989), 34–35; *Frederick Douglass' Paper,* December 25, 1851, October 2, 1851.

an "American Continental and West Indian League" to aid those who had fled slavery to settle on farms either in Canada or the West Indies. But there were hints even here that his proposal would meet with a cool reception. A resolution calling on slaves to "come out from under the jurisdiction of those wicked laws" of slavery and settle in Canada was vigorously opposed by Martin Delany and others as "contrary to the desires and wishes of those of us...who believe it to be impolite and contrary" to the policy of opposing both the Fugitive Slave Law and colonization.[23] Surprisingly, Anderson's proposal came up for discussion in places he would never have expected. Because of the wide circulation given his mission by the New York *Post*, and increasing calls for the removal of free blacks, the Jamaica scheme was explored at a meeting of blacks in Rush County, Indiana, a development that must have gratified Anderson, given that he had focused all his attention and energy on the East Coast and Canada. But the meeting at the small rural church came to the same conclusion as those in Buffalo and Toronto.[24]

The Rush Country meeting even declined to send a delegation to a "State Convention of People of Color," which met in Indianapolis on August 1st, anticipating there would be discussions on the merits of Liberian colonization. The convention met three days before a vote was to be taken on a revised state constitution, a vote that could have profound implications for the future of black Hoosiers. The vote was mandated by a constitutional convention, which met in Indianapolis from October 1850 to January 1851. After 126 days of debate, a good portion of it devoted to the rights of blacks to live in and enter the state, the convention had called for both the expulsion of blacks as well as restricting their future entry into the state. At one point in the proceedings, James Rariden of Wayne County offered a series of resolutions in praise of the Compromise of 1850. What the Compromise had to do with a convention meeting to reform the state's constitution Rariden did not say. Nevertheless, his resolution produced five days of windy and numbingly repetitive disquisitions. But Rariden, and those who supported the resolution, had a point to make – one that became clear when the convention next turned its attention to the issue of black exclusion: they saw the Compromise and colonization as two sides of the same coin. In his first comments on the motion to exclude blacks, Rariden railed against abolitionism, which he described as a "monomania" and a "disease of the mind." The presence of blacks only worsened the situation and he wondered if a return to normalcy between the North and South would necessarily require the extermination of blacks if there was "no better way to get rid of them." The country, he conceded, had not yet come to that

---

[23] *Voice of the Fugitive*, September 24, 1851; Floyd J. Miller, *The Search for a Black Nationality. Black Colonization and Emigration, 1787–1863* (Urbana, IL: 1975), 111–13.

[24] Centreville *True Democrat*, August 7, 1851. For leaders of the meeting see Stephen A. Vincent, *Southern Seed, Northern Soil: African American Farm Communities in the Midwest, 1765–1900* (Bloomington, IN: 1999), 55–58, 144.

point, but he called up the Puritan's treatment of the Indians as an example the convention may want to contemplate. Until then, he would give the legislature all the power it needed to come up with a solution that involved the expatriation of blacks to Liberia.

William Foster of Marion County added that blacks should be denied both the right to vote and to settle in the state. He questioned why anyone would want "these cattle amongst us." Such views made some members of the convention cringe. Edward May of DeKalb and Steuben counties, for example, supported granting blacks the right to vote under certain restrictions that he did not specify, because, he believed, they were "men constituted like ourselves by nature." This did not mean, however, that they should be granted social and political privileges. David Kilgore of Delaware County posed the question differently: Why was a European immigrant, he asked, who had "no feelings common with us, who never felt the pulse of liberty till he set foot upon our soil," why was such "a man to enjoy the opportunity and the right to vote and to hold office...whilst these rights are to be denied to the unfortunate black man, who has ten times more intelligence, and who has lived in the State of Indiana from his birth?" Others, such as Daniel Read of Monroe County, rejected such reasoning: blacks and mulattoes were not, and could never be, citizens and, as such, should not be encouraged to remain in the state.[25]

What then was to become of those blacks who had long been residents in the state and those who had settled there in the years immediately preceding the convention? Black immigration, went the response, posed an imminent danger. All around them states had expelled, or were making preparations to expel, their black populations. Kentucky's recent constitution had ordered the expulsion of freed slaves and free blacks who entered the state. In 1847, Illinois had prohibited the entry of blacks and many anticipated Ohio would soon adopt a similar ban. Where then were the "old, decrepit, and superannuated slaves" of Kentucky to go but to Indiana? Many spoke of an influx of blacks in recent years adding to what was already a dangerously large number. The fact that there were only 11, 262 blacks recorded in the 1850 census seemed to matter little. O. L. Gibson of Clarke County observed that within the last twelve months 150 "cast off slaves" had joined the estimated two thousand blacks living in the county he represented. If this problem were not address immediately, Gibson anticipated a time when the "State will be dotted all over with negro cabins – when the white man will be driven out of the State, and his place occupied by the African." The only way to prevent such an eventuality was to "enact stringent laws, or insert a clause in the Constitution prohibiting the future emigration of blacks." Such action was dictated by what all those in favor of a ban insisted was "self-preservation," a phrase that had been widely employed during the public debates over the Fugitive Slave Law.

[25] *Report of the Debates and Proceedings of the Convention for the Revision of the Constitution of the State of Indiana, 1850* (Indianapolis: 1850), 614, 574–75, 233, 245, 253, 440–41.

Schuyler Colfax, the South Bend representative and editor, however, dismissed the argument of self-preservation as nothing more than an effort to gild exclusion with "the tinsel of a seeming and temporary expediency."[26]

But self-preservation also required that something be done to persuade black residents to leave the state. O. L. Gibson spoke for many: policies had to be put in place that would compel black Hoosiers to see the merits of settling in Liberia. Gibson was convinced that they would not leave voluntarily. Like so many other advocates of colonization, he thought he saw the hand of Providence at work in slavery. In slavery, Africans were introduced to Christianity and civilization, making them "much better than they came." This experience obligated blacks to follow the dictates of nature and Providence and take the teachings gained in slavery back to Africa. Let Free States shut them out, Gibson declared, and they would have no choice but to accept colonization. There was no better scheme of philanthropy, he concluded, "no project better adapted to the amelioration of the African race, than African colonization." Africa, the "negro's home...the land of his fathers," a place on the verge of civilization, would benefit from an influx of black American settlers, A. F. Morrison of Marion County observed.[27]

A handful of petitions from Randolph, Grant, and Union counties failed to impress the convention, which, in the end, voted by a lopsided margin to ban black and mulatto entry into the state and in favor of colonization. The ban comprised the first of the four clauses of Article XIII. The others voided all contracts made with blacks, fined those who broke the law, and earmarked those fines to subsidize the state's colonization project. It also mandated that all blacks and mulattos register with the clerk of the county in which they lived. Article XIII, as James H. Madison has argued, erected a "constitutional wall surrounding the state and papered [it] with signs reading 'whites only.'" The electorate was given two separate votes; one on Article XIII, the other on the revised constitution. Three days before the vote on August 4, 1851, a speaker at the Negro State Convention in Indianapolis – the one that Rush County residents refused to attend – worried that those opposed to the ban could lose by a margin of thirty thousand. It was a stunning miscalculation. Voters overwhelmingly endorsed the call for exclusion and colonization: 113, 828 voted in favor of Article XIII, 21,873 against. In some counties, such as Knox and Marion, the vote was even more lopsided. In Putnam County, 96 percent of the electorate voted in favor. Only four counties – Randolph, with the highest

---

[26] Ibid., 247, 446–48; Don Carmony, *Indiana 1816–1850. The Pioneer Era* (Indianapolis: 1998), 787; Willard H. Smith, "Schuyler Colfax: Whig Editor, 1845–1853," *Indiana Magazine of History*, Vol. 34, No. 3 (September 1938); James H. Madison, *Hoosiers. A New History of Indiana* (Bloomington, IN: 2014), 143–44. The Illinois ban aimed to protect the state against a "swarm of Negroes from every state of the Union," a population that, they declared, was "the refuse of humanity." Arthur Charles Cole, ed., *The Constitutional Debates of 1847* (Springfield, IL: 1919), 860–63.

[27] *Report of the Debates and Proceedings*, 448, 452–53, 603–04.

ratio of black residents in the state, Elkhart, LaGrange, and Steuben, all in the far northern part of the state, where many New Englanders had settled – voted against. While it took Illinois legislators six years to pass its enabling legislation, the Indiana legislature took less than one year to adopt its version: the "Negro Exclusion Law."[28]

Few public voices were raised in opposition to Article XIII in the months leading up to the vote. The one major exception was the *True Democrat*, a Free-Soil newspaper published in the eastern part of the state with a strong Quaker presence. No one gave the white man the "title deed" to the state and "excluded everybody else," the editor observed. This was particularly poignant given the fact that it was the white man who forced blacks to share the country with them, to help him build its institutions and to fight his battles. How then could blacks be legally and morally denied a share of the country's spoils? But more to the point, the editor was convinced that exclusion was legally unenforceable. As it turned out, he was right. There were a number of violations of the law but only one resulted in a conviction and that would be overturned on appeal by the state supreme court. The case of John P. Brown illustrates the difficulty with the enforcement of such a law at a time in American history dominated by the expansive movements of people across state lines. Brown, a citizen of Ohio, visited Fort Wayne on business in July 1855 and was arrested for violating the "Negro Exclusion Law." At his hearing, Brown's counsel argued that, under the law, the ban on entry applied only to Negroes and mulattos. Although Brown was described as a mulatto in the arrest warrant, it was clear he was neither. In response, the state argued that the law covered anyone with one-eighth "negro blood." The case against Brown was dismissed on the grounds that the state had failed to prove that Brown was either a Negro or mulatto. Even the most ardent supporters of the law were forced to admit, not long after its enactment, that there was not a county in the state where it could be easily enforced.[29]

[28] Ibid., 2075; *Indiana State Journal*, July 31, August 6, 1851; James H. Madison, "Race, Law, and the Burdens of Indiana's History," in David J. Bodenhamer and Randall T. Shepherd, eds., *The History of Indiana Law* (Athens, OH: 2006), 44; Carmony, *Indiana 1816–1850*, 449–50; Emma Lou Thornbrough, *The Negro in Indiana. A Study of a Minority* (Indianapolis: 1957), 68; Nicole Etcheson, *The Emerging Midwest. Upland Southerners and the Political Culture of the Old Northwest, 1787–1861* (Bloomington, IN: 1996), 101; Nicole Etcheson, *A Generation at War: the Civil War Era in a Northern Community* (Lawrence, KA: 2011), 128–29; Madison, *Hoosiers*, 145–47; *The Minutes of the State Convention of the People of Color of the State of Indiana* (n.p., n.d.), 3. My thanks to Sebastian Page for a copy of the *Minutes*, which he found in the Colonial Office Papers, National Library, London.

[29] *True Democrat*, April 24, 1851, February 2, 1854; New York *Tribune*, August 13, 1855. For other cases see Thornbrough, *The Negro in Indiana*, 71–72; *Barkshire v. State*, 7 Ind. 389 (1856). My thanks to James H. Madison for this reference. *Indiana State Journal*, February 6, 1854; Cincinnati *Gazette*, January 18, 1858. Months earlier, John Carter, a resident of Madison, Jefferson County, for almost twenty years, was charged in the court of common pleas for violating the law. See Mark Allan Furnish, "A Rosetta Stone on Slavery's Doorstep: Eleutherian

It might not have been enforceable, but the adoption of Article XIII did persuade some black Hoosiers to look to a future elsewhere. One Cincinnati newspaper reported that steamers from Madison, Indiana, regularly carried black families fleeing the state. They appeared, the reporter observed, to be "persons of some property, having with them fine stocks of horses, mules, and milch cows." Although some black residents did register with their local clerks, many seemed to have ignored the regulation entirely. One editor reported that, throughout the state, Negroes had refused, as he put it, to "toe the mark."[30] To black Hoosiers the law mattered whether it was enforced or not. But they also very likely were influenced by the widespread discussion about expulsion and colonization that came to dominate political debate in the months following the constitutional convention. An editor across the Ohio River in Louisville, who had reprinted the New York *Post*'s articles on Anderson's Jamaican mission, opposed settlement in Liberia on the grounds that it was difficulty to get to, its economy was weak, and its business prospects poor. He also believed that it was impossible to move the entire black population across such vast distances. It was far more practical, he reasoned, for blacks to go to Jamaica, to which they were invited, where jobs were available and labor was needed, a place with a climate that "suit[ed] the black man," with a government that would help the "negro in his incompetency to govern himself." Such assistance was the only way to ensure success, as the editor had no confidence in "a colony of negroes with an independent government." His competitor in New Albany, directly across the river from Louisville, vehemently opposed such reasoning; if the state was simply interested in getting rid of the race, Jamaica or Canada would be the preferred option. Removal, which was once a philanthropic enterprise at the founding of the ACS, over time had become a political necessity hastened by the violent agitation of abolitionists. Blacks, then, had to be placed in a secure location free from the "evils and annoyances by which they are surrounded here." Neither Jamaica nor Canada could be permanent asylums; Canada because it was already showing signs of rejecting the influx of fugitive slaves following adoption of the Fugitive Slave Law, and Jamaica because the condition of those who settled there could "never be other than menial." As a long-term project, removal to Liberia also held out the prospect of opening up Africa to world trade, transforming its ports into "marts of commerce" and attracting "capital, enterprise, and labor." Liberia, the editor predicted, will prove if the race was "capable of self-government." With the training they had received in America, Liberia, he was convinced, offered the best hope for the race.[31]

College and the Lost Antislavery History of Jefferson County, Indiana," (PhD, Purdue University, 2014), 1–2.

[30] Cincinnati *Commercial*, June 8, 1853, in *National Era*, July 17, 1853. Over the next few years, there were periodic reports of black families leaving the state for Canada. *Indiana Journal*, September 26, 1853; Aurora *Independent Banner*, June 29, 1853.

[31] New Albany *Ledger*, August 16, September 16, 1851; *Indianapolis* Journal, September 25, 1851.

The New Albany editor spoke for many who saw in colonization the solution both to the increasingly heated political contest over slavery and the future of the free black population. In Indiana, an inactive state colonization society, first formed in 1829, showed signs of life following the hiring of Rev. James Mitchell as its secretary and agent in 1848. A Methodist minister born in Londonderry, Ireland, Mitchell became the driving force on the State Board of Colonization, which was mandated by Article XIII and made up of the leading figures in state government, including the governor. He very quickly became the face and the voice of the movement in the Midwest. He was its principal contact with the national office; he hired subagents and determined their salaries, traveled the region raising money and promoting the cause as well as managing the office in Indianapolis. But more importantly, he provided the local movement's intellectual heft. Slavery was an evil, he argued, because it "withholds knowledge" from the enslaved, keeps them in perpetual bondage, undermines the family, and traffics in the sale of humans. All around the world, wherever they were found, Africans were in a state of degradation. Free blacks in the United States were, however, the "most respectable class of Africans" precisely because they had been exposed to a "republican society." Yet even in America they suffered "civil and social disabilities"; they played no part in making laws, were taxed without representation, could not testify against whites in court, nor could they marry whites. America also had a special responsibility to promote this project because its republican traditions made it "the light of the world." It was the duty and responsibility of all "pious colored men" who continued to suffer under the weight of prejudice, therefore, to go to Liberia, which had been established by republican America. "[B]enevolent America" had a corresponding duty to aid in that mission. Liberian colonization, then, was part and parcel of the nation's domestic and international responsibility. But he pointed to other important features of Liberian colonization: it was a free-produce enterprise, a potentially economically viable country where coffee, sugar, and cotton, the staples of world trade, could be produced in such quantities by free labor so as to undermine slavery. All of this would, he predicted, simultaneously set in place a system of gradual emancipation in America and the consolidation of a viable nation in Africa where the emancipated would have free rein to develop their talent and demonstrate to the world the capabilities of the race.

But before any of this could be attained, the races needed to be separated. Separation, Mitchell maintained, was essential to both the success of the enterprise in Liberia and the future of the United States. History had shown that no nation could exist made up of two different and incompatible races as presently existed in America, where the stronger race refused to contemplate the possibility of race mixing. A "heterogeneous population that will not amalgamate," he predicted, will sooner or later become a "turbulent, restless and revolutionary population." There were only two possible remedies to this problem: either there was to be amalgamation or the races must separate. But the "dignified and upright *superior*" white man will not mix with the colored man even if he is moral and respectable because he is inferior. Under these circumstances, the separation and transportation of the inferior race elsewhere offered the only viable option. For the "poor colored man is the sickly tree that stands in the grove" overshadowed by "a stronger race that shoots up to the heavens and spreads its branches to the light – casting a destructive shade on all below." In an effort to drive home the viability of his proposal, Mitchell calculated that the cost to the country's exchequer would be considerably less than the funds expended in the recently concluded Mexican War, a cost, he predicted, that Americans would be willing to bear to save the land from the scourge of civil and race war.[32]

The vitriol so evident in the constitutional convention's discussion of the place of blacks in the state and the draconian measures adopted seemed to portend, if not civil strife, at least rising sectarianism. More significantly, developments in Indiana seemed to reflect what was going on in the country as a whole. On those grounds alone, Mitchell's solution seemed more than justified. Mitchell set about putting his plan into operation in the months after the formation of the State Board of Colonization in 1852. Under the terms of its formation, county treasurers were empowered to receive donations and bequests for the cause. The signs looked promising. Indiana was the only state to have made colonization a part of its organic law. Soon after, the state legislature granted the board and the reenergized colonization society an appropriation of $5,000. An even more positive sign was an apparent rise in pro-colonization sentiment – or so Mitchell thought – among black Hoosiers. Mitchell was buoyed by the departure of two large families in March 1850. The party was led by William Findley, who had established a prosperous barber shop with his partner Samuel Webster in Lafayette before moving a few miles south to Covington along the Wabash River. Webster would follow Findley to Liberia in November 1852. Findley became an important ally in Mitchell's effort to encourage black Hoosiers to move to Liberia, writing frequent letters from his new home and returning periodically to tour the Midwest promoting the cause. Webster never returned, but his letters to old Indiana friends found their way into local newspapers. Webster spoke for his former partner: the land around the St. Paul River where he had settled, he reported, was more beautiful and fertile than that along the Wabash; business in Monrovia was promising; and most importantly of all, there was money to be made in Liberia.[33]

---

[32] *Answers of the Agent of the Indiana Colonization Society to the Resolution of Inquiry on the Subject of African Colonization Passed by the House of Representatives of the General Assembly of the State of Indiana, on the 3rd of February, 1852* (Indianapolis: 1852), 17–18, 20, 23, 25, 27–34, 38. For Mitchell's background see his interview in the St. Louis *Globe-Democrat*, August 28, 1894. My thanks to Sebastian Page for a copy of the interview.

[33] *Report of the Secretary of the State Board of Colonization of the State of Indiana to the Governor for 1853* (Indianapolis: 1853), 8–11; Mary E. Anthrop, "The Road Less Travelled. Hoosier African Americans and Liberia," *Traces* (Winter 2007), 19; *African Repository*, May 1850, May

Even before the state had appropriated funds for colonization, Mitchell reached out to friendly ministers, pleading with them to use their July 4th sermons to raise support for the cause. His communications optimistically pointed to large numbers of "respectable colored persons" who were eager to migrate if only enough funds were available. Even on the eve of departure, when Mitchell had a firmer grip on the actual numbers, he consistently inflated the number of emigrants who were about to board ships. Such erroneous claims were repeated regularly throughout the decade. Mitchell knew better; all the signs pointed to open hostility among those who stood to benefit most from the cause he so avidly promoted. There were also moments of dark despondency. As he wrote to the national office, promoting the cause taxed both his energy and health. He found himself frequently away from home for long stretches of time, "rolling and tumbling over Rail Roads, puffed and blown along Rivers – dragged and hauled through storms of snow, rain and wind," with few rewards to show for his efforts. A supporter from Corydon, in the southern part of the state, gave a measure of the difficulty Mitchell faced: there were, he estimated, seventy-five to eighty blacks living in the country, all of them "opposed to emigrating to Liberia...or any where else."[34]

In an effort to improve the society's image among African Americans and encourage more of them to emigrate, Mitchell hired Rev. John McKay, a thirty-nine-year-old former slave who had "purchased himself." McKay toured the state for three months in an effort to raise funds for a projected mission as well as to seek out potential emigrants. Like so many other advocates of Liberian colonization, Mitchell calculated that positive reports by black visitors to Liberia would generate an increase in the number of applicants who wanted to leave. At the end of his tour, McKay had raised a paltry $185, the major proportion of which went toward covering traveling and other expenses, including his salary. This was not what Mitchell had expected. As a result, he looked for other means to finance McKay's mission. It appears that Mitchell may have mortgaged his home to cover part of the cost of the mission. On the eve of McKay's departure, Mitchell predicted that the trip would include forty Hoosiers. Gov. Joseph Wright was even more optimistic; he thought fifty or even sixty would accompany McKay. In the end, only twenty sailed with McKay in November 1853.[35]

1851; *Indiana State Journal*, February 18, 1852, February 25, 1853; Raquel l. Henry, "The Colonization Movement in Indiana, 1826–1864: A Struggle to Remove the African American," (PhD, Indiana University, 2008), 145, 153; Louisville *Courier*, January 24, 1852; Lafayette *Courier*, March 30, May 23, 1853.

[34] *Indiana State Journal*, July 5, 1851, June 16, 1854; James Mitchell to William McLain, Indianapolis, March 3, 1853. American Colonization Society (ACS) Papers; Hugh Neely to Dear Sir, Corydon, June 6, 1854, State Board of Colonization, Gov. Joseph A. Wright Papers, Box 3, Indiana State Archives, Indianapolis, Indiana.

[35] *Report of the Secretary of the State Board of Colonization*, 8–9, 23; New Albany *Ledger*, November 30, 1853; *Indiana State Journal*, October 10, 1853; *African Repository*, January

On his return, McKay reported glowingly on the economic conditions in Liberia, the health, beauty, and "great fertility" of the many settlements he visited, the relatively swift and easy acclimation process and mortality rates, which he declared were not as high as some had claimed. Moreover, both the "natives" and the government in Monrovia were eager to attract more emigrants and welcomed the contributions they would make to the prosperity of the nation.[36] Soon after his return, McKay went on another three-month tour of the state, reporting on his experiences in Liberia and encouraging blacks to consider joining the party of Hoosiers who had gone out with him. Mitchell and the Society were optimistic and encouraged that McKay, who had seen conditions in Liberia and had left persuaded of its potential, could not fail to impress those he met on the tour. "The colored people can be reached more successfully," Thornton Mills, Mitchell's successor, later observed, "by one of themselves, who has seen what he describes, than any other person." It was an approach that was employed, with differing degrees of success, by other colonization societies. Initially, there were reports that McKay had persuaded a significant number – estimated to be about fifty – to leave in October 1855. But then to the surprise of the board, McKay unexpectedly resigned. It was a replay of developments that had occurred almost ten years earlier when the society's black agent resigned under pressure from black opponents of colonization. The "adverse influence" on McKay was also felt by those who had initially expressed an interest in leaving, but who withdrew, leaving just eight families who, the board reported, were in "such poor health and destitute" that the mission had to be scrapped.[37]

The aborted 1855 mission spelled the doom of the plans of Indiana colonizationists. Mitchell soon resigned, frustrated by both the failure to attract emigrants in the numbers he had hoped, and disagreements with the board. His successor's stay was even shorter. He would also leave deeply frustrated by his inability to make any inroads into the black community. These failures contributed to crippling dissension in the state society. Worried the society would go out of business, the national office sent a mission to Indianapolis in an effort

1854; "Report of the Proceedings of the Indiana State Board of Colonization from March 24, 1853 to December 7, 1860." Indiana State Archives.

[36] *Report of the Rev. John McKay Colored Agent of the State Board of Colonization on Liberia* (Indianapolis: 1854), 5–10. McKay chose to ignore the devastating news of death that filtered back to Indiana following the settlement of the Tompkins family in Liberia. The family of six – Peter, his wife Harriet, and their four children – immigrated in February 1851. Less than a year later, Harriet reported the death of her husband and three of the children. Douglas F. Denne, "Letters from Liberia. The Story of the Tompkins Family," *Traces of Indiana and Midwest History*, Vol. 23 (Winter 2011), 30–35.

[37] "Report by Thornton Mills, Secretary of the Board of Colonization" in *Journal of the House of Representatives During the Thirty-Eighth Session of the General Assembly of the State of Indiana* (Indianapolis: 1855), 229–30; "Report of the Proceedings of the State Board of Colonization." See *Indiana State Journal*, February 16, 1855, for a report of a meeting of African Americans who condemned McKay.

to heal the divisions and, as one agent put it, to wake it out of its lethargy. The society, he reported, was at its "lowest ebb." The agent visited black barber shops and held prayer meetings with AME ministers, but to little effect. On a stop in Terre Haute only half a dozen people showed up to a meeting, even after extensive advertising in local newspapers and churches. In spite of his opponents' pledge never to rehire him, Mitchell returned to the helm of the society in 1859, working again with McKay, but with no better results. Again, there were predictions of an upsurge in interest among African Americans and again nothing came of them. As Mitchell lamented, the steam had gone out of the movement. Back in charge, his report, however, made for depressing reading; try as he might, he could not breathe new life into the organization. There was another "slight check" in the stream of emigrants, as he euphemistically put it, due in part to the failure of crops in Liberia, the "slander" directed at the Liberian government for what its critics thought was its support for a proposal to renew the slave trade, and the "embarrassed condition" of the Indiana state treasury. In customary fashion, Mitchell refused to acknowledge that much of the society's failures were directly attributable to the continued opposition of blacks. Not one black Hoosier applied to go to Liberia after 1856. It is also clear that his style of management, which some described as heavy handed, as well as disputes with the state society, exacerbated the problem. But the numbers told the story: between 1820 and 1860 only fifty-eight Hoosiers left for Liberia, fully three-quarters of them in the first few years of the 1850s. That "surge" had raised hopes that a new and more vibrant colonization society, led by a hardworking administrator, and backed by the generous support of the state, would turn the tide in favor of colonization. But in the end the society's inability to attract a regular flow of emigrants proved its undoing.[38]

The fact that few black Hoosiers left for Liberia in the wake of Article XIII is not, however, a true reflection of the reach and influence of the state law. Following the constitutional convention, Indiana's exclusionary law was frequently cited by those in favor of colonization, both black and white, as one of the reasons blacks should consider leaving the country. Others included the social and political upheaval caused by the adoption of the Fugitive Slave Law. The passage of stringent laws against free blacks in the North only added to the sense of crisis. Wisconsin and Iowa, for example, defeated attempts to give the vote to black men, Oregon excluded them, and Illinois imposed a set of restrictive black laws. William Sawyer, the representative of Auglaize

---

[38] Mitchell to McLain, Indianapolis, July 27, 1854, Thornton Mills to McLain, Indianapolis, February 5, 1857, Robert Finley to Dear Gurley, Indianapolis, February 28, March 3, 1857, John Says to McLain, Indianapolis, June 4, 1858, Says to R. R. Gurley, Terra Haute, June 26, 1858, all in the ACS Papers; *Report of the Secretary of the State Board of Colonization of the State of Indiana* (Indianapolis: 1859), 5, 11; Etcheson, *A Generation at War,* 130; Anthrop is more indecisive about the number of people who left. She put it at "fewer than a hundred." Anthrop, "The Road Less Travelled," 14; *Report on Colonization for 1863 to the State Board* (Indianapolis: 1864), 494–95.

County at the 1850 Ohio Constitutional Convention, summed up the mood of the time: America, he asserted unequivocally, was an "Anglo-Saxon nation" that did not welcome the presence of blacks. Arguments like these, as well as other indignities, prompted Samuel Williams, a forty-year-old AME minister and barber from Johnstown, Pennsylvania, to consider leaving. For four years he had voted in federal and state elections, until he was disenfranchised by an 1838 amendment to Pennsylvania's constitution that restricted the vote to white males. The dispute over the Fugitive Slave Law added to his distress – so much so that, by 1852, he had made up his mind to "find a new home some place in the world where the black man could be free." Earlier, the Alton [Illinois] Colored Baptist Association had commissioned Rev. Samuel Ball to visit and report on Liberia's suitability as a site of settlement. In a dispassionate, sometimes critical report to the association, Ball, nonetheless, praised the country as a place where blacks could settle free from the racial restrictions that dominated their lives. The four months spent in Liberia, he later told a St. Louis, Missouri, audience, was his first taste of true freedom.[39]

It was that search for freedom in the face of rising oppression and a resurgent colonizationism that prompted many blacks to contact their state colonization societies about the prospects of settling in Liberia. By the time these contacts were initiated, those wishing to leave had already made the decision to seek a future outside of America. James Theodore Holly was fairly typical. Born in Washington, DC, his family had moved first to Brooklyn, New York, then to Burlington, Vermont, hoping to escape racial strictures. He wrote to the ACS in the summer of 1850 that he was ready to settle in Liberia. Although he was trained as a shoemaker, he told the society, he had studied the classics so he could "discharge the high mission of a teacher in my fatherland." Holly had recently participated in a public debate with his elder brother on the merits of Liberian colonization. Now, he and two young friends were anxious to leave. Nothing came of Holly's overture to the ACS, but public debates of this sort were a regular occurrence in black communities in the early years of the decade. For a month in early 1853, for example, Harrisburg, Pennsylvania, blacks conducted a series of weekly debates on the topic: "Which offers the greatest inducements for a permanent home for the colored man, Africa or America." Thomas Morris Chester, a young man with "more than common abilities," as one local newspaper observed, spoke in favor of Africa. But later Chester would insist that his decision to leave America was not the result of

---

[39] Chicago *Tribune*, October 4, 1851; Lancaster *Examiner* and *Herald*, May 14, 1851, March 3, April 28, 1858; *Report of the Debates and Proceedings of the Convention for the Revision of the Constitution of the State of Ohio, 1850–51*, 2 Vols. (Columbus, OH: 1851), I, 56–57; Rev. Samuel Williams, *Four Years in Liberia. A Sketch of the Life of the Rev. Samuel Williams*, in Wilson Moses, ed., *Liberian Dreams, Back-to-Africa Narratives of the 1850s* (University Park, PA: 1998), 130–31; Samuel S. Ball, *Liberia. The Condition and Prospect of that Republic* (Alton, IL: 1848), 9–14; *Maryland Colonization Journal*, April 1850.

colonizationist influences but a "pure and preconcerted" conviction that the future of the "aliens of Africa" in America was in Africa. It was his passion for liberty that made it impossible for him to "submit to the insolent indignities and contemptuous conduct to which it has almost become natural for the colored people dishonorably to submit themselves." The alternative was life in a different country where freedom was guaranteed. For Chester that country was Liberia.[40]

To William Findley of Indiana the true measure of independence was the attainment of "rights and privileges as *broad* and as *liberal* as those enjoyed by the white citizens of the United States," something blacks had never enjoyed. If such independence could not be attained in the United States it must be sought elsewhere. Only in Liberia, a "Christian Republic," could the "colored man find a quiet and secure home." To stay and fight in America would be futile. Slavery, he had no doubt, would some day be "abolished by Divine Providence." But, he was equally convinced, it was not the will of Providence to grant blacks "perfect social equality *with the white race at this time.*" He was, therefore, no longer willing to wait on the white man's favors; instead he had chosen to follow "the example of Abraham who disliked strife" and who chose instead "separation as a remedy." Blacks, he concluded, should "separate from the white race, that we may be free and they enjoy peace; for doubtless, God had given this land to them."[41]

The young Hartford, Connecticut, Deguerrean artist, Augustus Washington, the son of a former slave and a woman of South Asian descent, who had been educated, first at Oneida Institute in upstate New York, and then briefly at Dartmouth College before settling in Hartford where he taught school for a while, spoke for many: black Americans, he declared, needed a "space to rise." In a widely reprinted statement, Washington argued that blacks needed to find a home where the "equality of rights and liberty" were assured and the mind unfettered. He had begun looking for such a space during the war with Mexico only to conclude, after years of careful thought, that Liberia was that place. Africa was the black man's natural home where, following his "highest and happiest destiny," he could help to redeem the continent. The victims of American oppression were destined, he predicted, to "plant in Africa a religion and morality more pure, and liberty more universal, than it has been the lot of any people to enjoy." Like so many others, Washington's decision to leave was influenced by the passage of increasingly restrictive federal and state laws.

[40] A copy of James Theodore Holly's letter can be found in the Black Abolitionists Papers (microfilm), Vol. 6: 14,894; Miller, *The Search for a Black Nationality*, 108–09; Harrisburg *Telegraph*, June 25, 1857; *Maryland Colonization Journal*, September 1854; Harrisburg *Borough Item*, February 10, 15, 23, 28, March 10, 22, 31, April 6, 1853; R. J. M. Blackett, *Thomas Morris Chester, Black Civil War Correspondent. His Dispatches from the Virginia Front* (Baton Rouge: 1989), 11–12.

[41] Findley's letter to James Mitchell is republished in McKay, *Report of Rev. John McKay*, 36–37.

Yet, in spite of these disabilities, he marveled that blacks continued to "cling
with deadly tenacity to a country that hates them, and offers them nothing but
chains, degradation, and slavery." Doing the work of redeeming Africa would,
in the long run, he argued, redound to the benefit of those who chose to stay
in America. Like others, he had come to the realization that blacks could not
achieve social and political equality in America; only "friendly and mutual separation" would provide them with the space to rise.[42]

It was only after such long and sometimes agonizing personal retrospection
and community debate that potential settlers, such as Washington, Williams,
Findley, and Chester, approached state and national colonization officers for
information on the cost of getting to Liberia, the sailing schedules, the possibility of financial assistance, the prospects for trade, and any other information
they thought was necessary to finalize their plans. Their justifications for leaving were as varied as their personalities. All of those discussed here would echo,
to some extent, the arguments long espoused by colonizationists. Findley chose
to follow the call of Providence. Washington narrowed the differences between
the agendas of abolitionists and colonizationists, insisting that both had contributed to the struggle against slavery but, in the end, based his decision on
what he thought were practical considerations and the need for the races to
separate. Chester came to his decision after careful examination of conditions
in America – a decision, he maintained, that had nothing to do with the pro-
gram of colonizationists. But his decision to go to Liberia could not have been
easily made, for it flew in the face of his family and the local black community's
cherished abolitionist traditions, which abhorred and rejected anything to do
with Liberia.

Many of those who decided to emigrate would leave either by themselves
or with their families. Others left as members of an organization – in Samuel
Williams' case, the organization was the Liberian Enterprise Company, a small
joint-stock company formed in middle Pennsylvania soon after he and Charles
Deputie of Hollidaysburg returned from a scouting mission to Liberia. The
group of thirty-two members sailed in 1853 with the financial backing of the
Pennsylvania Colonization Society (PCS), taking with them a steam sawmill
and "thousands of dollars' worth of goods." By the end of 1854, Williams
reported that the mill was fully operational and the sale of cut lumber brisk. He
anticipated repaying the loan from the society before it came due. But Williams
later had to admit that he had been much too optimistic. The company, unfortunately, had located the mill too far from potential markets. Transporting the
lumber they produced was also hampered by the country's poor infrastructure.
And to make matters worse, the Philadelphia merchants who had advanced
the company credit declared bankruptcy not long after the settlers had set up
business. These difficulties only exacerbated relations among members of the

---

[42] New York *Tribune*, July 9, 10, 1851; *Maryland Colonization Journal*, September 1851.

company. Within months of their arrival in Liberia, there were, as we shall see, signs that all was not well.[43]

Two years earlier, in May 1851, the Cambridge [Maryland] African Colonization Society, made up exclusively of blacks, had sent out two of its members, Rev. Benjamin Jenifer and Thomas Fuller, on a mission to Liberia. Their report spoke glowingly of the productivity of the country's rich soil; no man, they announced, could starve in Liberia. The climate was "mild and pleasant," and Monrovia was a "fine and flourishing town." They visited a number of schools in settlements and towns run by missionary societies. The existence of several literary and benevolent societies in these communities pointed to a vibrant intellectual culture. The people of Liberia seemed to live "as happy, and in the enjoyment of as good health as any people." On the whole, colonists were doing markedly better than if they had remained in America. Jenifer and Fuller recommended that free blacks migrate to this country of promise if they were truly committed to enjoying all "the rights and privileges of freemen." Although it is not clear what influence their report had on members of the Cambridge Society, months later the two were present at a contentious state convention in Baltimore that failed to agree on the merits of colonization. The dispute very likely put paid to the society's plans. In spite of repeated claims that he was on the verge of leaving for Liberia, Jenifer never did. Fuller, on the other hand, would become a leading figure in Liberian politics later in the decade.[44]

While groups such as the Liberian Enterprise Company and the Cambridge Society relied heavily on the financial support of their respective state colonization societies, there were others, such as the New York "Liberian Agricultural and Emigration Association," that tried to steer an independent course from the local society. The association was organized in October 1851 in the midst of the stormy debate over the Fugitive Slave Law. The driving force behind its formation was Lewis H. Putnam, who was born in North Carolina and who had lived for a while in Canada before moving to New York City, where he became active in aiding fugitive slaves and organizing resistance to the implementation of the law. It is not clear what triggered Putnam's interests in Liberia, but he seems to have first floated the idea of cooperation with J. B. Pinney and other leaders of the New York State Colonization Society (NYSCS) in 1848. Putnam probably offered his services as an independent recruiter of emigrants. Nothing came of his plans, however, until the political upheaval surrounding the enforcement of the Fugitive Slave Law once again raised questions about

---

[43] *Colonization Journal*, November 1853; *Maryland Colonization Journal*, February 1855; Williams, *Four Years in Liberia*, 141–43; Philadelphia *Public Ledger*, February 26, 1855.

[44] *Maryland Colonization Journal*, June 1851, December 1851, August 1852; Baltimore *Sun*, December 16, 1851; Hagerstown *Herald of Freedom*, June 4, 1851; *New York Colonization Journal*, May 1851, January 1852; Anita Aidt Guy, *Maryland's Persistent Pursuit to End Slavery, 1850–1864* (New York: 1997), 260–61.

the future of blacks in America. By mid-1851, Putnam had developed a scheme for what he called an "agricultural enterprise" in Liberia. In September, a meeting to discuss the worsening conditions caused by the "enactment of some recent acts of Congress," and which recommended the formation of an organization to protect the interests of African Americans, called on Putnam to report on his agricultural plans.[45]

The call was clearly orchestrated by Putnam, who was determined to establish himself as the leader of a black-led and innovative colonization society. "It was truly humiliating to think that every organization in existence which aims at the elevation of our race," he would later observe, was "under the management of those who cannot comprehend the difficulties under which we are laboring." The formation of the association had been announced earlier in the year. It planned to send out an advanced group to clear the land and construct cottages prior to the arrival of settlers. Each settler family would be provided with three acres of cleared land as well as farming implements and a cottage. Putnam announced that he was about to send out "provisions and tools" to start the process. He was not interested in attracting the sorts of settlers that had traditionally been sent to Liberia by the ACS and its state affiliates, he declared. As far as he was concerned, traditional colonizationists had relied too heavily on untutored and unskilled emancipated slaves. What Liberia most needed, the association argued, were skilled free blacks, "cultivated people to teach the uncultivated." This, Putnam predicted, would also soften the ACS's negative image among African Americans who had customarily rejected its claims and approach. Putnam called on those interested in his plans to send contributions directly to the association. Not surprisingly, the NYSCS worried that support normally sent to it was now being mistakenly diverted to the association. The association, J. B. Pinney felt it necessary to inform the public, was not the same as the society.[46]

At its first meeting – chaired by Elisha G. Jones, a barber and the future "home agent" of the association – it was announced that an agent had been selected to visit Liberia to determine where farms would be established and to prepare provisions for the arrival of emigrants. A Mr. Simons, opposed to the association's plans, reminded the meeting that the "colored people" did not want to emigrate and were committed instead to the belief that they had a "right to remain in America." By the time of the association's second meeting, black communities throughout the North were consumed by what had occurred at Christiana, Pennsylvania, and Syracuse, New York. The shoot-out at Christiana, which had result in the death of a slaveholder, and the dramatic rescue of the fugitive slave Jerry in Syracuse had sent shock waves throughout

---

[45] *New York Colonization Journal,* July 1860; New York *Tribune,* September 27, 1851, January 12, 1852; New York *Herald,* September 26, 1851.
[46] New York *Tribune,* March 4, 5, 1851; Rochester *Democrat,* December 12, 1851; New York *Herald,* October 21, 1851.

the country. As we have seen, blacks made abundantly clear their support for those in Christiana and Syracuse who had violated the law. Many communities in New York City and elsewhere organized meetings of support and collected funds to send to those who were under indictment. These new developments shifted the gaze of the black community away from Putnam's plans and may have prompted him publicly to disassociate the association from the ACS and the NYSCS. But how was that possible, many asked, if the association continued to make plans to establish its farms in Liberia? At a meeting chaired by William P. Powell and at which Samuel Cornish, George Downing, and others spoke, the association was castigated and ridiculed. Cornish accused Putnam of diverting money raised for the association to his personal use. He was not opposed to Putnam soliciting support from colonizationists so long as he did not "compromise the well-known sentiments of the colored people." Liberia, Cornish concluded, was the "last place" he would advise black people to go. Resolutions rejected the findings of the two earlier meetings and expressed continued opposition to colonization, whether promoted by the ACS or by "renegade colored men, made under the guise of an emigration society."[47]

Dismissing such criticism as unfounded, the association met again days later to consider a report from Putnam, who announced that the process of establishing farms in Liberia, begun in April, was progressing steadily. Liberia's problems stemmed largely from the fact that agriculture was woefully under-developed because its settlers were not provided with the resources they needed to succeed: "To send poor people to a country where there is no capital employed to develop its resources," he reasoned, "is imposing on them a task which nineteen out of twenty will fail to accomplish." That had been the cause of the economy's slow growth. The six-month support given by the ACS was demonstrably inadequate. What was needed was the establishment of viable agricultural settlements settled by skilled workers, the products of which would be sold on the international market.[48] Try as he might, Putnam could not overcome the conviction of anti-colonizationists that the association was, as Martin Delany put it, a scheme gotten up by J. B. Pinney and other New York colonizationists to hoodwink "some poor pitiable colored persons" who had loaned themselves "to the enemies of the race," a "hobby that colonization is riding all over the country." At the same time, Pinney and the leaders of the New York Society found themselves torn between the difficulty of rejecting associating with a potentially sympathetic black organization with a similar agenda, and the fear that the association was siphoning off funds that usually were theirs for the taking. The suspicion also lingered that Putnam was a charlatan who could not be trusted. For the remainder of the decade, Putnam and the NYSCS would conduct a series of bitter public disputes and legal challenges, the society accusing Putnam of being a "Negro Imposter" for collecting

---

47 New York *Herald*, October 3, 21, 1851.
48 New York *Herald*, October 21, 1851.

money under false pretenses, and for not having emigrated to Liberia as he had promised, and Putnam, in turn, suing the leaders of the society for defamation of character.[49]

Unfortunately for Putnam, political developments across the nation made black New Yorkers wary of the association's plan; it seemed to have all the hallmarks, opponents thought, of a Trojan horse. Following a meeting In October 1850 to welcome back James Hamlet, who had been redeemed from slavery with the aid of city merchants prominent in the movement to win public support for the Fugitive Slave Law, black New Yorkers formed the "Committee of Thirteen" to assist fugitive slaves and to protect their political interests. Not surprisingly, there were divisions over the best ways to address these new political challenges. A convention called by the committee the following March set out to address a wide range of issues, including the social and political condition of black New Yorkers, emigration, and the Fugitive Slave Law. As was his wont, the editor of the New York *Herald* thought he saw the deep, destructive, and sinister influence of abolitionists and political radicals on the meeting's agenda. The committee was preparing, he predicted, a "terrible collision between themselves and the whites, which would be attended with the most dreadful consequences." Never one to miss an opportunity to ridicule local black leaders, the editor dismissed them as "good artists in the way of opening oysters, blacking boots, starching, and whitewashing." The ridicule was unrelenting and unrestrained: the leaders were of mixed race, a blend of English, Irish, Scots, French, and German with "the dark fluid of Barbary, Guinea, Nigrita and Timbuctoo," who demonstrated as much intelligence as the "antirenters and socialists of any color." There were two great men in the state, he concluded sarcastically, white William Seward, the New York senator, "socialist, abolitionist and anti-renter," and black George Downing, of "the famous oyster cellar," whose views generally converged except on two or three points, when "the oysters have decidedly the advantage."[50]

If the report written and presented by James McCune Smith is an indication of the convention's deliberations, then it appears that much of the time was devoted to social issues internal to the black community. The Fugitive Slave Law and colonization were tangential. But the report did recommend a form of separation, reminiscent of Horace Greeley's. It suggested that blacks move to rural areas as farmers, businessmen, and mechanics. It also called for the establishment of a "mutual savings institution," explored the issue of rising house rents, the cost of fuel, and other domestic issues. The suggestion that blacks abstain from "policy gambling" generated a heated debate during which Smith bemoaned the fact that blacks were spending $100,000 annually on policy gambling. Gambling was so pervasive, he argued, much to the amusement

---

[49] Martin R. Delany, *The Condition, Elevation, Emigration and Destiny of the Colored People of the United States* (1852, rpr., New York: 1969), 33; *New York Colonization Journal*, July 1860.
[50] New York *Herald*, October 25, 1850, March 17, 23, 1851.

of many in the hall, that it was "changing the very physiognomy of the colored people." P. A. Bell, however, rose to Smith's defense: policy gambling had done more damage to the black community, he calculated, than the Fugitive Slave Law could ever hope to do. While the law may have resulted in the capture of six fugitives in the city since its passage, he had it from reliable sources that nineteen out of twenty blacks picked up for petty larceny had policy tickets in their possession. Gambling, he concluded, led inevitably to "robbery, licentiousness, drunkenness, and every vice and crime in the calendar." Although John L. Zuille wondered what abstinence from alcohol and gambling had to do with the need for a savings institution, the motion was carried. One suspects that the editor of the *Herald* allowed such discussions to pass without comment because they dominated the attention of the convention, leaving little time for the exploration of larger political issues.[51]

What the editor did not realize, or chose not to see because of his visceral distrust of black leaders and their abolitionist allies, was that, with the formation of the Committee of Thirteen, the black community had set in place an organization capable of focusing on multiple issues simultaneously, including, when the time came, the Fugitive Slave Law and colonization. Their opposition to Putnam's plans in the light of developments such as Indiana's exclusionary law would soon lead to heated exchanges in the pages of the New York *Tribune*, whose editor, Horace Greeley, had long been considered a friend of black causes but who now seemed to have thrown in his lot with colonizationists. The situation in the country, Greeley observed, was becoming deeply divisive and increasingly dangerous. Slaveholders and their merchant supporters in the city, on the one hand, thought blacks capable only of "polishing boots and picking cotton." On the other, philanthropists saw them only as "sufferers and victims" of white selfishness. The latter taught blacks "self satisfaction," while the former inculcated a sense of deep "despair." As a result, the majority of blacks were sunk in "debasement and gross sensuality." Blacks also believed that they should be granted political rights regardless of their station in society. While he was supportive of some political rights, Greeley would not countenance what he called familiarity for "Intermingling," which, he declared, was neither natural nor desirable. Wherever it had occurred between intellectually superior and inferior people it had led to debasement. The only solution was separation of the races. Colonization was "the means whereby the oppressed Races and Communities" could renew their "youth and strength." Separation, he anticipated, could also result in the establishment of a number of substantial rural settlements in America or elsewhere where blacks would have the freedom from white interference to work out their future, where, "in defiance of prejudice," they could prove themselves worthy of the enjoyment of "self government." Why, he wondered, if blacks thought the conditions under which

---

[51] New York *Herald*, March 19, 31, 1851.

they now lived were so deplorable did they continue to denounce the ACS and the option it offered? The attachment of African Americans to a country that continued to deny them their rights was a "fictitious and imaginary sentiment." He had no doubt that if a law similar to Indiana's was submitted to a vote in any Free State it would be adopted unanimously. Given these facts, why, he wondered, were blacks so adamantly opposed to colonization?[52]

Smith had an answer and offered to explain to Greeley the reasons why African Americans so defiantly opposed any attempt at expatriation. Why, Smith wondered, was Greeley now willing to undermine all the good work he had previously done to promote equality of rights and opposition to the Fugitive Slave Law? The editor declined the offer partly, one suspects, because he could not abide Smith's sarcastic tone, but also because, as he said, Smith was in no mood to offer a reasoned response. But Greeley did offer to open his newspaper to any other black man who could offer dispassionate solutions to the consequences of the Indiana vote – as well as the exclusionary policies adopted by other states. But Smith was not to be denied; he took his message elsewhere. His was a lesson in the history of black opposition to the ACS and its policies, which he characterized as having been always "spontaneous, decided and firm." The colonizationist solution was based on the mistaken assumption that the colored man was African and Africa was his natural home. Since the founding of the country, Smith observed, Europeans had "mingled [their] blood with the negro; thereby producing in our free blacks the most thoroughly mixed of the human species." There was a child playing on the floor as he wrote, "among whose forebears, some generations back, may be named Korymantee in Africa; Carib and Iroquois in America, Spanish, French and old Puritan in Europe; and this child has a white skin, grey eyes and flaxen hair." He called on Greeley to brush up on his ethnography and then tell him "why this child is to be classified with the African race." They were not "free blacks" either, for truly black men were "getting as scarce as Indians"; nor were they "colored people," for they "have every variety of complexion." These people were, Smith concluded, "Americans to the manor born."

Smith poured scorn on Greeley's unease about amalgamation. Not a night passes in the South, he wrote, when white men – from the planter to the "lowest Scotch-Irish" – were not found in the embrace of black women. There was nothing revolting to "Nature, to God, nor to themselves" in such relationships. In fact, they were simply obeying that "Higher Law of Progress which demands as its first condition, the free admixture of varieties of human kind." Like many streams flowing into an expanding river, admixture ensured man's continued development: it was "progress; isolation is retrogression." The evidence of this continued admixture was palpable: there were now only fifty thousand of

---

[52] New York *Tribune*, June 24, 1851, August 21, 1851. James Mitchell called on the ACS to connect Greeley's commentary to the recent passage of Indiana's exclusionary law for the benefit of colonization. Mitchell to McLain, Indianapolis, July 13, 1852. ACS Papers.

"unmixed blood" in a black population of more than three million. There were also signs that amalgamation was not uncommon in the North. He pointed to an increase in marriages between black men and white women in New York City, where white women could be seen carrying "yellow babies," as many as black women did in South Carolina. America's motto was prophetic. From many nations, "from the strong Saxon energy of the Englishman, from the cool sagacity and indomitable perseverance of the Scot, from the fresh and buoyant Irish, from the keen intellectual vivacity of the Gall, from the far-reaching subtle genius of the German, and, though last, not least, from the all-suffering, the all-enduring, the all-surviving and long-despised Negro, are made up the ONE of the American people." Colonization to Liberia, based as it was on racial separation, therefore, violated this law of progress. How, he asked, could a colony of "isolated blacks" evangelize Africa? What kind of civilization would they carry to Africa given their experiences in America? If any country was in need of improvement it was America: "Here is our duty, and we are bound to do it." Like Frederick Douglass, Smith also saw signs of political progress in states such as Massachusetts.[53]

Greeley did receive and publish a number of letters in response to his editorial, none of which supported leaving. "H.J.," for example, was optimistic about the future. He saw a "ray of hope that Truth is progressing, and that one day the fog and mist of prejudice that now lowers about us will be dissipated by the sunlight of Justice." Greeley could not fathom the source of such optimism. The evidence was indisputable; wherever equal rights for blacks were put to a popular vote it went down in resounding defeat. This was the reality confronting African Americans, and no arcane ethnographic analysis about the history of amalgamation, or the changes to suffrage laws in one state, could detract from the fact that conditions were getting worse rather than better. Moreover, Greeley reiterated, he had never advocated for the removal of all blacks to Africa, only that separation and settlement away from whites seemed the best option.[54]

Although Greeley's views lacked the stridency of many other colonizationists, the fact remained that free blacks for whom Smith, Douglass, and others spoke, were adamantly opposed to any form of expatriation, whatever its source. Not surprisingly, associations such as Lewis Putnam's in New York City, Samuel Williams' in Pennsylvania, and Benjamin Jenifer's in Cambridge,

[53] New York *Tribune*, August 22, 1851; *National Anti-Slavery Standard*, August 28, September 11, 1851. Downing had employed similar reasoning in an earlier report on emigration prepared for the Committee of Thirteen. The claim that blacks had an affinity for Africa was, he argued, "false." They did not trace their ancestry to Africa alone: "The blood of many nations course through our veins." America was blessed with many advantages, "far beyond those afforded in Africa, or anywhere else." Individuals have a right to go wherever they wish, but, he insisted, there will not be a wholesale "alienation of our people from their country." *National Anti-Slavery Standard*, March 27, 1851.
[54] New York *Tribune*, August 28, 30, 1851.

Maryland, made little headway among those it sought to attract. It appeared that, not long after the association's formation, Putnam was expelled by its board of directors for raising funds without their permission. It was, one unsympathetic commentator observed, the "hurling out of the Colonization Synagogue, the great master spirit, the *great father of the whole late scheme.*" Smith employed a different metaphor. Putnam had, he wrote, an insatiable appetite for money and so "bows down before a 'ragout' with oriental obeisance, and counts it canonized in that it will minister to that organ." According to Samuel Cornish, Putnam had already collected $3,000 from "citizens who were foolish enough to believe his representations." Putnam's claim that he was about to send out agents with the goods he had bought and collected was pure fiction, Downing asserted; the goods, in fact, had been shipped not by Putnam but by the NYSCS. But Putnam's expulsion seemed to have had little effect on his plans; he carried on as if he were the association. He sent out Abraham Caldwell, a whitewasher, and Elias Jones to Liberia in January 1852 to explore the best location for the establishment of farms. Jones tragically drowned soon after their arrival. Caldwell, who returned to the United States in November, reported that he had met with J. J. Roberts, Liberia's president, who had granted his request for sixty lots of ten acres each along the St. Paul's River on which to establish the farms. Before he left for home, Caldwell had cleared ten acres on which he also built a large store house. Caldwell's enthusiasm for the future of the settlements was expressed in the most curious terms: once well-provisioned emigrants settle, he predicted, "trees fall, houses go up, snakes leave, wild cows tremble, deer flee, and birds sing for joy." Soon after Caldwell's return, Putnam issued a revised and expanded plan, which he sent to the authorities in Virginia, Maryland, Ohio, and Indiana. He anticipated establishing thirty-one agricultural districts, one for each of the states of the Union, each state taking responsibility for the settlement of its district. Each district would accommodate three hundred families with their own farm. Ultimately, Putnam predicted, the projected 9,300 farms would accommodate 46,000 settlers, far surpassing anything the ACS or its affiliates had accomplished in the many years since the founding of the colony.[55]

Nothing came of Putnam's grand scheme although he continued to peddle it to anyone who would listen.[56] He was nothing if not persistent. Even though

[55] New York *Tribune*, January 12, 1852; *New York Colonization Journal*, January 1852, June 1852, April 1853, September 1853; *National Anti-Slavery Standard*, January 22, 1852; *Maryland Colonization Journal*, August 1852; Quincy *Herald*, September 19, 1853; H. H. Bell, "The Negro Emigration Movement, 1849–1854: A Phase of Negro Nationalism," *Phylon*, Vol. 20, No. 2 (Second Quarter, 1959), 137.

[56] In 1860, as the country moved toward war, Putnam dusted off his old scheme and approached the New Jersey senate with an emigration plan and request for appropriations to purchase farms in Liberia. See *Weekly Anglo-African*, March 10, 17, 1860. Lewis H. Putnam, *A Review of the Cause and Tendency of the Issues Between the Two Sections of the Country, With A Plan to Consolidate the Views of the People of the United States in Favor of Emigration to Liberia* (Albany, NY: 1859).

he had been expelled from the association he founded, Putnam continued to collect money from supporters of colonization in the face of strong public condemnation by both black New Yorkers and the NYSCS. Black opponents could ridicule Putnam, but he remained unbowed. The mission of Caldwell and Jones testified to his determination to bring the settlement to fruition. Here was a black-led plan of colonization that seemed to thumb its nose at traditional black antipathy as well as defy the public warnings of local colonizationists. All of the other proposed companies led by blacks relied heavily on the support and largesse of colonization societies. Not so Putnam's. He not only crossed swords with the New York society, he also insisted that he would establish a presence in Liberia free of ACS control. If they were mockingly skeptical of Putnam's plans, Smith, Cornish, Downing, and other adversaries were startled when in his annual message Washington Hunt, governor of New York, declared his approval of colonization plans, including Putnam's. The Committee of Thirteen immediately called on Hunt to "disavow the scheme." A hastily organized meeting in Albany, New York, warned of "traitors among us – coloured men allied with our oppressors," men who were willing to "sell the cause of our oppressed brethren, and forsake the land of our birth, and the glory of our moral greatness, by an ignominious flight to the pestilential shores of Africa." The meeting, chaired by J. W. C. Pennington, condemned the association as a "false and deceptive movement" that was as harmful to the interests of blacks as were traditional colonizationists, most of them avid supporters of the Fugitive Slave Law. The rumor that Hunt had also requested an appropriation to support colonization troubled the meeting. It was not something blacks had requested, they observed. In fact, the governor was well aware that they had "unceasingly protested against the whole scheme of colonization." They dismissed Hunt's call as "unchristian and unconstitutional" and pledged to vote against him in the next election, aware that his recent narrow victory was in part due to the support of blacks. A delegation visited Hunt at the conclusion of the meeting to express their opposition. They must have left assured, for the governor informed them that, although he saw colonization as an alternative for "some blacks who wanted to leave," he was opposed to any form of appropriation for colonization and would veto any bill containing one.[57]

Although Putnam continued to attract some financial support – enough, at least, to send Caldwell and Jones to Liberia – his opponents, in the end, carried the day. Opposition in New York City and elsewhere made it next to impossible

---

[57] *National Anti-Slavery Standard*, January 22, 1852; *New York Colonization Journal*, January 1852; Philip S. Foner, "History of the Black Americans from the Compromise of 1850 to the End of the Civil War," http://testaae.greenwood.com/doc_print?fileID+GR7967&chapterID+GR7967-88&path=books/greenwood; Philip S. Foner and George E. Walker, eds., *Proceedings of the Black State Conventions, 1840–1865*, 2 Vols. (Philadelphia: 1979), I, 86–87; *Rochester American*, January 19, 1852.

to sustain such colonization schemes. When, in late 1853, they sailed for what all thought was a new life in Liberia, members of the Pennsylvania Liberian Enterprise Company were fairly optimistic that their well-laid plans would produce the sort of success that had eluded others. Within six months, William Nesbit, one of the settlers, was back in Hollidaysburg eager to talk to anyone who would listen about the company's misjudged enterprise as well as the parlous state of the country. It is very likely that Nesbit had always been deeply skeptical of the enterprise. In fact, in a pamphlet published months later, he claimed to have signed on to the voyage as a way to "test" whether colonization was viable. A withering critique of Liberia, the colonizationists who promoted it, and African Americans who supported it, the pamphlet opened with a condemnation of the ACS as a "base pandering of the dough-faces to the inhuman spirit of Slavery." The colony had been established on the erroneous assumption that blacks did not belong in America, that America was a white man's country, that they were inferior, that they could not improve their condition if they remained in America – all in all it was a "scheme of the most consummate villainy." Claims made for Liberia were simply "egregious falsehoods." The country was a "little plague spot," a land of "wretchedness and desolation," and a "mean farce," ruled by a "cod-fish aristocracy," its laws a "burlesque on a free country." It was nothing more than "one magnificent swamp" in the main street of whose capital grass grew so high it could hide an elephant. Missionaries who lived off the support of their parent societies had been abject failures, converting, by Nesbit's calculations, less than two dozen natives. Nesbit also had an answer for those who offered the Pilgrims as an example of why African Americans should seek a new life in Liberia free from American oppression: in America, the Pilgrims had found a "congenial climate" and had only "to make peace with their neighbors." In contrast, the climate of Liberia was inhospitable, with a soil that could not produce the kinds of food needed to sustain the settlers. Nesbit concluded his critique with a series of letters written by members of the company, including the wife and son of Charles Deputie, one of its leaders, condemning the country and expressing a desire to leave.[58]

The pamphlet's findings were endorsed by Martin Delany, the state's leading opponent of the ACS and Liberia. He dismissed colonization as the most "pernicious and impudent of all schemes," and Liberia as a "Potter's Field into which the carcass of every emigrant who ventured there would most assuredly moulder in death." Delany highlighted for the reader what he considered Nesbit's major findings: the country was unhealthy, slavery had not been eradicated, and missionaries had been abject failures. The country was nothing more, he concluded, than a "miserable hovel of emancipated and

[58] William Nesbit, *Four Months in Liberia or African Colonization Exposed,* in Moses, *Liberian Dreams,* 88, 97, 105, 109–11, 124; *Colonization Journal,* November 1853.

superannuated slaves and deceived colored men, controlled by the intrigue of a conclave of upstart colored hirelings of the Slave Power of the United States."[59]

Nesbit's pamphlet seemed to have caught the PCS, who had given the company its blessing and financial support, off guard. Such descriptions were not what colonizationists had hoped for from someone following a visit to the country. Traditionally, visitors who were considering settling there spoke of the country as a place of considerable promise. Although it is difficult to measure what impact such positive reports had on potential emigrants, the consensus among colonizationists was that they were an invaluable aid to the movement. Nesbit's views, therefore, could not go unchallenged. They were "grossly and palpably erroneous," the editor of one colonization journal responded. Nesbit's pamphlet and Delany's introduction were the result of "disappointed ambition" that had produced "violent hostility...calumnies and slanders." Nesbit had unfairly accused emigrants of "laziness, roguery, and hypocrisy." He seemed perversely "ashamed of his own people," suggesting that they had no future unless they clung to the "stronger white race for support." His criticisms of the country's shortcomings were nothing more than "inveterate...misstatements," all of which led the editor to wonder if Nesbit was the author of the pamphlet, and, if he were, had it been written under the "frenzy" of the African fever. Delany's maliciousness was dismissed as nothing more than the parroting of old and unsubstantiated "gross slanders."[60]

Thomas Morris Chester tried to blunt the impact of Nesbit's pamphlet. He knew firsthand what life was like in Liberia, he told many public gatherings. He was the sort of committed settler of whom any colonizationist could be proud. He was temporarily back in the United States to further his education before returning to Liberia. Chester claimed he knew Nesbit even before the company had left for Liberia and implied that he was not to be trusted. He, therefore, was not surprised that Nesbit could produce a work of such "palpable falsehood ... unworthy of the table of any house, unless to show the baseness and ingratitude of the author." In his time in Liberia, Chester had seen no evidence of violence toward natives, the enslavement of Africans, the ignorance of government ministers, missionaries selling rum, or emigrants not permitted to leave. For thirty years Liberia had "contended victoriously with a savage foe at home, and defended herself triumphantly from a presumptuous enemy and an ignorant prejudice abroad." Fortunately, the young republic was "now beyond the baneful influence" of such enemies. Those, such as Nesbit, who opposed Liberia were arraying themselves against "the only source" that had "elevated the black man by his own exertions." Chester was proud of what Liberia had accomplished in its brief history as well as its potential as the future home of all black Americans. As he told J. B. Pinney of the New York society, soon after his arrival in Monrovia, when he stepped on "the soil of

[59] Ibid., 81–84
[60] *New York Colonization Journal*, September 1855.

[his] ancestors, the heavy weight of oppression fell" and he was now enjoying full social and political equality. There, he concluded, was the home of black people "where they may live in the enjoyment of all the rights and privileges of citizens."[61]

Other members of the Enterprise Company, including Samuel William, its leading figure, and Rev. D. H. Patterson, also published rejoinders but with little effect. If numbers matter, as most black opponents contended, then Nesbit had clearly carried the day, confirming what many black Pennsylvanians thought of colonization. In spite of frequent public statements that there were many more who wanted to leave than the PSA could accommodate, only fifteen emigrated in the years between the publication of Nesbit's pamphlet and the end of the decade, when the society succeeded in sending out 108 emigrants. But even these numbers belied the fact that in the forty years between 1820 and 1860 fewer than three hundred, out of a black population that had almost doubled during the same period to 57,000, went to Liberia. And if Chester was an example of those committed to the young republic, he seemed to have spent an inordinate amount of time away from it, either at school in Maine, or on frequent visits to Harrisburg. If, a usually sympathetic editor wanted to know, he liked Liberia so much why did he not spend more time there? More significantly for his efforts, Chester's frequent lectures on the achievements and promise of Liberia seemed to have had little impact on his audiences; while they did not love Liberia less, the editor surmised, they seemed to love America more.[62]

Even when schemes were initiated by blacks, as they were by the New York City association, black opposition proved fatal to all colonization plans. Such was also the case in Baltimore following the 1852 State Convention of the Free People of Color of Maryland. The convention had been called by James A. Hardy, an AME minister, and John H. Walker, a schoolteacher, to consider the condition of free blacks and their future prospects in America and to "contrast them with the inducements and prospects opened to us in Liberia, or *any other country.*" As the delegates approached the building for the start of the meeting they were confronted by "several hundred" opponents of colonization. Only a strong police presence prevented a "general melee." The opposition stemmed in part from rumors that the convention had been financed by the state colonization society, but it is also clear that it drew on a long tradition of black opposition to colonization in the city. Benjamin Jenifer, head of the

[61] Harrisburg *Herald* (n.d.), in *New York Colonization Journal*, August 1855; Harrisburg *Commercial Register*, January 28, 1854.

[62] Williams, *Four Years in Liberia*; Rev. D. H. Peterson, *The Looking-Glass Being a Report and Narration of the Life, Travels, and Labors of the Rev. Daniel H. Peterson*, in Moses, *Dreams of Liberia*; Lancaster *Examiner and Herald*, May 24, 1854; Burin, *Slavery and the Peculiar Solution*, 80, 95, 98; David W. Smith, *On the Edge of Freedom. The Fugitive Slave Issue in South Central Pennsylvania, 1820–1870* (New York: 2013), 238–39; *Pennsylvania Telegraph*, December 22, 1859, January 14, 1860.

Cambridge society, had second thoughts about remaining at the convention in the face of such opposition but, in the end, was persuaded to stay. During the first session, James A. Jones, a delegate from Kent County and a firm supporter of emigration to Africa, claimed he was threatened and had to ask for police protection. The opposition continued into the second day. Resolutions in support of emigration and Liberia were countered by an insistence that more pressure be put on the state legislature to grant blacks their rights. On the third day, opponents in the hall went further and called for the removal of all references to Liberia in previously adopted resolutions. The highlight of the proceedings was the speech by the elderly Charles Williamson who, over the years, it seemed, had tested the prospects of all possible sites of emigration. He had lived in Canada, Trinidad, and Haiti, he reported, but none of them seemed to have fulfilled his expectations. Now he was ready, at the advanced age of sixty-seven, to try Liberia, which, he declared, had as "fine or better climate, as regards atmosphere, than the West Indies." James Hardy concurred: the "garden-spot" of Liberia, he told his listeners, had been prepared for black people by Providence.[63]

Liberia might have been set aside for African Americans by Providence, but its beneficiaries seemed oblivious to the gift. In the face of a relentless and withering opposition, the convention leaders had to concede that their plans were stillborn. They ought not to have been surprised given the history of strong local opposition to colonization dating back to the founding of the ACS. As the first state expedition was being prepared in 1831, prospective emigrants were visited by opponents who warned them of the hardships in Africa that awaited them and the possibility that they might be sold into slavery. Opponents continued their campaign while the ship laid at anchor in a last-ditch attempt to dissuade those on board from going to a "certain death in Africa." When the ship did sail, nearly half of those who were scheduled to leave were not on board. Sometimes opponents also intercepted emigrants on their way to embarkation ports. Fourteen of the sixty-five former slaves from Tennessee and Kentucky were, as the colonization agent reported, "decoyed away" by an association of blacks and their abolitionist supporters as they passed through Pittsburgh, Pennsylvania, in the summer of 1836.[64]

The tradition of intercepting manumitted slaves as they passed through Free States on their way to catch the ship to Liberia continued into the 1850s. In

[63] *Maryland Colonization Journal*, August 1852; "Documents: Proceedings of the Convention of the Free Colored People of the State of Maryland Held in Baltimore, July, 26, 27, and 28, 1852," *Journal of Negro History*, Vol. 1, No. 3 (July 1916), 323–38.

[64] Penelope Campbell, "Some Notes on Frederick County's Participation in the Maryland Colonization Scheme," *Maryland Historical Magazine*, Vol. 66, No. 1 (Spring 1971), 56; Christopher Phillips, *Freedom's Port. The African American Community of Baltimore, 1790–1860* (Urbana, IL: 1997), 223; Christopher Phillips, "'The Dear Name of Home': Resistance to Colonization in Antebellum Baltimore," *Maryland Historical Magazine*, 91 (Summer 1996), 197; *Colonization Herald*, July 9, 23, 1836; Pittsburgh *Gazette*, June 10, 16, 1836.

1851, Andrew Harper of St. Louis freed his twenty-two slaves, all members of the same family headed by sixty-year-old Emerine Harper, on the condition they go to Liberia. Under the care of Rev. W. D. Shumate, secretary of the Missouri Colonization Society, the party's itinerary took them along the Ohio River to Pittsburgh, then over land to Philadelphia where they were to catch a train for Baltimore, the port of embarkation. Three weeks after leaving St. Louis, the party ran into trouble in Hollidaysburg, Pennsylvania. As Shumate reported, two of Emerine Harper's sons, one sixteen, the other fourteen, were approached by "two mulatto men" who persuaded them to abandon the family and head for "parts unknown." Evidently, the boys were warned that Liberia was a "graveyard of most of those who migrated thither, and a cruel oppressor of those who survived." The ACS did all it could to find the boys. William McLain, head of the Washington office, contacted Charles Deputie, a founding member of the Liberian Enterprise Company, as well as a prominent white supporters in the area, in an effort to locate them. Deputie tried to get word to the boys that their family was distressed by their departure and were worried they would "never see them again." Andrew Harper added to the pressure on the boys, relaying threats that he would hunt them down as fugitives under the terms of the Fugitive Slave Law and sell them South. But Deputie was having his own troubles with the local black community, who were opposed to his plans to go to Liberia and who were therefore not inclined to be cooperative. The boys were never found. By late summer, it was reported, one had gone to Pittsburgh, the other to Canada.[65]

The decision to leave their family was neither easy nor spontaneous. There may have been some resistance by the boys to the conditions of Harper's emancipation plans. One local newspaper reported that their departure had been delayed by what it described as "unavoidable circumstances." It is possible that the family were negotiating with Harper for better provisions. At the time of their departure, a reporter observed that the family was "abundantly well provided with the necessities for the voyage." Yet when the party arrived in Baltimore, McLain was horrified to find them destitute with "absolutely nothing in the world except the clothes they had on their backs."[66] But it is equally as likely that the two boys, if not other members of the family, had initially refused to go. There were frequent reports of the enslaved refusing to go to Liberia as a condition of manumission. When, in 1836, Alexander Donelson, Andrew Jackson's brother-in-law, freed, by will, eleven slaves on the condition

[65] *Missouri Republican,* April 2, May 13, 1852; *African Repository,* June 1852; W. D. Shumate to Dear Sir, Baltimore, April 20, 1852, Shumate to McLain, Fee Fee, MO, June 16, 22, 1852, McLain to Shumate, Washington, DC, April 24, June 18, 22, July 6, 1852, McLain to Rev. David McKenney, Washington, DC, April 23, 1852, Charles Deputie to McLain, Hollidaysburg, July 5, 1852, ACS Papers.
[66] *Missouri Republican,* April 2, 1852; McLain to Shumate, Washington, DC, June 22, 1852, ACS Papers.

that they go to Liberia, his executor reported that those who were to be freed did not "like the idea of colonization." Three years after the Harper family left St. Louis, Dr. Elijah McLean of nearby Franklin County, Missouri, reported that he had abandoned plans to send a "family of servants" to Liberia because the two eldest children rejected the offer. William Kennedy, a lawyer, former state senator and Maury County, Tennessee, slaveholder, ran into similar difficulties when in 1852 he drew up plans to send a group of his former slaves to Liberia. As he reported, many of them were reluctant to leave the people and the place they knew for the unknown of an African country. Some even "refused to be manumitted." They were also distrustful of the ACS. As a result, six or seven of them refused to leave, preferring the slavery they knew to the offer of freedom in Liberia. Finally, those who did consent to go did so only after they were assured that they would be settled among relatives who had left earlier. A couple of them also demanded they be allowed to return if they did not find conditions in Liberia to their taste. Every decision to return, William McLain knew, was a statement of the settlement's shortcomings. The return of disgruntled emigrants had a decided influence on those in America who were waiting for news of conditions in the country before deciding on leaving.[67]

Such demands by prospective emigrants bothered McLain, who knew from experience that only those strongly committed to the enterprise stood a chance of succeeding. He was also concerned by the not infrequent demand for a return passage home from settlers who were frustrated by conditions in Liberia. One of those who insisted he be allowed to return to Tennessee if he did not like what he saw in Liberia was thirty-five-year-old Cyrus, a blacksmith, who left in December 1853. Within a year, Kennedy had agreed to pay for Cyrus's return passage to America. Soon after his return in early 1856, McLain reported that Cyrus had fallen in "among abolitionists," was afraid to return to Tennessee, and was disinclined to ever return to Liberia. Instead, Cyrus headed for Ohio, where he planned to stay until he heard from Kennedy. One wonders whether Cyrus had used Kennedy's offer to go to Liberia as a means of getting his freedom without ever intending to stay there. As Kennedy knew, Cyrus could not safely return to Tennessee without obtaining testimonials from prominent whites. Kennedy would also have had to procure for him special dispensation allowing him to stay in the state. No such dispensation was forthcoming and Cyrus would not return to Tennessee until after the conclusion of the Civil War. For Cyrus, home mattered but only if the conditions were to his liking.[68]

[67] Stockley Donelson to Dear Sir, Nashville, August 15, 1835, Kennedy to McLain, Columbia, March 2, 1852, ACS Papers; *Missouri Republican*, December 11, 1855; Campbell, *Maryland in Africa*, 103–04; Nashville *Gazette* (n.d.), in Alton *Telegraph*, February 2, 1853; *African Repository*, February, March 1853; New Orleans *Picayune*, January 1, 4, 1853; Nashville *Union and American*, July 17, 1853.

[68] Kennedy to Cowan, Columbia, August 16, 1852, Kennedy to McLain, Columbia, March 28, May 3, 1853, April 17, 1855, March 14, 1856, McLain to Kennedy, Washington, DC, March 20,

The enslaved sometimes used the excitement surrounding the departure of emigrants, such as the Kennedy groups, to escape to a Free State. Just as Kennedy was making plans to send out the second group, Montgomery Bell, the premier iron maker in Tennessee at the time, and the owner of more than three hundred slaves, announced his intention to free some of his slaves and send them to Liberia, where they could use their skills to develop an iron industry. Like Kennedy, Bell had made plans to send out his slaves in separate groups. Just before the departure of the second, Bell decided to send his nephew George C. Bain to England to purchase the necessary machinery. While Bain was in Washington negotiating with the ACS, Bell entrusted $3,500 to Joe Hall and Jim Burris, two of his trusted slaves, who were to deliver the money to James Bell, another of Bell's nephews. Instead of taking the money to James Bell, Hall and Burris headed to a Free State. But before leaving, they mailed a portion of the money, possibly as much as $2,500, to the first group who had gone to Liberia. The rest they used to finance their escape. Montgomery Bell was convinced, as he stated in an advertisement that offered a reward for their capture, that Hall and Burris had planned their escape with the aid and "guidance of a white man" and "two low white women." Over the next few weeks, two white men – Gideon Davis, forty-eight, a farmer and former constable, and John Luther, thirty-four, a blacksmith – and one white woman, Mahala Johnson, all of Dickson County, where one of Bell's larger furnaces was located, were charged with harboring Hall and Burris. Davis fled the state, the case against Johnson was dismissed for a lack of evidence, and Luther was found guilty and sentenced to four years in the state penitentiary.[69]

The enslaved found many ways to stymie their masters' plans to send them to Liberia. As Eric Burin has shown, they sometimes refused the "offer of freedom in Africa," tried to slow the pace of emigration by requesting more information on Liberia, which was not always readily available, insisted that kin on other plantations be freed to go along with them, changed their minds on

1856, ACS Papers; *African Repository,* January 1854; Columbia *Herald and Mail,* December 10, 1875; Jill L. Garrett, *Obituaries From Tennessee Newspapers* (Greenville, SC: 1980), 200.

[69] Nashville *Union and American,* September 5, 1854; C. Johnson to McLain, Nashville, September 13, 1854, ACS Papers; Dickson County Circuit Court Records, 1855–1866, Dickson County Archives. Information on Davis can be found in a letter from Blanche E. Craft to Linder Parker, Derby, Kansas, July 14, 2003. My thanks to Linda Parker for sharing a copy of the letter with me. Charles A. Sherrill, *Tennessee Convicts. Early Records of the State Penitentiary, Vol. 2, 1850–1870* (Mt. Juliet, TN: 2002), 218. Luther was pardoned in December 1856. In early 1852, Joseph H. Harrison of Maryland freed Nancy Brown and two of her children on the condition they go to Liberia. He put them in the charge of Robert Plummer, who was to get them safely to the emigrant ship in Baltimore. As a precaution, Plummer transferred Brown's free papers to the captain of the schooner carrying them to Baltimore, fearful she might take the opportunity to run to Pennsylvania "or some other free state rather than go to Liberia." Brown may have managed to work around Plummer's precaution, for the family does not appear on the manifest of ships sailing in 1852. See Robert Plummer to Dear brother (n.p.), April 27, 1852, Maryland Colonization Society Papers, Maryland Historical Society, Baltimore, Maryland.

the way to the ports of embarkation, and many times returned to America.[70] Such resistance disrupted, if it did not always curtail, the plans of slaveholders and colonizationists. Prior to the decisions of Emerine Harper's two sons to leave the family in Hollidaysburg, Pennsylvania, W. D. Shumate was optimistic that the family's departure would spur an increase in settlers from the state. Few, however, left for Liberia in subsequent years. In fact, only sixty-two opted for Liberia in the 1850s. The number of departures fell depressingly short of expectations. Much was expected following Rev. Armistead Miller's return to Ohio from a tour in 1853. His glowing report on conditions in the country, however, influenced no one. As he reported, he could not persuade anyone else to join his family. "Not one solitary man moves," one colonizationist lamented; "all affect to believe Miller [has] been humbugged." Settlers, such as Miller, were dismissed by former friends as "fool[s] or knave[s] – as liar[s] or dupe[s]."[71]

Shumate's and Miller's failure to generate the sorts of numbers they had anticipated was undoubtedly due in part to a lack of funds. In spite of periodic appropriation from state governments, local societies were always strapped for cash. But it is also clear that opposition from the enslaved, bolstered, as it was, by a deep distrust of colonizationists' motives by free blacks and abolitionists, had a profound impact on the movement's ability to operate in the ways it wished. Even in Indiana, where the new state constitution endorsed colonization, where the state society had procured financial support from the legislature and had placed its organization in the capable hands of James Mitchell, little came of the effort to attract emigrants in the numbers colonizationists had hoped. The fact that a law had been adopted that penalized blacks who came into the state and used the "blood money" collected to support colonization only infuriated African Americans. As John Says, agent of the ACS, reported in the summer of 1858 after a brief visit to the state that the society hoped would breathe new life into the local affiliate, everywhere he went he found the movement universally reviled by those who were to be its beneficiaries. Blacks and their white supporters also kept up pressure on the legislature to amend the constitution to remove Article XIII. Although they were unsuccessful, their unrelenting opposition worked against the aims of the movement.[72]

They may not have been able to stop legislatures in many of the Free States from appropriating money for colonization, or in the case of Indiana to adopt a new constitution with increased restrictions on the rights of blacks, but

[70] Burin, *Slavery and the Peculiar Solution*, 21.
[71] Donnie D. Bellamy, "The Persistency of Colonization in Missouri," *Missouri Historical Review*, 72 (October 1977), 17.
[72] *Maryland Colonization Journal*, November 1854; John Says to R. R. Gurley, Indianapolis, June 8, 21, 1858. ACS Papers; *Journal of the House of Representatives of the State of Indiana During the Thirty-Ninth Session of the General Assembly* (Indianapolis: 1857), 381–82, 480.

African Americans did make it next to impossible for the movement to attract significant numbers of emigrants. Illinois is a case in point. In the years since Samuel S. Ball had reported on his visit to Liberia in 1848, very few blacks left the state for Monrovia. In 1858, an agent of the state society, which claimed among its members Abraham Lincoln, announced that a few "intelligent" blacks from Springfield and Jacksonville were planning to leave on the spring sailing. In the end, only eighteen opted for Liberia between 1858 and 1860.[73] At times, other states, including Maryland and Virginia, showed better results, but they were never enough to justify the amount of money and energy expended in persuading free blacks that their future lay in Liberia. Barbara Fields has estimated that, after thirty years, and an estimated expenditure of $200,000, fewer than five hundred Maryland emigrants lived in the state colony in Liberia.[74] In politics, as in sports, numbers mattered and the numbers attracted to Liberia were abysmal. Under pressure from free blacks and abolitionists and the reluctance of slaves to accept the boon of colonization, the project was doomed.

The ACS and its affiliates did what they could to counter the opposition. Those who did go were a vital, if ineffective, force in the campaign to persuade others to follow. Liberia, they insisted, was the home of the black man, a place where they could exercise the full range of their talents. "Here I stand erect and free, upon the soil of my ancestors," William H. Taylor, a Pennsylvania emigrant, wrote for the consumption of those he left behind, "and can truly say to all of my race, You that would be free, Africa is your home, and the only home where he that is tinctured with African blood can enjoy liberty." Colonizationists disseminated these letters in periodicals and local newspapers. The one from Adam White of Missouri was fairly standard. White – who had been freed by Edward Bates, later Abraham Lincoln's attorney general, and emigrated in 1854 – declared Liberia "one of God's favorite places on earth." These letters also devoted space to comments on the agricultural and mercantile potential of the country. Stephen Mitchee, who left St. Louis in early 1851, made it clear that he never regretted going to Liberia: "We all live well in Africa," he wrote. America was not "the home of the free colored people." Many of these letters, which were republished in newspapers sympathetic to the cause, favorably compared life in Liberia to conditions under which free blacks lived in cities such as Cincinnati and Baltimore. As such, they echoed traditional colonizationist reasons why blacks should seek their future in

---

[73] *Illinois State Register,* February 4, 1858; Springfield *Journal,* May 9, October 12, 15, 1859; *African Repository,* June 1858, December 1859, November 1860.

[74] Barbara Jeanne Fields, *Slavery and Freedom on the Middle Ground. Maryland During the Nineteenth Century* (New Haven: 1985), 10. One Baltimore newspaper reported in 1851 that twenty-five families, numbering about one hundred, were about to sail, but it is not clear how many of them were from the state, as Baltimore was a major port of embarkation. Baltimore *Sun,* March 19, May 12, June 4, 1851.

Liberia. It was a country ordained by God in his infinite wisdom for the black man, a place to which the crushed children of Africa should return, bringing with them Christianity and civilization.[75]

Few heeded the call. This failure deeply frustrated black advocates such as Thomas Morris Chester. African American views of Liberia, he wrote in frustration following the publication of William Nesbit's pamphlet, were "conceived in profound ignorance, displayed in a ludicrous presumption and nourished by an unnatural superstition." That may well have been true, but as Nesbit and others pointed out, even for someone as committed to the Liberian project as Chester was, the amount of time he spent in America suggested that he had some reservations about the country's ability to provide for his personal needs. Other advocates, such as James A. Hardy, John H. Walker, and Benjamin Jenifer of Maryland, all of who called on free blacks to emigrate, never left the United States. Only Thomas Fuller of the Cambridge society moved to Liberia permanently. No one was more eloquent on the providential role of Liberia than Hardy. It was, he told the 1852 Baltimore Convention, the "garden spot" prepared by providence for black people. God in his pity, wisdom, and goodness had opened the way for a part of her colored children, "pre-doomed by bloody superstition to altars of death, to be delivered from immolation and find an asylum under a form of ameliorated service in the bosom of this country; and here their children have been born, elevated and blessed under redeeming auspices. In the lapse of time, by the same benevolent Providence, many of this [sic] people have become free, and to such the voice of heaven emphatically speaks, thundering forth in invigorating terms 'Arise and depart for this is not your rest.' "[76]

No white colonizationist could have expressed the connections between America slavery and African redemption more eloquently. Yet, unlike Harriet Beecher Stowe's character George Harris, Hardy never took the opportunity to move to the "garden spot." Much to the consternation of blacks and white abolitionists who had followed closely Stowe's indictment of slavery as each chapter of what would become her bestselling novel was published serially, her decision to send the Harris family to Liberia, they thought, gave unnecessary credence to a movement they had long reviled. His soul, Harris said, yearned for "an African nationality." While he insisted that the black man had every right to enjoy the fruits of citizenship in America, he wanted "a country, a nation of my own." He was going to Liberia, Stowe had him say, "not as an Elysium of romance, but as to a *field of work*," where, as a "Christian patriot, a teacher of Christianity," he can work for "glorious Africa." Slavery, Stowe seemed to agree with colonizationists, was a training ground for black

[75] *New York Colonization Journal*, April 1853; Boonville *Observer*, March 8, 1856; Hannibal *Tri-Weekly Messenger*, February 26, 1853; *Missouri Republican*, February 2, 1856; Lafayette *Courier*, March 30, May 23, 1853; *Maryland Colonization Journal*, August 1852.
[76] *New York Colonization Journal*, August 1855; *Maryland Colonization Journal*, August 1852.

Americans, even someone such as Harris, whose "shade of color is so slight," to find fulfillment in an exodus to Africa.[77]

Blacks did not take up the proffered offer of a new life in Africa, colonizationists insisted, because they were ignorant of what was in their best interest. Their dogged determination to stay in America and compel it to grant them the rights enshrined in the Bill of Rights was a direct threat to the country as it wrestled over its future in the wake of the Mexican War. Henry Clay and other politicians had advocated a twined approach to resolve the problem: find a way to compromise over the issue of slavery and at the same time remove free blacks, one of the thorns in the side of the slave system as well as a subversive force in Free States. Like Elisha Whittlesey, many were convinced that, in the long run, this approach would lead both to freedom for the slaves and freedom from black people. If only free blacks and abolitionists would cease their agitation over emancipation and colonization, slaveholders would eventually manumit their slaves. Abolition was the black man's curse and opposition to colonization only hardened the minds of those slaveholders who were partial to freeing their slaves. Colonizationists, on the other hand, saw themselves as patient and practical; they had provided a colony that, over time, had grown and matured economically and politically, a welcoming place for all those willing to go. But try as they might, they failed to persuade an appreciable number of blacks that their future lay in Liberia or anywhere outside the United States. Even among those who acknowledged its missionary potential, Liberia could not overcome its image as a place of forced exile. While it won some support from slaveholders and free blacks, in the end, the colonizationist solution had little effect on the peculiar institution, attracted relatively few black settlers to Liberia, and failed to quell the widening political conflict over slavery.

---

[77] Harriett Beecher Stowe, *Uncle Tom's Cabin* (New York: 1961), 426–29.

PART II

FREEDOM'S FIRES BURN

# 4

# Missouri and Illinois

Eight slaves – Edmund, aged thirty-seven, Isaac, thirty-four, Joseph and Bernard, both twenty-six, William, twenty-four, Theodore, twenty-three, another also named Joseph, twenty-two, and the youngest, Henry, eighteen – fled the Valle lead mines at Ste. Genevieve, Missouri, in September 1852, crossed the Mississippi River and headed for Sparta, Illinois. Isaac and the younger Joseph were slaves of Amadee Valle of St. Louis, the owner of the mines. Bernard and Henry were owned by Lewis Bogy, a prominent lawyer and a man of considerable wealth. Edmund was the property of William Skewes, an English-born farmer who owned eight other slaves. Theodore was claimed by Noree Valle, quite likely a relative of Amadee. The older Joseph was one of thirteen slaves owned by farmer Antoine Janis. William was the property of Jonathan Smith, who lived close to the mines. At least six of the escapees were hired out to work at the mines. All, the owners felt the need to point out, spoke both English and French. Given the possible destination of the runaways, it is unlikely that their facility with French would have been of much use.[1]

The eight seemed to have operated without the aid of outsiders, although it is very likely that they were assisted by other African Americans, both slaves and those who were free, who lived nearby. That they headed for Sparta, across the river in Randolph County, suggests that they were aware of the existence of the small but active group of abolitionists who operated in the area and who, over the years, had sheltered slaves seeking freedom. One Missouri newspaper had reported earlier that there were several slaves from the area hiding in Sparta. If the escapees knew of this support system, so too did their masters, who dispatched five policemen to the town in an effort to intercept

---

[1] *Missouri Republican*, September 15, 1852; Population Schedules of the Seventh Census of the United States, 1850, Missouri, Ste. Genevieve County; Slave Schedules of the Seventh Census of the United States, 1850, Missouri, Ste. Genevieve County.

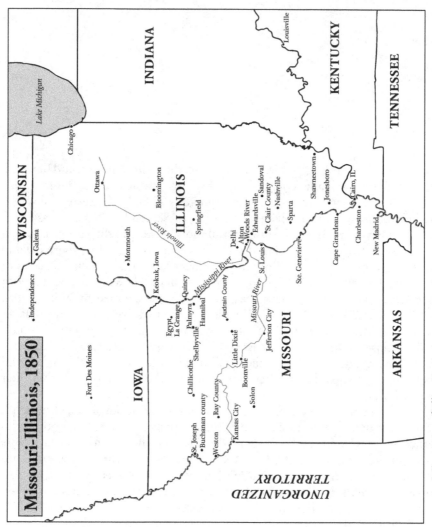

MAP 1. Missouri and Illinois.

them. The runaways gave their pursuers the slip, however, and headed north toward Alton, possibly to Rocky Fork, a small black rural settlement. While the others hid in the woods outside Upper Alton, Bernard, Theodore, and the younger Joseph went into town to buy food. There they were caught by three "white citizens" who were not associated with the Ste. Genevieve policemen, and taken to St. Louis, where they were placed in one of the city's slave pens. The others, meanwhile, continued north to Delhi, where they were betrayed by two white farmers, E. B. Way and W. A. Scott, who provided them with food and while they ate took possession of their weapons and arrested them. The five were also taken to St. Louis, where Way and Scott received a handsome reward of $1,000 each.[2]

It is not clear what became of the eight following their recapture but the story of their failed bid for freedom provides a window into the conflict over slavery in one of the zones of maximum conflict that existed on the borders between slave states and Free States. From Charleston north along the Mississippi River to Alexandra, in the area of the western Missouri River known as Little Dixie, and in the counties close to the Kansas Territory, particularly in the years after 1854 as the war between slaves and Free-Soil settlers heated up, slaves took every opportunity to reach freedom. Escapees also entered Illinois from the northwestern counties of Kentucky and from Tennessee further south. The Cumberland River was a major artery of escape for those fleeing slavery in Middle Tennessee. They escaped individually or in groups, some of which were made up of family members, others, as in the case of the Ste. Genevieve eight, comprising fellow workers. These group escapes were more likely to occur from areas closest to free territory. Slaveholders in St. Louis, Hannibal, and Palmyra on the Mississippi, in Lafayette, Jackson, Saline, and Callaway counties on the western reaches of the Missouri River, and in Platte and other counties directly opposite the Kansas Territory all experienced frequent group escapes. One Marion County proslavery organization reported the loss of fifteen slaves in one week from the area. A few months earlier an equal number escaped from Ray County, east of Kansas City. Nine slaves owned by a Major West of St. Louis left for "parts unknown" in July 1856. A few nights later, three abandoned John O'Fallon from the same city. Thirteen from different parts of Missouri passed through Chicago on the way to Canada in late 1853.[3] In May

---

[2] Cape Girardeau *Eagle* (n.d.), in Belleville *Advocate*, September 25, 1851; Chicago *Democrat*, September 26, 1851; *Liberator*, October 10, 1851; *Missouri Republican*, September 19, 22, 1852; St. Louis *News*, September 10, 1852, in New York *Tribune*, September 21, 1852; Alton *Weekly Courier*, September 22, 1852; Benjamin G. Merkel, "The Underground Railroad and the Missouri Borders, 1840–1860," *Missouri Historical Review*, XXVIII, No. 3 (April 1943), 282. On Rocky Fork see Cheryl Janifer LaRoche, *Free Black Communities and the Underground Railroad. The Geography of Resistance* (Urbana, IL: 2014).

[3] *Missouri Republican*, November 15, 1853; *Missouri Democrat*, July 16, 1856; Alton *Telegraph*, May 23, 1853; Merkel, "The Underground Railroad," 282; *Illinois State Register*, November 23, 1853. For another instance see *Illinois State Register*, April 7, 1855. See also R. Douglas Hurt,

1853, eighteen slaves (a "battalion," one newspaper called them) escaped from the western part of the state. Several of the eighteen were later caught short of their goal, but many did make good their escape. Less than a year later, nine left in one week from the same area of Little Dixie. In the northeastern part of the state, two of four from Palmyra were retaken by the sheriff outside Quincy, Illinois, in mid-1852. In one night, fifteen months later, eleven crossed over into Quincy and eluded their captors. A few months later, three who left were not so fortunate; they were retaken in Illinois and returned. These escapes from the area around Palmyra ceased for a while due no doubt to the vigilance of local authorities and slaveholders. By the summer of 1857, however, there was a resurgence of escapes from the area. This pattern was replicated in other parts of the state. While slaveholders did record some successes, they could not totally stem the wave of "stampedes." When one avenue of escape was cut off, as it was around Palmyra in 1854, fugitives devised different routes across the Mississippi River, choosing to head first to Iowa and then Chicago rather that follow the traditional route through Quincy. In November 1859, eleven took their leave from La Grange just north of Palmyra. The totality of individual escapes also came to be viewed as part of a wider collective activity.[4]

The frequency of escapes is reflected in the almost-daily advertisements that appeared in Missouri newspapers. Their sheer volume, especially from major centers such as St. Louis and smaller border cities, including Palmyra and Hannibal, suggests that the 1850 and 1860 censuses may have seriously undercounted the numbers who fled the state in the decade before the Civil War. Even if the census numbers were close to the mark, they failed to capture the sense of loss and vulnerability felt by slaveholders. While it is true that not all slaves who took leave of their masters planned to cross over into free territory, escapes, regardless of the cause or planned destination, were acts of dispossession as well as profound political statements of the slaves' awareness of the nature and meaning of freedom.[5] The evidence drawn from just one of the St. Louis dailies, the *Missouri Republican,* testifies to the frequency with which slaves sought to put distance between themselves and their masters. Advertisement for escapes, which appeared almost daily, were always detailed

*Agriculture and Slavery in Missouri's Little Dixie* (Columbia, MO: 1992), Harriet C. Frazier, *Runaways and Freed Missouri Slaves and Those Who Helped Them, 1763–1865* (Jefferson, NC: 2004) and Kristen Tegmeir Oertel, *Bleeding Borders. Race, Gender, and Violence in Pre-Civil War Kansas* (Baton Rouge: 2009).

4 Alton *Telegraph,* May 23, 1853; New Albany *Ledger,* June 8, 1853; Booneville *Observer,* May 6, 1854; Lexington *Express,* September 13, 1854; *Illinois State Register,* July 12, 1852; Hannibal *Courier,* November 10, 1853; *Missouri Whig,* July 13, September 13, 1854; Quincy *Herald,* August 7, 1854; New York *Tribune,* August 9, 1854; Hannibal *Messenger,* May 28, 1852, August 29, September 1, November 12, 1857; Hannibal *Journal,* June 2, 1853; *Illinois State Journal,* November 24, 1859.

5 Vincent Brown, *The Reaper's Garden. Death and Power in the World of Atlantic Slavery* (Cambridge, MA: 2008), 132; John Hope Franklin and Loren Schweninger, *Runaway Slaves. Rebels on the Plantation* (New York: 1999), 279.

in their description and offered rewards for the slave's recapture. These were frequently supplemented by brief news items that mentioned escapes but were not featured in advertisements. Some advertisements ran for months, others for a set period, only to reappear later in identical form, which suggests that masters believed runaways had not left the area. Others were convinced that escapees were heading for free territory. The levels of rewards varied depending on the slaveholder's estimation of the slave's value as well as the potential cost of recapture. When, for example, Jane escaped with her three children ages seven, six, and seven months in 1855, her St. Louis master, J. H. Gordon, offered the laughably low reward of $100 for their recapture. Two weeks later he thought better of it and doubled the reward. When that did not have the desired result, he raised it again, to $500.[6]

We should take masters at their word when they asserted that escapees were heading for free territory. When Nat, Jackson, and Jerry ran away from James L. Bell, nephew of Montgomery Bell, the Tennessee ironmaster, and possibly the largest slaveholder in the state, Bell took out advertisements for their escape not in Nashville but in Shawneetown, Illinois, and Louisville, Kentucky, newspapers, calculating that they may have been heading in either one of those directions.[7] Missouri slaveholders blanketed their local newspapers with announcements of escapes. Like Bell, they also took care to advertise in those cities and towns considered to be major exit points or possible destinations. It was not unusual to find advertisements in St. Louis newspapers for slaves who escaped from owners in Lexington close to the Kansas Territory border. At least after 1854 and the establishment of "free" settlements in the Kansas Territory, one would have expected slaves to head west. Yet masters continued to calculate that some slaves would choose either to gamble on the anonymity that a city the size of St. Louis provided, or use it as an exit point into Illinois. When, for example, four of Nathan Carter's slaves ran off from Lexington in May 1855, he placed advertisements in a St. Louis newspaper. Slave owners were not always as far off the mark as is suggested by the number of notices in the city's newspapers for recaptured slaves from other parts of the state. As a major port on the Mississippi River, St. Louis also attracted fugitives from many other parts of the Deep South.

The volume of advertisements is a reliable indicator of the frequency of escapes. Those published in the *Missouri Republican* for the years 1851–60 show an annual average of nearly forty slaves leaving their masters, a number that, in spite of some duplication, would surely climb if advertisements from the city's other dailies and weeklies were added to the mix. The tendency of

---

[6] *Missouri Republican,* September 28, October 9, 21, 1855. See *Missouri Democrat,* October 7, 1853, for an example of a short notice.

[7] *Southern Illinoisan,* June 30, 1854; Louisville *Journal,* May 27, 1854. Over the years, beginning as early as 1818, Montgomery Bell advertised for slaves who ran away in southern Illinois newspapers.

slaveholders to place advertisements in newspapers that reflected their political inclinations may complicate the picture, but only insofar as it tells us something about how determined they were to reclaim those who had taken flight. The pattern of escapes in St. Louis was replicated in other parts of the state. The frequency of escapes from Booneville and Lexington in 1853 and 1854, for example, spoke to the concerns of slaveholders in these communities. Some of those escaping Booneville, it appeared, sometimes attached themselves to immigrant wagons moving west, a development that understandably troubled slaveholders.[8]

Holding slaves in Missouri, as newspapers in many locales frequently declared, had become unpredictable, or as one editor put it in a guarded understatement, "the tenure of slave property [was] becoming very uncertain." Many saw the hand of outside abolitionists or internal auxiliaries of the Underground Railroad (UGRR) at work, inciting slaves to abandon their masters. There were frequent calls to the state legislature to further restrict the "privileges of negroes" and punish severely any "white man" who tampered with slaves. Patrols had to be strengthened and empowered to arrest any white man found associating with Negroes. One Cape Girardeau editor was convinced that abolitionists from outside the state had "hired secret agents" residing in the state to encourage escapes. Another editor, this one along the Missouri River, attributed an upsurge of escapes from the Booneville area in 1854 to a "spirit of insubordination among the slaves," which, he insisted, could only be "subdued by the most rigid discipline, and a strict enforcement of the police regulation."[9] Slaveholders agonized over the clandestine combination of recalcitrant slaves, outside abolitionists, and their agents within the state, both black and white. The constant flight of slaves sometimes got the better of observers. One reported that opponents of slavery in the western part of the state had devised an ingenious method of recognizing confederates: they signaled one another by removing from their vest pocket with their right hand a horseshoe-shaped leather object, tied to a length of string, from their left vest pocket, folding it over their left hand.[10] From this distance, it may appear that this observer had become unhinged, but to vulnerable slaveholders the ritual had all the hallmarks of a secret and clandestine operation.

Slaveholders had reasons to be worried. All around them were signs that opponents were at work "enticing" slaves to escape. St. Louis slaveholders' lives were complicated by a free black population that proved difficult

---

[8] Lexington *Express*, September 13, 1854; Booneville *Observer*, May 6, 1854.

[9] Cape Girardeau *Eagle*, August 30, 1850; Booneville *Observer*, September 9, 1854, in Albany (NY) *Journal*, September 19, 1854.

[10] *Missouri Brunswicker*, March 17, 1855, in Hannibal *Messenger*, March 27, 1855. Years later, Mark Twain recalled that abolitionists who came into Missouri to help slaves escape formed secret societies with "pass-words, grips, and signs." "A Scrap of Curious History," in Mark Twain, *What is Man? And Other Essays* (1906, rpr., New York: 1917), 217.

to control. Almost one-half of the state's free black population in 1861 lived in the city. Statistics from local courts recorded the almost-daily imposition of fines and expulsion of free blacks found in the city illegally. Authorities were convinced that they played a major role in the disappearance of slaves. The Union Association, an organization of free blacks and slaves formed in 1854, was, one newspaper suspected, akin to both a secret Masonic lodge and an abolitionist front that committed "nefarious deeds." The association had been preceded by the Knights of Liberty, an organization of free blacks formed sometime in 1846, which, it was suspected, worked to free slaves. The knights were very likely based at the First Baptist Church, the first black church in the city, which, until his death in 1854, was led by John Berry Meachum. Mary, John Berry's wife, carried on his activities after his death. Fugitive slave notices frequently mentioned that slaves disappeared on Sunday evenings following the end of church services. In May 1855 Mary was arrested, along with Judah Burrows and Isaac Breckenridge, two other free blacks, for arranging the escape of nine slaves from the city with the aid of unnamed black and white agents who managed to evade a police dragnet. The group was to be rowed across the river and once in Illinois placed in a wagon and taken to Chicago. Police got wind of the plot and were at the river's edge when the nine tried to cross. Five of the runaways were taken, one of whom confessed that they had met at Meachum's home to plan their escape. Yet in spite of the evidence, Meachum was acquitted. Churches such as Meachum's, one local editor worried, provided the organizational base for "nearly all the mischief concocted by the negroes in our midst." He had no doubt that First Baptist was the "headquarters of the underground railroad." The only way to curtail such activities, he concluded, was to shutter the black churches and provide "seats set apart for the colored fraternity in the white churches."[11]

Five years earlier, two possible allies of the Meachums, Benjamin Savage and Phillip Harris, were sentenced to ten and five years, respectively, in the state penitentiary for "enticing" slaves to escape from St. Louis. Savage, aged fifty and a prosperous barber, had been living in the city for seventeen years. Not much is known of the thirty-three-year-old Harris. Much of the evidence against them came from an unnamed visitor to Savage's shop who overheard the barber tell a customer that he had sent a telegram to Harris, who was in Chicago at the time, telling him to return home, as his mother was gravely

[11] Edward Hudlin, "African American Pioneers in St. Louis," Edwardsville *Intelligencer,* August 1, 2002. My thanks to Charlotte E. Johnson of Alton for a copy of this article. Lorenzo Green, Gary R. Kremer, and Antonio F. Holland, eds., *Missouri Black Heritage* (Columbia, MO: 1993), 96; *Missouri Democrat,* August 26, 29, 1854, May 23, 1855; *Missouri Republican,* May 22, 23, 1855, July 19, 1855; Chicago *Tribune,* May 25, 1855; Missouri *Intelligencer* (n.d.), in Chicago *Tribune,* June 21, 1855. Stephen Kantrowitz has suggested that fraternal organizations such as the knights played a critical role in the defense of black communities. See his *More Than Freedom. Fighting for Black Citizenship in a White Republic, 1829–1859* (New York: 2012), 144–50.

ill. The visitor apparently mistook this for a coded message. Harris was later accused of taking across the river a "light-skinned" slave woman who, in an effort to hide her identity, had worn a green veil. At his trial Harris produced a free black woman wearing an identical veil who he claimed was the woman with him on the ferry and who admitted to traveling with Harris across the river and back. The court was unconvinced. Years later, Harris claimed he was the victim of community hysteria caused by the rise in slave escapes from the city. As a result, the court, as well as the public, refused to consider the evidence he had offered in his defense. Within months of the verdict, a petition to the governor signed by "80 citizens of St. Louis" insisted that neither Savage nor Harris should be pardoned because they were at the center of a ring that, over the years, had taken out an estimated forty slaves from the city. The speed with which signatures to the petition were gathered and the vehemence of the language it employed suggest that, in some quarters of the city, there was a growing realization that something had to be done to stymie these activities. Harris was finally granted a pardon in 1853; Savage's came three years later following a flurry of petitions and letters to the governor, many from the same members of the jury who had found both men guilty. One described Savage as a "good hearted old man" who was very likely "the victim of circumstances," a rather belated admission that their conviction had been, as Harris had claimed, the result of the hysteria that had gripped the city.[12]

The jurors may have mellowed with time, but it was clear that the activities of Savage, Harris, the Meachums, and others caused city authorities considerable anxiety. In the years between the arrest of Savage and Harris and that of Mary Meachum, the authorities managed, partly through police vigilance and a measure of luck, to prevent a number of organized escapes. But each attempted escape, even when unsuccessful, confirmed the existence of a group of subversives bent on undermining the slave system. In November 1851, a scheme devised by an unnamed white man to spirit away a slave of Charles Farrell to Chicago was stymied when the slave betrayed the plan to his master. Two months later, two white women, Mary Ellis and Pamela Parker, were arrested and charged with abducting a slave girl belonging to Joseph Lemon. They were apparently the two ends of an abduction network; Ellis operating in St. Louis, Parker in Edwardsville, Illinois. In mid-1854, Frances Stames, a slave, was charged with abducting another slave. The captain of the steamer on which the two were traveling grew suspicious that Stames was not who

[12] *Missouri Republican*, September 21, 25, 1850; Louisville *Journal*, September 27, 1850; Petition, Box 5, Folder 33, Assistant Treasurer, US to Governor, St. Louis, 14 June, 1856, Box 8, Folder 67, Uriel Wright to Gov, St. Louis, 1 April, 1853, Box 6, Folder 20, all in Office of State Pardon Papers, 1837–1909, RG 5; Benjamin Savage to Governor Sterling Price, State Prison, Jefferson City, 7 August, 1854, Records of Gov. Sterling Price, 1853–1857, Missouri State Penitentiary Register of Inmates Received, all in the Missouri State Library and Archives, Jefferson City, Missouri.

he claimed to be and had him arrested and taken back to St. Louis. At his hearing in recorder court, Stames produced his free papers, was released, and left immediately for Chicago. Suspecting that the free papers were a forgery, a city policeman went after Stames, caught him in Bloomington, Illinois, and returned him to St. Louis.

Even in the face of such successes in preventing escapes, or recapturing those who had been abducted, one editor spoke of the presence of "abolitionist emissaries" who tampered with slaves and provided them with the means to escape. Negro stealers were defiantly taking slaves out by riverboat and rail. This "wholesale plunder" led one editor to speak of an "African exodus." While the rails of the UGRR in the city were laid by blacks, its conductors, those who were "constantly running off slaves," were white. An unnamed association of blacks in the city – very likely the Union Association or the Knights of Liberty – the editor knew, was in touch with white abolitionists in other states who provided them with money and advice. The headquarters of this "negro stealing" operation was located in Chicago. He had recently seen a letter from a slave woman who had escaped to Chicago informing other slaves that it was time to leave. All of this followed on the heels of an upsurge of stampedes from the city, including the escape of a group of fifteen to twenty, among whom were a "number of women and children." They evidently took leave on Sunday evening following church, crossed over to Illinoistown (now East St. Louis) where they were put on board a boat bound for Keokuk, Iowa, in "boxes marked as goods." From Keokuk they were taken to Wisconsin. The editor could not but be impressed by the planning and execution of these escapes. They show, he wrote, that "they have been most skilfully conducted." He must have been further impressed when soon after five slaves from the city arrived in Chicago – part of a contingent of seventeen escapees from other parts of the state.[13]

To the mix of free blacks such as the Meachums working to undermine the system from within must be added those who came into the state, the "thieving Abolitionists," as one editor fumed, "prowling in our midst." As in the case of those operating from within, it was not always easy to identify those who were the outside subversives, but to the slave system they represented one element of a larger threat. There were frequent reports from both sides of the Mississippi River of individuals who made sorties into Missouri to spirit away slaves. Those who managed to evade capture were usually categorized as "unnamed white men," on the mistaken assumption, and in spite of all the available evidence

[13] *Missouri Republican,* November 1, 1851, January 16, February 9, 1852, October 24, November 30, 1854; *Illinois State Register,* January 20, 1852; Louisville *Journal,* January 22, 1852; *Missouri Democrat,* June 8, October 24, November 1, 11, December 8, 1854; *Missouri Republican* (n.d.), in Chicago *Tribune,* September 2, 1854; New York *Times,* September 6, 1854. The pattern of escapes continued the following year. Eleven escaped, for instance, in February 1855 and six in one night two months later. See *Missouri Republican,* February 21, 22, 1855 and *Missouri Democrat,* February 22, April 4, 1855.

to the contrary, that slaves were incapable of acting on their own initiative. Those who knew better also knew that free blacks such as the Meachums were a major force in the movement to get slaves to freedom. An early 1855 report in a Cairo, Illinois, newspaper is representative. It gave an account of two runaways caught on a train near Sandoval and brought to Cairo. The slaves, the report took pains to point out, had been abandoned by an abolitionist – presumably a white man – who had helped them escape. Further north at Quincy there were reports of a group of "negro stealers" who prowled the streets and frequently crossed the river at night to "entice" slaves to escape. Not only did their actions anger Missouri farmers, they created instability in local trade, one editor calculated, undermining the town's ability to control commerce along the river. Were this not happening, the editor lamented, the town's population, wealth and prosperity would be "at least one-third greater than it is."[14]

Much of what we know about the activities of these subversives comes as a result of their failure to carry out their plans. Missouri State Circuit Court and penitentiary records provide some clues to the possible range of plans to aid slaves to escape. But even these are not a comprehensive indicator of the levels of outside interference. Of the nineteen lodged in the Missouri State Penitentiary for "enticing" or "decoying" slaves away during the 1850s, only one was born in Missouri. Benjamin Savage, for instance, was born in Pennsylvania but had been living in St. Louis for seventeen years and should, therefore, be considered a Missourian, but there was such a widespread belief that outsiders were at the heart of the problem that the prison records, which listed the place of birth of each inmate, confirmed what most thought they already knew. If further proof were needed, one only had to examine a few of the high-profile cases to confirm the existence of outside agitators. The first involved a thirty-six-year-old spinner from Massachusetts, Samuel Clements, and his thirty-one-year-old wife, Miriam, a seamstress, who was born in Maine. They were both charged with abducting two slaves – Barry, owned by William Spratt, and an unnamed slave owned by John J. Reese, from just outside Lexington in mid-July 1852. Evidently, the two had visited Miriam, who hatched the scheme to dress them as Indians and take them to the Osage nation in the Kansas Territory. They may have gotten as far as the "Osage hunting grounds" when they were taken and returned to Lexington. The Clements were each sentenced to the relatively short term of two years in the state penitentiary. Within weeks of her imprisonment, Miriam successfully petitioned members of the House and Senate Penitentiary Committee to be pardoned on the grounds that the state did not provide facilities for women prisoners. She also promised to leave the state if pardoned. The lack of such facilities must have worked in her favor, as she was released in January 1853, a mere five months after the failed abduction. Samuel was pardoned eighteen months later and left for Boston, where he was aided by that city's vigilance committee.[15]

In late 1853, Francis Moss, twenty-nine years old, and reputed to be a Canadian, was caught in Audrain County running off three slaves – Charles, Phillis, and Jesse – belonging to different Booneville masters. Moss was quickly tried and sentenced to five years in the state prison. The plot thickened when letters from Cincinnati, Ohio, and Macon – the report does not indicate if this is the Missouri or Georgia town – were intercepted at the Booneville post office addressed to Charles, one of the three slaves, which showed that he was not a slave but a free black named Robert Pelham who, as one local newspaper reported, "no doubt suffered himself to be sold, the more readily to succeed in enticing away slaves." If this seemed a little farfetched, the editor insisted that Charles' putative owner, Lofton Windsor, had only recently bought him from Ruben Bartlett, the St. Louis agent of a large Memphis, Tennessee, slave-trading company. Also found on Charles were notes in his own handwriting showing possible routes out of Missouri and distances between Alton, Illinois, and Detroit, Michigan, the major crossover point for fugitives entering Canada. As if to add further mystery to what was already an unusual case, the letters to Charles made mention of a "Lord Hamilton," which the editor presumed was Moss' code name. The mystery did not end there. Four years later, a letter from Moss' parents, Elizabeth and John Rowe, postmarked from Alton, pleaded with the governor of Missouri to pardon their "unfortunate son, known in the State Prison of Missouri as Francis Moss," which seemed to imply that Moss was not his real name.[16]

---

[15] Lexington *Express*, August 24, 1852; Circuit Court Case Files, Lafayette County, Boxes 10 and 27, State Journal, 1852, Box 6, General Assembly, Missouri State Penitentiary Register of Inmates Received, Office of the Secretary of State Pardon Papers, 1837–1909, RG5, Missouri Library and Archives; Vigilance Committee's Treasurer's Account Book, Siebert Collection, Harvard University in Black Abolitionist Papers (BAP), 6:10948.

[16] Hannibal *Messenger*, December 8, 17, 20, 1853; Booneville *Missourian* (n.d.), in Alton *Telegraph*, December 1, 1853; *State of Missouri v. Francis Moss*, Box 45, Folder 57, Circuit Court Case File; Missouri State Register of Inmates Received; the Rowes' letter can be found in the Office of the Secretary of State Pardon Papers, 1837–1909, Box 11, Folder 29, RG5, all in Missouri State Library and Archives. When a slave ran away from Cass County, Martin Gallagher, an Irish laborer, was suspected of being involved. He evidently admitted his involvement and asked for mercy. Gallagher was ordered to leave the state immediately and go to any state except the Kansas Territory. Two years later, eighteen-year-old Henry Ward Spencer – his first two names alone would have brought him under suspicion – who was born in Pennsylvania, led three slaves out of Pettis County, near the Kansas Territory line, taking five of the owner's horses with them and heading first to the Kansas Territory and then Iowa. *Cass County Gazette* (n.d.), in Hannibal *Messenger*, August 16, 1855. The same report was reprinted in the *Missouri Republican*, August 11, 1855; Booneville *Observer*, August 11, 1855; Chicago *Democrat*, October 28, 1857. James Patrick Morgans reports that route maps to the North were being distributed in central Missouri beginning in 1857. See his *The Underground Railroad on the Western Frontiers. Escapes from Missouri, Arkansas, Iowa and the Territories of Kansas, Nebraska and the Indian Nations, 1840–1865* (Jefferson, NC: 2010), 71.

Unfortunately, we know nothing about Charles (Robert Hamilton), but, as we have seen, free blacks were active agents in the movement. In many instances, particularly in St. Louis, they seemed to have worked alongside white agents. They ensured that the slave got across the river where white coworkers would accompany or direct the fugitive to either Chicago or Detroit. The case of John Cash in 1859 was not unusual. He was responsible for getting two slaves, Sophia and Corbella, across the river where they were to be met by unnamed white collaborators. Cash had supplied the women with men's clothes in an effort to conceal their identities. But the scheme unraveled when Cash's white collaborators failed to keep the appointed rendezvous. Four years earlier, forty-three-year-old William Smith, a laborer, was pursued by city policemen into Illinois where he was caught with Nancy, a sixteen-year-old slave belonging to W. T. Christy, four miles short of Alton. One city newspaper insisted that whites were involved, but that Smith had refused to divulge their names. Although Smith claimed he did not cross the river with Nancy, but in fact had met her on the road to Alton not long before the policemen appeared, he was convicted and sentenced to five years in the state penitentiary. Free blacks also acted on their own. Theodore Massey was caught before he even got to the river with a family of three in the spring of 1860. He had come under suspicion and was followed through alleyways as the group made their way to the river where they were to cross in a skiff.[17]

Free blacks sometimes acted independently of black organizations. Nonetheless, their presence and activities continued to cause considerable concern. In trying to control both their presence and activities, the authorities invariably overreacted, making frequent arrests and forcing them to prove they were not slaves on the lam. After a lengthy incarceration in the city jail on suspicion of being a fugitive slave, Nelson Lawson was finally brought to court on a writ of habeas corpus and freed only after he provided irrefutable evidence that he was a free man. Similarly, James A. Parker, a resident of St. Clair County, Illinois, just across the river from St. Louis, was taken up and imprisoned, as one newspaper put it, "for some time." Parker's problem stemmed from the fact that he had always been free and so could provide none of the traditional evidence needed in a slave state to prove one's status. He was only released following a hearing during which white witnesses from Illinois testified to his standing there. While on board a steamer from Cairo to St. Louis in January 1857, Miles Guba was arrested on suspicion of being a fugitive slave. When he could provide no evidence that he was free as he claimed, Guba was sent to jail where he languished for almost two years before he was brought

17 *Missouri Republican*, May 5, 1859, April 7, 1860, August 17, 18, November 18, 1856; *Missouri Democrat*, March 23, April 7, 1860, September 25, November 19, 1856; Senate Journal, Twentieth General Assembly, 1858–59, Box 12, Missouri State Library and Archives. John Johnson was similarly sentenced to five years for "running off slaves" in the days before the firing on Fort Sumter. See *Missouri Democrat*, April 1, 1861.

before a judge on a writ of habeas corpus and freed. These are just a few of the many examples drawn from St. Louis during the decade, testifying to the dangers free blacks faced in a city deeply suspicious of their presence and their proven involvement in aiding slaves to escape.[18]

Although there was a surreal quality to the Francis Moss case, it nonetheless provides a glimpse into both the planning that went into escapes as well as the system's ability to defend itself. Local courts were at the forefront of the defense against these incursions. A cursory look at St. Louis newspapers, which regularly carried court decisions, shows just how successful the system was in defending its interests. Published monthly, city and county jail statistics made regular reference to the number of runaway slaves recaptured as well as the number of free blacks found in the city without the requisite license. As far as the system was concerned, they were part and parcel of the same problem. Ellen and two of her children, Martha Jane and Esther, for example, were committed as runaways in May 1854. During one of the frequent spikes in the number of escapes between 1853 and 1854, twenty slaves were lodged in the city jail, waiting to be claimed by their master.[19] In a sample drawn from 1853–56 there are numerous and similar details of the system's successes against efforts by slaves, free blacks, and whites to undermine slavery in the city.

Slaveholders also devised a series of other measures to defend their interests. Following the capture of Francis Moss, it was reported that he had confessed and supplied local authorities with information on others who were involved in the local operations of the UGRR. Slaveholders here and elsewhere in the Border South were always eager to gather evidence on the membership and operations of local organizations. There were, however, painfully few recorded successes in identifying the mainstays of local organizations and there is no evidence that the information Moss gave his captors led to additional arrests or the dismantling of the organization to which he reputedly belonged. Not long after his capture, local slaveholders called a public meeting to devise plans to protect themselves against outside predators and their local collaborators. Similar actions were taken in other parts of the state that also experienced surges in escapes. Defense associations were organized along the Mississippi River from Cape Girardeau in the south to Hannibal and Palmyra in the north. In early 1853 a "pursuing committee" was formed in Marion County. It set up a patrol to detect abolitionist interference and to track down fugitives. It also offered rewards for the detection of abolitionists and their agents. At a later meeting, Ralls and Marion county slaveholders established a committee

---

[18] *Missouri Democrat,* June 25, October 1, 14, 1858. See also the case of James Edwards, covered in the *Missouri Democrat,* September 29, 30, October 19, 1853, and the *Missouri Republican,* September 30, October 3, 1853. Other cases are covered by the *Missouri Democrat,* September 11, 1856, and January 1, 29, 1857.

[19] *Missouri Republican,* January 11, May 24, 1854; *Missouri Democrat,* October 5, 1853, November 21, 1854.

of six from each county to track down fugitives and created a fund to defray the cost associated with recaptures. In the wake of a rising number of escapes from the Palmyra area in 1858, a public meeting pledged to bring the "nigger thieves to account" through the organization of a mutual protection society. The meeting also called for the expulsion of free blacks from the state. Months later, a vigilance committee was formed in New Madrid following a rise in the number of escapes from the area, the work, the committee was convinced, of "Abolitionists in their midst." They were also perturbed by the number of outsiders who had moved into the area recently and who, evidently, were not gainfully employed. A "law unto themselves," as the committee described itself unambiguously, it pledged to investigate any suspicious activities, interview the accused, and "inflict such punishment" as it deemed appropriate. It set up a system of patrols, demanded that passes issued to slaves specify the names of both the slave and the owner, as well as the place to be visited and the duration of the visit. Finally, the committee called on the state legislature to pass more stringent laws to protect slave property and to expel all free blacks from the state. While these meetings were usually called in response to specific sets of local concerns, regional and national political developments never failed to intrude. Those who attended the Boone County meeting to elect delegates to a proslavery convention to be held in Lexington in July 1855 were acutely aware of the impact of recent national developments on the slave system's ability to protect itself from the many-headed hydra of abolitionism. Resolutions condemned the recent Wisconsin Supreme Court decision that declared the Fugitive Slave Law unconstitutional. It and Massachusetts' personal liberty law were dismissed as evidence of "fanaticism, nullification and treason" aimed at creating discord among the people. The refusal of abolitionists and Free-Soil proponents to support enforcement of the Fugitive Slave Law, they insisted, was incompatible with the "spirit of the Union." Finally, the meeting condemned the efforts to flood the Kansas Territory with Free-State settlers.[20]

There was, at times, an element of desperation in some of these responses, the result, one suspects, of the vulnerability of slave property. Following an 1855 meeting to celebrate the emancipation of West Indian slaves in Quincy, attended by free blacks from across the river, a Palmyra editor expressed concern that they would return to Missouri imbued with the spirit of revolution and a determination to assist slaves to cut "their masters' throats." More vigorous means had to be employed in the face of such threats to slave property.

---

[20] Boonville *Observer* (n.d.), in Hannibal *Messenger,* December 8, 1853; Sherman. W. Savage, "The Contest Over Slavery Between Illinois and Missouri," *Journal of Negro History,* XXVIII, No. 3 (July 1943), 324; Oleta Prisloo, "The Case of 'The Dyed-in-the-Wool Abolitionists' in Mark Twain Country, Marion County, Missouri: An Examination of a Slaveholding Community's Response to Radical Abolitionism in the 1830s and 1840s," (PhD, University of Missouri-Columbia, 2003), 316; Quincy *Herald,* April 30, 1858; *Missouri Republican,* January 5, 1860. For reports on the Booneville and Lexington conventions see Boonville *Observer,* June 23, 30, July 1, 21, 1855, and *Missouri Republican,* June 4, 15, 21, July 10, 17, 1855.

There was no better place to start than by expelling all free blacks from the state. "Look at home," he warned slave owners in the area. "Black emissaries are among you burning with bloody instructions." It was a nice phrase freighted with multiple meanings, but others thought the editor was letting the situation get the better of him.[21] But the threat was real. As a consequence, anyone who dared to express abolitionist sentiments publicly had to be dealt with summarily. When, for example, Rev. David White of Pennsylvania preached a sermon in Chillicothe, Livingston County, in the spring of 1855 that many thought smacked of abolitionism, a public meeting declared its determination not to allow any preacher suspected of being partial to abolition into their community. The fact that White mentioned that he had once had a conversation with Frederick Douglass about conditions in slavery did not help his case. The meeting formed a vigilance committee to visit White and invite him to leave town. Almost simultaneously, a mob attacked the office of the Parkville *Luminary* – published in Weston, Platte County – because of its advocacy of Free-Soil policies, roughed up one of its editors, and dumped the press in the Missouri River. The newspaper was a "nuisance which has been endured too long." Its two editors were given three weeks to leave town or run the risk of joining the press in the river.[22]

As was the case in other border states, Missouri slaveholders felt particularly vulnerable in the wake of what they considered abolitionist depredations and the demonstrated willingness of the enslaved to seek their freedom. In response, they fashioned a set of responses that relied in part on a network of local protective associations, laws that controlled the movement of slaves and free blacks, the imposition of stiff penalties on those who interfered with their property, the intimidation of those who dared to express or propose abolition, and the establishment of a cadre of state and local police with the power to monitor what happened locally and to pursue runaways and those who assisted them into adjoining Free States. These measures found sympathy and support from the citizens of Illinois and particularly so after the Fugitive Slave Law lent additional political legitimacy to a tradition of "running down" slaves who had crossed into the state. The political geography of the state is crucial to an understanding of the history of fugitive renditions in Illinois. The southern portion of the state, known as Egypt, was generally hostile to the presence of blacks. Many of its original settlers were yeoman farmers from the South, and although one of the reasons for leaving was a desire to put some distance between themselves and an economy and society based on plantation

---

[21] Palmyra *Whig*, August 16, 1855; *Missouri Whig*, September 6, 1855. When "abolitionists" from Pike County, Illinois, abducted four slaves from Ralls County in 1860, a Hannibal editor appealed to mob violence as a way to quell the continued loss of slaves, even though the fugitives were retaken and returned. Hannibal *Messenger* (n. d.), in *Missouri Republican*, May 11, 1860.

[22] *Missouri Republican*, April 24, 1855; Alton *Courier*, April 23, 1855.

slavery, they were passionately opposed to the presence of African Americans in their midst. Egypt, one unsympathetic observer from the area recalled, was "emphatically a land of slavery...the hunting ground of the runaway negro," an area whose press was as "mute as a drumstick" when it came to the violence associated with the recapture of fugitives. The area, one distraught Free-Soil editor declared, was "little better than a province of Missouri." In fact, Missouri slaveholders frequently bought space in area newspapers to advertise for the recapture of runaways.[23]

But there was also a small and critical black presence in Egypt. When the Ste. Genevieve eight made their bid for freedom in 1852, the route they followed was not just geographically obvious, it also reflected an awareness of the presence of supporters in the area around Sparta, and in the black rural settlement near Woods River close to Alton. There were also black rural settlements further south, such as Miller Grove near Shawneetown, that were critical to the success of escapes. African Americans who settled in the small towns and rural areas of Egypt were, like their white counterparts, born in the surrounding slave states. While it is not always possible to identify all of the distinct black settlements, the records clearly show the existence of clusters of African Americans in the area that would play important roles in slave escapes. Of the 339 blacks who lived in Gallatin County on the Ohio River, for example, 191 were settled in clusters in Shawneetown, the majority of them born in Kentucky and Tennessee. The same holds true for the 104 African Americans living in Pope County across from Kentucky and south of Gallatin County. These settlements were a thorn in the side of those in the area who worked tirelessly to have them removed and slaveholders in the adjoining states who saw them as magnets for fugitive slaves. Benjamin Bond, lawyer, editor, and Whig representative to the 1847 State Constitutional Convention from Clinton County east of St. Louis, addressed the problems posed by the "little settlements of these free negroes" that had sprung up in the area and whose objective, he had no doubt, "was to aid slaves from the south to escape their masters."[24]

---

[23] Nicole Etcheson, *The Emerging Midwest: Upland Southerners and the Political Culture of the Old Northwest, 1789–1861* (Bloomington, IN: 1996); Chicago *Tribune*, November 4, 1859; Cleveland *Herald*, August 14, 1857; Cairo *Times*, November 22, 29, 1854, February 21, April 4, May 16, 1855; Allen C. Guelzo, "Houses Divided: Lincoln, Douglas, and the Political Landscape of 1858," *Journal of American History*, 94, No. 2 (September 2007), 391–417.

[24] Population Schedules of the Seventh Census of the United States, 1850, Illinois, Gallatin and Pope Counties; Arthur Charles Cole, ed., *The Constitutional Debates of 1847* (Springfield, IL: 1919), 202; LaRoche, *Free Black Communities and the Underground Railroad*, 43–56; Stephen Hahn likens these Northern black rural settlements to maroon communities found in several slave societies such as Jamaica, communities that existed on the fringes of plantations and aided and abetted slave escapes. The analogy is useful to a point but fails to take into consideration the fact that these settlements were in "free" territory and so had much more elbow room to operate politically. Stephen Hahn, *The Political Worlds of Slavery and Freedom* (Cambridge, MA: 2009), 24.

While Egypt was contested ground, it was also a place where little attention was given to the legal niceties of the Fugitive Slave Law. In fact, renditions usually occurred outside the remit of the law, without recourse to a hearing or the adjudication of a commissioner. Admittedly, the law was vague in this regard. Under Section 6, an owner or his agent could chose not to go before a commissioner for a warrant of arrest and instead seize the suspect "where the same can be done without process." But the law then required the fugitive to be taken before a commissioner or judge "to hear and determine the case of such claimant in a summary manner." There is no evidence that this was ever followed in Egypt. As a result, renditions were effected "without warrant or legal process" and were consequently usually violent.[25] Fairly typical was the case of a Mr. Sherwood of New Madrid County, Missouri, who received word in the fall of 1851 that one of his slaves who had escaped some time ago was hiding out near Sparta. Sherwood sent his son and "a number of others" to retrieve the slave. An armed group of abolitionists got wind of their plans and met the Missourians outside the town. Outnumbered, the Sherwood party returned empty handed. Sherwood's actions, one unsympathetic editor insisted, had violated both the spirit and intent of the Fugitive Slave Law and showed his and other slaveholders' willingness to use violence in the pursuit of runaway slaves.[26]

Cairo was the scene of a similar slave hunt in mid-1857 that would have turned deadly had blacks not resisted in numbers large enough to deter catchers. About fifty Missourians crossed into town in search of about a dozen slaves. They surrounded and tried to search a number of cabins but their African American occupants insisted on seeing a warrant. Shots were exchanged. Before they withdrew empty handed, one Missourian was injured and three arrested, including the ferryman who had brought them over the river.[27] But Missouri slaveholders relied on sympathetic whites opposed to the presence of blacks in the area to capture and return runaways even without the aid of catchers from across the river. The arrival of three fugitives near Nashville in early July 1857 came to a gruesome end. A large crowd set out in search of the fugitives and ran into them ten miles east of town. One of the escapees opened fire on the group but was shot and killed. The other two, however, managed to evade their pursuers. The person who had shot and killed the fugitive was taken into custody but discharged after a brief inquest. The following morning, other members of the group buried the slain fugitive, drumming on the coffin, one newspaper reported, to the tune of Stephen Foster's "Uncle Ned," which

---

[25] "Fugitive Slave Act 1850," www.nationalcenter.org/FugitiveSlaveAct.html; *Illinois State Journal*, July 30, 1857.

[26] Cape Girardeau *Eagle* (n.d.), in Belleville *Advocate*, September 25, 1851; Girardeau *Herald* (n.d.), in Chicago *Democrat*, September 26, 1851; *Liberator*, October 10, 1851.

[27] Cincinnati *Gazette*, July 27, 1857, in New York *Herald*, August 1, 1857; New York *Times*, August 1, 1857.

ended with the eerily appropriate phrase that the dead Negro had gone to the place where "good darkies go." A few hours later, the body of the slain slave was exhumed, his head cut off with an ax and "placed in a vessel of spirits" and sent back to Missouri.[28]

Although the Nashville incident was unique, violent confrontations continued throughout the decade. An attempt to recapture slaves from around Sparta in 1859 led to open clashes and death. Five slaves, three owned by D. M. Fox and two by John M. Gholson, left Fredericksburg (now Fredericktown), Madison County, in mid-September 1859, soon after a dozen other slaves had fled the area. A group organized to hunt them down headed for Sparta. Two days later, eleven members of the group positioned themselves on a bridge in an attempt to intercept the fugitives before they reached town. What they did not know was that the three fugitives had joined some of the others who had escaped earlier. Confronted by the slave catchers, the fugitives resisted. One of Gholson's slaves was shot and would later die; two of Fox's were injured. But the slave catchers left empty-handed, and their leader, Mr. Weatheringill, was arrested, charged with murder, and taken to jail in Chester. In response, a group of sixty from Madison and adjoining counties set out to free Weatheringill, but the mayor of Chester called for armed citizens to prevent his release. Forty responded to the mayor's call. Recognizing the possibility of a pitch battle between the groups, Fox pleaded with the Missourians to retreat and let the law take its course. His plea helped to diffuse the situation. But Fox was determined to pursue the two who had escaped the initial melee and were on their way to Chicago. He suspected that the slaves had been assisted by two Madison County residents, Thomas Snider, age thirty-six, and William Grooms, thirty-eight, who were both born in Kentucky. The two were arrested and taken before the Madison County Circuit Court, where they were both sentenced to five years for "decoying" slaves out of the state. Snider was pardoned in March 1864, Grooms four months later.[29]

Missouri slaveholders relied not just on random mobs but also on Illinois officials. Levi L. Lighter, Alexander County judge, along with local sheriffs, for example, was part of an organized effort that held suspected runaways in local jails and then placed advertisements in area newspapers calling on their masters to collect them. The suspicion lingered that many of those taken were not in fact fugitives but free blacks who, unable to prove their identity,

---

[28] Chicago *Tribune*, July 8, 1857; Cleveland *Herald*, August 10, 1857; Alton *Courier*, July 28, 1857; Nashville *Democrat* (n.d.), in Marietta *Intelligencia*, July 22, 1857; Chicago *Tribune* (n.d.), in Ashtabula *Sentinel*, August 6, 1857.

[29] *Illinois State Journal*, October 10, 1859; *Missouri Republican*, October 6, 1859; Alton *Courier* (n. d.), in Bloomington *Pantagraph*, September 30, 1859. See appendix 3 of Harriet C. Frazier, *Runaway and Freed Missouri Slaves*, 183; Grooms' wife, Mary, was later charged with bringing "instruments into jail to facilitate" her husband's escape. State of Missouri v Thomas Snider, State of Missouri v William Grooms, State of Missouri v Mary Grooms, Madison Circuit Court, Vol 2, 26, 108, 110, 116. Missouri State Archives.

were subsequently sold into slavery. There is no doubt that money was to be made from the return of runaways and kidnapped free blacks. In some instances it appears local authorities worked across state lines. Free blacks would be captured in Missouri, brought across the river, and placed in jail. Advertisements would then be published providing the kinds of physical descriptions commonly found in fugitive slave advertisements, making it easy for purported slaveholders to claim their lost property. If no one came forward after three months, the imprisoned would be sold into slavery. But these activities also had a wider political agenda: the control, and better yet, the expulsion of African Americans from the area. The 1853 Illinois "Black Law," like its 1852 Indiana counterpart, provided legal cover for many of these efforts. It had taken six years to pass this enabling legislation to enforce Article XIV of the state's 1847 revised constitution, which banned the entry of blacks into the state. When put to the voters, eighty-three of ninety-nine counties voted in favor. Driven largely by the concerns of politicians from the southern sector of the state, where the majority of African Americans lived, the law also imposed fines on nonresident blacks who remained in the state longer than ten days. If these fines were not paid they were to be sold at public auction to anyone who could pay the fine, and who, as a consequence, acquired the right to their labor for a specified length of time. It was the closest any state in the North came to the reinstitution of slavery.[30]

Support for the law in the legislature broke down almost entirely on sectional lines. Not one legislator from the northern sector of the state voted for it and only two from the central part supported it. Its adoption sparked a furious backlash. One Chicago editor denounced it as an "abomination" with no parallel even "on the coast of Barbary." His counterpart in the state capitol saw things differently. Whig opponents, such as the Chicago editor, were simply trumpeting old abolitionist canards in an effort to win political favor. The law did not reintroduce slavery, as many opponents claimed, but simply imprisoned and fined those who entered the state illegally, a necessity given that the state was being overrun by "pauper blacks" – usually superannuated slaves freed by their masters. Negroes were not citizens and so the state had every right to ban their entrance as it might that of "Indians and any other race of savages" if it found itself "liable to be overrun with them." The South should be compelled to support its Negroes until "they become such a burthen to them

[30] Alton *Courier*, August 15, 1857; Springfield *Register*, May 16, 1857; James P. Jones, "The Illinois Negro Law of 1853. Racism in a Free State," *Illinois Quarterly*, 40, No. 2 (Winter 1977), 6–9; Quincy *Herald*, February 21, March 7, 1853. While the law was not widely enforced, there were a number of occasions when blacks who were accused of being in the state illegally were sold at auction. See Alton *Telegraph*, June 28, 1853, Belleville *Advertiser*, April 22, 1857, and Nashville *Monitor* (n.d.), in Pittsburgh *Gazette*, July 9, 1853, for instances of the law's enforcement. In one recorded instance a Mr. Furness, who lived near Quincy, used the law to buy a suspected fugitive slave for a term of one month in order to protect him from being returned under the Fugitive Slave Law. See Quincy *Herald*, November 21, 1853.

that they will see the advantage of abolishing slavery." To allow the South to send its worn-out slaves to Illinois was to encourage the continuation of slavery. Bans such as Illinois', he anticipated, would ultimately encourage the South to end slavery. Then and only then will "the blacks begin to diminish, and a few generations will rid our country of this kind of population," for they could only exist in a state of slavery. "Feeble in intellect, repulsive in person, and addicted to improvidence and vice, they cannot but be overborne by the competition of white labor, where slavery is not legalized, and where the blacks are controlled by an intelligence superior to their own." It was a rather unconventional proposal to end slavery and ensure a future America free of all blacks. Yet unlike in Indiana, proponents of the law had little to say about what was to become of those who had resided in the state prior to the adoption of the new constitution. When it was rumored in 1855 that some were recommending repealing the law and granting blacks the privileges of citizenship, one southern Illinois editor flew into a rage: if that ever occurred he would be "for secession of the south-half, and the formation of it into a slave state." Thomas E. Milburn spoke for many white residents of Egypt: his ancestors had come to Illinois to avoid the "annoyance of negroes." No one that he knew wished their "posterity adulterated by mixing with the black African race." The fair skin of the "damsel with her rosy cheeks, and strait fair hair, her sparkling blue eyes, her fair visage, and her beautiful and delicate form, would then be changed by the African to a dark skin, a kinky head, thick lips, glaring eyes, and long heels."[31]

Milburn's overblown ethnographical analysis was a direct response to a series of resolutions adopted by a recent meeting of Methodist ministers that condemned both the Fugitive Slave Law and the Black Law. Shortly after the law's adoption, Free Democrats met at a convention in Ottawa to protest against it. A call for its repeal was also the driving force behind two Negro state conventions, the first in Chicago in 1853, the second in Alton three years later. In its address to the people of Illinois, the 1853 meeting insisted that they asked no special favors, only that they be "placed in a position" to defend themselves against the "scourge of despotism." Evenhanded justice would repeal the law, ensure their children were admitted to state schools, which their taxes financed, allow them to testify in court, and to vote in the land of their birth. The Alton meeting voted to establish a repeal association to work for the law's removal from the state's books.[32]

African Americans in middle Illinois, like those who lived in other areas of the state, sheltered, protected, and gave succor to runaway slaves. So, too, did a number of whites – both at major crossing points, such as Quincy, and in smaller towns away from the Mississippi River. As one local newspaper

---

[31] Chicago *Tribune*, February 24, 25, 1853; *Southern Illinoisan*, January 19, March 30, 1855.
[32] Alton *Telegraph*, May 7, 1853; Chicago *Tribune*, October 5, 14, 1853; Philip S. Foner and George E. Walker, *Proceedings of the Black State Conventions, 1840–1865*, 2 Vols. (Philadelphia: 1980), II, 54–82.

boasted, when Missourians came to the area in search of slaves, they had to keep one eye on the Quincy *Whig* and "the other on the colored population." These shelterers were vital to the successful operation of the UGRR in the state. While many were opposed to interfering with slave property in Slave States, they nonetheless felt duty bound to aid those who made it across the river. John Hossack, the Ottawa abolitionist, spoke for many: "I go not to Missouri to relieve oppressed humanity," he told a judge before he was sentenced for helping a fugitive escape, "for my duty has called me nearer home; but when He that directs the steps of men conducts a poor, oppressed, panting fugitive to my door, and there I hear his bitter cry, I dare not close my ear against it lest in my extremity I cry for mercy and shall not be heard." Others were motivated by less lofty moral and political considerations but nevertheless played equally important roles in the work of sheltering.[33]

In the middle belt of the state, an area roughly between Quincy in the north and Alton just upriver from St. Louis, slaveholders ran into stiffer opposition than they did in Egypt. There were rumors of the existence of what one reporter called a "formidable organization" to aid runaways in Quincy. When a black person from Knox County, Missouri, arrived in town and asked for directions to the home of Edward Turner, locals knew immediately that he was a fugitive slave aware of where he could receive assistance. African Americans in and around Alton, a substantial port on the Mississippi and a major crossing point for fugitives, established a comparable support network. When two St. Louis slaves – the property of the Chouteau family, prominent slaveholders in the city – arrived in town with a buggy they had stolen, blacks came to their assistance, placing them on a train bound for Chicago accompanied by two white men and a "Negro preacher." After the two left, Frederick Livers and Isam Walton, two blacks, hid the buggy on the outskirts of town. They were later charged with "secreting property" stolen in St. Louis. Both gave bond but the case collapsed when Livers fled town and the "principal witnesses" could not be found.[34]

But opponents of slavery did not have the field to themselves. In an effort to stem the flow of fugitives, St. Louis authorities employed spies in Alton and other towns along the river. This, in part, accounts for the successes slaveholders recorded. As a regular port of call for slaves on the run, Alton also attracted the attention of the St. Louis police. In late 1852, two policemen captured

---

[33] I have borrowed the term "shelterer" from Fernando Pico, who argued for their significance in a paper titled "Running Away and Finding Concealment: Runaway Slaves in Nineteenth-Century Puerto Rico," given at the Association of Caribbean Historians' annual meeting in Surinam in May 2008. Quincy *Whig* (n.d.), in *Missouri Whig*, July 27, 1854. Hossack's speech is reprinted in "Historical Notes," *Journal of the Illinois State Historical Society*, XLI, No. 1 (March 1948), 67–74.

[34] *Missouri Courier*, November 10, 17, 1853; Quincy *Herald*, November 24, 1851; Alton *Courier*, June 29, 1855, December 6, 1853; Alton *Telegraph*, December 13, 1853. For a history of the movement in the eight counties in and around Quincy see Owen W. Muelder, *The Underground Railroad in Western Illinois* (Jefferson, NC: 2008).

Johnson (no first name given) and took him to St. Louis. Apparently, Johnson was betrayed by a black couple with whom he had had a disagreement. But the action of the two policemen was, at least in the eyes of Thomas M. Hope, the mayor of Alton, an illegal act of kidnapping. They had forced "away from a free state, *privately,* without form of law, a man alleged, *but not proven to be,* a fugitive slave," Hope wrote L. M. Kennett, the mayor of St. Louis, in protest. Kennett insisted that he only heard about the incident after it had happened. He, nevertheless, excused the actions of the policemen on the rather spurious grounds that the marshal of St. Louis had the authority to grant policemen leave, and that it was during one of these leaves that the policemen, acting as private citizens, had made the arrest. More importantly, he maintained, it was the right of a citizen of Missouri to take his runaway slave "in Illinois and bring him home."[35]

Although, as in Egypt, fugitives were retaken without recourse to the law, only in this area of the state were cases adjudicated by commissioners and even then there were only three such hearings. The first occurred in Alton in 1853, the other two in Springfield in 1857 and 1860. In late 1851, Amanda Kitchell, a young slave from Shelby County, Tennessee, was brought to Alton by J. T. Leath, the son of her owner of the same name, where he evidently freed her. What no one knew was that young Leath had acted without his father's knowledge, which raises questions about his possible motives. A year later, Kitchell married Alfred Chavers. Three weeks after her marriage, Malcolm McCullon of Memphis seized Amanda and took her to the river to catch the St. Louis boat. Sometime after she fled Tennessee, McCullon had purchased Amanda from the elder Leath for $400. On their way to the river, a large black crowd responded to Amanda's cries, forcing McCullon to agree to take her before Levi Davis, the city's commissioner. Davis ruled in favor of MCullon and ordered Chavers' return. The decision stunned the black community. They rallied immediately, in an effort to prevent Amanda's return by offering to purchase her freedom. McCullon agreed, provided they could meet his extortionate asking price of $1,200. Much of the money to purchase her freedom came from the white community, but a few African Americans went to extreme lengths to complete the fund, including mortgaging what limited property they had. One of them, C. M. Howard, a merchant, wrote an almost plaintive letter detailing the sacrifices he and others had to make in order to raise the ransom price. As in other cases, such as Henry Long's in New York City, agreeing to such extortionate ransoms raised questions about the legitimacy of paying what many

---

[35] Alton *Courier,* November 30, December 17, 1852. There was a similar incident three months later when a slaveholder retook a slave from the black settlement near Wood River. *Missouri Republican,* March 5, 1853; Alton *Courier,* March 11, 1853. See also *Missouri Republican,* May 17, 1852, for an instance of the capture of a fugitive slave from a steamer on its way to Alton.

considered blood money. But confronted by the prospects of losing Amanda to slavery, the black community agreed to McCullon's demands.[36]

Hearings before commissioners provided the black community and their white supporters with opportunities to challenge the legality of the Fugitive Slave Law. They were not always successful, but by these challenges they also raised serious political questions about the law's legitimacy. They invariably drew on some of the best legal minds to contest the legality of warrants as well as the claims of slaveholders. All of this was played out in the two cases heard by Commissioner Stephen A. Corneau in the state capital in 1857 and 1860. In August 1857, forty-five-year-old Frederick Clements was caught seven miles outside Atlanta, Illinois, by Hiram McElroy, the son of his owner. Young McElroy was accompanied by US Marshal Dickson and Thomas Markham, who had been granted power of attorney to act for Clements' owner. William H. Herndon, Abraham Lincoln's law partner, and John H. Rosette, a Democrat turned Republican, appeared for Clements pro bono. They were opposed by Elliot Herndon, William's brother and a prominent local Democrat, and John A. McClernard. Even before the hearing could get underway, the brothers jousted over the ground rules. William insisted on seeing the authorization under which Clements was arrested. Elliot countered that nowhere in the law were suspected fugitives allowed counsel. "Nobody in the world," he maintained, had a "right to contest [an] owner's claim" to a Negro. If it wished, the court "may admit counsel as advisory to itself, but not as attorneys for the alleged slave." William argued that his sole aim was to ensure that the letter of the law had been followed, that the person making the arrest had a duly recognized power of attorney from "a proper court," and, if he did, that it be produced for examination by defense counsel. But as Elliot pointed out, this begged the question: If the law did not permit attorneys for the suspect, why would it allow William to examine or challenge the power of attorney? Furthermore, the Constitution, "common law...and the law of Congress" guaranteed the right of recapture. Corneau ruled that, as a courtesy, he would allow counsel for the suspect to examine the power of attorney at the point in the hearing when it was produced.

As the hearing began, William returned to the issue of the power of attorney's legitimacy. It did not conform, he argued, to the specific wording of the law, as Clements was designated a slave, not a "fugitive from labor." Nor did it show explicitly that slavery existed in Kentucky. Similar preemptive moves were employed regularly by defense counsels in many other hearings, each

[36] Alton *Courier,* January 21, 29, 1853; Alton *Telegraph,* January 26, 1853; *Illinois State Register,* January 20, 1853; Pittsburgh *Gazette,* January 27, February 9, 1853; *Kentucky Statesman,* January 25, 1853; *National Era,* February 10, 1853; *Alton General City Directory and Business Mirror for 1858* (Alton: 1858). My thanks to Charlotte E. Johnson of Alton for information on Amanda's maiden name; W. J. Norton, ed., *Centennial History of Madison County, Illinois and its People, 1812 to 1912,* www.idaillinois.org/cdm/ref/collection/edpl/id/11892

time unsuccessfully. Under cross examination, McElroy Jr. admitted that, over the years, Clements had been regularly granted permission to visit his wife, who was free and who lived across the Ohio River in Shawneetown, Illinois. William also produced a number of these passes signed by McElroy's overseer in order to show that Clements had long been permitted the freedom to enter a Free State. On his most recent trip he had traveled north of Shawneetown in order to be with his family, who had recently moved away. Corneau ruled against Clements – not on the larger issue of whether granting permission for a slave to visit or temporarily reside in a Free State made the slave free, but on the much narrower grounds that Clements had not been issued a free pass to make his most recent visit to his family.[37] William licked his wounds in a letter to Theodore Parker, the Massachusetts abolitionist, who tried to console him that the ruling against Clements was predictable, and his efforts "unavailing," because "on the side of the oppressor there was power." The Democrats, Parker explained, were in power and had the "same relation to progress in America that the Roman Catholic Church [did] in Europe." Things would only change when the party was "broken to fragments and ground to powder."[38]

The party was still in power in early 1860 when the same cast of legal characters was again in front of Corneau, this time in the case of thirty-five-year-old Edgar Canton, who was accused of escaping from slavery in Shelbyville, Missouri, in 1857. His owner, George Dickinson, had him arrested in Springfield in February 1860. Dickinson, however, did not have the appropriately executed documents, which provided William Herndon with an opening: he demanded that Dickinson prove Canton was his slave. As in the Clements case, Herndon also argued that Dickinson be required to prove that slavery existed in Missouri. If he could not, then his claim to Canton was baseless. Corneau had heard these arguments before and would have none of it and ruled in favor of Dickinson. Observers at the hearing were struck by what they thought was Canton's cavalier, if not slightly bemused, disposition during the course of the hearing. He seemed not to pay much attention to what was going on around him and throughout the proceedings wore a curious smirk on his face. Some thought he might have become unhinged. What no one could have known was that Canton was already making plans for another escape. On his way to St. Louis under guard, Canton pulled a knife that had been given him by one of his supporters and wounded one of the guards before he could be subdued. Once across the river, Canton was sold at auction for $1,500. But his new owner could not long hold him. One month later, he passed through Springfield on his way north, giving some of his friends what one newspaper

[37] *Illinois State Journal*, July 30, August 1, 3, 1857; *Illinois State Register*, August 1, 1857; Alton *Courier*, August 4, 1857.
[38] William Herndon to Theodore Parker, Springfield, August 4, 1847, Parker to Herndon, Newton Corner, August 9, 1857, L 05897, Lincoln Legal Papers, Abraham Lincoln Library, Springfield, Illinois.

described as "a hearty handshake," a clear demonstration of Canton's commitment to freedom and his determination not to be denied what he considered to be his right. Naturally, many believed that Canton's second escape had been facilitated by the St. Louis network of free blacks.[39]

Not long after he had settled in the apparent safety of Springfield's black community, Canton married and started a family. Once he was taken, members of the community offered to cover the cost of getting a white witness from Quincy who could prove that Canton was a free man. In fact, Herndon had written contacts in Quincy in an effort to identify the witness. But the commissioner's refusal to stay his decision put paid to the effort.[40] As with Canton, other fugitives managed to carve out a space of relative freedom for themselves in black communities throughout the northern third of the state. Chicago and other towns in the area developed a reputation as places that took care of fugitives who called these towns home. They married into the community, found jobs, some even started their own businesses secure in the knowledge that, in spite of the reach of the Fugitive Slave Law, few slaveholders would dare brave the opposition of black communities to capture them. Their sense of security could be measured by the fact that former owners sometimes knew where they were yet could not pry them loose. Peter Camden of St. Louis, for example, wrote an acquaintance in Chicago in June 1860 about two of his slaves, Fayette and Madison, and their brother Thomas, who belonged to another slaveholder. The three had escaped several years earlier and were now working in the city, Fayette as a drayman, and Madison at a carpet store. Camden had earlier made a trip to the city hoping to meet and persuade his two slaves to return to the comfort of their parents and other relatives. It is not clear if Camden's efforts produced the results he desired, but it is telling that his former slaves felt secure enough to remain in Chicago even after Camden knew where they were. In Ottawa, southwest of Chicago, a local "agent" of the UGRR felt secure enough to publish a card containing the names of those who had recently contributed to a fund that kept the "road running." He even invited all those interested in how they operated to visit the "depot" so he could demonstrate the "systematic working of our road." He was clearly thumbing his nose at the system, secure in the belief that no slaveholder would dare to reclaim his property from the town.[41]

As in so many areas of the North where they had established a life for themselves, fugitives fled Chicago by the score in the weeks following the passage

---

[39] *Illinois State Journal*, February 10, 13, 14, 17, 18, March 16, 1860. It was not the first instance of a fugitive being returned from the area only to reappear again. On this occasion the slave was taken a second time in Alton and returned to St. Louis. See Alton *Telegraph*, March 3, 11, 1853.

[40] William H. Herndon to Gentlemen, Springfield, February 11, 1860, L 05898, The Lincoln Legal Papers.

[41] Peter Camden to Dr. G. S. Case, St. Louis, June 4, 1860, Case Family Papers, Missouri Historical Society, St. Louis, Missouri; Ottawa *Republican*, June 18, 1859.

of the Fugitive Slave Law. Yet in the following months and years, the black community – and the city generally – reasserted its reputation as a place from which fugitives could not be taken. Following the return of Frederick Clements from Springfield, one of that city's Democratic newspapers devoted a lengthy editorial to the apparent political differences between Chicago and the state capital, the two largest cities in the state. Chicago, the editor observed, was "notorious" for its "mobs, riots, burglaries, murders [and] suicides and all crimes in the catalogue." It had, in fact, become "a successful rival to Sodom and Gomorrah," a place that had repudiated the Constitution and the acts of Congress. "Persons from the south, in pursuit of fugitive slaves, when they learned that fugitives had reached Chicago," the editor lamented, made "no further effort, well knowing that the dominant party there" – by which he meant the Republican Party – "will stop at nothing to defeat the arrest of a fugitive." By contrast, in Springfield, where "riots and mobs are unheard of, obedience to law and order" were among "the chief characteristics of its citizens." A Cairo observer went further: residents of Chicago were, he wrote, "undoubtedly the most riotous, mobocratic, law breaking people in this or any other State. Say niggers and slave-catchers in the same breath, and they are up in arms, ready for rapine and murder." In response to the failure to recapture a fugitive in 1851, an editor in Egypt simply severed Chicago from the rest of the state: "We of the South," he thundered, "do not regard Chicago as belonging to Illinois. It is a perfect *sink hole of abolition* as Boston or Cincinnati." Editors in the northern sector of the state responded in kind: they dismissed Egypt as nothing more than an extension of the slaveholding South. Even on the eve of the Civil War, observers in Missouri continued to lament the fact that it was next to impossible to recover fugitives once they made it to Chicago.[42]

There were times when even sympathetic Chicago observers were forced to concede that the black community was much too determined to resist enforcement of the law. They found explanations in the experiences of those who had settled in the city. "We cannot blame the colored men of this city," one editor observed, "for the jealousy with which they watch anything that looks like an attempt to take one of their color back to slavery, that bitter, crushing, terrible slavery, which so many of them suffered."[43] But at the same time, the editor was at a loss to understand why white men who should know better, and who had never endured the horrors of slavery, would allow themselves to be drawn into these acts of civil and political disobedience. The editor's quandary helps to explain why Chicago became a site of resistance to the law that so horrified observers from the southern part of the state and in Missouri. There were a few cases that came before the commissioner during the decade but none resulted in the return of a fugitive slave. As a result,

---

[42] *Illinois State Register,* August 3, 1857; Cairo *Times and Delta,* September 9, 1857; Chicago *Democrat,* July 11, 1851; *Missouri Republican,* January 16, 1861.

[43] Chicago *Tribune,* September 1, 1857.

abductions became the only avenue available to slaveholders. In this respect, the northern third of the state looked very much like Egypt: slaveholders did not rely on the law to effect returns. But unlike in Egypt, attempts to abduct fugitives from Chicago were met with stiff resistance. As we have seen, the city set a standard of resistance to the law within weeks of its passage when the city council, made up mostly of Free Democrats, adopted a resolution condemning the law and ordering city police to abstain from enforcing what it called an "unjust" law. Within days, Senator Stephen A. Douglas, in one of his patented marathon speeches, listened to by an estimated crowd in excess of four thousand, defended himself and the constitutionality of the law against critics and condemned the council's stand. An equally impressive and boisterous meeting, a week later, rejected Douglas' claims. Years later, following the election of James Buchanan to the presidency, supporters of the law made another abortive attempt to reverse the council's decision by proposing a revision to the city's charter that would force the mayor and city officers to obey and enforce all federal laws.[44]

Such official opposition to the law and its enforcement was buttressed by the revival and reorganization of the Western Anti-Slavery Society headquartered in the city. Plans were also put in place to collect donations to aid fugitives and their families leaving the city and those passing through town from other parts of the country on their way to Canada. At times, these organizations had their hands full catering to the pressing needs of escapees. It is not always easy to differentiate between these philanthropic activities and political action, as both were part and parcel of the local UGRR's operations. Whenever necessary, activists were able to call upon a wider circle of supporters. In mid-1854, for instance, following passage of the Kansas-Nebraska Act, the local movement responded to a "most astonishing rate" of increase in the number of fugitives passing through the city by augmenting the number of "conductors" to meet the demand and supplying "officers and passengers" with "iron" to defend against those who would interfere with operations.[45]

The driving force behind resistance to the law was the black community – both in the organizations it created and its ability to call out members of the community, on short notice, to resist attempts to retake fugitives. Within weeks of its passage, African Americans formed the Liberty Association to resist enforcement of the law and to protect those fugitives who made Chicago home. They worked closely with similar defense associations in St. Louis and

[44] Springfield *Register*, October 28, November 7, 1850; *Missouri Republican*, October 29, 1850; Chicago *Journal* (n.d.), in *Missouri Republican*, October 30, 1850; Scioto *Gazette*, October 29, 1850; www.enclycopedia.chicagohistory.org/pages/1430.html; Chicago *Tribune*, January 26, 1856, January 24, 1857; Stanley Campbell claims five fugitives were returned from the city, all "without due process of law. *The Slave Catchers. Enforcement of the Fugitive Slave Law, 1850–1860* (1968, rpr., New York: 1972), 199–206.
[45] Chicago *Democrat*, November 16, December 9, 1850; Chicago *Tribune*, June 7, 1854.

Detroit to protect and ensure the safe passage of fugitives to Canada. Members paid an initiation fee of 25 cents plus an additional weekly contribution of 10 cents. A portion of the funds collected went to cover expenses associated with supplying fugitives with clothes and food as well as the cost of getting them to safety. But some portion also went into paying for nightly patrols of the city. The patrols were divided into seven divisions, each composed of six men, whose duty it was to keep an eye on the city and ensure that slave catchers were prevented from reaching their prey. Bulletins from city newspapers frequently warned Southerners not to attempt to retake fugitives. Not only was the black community organized and well armed, one newspaper reported, but it was also sustained by "public sentiment," which supported its efforts to resist "all attempts against their liberty." These developments understandably worried supporters of the law. A city controlled by Democrats, in a state beholden to Stephen Douglas, was colluding with those who opposed a law that he had done so much to engineer through Congress. In late 1854, blacks formed another association – the Anti-Slavery Society of Chicago – to aid, as they said, fugitives to escape from the land of "slavery and prostitution to a land of Liberty and Virtue." It is not clear if this new society supplanted or supplemented the work of the Liberty Association. The results, nevertheless, were the same: slave catchers found it next to impossible to retrieve fugitives from the city. In late 1854, for example, two slave catchers from Missouri spent two months and an estimated $200 in a futile attempt to retake four slaves. Finally, one newspaper reported, "colored folks" got tired of their presence and "flogged both of them severely." Months later, a Kentucky master who came in search of his slaves was greeted by "stories of vengeance" and the "sad and doleful fate which had befallen those who had come [to town] slave hunting." The welcoming party also sent a deputation to a local lawyer who had agreed to take the case, informing him that there were "four hundred men here waiting to see the lawyer who depended on nigger-catching for his living."[46]

As in so many other locations in the North where fugitives had settled over the years, the passage of the law produced a flurry of activity that would set the tone of the city's response to enforcement. In the week following its adoption, a female fugitive, known only as Mitchell, voluntarily agreed to return with John Calvert, an agent of her St. Louis master. Concerned they may be followed, Calvert took a circuitous route along the Wabash River. As he had feared, they were pursued and overtaken by a group of African Americans near Bridgeport opposite Vincennes, Indiana. Mitchell was returned to Chicago and sent on to Canada. In this instance, the fugitive may have been protected, but the presence

---

[46] New Albany *Ledger*, November 8, 1850; Chicago *Tribune* (n.d.), in *Anti-Slavery Bugle*, August 20, 1853; *Southern Illinoisan*, September 9, 1853; Chicago *Tribune*, December 18, 30, 1852, March 7, August 15, 1855; Cleveland *Herald*, February 17, 1855; New York *Tribune*, August 18, 1855.

of slave catchers in the city also disrupted the lives of many. In search of his former slave, a Missouri slaveholder walked into a barber shop unaware that it was owned by the man he sought. While he was being shaved by an assistant, the fugitive, known only as Johnson, slipped away, presumably to Canada.[47]

When it was announced in early October 1850 that George Washington Meeker had accepted the position of commissioner, one local newspaper wondered how anyone could consent to such an appointment in a city that had made its views on the law abundantly clear. Within a year, Meeker was to sit in judgment in the first case heard in the city. Moses Johnson, a former slave owned by Crawford E. Smith of Lafayette County, east of Kansas City, Missouri, was captured by Samuel S. Martin, a local agent of the slaveholder, and two constables. Johnson was brought to the courthouse by the marshal and at least ten special assistants, three of them members of the US army. Additionally, the authorities called out five companies of militia, made up of the "most odious men to the colored population," in an attempt, one newspaper reported, to overawe potential rescuers. A large crowd of African Americans gathered outside the hearing room. Some attempted to enter the courthouse but were met by the "mayor and the City Marshal, together with a number of Police, as well as volunteers." They would maintain a vigil outside the courtroom, even at night, throughout the hearing. Johnson was defended by George Manierre, E. C. Larned, L. C. P. Frees, and Calvin DeWolf, leading figures in the local bar. DeWolf would later become a prominent judge in the city and continue to play a major role in cases involving fugitives. Manierre, who led the defense, objected to the affidavit under which Johnson was arrested, insisting it had not been issued by a proper court of record, and did not describe the person who was to be arrested. He also called for the rejection of the power of attorney, arguing that it was not properly certified. Meeker ruled that the latter could not be entered as evidence. It was a victory of sorts for the defense. But as I have shown in Chapter 2, the case turned on the affidavit's description of Johnson. Where it described him as 5' 5 ½" and "copper colored," the defense showed that he was both taller and "jet black." In the face of such discrepancies, Meeker ruled against the master. The defense's approach provided a template for many other defense teams in other parts of the North. The victory may also have persuaded slaveholders that they would have to rely on other means to reclaim their lost property. The use of the military raised disturbing questions about the best way to enforce the law. Were, one newspaper asked, "the guns and bayonets, swords and cannon of volunteer and enrolled companies of cities, states, and general government" necessary? Other cities in the North would deploy the military in similar ways, but in Chicago the authorities thought better of again using such heavy-handed tactics. But to some supporters of the law, especially those in Egypt, the failure to return Johnson in

[47] Chicago *Democrat*, November 1, 5, 6, 25, 1850; *Missouri Republican*, November 6, 1850.

spite of such a heavy military presence only went to prove that the city had become a cesspit of abolitionism.[48]

Not surprisingly, the black community celebrated what was, by any measure, a major victory. At two meetings held in the AME Church, they offered their thanks and raised funds to purchase two silver cups for the leaders of the defense team in appreciation for their services. Facing ostracism, those such as Samuel Martin, who had participated in the capture of Johnson, felt the need to issue a public apology. A year later, it was reported that landlords who had boarded the large military contingent were still waiting for payment from the government. Some landlords sued the deputy marshal in an effort to recover the money owed them. As in the case of the large military force called out to capture and hold those suspected of involvement in the shoot-out at Christiana, Pennsylvania, that resulted in the death of Samuel Gorsuch, the Maryland slaveholder, and the injury of others in the pursuing party, the government had yet to establish a mechanism for meeting the cost of enforcing the law.[49]

In the face of such concerted opposition, slaveholders generally shunned the city, opting instead to use slave catchers to nab and return runaways. But taking fugitives off the streets of the city was dangerous and usually unavailing. In September 1854, George Buchanan, his brother, John, and William Grant were commissioned by George Taylor and John H. Fellows of St. Louis to capture three fugitives, one of whom was William Turner. The thirty-year-old Turner was owned by Taylor, master of the steamer *Belfast*, which ran on the Mississippi River. Evidently, Turner had persuaded Taylor to buy him and allow him to be hired out so he could repay the captain. Turner did make some payments but escaped before repaying the full amount. According to Taylor, Turner wrote him from Chicago promising to meet his obligations but never did. At this point, Taylor decided to have Turner captured. The catchers brought with them all of the requisite papers. But a day after their arrival they ran into Turner on the street at a time when there were few people about. They gambled on capturing him rather that going first to a commissioner for a warrant. Turner resisted and seized one of his assailants' guns. Shots were exchanged but no one was injured. As the slave catchers later reported, Turner cried out and, in a matter of minutes, a large group of African Americans came to the fugitive's aid. Sensing the growing danger, the catchers decided to abandon their plans and take refuge in a tavern owned by someone they knew. But when they got there the proprietor, fearful of the crowd, refused to protect them. Officers arrived soon after and took the three into custody. Unable to

---

[48] Chicago *Democrat*, October 8, 1850, June 4, 5, 6, 7, 1851; *Western Citizen*, June 10, 1851; *Pennsylvania Freeman*, June 19, 1851; Springfield *Register*, June 9, 1851; *Missouri Republican*, June 10, 11, 1851; Kenosha *Telegraph* (n.d.), in *Western Citizen*, June 17, 1851; Shawneetown *Advertiser* (n.d.), in Chicago *Democrat*, July 11, 1851.

[49] *Western Citizen*, June 24, 1851; Chicago *Democrat*, July 19, 1852.

meet bail, the three were held until they could appear in court, charged with "attempting to create a riot" and kidnapping. They were defended by the district attorney, Thomas Hoyne, a Democrat and ally of Stephen Douglas. The prosecution was led by George Manierre. But before the case could be heard, Justice Treat of Springfield issued a writ of habeas corpus to be answered within twenty-four hours in the capital two hundred miles away. The prosecution was not informed until after the three had left town and so was unable to procure witnesses in time for the hearing. All of this occurred on the day a grand jury in Chicago had indicted the three. Treat ruled that the catchers were authorized to make an arrest "wherever and whenever they might find the victim," and were "to use such force" as they deemed necessary.[50]

Following the scuffle, Turner was sent off to Canada. The three slave catchers also managed to escape, not, as one local newspaper observed, by breaking "the bars of their cell" but by means of a writ of habeas corpus issued by a judge in Springfield. There were reports, admittedly from opponents of Stephen Douglas, that he had pressured Thomas Hoyne, his protégé, to find a way to bring a fugitive case to a hearing "to show that the law could be executed" in Chicago. That may explain why Hoyne took the unusual step of accompanying the slave catchers to Springfield for their hearing. If he could not hold Turner, the least he could do was deny opponents of the law the satisfaction of prosecuting slave catchers for kidnapping. The sheriff, C. P. Bradley, also came in for a share of criticism for not informing the prosecution of the writ from Springfield. Given the short time allowed to answer the writ, Bradley explained, he had done all he could to find Manierre, only to discover he was out of town. While he was opposed to slavery, Bradley made it clear that he was no abolitionist. Neither was he a slave catcher, nor an "apologist for slave catchers." But he was determined not to permit a "set of men to rescue from his custody any person legally committed" to him, if it could be prevented.[51]

To supporters of the law, Chicagoans had once again shown their true colors as "hypocritical thieves [and members] of that mob-ruled, treason-hatching city." After criticizing the three catchers for not following legal procedures, one St. Louis newspaper had, however, no doubt that, even if they had followed the law, the fugitive would not have been handed over. "Chicago," it observed, "has been so thoroughly abolitionized, the negroes have such entire possession of the sympathies of the people that they all combine to run off a slave."[52] Turner did not stay in Canada long; it appears he returned to Chicago soon after the excitement surrounding the case abated. Five years later, he found

[50] Chicago *Tribune*, September 11, 1854; Hannibal *Messenger*, September 19, 1854; New York *Tribune*, September 13, 1854; *National Era*, September 21, 1854; *Missouri Republican*, September 26, 1854; Chicago *Tribune* (n.d.), in New York *Tribune*, September 23, 1854.

[51] Chicago *Tribune*, September 14, 22, 1854; Pittsburgh *Gazette*, September 15, 1854.

[52] Palmyra *Whig*, September 21, 1854; *Missouri Republican* (n.d.), in Chicago *Tribune*, September 28, 1854.

himself at the center of another case, accused this time of colluding with the kidnapping of three young men: Washington Anderson, his brother James, and their cousin Henry Scott. Evidently, the three and Turner were hired to work on a farm in Michigan. Those who hired them bought agricultural equipment, as one newspaper reported, to "give color" to their plan. Turner soon returned to Chicago and reported that he had left the others on the farm. As it turned out, the Andersons and Scott were fugitives from St. Louis, owned by the family of D. M. Frost. Aware that it was next to impossible to retake fugitives from Chicago, Frost had hired two policemen from St. Louis to accompany him to Chicago, where he also made contact with Charles Noyes, the deputy marshal. Rather than going to the farm in Michigan, the three had been taken in irons and handed over to their master on Bloody Island, which sits in the middle of the Mississippi River opposite St. Louis. Noyes evidently was paid a handsome fee. Blacks in Chicago accused Turner of working with the kidnappers and threatened to lynch him. Turner pleaded with Noyes to imprison him for safekeeping. During the night, a mob made an unsuccessful attempt to take Turner out of his cell. Others who were friends of Turner were not so lucky; they were taken and flogged. Turner, Noyes, Charles W. Smith, about whom nothing is known, and a "young chap" – Charles Erdman of St. Louis, who had been in Chicago one week, and who, it was suspected, was there to identify the fugitives – were charged under a state law that considered it kidnapping when anyone was forcibly taken out of the state without first establishing a "claim according to the laws of the United States."[53]

The case against Erdman was dropped when it was shown that he was not involved with the removal of the three men. Noyes, one newspaper reported, slipped away unnoticed. As a consequence, the case against the kidnappers collapsed. It is not clear what became of Turner but it seems unlikely that he would have remained in the city. This was a most unusual case. There is no doubt that the Anderson brothers and Scott were fugitives. It appears Washington Anderson had been living in Chicago for "several years" following his escape. Sometime in the spring of 1859, he went into the southern part of the state, where he was captured and returned to St. Louis. Washington must have convinced his owner that he was glad to be back, for he was taken in without being punished. Early in June, he escaped again, taking a cousin, Henry, along. It seems likely that his capture in the spring was a cover for a plan to free Henry. Frost offered a combined reward of $1,850 for them. The fact that Washington had lived in Chicago for some time may explain why the black community saw their capture as a kidnapping. But given the community's history of protecting fugitives who settled in Chicago, it is unlikely that the community would have considered their capture anything but a kidnapping. The

53 Chicago *Democrat*, July 21, 23, 25, 1859; Chicago *Tribune*, July 21, 25, 1859; *Anti-Slavery Bugle*, July 30, August 6, 1859; *National Era*, August 4, 1859. The description of the three can be found in an advertisement for their escape in the *Missouri Republican*, June 6, 1859.

case was complicated even further by the fact that Frost published a lengthy account of his relationship with the three and the reasons for their recapture. Washington, he explained, had been known in St. Louis as a "gambler and a thief" who had left behind three wives. Frost discovered that he had married a fourth while in Chicago. An "expert pilferer of corn-cribs and hen-roosts," Washington first ran away at age sixteen. Henry Scott was no better. He had been convicted of larceny and flogged. Months earlier, he had been convicted of a similar crime in Indiana and sent to the state penitentiary from which he escaped to Chicago. Once in Chicago, Frost had hired additional "professional detectives," showing them the requisition for the slaves' recapture signed by the governor of Missouri as well as the record of their jail breaks. Frost also arranged a meeting with the fugitives, who, he reported, "were perfectly willing to come home," living as they were in abject poverty. They were not removed from the city by force, he informed the editor, but traveled with him back to St. Louis voluntarily. Neither did Charles Noyes forcibly remove the slaves, nor was Turner involved in any scheme to kidnap them. The recaptured slaves were not flogged, as had been reported, but were received "on their arrival home with new clothes, new blankets, plenty of money...tobacco, etc. etc." He decided not to retake Henry's older brother Governor Scott because he was married and was doing everything he could to provide for his family. "I concluded," Frost declared, "to leave him there as long as he chooses to behave himself." Frost explained why he had chosen not to resort to the law: "I entertain in common with many others, to not making my private affairs and losses assume the form of public nuisances. I did not then, nor do I now, consider that I had a moral right to place all the good people of Chicago in the dilemma of either endangering their lives in aiding me in a matter of no personal interest to themselves, or else of willingly violating the law of Congress."[54]

In successfully retaking his slaves, Frost could afford to be magnanimous, but his explanation was also self-serving. He had managed, with the support of others, to capture and return his slaves to St. Louis, something other slaveholders had been unable to do. It is also clear from testimony at the hearing into the charges of kidnapping that Frost had also worked with a railroad company to put on a special car in which he, Noyes, and the slaves traveled on their way to St. Louis. Yet in his closing comments he tipped his hat to the vigilance of black and white opponents of the law. Were it possible to retrieve his slaves by way of the law, Frost maintained that he would have pursued that option. That he could not force him to adopt a different course of action. His victory, however, troubled the black community. In a meeting at the Baptist Church they condemned Turner for his involvement and discussed ways to protect themselves against similar betrayals. Henry Oscar Wagoner, the forty-two-year-old former compositor at the *Western Citizen* and a hominy manufacturer, called

---

[54] Chicago *Democrat*, June 21, 1859; Chicago *Times*, August 3, 1859, in *Missouri Republican*, August 6, 1859.

for the appointment of a fifteen-member vigilance committee to investigate the kidnapping and to report to a subsequent meeting.[55]

The removal of the three St. Louis fugitives was a blow to the black community, many of whose leaders took it personally. After all, until then, their record of protecting fugitives who chose to stay in the city, or those passing through to Canada, had been unblemished. It was a community whose leaders had grown in stature and political sophistication in the years since the passage of the Fugitive Slave Law. They were led by, among others, Wagoner; John Jones, the merchant tailor, born in North Carolina of a free woman and a German father, who had moved to the city from Alton in 1845; William Johnson, a barber and the proprietor of a bathing and shaving saloon; and H. Ford Douglas, a former slave, the son of a slave woman and her owner who settled in the city in 1855. They built churches, created literary and debating societies called Negro convention meetings to challenge the state's Black Laws and other racial restrictions, opposed the policies and growing racial stridency of the Democratic Party and its state leader, Stephen Douglas, organized celebrations of West Indian emancipation, and, most pressingly, opposed enforcement of the Fugitive Slave Law.[56]

As in other cities, such as Pittsburgh and Boston, the black community sometimes acted independently of its leaders. The case of sixteen-year-old Charles Gantz is illustrative. As a young child, Gantz's mother had apprenticed him to Samuel Thompson, a farmer in Juniata County, Pennsylvania. In 1856, Thompson sold his farm to his brother and moved to Monmouth, Warren County, Illinois, leaving Charles in the care of his brother. When Thompson returned to Pennsylvania on a visit the following summer he found that Charles was being abused by a tenant on the farm. Thompson decided to take Charles with him to his home in Illinois. On the way, they stopped over in Chicago. Blacks got wind of their presence, and suspecting Thompson was a slaveholder returning a fugitive, demanded Charles' release. Calvin De Wolf, now a judge, heard of the brewing problem and asked Allen Pinkerton, who would later become famous for his detective agency, and who was considered a friend of the slave, to investigate. Pinkerton met with Thompson and Charles and left

[55] Chicago *Democrat*, July 25, 1859; Chicago *Tribune*, July 25, 1859; Christopher Robert Reed, *Black Chicago's First Century, Vol. 1, 1853–1900*,(Columbia, MO: 2005), 54, 78; Chicago City Directory (1853–54).

[56] Robert L. Harris Jr., "H. Ford Douglas: Afro-American Anti-Slavery Emigrationist," *Journal of Negro History*, 62, No. 3 (July 1977), 223; Reed, *Black Chicago's First Century*, 32, 58, 105; Arna Bontemps and Jack Conroy, *Anyplace But Here* (New York: 1966), 50; H. O. Wagoner to S. H. Kerfoot, Denver, September 27, 1884, Chicago Historical Society, Chicago, Illinois; Chicago City Directory (1849–50). In 1857 a meeting of African Americans led by Wagoner issued a public challenge to Douglas to debate Frederick Douglass as a way to address the "shameful abuse which is constantly being heaped upon us" by Douglas and the party he lead. Chicago *Democrat*, November 20, 1857, August 1, 1857; Chicago *Tribune*, August 1, 4, 1857, July 28, 1858.

convinced that they were who they said they were. Pinkerton and De Wolf tried to persuade the crowd gathered outside Thompson's hotel that Charles was free but they were unconvinced. The crowd surrounded the wagon, taking the two to the train station. Sensing danger, the wagon driver whipped his horses into a "furious pace," assailed by what one report called a "perfect storm of stones, mud and other missiles." Shots were also fired, although no one was hit. The wagon broke down a distance from the station, forcing Thompson and Charles to make their way on foot through side streets. Before the train could leave, the crowd caught up with the two. At this point, officers arrived and took Thompson and Charles to the watchhouse to protect them from the growing and angry crowd. They were later moved to a hotel. The following morning, Charles met with "several colored men" and convinced them that he was free. Some, however, were unpersuaded. On their way to the station with the sheriff the next day they were again confronted by a "number of colored men" who tried to seize Charles, forcing them back to the hotel. The matter was finally settled, and the two allowed to continue their journey, following a public hearing.[57]

Although this sort of action caused considerable anxiety among black community leaders and whites who supported the cause, it epitomized the community's vigilance and willingness to turn out in large numbers to protect fugitives. If, by their activity, slaveholders were forced to resort to measures outside the law, it seemed only logical, many blacks thought, to follow the maxim "better safe than sorry." They may have had to apologize to Samuel Thompson and Charles Grantz, but that was preferable to being deceived. This sort of vigilance was on display again in November 1860 in the midst of the presidential election when Stephen Friel Nuckolls, a Nebraskan slaveholder, tried to reclaim twenty-year-old Eliza Grayson, who had escaped with another of his slaves two years earlier. Nuckolls, the founder of Nebraska City, owned several mercantile stores, a city bank, and a railroad, as well as other businesses in and around the city. He was also a member of the territorial assembly and had voted not to abolish slavery following passage of the Kansas-Nebraska Act in 1854. Soon after her arrival in Chicago, Grayson had taken a job as a housekeeper in what one reporter described as an "infamous establishment" located in a part of town "thickly settled with colored people." She apparently told her story of escape to one of the "unfortunate white females of the house," who betrayed Grayson to Nuckolls. There, one wag recalled, was "hatched this pure desire to save the Union." On his way to Chicago, Nuckolls stopped

---

[57] Chicago events never seem to follow a simple or predictable course and need to be pieced together from a number of sources, some of them unsympathetic to the black community. Not surprisingly, a Cairo newspaper described the crowds who gathered outside the hotel as "black, yellow and white niggers." Chicago *Tribune*, September 1, 1857; Chicago *Democrat*, September 1, 1857; Chicago *Times*, September 1, 1857; Chicago *Press*, September 1, 1857; Detroit *Advertiser*, September 3, 1857; Cairo *Times and Delta*, September 9, 1857.

over in Springfield, where he obtained a warrant for Grayson's arrest from Commissioner Corneau. But he could find no one willing to execute the warrant. After some delay, the city commissioner appointed a special policeman to accompany Nuckolls to Grayson's place of work, where she was arrested. But she did not go quietly. In response to her screams a large crowd of African Americans followed. Grayson was placed in the armory for safekeeping, but the crowd kept watch. In a move to prevent her return, Calvin De Wolf issued a warrant for Grayson's arrest for "disorderly conduct." On the way to De Wolf's court to answer the summons, the crowd seized Grayson and sent her off to Canada. Nuckolls was taken to a hotel by police for his own protection. The ignominy of losing a slave worth an estimated $1,200 at the hands of a crowd of blacks was more than Nuckolls could take. He brought suit, but, interestingly, not against those responsible for freeing Grayson, but a group of nine whites, including George Anderson, the deputy sheriff, who had accompanied him to the armory to secure Grayson; De Wolf; Chancellor L. Jenks, who had read law with De Wolf and had issued the arrest warrant; as well as the sheriff. Bail was set at $2,500 for each of the accused. It is very likely that the outbreak of the Civil War worked against Nuckolls, for the case was finally dismissed in December 1861. It is just as likely that no one in the city could be found who was willing or dared to testify against the accused.[58]

Ottawa was another town in the northern sector of the state with an enviable record of sheltering fugitives. When on the rare occasions regular operations were disrupted by the capture of a fugitive slave, as they were at the end of 1851, the local arm of the UGRR was able to organize groups to track down the slave catchers and retake the fugitive.[59] It was a record that remained largely unchallenged until October 1859. The case had its origin in Egypt. In early October, John B. Jones of the town of Anna and J. Curtly, leaders of a gang of "Union County kidnappers," which included a former judge of the county as well as Jonesboro's former postmaster, abducted Jim Gray while he was working on a farm in Perry County and placed him on a train, intending to take him back to Union County. Fortunately for Gray, Benajah

[58] Chicago *Tribune,* November 13, 16, December 5, 1860; Chicago *Democrat* (n.d.), in Baltimore *Exchange,* November 17, 1860; *Anti-Slavery Bugle,* December 1, 1860; Chicago *Democrat,* November 20, 1860; *National Anti-Slavery Standard,* November 24, 1860; http://homepages.rootsweb.ancestry.com/-ahopkins/nuckolls/neb; http://undereverystone.blogspot .com/2013.12.01_archives.html (posted by Jim Craig); *The Fugitive Slave Law and Its Victims* (New York: 1861), 157–58, quoting the Omaha *News,* December 12, 1858, and Chicago *Journal* (n.d.), in *National Anti-Slavery Standard,* February 5, 1859. For the warrant of arrest issued by Corneau see Adams-Snyder, Box 4. United States Commissioner Docket, Abraham Lincoln Library; Morgans, *The Underground Railroad on the Western Frontier,* 99–102; James Patrick Morgans, *John Todd and the Underground Railroad. Biography of an Iowa Abolitionist* (Jefferson, NC: 2006), 92–95.
[59] See, for example, Chicago *Democrat,* October 21, 1851; Pittsburgh *Gazette,* November 1, 1851; *Liberator,* November 7, 1851.

G. Roots, a civil engineer, educator, and agriculturalist who had moved to the area from Connecticut twenty years earlier, was on the train. Roots seemed to have made a nuisance of himself protesting against Gray's capture. When Gray was placed in a jail in Jonesboro, Roots tried unsuccessfully to have a local judge rule that Gray was being held under an 1845 state law that had been declared unconstitutional by the state supreme court. Failing to get a response, Roots traveled north to Ottawa, where he persuaded State Supreme Court Justice John Caton to issue a writ of habeas corpus ordering the sheriff of Union County to produce Gray. Eight or ten men from Union County, along with Richard Phillips of Cape Girardeau, Missouri, who claimed Gray was his slave, traveled to Ottawa for the hearing. Phillips claimed to have bought the twenty-eight-year-old Gray from one of his sisters sometime around 1855 for $1,000 and that Gray had escaped the previous spring. Caton initially ruled in favor of Gray on the grounds that the law under which he was held was unconstitutional. What Caton did not know was that, on their way to Ottawa, the group had procured a warrant for Gray's arrest as an escaped slave from the Springfield commissioner, who also deputized the Union County sheriff to serve it. Unwilling to meddle in what was now a federal case, Caton ruled that the warrant was legitimate and remanded Gray to the custody of the Union County sheriff. While he was busy preparing the necessary papers, Gray took what one reporter called "leg bail" and was hurried off in a carriage to Canada.[60]

In the midst of a presidential campaign, and just as the country was coming to grips with the significance of what had happened at Harpers Ferry, a group of people at a meeting in Jonesboro pledged that, in the future, fugitives would be returned to their owners at all hazards. Supporters of Gray's rescue in Ottawa saw the Jonesboro meeting as a partisan attempt to boost Stephen Douglas' political standing. One Jonesboro newspaper acknowledged that Ottawa Democrats had offered their services to prevent Gray's escape. There was also growing pressure to sue unnamed Ottawa Republicans for aiding Gray. In the midst of this wrangling, a grand jury sitting in Ottawa began examining witnesses in late December. A week later, eight residents of Ottawa were indicted for their involvement in the rescue. They included Dr. Joseph Stout, a physician; and his brother James, a lawyer; Claudius. B. King, a sash and blind manufacturer; and his brother, Harvey, C. Campbell, a clerk; E. W. Chamberlin, a law student; S. P. Smith, about whom nothing is known; and the Scottish-born John Hossack, who had settled in Ottawa in 1849, where he had developed an extensive lumber and grain business. Richard Phillips, who

---

[60] Chicago *Tribune*, October 26, November 4, 30, December 12, 31, 1859, February 11, 1860; Chicago *Democrat*, October 26, 1859, March 1, 1860; Ottawa *Republican*, October 21, 29, November 5, 12, 1859, March 3, 1860; *Missouri Republican*, October 23, 1859; www.nps.gov/subjects/uhov/ntf_member/ntf_member_details. My thanks to Martin Crawford for tracking down information on Roots.

owned more than seventy slaves in 1860 and made it abundantly clear that he was willing to spend $8,000 to reclaim Gray, threatened to bring suit against those accused of rescuing Gray.[61]

The case was moved to Chicago in early January. Supporters in Ottawa organized a committee to keep in touch with the accused. The first to come to trial were Hossack and the two Stout brothers. On the first day of the trial, Judge Drummond threw out two of the counts but rejected a motion to quash the other two. James Stout was granted bail and returned to Ottawa. The other two refused and insisted on an immediate trial. But the city was apparently strapped for cash and unable to pay the jury. As a result of the delay, Hossack decided to accept bail and return home. Joseph Stout continued to refuse and remained in jail. Days later, the King brothers and Chamberlin surrendered and were taken to Chicago. Rather than challenge the testimony of witnesses who gave a full account of the escape from Caton's court, defense counsel chose to raise questions about both the nature of the warrant and its execution. Drummond did concede that the lack of a seal on the warrant was an "irregularity" but ruled that it was not enough to invalidate it. He even doubted that a seal was necessary for a "process issued by a United States officer." After deliberating for four hours, the jury hearing Joseph Stout's case remained deadlocked. He would be retried later and found guilty. His brother, who defended himself, was cleared. Hossack, who witnesses claimed held the reins of the horses tied to the wagon in which Gray escaped, was found guilty. He was sentenced to ten days in prison and fined $100. Dr. Stout was also sentenced to ten days and fined $50. Claudius King was given a one-day sentence and charged $10. It was later reported that S. P. Smith, who had been arrested somewhere in Michigan, pleaded guilty and was "suffered to go where he pleased."[62]

Even with the possible threat of a suit from Richard Phillips, these were laughably minor sentences. Drummond then poured salt on the wound by giving Hossack an opportunity to say a few words before he passed sentence. What followed was one of the most masterful and impassioned condemnations of the Fugitive Slave Law heard in a court of law, as poignant as Charles Langston's following his conviction for participating in the rescue of a fugitive in Wellington, Ohio, in 1858. The prosecution had insisted that, as a foreigner who had enjoyed political liberty and benefitted from the economic opportunities provided by his adopted country, Hossack, of all people, should have

[61] Ottawa *Republican*, November 5, 12, December 21, 24, 1859; Chicago *Tribune*, December 22, 28, 30, 1859; Chicago *Democrat*, December 30, 1859; Cleveland *Herald*, December 30, 1859; Rev. John H. Ryan, "A Chapter from the History of the Underground Railroad in Illinois. A Sketch of the Sturdy Abolitionist, John Hossack," *Journal of the Illinois State Historical Society*, 8, No. 1 (April 1915), 25, 29.

[62] Ottawa *Republican*, January 7, 14, 21, March 3, April 28, 1860; Chicago *Democrat*, January 5, March 1, 2, 3, 26, October 5, 1860; *Anti-Slavery Bugle*, March 26, 1860.

obeyed its laws. But why would someone, Hossack countered, who came from a land that was "never...conquered and where a slave never breathed" obey "wicked and ungodly laws" that "violated both the letter and spirit of the constitution." Given that he had escaped a land of "crushing aristocracy," how could he now be expected to support "a worse aristocracy." Hossack suggested a number of reasons why he should not be sentenced. First, he had been condemned for being an abolitionist, a group of people the prosecution seemed to despise. But he was proud to be put in the company of "Clarkson and Wilberforce" in his native land and "Washington and Franklin...in this boasted land of the free." Second, because the Fugitive Slave Law was "at variance with the spirit and letter of the constitution." Those who prostituted the Constitution in support of slavery were "traitors not only to the liberties of millions of enslaved countrymen, but traitors to the constitution itself, which they have sworn to support," which, he pointed out, never once mentions the word "slave." In addition, the Declaration of Independence promised to promote the happiness and welfare of the people by insisting that all men were created equal and endowed by their Creator with inalienable rights. But slavery compelled political parties to cringe before its dreadful power, "to creep in the dust," debauching "the Christianity of the nation," and bidding "a craven priesthood stand with golden rule in hand and defend the robbing of mothers of their babes and husbands of their wives."

Hossack then turned his guns on the Fugitive Slave Law. The article of the Constitution that required the return of fugitives from labor was, as many opponents of the law had argued, a compact between the states, and so gave Congress no authority to enact laws for its implementation. More damagingly to the rights of all, the law placed enforcement exclusively in the hands of one man from whose decisions there was to be no appeal, a man who was bribed to decide in favor of slaveholders. Third, under the Constitution, which provides for trials by jury, he should not be sentenced for openly flouting a law that did not provide due process. Slavery first consigns a man to the rank of property, then insists on a law that magnifies "slave property above all other property." Here Hossack adopted the trademark slogan of Garrisonian abolitionism: if slavery was guaranteed by the Constitution then that document was "a covenant with death and an agreement with hell." Fourth, the law was also at "variance with the law of God that commands us to love Him...and my neighbor." While he would never enter Missouri to encourage a slave to escape, if a fugitive came to his door, he was obligated, as a Christian, to give him aid and comfort. Concluding, Hossack refused to throw himself on the mercy of the court, for, he declared, "mercy...is kindness to the guilty" and he was guilty of no crime. Mercy is what one asked of God, justice is what he demanded from the court. Hossack looked to the future in his conclusion. He had no doubt that slavery was doomed, but he was also convinced that the country would have to pass through a "terrible conflict which the destruction of slavery must cost." He took comfort in the certainty that, when written, histories of the "great struggle" would proclaim the rescuers of Jim Gray as "having done honor to God, to humanity, and to themselves."[63]

Coming as it did in the midst of a pivotal presidential election, Hossack's was a bravura performance – one which had the potential to cause political discomfort for many in the Republican Party who counted on the state to help put Abraham Lincoln in the White House. Just as the trial was drawing to a close, the city swarmed with large crowds to hear Stephen Douglas. Democratic newspapers said next to nothing about the trial or the speech; Republicans temporized, unsure about the best way to handle such a politically charged trial, and worried about the political price they might pay for publicizing Hossack's speech. The editor of the *Tribune,* a supporter of the Republican Party, gave the trial limited coverage and delayed publishing Hossack's speech. Not so the editor of the *Democrat,* another supporter of Lincoln, who seemed relatively unconcerned about any political fallout. He published Hossack's speech three times in as many days. Its first publication, he reported, created a "marked sensation." All three issues in which the speech appeared sold out as quickly as they rolled off the press. This did not mean, the editor made clear, that he was advocating resistance to the law. In fact, the best way, he thought, to ensure its repeal was to enforce it honestly. The suffering of Hossack and his companions under the law, he predicted, would create "a state of feeling" that would ultimately "demand its repeal or modification." He called on the public to visit the prisoners and to contribute to a fund to cover the cost of the trial. "It will take paying as well as praying to get John Hossack out of jail," he observed matter-of-factly. Finally, he called on the Republican Party of Chicago to pay the exorbitant costs of the trials, estimated to be about $2,500 in each case. These costs were compounded daily, which meant that the prisoners would languish in jail until they were paid in full.[64]

A relief fund established to defray the cost of the trials attracted support from all parts of the North. Yet, according to the editor of the *Democrat,* leaders of the local Republican Party continued to remain indifferent to the continued imprisonment of "two sons of freedom [who were] suffering within the walls of the prison [while] cool, calculating, selfish, cowardly, and corrupt politicians [were] calculating what effect their liberation [might] have upon their own chances for office." The mayor offered to pay Hossack's fine; Deacon W. V. Coe offered to pay Joseph Stout's. George Manierre, the city's leading defender of accused fugitives, contributed $100. Visitors to the prison, including city policemen, contributed $105, mainly in small donations collected from those on their beats. It seemed only obvious to the editor that the Republican Central Committee should make up the difference. Separate meetings were called by the Anti-Slavery Society and African Americans for November 11th, at which money was collected for the fund. In fact, the editor called for stopping all

[63] Hossack's speech is reprinted in "Historical Notes," *Journal of the Illinois State Historical Society,* XLI, No. 1 (March 1948), 68–74; Chicago *Democrat,* October 5, 1860.
[64] Chicago *Democrat,* October 6, 8, 10, 1860.

contributions to the party until it acted. The Republican Central Committee, he insisted, should make up the difference and insure the immediate release of the prisoners. Hossack and Stout were finally freed ten days later.[65]

The determination to rescue Gray had also been influenced by an event that occurred a few days before the fugitive was brought before Judge Caton. A couple of meetings had denounced the presence of two slave catchers from St. Louis who were in town searching for a suspected fugitive name Berkley. But Berkley was not a fugitive; he was a victim of kidnapping. Formerly a slave in Virginia, he had been freed and settled in Ottawa sometime in 1852. In early 1859, he was hired, as so many others were at the time, to work on Pikes Peak. On his way there, Berkley was arrested in St. Joseph, Missouri, as a suspected fugitive slave and placed in the same jail as Dr. John Doy, who had been accused of running slaves to freedom from the Kansas Territory and Missouri. Berkley was sold to a Missouri farmer for $1,045 and soon after resold to a slave trader in St. Louis. There he was shackled to another slave and put on board a steamer bound for New Orleans. The two slipped their irons at Memphis, jumped overboard, and headed north, traveling through Tennessee and Kentucky, and arriving in Ottawa toward the end of 1859. Someone in town alerted connections in St. Louis of their return. The town had only recently ensured the safety of Berkley, and forced the slave catchers to leave, when Gray was brought into Caton's court.[66]

Although there were only a few cases of kidnapping in Illinois during the decade, free blacks such as Berkley were, nonetheless, in constant danger of being taken into slavery. As opponents of the Fugitive Slave Law had predicted, its lack of judicial guarantees increased the chances that kidnappers would go unpunished. It is also not easy to determine exactly how many free blacks were kidnapped, in part because opponents of the law tended to equate the capture of former slaves who had lived free for some time – as was the case of the Anderson brothers in Chicago – as kidnappings. But there undoubtedly were instances in which free blacks were taken out of the state, especially, as we have seen, by gangs operating in Egypt. One case was recorded in northern Illinois just as the trials against the Ottawa rescuers were drawing to a close. In September 1860, Jo Wilder came to Galena, in the far northwest of the state, recruiting black laborers to work on farms and a hotel in Fort Des Moines, Iowa. Joseph Jacobs, James Drayden, and Jerry Boyd, a "miner and day laborer," contracted to accompany Wilder to Iowa. Boyd was born a slave in Kentucky and had runaway to Cincinnati, where a brother secured his freedom. In the years since he had lived in Galena, Boyd had managed to raise sufficient funds to purchase his wife Mary's freedom. In 1860, the pair lived in rented accommodations along with Charlotte Alexander, a house servant, and a two-year-old white girl, the daughter of a servant living elsewhere in the city. Just before the family's departure, a

[65] Chicago *Democrat*, October 9, 11, 1860.
[66] Ottawa *Republican*, October 15, 22, 1859.

letter arrived from western Missouri raising suspicions about Wilder. Jacobs and Drayden, nonetheless, left by train for Independence, Iowa, where they were to meet their contact. No one was there to meet them when they arrived, so they returned home. The Boyd family left Galena by wagon. Soon after they crossed the Mississippi River, a stranger asked to join the party. When they turned south, Boyd grew suspicious of the stranger. Three days out of Galena, Boyd was shot and killed by the stranger just outside Solon, Johnson County, Missouri. The women were taken in the direction of St. Joseph, where Wilder and the stranger, his accomplice, were arrested on suspicion of abduction. Following an interview with Mary, the Mayor of St. Joseph, Reuben Middleton, contacted Galena with the details of the murder and arrest of the two kidnappers, whose real names were John Gooden, alias Jo Wilder, and Peter Boulton, both residents of Caldwell County. On their way to St. Joseph, Boulton had left Mary in Buchanan County, with his father-in-law, a Mr. Baker.

As it turned out, the kidnapping was in revenge for the loss of the Boulton family slaves in February 1853. Peter's father, Rice Boulton, who then lived near Dover, Kentucky, suspected that his nine slaves, a woman and her eight children and grandchildren, had been taken away on the UGRR. The family settled in Windsor, Ontario, from where the mother wrote Boulton that she had left because he had sold her two eldest daughters to slave traders. Apparently, Peter had earlier persuaded Baker to finance an unsuccessful attempt to recover the family's slaves. When that failed, Peter decided to compensate for the family's loss by kidnapping. Why or when he settled on the Boyd family is uncertain. Two Galena residents – Wellington Weigley, a lawyer, and Samuel Hughlett, a smelter – traveled to St. Joseph to testify at the trial, following which Boulton was committed to jail, charged with kidnapping. Gooden was placed in irons and handed over to Weigley and Hughlett to be returned to Galena, where he was to face charges of kidnapping and murder. Just outside St. Joseph, an armed group boarded the train in an attempt to free Gooden. During the commotion, Gooden slipped away and leapt from the moving train. Boulton was later released when he posted the $2,000 bail.[67]

The rescue in Ottawa, and the subsequent trials in Chicago, as well as the kidnapping and murder of Boyd brought to a rather tense end a decade of conflict over enforcement of the Fugitive Slave Law. The regular flow of slaves out of Missouri into Illinois, Iowa, and the Kansas Territory tested the ability and willingness of authorities to enforce it. It is impossible to calculate with any precision the numbers who, acting on their own, or with the aid of supporters, passed through Illinois on their way to Canada or who, as in the case of Edgar Catron, decided to make a new life for themselves in its urban black and rural communities. But slaveholders were equally determined to retake their property, even from places such as Ottawa, Chicago, and other towns

---

[67] *Missouri Courier*, May 5, 1853; *Missouri Republican*, October 16, 18, 1860; Galena *Courier*, October 26, 1860, in New York *Times*, November 6, 1860; H. Scott Wolfe, "The Fate of Jerimiah Boyd. A Tale of Kidnapping and Murder in Old Galena," www.lib.niu.edu/2004/iho40510.html

in northern Illinois that had in place effective systems of protection for fugitives. Slaveholders were much more successful in recapturing fugitives in Egypt because of its white inhabitants' general aversion to the presence of blacks. But even here black rural settlements provided a significant measure of protection for the fugitive. As a consequence, the conflict there sometimes degenerated into open and bloody violence. If one measure of the Fugitive Slave Law's effectiveness was the number of slaves retaken and returned as a consequence of hearings before commissioners, then it was woefully ineffective in this part of the country. There were less than a handful of hearings during the decade and in only one of these – the case involving Frederick Clements – was the suspect returned permanently. Others were either bought, as in the case of Amanda Chavers in Alton, returned only to escape again, as did Catron, or freed, as was Moses Johnson in Chicago. Gray may have been remanded, but he was rescued and sent to Canada. Stanley Campbell, who has done more than any other historian to quantify the effectiveness of the law, has identified twenty-five incidences involving forty slaves that came to some resolution in Illinois during the decade.[68] But his numbers remain speculative, mainly because he does not separate kidnappings from fugitive renditions. The constant lament of Missouri slaveholders that slaves were regularly on the run or that they were being "enticed" away by increasingly active opponents both from outside and inside the state suggests that it was impossible to stem the flow of runaways.

The mechanisms put in place to curtail escapes met with some success, but, over the course of the decade, proved largely unavailing. Two incidents at the close of the decade speak to the levels of frustration felt by slaveholders as well as the impact that the constant loss of slaves had on the debate over the future of slavery in Missouri – a state, admittedly, inching away from slavery as the decade came to a close. A sixty-year-old woman, her two sons, one daughter, and one young child, very likely a grandchild, escaped from St. Louis in late summer 1859 while their master was away in Baltimore. Reporters wondered whether the elderly woman could have devised such a plan of escape without aid from outside. In fact, there was a suspicion that the family had been previously "tampered with by white men." But the reporter had no doubt that "captivating stories of freedom and life in Canada, breathed into their willing ears by some Abolitionists [had] induced them to take the step they did," to leave the comforts of home for an unknown life in a cold and cheerless land. Months earlier, after it was reported that John Brown had arrived in Chicago with a large number of slaves on their way to Canada, one newspaper saw a connection between the continuous "Negro exodus from Missouri," and the "stream of emigrants to the South, and another to the North, bearing away our slaves at a rate that will soon destroy the last vestige of the institution, and leave us entirely niggerless."[69]

---

[68] Campbell, *The Slave Catchers*, 199–206.
[69] *Missouri Democrat*, August 27, 1860; St. Louis *News*, November 9, 1859, in Chicago *Tribune*, November 11, 1859.

# 5

# Western Kentucky and Indiana

When thirty-one-year-old James Armstrong, a valued slave, crossed the Ohio River in a bid for freedom on October 8, 1853, James Rudd, his master, a wealthy Louisville merchant, responded immediately, sending two members of his family, accompanied by a slave catcher from Hamlet Services, in hot pursuit. Armstrong did not get far into Indiana; he was soon caught and returned at a cost of $135 to Rudd in jail fees and other expenses. Almost two months to the day after his first escape, Armstrong was on the run again, this time in the company of Edward, a slave of Christopher Beeler. They were assisted by Moses Bard, a black barber sometimes known as Moses Hurst, and Shadrach Henderson, a black boatman, both residents of New Albany, Indiana, across the river from Louisville. The four headed first to New Albany and then north to Salem, Washington County. For some inexplicable reason, they doubled back to New Albany and took refuge in the basement of the Presbyterian Theological Seminary, where they were arrested by Louisville police on December 18, 1853. Armstrong's recovery cost Rudd $342, the bulk of which – $250 – was payment of an advertised reward. Rudd also confiscated $83 found on Armstrong at the time of his recapture. Worried that Armstrong's actions would affect the disposition of his forty-six other slaves, and clearly peeved by Armstrong's determination to be free, Rudd sold the recalcitrant slave in March 1854 for $1,600, a handsome profit, all things considered.[1]

Armstrong's escapes bring into sharp relief a number of issues associated with the flight of the enslaved from the area, and all along the border between

---

[1] Account Book 1830–1860, James Rudd Papers, Filson Historical Society, Louisville, Kentucky. My thanks to Pen Bogart for bringing this to my attention. It is not clear if Armstrong was one of the many slaves Rudd hired out around the city. See Matthew Salafia, *Slavery's Borderland. Freedom and Bondage Along the Ohio River* (Philadelphia: 2013), 209. Pamela R. Peters, "Gateway to Freedom. New Albany, Floyd County, Indiana," 21–26. My thanks to Pamela Peters for a copy of this essay. Louisville *Courier*, December 24, 1853.

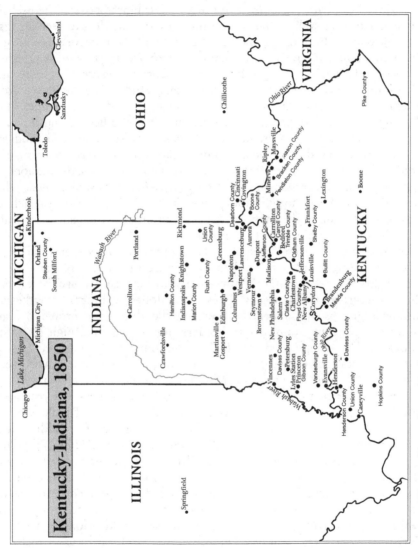

MAP 2. Western Kentucky and Indiana.

slavery and freedom. Armstrong, it seemed, had taken the initiative, at least in the first instance, to flee his master, to emancipate himself, and when that did not succeed, to seek assistance from those he knew had a reputation for aiding those seeking freedom. The sheer volume of advertisements in local newspapers offering rewards for escaped slaves speaks to the determination of the enslaved to be free, or at least to put some distance between themselves and their masters, as well as the commitment of slaveholders to recover lost property. J. Blaine Hudson has calculated that of all the fugitive slave advertisements he compiled covering the years 1788 to 1861, 42 percent referred to escapes in the years 1850–59. If, as Pen Bogart has estimated, three out of every four escapes were never advertised, then Hudson's findings are even more telling. Bogart also acknowledges that the estimated 1,316 escapes during the 1850s was a dramatic increase over the 434 who fled during the previous decade. The numbers were not only larger, but also pointed, as Hudson shows, to a worrying development as far as slaveholders were concerned: a marked increase in the number of those who escaped as families, the number of women – especially older women – and children involved, as well as those who escaped in groups. Even more troubling was the revelation that slaves such as Armstrong could call on the support of others, in his case free black residents of New Albany, to get him out of Louisville.[2]

A review of escapes from Louisville covering the period between June 1852 and October 1854 paints a more detailed picture of the nature and extent of these flights for freedom. Of the fifty-two who escaped, twenty-three were caught and returned. Of these only six escaped alone; the others left either as families or in groups whose members were unrelated. It is this profile of fugitive slave escapes that troubled slaveholders, for it suggested high levels of coordination. The group of ten who fled in December 1853 consisted of two unrelated families, one of five, the other of three, plus two others who were not identified. The first led by Henry Morehead, twenty-eight, his wife Mary, twenty-two, and their three children all under the age of five – the youngest, remarkably, only seven months old – were claimed by William Riddle, who in 1850 owned twenty-one slaves. Problems may have started for Riddle when he discovered that Morehead was attending school at night. Riddle had police break up the school. Morehead later decided to escape when he got word that Riddle was planning to sell his wife and children. Riddle unsuccessfully pursued the family into Indiana, offering a reward of $500. The Moreheads later settled in London, Ontario. The family name of the second group is not known, but it was made up of a man, woman, and child belonging to John O. Harrison. None were returned. The previous year, Charles Q. Armstrong

[2] J. Blaine Hudson, *Fugitive Slaves and the Underground Railroad in Kentucky Borderland* (Jefferson, NC: 2002), 33, 48; Pen Bogart, "Making Their Way to Freedom: Runaway Slave Advertisements from Louisville Newspapers, 1788–1860," 3, 7, 11, 39. My thanks to Bogart for a copy of his essay.

offered a reward of $300 for Mary, aged twenty-five, and her three children, Sam, nine, Joe, seven, and an unnamed child, aged two. They were, Armstrong thought, accompanied by another slave named Edda, aged eighteen, and two unnamed white men, for whom he offered a reward of $100 each. One local newspaper considered it one of the "boldest cases of kidnapping." Armstrong reported that the two white men had been regular visitors to his home over the previous weeks, during which they must have communicated with Mary. They were the ones who hired a hack to take Mary's baggage to the ferry. Mary and the children were retaken at a "Negro's house" in Charlestown, Indiana, and returned. Nothing more was heard of the white men. Mary later testified in police court that she and her family were taken across the river to Jeffersonville not by white men but by Reuben Johnson, a free black, who handed them over to another unnamed black man who took them by coach north of the town. Johnson, who was described by a clearly unsympathetic reporter as a "*barbarous*, smoothed tongue ... hard drinking trifling fellow*," was held over for trial. As it turned out, Edda never left the city, but had hidden out in the home of a friend, where she was caught weeks later. The case suggests the existence of temporary alliances, if not permanent organizations, of free blacks and whites working together to help the enslaved escape.[3]

Not a few of these runaways, such as the unnamed three who crossed the river in a skiff in June 1852, had hired out their time with the permission of their owners and used the "considerable money" earned to finance their escape. They were traced by slave catchers to Knightstown, east of Indianapolis, Indiana, but gave their pursuers the slip and headed for Toledo, Ohio, where they boarded a steamer for Detroit. In an effort to head them off, the slave-catchers sent a telegram to the deputy sheriff of Detroit, who responded that the fugitives, who he erroneously believed were fugitives from justice, had been taken into custody. When the catchers arrived in Detroit, however, they were informed, much to their dismay, that the slaves had broken out of jail and crossed into Canada with the support of a large crowd of "excited colored people." One rather incredulous Louisville editor reported that the slave catchers were forced to return empty handed and with a "poor opinion of the strength of the Detroit jail." Catchers had a measure of redemption two months later, however, when they went in search of seven slaves who had fled from a Mr. Ashburn. Two of them, Luther and Jim, were retaken after a shootout in southern Indiana, during which Luther was injured. Nothing was heard of the other five. In some instances, those fleeing did not make it over the river. In May 1854, a white man and a woman, her face covered by a veil, boarded a steamer on their way to Madison, Indiana. When the clerk went below to

---

[3] Louisville *Courier*, December 3, 5, 9, 17, 1853, August 20, 24, 1852, February 11, 1853; Louisville *Journal*, August 20, September 15, 1852; Bogart, "Making Their Way to Freedom," 11, 30; Benjamin Drew, *A North Side View of Slavery* (1856, rpr., New York: 1969), 180–82.

collect the fares, the man paid and then reached behind the woman's back to take a bank note out of her hand. The clerk grew suspicious and insisted that the woman remove her veil, after which it was discovered that she was a slave of a Mrs. Woolfolk of Louisville.[4]

Although the authorities recorded some successes, they, nonetheless, seemed incapable of fashioning a response that could completely stem the tide of escapes. As the frequency of group escapes continued into 1855, one editor despaired: our city, he lamented, seemed to be "infested with a class of negro stealers, who are becoming very obnoxious." In May, Henry, who was owned by Mrs. Cocke, and his wife Violet and their two children, who were owned by Mr. Jack, were driven by an unnamed black man, owned by Judge Nicholas, to the ferry landing in Portland, on the outskirts of the city. The hack was filled with their personal belongings and food. Before they could transfer their belongings to a skiff, they were intercepted by the watchman at Portland. Two weeks later, a group of six did manage to get to New Albany, but were caught by the "honest citizens" of Floyd County. When seven ran away over one week-end in September, the same editor lamented that not a night passes without "one or more running away," symptomatic, he observed, of a "regular and constant stampede" out of the city. The problem continued unabated throughout the decade. The eight who left in one night in April 1858 were part of a "daily and nightly" occurrence during which slaves went off "one, two, three, or a dozen at a time," spurred on by a growing number of abolitionists and "Black Republicans," who were as "thick in these parts as wolves in a prairie." One year later, policeman Dick Moore recovered slaves worth in excess of $6,000 in one month, for which he was paid, in the case of two of them, a handsome reward of $500. Few took much comfort in such successes. Left unsaid was the implied suggestion that slaveholders may have lost just as much, if not more, than they recovered.[5]

Losses along the river from counties to the east of Louisville, while not as dramatic or extensive, were just as worrying. There were regular group escapes out of Boone, Carroll, and Trimble counties, crossing at Lawrenceburg and Aurora, Dearborn County, Madison, Jefferson County, and other points along the Ohio River into Indiana. The three who left R. Wickliffe of Trimble County in August 1853 and were followed to Madison escaped following a shoot-out. Within a month, another eight escaped from the same county and were followed to Madison, where seven were recaptured. By the middle of the decade, one Madison newspaper reported, slaves were fleeing almost

[4] Louisville *Courier*, June 12, 1852, August 26, 28, 1852; Detroit *Tribune*, June 4, 1852; New York *Tribune*, June 9, 1852; Cincinnati *Commercial*, May 16, 1854; New Albany *Ledger*, May 17, 1854.
[5] Louisville *Courier*, March 3, May 15, June 30, September 25, 1855, May 3, 1858, August 10, 1859; Louisville *Journal*, August 10, 1859; New Albany *Ledger*, August 10, 1859; Hudson, *Fugitive Slaves and the Underground Railroad*, 50.

daily from Trimble County. Two fugitives, who were aided by members of the Underground Railroad (UGRR) in Madison, were followed and overtaken by seven slave catchers near Dupont, fifteen miles north of the river. They were subsequently freed by another group of UGRR operatives. About the same time, a Carrollton newspaper recorded the escape of five slaves from a county to the south, all of whom made it safely to Canada. When wintry weather caused the river to freeze in early 1856, slaves used the "ice bridge" to escape. The result, one reporter estimated, was a considerable loss to the "industrial capital of the slave states."[6]

Basing his estimates almost exclusively on reports out of Henderson, Union, and Daviess counties in the Lower Ohio Valley, one historian has estimated that very few slaves escaped from these western counties. As a consequence of the continued expansion of slavery in the area, especially in counties such as Henderson, during the 1840s, logic would suggest that there would be a corresponding increase in flights from the area. Although admittedly difficult to quantify, William Cockrum's account of UGRR activities in southwest Indiana points to a number of group escapes from across the river. Reports out of Indiana reinforce Cockrum's claims. Many of these reports, not surprisingly, dealt with recaptures, but they also provide a fuller picture of the extent of the problem slaveholders in the area faced. While some escapes may have originated in states further to the south, arrests around Vincennes, Indiana, on the Wabash River, a principal avenue of escape, suggest the numbers leaving the Lower Ohio River Valley were larger than previously thought. Early in 1851, officials in Vincennes pleaded with the federal government to appoint a commissioner to deal with the troubling number of fugitive slaves caught in or near the city. There were reports in September 1853 of two groups of escapees, one involving four slaves, followed the next day by another of six. They had for some time been "laying in supplies" and left with permission to attend a frolic a couple of miles away. They were finally caught in Daviess County, east of Vincennes. When John Moore was finally appointed commissioner, he ran into a storm of protest following his decision in 1854 to remand George Givens, who had escaped Union County six years earlier. The following year, eight were taken at the black settlement known as Africa as they tried to board an Evansville and Crawfordsville train. They were returned to Evansville by the conductor and sent back to Henderson, the conductor receiving an estimated $900 for what a local newspaper called "a tall day's work." There was a reported stampede of slaves over a two-week period from Hopkins County in September 1858, involving at least nine slaves, plus what one observer rather

⁶ Louisville *Courier,* August 27, 1853; Cleveland *Herald,* September 2, 1853; *Liberator,* September 9, 1853; New Albany *Ledger,* September 17, 1853; Madison *Banner* (n.d.), in Evansville *Journal,* September 10, 1855; Carrollton *Times* (n.d.), in Louisville *Courier,* June 5, 1855; Lawrenceburg *Independent Press,* May 18, 1853; Dearborn *Register,* February 15, 1856; Madison *Courier,* July 28, 1856.

vaguely described as "several others." Nearly two years later, three were taken outside Vincennes on their way to Canada. Two of four fugitives from the area were captured at the home of a white man in Princeton, Gibson County, by John Gavitt, the sheriff of Evansville; a third was later seized in Illinois across the river from New Harmony. Nothing is known of what became of the fourth. The one major successful escape from the area occurred in early 1855 when three fugitives managed, on their second attempt, to make it to Canada via Ashtabula, Ohio.[7]

There is no way to tell if James Armstrong, or any of the others who fled, had a destination in mind. There is evidence to suggest, however, that here, as elsewhere along the divide between slavery and freedom, that not a few escapees opted to settle a safe distance away from the place of their enslavement but yet close enough to those they left behind. The black settlements that were established over the years close to the river in southern Indiana suggest that former slaves were keen to stay in touch with family and friends. But the passage of the Fugitive Slave Law, and Indiana's "Negro Exclusion Law" of 1852 – the enabling legislation of Article XIII of the 1851 Indiana Constitution, which prohibited the settlement of African Americans in the state – resulted in the dismantling of a few of these settlements. Former occupants moved further north into the state and into Michigan. An untold number also set their sights on Canada. In fact, Moses Bard had offered to get James Armstrong and Edward to Canada. Word of the Canadian refuge and the best ways to get there filtered back to Kentucky through word of mouth and through letters written by former slaves to family and friends who were left behind. The unnamed slaves who escaped in late 1857 only to return a few months later for what one newspaper described as a "brief visit" would have carried word of the benefits of freedom in Canada. It appears that both Bard and Shadrach Henderson had spent time in Canada. One Cincinnati newspaper described them as Canadian citizens, "having emigrated there some years ago from New Albany." They had returned to the area, the same newspaper reported, "to assist some colored friends off by the underground line." George Washington Carter, a barber who owned considerable property in New Albany

[7] John Michael Crane Jr., "Slavery on the Edge of Freedom: The Lower Ohio Valley in the Antebellum and Civil War Era," (PhD, Vanderbilt University, 2009), 123, 137; Salafia, *Slavery's Borderland*, 209; William M. Cockrum, *History of the Underground Railroad As It Was Conducted by the Anti-Slavery League* (1915, rpr., New York: 1969); Darrel E. Bigham, *On Jordon's Banks. Emancipation and Its Aftermath in the Ohio River Valley* (Lexington,KY: 2006), 15; Henderson *Reporter* (n.d.), in *Liberator*, September 23, 1853; Ripley *Bee*, July 23, 1853; New Albany *Ledger*, June 19, 1854; Vincennes *Gazette*, September 26, 1855; Evansville *Journal*, August 11, 19, 1853, February 15, 1854, September 27, 1855; *Western Sun*, June 12, 1858; Hopkinsville *Press* (n.d.), in Louisville *Courier*, September 2, 1858; Madison *Courier*, September 4, 1858. There were reports that five fugitives from Henderson were captured near Vincennes in August 1859. Evansville *Journal*, August 23, 1859; Ashtabula *Sentinel*, March 29, 1853.

and an ally of Bard and Henderson, traveled frequently to Canada, where two of his sons were being educated.[8]

Whatever the source of the information, it is clear that slaves contemplating escape were well informed about conditions and opportunities in Canada. One correspondent of a Massachusetts newspaper recalled a conversation with a Louisville slave in his hotel room who inquired if he had ever been to Canada. The slave was convinced that the living conditions of African Americans there were considerably better, or as he put it, they were living "real smart." The slave also spoke of efforts by slaveholders and city authorities to disabuse slaves of misplaced notions about the benefits of living in freedom in Canada. Slaves were told that fugitives who made it there were abandoned to fend for themselves and experienced such high levels of starvation that they had "to eat one another." Proponents of slavery took every effort to paint Canada as a cold, unhealthy wilderness, a place where black people could find neither comfort nor the welcoming embrace of family and friends. But these messages fell on deaf ears. Slaveholders latched onto and reprinted stories of former escapees who chose to return to Kentucky. On Tom's return, for instance, it was reported that he found that "freedom in Canada was worse, far worse, than slavery in Kentucky...that a free nigger had to work harder...and eat less than in slavery...that freedom was a humbug and...his home in Louisville [was] far preferable." When a Dr. Robert Vaughn went to Chatham, Canada, in an unsuccessful attempt to persuade his former slave to return, he reported that life in the black settlements was "miserable in the extreme."[9]

Runaways who made it safely to Canada wrote frequently to friends and family left behind, extolling the benefits of the country. Authorities in Louisville did all they could to stem the flow of such letters. In this they had some success, building several cases against local opponents of slavery on letters from the Free States and Canada found in their possession. During a raid on the home of John C. Long, described as a "crippled white dyer and scourer," who had agreed to help Alfred, a slave of Mrs. Pierce Butler, escape, the police found a cigar box filled with letters from Long's brother, who had lived in Westport and Chillicothe, Ohio, in which he asked for a description of Alfred he could include in a free pass that would allow Alfred to travel to Canada unmolested. On the back of one of the letters Long had copied the details to be included on the pass.[10] Reports of such incidences, which were given ample coverage in

---

[8] Louisville *Courier,* January 11, 1858, December 24, 1853; Cincinnati *Commercial* (n.d.), in *Pennsylvania Freeman,* January 12, 1854; Pamela R. Peters, *The Underground Railroad in Floyd County, Indiana* (Jefferson, NC: 2001), 81–83, 124–26. On black settlements in southern Indiana see Xenia E. Cord, "Free Black Rural Communities in Indiana. A Selected Annotated Bibliography," 4, typescript, Indiana Historical Society, Indianapolis, Indiana.

[9] Springfield *Republican,* December 12, 1857; Louisville *Courier,* July 19, October 28, 1857.

[10] Louisville *Courier,* October 6, 8, 12, 16, November 5, 1855. Long's case dragged on for almost one year before he was sentenced to four years in the state penitentiary. On appeal he was granted a second trial, which resulted in a hung jury. Louisville *Journal,* October 22, 23, 1856;

local newspapers, rather than dissuade slaves from leaving, only added to the allure of Canada.

James Armstrong's first failed attempt to escape might have prompted him to seek the assistance of Moses Bard and Shadrach Henderson. Even if many slaves took the initiative to escape without the aid of others, the evidence points to the existence of a group of individuals, black and white, men and women, free and enslaved, some residents of the city, others who lived across the river in Jeffersonville and New Albany, and others who were outsiders, all of who played a pivotal role in the movement to get slaves out of the city. Some acted alone, others as part of a wider but amorphous network that proved as difficult for local authorities to pin down as it has been for historians trying to piece together the complexities of this form of resistance to slavery. At the heart of the network was a free black population in the city, which, when combined with those in New Albany and Jeffersonville, was as large as that of the Cincinnati, Ohio, metropolitan area. Something similar, if not as extensive, existed in and around Madison, Indiana, to the east. There, an organized and efficient network had been active until 1846, when some of its most active members decided to move their operation elsewhere. George Baptiste, for instance, relocated to Detroit. Elijah Anderson shifted his operations upriver to Lawrenceburg, Indiana, where he maintained extensive communications with colleagues in Sandusky, Ohio. He also kept a second home in Detroit. Following the breakup of the Madison network, activities in the area were sustained by Chapham Harris, who ran operations from his forty-acre farm three miles outside the city. He worked closely with Richard Daly, a slave in Carroll County, Kentucky, until Daly escaped with his family in October 1857. Operations in the Lower Ohio River Valley, as Michael Crane has shown, were much smaller.[11] These clandestine operations to the east and west of Louisville were a thorn in the side of local authorities.

Louisville authorities were frustrated in their efforts to break up what they saw as a ring of conspirators. They did succeed in bringing some individuals to heel, but the goal of destroying the cell proved singularly elusive. Knowing

Louisville *Courier,* October 21, 1856; J. Blaine Hudson, "Crossing the 'Dark Line': Fugitive Slaves and the Underground Railroad in Louisville and North-Central Kentucky," *Filson Historical Quarterly,* 75 (2001), 50–52.

[11] Hudson, *Fugitive Slaves and the Underground Railroad in the Kentucky Borderland,* 25; Rush R. Sloane, "The Underground Railroad of the Firelands," *The Firelands Pioneer,* 5 (1888), 44; Diane Perine Coon, "Reconstructing the Underground Railroad Crossings at Madison, Indiana," typescript in the Madison-Jefferson County Public Library; John W. Blassingame, *Slave Testimony. Two Centuries of Letters, Speeches, Interviews and Autobiographies* (Baton Rouge: 1997), 519–21; Salafia, *Slavery's Borderland,* 165; Bigham, *On Jordon's Banks,* 23; Crane, "Slavery on the Edge of Freedom," 123; Mark Allan Furnish, "A Rosetta Stone on Slavery's Doorsteps: Eluatherian College and the Lost History of Jefferson County, Indiana," (PhD, Purdue University, 2014) who challenges the view that the cell was destroyed as a result of an attack on the black community.

the dangers involved, these individuals deliberately avoided the creation of formally structured organizations and instead chose to act in small groups that disbanded and went their separate ways soon after a plan was effected. Each escape, especially those involving groups of slaves, was generally seen as the work of the UGRR. But no one seemed to know who its members were, how its operations were financed, or even how slaves managed to slip through the cordon of policemen and watchmen appointed expressly to prevent escapes. Laws were passed prohibiting ferry operators from taking blacks across the river unless they could show required documents. Skiffs had to be secured and oars removed. Recaptured slaves were promptly taken to police court in an effort to determine who had provided assistance. When, for instance, James Armstrong was captured the second time, Moses Bard and Shadrach Henderson were arrested in Cincinnati, brought back to Louisville, and examined in police court. Although Henderson did implicate a prominent free black resident of Louisville, the examination failed to prove that he was involved in the failed escape. As a precaution, Henderson was held in prison under suspicion of involvement in another unrelated escape. At the same time, Bard was held over to appear at the next session of the circuit court. Yet no one seemed to be able to decipher exactly how the local UGRR operated or who its operatives were. No impartial observer could have examined the pattern and frequency of escapes and not come to the reasonable conclusion that there must have been a measure of coordination. It is the nature of that collusion that proved so elusive and at times drove the authorities to distraction. The frustration is evident in the tone of editorials following periods of heightened escapes. "Our city," one newspaper lamented, following a bout of group escapes, "seems infested with a class of negro stealers, who are becoming very obnoxious." On another occasion, the same editor wrote of the existence of a "gang of scoundrels...who are engaged in the running off of negroes."[12]

There were slaves who helped other slaves escape yet chose to remain behind. Leonard, a slave of John Moore, was accused of helping "Old Ben." In an effort not to raise suspicion, Ben was to cross the river in the company of a group of white boys. While the authorities were able to stymie the efforts of Leonard and Ben, they consistently failed to unravel the system developed by Ralph, the slave of Roman Catholic Bishop Spaulding, who for many years was suspected of helping slaves escape. On one occasion, Ralph was arrested for assisting four slaves owned by different Louisville residents in an unsuccessful escape attempt. The four were caught in a hack driven by a "boy named Carrol" as it neared the river. Although Ralph was given thirty lashes for his involvement in the plot, questions about a wider scheme remained frustratingly unanswered.[13]

---

[12] Louisville *Courier*, December 24, 1853, March 12, 1855, December 4, 1856.
[13] Louisville *Courier*, August 21, 25, 1855, September 20, 1853, January 8, 1857, May 31, 1851. There is a John Moore in District 2 who owned twenty-one slaves but there is no way of proving that this is the same person who owned Ben.

There were white women and men, as well as free blacks, who aided escapes. At times there was some coordination between them, but its extent and duration is not always easy to determine. Mary Affleck, a white dressmaker, for instance, was accused in 1854 of "enticing" Henry, a slave of Dr. Gross, to escape. Evidently, Affleck bought two train tickets from an agent of the Jeffersonville Railroad Company at its office using the name Mrs. Watts. She also made arrangements for a hack to pick up Henry near dawn and take him to the ferry. It is not clear what went wrong, but Henry was caught and Affleck arrested at her home for what one newspaper gleefully described as the "latest and cutest abolitionist dodge." When Affleck's home was searched the police found receipts for a box and two trunks that had been sent to Chatham, Canada. The fact that Affleck bought two tickets suggests that she or someone else intended to travel with Henry. If she did intend to travel with Henry, it raises questions about a possible relationship that went beyond simply aiding a slave to escape, the sort of relationship which flew in the face of both law and convention. Months earlier, Sarah Ann Lucas – who was born in Ohio, and later settled in New Albany – was accused of assisting Amanda, a slave of Benjamin J. Adams, to cross over to New Albany, where she was registered as Mary Jackson, a free person born in Ohio. Lucas owned two houses, one in New Albany, the other in Louisville. She was arrested during a visit to Louisville in January 1854 and charged with aiding in Amanda's escape. The authorities, however, could not prove that she was involved and so the case against her was dropped. But she was held to bail of $600 for good behavior for one year. Holding someone over to good behavior was standard practice in cases where the evidence of collusion was inconclusive. It was also an expression of frustration, of an inability to tie a suspect to an escape. Nothing is known of what became of Amanda.[14]

Blacks and whites frequently collaborated. When Mary escaped from J. G. Mather, the owner of a furnishings store, in December 1853, she was hidden in the home of Georgina Stephenson, a free woman of color, then taken to Dudley C. Jones, a free black cabinetmaker, where she was dressed as a boy and was about to be transferred to the home of another free black when they were all apprehended. Mary's testimony in police court implicated Jones, who was sent to jail to await trial at the next sitting of the circuit court. There is no evidence that Jones was ever brought to trial. But Stephenson was sentenced to two years in the state penitentiary. The police had William Lewis, a forty-five-year-old carpenter, and Dick Buckner, a free black laborer, under

[14] Louisville *Journal*, April 7, 1854; Louisville *Courier*, April 7, 8, 10, 1854; *Liberator*, May 12, 1854; *Pennsylvania Freeman*, May 4, 1854; Peters, "Gateway to Freedom," 16–17; Hudson, "Crossing the 'Dark Line,'" 49. Henry and Mary Messler, described as an indigent white couple, were arrested for harboring Peter, a slave of B. E. Pollard, in their home for three weeks before he was discovered by police. So, too, was Mary McCarty described as a "middle aged white woman." Both reports implied that they were waiting for an opportunity to get the slaves across the river. Louisville *Courier*, July 19, 1853.

surveillance for some time after two slaves, Buckner's stepdaughter and her child, escaped, were caught, and returned in February 1858. A trunk filled with women's clothes was found in Lewis' room, as well as a daguerreotype of the child. Several railroad tickets, a carpetbag of clothes, and a bible and books belonging to Harrison Laville, who had fled with his wife and daughter to Canada earlier, were found at Buckner's. They also retrieved a letter from J. Wesley Ray, a fugitive slave from Shelby County now living in Chatham, thanking Buckner for forwarding his cloak. It was discovered that Buckner also kept a copybook in which he listed the names of slaves, many of whom had escaped recently. Both Lewis and Buckner were described by one reporter as secret agents of the Republican Party and "conductors of the Underground Railroad," major threats to slave interests in the city. They were both sentenced to two years in the state penitentiary.[15]

The majority of cases heard in police and circuit court involved free blacks. George Akin, for instance, was brought to police court on suspicions of encouraging Jim, a slave of James T. Thompson, to escape. Jim testified that Aiken was to row him across to New Albany. When caught, Jim was "loaded down with plunder" – all the clothes he possessed including three pairs of pants, two coats, and four shirts. But because Aiken was not caught in the act the courts could do no more than hold him over to good behavior for one year at $500. In early 1855, William Jeter was charged with attempting to run off Celia, a slave of a Mr. Young of Shelby County. Celia had been hired out in Louisville, where she formed a relationship with Clairborne Overstreet, a free black. When Celia and Overstreet got word that Young was planning not to renew the hire, they made plans to escape. But Young got wind of their plans and while Overstreet was in Jeffersonville buying train tickets for their escape to Canada the master had Celia arrested at Jeter's home.[16]

No other free black frustrated local officials more than James Cunningham, a musician who, according to the census, was born either in England or Bermuda. A man of considerable means, Cunningham was described by one local newspaper, rather dismissively, as "the well-known Professor of the polite art of dancing." For many years, Cunningham had provided entertainment on passenger steamers traveling the Ohio River and, it appears, used his connections on both sides of the river to help slaves escape. In fact, Cunningham may have been at the center of a small cell of subversives that included William Harding, a black riverboat steward, and George Washington Carter, both residents of New Albany. Cunningham, Harding, and others traveled unannounced to Pittsburgh in 1852 to attend the Free-Soil Party meeting, where they met Frederick Douglass, Martin Delany, and Henry Highland Garnet and

---

[15] Louisville *Courier,* December 9, 17, 19, 20, 1853, August 18, 20, 1858; Louisville *Journal,* August 14, 16, 17, 18, October 28, 1858; Register of Prisoners, 1855–1861, Kentucky State Library and Archives, Frankfort, Kentucky.

[16] Louisville *Courier,* October 25, 1853, January 12, 1855.

other leading black figures in the party. They also took out a subscription to Douglass' newspaper, which they had posted to Harding in New Albany to circumvent the prohibition against abolitionist materials in Louisville. Harding got the newspaper to Cunningham by rowing it across the river and hiding it among the sheet music in Cunningham's piano. Cunningham was suspected of having a hand in many escapes from Louisville in the early part of the decade, including that of James Armstrong, whose clothes were found at his home. The police also found letters from Calvin Fairbank to Cunningham and his wife following Fairbank's capture for helping a slave escape in 1851. He was also suspected of being involved with Moses Bard and Shadrach Henderson. In fact, it was Henderson who implicated Cunningham in Armstrong's attempted escape. But try as they might the authorities could not lay "the ropes on him," as one reporter ominously put it. When, in 1855, Cunningham visited the court in support of a friend – a rather brazen act of defiance given that he was under surveillance – he was arrested on suspicion of aiding an unspecified number of slaves escape. It was an act of desperation, for the police had no evidence to tie Cunningham or his wife directly to any specific escape. Instead, he was charged with assisting an unspecified number of unnamed slaves to flee. Not surprisingly, the case had to be dismissed for a lack of evidence. But in an effort to intimidate him, Cunningham was forced to post bail of $500 and to be on good behavior for one year.[17]

Cases involving cooperation between men and women across racial lines pushed up against the laws, rules, and traditions laid down by slave societies. They also grated on racial sensibilities, as they sometimes involved amorous relationships that threatened to undermine the racial order. They spoke to a potential for the sort of social disorder that could subvert the system. Testimony and reports of William Lewis' involvement in the attempted escape of Dick Buckner's stepdaughter took pains to point out that he was seen frequently with black women in public and that many of them visited his rooms. As his landlord testified, "negro women [were] in constant habit of going into his room at unusual hours." The testimony got so graphic that the judge felt the need to step in and stop what he thought were unnecessarily prurient details. In 1858, the city seemed transfixed by the story of two outsiders, W. Mottley, a white man, and Mahala Harris, a free black woman, on their way west from Richmond, Virginia. The chief of police grew suspicious, had them arrested, and cabled Richmond for information. Harris and Mottley, who it was claimed had "plenty of money," easily made bail and crossed the river to Jeffersonville, where they rented rooms. The authorities in Richmond responded promptly

---

[17] W. H. Gibson, Sr., *History of the United Brothers of Friendship and Sisters of the Mysterious Ten in Two Parts. A Negro Order* (Louisville, KY: 1897), 30–34; Louisville *Journal*, April 6, 1855; Louisville *Courier*, April 6, June 22, 1855; Peters, "Gateway to Freedom," 28–29; Peters, *The Underground Railroad in Floyd County, Indiana*, 123–24. My thanks to Pen Bogart for information on Cunningham.

that Mottley had abandoned his wife and six children in destitute conditions. The police chief threatened to arrest Mottley a second time if he "did not disgorge some of his money for the benefit of his wife." Mottley was forced to hand over $900 of the $1,000 in his possession.[18] On this occasion, the cad had met his match, and, it appeared, society's standards had been upheld.

But a couple of years earlier the police's investigative abilities were tested by a fugitive case that involved proven sexual relations across racial lines. Rachel, twenty-six, described as "a lady of light color" and the only slave of John C. Wetherley, a fifty-year-old grocer, escaped to Chatham, Canada, in November 1856 with the assistance of F. George Cope, a well-known white grocer who had moved to the city from Philadelphia some years earlier. Cope evidently had written Rachel a pass and arranged to have her accompanied by an unnamed white man. Rachel had long taken in washing for Cope. But there was clearly more to the relationship, for, according to witnesses, she was also a frequent visitor to Cope's home, where she was in the habit of spending an inordinate amount of time, long enough, one witness recalled rather quaintly, "to transact any business they might have to do." During these visits Cope would follow her upstairs when she went to put away his clothes. But this witness rather sheepishly refused to "say what they did" while upstairs, leaving it to the imagination of the packed courthouse. Cope later admitted that Rachel had become his "wife under Heaven," and that their "sacred vows" were registered "before God and the throng that surrounds the throne of angels." They had planned Rachel's escape with the understanding that, once the excitement caused by her escape blew over, he would close up shop and join her in Canada. As he told her in one letter, he was deeply in love – so much so that he had "lost all interest in business of any kind."

Two weeks after Rachel's escape, Cope sent her a package containing flannels, bars of soap, yarn, stockings, boxes of sardines, perfume, hair oil, and a Bible, in which he wrote "to Rachel, by her affectionate husband, George." Cope also contacted William Gilchrist, a free black former resident of Louisville now living in Chatham, who frequently visited his old home and was suspected of involvement in the UGRR. But Cope's love may have been misplaced. In August 1857, John Wetherley made a trip to Chatham in an unsuccessful effort to persuade Rachel to return. Although she declined, she handed over Cope's letters and the Bible he had sent her. It is likely Rachel had formed a new relationship in Chatham and so wished to sever connections with Cope. The two letters became the basis of Wetherley's suit against Cope for the abduction of his slave. Cope was examined in police court and later sent to trial in circuit court. The result of the case, which was not heard until January 1859, turned on a close examination of Cope's handwriting. In spite of all the evidence linking the two romantically, the jury deadlocked on whether Cope had participated in

---

[18] Louisville *Journal*, May, 14, 1858.

the escape because, according to one wag, there were too many "amalgamating and kidnapping difficulties" that could not be resolved. Cope faced a second trial in October and again the jury could not agree on his guilt or innocence, by which time he had languished in prison for two years.[19] Such relationships across the racial divide were taboo and the guardians of social conventions in both the South and the North did all they could to prevent them.

The perennial concern about the existence of a UGRR cell in the city masked a larger concern about the level of outside interference, much of which, it was assumed, was the work of unidentified white men. The worse fears of slaveholders were confirmed in November 1851 when Calvin Fairbank, a Vermont-born and Oberlin-trained minister, was picked up in Jeffersonville for helping Tamar, a twenty-five-year-old slave of Alfred. L. Shotwell, a commercial merchant, escape. This was Fairbank's second brush with Kentucky law. In 1844, not long after his graduation, he and Delia Webster, who had also briefly attended Oberlin, and with whom he ran a school in Lexington, Kentucky, were convicted of helping Lewis Hayden, his wife, Harriet, and their son, Jo, escape. Their route took them through Maysville, Kentucky, across the river to Ripley, Ohio, and then on to Canada. Webster was sentenced to two, Fairbank to fifteen years in the state penitentiary. Webster was pardoned five weeks later. Fairbank served four years before he was released. Within a few years, both were back in the area. She moved to Madison, Indiana, where she planned to open a school. She also bought a farm in Trimble County, Kentucky, across the river from Madison, which she planned to cultivate using free labor but which many slaveholders believed, with some justification, was to be a base from which to siphon off slaves. Fairbank returned in 1851, ostensibly to retrieve the remains of his father who had died, and was buried, in Kentucky while trying to obtain a pardon for his son. But it was clear that Fairbank's return had more to do with his deep-seated commitment to undermine the system by helping slaves to reach free territory.

It is not entirely clear how or when Fairbank made contact with Tamar. Witnesses at his trial recalled seeing him in the streets outside the Baptist church that Tamar attended. In fact, Fairbank had written William Lloyd Garrison in October, reporting on his visit to slave pens in the city from which "young men and women, who seem fit for refined society" were sold. But Fairbank also pledged not to become involved; he had every intention, he wrote, of keeping out of "the lion's jaws." "Humanitas," who claimed to have been in the area three weeks after Fairbank's arrest, offered a slightly different explanation: Fairbank had only decided to cross over from Jeffersonville, he

---

[19] Louisville *Courier*, August 28, 29, 31, 1857, January 19, 21, 1859; Louisville *Journal*, January 19, 20, 21, October 17, 18, 19, 1859. For a discussion of the impact of similar relationships in Britain at the end of the eighteenth century see Catherine Molineux, "Britain's Rebel Slaves," a paper presented at Vanderbilt Dialogues: A Law School-Department of History Workshop, April 3, 2009.

wrote his local newspaper, when he got word that a slave woman was seeking help to escape. Whatever the proximate reasons leading up to his involvement, Fairbank met Tamar in Louisville, and rowed her across the river to Jeffersonville in a leaky skiff. There he rented a buggy, he told the owner, to take them to Charlestown, to the northeast. Their plan was to travel northwest to Salem, where Tamar would catch a train for Indianapolis. On the way, the buggy broke down and Fairbank had to seek assistance. Those who came to his aid would later testify that he was seen traveling with a woman who fit Tamar's description. That phase of the plan completed, Fairbank returned to Jeffersonville, intending to leave the next day to retrieve his father's remains. By this time, Louisville police had crossed the river and were making inquiries when Fairbank was spotted outside the hostler's stables and arrested after a scuffle. As if to add to the drama of the case, when captured Fairbank at first refused to give his name. When he finally relented, he claimed to be James S. King. But Fairbank was recognized by witnesses who saw him in town before Tamar's disappearance. He was examined and sent to trial in the March sitting of the circuit court.

Webster's arrival by steamer soon after Fairbank's arrest raised fears that they were again acting in concert. As it turned out, her arrival was purely coincidental. The history of their connections, however, was so compelling that observers saw a conspiracy. As a result, Webster felt it necessary to distance herself publicly from Fairbank's actions. "I was surprised and grieved," she wrote for public consumption, "that a man of his profession should condescend to lay himself liable to censure from those who had befriended him. But I regret most of all his seeming want of honor and moral obligation." What many at first did not realize was that Laura Haviland, an abolitionist with long-standing connections to the UGRR, who, at the time, was in Cincinnati and had tried to dissuade Fairbank from going to Kentucky, had arrived with clothing and blankets for the prisoner. It was mistakenly assumed at first that she was Webster. Although she was allowed to visit Fairbank in jail, public reaction to her presence and opposition to her mission, forced her to leave town soon after. The combination of Webster's denunciation and Haviland's forced departure depressed Fairbank. He found himself alone with no visitors in the three months between Haviland's departure and his trial. As he told Frederick Douglass, he was left "rolling the ball all alone."

As far as Fairbank was concerned, his capture in Jeffersonville was illegal, both under the Fugitive Slave Law and the laws of Indiana. He and his supporters insisted that police from a Slave State had no legal authority to arrest someone in a Free State, even if the person was suspected of helping slaves escape. If an arrest was to be made, he argued erroneously, it had to be done by Indiana authorities, who would have to await a request from the governor of Kentucky before the prisoner could be legally extradited. Although the law passed in 1850 did not specifically envisage a police force from a Southern state arresting suspects in a Free State, it did permit duly constituted Southern slave catchers to apprehend runaway slaves. But Fairbank was right in one respect: the law did not permit Southern police officers to make arrests in Free States without warrants from a court. Fairbank's was a novel argument that had little chance of swaying a jury of Louisville residents troubled by interference with slave property from outsiders. Fairbank did not realize that the law's remit had expanded in the short time since its passage to include actions such as those of the Louisville police, so long as they did not lead to public disorder. As far as Louisville prosecutors were concerned, abducting slaves "was one of the highest crimes known to the law," a crime that had to be "driven from the State and country, or the State [would] be disrupted, and society unhinged and broken up." The perpetration of such crimes, according to one Northern editor, had "caused so much ill feeling in one portion of the Union against another portion," that "the friends of order and the Union" had been laboring sedulously trying to arrest such activities. The jury took less than twenty minutes to convict Fairbank of aiding in the escape of Tamar. He was sentenced to fifteen years in the state penitentiary, where he would languish until pardoned in 1864.[20]

Alfred Shotwell might have taken comfort in Fairbank's conviction and punishment, but he never managed to recapture Tamar, in spite of his best efforts. One historian has estimated that he spent much more money trying to reclaim her than she was worth. To the impartial observer, such actions seemed impractical, even irrational. Surely, there came a point when a rational person would conclude that a reclamation was not worth the expenditure in either time or money. But to slaveholders such as Shotwell, who in 1860 owned ten slaves, the loss of a slave mattered economically, personally, and even politically. Tamar had been allowed to hire herself out over the years and, as a consequence, had lived relatively freely. In return, Shotwell was guaranteed a regular income. The arrangement also provided Shotwell the comfort of knowing that he was a benevolent master – one who permitted his slave a large measure of freedom. Consequently, Tamar's decision to flee – and it was her decision – denied him a guaranteed income and at the same time shattered illusions of authority and control. It was also an act of betrayal that very likely diminished Shotwell's standing in the community, where a slaveholder's ability to control the actions of those he owned mattered. Outside interference further undermined such authority. Regardless of the number of slaves they owned, most slaveholders reacted similarly when one of their slaves escaped. As property, slaves had to be reclaimed at all cost. It was the same calculation that drove James Rudd to

[20] Louisville *Courier*, November 11, 17, 18, 19, 27, 1851, February 25, 1852; Louisville *Journal*, November 18, December 8, 1851; *Liberator*, November 7, December 12, 1851, January 23, March 5, 12, April 23, 1852. Many of these issues of the *Liberator* contain reprints of articles from *Frederick Douglass' Paper*, the Worcester *Spy*, and the *Ohio Times*. New Albany *Ledger*, November 19, 1851; Toledo *Blade*, March 9, 1852; Randolph Paul Runyon, *Delia Webster and the Underground Railroad* (Lexington, KY: 1996), 11–21, 62–65, 126, 153, 159, 161–62; Calvin Fairbank, *Rev. Calvin Fairbank During Slavery Times* (1890, rpr., New York: 1969), 46–53, 56–57.

invest considerable sums in the recapture of James Armstrong and to sell him when the slave's recalcitrance seemed to endanger Rudd's authority as well as his investments by possibly influencing others to leave.

Louisville suffered one other recorded instance of outside white interference with slave property. In early 1856, twenty-year-old Mary Jane, a slave of Joseph Newland, a merchant, was caught on the ferry as it docked in New Albany. According to one report, she was "gorgeously attired," dressed in a "rich black silk robe," hung with "floating flounces" with a "magnificent fur" draped across her shoulders and her face covered with a "thick green veil," a disguise of choice, it seems, of many "fair-skinned" enslaved women trying to reach free territory. All on board the ferry thought Mary Jane was white, until her companion, Elisha Hyller, a white man from New York, recklessly lifted the veil and kissed her as they were about to disembark, convinced, one supposes, that they had made it safely across the river. Mary Jane was arrested immediately. Hyller, however, continued into New Albany, where he was later arrested. Two train tickets to Michigan City and Detroit were found on him, as well as money, which, Newland testified, belonged to Mary Jane. Like James Armstrong, Mary Jane might have been covering the cost of her escape. It was, Newland pointed out, her second escape attempt. Hyller was held at $1,200 bail, to appear before the circuit court in January 1857. The case, however, was continued to October, but there are no reports of its resolution.[21]

East of Louisville, Delia Webster quickly ran afoul of slaveholders. As they had anticipated, a number of slaves escaped from the area following her purchase of a farm in Trimble County. A meeting of Oldham County slaveholders in February 1854 declared that, since her arrival, several slaves had "run off from their masters." Some estimates put the number at twenty, costing slaveholders as much as twenty to thirty thousand dollars. The only way to solve this problem was to insist she leave the state. Weeks later, Webster received an ultimatum from a committee of her neighbors: she must either agree to sell her farm and leave the area immediately or she would be "mobbed at the dead of night," her fences torn down, her animals slain, her barn and outhouses burned, her "dwelling houses blown up, and yourself assassinated." Neither man nor beast was to be spared. Webster was subsequently arrested on suspicion of helping slaves escape and placed in a cell without heating at a time of year when the temperature was unseasonably cold. She was finally released following a hearing in a nearby county on the grounds that her arrest was illegal and unwarranted. Webster temporarily returned to the farm, where she supervised spring planting before leaving for the relative safety of Madison, Indiana. Her experiences, her biographer has written, finally convinced her that the "days

---

[21] Louisville *Democrat* (n.d.), in Evansville *Journal*, February 23, 1856, and Chicago *Tribune*, February 26, 1856; Louisville *Journal*, February 20, 1856, January 16, May 12, October 15, 1857; Louisville *Courier*, February 21, 22, 1856; Hudson, *Fugitive Slaves and the Underground Railroad in the Kentucky Borderland*, 80.

of her farm's usefulness were finally over." In early summer, an arrest warrant for her involvement in the 1844 escape of Harriet and Jo Hayden arrived from Lexington. Evidently, her earlier conviction had only addressed her part in Lewis Hayden's escape. Webster took refuge in Indiana, where she was held in jail under an extradition request from the governor of Kentucky. The hearing, however, resulted in her release. For the rest of the decade, Webster continued to be a thorn in the side of Trimble County slaveholders.[22]

Late one night in late May 1854, Thomas Brown, a fifty-seven-year old Irishman, passed through Evansville, Indiana, after delivering three female slaves at "the Canada depot in Petersburg," Pike County, the "Southern terminus" of the UGRR in the southwestern part of the state. According to one reporter, this route afforded the fastest and most secure means of getting fugitives to Canada, sometimes in less than three days and nights, faster, he estimated, than other known routes.[23] Brown and his wife had earlier lived in Indianapolis, moving later to Cincinnati before finally settling in Henderson County in the Lower Ohio River Valley in spring 1850 with their two young daughters. Mrs. Brown set up a millinery store in Henderson and Thomas peddled her wares from a small covered wagon in northern Kentucky and across the river in southern Indiana. Drawn by two horses, the wagon's curtains could be lowered to protect the goods and conceal anything else Brown may be carrying, or as one reporter put it, the wagon was "well adapted to [the] business, either [of] negro stealing or notion peddling." Not long after the Browns' arrival, slaves began to disappear in significant numbers from Union, Henderson, Hopkins, and Daviess counties. Thomas soon came under suspicion. On his way back from Petersburg, he was followed by Marshal John Ward and Sheriff John Gavitt of Evansville into Kentucky. Confronted, Brown drew his revolver and "defied the officers to take him." He was captured later at his home by a "large band of ruffians" led by Ward and Gavitt and sent to Union County accused of aiding the three slaves' escape for which Brown was reputedly paid $200 by a "free negro" living in the vicinity of Petersburg.

Following Brown's arrest, an indignation meeting of area slaveholders led by Archibald Dixon, a former lieutenant governor of Kentucky, and later chosen to fill the unexpired Senate term of Henry Clay following his death in 1852, and A. J. Henderson, like Dixon a prominent slaveholder, raised $100 as an expression of thanks to Ward and Gavitt. The meeting promised an additional $400 if Brown were convicted, and elected a committee to visit Mrs. Brown to

---

[22] Frankfort *Commonwealth*, February 27, 1854; Louisville *Courier*, March 18, 1854; Indianapolis *Journal*, March 18, 1854; New Albany *Ledger*, March 17, June 23, 1854; Madison *Courier*, August 16, 1854; Louisville *Journal*, July 6, 23, 24, 1854; New York *Times*, July 24, 1854. An account of Webster's activities following Fairbank's conviction is covered in Runyou, *Delia Webster*, 184–203.

[23] Petersburg is at the center of much of Cockrum's account of UGRR activity in southwest Indiana. Cockrum's *History of the Underground Railroad*, 16, 80.

persuade her to leave the state. She and her daughters moved first to Princeton in Gibson County, Indiana, and later to Indianapolis, where she eventually opened a millinery store. Brown was held in the Morganfield prison for twelve months before his case was heard, a prison notorious, even by contemporary standards, for its filth and lack of amenities. Many suspected the delay gave the state time and opportunity to find witnesses willing to implicate Brown in the escape. When he was finally brought to trial, Brown was convicted on the testimony of an odd cast of witnesses. James Steele, an African American from Gibson County, Indiana, described by a Brown supporter as an "inordinately avaricious" and "inferior yellow looking, woolly-headed, ignorant fellow," was bought off, many suspected, by Kentucky slaveholders. The prosecution also called on a fourteen-year-old Irish boy living with a black family in Evansville and a Mexican with the unlikely name of John Cassday, both of whom had been sent into Kentucky to retrieve horses and who seemed, from their testimony, to have run into Brown at every turn. Brown claimed that Cassday was in fact an Indian who described himself as a Mexican because, under Kentucky law, Indians could not testify against white men.

Brown was convicted and sent to the state penitentiary, where he met a number of other abductors, including Fairbank. If the Morganfield prison was described as a "Calcutta Hole," the penitentiary in Frankfort was little better. Brown was forced to labor beyond his physical capabilities and age, was sometimes flogged with the cat-o'-nine-tails, and had two teeth knocked out when he protested the treatment meted out to another prisoner. Fairbank confirmed the harsh treatment meted out to abductors in the state penitentiary. Counting every blow, Fairbank claimed that he received "thirty-five thousand, one hundred and five stripes from a leather strap" between 1854 and 1862. Brown was finally released in May 1857, having served his full sentence. He joined his family in Indianapolis, where friends and supporters organized a meeting to welcome him home. Brown insisted that he was innocent of the charges, although he admitted that "where he found a poor slave running for freedom, naked and hungry," he took him in, fed, and clothed him. In spite of the many hardships he and his family had endured, Brown told the meeting, they remained committed to helping the "suffering slaves of Kentucky."[24]

Weeks after Brown's arrest, Eli Bryant, a white resident of Evansville, was asked by a Mrs. Carter to go to Kentucky to fetch her son, a free black, so he

---

[24] New York *Tribune*, November 3, 1855; *Free Democrat*, July 6, 1854; Indianapolis *Journal*, May 25, June 12, 1857; J. Winston Coleman, *Slavery Times in Kentucky* (Chapel Hill, NC: 1940), 215; Crane, "Slavery on the Edge of Freedom," 140–42; Thomas Brown, *Brown's Three Years in the Kentucky Prisons, From May 30, 1854, to May 18, 1857* (Indianapolis: 1857) in Paul Finkelman, ed., *Slave Rebels, Abolitionists and Southern Courts. The Pamphlet Literature, Series IV, Vol. 2* (New York: 1988), 603–19; Fairbank, *Rev. Calvin Fairbank*, 11; James M. Pritchard, "Into the Fiery Furness. Anti-Slavery Prisoners in the Kentucky State Penitentiary, 1844–1870." My thanks to Pritchard for a copy of his paper. Union County Circuit Court Records, Box 80, Bundle 392. My thanks to Michael Crane for a copy of the court records.

could visit his sister, who was seriously ill. Why the son could not cross into Indiana on his own is unclear. Bryant and the son were arrested in Henderson, the boy on suspicion that he was a fugitive slave, and Bryant as an agent of the UGRR. The son was soon cleared, but Bryant was kept in prison for six months then released on a bond of $1,000 and the promise never to return to Kentucky. Described as a "poor man," Bryant was forced to go on a begging tour to raise money to pay his lawyer's fees and other debts he had incurred while in prison.[25] Henry Vinson, a free black, had also been accused of collusion with Brown, but was released for a lack of evidence. In both cases, the authorities in Union County adopted an approach that, by 1854, had become common practice: when in doubt, suspects were held on suspicion of aiding unspecified slaves to escape. It was admittedly unusual to hold someone for as long as Brown and Bryant were, but those who had lost slaves were determined to do whatever it took to protect their property. The fact that Brown was not caught with slaves, either in Indiana or Kentucky, mattered little. Having come under suspicion, the "outsider" had to be captured and punished. If, in Fairbank's case, Louisville police officers had captured him in Jeffersonville without a warrant, in Brown's case, he was taken by Evansville police in Kentucky without even the pretense of a warrant. In an effort to stem the tide of escapes, state lines had become legally porous in these borderland areas. Although Brown had offered the standard defense of his actions – namely, that he had not interfered with slave property but had simply followed biblical dictates to help the poor and feed the hungry – his willingness to use violence to defend himself when confronted by John Ward and John Gavitt was fairly typical.

Slaves were also assisted by African Americans from outside the state. In May 1860 the Louisville police arrested A. H. Scott and John Henry at a local hotel. They had been in town almost four weeks. Scott claimed to be a painter from Covington, Kentucky; Henry, described as a mulatto, admitted that he had escaped from Macon, Georgia. Scott, who at first was thought to be white, turned out to also be a fugitive from Georgia, a fact which raises intriguing questions about the system's ability to identify the race of potential subversives. But what worried the authorities even more was the discovery of daguerreotypes of black men and women in Henry's possession, suggesting that the two had targeted specific slaves for assistance. This was not the first time, as we have seen, that photographic images of slaves had been found on those suspected of assisting slaves to escape. At a time when the reproduction of such images was becoming increasingly popular and cheap, opponents of slavery, it appears, had availed themselves of the most recent technological advances to subvert the system's ability to protect itself. But where these prints were made, and who provided them, remains a mystery. This was a particularly troubling development – much more significant, the police seemed to think,

[25] Indianapolis *Journal*, July 30, 1855.

than the discovery of the book found at Dick Buckner's home listing the names of slaves, many of whom had disappeared.[26]

As the Thomas Brown case demonstrates, violent confrontations over the recovery of slaves had grown increasingly common in the wake of the Fugitive Slave Law. These were violent times and violent places. In September 1857, Charles, a skilled blacksmith and the slave of Dr. C. H. Ditto of Brandenburg, Meade County, a few miles west of Louisville, crossed the river into Harrison County, Indiana, as he had done many times before, to shoe horses. This time he did not return, instead going north to Corydon and then to Brownstown, where he caught a train on his way to Canada. He was assisted by Charles Bell, whose father David owned and operated the ferry between Brandenburg and Mauckport, Indiana. Working with Charles Bell was the Maryland-born Oswell Wright, an African American who had immigrated with the Bell family to Indiana in 1829. Wright lived in Corydon and was responsible for getting Charles to Brownstown. Ditto flooded Brownstown with posters and handbills in an effort to intercept Charles. They failed to stop his flight, but they did produce a couple of witnesses who claimed to have seen Wright and Charles together. Wright, they claimed, had informed them that the Bells were involved in the escape and were planning to bring out Charles' wife Mary Ann. Two weeks after Charles' escape, David Bell, aged seventy, Charles Bell, and Oswell Wright were kidnapped by a group of Kentuckians and taken to jail across the river. They were indicted for assisting in the escape of Charles and were sent to jail to await trial.

Horace Bell, twenty-eight, and his older brother John, who had immigrated to California at the height of the gold rush, returned to Indiana when they got word of their father's imprisonment, and hired an attorney to defend the three. Horace Bell had developed a reputation as a man of action. Soon after arriving in California, he joined the ranks of William Walker's disastrous filibustering expedition to Nicaragua, at the end of which he was one of only a handful of survivors of a harebrained scheme that had gone terribly wrong. When the case was postponed, the Bell brothers took matters into their own hands, went to Brandenburg, and forced the jailer, at gunpoint, to release their father and brother. Evidently, Oswell Wright and been moved to another jail and so was not rescued. The Bells were pursued and shots were exchanged as they crossed the river. Days after the rescue of his father and brother, Horace Bell was nabbed in the streets of New Albany by five well-armed men who disarmed him and took him to Louisville, where he was transferred, during the night, to Brandenburg. A public meeting in New Albany denounced the invasion from across the river and demanded Horace's immediate release. Nothing, a New Albany editor insisted, could "palliate" kidnapping. There were methods under the law that Kentuckians could have used to ensure Horace was brought to

---

[26] Louisville *Journal*, May 9, 1860; Louisville *Courier,* May 9, 10, 1860.

trial. In fact, the editor took pains to point out that the dispute had nothing to do with slavery. It was simply a "violation of our rights as an independent commonwealth." Relations between the two states had always been cordial, he observed. In fact, the people of Floyd and Harrison counties had done everything asked of them to ensure that the laws of "the constitutional compact" had been executed. A meeting in Louisville came to similar conclusions and city editors did what they could to diffuse a dispute that had the potential to disrupt relations between the cities. But the situation spiraled out of control when it was discovered that Horace had been moved out of Brandenburg to a safer location. Supporters decided that Horace had to be rescued. The governor of Kentucky got wind of their plans and called out the Kentucky legion and the Meade County Rangers. Twenty-five from New Albany, armed with "muskets, pistols, a swivel and ammunition," boarded a rented ferry to Brandenburg. They were joined by a larger group from Harrison County who traveled overland. Disaster was averted, however, when a committee of Brandenburg citizens offered to meet with a committee of the "invaders." The two sides quickly struck an agreement: Horace would plead guilty, with bail set at $750, to appear in November. Sureties would be provided by the Brandenburg group. Soon after his release, Horace returned to California. Those who posted the bond guaranteeing his appearance were later released from the payment by the governor.[27]

Ironically, in the excitement over the kidnapping and release of Horace Bell, Oswell Wright seemed to have been forgotten. While the charges against David and Charles Bell for aiding in the escape of Charles were dropped and Horace Bell was given a hero's welcome on his return to New Albany, Wright was tried and sentenced to five years in the state penitentiary, where he remained until he was released in June 1864 at the age of forty-five.[28] There he would have

[27] New Albany *Ledger,* October 25, 27, 29, 30, November 2, 1858; Louisville *Democrat* (n.d.), in New Albany *Ledger,* October 26, 1858; Louisville *Journal,* October 25, 26, 27, 28, 30, 1858; Louisville *Courier,* November 1, 4, 1858; Evansville *Journal,* October 27, 28, 29, 1858; Ripley *Bee,* October 30, 1858; *Anti-Slavery Bugle,* October 30, 1858; Maxine F. Brown, "The Role of Free Blacks in Indiana's Underground Railroad. The Case of Floyd, Harrison and Washington Counties," (Report prepared for the Indiana Department of Natural Resources, Division of Historic Preservation and Archeology, n.d.); Earl O. Saulman, "Blacks in Harrison County, Indiana. A History," (typescript copy in the Corydon Public Library); Peters, *The Underground Railroad in Floyd County, Indiana,* 86; Charles H. Money, "The Fugitive Slave Law of 1850 in Indiana," *Indiana Magazine of History,* XVII (September 1921), 287–97; Stanley Harrold, *Border War, Fighting Over Slavery before the Civil War* (Chapel Hill, NC: 2010), 181–82.; Benjamin S. Harrison, *Fortune Favors the Brave. The Life and Times of Horace Bell, Pioneer Californian* (Los Angeles: 1953), 75–85. For William Walker see Robert E. May, *The Southern Dream of a Caribbean Empire, 1854–1861* (Baton Rouge: 1973), 77–110.
[28] Brown, "The Role of Free Blacks in Indiana's Underground Railroad," 3–10; "Register of Prisoners Confined in the Kentucky Penitentiary, 1855–1861." Following Horace's release, "Chapman's Varieties," a New Albany theater company, put on a drama, "Horace Bell," which drew enthusiastic audiences and positive reviews from the press. New Albany *Ledger,* October 30, 1858.

met, as Thomas Brown did, others who were imprisoned for assisting slaves to escape. One of these was the blacksmith Elijah Anderson, a major figure in the UGRR cell operating out of Madison, Indiana, in the 1840s. As we have seen, Anderson later moved his center of operations upriver to Lawrenceburg, Dearborn County, close to the Ohio state line, where he continued to funnel escapees through Sandusky and Detroit to Canada. In 1855, a Sandusky coworker estimated that Anderson had led eight hundred slaves to safety since the passage of the Fugitive Slave Law using the Cincinnati and Cleveland Railroad. In 1856, Anderson was caught in Kentucky, where he had gone to take out the wife and four daughters of a freed man. His capture may have simply been the result of bad luck, but many suspected that he had been betrayed. The day of his capture, William Anderson, a black minster and a member of the Madison cell of the UGRR, and no relation of Elijah's, was released by a Kentucky court. When arrested, William was found carrying incendiary abolitionist literature in his carpetbag. He was taken to trial in Louisville, where witnesses claimed he had been involved in assisting slaves out of Kentucky. But no evidence was provided linking him directly to any one escape. As in so many other similar cases where connections could not be proven, William was forced to post a hefty bond guaranteeing good behavior before he was released. But what seemed to weigh equally heavily against him was his active involvement in an unsuccessful effort to elect a Republican governor of Indiana. With the elections over, one reporter speculated, the "drunken old negro" who had been hired by the Republican Party had turned his attention to stealing slaves. Even an otherwise sympathetic "Native of Indiana" dismissed such reasoning as sheer nonsense. Why, he seemed to imply, would the Republican Party hire "a silly and harmless old darky, who hardly knows enough to go in when it rains? And the report that 'he is a leading Abolitionist preacher of the Methodist Episcopal Church North,' and all that, is rich enough to give an ostrich a sour stomach."[29]

When Elijah Anderson was first arrested in Carrollton, Kentucky, he had in his possession, according to one report, a "quantity of Canadian and Detroit

[29] Sloan, "The Underground Railroad of the Firelands," 44; John Tibbets, "Reminiscences of Slavery Times Written by Grandfather Tibbetts in his 70th Year." My thanks to the late Gwen Crenshaw, who studied with me at Indiana University, for a copy of the Tibbetts' reminiscences. Louisville *Courier*, December 15, 1856; Louisville *Journal*, December 15, 1856; Madison *Courier*, May 30, August 30, December 16, 31, 1856, January 2, 1857; New York *Tribune*, December 22, 1856; Fergus M. Bordewich, *Bound for Canaan. The Underground Railroad and the War for the Soul of America* (New York: 2005), 202–06; Keith P. Griffler, *Front Line of Freedom. African Americans and the Forging of the Underground Railroad in the Ohio Valley* (Lexington, KY: 2004), 115–17. It appears Kentucky authorities had targeted the leaders of the movement in Madison. In November, Chapman Harris was arrested in Louisville, reportedly with a bowie knife, pistol, "lucifer matches," and "power and ball in abundance" on him. He was held to bail at $200 for good behavior for six months and told to leave the state in five minutes. Undated Louisville newspaper clipping in the Chapham Harris folder, Madison-Jefferson County Public Library; Louisville *Journal*, November 25, 1856.

money" which, it implied, was to be used to get slaves to freedom. He was released for a lack of evidence but immediately rearrested and taken for trial in the Bedford Circuit Court, where he was found guilty of running off two slaves from Trimble County and sentenced to eight years and eight months in the state penitentiary, a rather unusual term of imprisonment. No one else incarcerated in the state prison for assisting slaves to escape received a sentence that included additional months. Elijah was found dead in his cell "the day Lincoln delivered his inaugural address" from what was described as an inflammation of the membrane of the heart. The coincidence of William Anderson's release and Elijah's imprisonment on the same day raised suspicion among many African Americans that William had betrayed Elijah. William, Keith Griffler has written, became the "unsuspecting victim of the desire for retribution." William maintained that he had been falsely accused. By implicating him in the arrest, William speculated, friends of Elijah's were hoping to win his release. Had he been the cause of Elijah's arrest, William argued in his defense, the authorities surely would have held him as a material witness.[30]

All along the southern shore of the Ohio River slaveholders felt particularly vulnerable to the continuous loss of slaves and what they believed were depredations committed by outsiders. In places such as Mason, Bracken, Pendleton, and Boone counties close to Cincinnati, and in the Lower Ohio River Valley, they formed associations to protect their property from outside interference and to limit what one observer called a "leave-taking fever" among the slaves. The eastern association, which first met in Minerva in November 1852, as well as a similar, if smaller, organization, formed in Henderson in August 1855 in the wake of the Thomas Brown case, had as their objective the security of slaves in those areas. At about the same time as the formation of the Henderson association, five special river patrols were appointed to police "stretches of the Ohio River shoreline." The insecurity of slave property along the river was worsened by the free flow of trade and communications in the area. Fairbank's capture was proof enough – if proof was ever needed – that the authorities had to be vigilant if they wished to exclude abolitionists, lecturers, itinerant peddlers, and missionaries who came spreading their "poisonous sentiments" against slavery. Although Louisville slaveholders did not follow the course adopted by their Mason and Henderson counterparts, they did devise their own system of defense. Faced with recalcitrant slaves, some slaveholders, such as James Rudd, chose to cut their losses and sell the offending slave. Dr. Henry Bullitt, a wealthy hemp plantation owner in Jefferson County, for instance, decided to sell Charles, convinced he was about to be "seduced off by the

---

[30] Louisville *Courier*, December 19, 1856, June 19, 1857; Louisville *Journal*, December 19, 1856, June 19, 1856; Madison *Courier*, June 20, 1857; Pritchard, "Into the Fiery Furnace," 13. Curiously, Elijah's name does not appear in the Register of Prisoners. William J. Anderson, *Life and Narrative of William J. Anderson* (Chicago: 1857), 57; Griffler, *Front Line of Freedom*, 115; Furnish, "A Rosetta Stone on Slavery's Doorsteps," 302.

conductors of the underground railroad," who, he wrote his wife, were "constantly at their dirty work." These individual precautions were reinforced by an extensive policing system developed by the city over the years. By the mid-1850s the city employed a police chief, a night police division, as well as several detectives. There were also sheriffs and watchmen. These were supplemented by a wide array of sentries, captains and clerks on steamers, and neighborhood informants, all of whom had the power to stop and apprehend suspects. At the back of this policing system was a slew of state and local ordinances that required ferrymen and stewards on steamers, under pain of substantial fines, to ensure that only African Americans with the requisite documents were allowed on board, and a court system, both police and circuit, that worked in tandem to adjudicate cases. As we have seen, those suspected of assisting slaves to escape, or even harboring them, were brought to court. While the courts played a pivotal role in defending the system, the rate at which suspects were convicted was surprisingly low. The one recourse available when conviction proved unlikely was to hold the suspect over to good behavior at a cost that many must have found prohibitive.[31]

Whatever impediments the system threw up, slaves continued to escape into Indiana on their own initiative or with the aid of free blacks and sympathetic whites. In the fall of 1853, Jim, a slave of James T. Thompson, was caught by local police officers on his way to the river. Suspecting that he had an accomplice, the police dressed another black man in Jim's clothes and sent him to the river. But the suspect, George Akin, a free black, saw through the ruse and walked away. As we have seen, Akin was brought to police court anyway, but the police failed to tie him directly to the plot and had to release him with bail set at $500. Toward the end of the decade, local editors could do no more than wring their hands as slaves continued to escape "one, two, three or a dozen at a time." Jim could have crossed the river by ferry or skiff to either New Albany or Jeffersonville, where he would have boarded a train to either Salem or Seymour before making a connection to Indianapolis or Cincinnati, or he could have gone by boat first to Madison, then on to Cincinnati. Attempts to travel by steamer were frequently thwarted by vigilant stewards and clerks. Louisville police also went regularly to Madison and Cincinnati to arrest both fugitives and those suspected of assisting them.[32]

Even when escapees made it to Indiana they were confronted by railroad agents as well as white Hoosiers sympathetic to slavery or eager to reap the sometimes lucrative rewards offered for the recapture of fugitives. When Obadiah Buckner sued the Jeffersonville and Indianapolis Railroad Company

---

[31] The Minerva meeting is discussed in the following chapter. For the Henderson association see Louisville *Courier,* September 5, 1855; Evansville *Journal,* September 28, 1855; Henry Bullitt to Sallie, Louisville, February 5, 1858. Bullitt Papers, Filson Historical Society; Crane, "Slavery on the Edge of Freedom," 135.

[32] Louisville *Courier,* October 25, 1853, April 29, 1858.

for refusing to carry him because he could not provide evidence that he was free, he was awarded $20 by a justice of the peace. The company immediately appealed to Judge Bucknell of the Clarke County Circuit Court, who reversed the decision, ruling that, because Article XIII of the new state constitution denied Negroes the rights of citizens, the restriction imposed on Buckner was not unreasonable. To Louisville observers, Bucknell's decision had wider significance for Kentuckians; a negative ruling could have materially affected "the safety of their slave property." Had the case not been won on appeal, one Louisville editor surmised, there would have been no need for a UGRR; fugitive slaves could have used the railroad unimpeded. Those opposed to Bucknell's ruling suspected that the railroad had adopted the policy of requiring African Americans, even those such as Buckner, who were free, to show their free papers, because the majority of its shares were held by Louisville investors. Other railroad companies in the area did not adopt similar policies, although periodically during the decade they did impose restrictions as a direct response to a spike in the number of fugitives who used the rail systems to reach deep into Indiana. Ferry companies also adopted similar measures. Late in the decade, owners of the Portland and New Albany ferry, for example, announced that black drivers of hacks, drays, and wagons would not be permitted to board their ferry unless they were traveling with their owners or were properly "vouched for, or [had] a pass."[33]

In Clarke County and elsewhere in southern Indiana there were what was described as "small posses" who caught and returned fugitive slaves for which they were paid handsome rewards. In Madison, fugitive slaves and those who assisted them had to run a gauntlet laid down by Wright Rea, the local sheriff. John Gavitt, his counterpart in Vanderburgh County, proudly boasted of having returned thirty to forty fugitives by 1854. A local editor warned slaves to avoid Evansville, where they would find it "impossible to elude the vigilance of our Evansville officers." Within three years the entire black population of the county was under siege. The precipitating event was a dispute between the Lyles, a black family, and a white neighbor, Thomas Edmonds, over a pig owned by the Lyles that had destroyed Edmonds' crops. When Edmonds tried to capture the pig he was shot and seriously hurt. The Lyles' home, part of a rural community of about two hundred blacks in Union Township, was attacked by about seventy-five armed whites. The Lyles were able to repulse the initial assault, during which three whites were seriously injured, as was the brothers' mother. The next day, a larger group of whites gathered to "drive out and exterminate the blacks." Sheriff Gavitt defused the situation by promising to persuade the Lyles to leave, which they did, joining members of their extended family at Lyles Station, a black settlement to the north in Gibson County. In

---

[33] Louisville *Courier*, August 14, 1854; New York *Tribune*, August 8, 18, November 21, 1854; *Anti-Slavery Bugle*, December 2, 1854; *National Era*, December 7, 1854; New Albany *Ledger*, July 29, 1859.

the summer of 1860, a notice warned those blacks, whom it described as "lazy, worthless, drunken and thieving," many of them expelled from other cities and towns in the state, to leave within five days.[34] Evansville was not safe for African Americans – slave or free.

Kentucky slaveholders depended on and worked closely with the residents of Evansville and other southern Indiana towns and cities. An incident that occurred in 1858 was fairly typical of such cooperation. Three slaves – Smallwood, Lindsey, and Isaac – escaped from N. M. Hicks of Henderson County. Hicks sent out posters and handbills offering a $500 reward for their recapture. He also crossed the river with two other Kentuckians in pursuit of the fugitives. In Evansville he hired John P. Evans and a number of others at $5 per day. Evans was also supplied with a horse. The group divided teams, each one going in a different direction hoping to increase their chances of capturing the runaways. The group, including Hicks, Evans, and the two Kentuckians, set a trap for the three fugitives eight miles outside Vincennes on the route of the Evansville and Central Railroad, where the three were recaptured. Evans soon after brought suit against Hicks, claiming he had only received $30 in per diem payments and none of the advertised reward. In his defense, Hicks insisted that Evans had approached him in Evansville and offered his services at the agreed per diem rate. The other Hoosiers, he pointed out, were hired at the same rate. Hicks prevailed. The case demonstrates the extent and levels of cooperation between slaveholders anxious to reclaim their property and those who stood to benefit financially from the hunt for fugitives. By "law and custom," Michael Crane has argued, "slavery's borders extended well beyond the Ohio River."[35]

The greatest danger of recapture, not surprisingly, lay in southern Indiana. Those who made it past the middle portion of the state stood a better chance of reaching their goal. Of the dozens of recaptures identified only a couple seemed to have occurred north of Indianapolis. A few months after the passage of the Fugitive Slave Law, a mother, aged fifty-five, her thirty-five-year-old daughter, and the daughter's son, aged eight, were lured across the river "under pretext of receiving money coming to them." The family, claimed by Dennis Tramell of Fort Smith, Arkansas, had been living in New Albany for about four months. The three were taken by their captors on a steamboat bound for Arkansas but were rescued by locals at Caseyville in southwest Kentucky, along the Ohio River, where they had lived before moving to New Albany.

---

[34] Evansville *Journal*, July 22, 23, 24, 27, 28, 29, 30, August 1, 1857, April 16, 21, 1858; Sandusky *Commercial Register*, July 31, 1857; *Anti-Slavery Bugle*, August 22, 1860; Darrel. E. Bigham, *We Ask Only a Fair Trial. A History of the Black Community of Evansville, Indiana* (Bloomington, IN: 1987), 14–15. My thanks to Pat Sides, Archivist, Willard Library, Evansville and Darrel Bigham for information on this event. On Lyles Station see Carl C. Lyles, Sr., *Lyles Station Yesterday & Today* (Evansville: 1984).

[35] New York *Tribune*, August 28, 1854; Evansville *Journal*, February 15, 1854; John P. Evans v. H. M. Hicks, Henderson Circuit Court Equity File. My thanks to Michael Crane for his notes on the case. Crane, "Slavery on the Edge of Freedom," 44, 137–39.

A "number of medical gentlemen" who examined the mother concluded that she did not have a "trace of African blood in her veins." In fact, her grandson had been attending school in New Albany with white children. The head of the family, who was born in Baltimore, had moved with her husband to Arkansas, where she and her daughter were abducted by Indians who murdered her husband. Tramell continued to insist that the family were slaves. After a hearing in New Albany, they were extradited to Kentucky, from which Tramell hoped to return them to Arkansas. The decision aroused considerable opposition on both sides of the river, not, according to one editor, because of resistance to enforcing the Fugitive Slave Law, but because they were "Anglo-Saxon." A public meeting in New Albany, chaired by the mayor, raised a portion of the $600 ransom Tramell demanded; the balance came from Louisville. This was, as one New Albany editor put it in what must be one of the great understatements, "the most singular and interesting case," one that excited great curiosity and was covered in newspapers in New York, Philadelphia, and Washington, DC. The message of the case, he insisted, was the levels of sympathy shown by the citizens of Indiana and Kentucky, a Free and Slave State, for the family. In Caseyville, he wrote, a "slave-holding mob" had taken them away from the claimant, who was threatened with "summary vengeance." He was proud that "our citizens acted as they did. Under very aggravating circumstances they had exhibited their respect for the law; and in so promptly subscribing for the liberation of these persons, have shown that they are not insensible to the calls of benevolence and charity." This was not just an interesting case – it was bizarre, if for no other reason than the family was considered, by all who knew them, to be white. No one seemed to question the judge's decision to remand the three to Tramell in the face of overwhelming evidence that they were white or even why those interested in gaining the family's release would have agreed to pay the ransom. Not even abolitionists, who made much of the case as part of their criticism of the Fugitive Slave Law, used it to discuss the likelihood that whites could and did sometimes become victims of slavery. The story's final irony may very well be that, like so many other fugitives who were recaptured, the names of the family members were never revealed.[36]

Months later, Mitchum, otherwise known as Stephens, a blacksmith, was captured near Vernon, where he lived with his wife and four children. He was claimed by George W. Mason of Daviess County, Kentucky, from whom he had escaped nineteen years earlier. Taken before a local justice of the peace,

---

[36] New Albany *Ledger*, November 12, 15, 27, 30, 1850; New York *Tribune*, December 2, 1850; Louisville *Journal* (n.d.), in New Albany *Ledger*, December 2, 3, 1850; New Albany *Bulletin* (n.d.), in New York *Tribune*, December 12, 1850; *National Era*, December 12, 1850; Madison *Courier*, December 4, 1850; Lexington *Observer & Republican*, December 4, 1850; Maysville *Eagle*, December 3, 1850; Money, "The Fugitive Slave Law of 1850 in Indiana," 270–72; Peters, *The Underground Railroad in Floyd County, Indiana*, 11–12.

Mitchum's lawyers called for a dismissal on the grounds that only commissioners and judges could adjudicate cases under the terms of the Fugitive Slave Law. The justice of the peace rejected their objections and proceeded with the hearing, ruling in favor of Mason solely on the evidence of a witness for the slaveholder who admitted that he had not seen Mitchum since his escape, but who had no doubt that he was the slave claimed. Critics of the law had insisted, from its inception, that, because it did not recognize statutes of limitation, individuals such as Mitchum who were, for all intents and purposes, free, could be re-enslaved. Months later, Martha Rouse, thirty-five, was kidnapped from the small black settlement near New Philadelphia, Washington County, north of Jeffersonville, by five white men, while her husband, Charles, was away working on their farm. Martha had escaped ten years earlier and settled in New Albany, where she met and married Charles, who was unaware that she had ever been a slave. They later moved to New Philadelphia. A group of whites from the area followed and caught up with the kidnappers in Jeffersonville and agreed to their $600 ransom demand. The kidnappers, however, insisted they would only conclude the negotiations in Louisville. Once there, they reneged on their promise and nothing more was heard of Martha.[37]

Technically, these were cases that came under the purview of the Fugitive Slave Law, but as far as the communities from which Mitchum and Rouse were taken were concerned they were kidnappings. As in other Free States, the danger of being kidnapped in Indiana was real. In an incident eerily similar to that of Solomon Northup – who was kidnapped, in 1841, from upstate New York and sold into slavery in Louisiana, where he spent twelve years before regaining his freedom – Eli Terry, a free black, living in Hamilton County, had accompanied his employer, James Carter, on a business trip in 1842 to St. Louis, where Terry was taken and sold into slavery in Texas. In 1849, the yearly meeting of Friends of Indiana got word of his whereabouts and sent a delegation to Texas, who, "after considerable difficulties," won his release in late 1850. Other cases of kidnapping occurred closer to home. James Cotes, a resident of Gibson County, was taken off of a train in Jeffersonville, in May 1854, on his way home from a business trip. He was beaten, cut, and subdued in full view of travelers at the train station. On the way across the river to Louisville, he was recognized by the steamboat captain, who intervened and had the kidnappers arrested. A month later, a crowd in Columbus forced suspected kidnappers to release a boy they had in their custody. And four men were indicted in Greensburg, in the spring of 1855, for kidnapping two men and selling them in Kentucky. Two of the accused fled the state; the others were brought to trial in October but

---

[37] Madison *Courier,* March 5, 1851; Madison *Banner* (n.d.), in *Anti-Slavery Bugle,* March 29, 1851; Emma Lou Thornbrough, *The Negro in Indiana. The Study of a Minority* (Indianapolis: 1957), 107–09; Coy D. Robbins, *Reclaiming African Heritage at Salem, Indiana* (Bowie, MD: 1995), 103; Money, "The Fugitive Slave Law of 1850 in Indiana," 272–73.

were freed on the grounds that the state's anti-kidnapping laws conflicted with the Fugitive Slave Law, which, the judge ruled, took precedence.[38]

When, in 1857, Elijah Wilson and his wife, residents of Gibson County, arrived in Martinsville, Morgan County, on their way home after a visit to Canada, they were arrested by two lawyers, Warren P. Quick and Robert E. Evans, assisted by Velonious H. Cummings, a cabinetmaker, as suspected fugitive slaves. The three took the Wilsons to the home of an acquaintance, where they tried to cajole them into admitting they were fugitive slaves. When that failed, they offered the town jailer $10 to use his brace of horses and wagon to take the two to Edinburgh, where they planned to catch a train to Louisville. The jailer, however, refused to become involved. They then tried unsuccessfully to hire a wagon to take the Wilsons to Gosport, where they could catch a train. Failing to generate any interest in their plans, the three finally released the Wilsons. They were arrested, soon after, for attempted kidnapping. The hearing was moved to an adjoining township but the prosecution was unable to attend because the White River was blocked by ice. When the case did come to trial, the charges were dismissed, the judge giving them what a local editor called the "rogue's refuge, the legal doctrine of 'doubt.' " The editor, who had some rather disparaging things to say about Elijah Wilson, dismissing him as a "poor half-witted mulatto," was, nonetheless, very critical of those who participated in the kidnapping. He was stunned that Quick saw nothing wrong with what he and the others had done. "I'm a democrat," Quick ranted at the editor, "and I believe in slavery. By G-d slavery is RIGHT, and I would like to see it extended into every d – b state in the Union. I could walk up to the ballot box, with my hand upon my heart, and vote to make Indiana a slave state....What is the d – b nigger made for? Why, to be a slave to the whites, and I hope to see the time when I can own niggers....I have travelled in the slave states, and seen the benefits of slavery, and I believe every state ought to recognize the institution. Slavery is the natural condition of every d – b nigger." The editor seemed a little surprised that the incident had taken such a partisan turn. After all, kidnapping was illegal. But Quick spoke for many who believed that Indiana was best served if African Americans were persuaded or forced to leave the state. But the fact that he and the others had violated the state's anti-kidnapping law, in effect since 1810, and had gone unpunished was further confirmation of the general hostility to the presence of blacks in Indiana.[39]

---

[38] Pittsburgh *Gazette*, November 22, 1850; New Albany *Ledger*, April 20, 1854; *The Fugitive Slave Law and Its Victims* (New York: 1861), 39, 48; Thornbrough, *The Negro in Indiana*, 102.

[39] Franklin *Republican* (n.d.), in Indianapolis *Journal*, February 11, 1857; *Morgan Gazette*, February 7, 14, 21, 28, 1857. Unfortunately, there are no extant copies of the town's Democratic newspaper, which may have put a different political slant on the incident. See Emma Lou Thornbrough, "Indiana and Fugitive Slave Legislation," *Indiana Magazine of History*, L, No. 3 (September 1954), 214–18 for a discussion of the ways Indiana's anti-kidnapping laws changed in the first two decades of the state's history.

The arrest in Indianapolis of John Freeman in June 1853 exposed the unwillingness or inability of federal and state authorities to curb kidnapping, as well as the general antipathy to the presence of African Americans in the state. Freeman had moved to Indianapolis in 1844 from Georgia, where he was born free. In the years since his arrival he had married and amassed a considerable fortune, which, it was estimated, made him the richest black man in the state. According to Rev. Henry Ward Beecher, who knew him well, Freeman was "universally respected" in the city. Yet when Rev. Pleasant Ellington, a Methodist minister and Missouri slaveholder, claimed that Freeman was his former slave Sam, who had escaped from Kentucky in 1836, the authorities visited Freeman at home and persuaded him to accompany them to the office of the justice of the peace as a witness in an unrelated case. Freeman was taken instead to Commissioner Squire Sullivan's office, where he was charged with being a fugitive slave. Lawyers for Freeman swore out a writ of habeas corpus in circuit court, arguing that until such time as the commissioner decided Freeman's fate the assumption was that he was free and, as a consequence, a state court had the power to address the issue of his freedom. It should not be taken for granted, they argued, that a mere claim was sufficient to keep Freeman in prison. Until the claim could be proven, the state court could and should continue to hear his appeal. No federal authority, they insisted, could seize a free man. It had no more right to do so than a state court had to dismiss a fugitive slave. They did concede that the moment it appeared a seized man was a slave the state's jurisdictions ended. Similarly, if it appeared a seized man was free the jurisdiction of the federal courts ceased. State courts, they argued, were equally competent to address the issue of a person's free or slave status. The judge ruled, however, that all he could decide was whether Freeman was being held legally and by the right authorities. He, therefore, remanded Freeman to the custody of US Marshal John Larne Robinson, who was ordered to hold the accused until Commissioner Sullivan could arrange a hearing. Freeman's lead attorney, John L. Ketcham, called for a delay so witnesses could be brought from the South. Sullivan agreed to a delay of nine weeks, an unprecedented concession – one that was not to be repeated in any other fugitive case. The fact that Freeman was well known in the city may have persuaded the commissioner to grant such a lengthy delay. But he would not accede to the request to release Freeman, even after some of the city's most prominent figures offered to guarantee a substantial bail. Concerned that the city jail was not secure, and worried that blacks were considering a rescue attempt, Robinson made plans to move his prisoner to Madison, which would have taken Freeman away from his family and made consultation with his lawyers next to impossible. Robinson at first rejected counteroffers by Freeman's friends to cover the cost of hiring additional guards at the city jail, and only relented when Freeman agreed to pay the daily jail fee of $3 himself.

While the defense team was awaiting the arrival of witnesses from Georgia, Robinson permitted Ellington and a couple of his witnesses to visit Freeman's cell, where the prisoner was subjected to a physical examination for signs of scars and other body marks that could substantiate the slaveholder's claim. This was not only unusual, it was a brazen attempt to preempt the normal forms of identification that usually occurred during a hearing. Given that the hearing had been postponed, neither Ellington nor his witnesses had until then an opportunity to claim that marks on Freeman's body identified him as the fugitive slave Sam. Allowing the visit to Freeman's cell, Robinson, in effect, had provided the claimant with the means to identify any marks that could be used during the hearing. During the postponement, Freeman's attorneys were busy gathering witnesses. Ketcham visited Georgia and, by mid-July, had returned with Leroy Patillo of Monroe, Georgia, who knew Freeman and knew he was free. By the start of the hearing, five additional witnesses had arrived from Georgia to buttress Freeman's defense. Ellington also brought witnesses to the hearing, including C. M. Jennings, a merchant from Wetumpka, Alabama, and four others from Walton County, Georgia. In addition to the witnesses from Georgia, one of Freeman's attorneys, accompanied by a slaveholder from Kentucky, had gone to Malden, Canada, to interview Sam. They were able to identify the marks on Sam's body – a burn on his left leg below the knee, scars on his back above his shoulder, marks on his left wrist and elbow, his small ears and his "singular feet," on which one toe on each foot were much longer than the others. Sam was also "tall, jet black and full chested" compared to Freeman, who was "six inches shorter, low, heavy-set and was a muddy brown color." When Ellington's son visited Freeman in jail and admitted that he did not recognize the prisoner, his father's case collapsed in the face of irrefutable evidence.[40]

Freeman was forced to dispose of much of his property to meet the cost of his defense. Because the law made no provisions for compensation for those wrongly accused of being fugitive slaves, Freeman had no alternative but to sue Ellington, which he did, claiming $10,000 in damages. The courts, however, awarded him a mere $2,000. But even this he could not collect, as Ellington quickly put his property out of reach. A correspondent from Platte County, in western Missouri, wrote that Ellington had sent his slaves to "parts unknown" and disposed of the rest of his property. Ellington, he wrote, claimed that abolitionists in Indianapolis had robbed him of his property by sending Sam to

[40] Indianapolis *Journal*, June 23, 24, 25, 28, September 3, 22, 23, 1853; Indianapolis *Sentinel*, June 30, July 18, 25, September 1, 3, 1853; *Free Democrat*, September 1, 1853; New York *Independent* (n.d.), in *Liberator*, July 29, 1853; New York *Tribune*, November 16, 1853; *National Era*, July 28, September 15, 1853; New Albany *Ledger*, June 25, 29, 1853; Toledo *Blade*, March 3, 1854; Money, "The Fugitive Slave Law of 1850 in Indiana," 189–91; Gwen J. Crenshaw, "Brother John Freeman's Homecoming Celebration: The Black Reaction to the Freeman Case and the Fugitive Slave Law of 1850," *Black History News and Notes* (February 2003); Dean Kotlowski, "'The Jordon Is a Hard Road to Travel'; Hoosier Responses to Fugitive Slave Cases, 1850–1860," *International Social Science Review*, 79, Nos. 3 & 4 (2003), 75–77; Thornbrough, *The Negro in Indiana*, 115–18.

Canada, substituting him with Freeman, and then sending to Georgia for witnesses to prove Freeman was free. Freeman then turned his sights on Robinson. He accused the US marshal of extortion for forcing him to meet the cost of his imprisonment while awaiting the hearing before the commissioner. Freeman had refused to be transferred to Madison, fearing that, once on the way, there was nothing to stop Robinson from taking him into a Slave State. Furthermore, he pointed out, the Indianapolis jail was secure and so did not need special guards. He also accused Robinson of allowing illegal bodily examinations by Ellington. Freeman at first had refused to be examined but then relented when Robinson threatened to use force. During one of the examinations, Robinson had rapped him on the legs with a cane and demanded he raise his pants legs. On another visit, the jailer, a deputy marshal, and Robinson had ordered Freeman to strip. Later, the deputy marshal publicly apologized for his part in the forced examination. One of the prosecuting attorneys, J. A. Linton, however, denied that Freeman was ever touched during Ellington's visit to the jail. More importantly, he argued that the examinations were in order, for the claimant had every right to examine Freeman's body for scars, "as the question of *identity* was the material question in the case." Robinson, he concluded, had acted properly, for, at the time, the law considered Freeman a fugitive slave. As such, Robinson could not deny the claimant his legal right to examine the suspect.[41]

Indiana senator Jesse Bright came to Robinson's defense with a recommendation to Attorney General Caleb Cushing that the federal government show its support by covering Robinson's attorney fees and possibly moving the case to federal court. In opposition, a large meeting of Free Democrats of Rush County, Robinson's county of residence, condemned the marshal for forcing Freeman to strip and in doing so "prostituting his high and responsible office to the detestable crime of kidnapping." The meeting called on the president to remove Robinson. A Democrat, Robinson had voted against passage of the Fugitive Slave Law while in Congress. Later, he was appointed marshal by President Pierce with the full support of the Democratic Party in Washington and Indiana. In his own defense, Robinson maintained that the fees to cover the guards while Freeman was in jail were not determined by him. Worried that he would be held liable under the Fugitive Slave Law if Freeman were rescued, he decided to move him to a more secure jail in Madison. Hearing this, Freeman's lawyer offered to pay for the guard. Robertson left the final arrangements to his deputy. Had his plans not been opposed, he estimated Freeman could have been held in a secure facility for 40 cents per day. It was Ketchum who had suggested the $3 daily fee to keep Freeman in Indianapolis. Nowhere in his letter does Robinson mention that he planned to move Freeman to a jail on the Ohio River, which, not surprisingly, raised suspicions about his intentions. He

[41] *Free Democrat*, March 2, 16, 1854.

also insisted that at no time did he force Freeman to strip. He did admit asking Freeman to raise his pants legs and to show his shoulder without mentioning why he had made such a request. He had kept his superiors in Washington fully appraised of his actions and they, including the president, had approved of what he had done. Freeman's suit was taken to the state supreme court, which upheld his right to sue the US official, since stripping a prisoner and extorting jail fees, the judges ruled, were unlawful. The court, however, dismissed the suit on the grounds that the case should have been brought in Rush County, where Robinson resided, and not Marion County, where Freeman was imprisoned.[42]

The failure to win either suit left Freeman mired in debt. Friends in Indianapolis established a fund under the care of Calvin Fletcher, a prominent lawyer and banker. Freeman also reported receiving support from elsewhere. But neither the fund nor the outside support was large enough to cover his debt. He also tried to raise additional support during a tour of the Midwest, but this netted only small sums. As a result, the cost of his defense and his inability to recoup the monies he had expended to fight his extradition forced Freeman to liquidate most of his property, including his restaurant. For a while he worked as a painter and laborer. Later, he ran a small oyster bar until he and his wife decided to immigrate to Canada in the early years of the Civil War. They would later resettle in Topeka, Kansas.[43]

As in so many other cases, Freeman's imprisonment reignited a furious debate about the constitutionality, limits, and implementation of the Fugitive Slave Law. Following his release, a meeting of African Americans condemned the law under which such an outrage was permitted as a "disgrace to the Republic; a crime against the humanity of the age; [and] a violation of the laws of God." They called for the law's repeal. Others, including the editor of the Fort Wayne *Sentinel,* would not go that far, although he called for amendments to give "greater protection to free persons of color." As it now stood, he insisted, any free black was liable to be dragged into slavery. Had he not money and friends, the editor had no doubt Freeman would have been sent into slavery. Freeman was not freed by the mercy of the law, Dr. Samuel W. Ritchie, a graduate of Rush Medical College, wrote, but because of "the unprecedented delay for the procurement of testimony which was not contemplated" by it. One irony that did not escape George Julian, a leader of the Free-Soil movement, was the speed with which Southerners came to Freeman's defense while Northern "serviles and flunkys" worked to send a free man into slavery. But

---

[42] New York *Tribune,* November 16, 1853; Indianapolis *Journal,* November 23, 1853; *National Era,* October 6, 1853; *Free Democrat,* February 16, 1854; Money, "The Fugitive Slave Law of 1850 in Indiana," 184; Thornbrough, *The Negro in Indiana,* 117; Freeman v. Robinson, 7 Indiana 321, Supreme Court of Indiana (November 1855).

[43] Pittsburgh *Gazette,* August 13, 1855; Cleveland *True Democrat,* September 7, 1853; Crenshaw, "Brother John Freeman's Homecoming Celebration," 7; Gayle Thornbrough, et al., eds., *The Diary of Calvin Fletcher,* 9 Vols. (Indianapolis: 1977), V, 81; *Free Democrat,* March 16, 1854.

others wondered what alternatives were available to the authorities once Freeman was accused of being a fugitive. The right of rendition was not only guaranteed under the Fugitive Slave Law, it was mandated by the Constitution. Ignoring all the evidence to the contrary, this observer believed that the law did afford ample "protection to the free colored man." Freeman would have found such arguments perverse and a danger to the already limited rights of blacks. So did others. Recognizing the danger, more than seventy blacks left the state for Canada in the days after Freeman's imprisonment. One of them, Thomas Hedgebeth, a free black, who had migrated to Indiana from North Carolina a number of years earlier, decided to leave, he told Benjamin Drew, to "escape the oppression of the laws upon the colored man."[44]

Eighteen months after John Freeman was released from the Indianapolis prison, Marshal Robinson was involved in another case, this one in northeast Indiana. And as in the Freeman case, this one was also without precedent in any Free State. In August 1853, three young slaves – Tom, Jim, and Alfred – escaped from a plantation in Trimble County, Kentucky, seven miles across the river from Madison. Tom and Jim were owned by Daniel M. Payne of Trimble County, Alfred by Mortimer W. Roberts. Daniel Payne's son, Wellington, trailed the three through Madison, first to Napoleon, a small town in Ripley County, then later to Richmond, close to the Ohio state line, where he lost track of them. The three, along with other suspected fugitive slaves, were later seen in Orland, in the far northeast of the state, on their way to Michigan. Concerned about the rising number of fugitives passing through the area at the time, Robinson brought suit against Benjamin Waterhouse and three others for harboring, concealing, and preventing the recovery of fugitive slaves. Waterhouse, who migrated to the area with his brother, John, from Oswego County, New York, had settled in South Milford, LaGrange County, which boasted a strong UGRR cell. John later moved to a farm in Kinderhook, just across the state line in Michigan. Lawyers for the four moved to have the indictments dismissed on the grounds that they lacked specifics; they did not show that the Negroes seen in the area at the time were fugitives, and, if they were, did not say who their owners were. The indictments were also unusual in that they were not the result of a slaveholder or his agent following and claiming an escapee, but were, as one editor observed, the "business...of northern parentage."

The indictments were dismissed, but Robinson promptly empaneled a new grand jury, which reinstated them. The marshal also took the unusual step of financing a search for evidence to substantiate the indictments. He provided $50 to his deputy, Dr. Madison M. Marsh, to visit Kentucky and persuade

[44] *Free Democrat*, September 1, 1853; Crenshaw, "Brother John Freeman's Homecoming Celebration," 5; Indianapolis *Sentinel*, September 1, 1853; Fort Wayne *Sentinel* (n.d.), in Indianapolis *Journal*, September 8, 1853; *National Era*, September 15, 1853; George W. Julien, *Political Recollections, 1840 to 1872* (1884, rpr., New York: 1970), 135; Benjamin Drew, *A North-Side View of Slavery* (1856, rpr., New York: 1968), 276–79.

Payne to pursue the case by accompanying him to Canada to locate the slaves. Marsh took along Cyrus Fillmore, brother of the former president of the United States, who claimed to have seen the slaves on Benjamin Waterhouse's wagon as they passed through Steuben County. March was a particularly zealous deputy. He was described as the "most outspoken of the pro-slavery men in the county." Marsh, Fillmore, and Wellington Payne did visit Windsor, Canada, where they met and interviewed Tom.

The case was heard in Indianapolis in November 1854 before Judge E. M. Huntington. In an obvious effort to win a conviction, the indictments provided the most expansive definitions of harboring and concealing. Under the former, Waterhouse was accused of receiving "clandestinely and without lawful authority" the three fugitives. Concealing was interpreted to mean to "hide, secrete, keep secret, cover, disguise, withdraw from observation or keep from sight." If, the indictments concluded, "the slaves were transported towards Canada by the defendant whereby their services had been lost to their master it is a case of harboring and concealing within the meaning of the statute." But even under this broad interpretation, the prosecution found it next to impossible to prove that Waterhouse had harbored, concealed, or transported the fugitives to safety. Cyrus Fillmore was the only person to claim that he had seen the three in Waterhouse's wagon and to have identified one of them as Tom, whom he later met during his visit to Canada. Under cross examination it became clear that the prosecution's star witness had gotten only a fleeting glimpse of the Negroes as they passed. He was not even certain how many were in the wagon at the time. He would come in for some harsh treatment from unsympathetic editors, one of whom wondered whether a brother of Washington, or any other president for that matter, would have lowered himself to become a slave catcher for the petty pittance of $3 plus expenses. The editor observed that he had known many doughfaces in his lifetime, but "they were brave and honorable men in comparison with Indiana Fillmore." Complicating the prosecution's case further was Waterhouse's son's insistence that Fillmore could not have seen the fugitives with his father, for the people he usually carried were free blacks who regularly passed through the area. His testimony challenged Fillmore to differentiate between who he thought were fugitives and who he thought were free blacks.

The jury, however, found Waterhouse guilty on one count, but recommended leniency. Taking the recommendation seriously, Judge Huntington sentenced Waterhouse to pay a fine of $50 and serve one hour in jail, which he was allowed to spend in the custody of the marshal in the courthouse as the sentencing documents were being prepared. The government was also required to pay the cost of the trial. There were other instances when the convicted were given comparatively light sentences, but none required the government to cover the cost of the case. It is very likely that the unusually light sentence was the only way to secure a conviction. The prospect of Waterhouse going to prison, one observer suggested, would have resulted in an acquittal. Others thought the jury had done its job; it was the judge, clearly sympathetic to the accused, who had imposed such an absurdly lenient sentence.[45]

Aspects of this case raise more questions than they answer. It appears that Washington clearly had a hand in the case coming to trial. Determined to confront those who openly violated the law, members of the administration insisted on the prosecution of the Steuben County abolitionists. Successive Democratic administrations took a similar line in Boston, Chicago, Oberlin, and elsewhere, in an effort to send a message to black opponents and white abolitionists that they would pay a price for their resistance. If Robinson's actions were meant to intimidate local abolitionists, they failed miserably. In the midst of the trial, two groups of fugitives, one of seventeen, the other of five, passed through Orland. There is no doubt that Daniel Payne was pressured to pursue the case against Waterhouse and the others by Robinson, whose expenses were fully covered by the national treasury. In his defense, Waterhouse's attorney mocked the notion that someone could be accused of harboring a fugitive slave when no one was pursuing him. There was no evidence that the persons seen in Orland were escaped slaves. Surprisingly, Judge Huntington dismissed these questions as irrelevant; fugitives, he ruled expansively, and without the benefit of evidence, were those black persons seen in Indiana who were known to be slaves in Kentucky. But the identity of those Fillmore caught a fleeting glance of, at some distance, could not be positively identified. As far as one unsympathetic editor was concerned, Waterhouse must have known that those he was carrying were escaped slaves. All that was necessary, in that case, was to demonstrate that, by his actions, Waterhouse meant "to prevent discovery," a rather imprecise yardstick by which to measure guilt. At no time did the prosecution prove the point that those traveling with Waterhouse were fugitive slaves. The abolitionists may have lost the case, but in the court of public opinion, in Steuben County and other sections of northeast Indiana, they were seen as victims of an unwarranted prosecution.[46]

---

[45] *Free Democrat,* December 14, 21, 28, 1854, May 25, June 6, 8, 1855; Indianapolis *Journal,* December 13, 22, 1854, January 15, 1855; Fort Wayne *Standard,* December 28, 1854, January 4, 25, 1855; New York *Tribune,* December 17, 18, 1854; *Anti-Slavery Bugle,* December 23, 25, 1854; New York *Herald,* January 25, 1855; May Term 1853 Case, United States vs. Benjamin B. Waterhouse, Mixed Case Files, 1838–1913, General Record, 1819–1958, Records of the United States District Court of the Southern District of Indiana, Indianapolis Division, RG 21, National Archives, Great Lakes Region, Chicago; Money, "The Fugitive Slave Case of 1850 in Indiana," 275; Harvey W. Morley, *The 1855 History of Steuben County, Indiana* (n.p.: 1956), 355–56. At the outbreak of the Civil War, Marsh enlisted with the Confederate army and died fighting against the Union. My thanks to Peg Dilbone for a copy of Morley and for sharing her vast knowledge of the history of the area. Jeannie Regan-Dinius, "Federal Court Cases: Holdings at the National Archives, Chicago." My thanks to Regan-Dinius for a copy of her essay. Kotlowski, "'The Jordon Is a Hard Road to Travel,'" 77–78.

[46] John Law to Caleb Cushing, Vincennes, March 16, 1855. Letters Received by the Attorney General, 1809–1870, Northern Law and Order, Reel 5; *Anti-Slavery Bugle,* November 25, 1854; Indianapolis *Journal,* December 22, 1854; *Free Democrat,* December 28, 1854.

The last major fugitive slave case heard in Indiana occurred in Indianapolis in November 1857. John West (or Weston) was arrested in Naples, west of Springfield, Illinois, where he had been living for some time, by Austin W. Vallandingham of Frankfort, Kentucky, his son, and an agent. Vallandingham claimed West had escaped from Louisville in 1854, where he had been hired to work as a fireman on Ohio and Mississippi River steamers. On their way back to Louisville by train, the group had to make a connection in Indianapolis. Samuel Williams, an African American, got wind of their presence and filed an affidavit in the court of common pleas, seeking West's freedom. They also hired a group of prominent lawyers, including George W. Julian and John Coburn, to represent West. Vallandingham's lawyers questioned whether, under Indiana law, a black man could seek a writ against a white man. Judge William J. Wallace ruled that Williams could and freed West. These were "strange times," one city editor marveled, when an "officer would, upon the affidavit of a negro, who complains of no personal injury to himself, but to another, should issue a writ for the arrest of a white man." As West was leaving Wallace's court he was arrested under a warrant issued by Commissioner John H. Rea. Julian and Coburn moved to have the warrant squashed on the grounds that Vallandingham had provided no evidence that West was his slave at the time of his escape, that the Kentucky documents presented to Rea were not properly authenticated, and, finally, that the documents did not give the fugitive's name. In an interesting twist, they also insisted that Vallandingham had violated Article XIII of the Indiana State Constitution by bringing a Negro into the state. Conceding that the documents were deficient, Rea, nonetheless, dismissed the motion to reject the warrant and proceeded with the hearing. Coburn argued that, under the recent Dred Scott ruling, the Supreme Court of the United States had ruled that a slave carried or allowed to go into a Free State was considered free as long as he did not voluntarily return to a Slave State. In the two years that West had worked on the steamer, he had entered Indiana and Illinois on many occasions. Vallandingham, or anyone else, who hired a slave to work on an Ohio River steamer must have done so with the clear knowledge that the slave would have cause to enter the adjoining Free States. Witnesses for Vallandingham claimed that they knew West and his family, all of whom were slaves. In his summation, Julian left no doubt about what he thought the black crowd that packed the hearing room should do if the ruling went against West. "The fugitive act," he thundered, "is a godless law, it is an unutterably infernal law and if its provisions are carried out, it will drag God Almighty from his throne, and inaugurate the reign of the devil upon earth."[47]

In explaining his decision to return West, Rea insisted that the commissioner's role was a ministerial, not a judicial, one. As such, he did not have the authority

---

[47] Indianapolis *Sentinel*, December 3, 1857; Julian is quoted in Money, "The Fugitive Slave Law of 1850 in Indiana," 263.

to decide if, by bringing or allowing West into a Free State, Vallandingham, in effect, had made him free. Rea then fell back on a bit of legally questionable reasoning frequently relied on by other commissioners and not a few Supreme Court justices: his decision, he announced, was not final. "[E]very person so returned may then take his case to court and jury, try the merits and ascertain the fact of his being a slave" in the state in which he resides. Marshal Robinson immediately got together a posse of forty to escort West back to Kentucky. One editor tried to embarrass or possibly intimidate members of the posse, whom he sarcastically dismissed as "patriotic individuals...who sacrificed their domestic comforts at the rate of $2 a day in order to bow in servility to slavery and nigger drivers," by publishing their names. In an effort to delay his return, West's supporters filed a writ of habeas corpus with Judge Wallace, who ruled that Rea's certificate of return was final under the law and that he could not discharge a person once he was in the custody of a federal officer.[48]

Once Wallace ruled that he could not reverse the commissioner's decision, a dozen or more of West's supporters, including Julian, hatched a scheme to free him. Two or three of them were to ask the jailer to let them say goodbye to West. While one of them was speaking to the jailer, West would race through the door, mount a waiting horse and make his escape. When the jailer refused to allow the interview, the plotters improvised. While Deputy Marshal Jesse D. Carmichael was adjusting the reins of the horses, West leapt from the wagon on which he was sitting, mounted a horse, and headed for nearby woods. But West did not know the quickest way out of the woods or his way around the city. According to Julian, West was also not a very good horseman. To add to his problems, West had mounted a slower horse than the one provided. He was quickly recaptured by Carmichael, placed in irons, and put on a Louisville-bound train. Fearing another rescue attempt, the president of the Jefferson railroad – the very same railroad that was sued by Obadiah Buckner for refusing to carry him without documents proving he was free – stationed guards on the railroad for twenty miles outside Indianapolis to preempt threats to destroy the tracks. Three miles beyond the city, the guards found rails and cross ties stacked on the tracks. A mile on, the train was again brought to a standstill so guards could remove an even larger impediment. In spite of these efforts, West was returned.[49]

The black community's effort to rescue West may have fizzled in the face of an overwhelming police presence and the railroad's vigilance, but it was one about which they were proud. So was Julian. It was, he later boasted, the only felony in which he ever became involved. One local editor took a different view

[48] Rea quoted in Money, Ibid., 265; Indianapolis *Journal*, December 12, 1857.

[49] Indianapolis *Journal*, November 28, 30, December 1, 2, 3, 4, 5, 7, 8, 10, 14, 1857; Indianapolis *Sentinel*, December 3, 7, 8, 1857; Madison *Journal*, November 27, 1857; Louisville *Journal*, December 4, 5, 1857; New York *Tribune*, December 14, 1857; Chicago *Tribune*, December 5, 8, 1857; Anti-Slavery Bugle, December 19, 1857; Stanley W. Campbell, *The Slave Catchers. Enforcement of the Fugitive Slave Law, 1850–1860* (New York: 1968), 132–33.

of Julian's involvement: he was a traitor who, by his actions, "morally, at least, put himself in open rebellion against the government," for which he merited five years in the state penitentiary. Such a sentence should be carried out for the "peace of the loyal state of Indiana, for the welfare of the whole Union, and for the happiness of the whole world, including niggers." At least as far as this editor was concerned, the return of West sent an unmistakable message to Kentucky, and the entire South: in Indiana the law was being "impartially administered."[50]

The editor may have been comforted by the thought that West's return demonstrated the state's commitment to the enforcement of the law and the maintenance of the Union. Others were not so sure. That same year, T. F. Bethell submitted a bill to the state House aimed at making the application of the Fugitive Slave Law more efficient. Anyone who found a "Negro or mulatto" in the state, who he suspected was a fugitive slave, could arrest him and take him before a commissioner or a justice of the peace. If the suspect could not produce "free papers" he would be jailed for thirty days. If, during that time, the owner or his agent could show, by means of a habeas corpus trial, that the person being held was a fugitive from slavery, he would be handed over "after all the costs [had] been paid." If, at the end of thirty days, no one claimed the suspect, he was to be released "at the cost of the informant." None of this, Bethell maintained, was to be construed as an impediment to a slave passing through the state on "legitimate business for his master" if he had a written pass. Nothing came of Bethell's bill but its submission reflected a lingering concern among supporters of the Fugitive Slave Law that a more efficient system of enforcement had to be developed to address the continuing influx of and passage of fugitive slaves through the state. With an eye to the problem faced by slaveholders such as Vallandingham, Bethell's bill also recognized that slaves were important cogs in commercial connections between the states.[51]

What successes Kentucky slaveholders had in retaking their slaves in Indiana, when coupled with precautions taken at home to stem the flow of escapes, did little to curb escapes; they continued to leave in troubling numbers. Slaveholders knew that the number of recaptures were outstripped by those who made it safely into Indiana and beyond. Periodically, Indiana newspapers partial to the movement reported on the thriving business of the UGRR. At one point, in 1853, an editor expressed surprise at the rising number of passengers carried on the UGRR and pointed out that the movement had been forced to open new branches to meet the increased demand. As in other Border States, the value of slaves lost to Kentucky slaveholders defies close calculation. Negro property across the river was "very uncertain and unsecure," according to one Madison

[50] Julian, *Political Recollections*, 164; Patrick W. Riddleberger, *George Washington Julian, Radical Reformer* (Indianapolis: 1966), 118–19; Indianapolis *Sentinel*, December 7, 1857.
[51] A copy of the proposed bill is in the Bethell-Warren Papers, Box 1, Folder 3, Indiana Historical Society, Indianapolis.

observer, who also worried that Kentucky slaveholders seemed to "place but little value upon their negroes," as they were likely to leave them at any time. Further east along the river, the editor of an Indiana Democratic newspaper tried to put a figure on these losses following a spike in escapes: since 1850, he observed, escapes had been "steady [and] incessant." If, he speculated, a "good servant" fetched $1,000, the loss to the "industrial capital of the slave states" had to have approximated $30 million. If the five thousand to ten thousand fugitives who chose to remain in the Free States, "postponing further flight until the exigencies of pursuit warrant it," were added to the mix, the accumulated losses resulted in a significant "depletion [of] slave holding interest." A Louisville editor tried to be a little more precise in his calculation of these losses: by 1853, he estimated, two thousand slaves had fled the area at a loss of $2 million. But even this was no exaggeration if Pen Bogart's estimation of the number of slaves who fled Louisville during the decade is accurate. Whatever the legitimacy and accuracy of these figures, Louisville slaveholders and their counterparts along the river were in no doubt that the loss of slave property increased the cost of doing business. Not only did the cost of reclaiming a slave increase over the decade, as James Rudd discovered, but slaveholders in adjoining counties were growing increasingly reluctant to hire their slaves in Louisville, which in 1857, one observer calculated, resulted in "a great advance in the price of hire of slaves this season." It is possible that slaveholders inflated their losses in an effort to pressure governments on both sides of the river to improve their detection and policing systems. But given what we have seen, one wonders what else local and state governments as well as slaveholders could have done to stanch the bleeding. Together, slaves who decided to escape, and those who assisted them, comprised the local arm of the UGRR. Their actions came increasingly to influence the terms of the debate over the future of slavery locally and across the state as well as in discussions about the future of African Americans in Indiana. Where formerly such activity was seen as the work of a few, something that could be controlled locally, by the close of the decade the increasing number of attempted flights came to be interpreted as the work of a clandestine group of internal subversives and outside abolitionists spurred on by Free-Soil advocates and the Republican Party. Working in tandem, they were, as one editor declared, the "curse of the South."[52]

---

[52] Indianapolis *Journal*, December 7, 1854; Lafayette *Journal* (n.d.), in New Albany *Ledger*, November 10, 1859; Louisville *Journal*, November 11, 1859; *Free Democrat*, May 5, 1855; Louisville *Democrat*, October 26, 1857, in New York *Tribune*, November 2, 1857; *Ohio State Journal*, October 30, 1857; Dearborn *Register*, February 15, 1856; Louisville *Times* (n.d.), in Madison *Courier*, December 27, 1853; Louisville *Courier*, January 8, 1857, May 3, 1858.

6

# Eastern Kentucky and Ohio

As the former slave, Josiah Henson, recalled, he faced a tricky dilemma when in 1825 he arrived with a boatload of fellow slaves in Cincinnati. He had been directed by his Maryland master to take the slaves to a plantation in western Kentucky. When their boat docked in Cincinnati, the "colored people" suggested that the group "remain with them," using, Henson recalled, "all the arguments now so familiar to induce slaves to quit their masters." But Henson felt honor bound to complete the task he was assigned. Years later, when he did decide to escape from slavery in Daviess County, Kentucky, Henson headed to the black community in Cincinnati, which protected him and guided him to the shores of Lake Erie from which he sailed to Canada. Blacks in the city were not the only ones who tried to persuade Henson and the group of slaves to leave. Wherever they stopped along the northern banks of the Ohio River they were met with similar receptions.[1]

Situated as they were – almost directly opposite towns and villages on the other side of the river – Henson's possible ports of call became geographically significant in the evolving political dispute over fugitive slaves. They provided places of protection and rest for slaves on the run from the northern counties of Kentucky. Those fleeing Boone, Kenton, and Campbell counties through Covington usually headed first for Cincinnati, although in some instances slaves leaving Boone County opted to cross the river into Indiana at Lawrenceburg or Aurora. From Bracken, Mason, and Lewis counties they traveled through Maysville before heading for the safety of Ripley, Ohio. Ironton, along the river, east of Ripley, provided similar support for those from Greenup County, Kentucky, and Cabell County, Virginia. These river towns were also

---

[1] Josiah Henson, *The Life of Josiah Henson, Formerly a Slave, Now an Inhabitant of Canada as Narrated by Himself*, in Yuval Taylor, ed., *I Was Born a Slave. An Anthology of Classic Slave Narratives Vol. 1, 1772–1849* (Chicago: 1999), 733–34, 745.

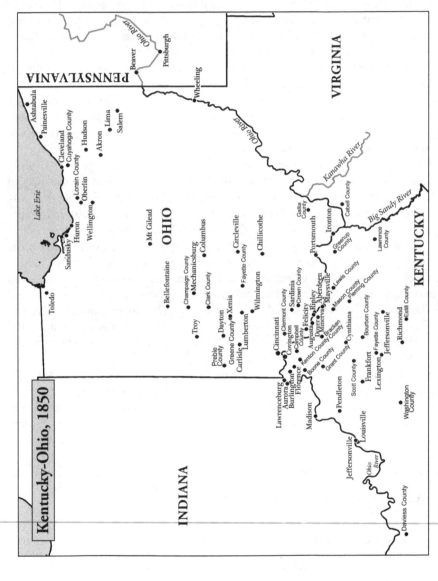

MAP 3. Eastern Kentucky and Ohio.

the departure points for those who went south to help slaves escape. Equally significant were the black rural settlements close to the river in southern Ohio, which, as one historian has argued, became meccas attracting fugitives from eastern Kentucky. Poke Patch, north of Ironton, and twenty miles from the river, was a vital link in the system of escape routes leading through Lawrence and Gallia counties. There, the barber, Gabe Johnson, and the day laborer, John Ditcher, who were the principal operators in the settlement, and very likely members of an African American organization called the "Order of Twelve," worked closely with sympathetic whites such as John Campbell, founder of Ironton. The same was true in Ripley, one of "the busiest shipping points" on the river and a few miles west of Maysville. Perched high on a hill back of the town stood the home of Presbyterian minister John Rankin, who kept a light burning in his window that could be seen for miles across the river. Beginning in 1849, after he had settled in Ripley, John Parker, the former slave and foundry owner, whose home was situated on the river's edge, was usually the first to welcome fugitives to the town. A black settlement, on the side of a hill overlooking the town, provided protection, as did the Gist settlements in Sardinia, north of Ripley. Free blacks in these settlements, one frustrated Maysville editor declared, acted as the "sentinels and agents of Ripley slave stealers." When, in the spring of 1852, four slaves escaped from Dover on the river east of Maysville, they were followed by an armed search party, which was forced to return empty handed. The fugitives were evidently accompanied by an unnamed free black who had bought his freedom a few years earlier, and who had returned to the area under the guise of a tobacco salesman to take out his wife and their two children, as well as two friends. It was impossible, the editor lamented, to retake fugitives once they made it to Ripley; they "might just as well be in Canada," he despaired.[2]

The escape of the four from Dover ushered in a period of what one newspaper called a "leave-taking fever" that deeply troubled slaveholders in the area. In September alone, forty-eight slaves escaped. One slaveholder estimated that another twenty-two had fled the month before. Of the five men, one woman,

---

[2] Darleen Innis, "Poke Patch Station," transcript, Lawrence County Public Library; Herbert H. Scott, "The Pioneer People of Poke Patch," transcript, Lawrence County Library; W. H. Siebert interview with Gabe N. Johnson, Lawrence County, September 30, 1894. Copy in Lawrence County Public Library; Louisville *Courier*, December 18, 1860; Ironton *Register*, October 31, 1878; Keith P. Griffler, *Front Line of Freedom. African Americans and the Forging of the Underground Railroad in the Ohio Valley* (Lexington, KY: 2004), 93; Cheryl Janifer LaRoche, *Free Black Communities and the Underground Railroad. The Geography of Resistance* (Urbana, IL: 2014), 74–75; Ann Hagedorn, *Beyond the River. The Untold Story of the Heroes of the Underground Railroad* (New York: 2002), 11–13, 88, 222, 231–37; Stuart Seely Sprague, ed., *His Promised Land. The Autobiography of John A. Parker, Former Slave and Conductor of the Underground Railroad* (New York: 1996), 95; Maysville *Eagle* (n.d.), in Scioto *Gazette*, March 25, 1852; Louisville *Journal*, April 23, 1852; *Anti-Slavery Bugle*, April 3, 1852; *Liberator*, April 16, 1852.

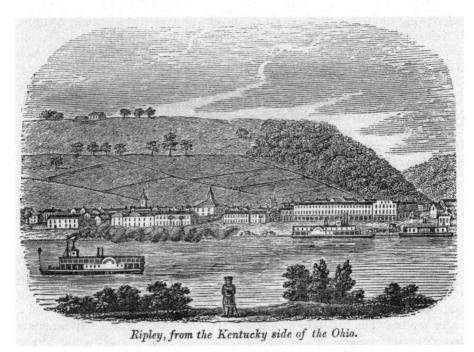

*Ripley, from the Kentucky side of the Ohio.*

FIGURE 2. Ripley from the Kentucky Side of the Ohio. (Courtesy of the Union Township Public Library)

and two children, belonging to different slaveholders in Mason County, who escaped on October 7th, none were retaken. Days later, nine slaves belonging to Joseph Taylor fled into Brown and Clermont counties, in Ohio, followed by a search party of one hundred Kentuckians, who returned empty handed. Weeks later, thirty-one who left Augusta and Dover were traced to Ripley, where they were protected by blacks "armed with guns and who surrounded the hotel where the Kentuckians" were staying. Immediately on arrival, the search party had headed for John Parker's house. Again, they could find none of the fugitives. Later, a group of whites crossed the river with a black man, William Carter, who went directly to Parker's claiming he was a fugitive in need of help to get his family out of slavery. The ruse failed and the group of whites was forced to hurry back across the river. Five of the thirty-one decided against staying in Ripley temporarily. Of the remainder, three were retaken almost immediately; many of the others were recaptured later, forty miles into Ohio. Of the forty-eight who had escaped almost half, it seemed, had made it to safety.[3]

[3] Louisville *Courier*, October 2, 4, 12, 1852; Louisville *Journal*, September 11, 1852, Maysville *Eagle* (n.d.), in *Liberator*, September 24, 1852; Maysville *Eagle*, October 9, 1852; *Voice of the*

Growing understandably alarmed, slaveholders in the adjoining counties of Kentucky met in Minerva, Bracken County, in early November 1852, and agreed to the formation of an association to protect themselves against such loses. They agreed to take a census of slaves owned by members, to support only the recapture of members' slaves, to establish what it called a pursuing committee supported by a permanent fund, and to set levels of rewards for those in Free States who aided in the recapture of escapees – $200 would be paid for those over sixteen years of age, $100 for those younger, and $50 for information leading to the recapture of fugitives. The meeting also called on the state to strengthen slave patrols in border counties. For those who made it past this cordon, the association hired a former resident of Kentucky, who now lived in Sandusky, Ohio, on Lake Erie, at a monthly salary of $30, to keep a watch for fugitives trying to cross into Canada.[4] One unnamed local slaveholder, however, did not wait for the association to begin operations. In late October, he left for Sandusky and Malden, Canada, in search of his lost slaves. In interviews with the captain of the *Arrow*, a steamer with a long record of ferrying fugitives across the lake, he discovered that more than two hundred fugitives from Kentucky had landed in Canada recently. On the steamer to Malden, he also interrogated fugitives, whose answers to some questions were understandably guarded, but on others surprisingly forthcoming. His attempts to discover if free blacks or whites from Ohio had advised slaves on "the course to pursue" solicited, he reported, no "satisfactory answer." But he was left in no doubt that a large number of slaves were keen to leave and, in fact, others were planning an "awful lumbering of the darkies to the free grounds" next summer.[5]

There were a few escapes the following summer, but nothing compared to the numbers of 1852. Evidently, twenty-eight escaped in April, twenty-five of them from Boone County. A family of five was caught trying to cross the river below Maysville in early July. Four slaves – two men, a boy and a girl – accompanied by an unnamed white man, fled Fleming County, south of Maysville, a few days later. The well-armed group was tracked to Wilmington, Ohio, just north of Cincinnati, where the two children were wounded in a firefight and the white man beaten within an inch of his life. Only the boy was returned.[6] The drop in escapes may have been the result of the Minerva Association's

*Fugitive*, October 21, 1852; Maysville *Eagle* (n.d.), in *National Anti-Slavery Standard*, November 4, 1852; Ashtabula *Sentinel*, October 30, 1852; New York *Tribune*, November 27, 1852.

4  Cincinnati *Gazette*, November 22, 1852; *Ohio State Journal*, November 24, 1852; *Anti-Slavery Bugle*, December 11, 18, 1852; *Pennsylvania Freeman*, December 16, 1852. The leadership of the association, its president, James Pepper, and secretaries, Thomas B. Stephenson, J. T. Bradford, and L. Hawkins, owned few slaves. Of the four, Pepper owned the largest number: eleven.

5  New York *Tribune*, November 27, 1852; *Liberator*, December 17, 1852.

6  Louisville *Courier*, July 9, 1853; Ripley *Bee*, July 23, 1853; Maysville *Eagle*, July 12, 1853; *Indiana Journal*, July 18, 1853; Pittsburgh *Gazette*, July 19, 1853; New York *Tribune*, July 28, 1853.

enhanced vigilance. But the state's decision to bolster its protective defenses also contributed to the reduction in the number of escapes. Two years earlier, the state legislature had passed a law making it illegal for ferrymen to take slaves across the river unless they were in the company of their owners or were with someone certified to travel with them. The penalties for violating the law were steep: the boat could be seized and the owner's "ferry rights" canceled. He could also be fined $200 and be held liable for the value of the slave. In order to prevent "wholesale escapes" of the sort that occurred in 1852, patrols of "sober and discreet citizens not exceeding thirty" were appointed "to guard and watch the places of crossing the river" and to keep an eye on "all water crafts" on the Kentucky side of the river. As John Parker recalled, the woods were usually heavily patrolled, river crossings watched, and boats pulled out of the water at night, padlocked and their oars removed.[7]

The Minerva Association's response to the dramatic escapes of 1852 may have been partly responsible for the decision to prosecute Rush R. Sloane, a Sandusky lawyer and abolitionist, for his involvement in the rescue of three Kentucky slaves. Seven fugitives – two men, two women, and three children, one of them eight months old – arrived by train in Sandusky, in late October 1852, and were about to board a steamer bound for Detroit when they were captured by Oliver Rice, the city marshal, and taken to the mayor's office. In an act of supreme sacrifice, the mother of the eight-month-old child broke away temporarily from her captors, walked a short distance, and placed the child on the ground before returning to the group. Later, the child was brought to her in prison, but she refused to acknowledge it as hers. Soon after the fugitives were taken, three members of the local arm of the UGRR – S. E. Hitchcock, a commission merchant, John B. Lott, a black barber, and John Irvine, a master carpenter and builder – persuaded Rush Sloane to act as the fugitives' attorney. Sloane confronted the two slave catchers, who between them apparently held twenty-five unsigned powers of attorney from Kentucky slaveholders. Sloane demanded to see the warrants or writs under which the arrests were made. When the slave catchers could produce neither, Sloane announced to those gathered in the mayor's office that the fugitives were not being held under the proper authority. They were rushed immediately from the room by a group of armed black men led by John Lott and hurried to a boat that was about to sail for Canada. The slave catchers could not find a ship captain willing to follow. They instead left for Huron, where they hoped to hire a boat.

As the group was leaving the mayor's office, Lewis F. Weiner, claiming three of the slaves, approached Sloane with evidence of ownership and a warning that he intended to sue him if they were lost. The case finally came to trial in Columbus, Ohio, two years after the rescue. Weiner was joined in the suit by Charles M. Gibson, who claimed damages of $17,000 for the loss of his

[7] *Liberator*, February 14, 1851; J. Winston Coleman, *Slavery Times in Kentucky* (Chapel Hill, NC: 1940), 101; Hagedorn, *Beyond the River*, 253; Sprague, *His Promised Land*, 72.

property. The case was heard by US District Court Judge Humphrey H. Leavitt, who had already established a reputation as a particularly stern opponent of those involved in the rescue and protection of fugitive slaves. The jury hearing the Gibson case rejected his claim for damages on the grounds that the powers of attorney used by the slave catchers were defective. In his instruction to the jury in the Weiner case, Leavitt pointed out that the suit was brought under Section 7 of the 1850 Fugitive Slave Law: a person who knowingly and willingly obstructed, hindered, or prevented a "claimant or [his] agent" from arresting a fugitive "either with or without process" was liable to a fine not exceeding $1,000 for each fugitive and to "imprisonment not exceeding six months." Although thirteen of Sandusky's "most worthy and respectable citizens" testified for the defense and, as Leavitt readily admitted, the city marshal's testimony contained multiple errors and so was inadmissible, he insisted that Sloane must have known that those under arrest were fugitives from slavery. The fact that there was no warrant from a commissioner, and the slave catchers were not in possession of appropriate powers of attorney, did not detract from the logical supposition, Leavitt reasoned, that Sloane must have known they were slaves. The jury ruled in favor of Weiner, and Leavitt set damages, under the law, at $3,000 plus cost, which amounted to an additional $393. Sandusky reacted to the verdict and fines with stunned disbelief. As one sympathetic editor saw it, Sloane had been prosecuted under a law that was not only "unjust in itself, but, in this instance at least, most wrongfully administered." It was also the most flagrant violation of "justice, LAW and right that ever blackened the pages of a judicial record." Immediately following the decision, a public meeting in Sandusky of Sloane's supporters set up a committee to raise funds to cover the fines. While he was willing to accept support to cover court costs, Sloane insisted that he must be solely responsible for paying the damages. Anyone who openly defied the law, who believed it violated all principles of justice, must be willing, he informed supporters, to suffer the consequences of his actions.[8]

Although he had to wait two years before the case was heard, Weiner must have left Columbus satisfied that the law had worked as it was intended. Fellow slaveholders in Kentucky also took some comfort in the outcome. Nonetheless, the Mason County slaveholder's discussion with the fugitive on the boat to Malden raised an issue that would continue to tax the resources of the Minerva

---

[8] Sandusky *Commercial Register,* October 21, 1852, October 28, 31, November 2, December 5, 16, 23, 25, 1854; New York *Tribune,* October 27, 1852; *Liberator,* October 29, November 5, 1852; New Albany *Ledger,* November 9, 1852; Ashtabula *Sentinel,* January 25, 1855; *The Federal Cases. Comprising Cases Argued and Determined in the Circuit and District Courts of the United States, Book* 29 (St. Paul: 1897); Rush R. Sloane, "The Underground Railroad in the Firelands," *The Fireland Pioneer,* V (1888), 46–49; Stanley W. Campbell, *The Slave Catchers. Enforcement of the Fugitive Slave Law* (New York: 1968), 137–38; Tom Carlarco, *People of the Underground Railroad. A Biographical Dictionary* (Westport, CT: 2008) www.accessible.com/search/fhist.htw?CiwebHitsFile=%2Faccessible%Ftext%2Ffree

Association as well as fellow slaveholders in other parts of the state: how best to stop the continued flight of slaves and the support they received from free black and white "outsiders." The Reverend Henry M. Dennison, who lost a slave in Columbus, Ohio, in 1855, posed the issue in the starkest terms possible: the abolitionists not only engineered the escape of his slave, they also "scattered incendiary pamphlets, and sent wily and disguised emissaries throughout the whole South...to excite the lowest and most ignorant class of the Southern people to discontent, sedition and revolt." John Parker confirmed Dennison's worse fears: escaping slaves, he recalled, passed through Ripley almost nightly, supported by a "number of men" who regularly crossed the river to bring them out. Parker should have known; he was one of them. The group would also have included John Fairfield (a possible nom de guerre), the son of a wealthy Virginia slaveholder, who for two decades, beginning in the 1830s, used his inheritance to lead slaves to freedom from different parts of the South, including Virginia, Kentucky, and Missouri. Levi Coffin, a leader of the UGRR in Cincinnati who knew Fairfield well, described him as a "wicked man, daring and reckless in his actions, yet faithful to the trust reposed in him, and benevolent to the poor." Coffin did not endorse Fairfield's "mode of action," and tried to persuade him to discontinue his activities, yet felt an abiding respect for the subversive's commitment to undermining the slave system.[9]

The signs of outside, and inside, interference were unmistakable. In late 1850, John Portman, a white man from near Carlisle, Ohio, and an unnamed black man from the same town were intercepted at a steamer landing between Maysville and Aberdeen when a ferryman, as he was obligated by law to do, inquired if the black man traveling with them was free. It seemed a simple, unthreatening question – one the two should have anticipated. Portman answered that he was free and his companion, almost simultaneously, that he was not. The plot fizzled and they were both taken into custody. R. A. Graham of Preble County, Ohio, arrived in Cynthiana, Harrison County, Kentucky, in August 1854 peddling a "patent plow." He immediately gained access to plantation owners interested in the new invention. Graham, who was also a preacher, was invited to preach to white congregations as well as at the African Methodist Church, where in his sermon he spoke of plans by Ohioans to free slaves in his audience. Graham had to be locked up in the local jail for his own protection. The next day, with his face blackened, he was marched out of town. When days later a fugitive was "decoyed" away by two white peddlers in their covered wagon, it seemed to confirm Graham's report that Ohio abolitionists

---

[9] Sprague, *His Promised Land*, 71, 106; Griffler, *Front Line of Freedom*, 58–59; Hagedorn, *Beyond the River*, 256–57; William H. Siebert, *The Underground Railroad From Slavery to Freedom* (1898, rpr., New York: 2006), 153–54; Fergus M. Bordewich, *Bound for Canaan. The Underground Railroad and the War for the Soul of America* (New York: 2005), 346; Levi Coffin, *Reminiscences* (1898, rpr., New York: 1968), 428–46; M. B. Butler, *My Story of the Civil War and the Underground Railroad* (Indianapolis: 1914), 181–83.

had established a fund out of which, evidently, peddlers were to be paid $50 for each slave removed.[10]

Free black Kentuckians may not have received payment from outside organizations, but they were nonetheless deeply implicated in the effort to get slaves to free territory. A seventy- year-old baker, known fondly in Mason County as Doctor Perkins, was sentenced to three years in the state penitentiary in 1852 for taking a slave of Blackstone Rankin across the river. Pleas for a pardon based on his age were rejected by the governor even though Perkins promised to leave the state if he were freed. Perkins died in prison in September 1854, less than one year after his incarceration. Weeks after Perkins' capture, Henry Ramsey and his brother Isaac were brought before Bracken County Circuit Court, charged with aiding a slave of Walter Lynn to escape. The jury acquitted Isaac and could not agree on Henry's guilt. In the summer of 1856, George Williams was taken from his home in Brown County, Ohio, by a group of armed Kentuckians, and taken to Mason County, where he was charged with enticing several of Dr. James McDowell's slaves to escape. Williams claimed his confession was coerced at knife point. He also insisted that he was not with the slaves when arrested. His request for a new trial was denied and Williams was sentenced to fifteen years in the state penitentiary, where he died three years later, apparently of consumption, at age thirty-five.[11]

Included in this group of subversives were fugitives or former freed slaves who returned either to take out other slaves or to reclaim family members still in slavery. An unnamed former slave of Warren B. Rogers of Bourbon County, who had fled to Canada in the fall of 1857, returned less than one year later

---

[10] Ripley *Bee*, November 23, 1850: Maysville *Eagle*, November 12, 1850; *Western Citizen*, August 18, 1854, Paris *Citizen* (n.d.), in Louisville *Journal*, August 19, 1854; Cynthiana *News*, August 17, 1854, in *Kentucky Statesman*, August 18, 1854; Harrodsburg *Ploughboy* (n.d.), in Louisville *Journal*, August 22, 1854; New York *Tribune*, August 28, 1854. There were many other instances of white subversives entering the state. One of the most dramatic involved a Mr. Pullman, who, it was reported, had connections in Cincinnati. In mid-1855, he was caught taking out three slaves from Jessamine County, south of Lexington. When Pullman broke loose from his captors he was shot in the back, but, surprisingly, got to his feet and fled towards the Kentucky River, where he fell over a cliff forty-seven feet above the river. Impressed, one report acknowledged that he was "endowed with more than mortal vigor." Readers of the encounter were left with the impression that Pullman might have survived the fall. Louisville *Courier*, June, 16, 1855. The report of the incident was republished widely. See, for example, Chicago *Tribune*, June 22, 1855, and Cleveland *Herald*, June 19, 1855.

[11] Ripley *Bee*, November 26, 1853; New York *Tribune*, November 28, 1853; Covington *Journal*, November 26, 1853; *Anti-Slavery Bugle*, December 10, 1853; Mason County Circuit Court of Justice, Case Files, Kentucky Department of Libraries and Archives, Frankfort, Kentucky; "Slavery in Mason County, Kentucky: A Century of Records, 1788–1882, 2 vols., Vol. II, 161" compiled by Caroline R. Miller, Maysville, Kentucky, National Underground Railroad Museum, 2001; "African American Records, Bracken County, Kentucky 1797–1919, 2 vols.," compiled by Caroline R. Miller, Bracken County Historical Society, 1999, 338; James Pritchard, "Into the Fiery Furnace: Anti-Slavery Prisoners in Kentucky State Penitentiary, 1844–1870," 4. My thanks to Pritchard for a copy of his very informative paper; Hagedorn, *Beyond the River*, 255.

and took out two slaves, one belonging to Joseph Wilson, the other to Rogers. It is quite likely that they were related to the former slave. The three were tracked down by a "party of Irishmen." Shots were exchanged, during which one of the pursuers was injured and Rogers's slave killed. Wilson's slave was captured, as was the "Canadian," who subsequently gave his captors the slip and disappeared. In the fall of 1858, Julett Miles, a former slave in Bracken County, who had settled in Felicity, Ohio, sixteen miles from her former home, returned to Kentucky in an effort to take out her ten children and grandchildren when she got word that they were about to be sold and sent to New Orleans. Owned by his father, Miles had been John G. Fee's nursemaid. Fee, the future founder of Berea College, was a prominent opponent of slavery. When, in 1847, Fee got word that his father planned to sell Miles, he bought her and set her free, a decision that caused a permanent rift between father and son. Miles, however, continued to work for the senior Fee until she moved to Ohio in 1854. Over the years, those of Miles' family still in slavery were owned by a number of Mason and Bracken County slaveholders. On her return, Miles was caught and, following a series of trials, convicted for attempting to "entice away" slaves. In spite of his efforts, Fee was unable to raise bail and Miles was sentenced to the state prison for three years, where she died in August 1859. The cause of death was listed as "stomach inflammation," which suggests that she either poisoned herself or was poisoned.[12]

As in other Border States, the courts and prisons of Kentucky were a significant, if not the only, line of defense against efforts to undermine slavery by aiding slaves to leave. James Pritchard's study of the Kentucky penitentiary records shows that, between 1844 and 1870, forty-four men and women were incarcerated for "assisting slaves to run away," sixteen of them in the 1850s. Of the forty-four, twenty-four were white. Seven were born in Kentucky or other slave states, ten in Free States, and seven were classified as foreign-born. With the exception of Isaac Barber, the physician, and Calvin Fairbank, the Oberlin-trained minister, the majority were either laborers, tradesmen, or farmers. All of the African Americans, with the exception of John Russell, were born in Ohio. Of the seven African Americans whose occupations were listed, five were laborers, two were coopers, and one was a blacksmith. Surprisingly, six of the forty-four were over the age of sixty; Doctor Perkins, as we have seen, was seventy. An 1830 law mandated sentences of two to twenty years for "seducing or enticing" slaves to escape. Those convicted of "persuading" slaves to run away faced sentences of one to five years under an 1845 amendment to the 1830 law. It is not clear who determined what charges were brought against the accused. The length of sentence for those convicted of "seducing or enticing" also seems arbitrary. The record from other states shows that multiple charges, including

---

[12] *Western Citizen*, August 6, 1858; Ripley *Bee*, November 13, 1858; New York *Tribune*, March 28, 1859; Victor B. Howard, *The Evangelical War Against Slavery and Caste. The Life and Times of John G. Fee* (Selinsgrove, PA: 1996), 60, 114–16; Pritchard, "Into the Fiery Furnace" 11–12.

enticing, seducing, abducting, assisting, and persuading were usually leveled at the accused in the hope that one would stick. Foley Stephens, aged twenty-six, was sentenced in 1857 to ten years for "enticing." Two years earlier, William Pistor, aged twenty-five, who was born in Germany, received two years for the same crime. William Dixon, twenty-one, English-born, received ten years for "abducting," while Paul Coleman, aged thirty-five, who was black, was sentenced to five years for "assisting." It is not clear what the differences between the two charges were. Of those imprisoned, twenty served their time, fourteen were pardoned, and eight died in prison, including Doctor Perkins and Julett Miles. One, William H. Davis, aged sixty-one, escaped, and another, William Dixon, had his sentence overturned by the Kentucky Supreme Court. The records contain little information on Susan Woods, twenty-six, the only woman to be convicted of "aiding" slaves to escape.[13]

While not all of those incarcerated in the state penitentiary were involved in cases from eastern Kentucky, neither the courts nor the activities of individual slaveholders could stem the flow of slaves from the area. In the years after the formation of the Minerva Association in late 1852, slaves continued to enter southern Ohio between Ironton and Ripley. When thirty fled Mason County in January 1860, the authorities could find no signs that they had crossed the river. While local authorities suspected that they were being hidden by free blacks in Maysville, no one could be certain that they had not slipped through the cordon.[14] Here, as in other parts of the state, the river provided little protection for slaveholders. Although impassible at times, it was never a serious impediment to those who were determined to escape. In fact, one observer dismissed it as nothing more than an ineffective fence along "our great plantations, which thousands of breachy slaves jump over every year, and defy hound, hunter, and the government to boot, to bring them back." When the river froze in winter, as it frequently did during the 1850s, slaves ignored the elements to take advantage of what one wag called its "constitutional freezing," to cross into Ohio. Five slaves from Mason County did exactly that using sleighs in 1856. Neither the sleigh, the horses that they used to get to the river, nor the slaves themselves were heard from again. Lucy Stone Blackwell, the Ohio abolitionist, reported that 175 fugitives had crossed on the ice in one three-month period during the winter of 1856. The problem of slave escapes so bothered the authorities that, when, in 1856, Kentucky chartered a company

---

[13] Pritchard "Into the Fiery Furnace." See also William C. Sneed, *A Report on the History and Mode of Management of the Kentucky Penitentiary, from Its Origins in 1798, to March 1, 1860* (Frankfort, KY: 1860), which is a useful supplement to Pritchard's analysis.

[14] Louisville *Courier*, January 9, 1860. For reports of other escapes from the area, some of which were ultimately foiled, see *Anti-Slavery Bugle*, October 8, 1853, October 21, 1854, October 10, 1857; Maysville *Eagle* (n.d.), in New Albany *Ledger*, June 26, 1854; Cincinnati *Gazette*, November 4, 1856; *Liberator*, November 14, 1856; Evansville *Journal*, September 28, 1857; Cleveland *Herald*, September 28, 1857, Maysville *Eagle*, September 22, 1857.

to build a suspension bridge across the river, the company was made liable for any slaves who escaped across it.[15]

But of all the cities and towns along the northern bank of the Ohio River, Cincinnati – because of its location and its stature as a major commercial center with substantial links to Kentucky and Virginia, the size of its black population, which, in 1850, stood in excess of three thousand, that community's well-established organizations, supported by a vibrant antislavery tradition – became a magnet for slaves seeking freedom. It was also a major port of call in the domestic slave trade. As the captain of the steamer *Tropic,* carrying a number of slaves for the New Orleans slave market, put it during a hearing to free some of his cargo, the "transportation of slaves was part of the regular business of steamboats on the Ohio River." At low water on the Kentucky side it was customary for slave boats to land at one of the Cincinnati wharves and immediately ferry their human cargo in skiffs to Covington, where they could be kept away from prying abolitionists until sailing time.[16] Not surprisingly, Cincinnati was the obvious crossing point for slaves fleeing Kentucky counties, such as Boone, Kenton, and Campbell directly opposite the city, and Grant and Pendleton further south. In the summer of 1854, for example, twenty-three slaves from Grant and adjoining counties lashed a number of canoes together, rowed down the Licking River into the Ohio before making their way to the northern part of the city, where they were run off on the UGRR. Twenty-five escaped from different Boone County masters in April 1853. It was reported that the leader of this organized escape had read an installment of *Uncle Tom's Cabin* to the group weeks before the date of their departure. But Cincinnati was also the preferred destination of slaves fleeing other parts of Kentucky. Slaves escaping from Louisville, for instance, sometimes opted for a more circuitous route, bypassing Jeffersonville, Indiana, directly across the river, heading instead for Cincinnati through Madison, Indiana. In the spring of 1855, a group of slaves from different parts of Kentucky – four from Union County in the west opposite Evansville, Indiana, five from Bracken County, opposite Ripley in the east, and two from Boone County, south of Covington – floated down the Licking River to freedom. They may have come together purely by chance during their respective escapes, but it is just as likely that their arrival in Cincinnati was planned. The number of advertisements that appeared in the Covington *Journal* from masters in different parts of Kentucky suggests that they were reasonably sure that escapees were heading for Cincinnati.[17]

[15] *Liberator,* February 4, 1853, March 7, 1856; New York *Tribune,* March 21, 1856; Carrolton *Times* (n.d.), in Maysville *Eagle,* June 7, 1855; Cleveland *Herald,* February 16, 1856; Hagedorn, *Beyond the River,* 254.

[16] Cincinnati *Gazette,* August 27, 1853, July 6, 1853; Cincinnati *Atlas* (n.d.), in Cleveland *Herald,* July 7, 1853.

[17] Nikki Taylor, *Frontiers of Freedom: Cincinnati's Black Community, 1802–1868* (Athens, OH: 2005); James Oliver Horton and Stacy Flaherty, "Black Leadership in Antebellum Cincinnati," in Henry Louis Taylor Jr., ed., *Race and the City. Work, Community, and Protest in*

There is no way of knowing with any certainty how many slaves escaped along this section of the Ohio River during the 1850s. One unidentified Southern newspaper estimated that, in the twelve months prior to June 1850, roughly 143 slaves escaped from Kentucky. Local observers, particularly those who were committed to enforcement of the Fugitive Slave Law, were convinced that the numbers of escapes through Cincinnati were increasing at an alarming rate, many more than the public imagined. So frequent were these escapes that one newspaper saw little benefit in recording each of them. By the end of 1853, a Covington observer, clearly worried by the steady stream of escapes, could see no end in sight, as "the facilities for escape north had multiplied." There seemed to be no "remedy for the evil," nor did the "utmost vigilance, and the kindest treatment" stem the flow. Some of these observations may have been deliberately alarmist and meant to prod local authorities on each side of the river to coordinate their efforts to address the problem. No one could dispute the fact that the rising number and frequency of escapes was real indeed. Individual escapes were alarming enough, but it was the frequency and apparent coordination of group escapes that caused the most concern. In this, slaveholders along this section of the river were not alone; all along the divide between slavery and freedom, especially in those areas closest to free territory, slaves continued to escape in groups. In November 1852, three slaves – two men and one woman – escaped into Lawrenceburg, Indiana, made their way north through Ohio to Dayton, then on to Bellefontaine, where they were tracked by their owner, who arrived too late to retake them. In May 1853, twenty-five escaped from Boone County; in June, ten from Newport; in August, eleven from Boone, of whom five were returned; and in December, five from Covington. Later in December, thirteen escapees from Covington passed through Detroit, although it is not clear if that group included the five who had left earlier the same month. The pattern continued into 1854 when it was reported that twenty-three fled from Grant County in June; twenty-one in the same month from Pendleton, followed two months later by another seven; nine from Boone County in September; and eight from Bourbon County later in the year. In early 1854, Rev. H. H. Hawkins, a former fugitive slave from Kentucky, who was then living in Canada, and who was in Cincinnati raising money to buy his freedom, estimated that there were about four hundred former slaves who had lived within a radius of one hundred miles from Cincinnati now settled in Canada West.[18]

*Cincinnati, 1820–1970* (Urbana, IL: 1993), 76; Henry Louis Taylor and Vicky Dula, "The Black Residential Experience and Community Formation in Antebellum Cincinnati," in Taylor, ed., Ibid., 99, 115; Adam Lowry Rankin, "Autobiography of Rev. Adam Lowry Rankin," typescript, Rankin Papers, Stanford University, a copy of which is in the Ripley Public Library; Aurora *Independent Banner,* April 13, 1853; New Albany *Ledger,* April 14, 1853; *Liberator,* February 4, 1853, March 7, 1856; Cincinnati *Gazette,* June 15, 1854, April 19, 1855; Evansville *Journal,* June 19, 1854; *National Era,* June 22, 1854. For advertisements see Covington *Journal,* October 14, November 2, 4, 11, 1854.
[18] Cincinnati *Gazette,* December 2, 1851, October 25, 1852, April 20, June 22, 1853, June 15, 1854; Cincinnati *Enquirer* (n.d.), in *Pennsylvania Freeman,* December 16, 1852; Cincinnati

Slaveholders could be their own worst enemies. Sometime in the mid-1840s, Joshua Zimmerman of Boone County had settled Billy and seven or eight of Billy's family members on a farm he had bought for them in Ohio. During the 1850 Christmas holidays, he gave nine of his slaves – members of Billy's family – permission to visit him, providing them with the necessary passes, horses, and a wagon. Soon after they arrived at Billy's, they wrote Zimmerman, offering to return the horses and wagon but letting him know, in no uncertain terms, that they had every intention of remaining in free territory. It is not clear if Zimmerman made any effort to recapture these slaves. But then Zimmerman was an unusual slave master who was either supremely confident or stunningly indifferent in his relationship with his slaves. It is also likely that he was being practical, fully aware that the cost of recapture normally exceeded the value of the fugitives sought. But the majority of those who lost slaves took a completely different approach. More typical was the response of the masters of the nine slaves from near Burlington, Boone County, who escaped in June 1854. They included Shadrach, aged sixty, his wife Susan, thirty-nine, and her two sons, Wesley, nine, and John, three. They were joined by Lewis, aged twenty-four, Lee, twenty-one, and his wife Amanda, twenty-six, and her three-year-old daughter Sarah. Interestingly, Lee was owned by two minors, Elizabeth Ann Blackenbaker, aged eleven, and her younger brother, Jasper, eight. The group was hidden in a barn on the outskirts of Cincinnati, but before they could be moved they were betrayed by John Gyser, an African American, for the $1,000 advertised reward. Shadrach had decided to flee with his family when he got word that he was about to be sold. His owner, Jonas Crisler, was deeply offended that a slave he had owned for nearly twenty-five years, and whom he had treated kindly, would not have approached him first with his concerns. As a result, Crisler decided that he wanted nothing more to do with such an ungrateful slave and planned to sell Shadrach if he could.[19]

There is no way of knowing how many of those who crossed over at Cincinnati decided to stay there, opting for the anonymity and protection afforded by the black community and the UGRR network, how many headed further north, or what percentage chose to go directly to Canada through Sandusky and Detroit. How many of the twenty-three escapees from Grant and surrounding counties who arrived in Canada in June 1854, for instance, came directly from eastern Kentucky, or what number of them spent time working on farms in middle and northern Ohio before moving on, remains a

*Enquirer,* June 2, 22, 1853; Covington *Journal,* March 1, 1851, February 15, 1852, August 20, December 10, 1853, October 4, November 4, 11, 1854; New Albany *Ledger,* June 27, 1854; Louisville *Courier,* April 10, 1853; *Liberator,* May 6, 1853; *National Anti-Slavery Standard,* June 19, 1851, June 24, 1854; Sandusky *Commercial Register,* February 22, 1854.

[19] Cincinnati *Nonpariel* (n.d.), in *National Anti-Slavery Standard,* January 30, 1851; Cincinnati *Commercial,* April 19, 1855; Cincinnati *Gazette,* June 15, 16, 19, 1854; *Pennsylvania Freeman,* June 22, 1854; Population Schedules of the Seventh Census of the United States, 1850, Kentucky, Boone County; see also the Slave Schedules for Boone County, 1850.

mystery. As in other locations along the slavery divide, there were also serial escapes – that is, family members who chose to leave, not as Shadrach did, as a group, but one or two at a time, as in the case of the mother and her five daughters who passed through Cincinnati from Covington in early 1857, leaving her husband and son behind. One of her daughters had preceded them. But if the action of slave families in other Border States is any indication, the owners of the father and son could count the days before they left.[20] There is no evidence to suggest that these slaves did not act on their own initiative. The decision to leave, as in the case of the group that read the extract from *Uncle Tom's Cabin*, was theirs to make and they made it. The group of slaves from different parts of the state who floated down the Licking River also seemed to have acted on their own, although we have no idea how they got together or when they planned to make the break for freedom.

Slaveholders, and local and state authorities, did all they could to curtail escapes, at times forming protective associations, such as the one at Minerva, which hired patrols to track fugitives on their way to the river and employed slave catchers to seek out escapees once they made it across the river. As we have seen, the Minerva Association also employed someone in Sandusky to look out for fugitives trying to cross the lake into Canada. Reports of recaptures frequently mentioned the role of local spies in ferreting out fugitives. Even in Ashtabula County, on Lake Erie, which one historian described as a "no-man's land" for slave catchers, there was reputed to be an organization known as the "Knights of the Golden Circle," which kept a close lookout for fugitives passing through the area. Rewards were substantial. The one offered by the owner of Shadrach and his family appealed to Ohioans, white and black. Once caught, fugitives could be hurried back, if taken close to the river, or brought before a commissioner or judge. Commissioners, especially those in Cincinnati, almost invariably ruled in favor of masters. There were, however, times when the most vigilant of masters were flummoxed by racial identities of their own making. In the fall of 1850, an unnamed fugitive, described as a "bright mulatto," escaped from Scott County and managed to get through Covington undetected because those on watch at the river thought he was white. He was betrayed, however, by a white man in Cincinnati who offered to get him to Canada.[21]

Blacks and white allies in Cincinnati provided protection for escapees while they were in the city and guided them to safety further north. One Columbus editor, speaking for many of those opposed to efforts to subvert the law, railed

---

[20] Cincinnati *Gazette*, June 15, 1854; *Free Presbyterian*, March 11, 1857; the quarterly report of the Cleveland "Committee of Nine," a black organization, reported in September 1854 the arrival of 176. An earlier report mentioned the arrival of forty fugitives in one week. *Anti-Slavery Bugle*, September 16, 1854; *Liberator*, October 29, 1852.

[21] Robert H. Fuller, *Underground to Freedom. An Account of the Anti-Slavery Activities in Ashtabula County Prior to the Civil War* (Jefferson, OH: 1977), 6, 17; Covington *Journal*, October 19, 1850.

against what he called "smelling committees," who had developed a system for identifying fugitives in their midst. White Southerners traveling with "servants" were subjected to "the prying insolence of some of our negroes, or their over-zealous white sympathizers, and [to being] brought before our courts to answer" why they dared "to pass through the State or stop in it" with their slaves. In this case, the slaveholder, who had lost his slave, described members of the "smelling committee" as made up exclusively of black women – "birds of ill omen," he called them. Whites and blacks traveling together were enough to raise suspicion. Slaveholders were frequently warned not to bring their slaves with them when visiting the North. But this was not always possible. A slaveholder relocating with his property from Virginia to Missouri, for example, could not always avoid passing through or stopping, if only for a while, in Ohio. Some traveling by river tried to avoid Cincinnati by docking instead in Covington. The same was true, as we shall see, for those traveling by rail through middle and northern Ohio. There were occasions when free blacks accompanying whites were mistaken for slaves and spirited away by these "committees." The precautions taken by Charles E. Stewart, traveling from Mississippi with a group of slaves he had manumitted, points to some of the defenses slaveholders devised. Soon after landing in Cincinnati, Stewart went before the Court of Common Pleas, where he produced the deeds of manumission. Had he not done so, it is very likely his former slaves would have been seized. While some of the leaders of these black groups can be identified, we know little about their structure, size, or membership. What we do know is that they existed in many parts of the state, mainly in large cities, but also had a presence in smaller communities such as Ironton, Oberlin, Circleville, just north of Chillicothe, and Painesville along the lake. In Cincinnati, the group was known as the "Life Guard," in Cleveland, the "Committee of Nine." Under the leadership of Gad Worthington, a porter, the Cleveland group organized frequent "grand Underground Railroad" entertainments, the proceeds going to aid fugitive slaves. By the end of the decade there was also a "Fugitive Aid Society," which possibly worked in tandem with the Committee of Nine, and which was led by William E. Ambush, a barber. In both Cincinnati and Cleveland there were also colored ladies anti-slavery sewing societies – offshoots of similar societies led by prominent white abolitionists. The Cincinnati Anti-Slavery Sewing Circle was organized by Sarah Otis Ernst and through its annual fairs raised money to support both the Western Anti-Slavery Society as well as the work of aiding fugitive slaves. The Cleveland Colored Ladies Benevolent Sewing Society was formed not long after the passage of the Fugitive Slave Law and maintained an active presence throughout the decade. It is very likely that the activities of the Cincinnati groups were coordinated with those of the city's vigilance committee.[22]

[22] *Ohio Statesman*, March 16, May 29, 1855; Cincinnati *Gazette*, May 21, 1854; New York *Tribune*, July 21, 1854; *Ohio State Journal*, July 24, 1854; Scioto *Gazette*, April 10, August

The Life Guard and its supporters kept a close watch on the river wharves and hotels, many of whose employees were African American, for fugitives in need of assistance and for slaveholders and their agents whose activities had to be stymied. In midsummer 1857, a Mr. Warren of Memphis arrived at the Dennison House with a well-dressed black boy. The boy took rooms at the Dumas House, the city's leading black hotel. This immediately raised suspicion, and a "conclave of blacks," worried that the boy was on the lookout for fugitives, interrogated him. Insisting he could prove his innocence, the boy got word to his master, who contacted the police. When the police arrived at the hotel they found the African Americans armed and arrested them, which gave the boy time to slip away. Were he found guilty, it was reported, he would have been given one hundred lashes. The episode points to the levels black Cincinnatians were willing to go to to protect their community from slave catchers and, as we shall see, kidnappers. The work of this conclave – and others of its kind in other areas of the state – was reinforced by large crowds that quickly gathered whenever the community seemed threatened or when, as in March 1855, a group of sixteen slaves on their way from Wheeling, Virginia, to St. Louis on the steamer *Falls River* docked at a city wharf. A crowd of African Americans, along with a few whites, tried unsuccessfully to free them by storming the steamer. Sensing further trouble, the slaveholder hurried the group to Covington just ahead of a writ of habeas corpus obtained by Henry B. Blackwell, a white wholesale merchant and abolitionist. The conclave was a presence during almost every fugitive case that came to court, a presence which sometimes even intimidated court officials and the police. They were also marshaled to prevent fugitives from being returned south without first having a hearing. When a father, mother, and child, suspected fugitives, were seized by a group of slave catchers who planned to take them over the river, the catchers were attacked and the fugitives rescued by an unidentified "party." Even when the courts ruled in favor of slave masters, as occurred in the case of George McQuery, in 1853, a "large number of excited citizens and colored men" followed the heavily armed guards and city constables to the river. Shouts of "fugitives" or "kidnappers" were guaranteed to attract large and protective crowds. Occasionally, these situations threatened to spin out of control. The efforts of a group of blacks to stop the kidnapping of John Watkins in 1853 were opposed by a "party of Irishmen," friends of the hack driver taking Watkins to the wharf. Watkins had been arrested in September for committing

1, 8, 1854, April 27, 1855; Cleveland *Leader,* February 18, August 1, 1855, February 4, 1856, February 4, 1860; *Spear, Denison and Company's Cleveland City Directory for 1856* (Cleveland: 1856); for Ernst see Stacey Robertson, *Hearts Beating for Liberty: Women Abolitionists in the Old Northwest* (Chapel Hill, NC: 2010). In her annual report, Mrs. Straight, president of the Cincinnati Anti-Slavery Sewing Circle, painted a rather gloomy picture of the state of abolitionism in the city. The one bright spot was the work of the vigilance committee, which, she observed, remained vibrant. Ashtabula *Sentinel,* February 26, 1857.

"an outrage upon the person of a young woman." But the judge released Watkins for a lack of evidence. As he was leaving the station house, however, Watkins was rearrested, this time for stealing a watch. He was placed in a carriage driven by Frank Green, described as an "Irishman," which headed for the river. It was Watkin's screams that brought the crowd of blacks to his rescue. Pistols were discharged and stones thrown before Watkins was returned to prison for safekeeping. At a subsequent hearing, it was finally agreed that the claim that Watkins was a fugitive was pure fabrication and he was released.[23]

Such vigilance was born of a deep and abiding vulnerability. All blacks, free or formerly enslaved, faced the very real prospect of being taken up and sent across the river. George Brown, owner of a barbershop, and a resident of the city for many years, was arrested in 1853 on suspicion that he was a fugitive slave. Brown insisted that he was born free in Vincennes, Indiana. Jeremiah S. Ballenger claimed that he was his former slave, Moses, who had escaped from Maysville ten years earlier. Brown was fortunate: someone who had known him as a boy happened to be on a visit to the city at the time and testified on his behalf. But Brown also had to use all of his influence and a substantial amount of his own money to have his name cleared. By the 1850s, Cincinnati was also an important center of manumission. Slaveholders who wished to free their slaves used the city courts to legalize these transactions. There were more than ninety such cases in 1858 alone. But manumission in the city was no guarantee of permanent freedom. Proof of one's freedom rested entirely on those accused of being fugitives. When Charles Bodman, a resident of the city, inherited three slaves from an uncle in 1858, he had them manumitted in a local court. Before granting them their freedom the judge felt constrained to warn them to carry their manumission papers with them at all times.[24]

But nothing expressed their vulnerability more than the possibility of being kidnapped and spirited across the river. As opponents of the Fugitive Slave Law had warned before its passage, and continued to do so after its adoption, the absence of habeas corpus guarantees was likely to result in an increase in kidnappings. The assurance of Supreme Court judges and the attorney general that the right of habeas corpus was unaffected by the law provided little comfort. Some local observers were largely unmoved by these warnings. While opposed to the law, the editor of the Cincinnati *Gazette* was convinced that the rights of free men would not be violated and boldly declared, "There will be no kidnapping." Another editor, this one in Columbus, dismissed the concerns expressed by a meeting of African Americans that the law would actually encourage kidnappings as too alarmist. Most of "our citizens," he countered, "are so thoroughly opposed to kidnapping, and so sensitive on the subject, that

[23] Cincinnati *Gazette*, July 12, 1857, March 19, 20, 1855, September 9, 13, 1853; Cincinnati *Nonpariel* (n.d.), in Cleveland *Herald,* December 13, 1852; *Anti-Slavery Bugle*, August 27, 1853; Cincinnati *Commercial*, March 19, 20, 1855; Cincinnati *Enquirer,* September 13, 1853.
[24] *Anti-Slavery Bugle*, October 1, 1853; Cincinnati *Gazette*, March 9, 23, April 17, 1858.

any attempt of the kind here would fail, and the persons attempting such a game would hardly escape the vengeance of summary Lynch law." The editors would come to rue such optimism over the next few months and years, as African Americans continued to face the very real threat of kidnapping. In the wake of the failed attempt to kidnap Isaac Williams in the fall of 1852, the Cincinnati police estimated that there had been twelve such attempts in the previous three months. Unsuspecting young black boys were frequent targets, lured away by promises of jobs somewhere along the river. Alfred Logan, eleven, who had been freed in Kentucky, and William Ralls, fourteen, a free black resident of Mt. Vernon, Ohio, for example, were hired in 1856 by John Orr to work on his farm fifteen miles from Cincinnati. Orr's scheme only unraveled when he tried to sell the boys to slave traders in St. Louis, Missouri. Evidently, Orr had earlier escaped from a Hannibal, Missouri, jail, where he was being held on a similar charge. It took a requisition from Ohio's governor to his counterpart in Missouri, and a mission by David Anderson, who journeyed to St. Louis with Logan's free papers, to have him freed. The situation was complicated in part because, when questioned about where he was manumitted, Logan had given his place of birth, not where he was freed. Even before Anderson arrived in St. Louis, Ralls had been released and Orr had once again escaped. Two years earlier, a nine-year-old orphan, John Nelson, was persuaded to join two unnamed black men on a boat going up the river. Nelson jumped ship at Ripley and made his way back to Cincinnati when he overheard the men planning to sell him for $300. He was followed by the two kidnappers, who attempted to recapture him, but was saved when his cries alerted a number of dockhands. It is not clear what became of the kidnappers, but, as one observer reported, the incident "created much feeling among our colored people."[25]

While a handful of African Americans were involved in kidnappings in the city, as they were in other parts of the North, the danger emanated largely from organized groups of whites. In mid-1859, Michael Weaver and William Stewart abducted James Waggoner and took him over the river to Newport, where he was jailed on suspicion of being a fugitive. Weaver and Stewart were arrested and charged with kidnapping, but were released when no one appeared to testify against them. Unable to prove that he was free, Waggoner languished in jail until his sale was announced in order the cover the cost of his incarceration. He was sold for $700 and sent to a slave pen in Lexington. Sometime in the fall, information came to light that Waggoner was, in fact, born free, as he had maintained all along, in Brown County, Ohio, in 1840. His father, Peter, had been freed by will and moved to Ohio at a time when his former owner's will was being contested by surviving family members. It took

[25] Cincinnati *Gazette*, October 17, 1850, June 10, 1854, March 14, 15, 1856; *Ohio State Journal*, October 16, 1850; Cincinnati *Commercial*, March 12, 13, 14, 15, 17, 1856; Hannibal *Messenger*, March 15, 27, 1856; *Missouri Democrat*, March 20, 27, 1856; *Pennsylvania Freeman*, October 2, 1852; Cleveland *Herald*, March 14, 1856; Cincinnati *Enquirer*, June 10, 1854.

the persistence of supporters in Cincinnati, as well as a number of concerned citizens in Newport and Covington, who, as the case progressed through the courts, came to question whether Waggoner was ever a slave. Collections had to be taken up in black churches to cover the cost of the trials. Ohio congressman Joshua Giddings condemned the kidnapping as "a dastardly submission, disgraceful" to the state, and thundered that Newport ought to be left in ashes for allowing "the pirates of that city to enslave a freeman of Cincinnati." A few months earlier, Weaver and Stewart had been involved in another kidnapping case, during which they attempted to extort money from a Virginia slaveholder for the return of a former slave.[26]

Overall, those involved in kidnapping managed to escape prosecution. One remarkable exception concerned Henrietta Wood, who was kidnapped and sold into slavery in Kentucky in 1853. Wood had been a slave in Louisville until 1847, when her owner manumitted her in Cincinnati. Family members of her former owner, however, were never reconciled to her manumission. Sometime in early 1853, they sold Wood, without her knowledge, for the suspiciously low price of $300, to Frank Rust. In June 1853, Rust, John Gilbert, and Rebecca Boyd, for whom Wood worked at a boardinghouse in the northeastern section of the city, tricked Wood into going over to Covington, where she was taken into custody, carried first to Florence, then Lexington and Frankfort, where she was handed over to Zebulon Ward, director of the state penitentiary. Wood was later sold to slave traders, Pullum & Griffin, who took her to Natchez, where she was sold to Girard Brandon, a Mississippi slaveholder, for $1,050. As Union forces encircled Vicksburg, at the height of the Civil War, Brandon fled the city, taking five hundred of his slaves with him to Texas, where Wood remained until 1868, when word finally reached them that they were free. Wood returned to Natchez, where she spent the next few years working for Brandon. She then returned to Cincinnati. Those who had claimed her as a slave, and sent her deeper into slavery, underestimated Wood's resourcefulness. When she was first kidnapped she had tried unsuccessfully to have her claim to freedom adjudicated by Kentucky courts. Sometime after her return to Cincinnati, Wood, now in her sixties, got word that Zebulon Ward, now a man of some wealth, was in Ohio to attend the horse races. Wood brought suit against him, claiming damages of $20,000 for what she estimated were potential lost earnings during her years in slavery. The case was not heard until 1878, when the court awarded Wood $2,500 in damages – much less than she had hoped. From its start in 1853, there was something very odd about the entire episode, or as one Kentucky newspaper aptly put it, there was "a screw

[26] Cincinnati *Gazette*, June 5, 6, 7, 8, 19, 1860, August 16, 17, 20, 23, 24, 1860, October 20, 25, 1859; Cincinnati *Commercial*, October 20, 1859. Giddings is quoted in John A. Vacha, "The Case of Sara Lucy Bagby. A Late Gesture," *Ohio History*, 76, No. 4 (1967), 223. For other African Americans involved in kidnapping see the case of Robert Russell in Hagedorn, *Beyond the River*, 252–53.

loose somewhere." In one respect, there was nothing unusual about Wood's kidnapping. What is telling, however, was her determination to prove that she was falsely taken and her struggle to procure some form of reparations for her years of re-enslavement.[27]

These cases were not exceptional. There were countless other cases of kidnapping across the state, although it is not always easy to determine the exact number, in part because opponents of slavery tended to describe most captures of suspected fugitives as kidnappings. While *The Fugitive Slave Law and Its Victims,* a survey of fugitive slave incidents put together by New York City abolitionists in the weeks before the outbreak of the Civil War, provides a useful compilation of cases in Ohio and elsewhere, it tends to distort the record of kidnappings by conflating the two. But the number of kidnappings (or attempted kidnappings) compiled from local newspapers suggests that the New York abolitionists were not far off the mark. Kidnappings were frequent and occurred in many parts of the state, although, not surprisingly, the majority were recorded in southern counties. Isaac Hensley, his wife, and four children were taken from their home in Sardinia, Brown County, and carried to Maysville in 1853. John Watkins was arrested, in 1853, on the pretext of having stolen a watch in Cincinnati, but was rescued by a crowd of African Americans when his captors tried to get him across the river. James Worthington, an Akron barber, just managed to escape the clutches of kidnappers in 1853. Cook (no first name given) was taken from a village near Xenia, clubbed, and left for dead on the side of the road as he was being driven south on the way to Cincinnati in 1854. Like Henrietta Wood, Jane Moore of Cincinnati was taken across the river to Covington by her employer in November 1854. Fortunately for Moore, the mayor of Covington freed her. Three years later, Benjamin Chelsom, a freed slave, formerly of Lexington, Kentucky, was lured across the river by his former owner with the aid of an unnamed free black and sent into slavery in Estill County, Kentucky. There seemed to be a spike in the number of cases in 1859 in Chillicothe, Portsmouth, and Cincinnati. Gangs of kidnappers appeared to have operated quite freely in counties close to the river. One such gang operated out of Mason County, Kentucky, stealing free blacks in Ohio and selling them in Maysville. They also enticed slaves to escape, only to sell them to slave traders. The problem became so acute that, in 1860, the state of Ohio felt the need to adopt a law to prevent kidnapping. As one editorial observed, kidnapping had become the "most profitable, tempting, and only

[27] Cincinnati *Gazette,* June 3, 7, 23, 1854; *Kentucky News* (n.d.), in *Anti-Slavery Bugle,* January 14, 1854; Cincinnati *Enquirer,* June 3, 1853; Nashville *Union and American,* January 18, 1871; Ripley *Bee,* March 6, 20, 1879; *Stark County Democrat,* April 18, 1878; Cincinnati *Commercial,* April 2, 1876; T. D. Clark, "The Slave Trade Between Kentucky and the Cotton Kingdom," *Mississippi Valley Historical Review,* 21, No. 3 (December 1934), 333; www .encyclopediaofarkansas.net/encyclopedia/entry-detail.aspx?entryID=4153&m. My thanks to Caleb McDaniel, who is working on a biography of Wood, for sharing some of these sources with me.

kind of robbery that can be carried on without danger."²⁸ So much for the insistence of other editors in 1850 that there was little danger from kidnapping.

Even more troubling was the fact that it was not always easy to differentiate between a kidnapping and an abduction, which, under the law, was permissible if it did not result in public disorder. Opponents of the law had every reason to believe that the rendition of the Marshall and Burns families in the fall of 1860 was, in fact, a kidnapping. Thomas Marshall, his wife, and child, and Henry Burns, along with his wife and infant, were bundled into the night train bound for Cincinnati near Sandusky by a posse of about a dozen. Burns had moved into the area nine months earlier, rented fifty acres, and built his family a home. Nothing is known of the Marshalls or how long they had lived in the area. Burns' neighbors, all of whom were black, attempted to intercept the train at its normal stop in Centralia, but they were foiled when it made an unanticipated stop earlier at a shunting where the captives were placed in a darkened car attached to the back of the train. Later, the conductor reported that he had been approached by someone he took to be a police officer from Cincinnati to make the stop to take on board six or eight passengers, "mail robbers and counterfeiters," not, as he pointed out, a particularly unusual request. The additional car, he reported, which was kept locked and was not intended for the use of the public, had been added by the superintendent of the railroad company. The posse was given the keys to the car by the brakeman. It was not until the conductor went to the car to collect the fares that he realized the passengers were black and, he suspected, fugitive slaves. As the train made its way south, the conductor was shown what he and others believed were legal documents signed by a Cincinnati official. Opposed as he was to the rendition of fugitive slaves, the conductor wired ahead to friends in an unsuccessful attempt to have a local judge issue a writ of habeas corpus. The families, who at this point were reported to be fugitive slaves from Mason County, Kentucky, were taken from Cincinnati to Lexington, where they were lodged in the slave pen owned by Lewis E. Robards, "a rendezvous," one historian has written, "for a gang of kidnappers and nigger thieves that operated along the Ohio River,"

²⁸ Cincinnati *Gazette* (n.d.), in Scioto *Gazette*, September 29, 1853; Maysville *Eagle* (n.d.), in *Anti-Slavery Bugle*, October 1, 1853, June 3, 17, 1854; Ripley *Bee*, September 24, 1853; Cincinnati *Gazette*, September 9, 13, 1853, November 15, 1854; Cincinnati *Enquirer*, September 13, 1853; Cincinnati *Gazette* (n.d.), in New York *Times*, November 25, 1854; Xenia *Torch-Light*, May 31, June 7, 14, 21, 1854; *Ohio State Journal*, June 2, 1854, February 26, 1860; Cincinnati *Gazette*, August 29, 30, 1859; Cincinnati *Commercial*, August 29, 1859; Chillicothe *Gazette*, October 11, 1859, in Cleveland *Herald*, October 17, 1859; Portsmouth *Tribune* (n.d.), in Cleveland *Herald*, October 22, 1859; Chicago *Democrat*, October 19, 1859; Cleveland *Leader*, October 18, 1859; Scioto *Gazette*, October 13, 1859, in New York *Tribune*, October 19, 1859; Marietta *Intelligencer*, October 20, 1859; Sandusky *Commercial Register*, January 17, 1860; Scioto *Gazette*, January 10, 1860; Baltimore *Sun*, November 25, 1854; Washington *Republican* (n.d.), in *New York Colonization Journal*, February 1855.

and the very pen where Henrietta Wood was held for a while before she was sent to the state prison.[29]

The case raises a number of interesting questions, not the least of which is the level of collusion between the authorities in Cincinnati and officers of the railroad company, if not the company itself. The darkened and locked railroad car suggests that the railroad superintendent was complicit in the abduction of the families. If signed by a Cincinnati official, the document shown to the conductor raises question about the reach of the commissioner's remit. Surely, Sandusky was out of his jurisdiction. Whereas in the past, slaveholders sought arrest warrants from a commissioner in the district in which they suspected fugitives had settled, by the end of the decade all that was needed was a signed warrant from a commissioner in any location. Practice, in effect, had widened the power and reach of commissioners. But there were other questions raised by the case: initial reports insisted that the posse had been led by US Marshal Manson of Cincinnati, operating with a warrant issued by a city commissioner. As it turned out, the marshal was sick and in bed at the time and the commissioner was out of town and so could not have signed the warrant. Nothing in this case conformed to the requirements of the law.

The city's African American organizations and their counterparts elsewhere in the state, as well as their white supporters, did what they could to protect the black community against such assaults on their rights and freedoms. Following adoption of the Fugitive Slave Law, the courts, both federal and state, became the site of an increasingly acrimonious contest over the competing rights of slaveholders to reclaim their property and those of blacks to maintain their freedom in a Free State. Not surprisingly, Ohio, and particularly Cincinnati, was on the front line of this struggle. Throughout the decade, the competing drama involving fugitives and slaveholders was played out in the courts and commissioners' hearing rooms. In some cases, former slaves had been living as free men in the state for many years; in others, they were dragged into court soon after they made it across the river. Reclamation stood a much better chance of success in federal courts. Chances of subverting such claims improved considerably if opponents of slavery could get cases moved to state courts, where, before sympathetic judges, lawyers could build their defenses on the argument that all who lived in a Free State, regardless of the length of their residency, had to be considered free until proven otherwise. Teams of antislavery lawyers worked pro bono. In Cincinnati, they were led by John Jolliffe. Born into a Quaker family in Virginia, Jolliffe moved to Ohio in 1827, where he quickly became active in the abolitionist movement. He would lead

[29] Sandusky *Commercial Register,* October 15, 16, 17, 20, 1860; Louisville *Courier,* October 16, 1860; Coleman, *Slavery Times in Kentucky,* 210; Sloane, "The Underground Railroad in the Firelands," 87–88. Sloane's version of the capture is different in many significant details. He calls Burns Bennett and mentions that the Marshalls had four children, the Burns three, and in the posse's haste to get the families away, one of the children was left behind.

the defense team in almost every fugitive slave case heard in the city during the 1850s. By the start of the Civil War, he had devoted almost twenty years to the legal fight against slavery and the protection of fugitive slaves.[30] Jolliffe and his team usually faced groups of well-funded and skilled lawyers committed to the defense of federal law and the protection of slave property.

Given its location, it is surprising that it took almost three years before the first case was heard in Ohio. Compared to other border regions, Ohio seemed particularly tardy in this regard. In June 1850, nineteen-year-old Lewis – sometimes spelled Louis – escaped from his Fleming County master, Alexander Marshall. Lewis was tracked to Cincinnati but slipped passed his pursuers and headed for Columbus, where he lived until he was captured in the fall of 1853 by US Marshal Manuel Dryden of Cincinnati. Friends in Columbus immediately alerted Jolliffe, and Dryden was arrested for kidnapping soon after he returned to Cincinnati. At the hearing before Commissioner S. S. Carpenter, Lewis was defended by Jolliffe and Rutherford B. Hayes, the future president of the United States. Although witnesses for Marshall claimed to have known Lewis as a slave, and Dryden produced an affidavit from Marshall, the defense insisted that Lewis was, by legal precedent, free, because he had come into the state with his master's consent. Normally, the weight of the plaintiff's evidence would have been sufficient grounds for ordering Lewis back into slavery immediately. But surprisingly, Carpenter agreed to a full, rather than an expedited, hearing. Carpenter may have either been partial to Lewis or intimidated by the large number of blacks who daily crowded the hearing room. While Carpenter was preparing his decision on the defense's motion for a full hearing, Lewis slipped out of the courtroom largely unnoticed and into the street to the cheers of "the crowded audience." The hearing was suspended until the marshal could find Lewis. But Lewis was nowhere to be found; he was being hidden in a series of safe houses by members of the UGRR. Weeks later, he was slipped out of town dressed as a woman and sent first to Sandusky and then Detroit before heading for Canada under the name William Alexander.[31]

The Lewis case was just one of a number of high-profile cases adjudicated in or with connections to Cincinnati during the decade. Months before Lewis' escape, George Washington McQuery, a suspected fugitive from Washington County, Kentucky, was taken before Carpenter. He had escaped in 1849 with three other slaves, and lived for a while in Indiana before settling in Troy, Ohio, where he worked on a canal boat, and where he married and started a

[30] For Jolliffe see Steven Weisenburger, *Modern Medea. A Family Story of Slavery and Child Murder from the Old South* (New York: 1998), 91–93, 283; Hagedorn, *Beyond the River*, 188–89.

[31] Cincinnati *Gazette*, October 21, 1853; Cincinnati *Commercial*, October 18, 19, 21, 1853; Cincinnati *Enquirer*, October 22, 1853; *Anti-Slavery Bugle*, November 5, 1853; Detroit *Democrat* (n.d.), in *Missouri Democrat*, November 26, 1853; Sloane, "The Underground Railroad of the Firelands," 46; Wilbur Henry Siebert, *The Mysteries of Ohio's Underground Railroad* (Columbus, OH: 1951), 53; Coffin, *Reminiscences*, 548–54; Stephen Middleton, "The

family. His whereabouts were betrayed by a coworker. The twenty-eight-year-old McQuery was picked up by his former owner, Henry Miller, without a warrant and taken to Dayton, where he was put in the hands of a US marshal. His supporters applied for a writ of habeas corpus from the local probate judge, who refused to act on the grounds that McQuery was already in the hands of a competent federal officer. He was taken to Cincinnati, but before Carpenter could act, Peter H. Clark, the African American schoolteacher and active member of the black community, intervened and applied to Supreme Court Justice John McLean, who was on his circuit in the city, for a writ of habeas corpus. McQuery was defended by Jolliffe and James G. Birney, the former slaveholder turned abolitionist. Four witnesses, including Miller's son, claimed to have known McQuery as a slave. McLean was eager to reaffirm his view of the law's constitutionality. He preemptively brushed aside Jolliffe's efforts to question the law's constitutionality and Birney's call for a continuance. The judge used his summation to reject the battery of arguments used by defense counsels and to rule that the law was constitutional. History shows, McLean declared, as he had done earlier in Philadelphia, that the issue of slave rendition played a critical role in the discussions of future relations between the states following the Revolution. It was an issue that was "deeply interesting to the slave States." Its resolution helped to cement the federal compact. Consequently, courts had no power to overrule such political arrangements. The power to do so resided exclusively with the people and their representatives. No state acting independently, therefore, could impede the constitutional requirement to deliver up fugitives from labor. The issue, McLean ruled, turned not on whether the fugitive is "a slave or a freeman, but whether he owes service to the claimant." He rejected the argument that the differential pay to commissioners constituted a bribe. It was, he insisted, nothing more than "compensation to the commissioners for making a statement of the case, which includes the facts proved, and to which his certificate is annexed. In cases where the witnesses are numerous, and the investigation takes up several days, five dollars would scarcely be a compensation for the statement required." McLean concluded with an observation, which he must have known was totally impractical, but one to which many defenders of the law were deeply attached: being remanded did not preclude a slave from making his case "to a court in a slave State," which, as a rule, acted "with fairness and impartiality." McLean was on firm legal ground, but he could not have been surprised that his reasoning generated a number of critical responses. J. P. Blanchard, for instance, dismissed as a total non sequitur the justice's contention that if the law was not enforced the social and political fabric of the country would unravel. He also questioned, as so many

Fugitive Slave Crisis in Cincinnati, 1850–1860: Resistance, Enforcement and Black Refugees," *Journal of Negro History*, 72, Nos. 1 & 2 (Winter/Spring 1987), 26; Weisenberger, *Modern Medea*, 104–06. Carpenter tended his resignation soon after, arguing that, under the law, the office of commissioner was "judicial" and so unconstitutional.

other opponents of the law had done, whether Congress had the power, under the Constitution, to legislate on such matters as slave renditions. If it did not, as he believed, then the law was unconstitutional. Furthermore, if comity was the legal glue that held the country together, Blanchard wondered how South Carolina could enact laws under which it imprisoned black seamen, free citizens of Northern states, and yet not face any legal sanctions.[32]

McQuery was returned to slavery, but McLean's was not to be the final word on the law's constitutionality. Almost two years later, opponents of the law would record their only legal victory. The case involved sixteen-year-old Rosetta Armistead, a slave of Rev. Henry Dennison, an Episcopalian priest formerly of Virginia, now a resident of Louisville, Kentucky, and the son-in-law of former president John Tyler. Following the death of his wife, Dennison asked a friend, a Dr. Miller, to take Rosetta back to Virginia so she could be with Dennison's family. Because the river was frozen near Cincinnati, Miller decided to travel by train through Columbus. While waiting for their connection, the black community got wind of their presence. Rev. William B. Ferguson, a black Baptist minister, moved quickly to have the slave brought before a probate judge under a writ of habeas corpus. At the hearing, the judge asked Rosetta if she wished to continue with Miller to Virginia or if she preferred to be free in Ohio. Once she expressed a desire to be free, the judge promptly assigned her a guardian – Lewis G. Van Slyke, a local abolitionist – as was required by law. Van Slyke then arranged for Rosetta to be employed in the home of James H. Coulter, a homeopathic doctor. Once he got word of the judge's decision, Dennison hurried to Columbus and demanded an interview with Rosetta, during which she reiterated her wish to be free. Following the interview, Dennison left for Cincinnati, where he had earlier obtained an arrest warrant from Commissioner John L. Pendery. Two Cincinnati officers subsequently traveled to Columbus, where they seized Rosetta, placed her in a carriage, and headed for the train station, followed by "several citizens," including Van Slyke. Before boarding the train, Van Slyke wired supporters in Cincinnati, warning them of Rosetta's arrest. In Cincinnati, Van Slyke obtained a writ of habeas corpus from Judge Parker of the Court of Common Pleas, who ordered the sheriff to hand over Rosetta to Van Slyke. US Marshal H. H. Robinson, proprietor of the Cincinnati *Enquirer,* and an ardent proslavery Democrat, however, refused to hand her over. In response, Parker ruled both Robinson and Dennison in contempt of court. Robinson was arrested but immediately freed by Judge McLean on appeal. In his decision, Commissioner Pendery condemned Rosetta's lawyers, including Salmon Chase and Rutherford B. Hayes, for working to bring

---

[32] Cincinnati *Gazette,* August 17, 18, 1853; Cincinnati *Enquirer,* August 17, 1853; Cincinnati *Commercial,* August 29, 1853; New York *Times,* August 22, 1853; *Anti-Slavery Bugle,* August 20, 27, 1853; *National Anti-Slavery Standard,* October 13, 22, 1853; Weisenburger, *Modern Medea,* 102–03; Campbell, *The Slave Catchers,* 121–23; *The Fugitive Slave and Its Victims* (New York: 1861), 28.

state and federal courts into conflict in an effort to undermine the Fugitive Slave Law. Then, in a surprise move, he ordered Rosetta free on the grounds that she had been brought into the state with the consent of her owner.[33]

Dennison, however, did not accept Pendery's judgment quietly. In a letter to the *Ohio Statesman*, a Democratic newspaper, he condemned the actions of the Columbus black community, its white allies, and those who brought suit demanding Rosetta's freedom as "men stealing Abolitionists." Their action had separated Rosetta from those "most attached to her true interests" and from "the home of her childhood and the arms of her parents, her brothers and sisters." His wife, who had died in June 1854, was devoted to Rosetta, had taught her to sew, and had begun to teach her to read. The actions of opponents violated the Constitution, defied the "injunction of Holy Writ, and pronounced the Bible a forgery, and God...a tyrant." As a "Northern man with Southern feelings," someone who was born and educated in Pennsylvania and had attended seminary in Maryland – a true American, he seemed to imply – Dennison was convinced that, if allowed to continue, these abolitionist activities would ultimately destroy the Union. In response, the city's Whig newspaper wondered where in the South a Northerner would be allowed to express views critical of slavery as Dennison had been permitted to berate and falsely accuse Northerners of undermining the Constitution and country. "Is there an intelligent person," it wondered, "who supposes an antislavery man could go to Richmond or Nashville, and publish such an attack upon the Courts and the people ... without subjecting himself...to the fury of a pro-slavery mob." The question needed no answer. Were such a thing possible, the editor seemed to suggest, it would indeed be the ultimate expression of comity.[34]

Antislavery forces in Ohio would not win another case in the years leading up to the Civil War. The Rosetta case had taught opponents an invaluable lesson about ways to counter claims that slaves were made free merely by being brought or allowed to come into the state with the consent of their owners. After all, in Ohio, as was the case all along the divide between slavery and freedom, slaves frequently crossed into free territory to do business for their owners, a tradition vital to continued commercial relations between the sections. To allow the Rosetta ruling to establish a precedent would undermine these ties. The successful resolution of the Armistead case was soon overshadowed by a bloody and gruesome confrontation between a slave mother and slave catchers in Cincinnati in late January 1856. Eight slaves – Simon Garner, fifty-five,

---

[33] *Ohio State Journal*, March 12, 15, 23, 24, 25, 26, 31, April 4, 7, 11, 1855; *Ohio Statesman*, March 13, 16, 20, 1855; Cincinnati *Commercial*, March 26, 27, 28, 29, 30, 31, April 2, 3, 4, 5, 19, 1855; Cincinnati *Gazette*, March 26, 28, 29, 1855; Cleveland *Herald*, March 21, 1855; *National Era*, April 12, 1855; John Nivens, et al., eds., *The Salmon P. Chase Papers, Vol. I, Journals, 1829–1872*, n. 56 (Kent, OH: 1993), 244; Paul Finkelman, *An Imperfect Union. Slavery, Federalism, and Comity* (Chapel Hill, NC: 1981), 175–77.

[34] *Ohio Statesman*, March 16, 1855; *Ohio State Journal*, March 21, 1855.

his son of the same name, aged twenty-five, and Mary Garner, fifty, belonging to James Mitchell, Margaret (Peggy) Garner, twenty-two, and her four children, Tom, Sam, Cilla, and Mary, owned by Archibald K. Gaines – escaped from Boone County, eighteen miles from Covington, crossed the frozen river into Cincinnati, where they hid out at the home of a former slave and relative, Joseph Kite. The fugitives were tracked to Kite's home by a force of US marshals and Kentucky officers. Trapped, and determined not to be retaken, Margaret (Peggy) Garner cut the throat of Mary, her two-year-old daughter and was about to slay another of her children when she was stopped. News of Mary's death shocked the country. It was either a cold-blooded murder or an act of desperate courage and defiance. The mother who had abandoned her infant in Sandusky as she was about to be taken into custody was understandable, as was the bloody resistance at Christiana, but the decision to kill one's child rather than see it returned to slavery was an act, many believed, born of sheer desperation, the result of a mother driven mad by an inhumane and oppressive system of exploitation. Lucy Stone spoke for many opponents of slavery: "If in her deep maternal love she felt the impulse to send her child back to God, to save it from coming woe, who shall say she had no right to do so?" Margaret's actions, one editor contended, were not that of a crazed slave but of a human being with "all the feelings, instincts and aspirations of men," who, like all men, "yearn for freedom." Like the Roman Virginius, Margaret chose to kill her daughter rather than have her exposed to the horrors of slavery. Others disagreed. Margaret was no hero. Hers was a "deed of blood," an "act of a crazed and frenzied negress," and "altogether unprecedented," made more "inexplicable and unusual" by the fact that fugitives frequently chose to return voluntarily to the "house of bondage" after experiencing the blessings of freedom in the North and Canada.[35]

Three hearings were held in quick succession: a coroner's inquest into the murder; a habeas corpus hearing before Probate Court Judge John Burgoyne at which John Jolliffe argued, as he had done in previous cases, that the slaves had been permitted, on many occasions, to come into Cincinnati with their owner's consent; and a traditional fugitive slave hearing before Commissioner Pendery. What followed was a bizarre legal wrangling over who should hold the prisoners, and which case should take precedent – the criminal case, under Ohio law, for murder, or the case of rendition under federal law. Surrounding it all was the fear that the fugitives might be spirited away with the collusion of local sympathizers and a police force operating under legal cover of sympathetic state judges. The cases, Steven Weisenburger has argued, exposed

---

[35] Weisenburger, *Modern Medea*, 87–88; Nikki M. Taylor, *Driven Toward Madness. The Fugitive Slave Margaret Garner and the Tragedy on the Ohio* (Athens, OH: 2016), 7–23, 78–79; Mark Reinhardt, *Who Speaks for Margaret Garner* (Minneapolis: 2010), 35–37; Cincinnati *Gazette*, February 14, 1856; Cincinnati *Enquirer*, January 30, March 2, 1856; New York *Tribune*, February 8, 1856.

political differences rubbed raw by heightened tensions over the issue of slavery among many of the main players: judges, sheriffs, marshals, and editors. Large crowds made up mainly of African Americans were present throughout the trials and whenever the family was taken from jail to the courthouse. Black women were particularly vocal. When an officer ordered them to make way, one was reported to have responded: "D – n you! D – n you. I'm free born, half white, and as good as any white-livered b – h in Ohio!" Three days after the murder, the Cincinnati *Commercial's* call for a public meeting was dismissed by the *Enquirer* as an attempt to "overawe and intimidate the Court." Concerned that such a meeting would inflame public sentiment and encourage further violations of the law, the usually sympathetic *Gazette* suggested that the best approach would be to work through the courts for the slaves' freedom, and, should that fail, to start a subscription to purchase their freedom. This would aid the Garner family "materially," and, even more importantly, lower the political temperature and defuse political tensions. This was a potential tinderbox. Irate black crowds confronted a large contingent of police and groups of what one newspaper described as gaunt Kentuckians with "small red, sunken eye[s], hollow cheeks and sharp chin[s]."[36]

At the hearing before Pendery, Jolliffe attacked from two directions: he brought witnesses who testified that the slaves were allowed into Ohio on many occasions and so were free, and he railed against the Fugitive Slave Law as unconstitutional. In this case, the law had driven a "frantic mother to murder her own child, rather than see it carried back to the seething hell of American slavery." The execution of the law required "human hearts to be wrong and human blood to be spilt." Francis T. Chambers, formerly of Mason County, a friend of the Gaines family, and a Democratic Party stalwart, countered that the slaves had never been permitted to come into Ohio. The claim was an attempt, he insisted, to circumvent the ban on testimony of fugitives by getting someone else to speak on the slaves' behalf. Pendery agreed: such testimony was inadmissible under the law. The commissioner ruled against the Garners and they were returned promptly in a buggy under heavy guard, led by Hiram H. Robinson "surrounded by a number of deputy Marshals." Large crowds followed in silence, one reporter observed, as if they were "attending the funeral of the sovereignty of the State of Ohio." Slaveholders and supporters began celebrating even before the ferry got across the river. Once the slaves were safely in the Covington jail, the celebrations continued at a local hotel with speeches and cheers for visitors from Ohio. But not for Edmond Bibb, a reporter for the *Gazette,* who was assaulted. Bleeding and semiconscious, he only escaped when a former deputy marshal from Cincinnati, and a group of Ohioans, "drew their shooters and ordered the Kentuckians to stand back."[37]

The decision to return the Garners came at the end of lengthy and costly hearings lasting twenty-nine days. It is estimated that Archibald Gaines spent $1,000 on the case – not an unusually large amount. But Hiram H. Robinson's "battalion-strength posse," armed with repeating rifles and pistols, added to the overall cost. So, too, were the four hundred special deputies who were sworn in for the length of the trial at $200 per day. Each of them was issued a certificate guaranteeing payment. Many of these, it was reported, were discounted at local bars and eateries at $16 each. Those who bought them stood to pocket a handsome profit. Evidently, they were being sold to people who "never had any money for such investment before." Who buyers worked with, or for whom, was not known, but it was presumed that "the person who furnished the funds knew there was secret service money enough to pay all the expenses." Evidently, Robinson had gone to Washington, DC, to consult with Elisha Whittlesey, the comptroller of the Treasury, the responsible agent for the disbursement of funds in such cases. But officials in the department were troubled by the rumored discounting of certificates and dispatched an agent to investigate Robinson's claim for $22,000 in expenses. A local correspondent estimated that there were actually five hundred marshals – not the four hundred as earlier reported – many of whom did nothing during the trial. No more than 250 of them were actually present at the "trial on any one day, and a great many," who held warrants, "never saw the inside of the court room." There were accusations that many were filing claims for "false mileage and witness fees." The suspicions of embezzlement and payments to policemen were never resolved and continued to be an item for discussion in the local press well into 1857.[38]

A byzantine case of cat and mouse between Archibald Gaines, Ohio Governor Salmon Chase, and Charles Morehead, governor of Kentucky, over the return of Margaret Garner to face trial for the murder of her child in Ohio dragged on in the weeks following Pendery's decision. It was preferable, supporters seem to think, that Margaret face lengthy imprisonment for murder in an Ohio prison than life in slavery. Gaines had promised to defer selling Margaret south until Chase had made a decision on whether he would request Margaret's extradition. But Chase did not act immediately and Gaines used the delay to transport Margaret and her child, Cilla, to Arkansas. On the way,

---

[37] Weisenburger, *Modern Medea*, 199–200; Taylor, *Driven Toward Madness*, 86; Cincinnati *Gazette*, February 1, 12, 29, 1856; Covington *Journal*, March 1, 8, 1856; Cincinnati *Enquirer*, February 2, 1856.

[38] Weisenburger, *Modern Medea*, 192, 195, 202, 230, 235; Cincinnati *Gazette*, March 5, April 3, 1856, June 3, 1857; New York *Tribune*, April 23, 1856. I have been unable to find – nor has Weisenburger, who has written the definitive study of the case been able to find – the Treasury reports. Those held in the National Archives seem to have ceased in 1854.

there was a dreadful collision between the boat on which Margaret was traveling and another steamer. In the panic that ensued, Margaret and Cilla fell overboard. Margaret was rescued, but Cilla was never found.[39] Some suspected that Margaret had finally accomplished what she had set out to do when cornered in Cincinnati.

In a series of eight articles addressed "to the People of Cincinnati," a Kentucky slaveholder, writing under the nom de plume "Justice," tried to make sense of the Garner case. Seven of the eight articles were devoted to traditional justifications of slavery on constitutional and biblical grounds. But the first was a shot across the bow, a warning that the actions of opponents in the Garner and other fugitive slave cases had made the Fugitive Slave Law a "nullity," and, in so doing, threatened the future of the Union. "Every pretext, and artifice, and subterfuge, that dishonest ingenuity could conceive and suggest, was tried to prevent the execution of the law, deny justice and produce delay" and increase the cost of litigation. "Vile incendiary speeches, and publications" were made and scattered throughout the city "to excite the evil passions of deluded fanatics, runaway negroes, and thieving pretenders, to violence and blood." Margaret Garner, he insisted, was no Roman hero but a "very common, cross tempered, flat nosed, thick lipped negro woman, whose father was a very bad character," a man from whom she learned her "devilish temper." If the leading citizens did not publicly demonstrate aversion to the activities of these fanatics, the future of the Union was indeed doubtful, for, as it now stood, the Fugitive Slave Law was "utterly valueless to the slaveholding States, who's wrong it was made to remedy." The Union, he concluded, "was no longer perfect."[40]

One wonders what "Justice" thought was needed to save the Union. Surely, the record of cases to date in Ohio generally favored the claims of slaveholders. With the exception of the Rosetta Armistead case, all the decisions had gone against opponents of the Fugitive Slave Law, to say nothing of the fugitives themselves. But it was also clear to "Justice," or any other observer, that slaves continued to flee across the river and to receive shelter and aid from opponents of slavery. The next significant case to come to trial involved Irvin and Angeline Broadhus, who escaped from C. A. Withers of Covington and took refuge in an apartment in Cincinnati rented by William Connelly, a thirty-year-old reporter for the Cincinnati *Commercial*. The fugitives were retaken after a violent confrontation with the sheriff and his posse, during which Irvin was shot and one of the arresting officers injured. They were brought before Commissioner Newhall and, after a brief hearing, taken to Covington. Irvin died soon after and Angeline was sold to a Richmond, Kentucky, slaveholder. Soon after their arrest, Connelly disappeared. In early 1858, the city authorities got word that

---

[39] Weisenburger, *Modern Medea*, 230; Taylor, *Driven Toward Madness*, 86–88; *National Era*, March 20, 1856.
[40] Covington *Journal*, March 22, 29, April 5, 12, May 31, June 21, 28, August 2, 1856.

he was working at the New York *Sun*. He was arrested there and returned to Cincinnati to stand trial.

The case against Connelly turned on whether he knew the Broadhuses were fugitives. He insisted that he did not, because, over the years, they had frequently visited Ohio with their owner's consent. It is not clear how Connelly could have known this unless he was in touch with the slaves prior to their decision to escape. It also appears that Connelly never lived in the apartment he rented. Prosecutors wondered why Connelly needed so large an apartment when his family lived elsewhere. The implication was that he was a member of the city's UGRR and had rented the apartment as one of the organization's safe houses. Connelly was also frequently seen carrying food to the apartment, which prosecutors suggested was evidence of a wider conspiracy. The case brought together some of the leading legal lights in the city. Connelly was defended by John Bernhard Stallo, the German Hegelian and author, and Thomas Corwin, the former governor, Whig senator, and secretary of the Treasury under Millard Fillmore. The lead prosecutor was Stanley Matthews, a former editor, the US attorney for the southern district of Ohio, and a future member of the Supreme Court.[41]

Throughout the trial, the lead attorneys on both sides kept the packed courthouse riveted with arguments spiced with arcane points of law and not a little of the dramatic. Corwin gave a bravura summation sprinkled with humorous asides and biting sarcasm. In a stiflingly hot courtroom, he took frequent and dramatic pauses to swig from a flask, which reporters suspected contained something other than water. After each draft he would turn to the jury and declare: "That's not bad. I saw you cast a wishful eye on it." But Corwin saved his best barbs for Commissioner Newhall, who he knew had only recently arrived in the city from South Carolina. He mocked the commissioner for his tendency to issue warrants speedily, convinced that the future of the Republic rested on the recapture of fugitives – "the chosen instruments of the devil to break up the Union and spread misery all over the world." Matthews held his own. Corwin's sarcasm was wide of the mark, for cases such as the Broadhuses', he warned, had deep political resonances; every message sent to Kentucky, from the words of the governor to the verdict of a jury like Connelly's, should be one of "peace, love and goodwill."[42]

[41] On Stello see Philip F Gura, *American Transcendentalism. A History* (New York: 2007), 271 and New York *Times*, January 20, 1909. On Corwin's views on slavery and free soil see Michael F. Holt, *The Rise and Fall of the American Whig Party. Jacksonian Politics and the Onset of the Civil War* (New York: 1999), 265–67. Many abolitionists considered Matthews a turncoat. A former associate of Gamaliel Bailey, editor of the *National Era*, he was, by the 1850s, as one correspondent graphically put it, "eating soup with the Devil" and using "a very short spoon to do it with." Boston *Bee* (n.d.), in *Liberator*, July 2, 1858, and Ashtabula *Sentinel*, April 22, 1858.

[42] Cincinnati *Gazette*, May 8, 17, 1858; Cincinnati *Commercial*, May 8, 9, 15, 25, 1858; New York *Tribune*, April 6, 7, 1858.

By pointing to the consequences of this and other fugitive slave cases, Matthews put his finger on what drove the debate over the larger significance of the Fugitive Slave Law. Connelly was found guilty, which should have mollified those concerned about the maintenance of the law and, by their calculations, the future of the country. But the air went out of their sails when Judge Leavitt, no friend of abolitionists, who had levied heavy fines on Rush Sloane a few years earlier, announced Connelly's sentence: twenty days in prison and a charge of $10, a slap on the wrist for such a major crime. Connelly's supporters rejoiced. Such leniency seemed to mock proponents of the law as well as slaveholders. This was not a message of peace, love, and goodwill. The prisoner's jail, one observer reported, became "a reception room, where went men and women to do honor to the principle through the person of the representative." Visitors to Connelly's cell included "delegates from Methodist and Unitarian conventions meeting in the City." Levi Coffin recalled that the jailer got so tired locking and unlocking the jail door for visitors that he left it open permanently. The prisoner was provided with all possible comforts by his visitors – a bedstead and bedding, table and chairs, and food, including "strawberries, pastries and other delicacies." On the day of his release, a constant rain blanketed the city. German social and political organizations, including the Turnverein and Arbiter Verein, requested that the jailer postpone Connelly's release by a few hours. Hopefully, the rain would let up and they could be there to greet him in full force. Six hundred Germans and other supporters marched to the jail accompanied by a band, banner, and torches. Connelly was escorted to a packed Turner Hall, where speeches were delivered by Stello, Corwin, George Thompson, and others. In a curious twist of history, while Thompson was a student in Quincy, Illinois, years earlier, he and a couple of his classmates had crossed the Mississippi River in an effort to help slaves escape. They were caught and given lengthy sentences for "enticing" slaves to escape. He later accompanied the Mendian Africans, who had led the successful rebellion on the slave ship *Amistad,* back to Sierra Leone as a representative of the American Missionary Association. Thompson happened to be in the city raising money for the mission when Connelly was released.[43]

At the meeting, Connelly announced that he would explain the workings of the UGRR in a lecture at a local black church the following evening. It was the sort of information opponents of the largely secret organization had been seeking for years. Such an exposé from someone in the know could be a prelude

---

[43] Cincinnati *Gazette,* May 18, 19, June 12, 1858; Cincinnati *Commercial,* May 24, June 12, 1858; *Liberator,* July 2, 1858; Larry Gara, "The Fugitive Slave Law in the Eastern Ohio Valley," *Ohio History,* 72, No. 2 (April 1963), 124–25; Coffin, *Reminiscences,* 582–88. Connelly returned to his job at the New York *Sun* soon after. On Thompson see Joseph Yannelli, "George Thompson among the Africans. Empathy, Authority, and Insanity in the Age of Abolition," *Journal of American History,* 96, No. 4 (March 2010), 979–1000. Interestingly, the *Sun* carried only a brief report of the case and did not even mention Connelly's capture in the city. See *Liberator,* July 30, 1858.

to dismantling what many considered the nation's principal domestic enemy, a group responsible for undermining one of the pillars of the liberal democratic state: private property in slaves. Not surprisingly, supporters of the UGRR worried about the consequences should Connelly expose the details of how the local organization functioned – its methods of operation, its financing, its lines of communication across the Ohio River, the series of safe houses it had established in the city, and the people who made it all work. It is very likely that Connelly thought better of his plans, or was pressured not to say much about what he knew, for he told his audience very little that was revealing. He did, however, point to some features of the movement that have continued to intrigue historians. The majority of its conductors, he estimated, were born in the South and many non-slaveholding whites sympathized with the organization. While some of these Southerners became involved for the sheer excitement of it, others knew there was money to be made in getting slaves across the river. "These Conductors," he declared, "hate Slavery, but generally have the vices of their Southern education, and are not always particularly moral." He also made reference to instances of whites, even some who had been imprisoned, returning to the work of the movement after their release. There was little here to comfort slaveholders.[44]

Almost a year before the sheriff laid siege to the apartment where the Broadhuses were hiding, Commissioner Newhall had issued a warrant for the arrest of Charles and Edward Taylor, Russell Hyde, and Hiram Guttridge of Champaign County for sheltering and protecting thirty-six-year-old Addison White, who had escaped from Fleming County, Kentucky, in the summer of 1856. Since then, he had been employed on a farm outside Mechanicsburg, west of Columbus, owned by Udney Hyde, a native of Vermont who was involved in the activities of the local UGRR. Daniel White, Addison's owner, became aware of his whereabouts from letters Addison had written his wife, a free black woman, who was still living in Kentucky. Daniel White, along with a number of Kentuckians, two US deputies from Cincinnati, and the deputy marshal of Urbana, descended on the Hyde farm in April 1857. Addison armed and barricaded himself in a loft and fired on pursuers as they attempted to enter the loft. By this point, a large crowd of armed neighbors had assembled outside the farm. Daniel White and the others thought better of continuing the siege and promptly left the area. Weeks later, Deputy Marshal B. P. Churchill and eleven assistants returned to Mechanicsburg with Newhall's warrant. No one could explain to local folks why it took twelve officers to arrest four men who, unlike Addison, made it clear they had no intention of resisting. Opponents, however, swore out a writ of habeas corpus with a local judge, but before it could be served Churchill and his posse left the county with their prisoners. What followed was a race to Cincinnati with the posse pursued every step of the way.

---

[44] Cincinnati *Gazette*, May 19, 1858.

Another writ was obtained in Clark County, but Churchill refused to hand over his prisoners. A third writ was procured in Greene County. This time, Sheriff John E. Lyton – with the backing of a crowd in excess of three hundred, many of them women – seized Churchill and his deputies near Lumberton following an exchange of gunfire. They were taken to Springfield to stand trial, but before it could begin they were freed through a writ signed by Judge Humphrey H. Leavitt, sitting in Cincinnati. Lawyers for Churchill argued that, as the law of the land, the Fugitive Slave Law vested the power to make such arrests in the hands of US marshals, not local officials. Because federal law trumped state and local ordinances, writs issued by local courts could not be served on federal officers during the course of their assigned duties. Because such writs were of "no weight," and had been issued "under false premises," they must not be obeyed. Leavitt agreed; the aim of the county writs, their execution, and the action of those opposed to the marshal were, he ruled, in themselves acts of "political nullification." The law of the United States could not be evaded, either by violence, "which is rebellion, or by the spacious pretenses of law." The case against those accused of participating in the attempted "rescue" was heard in July. The defense insisted that, as a sovereign state, Ohio had the power to issue writs for the arrest of Churchill and the others. The charges against Hyde and Guttridge were dismissed, however, and the Taylors' hearing was postponed until October. The case against the Taylors limped through the courts until April 1858, when it was abandoned by the district attorney. The pressure to prosecute the case came directly from the Buchanan administration in Washington, DC. District Attorney John H. O'Neill concurred: resistance to the law, he told his superiors, was the work of "traitors in Ohio" led by Republicans. If the government did not show resolve, it "will be hereafter wholly impossible to execute any process in Ohio in the slightest degree connected with the Fugitive Slave Law." In the meantime, local supporters raised $950 to ransom Addison, who later settled in Mechanicsburg.[45]

Of the major cases heard in Ohio during the decade, the one involving Addison White represented an apparent shift away from Cincinnati and southern counties to the northern tier of the state. Although fugitive slave cases

[45] Cincinnati *Gazette*, May 29, 30, June 1, 2, 13, 17, 18, 26, July 10, 11, 13, August 1, 3, 1857, April 21, 1858; *Ohio State Democrat*, June 11, 1857; *Anti-Slavery Bugle*, June 6, 13, 1857; Xenia *Torch-Light*, June 3, August 5, 1857; Ashtabula *Sentinel*, June 4, 11, August 13, 1857; *Ohio State Journal*, June 30, 1857; Chicago *Tribune*, June 2, 1857; *Liberator*, July 17, August 14, 1857; Middleton, "The Fugitive Slave Crisis in Cincinnati," 29; Campbell, *The Slave Catchers*, 161–64; Siebert, *The Underground Railroad*, 334–35; Ralph M. Watts, "History of the Underground Railroad in Mechanicsburg," *Ohio Archeological and Historical Society Publication*, XLIII (1934), 233–51; Benjamin F. Prince, "The Rescue Case of 1857," *Ohio Archeological and Historical Society Publication*, XVI (1907), 292–308; John H. O'Neill to J. S. Black, Cincinnati, May 30, 1857. Letters received by the Attorney General, 1809–1870, National Law and Order, Reel 16.

continued to be adjudicated in Cincinnati courts and commissioners' hearing rooms, those with the greatest political impact, after 1857, occurred in the area north of Columbus. The most dramatic of these involved John Price, who was nabbed in September 1858 by slave catchers from Mason County, Kentucky, outside Oberlin, and hurried off to Wellington, a village nine miles to the south, to catch the late afternoon train for Columbus. Price had escaped from John G. Bacon in the company of two others across the frozen river in January 1856. They made their way to Oberlin, a college town that welcomed fugitives. During the 1850s, these fugitives from slavery helped to swell the town's black population by almost 300 percent. Oberlin was, as some locals proudly boasted, a "city of refuge" for fugitives. John Bacon had gotten wind of Price's whereabouts and commissioned his neighbor, Anderson Jennings, to capture Price. Jennings, in turn, hired Richard P. Mitchell, who had worked for him as an overseer. On their way to Oberlin, they were joined by Jacob Lowe, a US deputy marshal of Columbus, and Samuel Davis, that city's part-time jailer and deputy sheriff. In Oberlin, Jennings persuaded Shakespeare Boynton, the thirteen-year-old son of a prominent landowner, to join in their plans to capture Price. Young Boynton was to offer Price a job on his father's farm harvesting crops. On the way to the farm, the wagon in which Price and Boynton were traveling was overtaken by Jennings and Mitchell. Price was bundled into a carriage and the three headed for Wellington. News of Price's capture spread quickly throughout the town and a large crowd, estimated at two hundred, followed. Almost every horse was commandeered. "Farmers' wagons, private carriages and every hack in the town were chartered." It took only fifteen minutes for the crowd to gather in the village square "armed with weapons of death." One of those in the chase was Charles Langston, a forty-one-year-old teacher and school principal, the son of a slave mother and a Virginia slaveholder who had freed Charles and his two brothers and divided his property among the three. After their parents' death in 1834, the three had settled in Ohio.

The carriage carrying Price arrived in Wellington with time to spare before the departure of the five o'clock train. Jennings took rooms in the only hotel in the village, but grew alarmed by the large crowds milling about following a fire. As a precaution, he moved Price to a room in the attic. Soon after, the crowds in the street were augmented by the large contingent from Oberlin, who immediately surrounded the hotel and demanded Price's release. Langston and the others tried to procure a writ of habeas corpus as well as persuade the town sheriff to arrest Jennings and the others as kidnappers. He even tried to negotiate with Jennings for the release of his captive. When this failed, the crowd rushed the hotel, took Price, and carried him back to Oberlin in a carriage driven by Simeon Bushnell, a white bookseller. Price was hidden for a while in the home of James Fairchild, president of the college, and later sent to Canada. On their return to Oberlin, a crowd gathered outside the post office and pledged that "whosoever laid hands on a black man in this community, no matter what the color of the authority, would do so at the peril of their life."[46]

The authorities had other ideas. A grand jury, which convened in mid-October in Cleveland, a heavily Republican city, was made up exclusively of Democrats, including Shakespeare Boynton's father, and presided over by Judge Hiram Willson, who made it abundantly clear that he found abolitionist dogma repugnant. The grand jury indicted thirty-seven for violating the Fugitive Slave Law – twenty-five from Oberlin, the others from Wellington. Among those from Oberlin were twelve blacks, including Charles Langston; John Copeland, who would later gain fame as part of John Brown's group that attacked the federal arsenal at Harpers Ferry; John Watson; and O. S. B. Wall, a shoemaker and Langston's brother-in- law. Among the white defenders were Simeon Bushnell, who had driven the carriage that took Price back to Oberlin, and Ansel Lyman, who had raised the alarm following Price's capture. Also included were Henry Peck, a professor at the college; James Fitch, a bookstore proprietor; and Ralph Plumb, a lawyer, for aiding and abetting, although none were present at the rescue. Jerry Fox, Thomas Gena, and John Hartwell – fugitive slaves – were also indicted but never apprehended.[47]

What Steven Lubet has aptly described as the "longest, and most radically politicized fugitive slave trial of the antebellum era" began in Cleveland in April 1859. The defense team of Rufus Spalding, Albert Gallatin Riddle, Franklin Backus, and Seneca O. Griswold – "four of Ohio's most prominent attorneys" – faced US Attorney George Belden, a Democrat and supporter of the Fugitive Slave Law, who insisted that rescues were acts of treason, and George Bliss, "a former judge and Democratic congressman." Belden was under pressure from Washington to prosecute the case against the abolitionists and anti-administration Republicans fully. The small abolitionist town should not be allowed to set a precedent and go unpunished, nor should the defenders be allowed to "expose the iniquity of slavery" unopposed. Bushnell was the first to come to trial. As in other cases of its kind, the defense questioned the legitimacy of the power of attorney given to Jennings, whether Price's admission

[46] For details of the rescue see Steven Lubet, *Fugitive Justice. Runaways, Rescuers and Slavery on Trial* (Cambridge, MA: 2010), 238–41, 244–47; Nat Brandt, *The Town that Started the Civil War* (New York: 1990), 87–111; J. Brent Morris, *Oberlin. Hotbed of Abolitionism. College, Community, and the Fight for Freedom and Equality in Antebellum America* (Chapel Hill, NC: 2014), 208–11; William Cheek and Aimee Lee Cheek, *John Mercer Langston and the Fight for Black Freedom, 1829–1865* (Urbana, IL: 1989), 317; New York *Tribune*, September 18, 1858; Cleveland *Leader*, April 6, 1859. For biographical information of Charles Langston see Frederick J. Blue, *No Taint of Compromise. Crusaders in Antislavery Politics* (Baton Rouge: 2005), 65–66.

[47] Brandt, *The Town that Started the Civil War*, 71, 75, 115, 129; Lubet, *Fugitive Justice*, 250; for Wall see Daniel J. Sharfstein, *The Invisible Line: Three American Families and the Secret Journey from Black to White* (New York: 2011).

FIGURE 3. The Oberlin Rescuers at Cuyahoga Co. Jail, April 1859. (Courtesy of the Oberlin College Archives)

in Wellington that he was a slave, and had escaped, was voluntarily given or forced, or even if such an admission was reliable and admissible, and whether the person described in the warrant was Price. These questions of identification, as we have seen in other cases, were meant to poke holes in the claims of owners who seemed incapable of describing the true color of fugitives. Judge Willson put paid to all questions about identity: a "dark complexion, wooly head, and flat nose," he ruled, "with possession and claim of ownership, do afford *prima facie* evidence of the slavery and ownership charged." Bushnell was found guilty and sentenced to sixty days in prison and fined $600 plus cost.[48]

---

[48] Lubet, *Fugitive Justice*, 259–65, 294; the judge's quotation can be found on p. 272; Brandt, *The Town that Started the Civil War*, 147; Cleveland *Leader*, May 13, 1859.

Charles Langston was the next to come to trial. He, too, was found guilty, but before he could be sentenced Judge Willson asked if Langston had anything to say. That was a mistake. If one of the trial's intents was to condemn the actions of the rescuers and, by extension, the abolitionist traditions of Oberlin, then Willson erred in providing Langston with such an opening. What followed was one of the most poignant indictments of the country's treatment of black people. Langston's opening sentences set the tone. This was the first time, Langston admitted, that he had appeared in court for violating the laws of the country. He asked no favors of the court, nor did he believe that anything he said would influence the judge's "predetermined line of action," for the entire machinery of government was "constituted to oppress and outrage colored men." The forcible capture of Price disturbed the peace and tranquility of the town's black population, a population made up of those who, in the face of much suffering, had managed to purchase their freedom, those who were the recipients of the kindness of caring masters who had consented to set them free, and those who, by sheer will and to their "everlasting honor," escaped the plantation, "eluded the blood-thirsty patrols," evaded bloodhounds, swam across swollen rivers, reaching, at last, "through incredible difficulties, what they, in their delusion, supposed to be free soil." By these measures, Price had a right to his liberty "under the laws of God, under the laws of Nature, and under the Declaration of American Independence." The slave catchers had violated those "laws" by their actions. Langston was proud to identify with Price, a man of his race. Empathy with the oppressed, he had long learned, was part of his patrimony, handed down to him by his father, who had fought in the Revolutionary War, which established the principle that "*all* men have a right to life and liberty." That is why he went to the aid of Price. In addition, if under Ohio's laws all men living in the state were presumed to be free, then Jennings ought to have gone before state authorities and proved the contrary. Under the circumstances, and as a citizen of Ohio, Langston felt an obligation to do what he could to ensure justice was done. The law under which he was arraigned, therefore, was an "unjust one, one made to crush the colored man, and one that outrages every feeling of Humanity, as well as every rule of Right." In so doing, it had turned him into "an *outlaw of the United States*." For these and other reasons, Langston insisted, he should not be sentenced. Furthermore, it was obvious to any unbiased observer that he was not tried by an impartial jury of his peers, a guarantee enshrined in the Constitution. His jury shared all the "deeply fixed *prejudices*" that had long oppressed the "colored man." He was tried instead by "a jury who were prejudiced; before a Court that was prejudiced; prosecuted by an officer who was prejudiced, and defended, though ably, by counsel that were prejudiced." There was, in fact, not a "spot in this wide country" where a black man might "dare to ask a mercy of a white man." Were he to visit Philadelphia Hall, that symbol of the struggle for independence and say to a United States marshal that his father was a "revolutionary soldier; that he served under Lafayette, and fought through the whole war; and that he always told me that he fought for *my* freedom as much as for his own;…he would sneer at me, and clutch me with his bloody fingers, and say he had a *right* to take me as a slave," for, quoting the dictum of the chief justice of the Supreme Court in the recent Dred Scott decision, "black men had no rights which white men were bound to respect." Langston maintained that he had acted properly and within the law when, in Wellington, he demanded that Price be accorded a hearing before he was taken south. If, he warned, accused blacks were not granted such basic rights, then they would inevitably and understandably be "thrown back upon those last defenses of our rights, which cannot be taken from us, and which God gave us that we need not be slaves." Were Willson in his position, Langston had no doubt that he would have acted as he had done that day in Wellington.[49]

Although Willson thought Langston had done the court an injustice, he was obviously moved enough to impose a light sentence – twenty days in the Cuyahoga County jail and a fine of $100. Those who heard the speech in the packed courthouse were deeply impressed with the range of Langston's indictment of the country, his passionate opposition to laws he considered unconstitutional, as well as his commitment to the struggle to remove all barriers to racial equality. In the assessment of one sympathetic editor, the speech was "manly…eloquent [and] withering," one that "will live in history" and one that the "children of the free states will read…in their school books, and will execrate the memory of the court, the jury who consigned such men to fine and imprisonment, for a crime so God like." Langston, the editor continued, had stood in the presence of the "federal court despotism, and like Paul of old, spoke words of truth and soberness." Years later, his brother, John Mercer, remembered the speech as being "powerful and matchless…wonderful in the breath of [its] views, masterly and unanswerable in logic, and law, commanding and irresistible in its delivery and effects."[50]

But the prosecution had only dispensed with two of the many cases still waiting to be heard. Before Belden could call the next case, however, a grand jury in Lorain County, home of Oberlin, had brought charges of kidnapping against Jennings, Lowe, and Mitchell. Their trial was set for July. In the meantime, supporters of the rescuers appealed to the state supreme court for writs of habeas corpus, a direct challenge to the constitutionality of the Fugitive Slave Law. Given that five Republicans sat on the court and its chief justice, Joseph Swan, was a known abolitionist, there was a general expectation that its ruling would favor the accused. But they were to be disappointed; the court ruled 3–2 against granting the writ. Even before the court had handed down its decision, word came from Washington that, while it was important that

[49] For a copy of Langston's speech see www.oberlin.edu/external/EOG/Oberlin-Wellington_rescue/c.langstonspeech.htm

[50] Cleveland *Leader*, May 13, 1859; John Mercer Langston, *From the Virginia Plantation to the National Capitol* (1884, rpr., New York: 1969), 187.

"public peace" be maintained and state authorities not offended, everything had to be done to ensure that the prisoners were not rescued or freed by judges. Either result would send a message to the country that federal law was unenforceable in the district. If the state supreme court was "imposed upon" to issue a writ of habeas corpus, Matthew Johnson, US marshal for the northern district of Ohio, was ordered by his superiors in Washington to respectfully decline to produce the prisoners. No state court, he was told, had the power to free prisoners in a case of this sort. Such powers belonged exclusively to federal courts. Should the state court attempt to take the prisoners, it would be an act of "lawless violence." Had the state supreme court ruled in favor of the rescuers, it appears the federal government was at least willing to contemplate an assertion of its absolute authority. The action of the Lorain County grand jury, however, produced a stalemate, which forced the hands of the prosecutors in Cleveland and, by extension, the federal government. A deal had to be struck to overcome the stalemate: the charges against the kidnappers would be dropped, it was agreed, if those against the rescuers, who were yet to be tried, were abandoned. The rescuers, Lubet concludes, had "worn down the federal government and emerged from jail with their principles intact." Langston was released the first day of June, Bushnell six weeks later.[51]

The rescue, the Cheeks have argued, injected "new emotional fervor into the anti-slavery movement," reinvigorated "the Ohio black movement," and critically affected "the Republican Party's evolution and standing in Ohio – and by extension, in the North." Almost twelve thousand attending a public meeting in a square not far from where the rescuers were being held in May, the day before the state supreme court would meet, heard speeches by Joshua Giddings, John Mercer Langston, and Rufus Spalding, the defense counsel. Giddings had long called for open resistance to the Fugitive Slave Law and did so again in his own inimitable style. Langston made his opposition to the law and the Democratic Party abundantly clear. Both had to be openly defied and defeated and the men held behind the jail walls liberated. Langston had been at the forefront of the effort to push the Republican Party in a more radical direction – one that opposed slavery – and insisted that Ohio's African Americans be granted all the rights of citizenship. The rescue was both an opportunity to undermine the law and pull the party back from its drift towards conservatism. He and Charles had also been major players in the establishment of the state's Negro Convention meetings. Its first, held in Columbus in January 1850, set out a wide-ranging political and social agenda. They created the "Ohio Colored American League" to agitate for the vote and the removal of the state's Black Laws. They also selected agents to canvass the state to resist "every form

[51] Lubet, *Fugitive Justice*, 298, 303–04, 309–13; Brandt, *The Town that Started the Civil War*, 221, 240; Blue, *No Taint of Compromise*, 84; J. S. Black to Matthew Johnson, Washington, DC. April 26, 1859, Letters Sent by the Department of Justice, General and Miscellaneous, 1818–1904, M699 (Microfilm, Roll 3).

of oppression and proscription," any laws that curtailed "the natural rights of man," the evils of slavery, and restrictions on the rights of the 25,000 "half freemen of Ohio." These themes were reiterated and expanded on in subsequent meetings. In the wake of the rescue, John Mercer called on the 1858 convention, chaired by Charles, to "trample the fugitive slave act under foot, as they had recently done in Wellington," and to destroy the Democratic Party. Peter H. Clark of Cincinnati was less sanguine that the Republicans would be any better. In their effort to become a national party, he observed, they had been growing increasingly conservative. The convention endorsed the actions of the rescuers, denounced the Fugitive Slave Law and the Dred Scott ruling as "huge outrages." The meeting also formed the "Ohio State Anti-Slavery Society" with John Mercer Langston as president, and pledged to work for the abolition of slavery and the repeal of all laws that "make a distinction on account of color."[52]

If the Ohio State Anti-Slavery Society, headquartered in Cleveland, was organized in part to prevent slave returns, then the members were taken by surprise when, in November 1859, Henry Seaton was spirited away from the city "without the knowledge of any person excepting those who did the work," hurried to Cincinnati, where, following a brief hearing, he was taken to Covington. The twenty-four-year-old Seaton had escaped from Greenup County, Kentucky, through Ironton, Ohio, in July 1859, and had settled in Cleveland. Evidently, Seaton was betrayed by George Hartman, a white man, who offered to either get him to Canada or find him a job in Oberlin. Seaton did not know that Hartman was working with Deputy Marshal Mason of Cincinnati, who had a warrant for the fugitive's arrest. When Hartman returned to Cleveland following Seaton's abduction, richer by $300, he was greeted by angry black crowds. He was subsequently brought before police court charged with abduction but was found innocent. African Americans packed the courtroom during the hearing and followed Hartman after he was released. He was forced to take refuge in the city jail to avoid the irate black crowds. Hartman, whom one newspaper described as "industrious, honest and attentive to business," slipped out of town on a train bound for Columbus under the cover of darkness, his "prospects for life in Cleveland" ruined, according to one observer, by his participation in the abduction of Seaton.[53]

---

[52] Cheek and Cheek, *John Mercer Langston and the Fight for Black Freedom*, 320–27; Morris, *Hotbed of Abolitionism*, 213; Lubet, *Fugitive Justice*, 302–03; Philip S. Foner and George E. Walker, eds., *Proceedings of the Black State Conventions, 1840–1865*, 2 Vols., (Philadelphia: 1979), I, 241–52, 334–41. On Clark see Nikki M. Taylor, *America's First Black Socialist. The Radical Life of Peter H. Clark* (Lexington, KY: 2013); Philip S. Foner, *Essays in Afro-American History* (Philadelphia: 1978), 154–77; Lawrence Grossman, "In His Veins Coursed No Bootlicking Blood. The Career of Peter H. Clark," *Ohio History*, 86, No. 2 (Spring 1977).

[53] Cincinnati *Gazette*, November 12, 1859; Cincinnati *Commercial*, November 12, 1859; Cleveland *Leader*, November 14, 15, 16, 1859; Ironton *Register*, November 24, December 1, 1859; Campbell, *The Slave Catchers*, 135.

The abduction came as a shock largely because since 1850 the city had been generally free of the turmoil associated with such renditions. The general support given the Oberlin-Wellington rescuers throughout their trials and incarceration and the fact that, by the end of the decade, the city had become a Republican Party stronghold, made it a relatively safe haven for former slaves. It also continued to be a major transshipment point for fugitives heading for Canada. Reports of large numbers of fugitives passing through the city were common. In the last few weeks of 1856, for example, an estimated seventy-eight escapees from Kentucky, Virginia, Georgia, and South Carolina had passed through the city. As one newspaper put it, those who chose to stay felt relatively safe protected by the black defense committees, which first came into existence following passage of the Fugitive Slave Law.[54]

Organizations such as the Fugitive Aid Society acted as both protective and welfare associations, shepherding fugitives through the city on their way to Canada, or finding jobs and shelter for those who chose to stay. In October 1860, the society found a job, first at the home of A. G. Riddle, the Republican congressman-elect, and then at L. A. Benton's, for Sara Lucy Bagby, who had recently arrived from Wheeling, Virginia. Bagby, twenty-eight, had escaped from John Goshorn, a real estate dealer, going up the Ohio River through Beaver to Pittsburgh, Pennsylvania. Bagby claimed she had been taken to Pennsylvania by Goshorn's granddaughter, Isabella, and so was therefore free. Goshorn, who had bought her in Richmond in 1852 for $600, insisted that she had never been taken into Pennsylvania but, in fact, had escaped there. Sometime in 1857, Goshorn had transferred Lucy (as she was commonly known) to his son William. Following a tip from a black person, the Goshorns tracked Lucy to Cleveland, where she was arrested at the home of L. A. Benton, with the aid of two deputy marshals. The capture riled the black community, who turned out in force outside the jail where she was being held, around the courthouse during a habeas corpus hearing, and, later, at the hearing before the commissioner. There were reports that eight armed blacks had been arrested, four from Oberlin, including John Wall, a brother of O. S. B. Wall, one of the Oberlin-Wellington rescuers. A number of women were also arrested, one for throwing snuff, and another for sprinkling pepper in the faces of the police. At a habeas corpus hearing before Probate Judge D. R. Tilden, Lucy was defended by R. P. Spalding, one of the Oberlin-Wellington rescuers' defense counsel; A. G. Riddle, for whom she had worked; and C. W. Palmer. Spalding requested a delay so he could visit Wheeling to determine if Lucy had ever been brought into a Free State by the family. On his return, he reported that, as the Goshorns maintained, Lucy had not been taken into Pennsylvania. Lucy was remanded to Wheeling under heavy guard. Some in the city were determined to prevent

---

[54] Cleveland *Leader*, June 16, December 8, 1856, January 13, 1857; Maysville *Eagle*, December 13, 1856.

her return. An unnamed armed white man and a black man boarded the train carrying Lucy at Hudson just outside Akron. They carried iron bars, which were to be used to decouple the carriage in which she was held. They were to be joined at Lima (today Limaville) by a group of forty well-armed African Americans. Anticipating trouble, the conductor decided not to make the customary stop at Lima. His decision prevented what could have been a bloody clash. Lucy was successfully returned to the Goshorns.[55]

On the surface, the Armistead, Broadhus, White, Bagby, and all the other cases that came to court concerned the legal right of slaveholders to reclaim their property. But running through all of them were considerations of larger political significance: to avert the danger of "political nullification," as Judge Humphreys Leavitt put it. The threat of dislocation loomed increasingly large as the decade progressed. Following Rosetta Armistead's release, a meeting in Jeffersonville, Kentucky, lamented the action of Northern courts that disregarded the rights of American citizens, rendered their property "fatally insecure," and interfered with the commercial interests of Southerners. The meeting called on the Kentucky legislature to appropriate funds to compensate Rev. Henry Dennison for the loss of his slave and to cover the cost of the two suits pending against him in Ohio. They also called for mass meetings throughout the state to support the effort and to protest the actions of the Ohio court. Although there is no evidence that other meetings were held, or that the Kentucky legislature ever considered appropriating funds to support Dennison, the Louisville meeting speaks to the ways the continuous flow of fugitive slaves into Ohio had the potential to affect political and commercial relations between the two states. When, in 1857, an antislavery majority in the Ohio legislature imposed criminal penalties on anyone who came into the state with the intent "to hold or control...any other person as a slave," the political fallout from the effort to recapture escaping slaves was confirmed. Although this piece of legislation was reversed by the legislature when it fell into Democratic hands, no one in Kentucky could ignore the fact that the security of their property rested, in large part, on the whims of the Ohio electorate.[56]

Freedom of movement for Southerners traveling through Free States with slaves was at the heart of the crisis over the Fugitive Slave Law. Slaveholders who chose to ignore all the warning signs found themselves in danger and their property vulnerable. This was amply demonstrated in 1854 when a delegation from the annual meeting of the Western Anti-Slavery Society boarded a train in

---

[55] Cleveland *Herald*, January 19, 21, 25, 28, February 12, 1861; Cleveland *Leader*, January 21, 22, 24, 25, February 1, 14, 1861; Ashtabula *Sentinel*, January 23, 30, 1861; Wheeling *Intelligencer*, November 28, December 10, 1860, January 23, 25, 26, 1861; Vacha, "The Case of Sara Lucy Bagby," covers the case in detail. John Malvin, *Autobiography of John Malvin. A Narrative* (Cleveland: 1879), 37–39; www.lva.virginia.gov/public/trailblazers/2010/honoree.asp?bro=3; www.ohiocountylibrary.org/wheeling-history/4287

[56] Cincinnati *Commercial*, April 19, 1855; Finkelman, *An Imperfect Union*, 177.

Salem, Ohio, where the meeting was in session, and removed a young slave girl
from the arms of Mrs. J. J. Robinson, who was on her way back to Memphis,
Tennessee, from North Carolina with her husband. The group was led by,
among others, Henry H. Blackwell, the Cincinnati merchant; Dr. Abraham
Brooke, a founding member of the Society for Universal Inquiry and Reform;
and an unnamed black man. According to Robinson, the girl, who had only
recently been given to his wife by her parents in North Carolina, had been
violently removed from the train by a group of blacks headed by Blackwell.
Soon after, the rescuers called a public meeting, to be attended by the girl, at
which she was renamed Abbey Kelley Salem. A subscription was also started
for her education. On his way through Cincinnati, Robinson threatened both
to bring suit against Blackwell for injuring his wife and to organize a boycott
against his wholesale hardware business once he got back to Memphis. Some
in Cincinnati, including the chamber of commerce, supported the call for a
boycott. A public meeting in Memphis in mid-September condemned the brutal
assault on the Robinsons and the robbery of their "rightful property" by a mob
headed by a person from a city whose "commercial intercourse" with Memphis
was worth millions annually. Unless Cincinnati publicly repudiated Blackwell's
actions, the meeting threatened to "break up the commercial intercourse"
between the two cities and divert its trade elsewhere. The meeting also called
on other Southern states to join the proposed boycott and demanded that the
city government create "special River Police" to check all boats from Cincinnati
and to enforce all municipal laws "in regard to free negroes." Finally, it pledged
to set up a "Correspondence Committee" to communicate with other Southern
states. Another meeting in nearby Fayette County evidently offered a reward of
$1,000 for Blackwell's capture.[57]

In spite of actions such as the Salem rescue, the authorities did what they
could to ensure that the law was fully enforced and that Southerners traveling through the state did not lose their property. Following the Salem rescue,
Abraham Brooke claimed that railroads in the area regularly carried slaves traveling with their owners. Local, state, and federal authorities developed a policing system that aimed to overwhelm the opposition, ensure the return of fugitive
slaves, and prevent rescues. Enforcement was, however, an expensive proposi-
tion. Under the law, the federal government was required to foot the bill for all
renditions if there was any hint of a rescue. There were also costs associated
with hearings. As we have seen, during the twenty-nine-day trial of Margaret

[57] Homestead *Journal*, August 30, 1854; *Anti-Slavery Bugle*, September 9, 30, 1854; Salem
*Democrat* (n.d.), in *Anti-Slavery Bugle*, October 14, 1854; *Ohio State Journal*, September 1,
1854; Cleveland *Leader*, August 30, September 2, 1854; New York *Tribune*, September 1, 1854;
Louisville *Journal*, September 1, 23, 1854; Baltimore *Sun*, September 2, 1854; Memphis *Appeal*,
September 10, 23, 1854; Covington *Journal*, September 30, 1854; Robertson, *Hearts Beating for
Liberty*, 161–63; A. Brooke to Valentine Nicholson, Marlboro, September 23, 1859, Valentine
Nicholson Transcripts, M642B1F2, Indiana Historical Society; Thomas D. Hamm, *God's
Government Begun the Society for Universal Inquiry and Reform, 1842–1846* (Bloomington,
IN: 1995), 42–49.

Garner, the US marshal, H. H. Robinson, had at his disposal a force of four hundred special deputies who were armed with repeating rifles and pistols costing the federal government an estimated $22,400. The Connelly trial apparently cost the government $5,000. In a moment of rare understatement, one editor observed that there was "nothing *cheap* about the Fugitive Slave Law."[58]

Over the decade, the commissioners, particularly those in Cincinnati, extended the reach of their remit in ways that, at times, seem to skirt the intent, if not the spirit, of the law. By the end of the decade, the boundary of the southern district of Ohio seemed to have drifted northward beyond Columbus. All a slaveholder searching for a fugitive whom he knew to be living in a northern district needed to do was procure a writ from a sympathetic commissioner – and there were many of those – in Cincinnati. The case of John Rice, also known as John Tyler, was fairly typical. Rice had escaped from Cabell County, Virginia, in December 1854 and settled in Mt. Gilead, Murrow County, Ohio, where he married and started a family. In October 1859, Rice and another African American, Henry Alfred, were hired by someone calling himself D. C. Watson to work for him in a "refreshment saloon" that he was about to open in Columbus. As it turned out, Watson was working with Cincinnati Deputy Marshal William L. Manson, who had a warrant for Rice's arrest. Manson calculated that it would be easier to take Rice in Columbus once he was removed from the security of friends in Mt. Gilead. But Manson should have anticipated that Rice, who is described as a large man standing over six feet tall and weighing two hundred pounds, would not go quietly. It took Manson, his deputies, and Watson more than a half hour to subdue Rice, and then only with the assistance of onlookers. Once subdued, Rice was taken to the station to catch the train bound for Cincinnati. Many in the crowd on the platform challenged Manson's actions. He responded that Rice was a suspected thief. By this time, a writ of habeas corpus had been obtained by a group of sympathizers in Columbus. The sheriff was unable, however, to serve it, as Manson had locked himself and his prisoner in a closet at the front of the train and posted an armed guard outside. Promptly on arrival in Cincinnati, Rice was taken before Commissioner Newhall, who refused to allow attorneys to act for the fugitive. Rice claimed that he was free and insisted that there were witnesses in Morrow County who could corroborate his claim, but the commissioner refused to delay the hearing or allow witnesses who testified for the owner to be cross-examined. After a brief hearing, Newhall remanded Rice to Covington, where he was taken by a large police force made up of "several members of the Independent Detective Police" headed by Marshal H. H. Robinson, who had returned Margaret Garner to her owner three years earlier.[59]

[58] Cincinnati *Gazette,* March 5, 1856, April, 3, 16, 1858; Ashtabula *Sentinel,* April 22, 1858; *Liberator,* July 30, 1858; Weisenburger, *Modern Medea,* 195.
[59] *Ohio State Journal,* October 29, 31, November 2, 4, 1859; Cleveland *Herald,* October 31, 1859; Cleveland *Leader,* November 1, 1859; Xenia *Torch-Light,* November 2, 1859; Cincinnati *Gazette,* October 29, 31, November 9, 17, 1859; Cincinnati *Commercial,* October 29, 1859.

To function effectively, the Fugitive Slave Law required federal and local authorities to work in tandem: commissioners willing to issue arrest warrants for fugitives beyond their jurisdiction, to arrange expedited hearings, and to employ large police forces, which were meant to awe the opposition. By the end of the decade, those, such as John Jolliffe, who volunteered their services to defend fugitives and raised questions about the law's constitutionality, found the going increasingly tough. The rejection of such arguments by commissioners had become routine. Even so, one could not imagine Jollife ever abandoning these claims, or following the line of political expediency followed by Lucy Bagby's lawyers. He persisted in the face of overwhelming odds, demanding suspected fugitives be given a thorough hearing. Opponents recorded some early successes – the escape of Lewis from the Cincinnati court and winning the freedom of Rosetta Armistead. But in the years after 1857, all suspects brought before commissioners or judges were returned and none rescued.[60] But the authorities did not have it all their own way. Even in defeat, judges were persuaded, as in the cases of Charles Langston and William Connelly, to impose laughably lenient judgments. More significantly, all the evidence points to a continued flow of fugitives from eastern Kentucky and Virginia who made it to safety either in the northern part of the state or Canada. For every John Rice who was taken and returned, there were countless unnamed slaves who made it to freedom.

---

[60] Cincinnati *Gazette*, November 15, 1859, December 26, 1860; Cincinnati *Commercial*, November 15, 1859; *Ohio State Journal*, December 19, 1859.

# 7

## Southeast Pennsylvania

As Congress put the finishing touches on the Fugitive Slave Law in August 1850, eight slaves from Clarke County in Virginia's Shenandoah Valley arrived in Harrisburg, Pennsylvania, followed closely by their owners and slave catchers. Three of the eight – Samuel Wilson, George Brocks, and Billy – broke their journey in the city; the others chose to move on further north. The choice to stay in the city was not unusual. The state capital, with a significant black population – at 10 percent, the largest of any city in the state – was close to the western end of an arc of contested sites of freedom stretching from Franklin County east through Columbia on the Susquehanna River, which emptied into the Chesapeake Bay, then further east through Lancaster to West Chester and Philadelphia. For years, it had been a destination for those seeking freedom. An estimated 150 fugitive slaves made the capital city their home in 1850. The topography of the area, with its mountain ranges running southwest to northeast, was in places remote enough to provide inaccessible sanctuaries for those fleeing slavery in northwest Maryland and the Shenandoah Valley. Pockets of black rural and urban settlements could be found in and around Christiana, Mercersburg, Chambersburg, Gettysburg, Carlisle, York, West Chester, and elsewhere. They and the many Quaker settlements in the area had long been magnets for those fleeing slavery. Columbia, primarily because of its location, and an "insatiable demand for cheap labor," mainly in its lumberyards, according to Carl Oblinger, "attracted fugitive slaves and manumitted blacks fleeing the Border slave states." An observer who knew the place well recalled that, during the rafting season, much of the work of stacking and transporting an estimated fifty million feet of lumber on rafts to Baltimore, Philadelphia, and Wilmington was done by African Americans. As early as the 1830s, these black communities had formed societies to protect themselves and the fugitive slaves who resided there. Formed in December 1840, the Gettysburg "Slave Refuge Society" assisted fleeing slaves, providing them with shelter, clothing, food, and

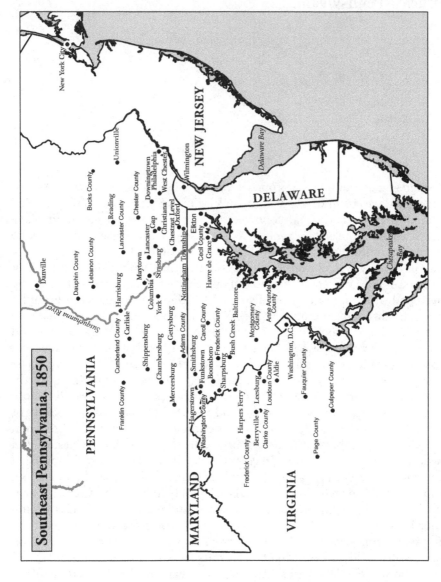

MAP 4. Southeast Pennsylvania.

transportation. Not surprisingly, slaveholders who lost slaves descended on the area in the hopes of reclaiming their property. This region of refuge, David Smith has observed, was also "honeycombed with slave catchers."[1]

With its rail links to places further north and east to Philadelphia, Harrisburg had become, by 1850, a destination for many fleeing slavery in Washington, Frederick, and Carroll counties, Maryland, and the northern Virginia counties of Loudoun, Clarke, Fauquier, and Frederick. Wilson, Brocks, Billy, and the others from Virginia very likely passed through one of Maryland's northwest counties on their way to Harrisburg. The Hagerstown and Frederick newspapers regularly carried sheriff notices of fleeing slaves from Virginia and other parts of Maryland intercepted on their way to Pennsylvania. In fact, these notices outnumbered traditional fugitive slave advertisements from local slaveholders, giving the false impression that few slaves fled the area. Of the seventeen advertisements that appeared in the Hagerstown newspaper between 1852 and 1858, for example, fifteen were sheriff notices announcing the capture of suspected fugitive slaves and calling on their masters to retrieve them. With the exception of two, all of those captured were from outside Hagerstown, many of them from other parts of the state and northern Virginia. Of the thirteen slaves who escaped from Loudoun County, Virginia, in June 1858, seven were recaptured after a shoot-out, two near Boonsboro, south of Hagerstown, and five near Smithsburg to the northeast. The others, the editor suspected, were holed up in the mountains. The same was true of Frederick. When, in September 1856, twenty-year-old Rachael, her husband, John Tate, twenty-three, his brother, Henry, twenty-one, and nineteen-year-old William Smith, who was not related, left Leesburg, Loudoun County, Virginia, and were joined by a number of others who were not named, their masters took out advertisements in the Frederick newspaper. Those hoping to intercept escaped slaves before they reached the Pennsylvania line descended on Hagerstown, Frederick, and adjoining towns. James Pembroke, who came of age on a large farm owned by Frisby Tilghman near Hagerstown, recalled that the town was a favorite haunt of slave catchers. But it was also contested ground. In 1847, an armed band of blacks unsuccessfully attacked the town jail in an attempt to free a group of fugitive slaves who were awaiting the arrival of their masters.[2]

---

[1] Carl Douglas Oblinger, "New Freedoms, Old Miseries: The Emergence and Disruption of Black Communities in Southeastern Pennsylvania, 1780–1860," (PhD, Lehigh University, 1988), 90–91; New York *Tribune*, May 9, 1853; David G. Smith, *On the Edge of Freedom. The Fugitive Slave Issue in South Central Pennsylvania, 1820–1870* (New York: 2013), 12–13, 17, 27–29, 32; Todd Mealy, *Biography of an Antislavery City: Antislavery Advocates, Abolitionists, and Underground Railroad Activities in Harrisburg, PA* (Baltimore: 2007), 33, 37; Gerald G. Eggert, "'Two Steps Forward, A Step-and-a-Half Back': Harrisburg's African American Community in the Nineteenth Century," *Pennsylvania History*, 58, No. 1 (January 1991), 1.

[2] Hagerstown *Herald of Freedom and Torchlight*, June 30, 1858; Frederick *Examiner*, October 9, 1850, June 14, 1854, September 24, 1856. For other examples see Hagerstown *Herald of Freedom and Torchlight*, September 20, 1854, November 28, 1855; Washington, DC, *Evening Star*, September 5, 1859; R. J. M. Blackett, *Beating Against the Barriers. Biographical Essays*

Northwest Maryland slaveholders rarely advertised their losses in local newspapers. Years later, Robert Cantwell of Elkton, Cecil County, further to the east, offered a possible explanation at a hearing in Philadelphia. When asked if the owner had advertised the loss of his slave he replied: "We do not make much stir about our slaves when they first go, as it is no use, until we hear something about them." When they did advertise, it usually involved the dramatic escapes of companies of slaves. Again, because of gaps in the run of available newspapers it is next to impossible to piece together a comprehensive account of the losses from the area. But what is clear is that the size and frequency of group escapes from northwest Maryland was comparable to those from other areas along the slavery divide. A family of thirteen fled the area for Pennsylvania in August 1852. They included Peter, forty-eight, his wife Cassa, forty-four, Cassa's daughter Charlotte, twenty-one, and ten others ranging in age from Elbert, nineteen, to Benjamin, an infant. Although the advertisement for their recapture did not state so explicitly, all indications are that they were members of the same family. In spite of early reports of their recapture in southeastern Pennsylvania, Peter, Cassa, and their family arrived safely in Harrisburg.[3] Two months later, the majority of Elias Cheney's twenty-seven slaves and one of Alexander Mitchell's eight slaves left the area together. They were followed to Lancaster, Pennsylvania, by Cheney's son, who returned home empty handed. One abolitionist editor allowed the successful escapes to get the better of him; the slave catchers, he rejoiced, could not find the "absquatulated party."[4]

These group escapes continued throughout the decade. The three who passed through Adams County, Pennsylvania, in October 1854, successfully eluded slave catchers who trailed them to Harrisburg. A second, consisting of a man, his wife, and child, and an unattached man, were caught by locals in Adams County. The man gave their captors the slip soon after, and the husband, with the aid of his wife, jumped from the wagon on its return trip through Gettysburg. While the slave catchers scurried about Gettysburg in a fruitless effort to get local authorities to hold the captives in the town's jail, the woman and child escaped. Owen Taylor, thirty-one, his wife Mary, and their son Edward left with Taylor's brother, his wife, and two children and Benjamin, another Taylor brother, during the Easter holidays in 1856 using a carriage and horses owned by Henry Fiery, Owen's owner. They headed first to Chambersburg, then to Harrisburg, where they caught the train bound for Philadelphia. They were

*in Nineteenth-Century Afro-American History* (Baton Rouge: 1986), 4; Elwood L. Bridner, Jr., "The Fugitive Slaves of Maryland," *Maryland Historical Magazine,* LXVI, No. 1 (Spring 1971), 49.

[3] *Pennsylvania Freeman,* July 28, 1853; Hagerstown *Herald of Freedom and Torchlight,* August 8, 18, 1852; Baltimore *Sun,* August 14, 1852; *Pennsylvania Freeman,* August 18, 1852.

[4] Hagerstown *Herald of Freedom and Torchlight,* October 20, 1852; Baltimore *Sun,* October 21, 1852; *Pennsylvania Freeman,* November 18, 1852.

followed to Harrisburg by Fiery's son, who approached Joseph C. Bustill, a black schoolteacher, and head of the local fugitive aid society, with an offer to free Owen in one year, and the others in what he called "proportional time" if they returned, or alternatively to free them all for $1,300. Bustill took pleasure in stringing Fiery along in the hope that he would be forced to "spend a few more dollars, and if possible get a little sicker of this bad job." Fiery later returned to Harrisburg, only to learn that the fugitives had made it safely to Canada. A couple of months later, another eight left on a buggy drawn by two horses from the stables of Lewis Snider of Hagerstown. They were tracked down before they made it to the Pennsylvania line but put up what one newspaper called a "stout resistance," forcing the slave catchers to retreat. They also took with them "valuable silks and other dresses, breast pins, ear-rings, finger-rings, bracelets," and other items valued at more than $300, which were recovered in Pennsylvania one week later. The assumption was that this was an act of dispossession, or to borrow a phrase from E. P. Thompson, these slaves had an "alternative notion of possession." But we will never know why they chose to leave them behind once they got to Pennsylvania, in a place where they could be found, except that the discovery of the "valuables" was meant to throw the slave catchers off their trail. Whatever their intent, they eluded their captors. There were fewer such escapes from the area around Frederick, but here, too, there were many group escapes, such as the one involving ten slaves who left in one night in May 1860.[5]

Local slaveholders did record some successes. In May 1854, Stephen Pembroke, the fifty-year-old brother of James Pembroke, now known as the Rev. James W. C. Pennington, who had escaped in October 1827, and Stephen's sons, Robert, aged seventeen, and Jacob, twenty, escaped from Sharpsburg to the west of Hagerstown. They were owned by Jacob H. Grove, a farmer, and David Smith, a shoemaker, both minor slaveholders. From Sharpsburg they traveled to Philadelphia, where they and nine others from Maryland and Virginia were hidden by William Still and the city's vigilance committee. Concerned that so large a group would attract too much attention, Still had them dispatched

---

[5] Gettysburg *Sentinel* (n.d.), in Indianapolis *Free Democrat*, July 6, 1854; Hagerstown *Herald of Freedom and Torchlight*, June 28, 1854, March 9, May 28, June 4, 1856; William Still, *The Underground Railroad* (1872, rpr., Chicago: 1970), 331–34; *National Anti-Slavery Standard*, July 5, 1856; Philadelphia Vigilance Committee, Journal C. Black Abolitionist Papers, 7:13587; Frederick *Examiner*, May 30, 1860; *Adams Sentinel*, June 4, 1860; E. P. Thompson, *Customs in Common* (New York: 1991), 184. For examples of other group escapes see Hagerstown *Herald of Freedom and Torchlight*, May 27, 1857, *National Anti-Slavery Standard*, June 6, 1857, Montgomery County *Sun*, May 29, 1857, Gettysburg *Republican Compiler*, October 14, 1850, and Baltimore *Sun*, October 7, 1850. In early January 1860, Mrs. M. E. Poole of Libertytown, Frederick County, got wind that the father of two children she owned was planning to take them away. Poole insisted that one of the children sleep on the floor in her room overnight. In the morning when she removed the blanket all she found was a "rag baby." *Adams Sentinel*, January 30, 1860; Frederick *Examiner* (n.d.), in Baltimore *Sun*, January 26, 1860.

in different directions so as to minimize possible recapture. Pennington was notified to expect the arrival of his family in New York City and warned that Grove and Smith may be close behind. Still's was no idle warning, for Grove and Smith, with the aid of Baltimore slave catchers, were on the trail of the Pembrokes. In fact, unbeknownst to either group, the Pembrokes and their pursuers had traveled on the same train from Philadelphia to New York City. The three were met by Pennington and hurried off to what was assumed to be a safe house. But the slave catchers, with the aid of local officials, soon discovered its location. Armed with a warrant for their arrest, the police broke into the home at three o'clock in the morning and removed the Pembrokes. Five hours later, and long before the local vigilance committee could arrange legal representation, the fugitives were brought before the commissioner and summarily ordered returned to Maryland. Pennington had been initially informed that the hearing would be held at eleven o'clock in the morning. The authorities were obviously stalling for time, hoping to get the fugitives out of the city before the black community could respond. But word of their capture leaked out and a large crowd gathered outside the courthouse. Aware of the threat of a possible rescue attempt, city officials ordered a large posse to escort the Pembrokes out of town. The crowd followed the posse to the New Jersey state line, looking, unsuccessfully, for an opportunity to spirit them away. In New Jersey, the Pembrokes were handed over to a local police force, who placed them on a train bound for Baltimore. Seven days after their escape from Sharpsburg, the three found themselves occupants of a Baltimore slave pen.

The recapture of the Pembrokes was a devastating blow to the reputation of the Philadelphia and New York City vigilance committees, whose record of protecting their charges had been, until then, almost unblemished. For some time after, the Philadelphia committee refused to send fugitives through New York City, preferring instead to use the line running through Elmira, New York, which they believed was more carefully monitored and secure. Still was particularly critical of the way the Pembrokes were guarded once they got to New York City. Warned that slave catchers were following, Pennington had ample time to move the three out of the city to a safer location. But the joy of seeing his brother after nearly thirty years may have caused Pennington to drop his guard.

The day after the Pembrokes were taken, Pennington's church was packed with an audience eager to explore their next course of action. The meeting decided on raising a subscription to purchase Stephen and his sons. Four weeks later, Pennington received a reply from Grove, offering to sell Stephen if the price were right. Pennington responded by offering $600. Recognizing a good thing when he saw it, Grove insisted that the purchase price also include expenses he had incurred in retaking Stephen. When the transaction was finally completed toward the end of June, the price had climbed to $1,373, much of which Pennington raised through public subscription. The elation surrounding Stephen's return to New York City was understandably subdued. Almost

$1,400 had been wasted when, with a bit more care, the fugitives could have been protected. Additionally, the joy surrounding Stephen's return was tempered with the news that Robert and Jacob had been sold to a North Carolina lumber merchant soon after they arrived in Baltimore. Their owner obviously had no intention of risking another escape.[6]

Area slaveholders also managed to recapture a number of escapees before they made it out of the state, or not long after they got to Pennsylvania, by employing a combination of police forces and slave catchers in and out of the state. The eight who fled Washington County in May 1858, for instance, were retaken near Shippensburg, Pennsylvania, by slave catchers who were paid a handsome reward of $800. It is not known if they were retaken by slave catchers who tracked them from Maryland or by a group of Pennsylvanians. In late 1854, John H. Pope, a Frederick cigar maker and policeman, announced the formation of an "Independent Police and Detective" force in northwestern Maryland made up of what he called an "efficient corps of spies" to detect and capture escaping slaves. He also had in place "the most experienced men of the mountain...along the Northern frontier of this State, throughout Pennsylvania" as well as an effective "line of detectives" from Maryland to the "Canadian frontier." Pope charged $10 in advance for "advertising and telegraphing runaways" and announced that he had the full support of area slaveholders. But Pope faced a problem: he could do nothing once escapees made it to Canada. In early 1855, he wrote Montreal's chief of police with a plan to reclaim the "vast numbers of slaves" who escaped to Canada and so fell outside "the pale of the Fugitive Slave Law." Once there, he acknowledged, they could only be retaken by "cunning together with skill." Pope was, therefore, looking for an "efficient person," someone willing to induce fugitives close to the border, where he and his men could nab them. Those who participated, he promised, would share in the very lucrative rewards offered by slaveholders eager to reclaim their valuable property. Pope's letter must have stunned the Montreal police chief, who passed it on to a local newspaper, which published it. Within a matter of days, newspapers in both Canada and the Free States reprinted Pope's proposal, heaping scorn on the plan, dismissing it as "unmitigated trash" and balderdash. But Pope was not to be deterred. In a public response, he ridiculed Britain's commitment to break the chains of the "tawny Ethiop in slavery" while keeping the "noble Celt in chains." Were he so

---

[6] Hagerstown *Herald of Freedom and Torchlight*, May 31, 1854; *Pennsylvania Freeman*, June 1, 1854; Still, *The Underground Railroad*, 169–74; John Blassingame, ed., *Slave Testimony. Two Centuries of Letters, Speeches, Interviews, and Autobiographies* (Baton Rouge: 1977), 169; *Frederick Douglass' Paper*, March 16, 1855; Baltimore *Sun*, May 29, 1854; Eric Foner, *Gateway to Freedom. The Hidden History of the Underground Railroad* (New York: 2014), 169–70. In May 1860 slave catchers also retrieved two fugitives from Frederick County in New York City before, as one local newspaper put it, the "freedom-shreikers" knew it. Frederick *Examiner*, May 9, 1860.

inclined, he boasted, he could invade and overrun Canada with his trusted dog and "six good mountain riflemen."[7]

Nothing came of Pope's grand scheme to retrieve escaped slaves once they had reached the security of Canada, although the evidence suggests that he continued to play an active role in reclaiming fugitives from the area. He also worked to curtail the activities of a gang of local kidnappers who first enticed slaves to escape, then had the fugitives caught by co-conspirators who sold them to slave traders. The gang was effectively dismantled, in late November 1854, when three of its leaders were tried and convicted of kidnapping. One of them, John Shaw, turned state's witness against Zachariah Shaw, who was sentenced to six years and two months in the state penitentiary, and James Morgan, who first successfully petitioned to have his case moved to Carroll County, then fled before his case could be heard, leaving behind property "more than sufficient to pay five times the amount" of his bail.[8]

Slaveholders also kept a close watch on free blacks who they believed represented the gravest threat to the system and who, they suspected, were the driving force behind many of the escapes from the area. Jesse Rawlins, a free black, was caught not long after two married slaves escaped from Frederick in the fall of 1854 in a carriage he had hired. They were retaken by their master in York, Pennsylvania, while waiting for a train to Harrisburg. Rawlins, however, was found not guilty. Mary Richardson and her sister Rachel Richardson were brought to court on similar charges. Rachel was found not guilty, but there is no report on the outcome of Mary's trial. Dan Thomas, a Hagerstown waiter, was recognized on a Washington, DC, train by a local judge as the fellow "who had decoyed some nine or ten slaves from their masters" in Funkstown. Thomas, the "pert free negro," as one newspaper described him, had slipped out of town soon after the slaves absconded. Thomas very likely faced a penalty similar to the one imposed on the three unnamed free blacks who were sold into slavery at public auction for aiding slaves to escape from Frederick County. Under an 1858 state law, the proceeds from such sales went first to cover the cost of the trial, secondly to indemnify masters for their losses, and thirdly, should there be any money left over, to the "families of the convicted parties." At one of these public auctions held outside the city jail on Christmas day 1860, a number of free blacks convicted of aiding slaves to escape were

[7] Hamilton *Spectator* (n.d.), in Chicago *Tribune*, January 25, 1855; Baltimore *Sun*, January 18, 1855; Montreal *Gazette* (n.d.), in *Western Planet*, January 24, 1855; Montreal *Gazette* (n.d.), in Rochester *Union*, February 8, 1855; William's *Frederick Directory, City Guide and Business Mirror* (Frederick: 1859).

[8] Frederick *Examiner*, November 22, December 13, 1854, March 7, 14, 1855; Frederick *Herald* (n.d.), in *Virginian Messenger*, December 2, 1854; T. I. C. Williams and Folger McKinsey, *History of Frederick County, Maryland* (Baltimore: 1967), 220–21; Annapolis *Gazette*, November 30, 1854. (My thanks to Kate Larson for this reference.) Minute Book, Frederick County Circuit Court, 1855, Maryland State Archives, Annapolis, Maryland. My thanks to Dean Herrin for some of the details.

themselves sold into slavery. Frederick Thomas Pinkney was sold out of state for twelve years, the purchaser paying $50; Harriet Ann Green was sold out of state for ten years for $25; Grafton Little was sold in state for five years for $100; Magdalena Howard was sold in state for three years for $50; and Henry Warner was sold in state for two years for $42. A local editor was surprised by how little they fetched – a reflection, he thought, of the ways the continuing political troubles over slavery had depreciated their potential value.[9]

The prosecution of free blacks, however, did little to ease the disquiet caused by their growing presence in the state and the undeniably troubling role they played in slave escapes. Calls to reduce their presence were resisted for fear that their removal would have damaging consequences to the state's economy, which was heavily reliant on their labor. This tension and ambivalence was captured nicely in reports on the 1854 "Negro Jubilee" in Frederick. A group of nine hundred from Baltimore arrived at nine o'clock in the morning in decorated carriages, stages, buggies, and omnibuses accompanied by a band. They paraded through the town on their way to a picnic on Derr Island in the Monocracy River, supervised by one policeman. Another group of six hundred, accompanied by a band, went by rail to Bush Creek under the supervision of another policeman. Both groups – the implication is that they were made up of free blacks and the enslaved – it was reported, enjoyed themselves. At the end of the day, they met and together marched through town. The peaceful gathering and the lack of alcohol, one editor chortled, was a direct refutation of the carping, "incendiary abolitionists" who, he was sure, would ignore the scenes of "unalloyed happiness" of the "sable sons of Africa" in the midst of slavery. Such displays should not only upset their "cherished theories about the suffering and oppression of the 'wretched slaves' " but abate their "vindictiveness against 'merciless slaveholders.' " Yet, the editor was unwilling to sanction such festivities for the simple reason that they violated the laws against Negro assemblies and were potentially injurious to the peace of society. He was not averse to expressions of "reasonable pleasures." After all, they already had "abundant opportunities for indulgence and recreation," and were "happier, better fed, clothed and cared for," and toiled less than any of "their race in the Northern States." On the contrary, his reluctance to encourage such assemblies

[9] Lancaster *Examiner and Herald*, November 24, 1858; *Adams Sentinel*, November 29, 1858; Hagerstown *Herald of Freedom and Torchlight*, October 11, 1854, November 17, December 12, 1858; Williams and McKinsey, *History of Frederick County, Maryland*, 221; Frederick County Circuit Court, Minutes 1860, Maryland State Archives; Frederick *Examiner*, September 13, November 15, 1854, October 24, November 14, December 12, 26, 1860; Frederick *Herald*, December 4, 1860; Baltimore *Sun*, September 13, 1854; Washington *Star*, October 4, 1854. Free blacks were also sold for minor crimes such as stealing. An 1858 law also aimed to reduce overcrowding in the state penitentiary by radically altering the way free blacks were punished. It opted for selling those convicted to slavery in and out of state for fixed periods. This resulted in a drop in black inmates by as much as 50 percent. Christopher Phillips, *Freedom's Port. The African American Community of Baltimore, 1790–1860* (Urbana, IL: 1997), 204–05.

was due entirely to the "outrageous interference with the rights of property by abolitionists." It was such interference – a conflation of the actions of outside abolitionists with those of local free blacks – that caused slaveholders to "be suspicious, and compels them to circumscribe the license of servants," worried about the potential mischief such events could cause. The fact that it took only two policemen to maintain order did not ease the editor's worries.[10]

Such concerns, and the prosecution of free blacks, did little to stop the hemorrhaging of escapes. A few slaveholders simply threw up their arms and refused to go after fugitives. When, in late 1854, a "valuable negro" belonging to Henry McCauley of Hagerstown escaped, no attempt was made to retake him, leaving the local editor to speculate on whether such a reaction stole the thunder of abolitionists by abandoning the escapee to "scratch for himself among the *free dirt* of Pennsylvania." It was a theme the editor continued to explore as escapes mounted. After a visit to Pennsylvania, he reported seeing more "dirty, ragged, abject, knavish-looking negroes in one day in Chambersburg" than he had seen in a month in Hagerstown. Once beyond the reach of their master, those who had escaped were promptly abandoned by their so-called friends in a "strange place and among a strange people" where they were at "*liberty* to work," if they could find anything to do, as well as at "*liberty* to *starve*" if they could not. Unprepared for freedom, they were "cheated, abused and discarded...until finally the gloom of despair" settled upon their "weak and untutored minds" and they sank to "the lowest depths of degradation, crime and poverty," dragging out "a miserable existence in the purlieus of some large town or city in this country or Canada" among "the hordes of debased and squalid creatures who infest these places, and furnish the Penitentiaries and Almshouses with their annual compliment of inmates, or the Pestilence with its first victims." Finding themselves in such squalid conditions, many escapees, he was convinced, would anxiously return if only they could afford the cost or if their former masters guaranteed that they would not be sold further south. It was a view he repeated frequently, as if trying to prod masters to give such aid and assurances, or to convince himself such options were possible. He even quoted from a letter purportedly written from Chatham, Canada, by a woman who had escaped with her children from Harpers Ferry in late 1852, in which she longed for the day when she could return to the friends and places she knew, for in Canada, she wrote plaintively, there was nothing but "hard times and bad darkies."[11]

Not only were these views a direct condemnation of abolitionists and those who persuaded slaves to escape only to abandon them to a miserable existence, they were also an expression of genuine alarm at the financial as well as emotional costs of continued and sometimes dramatic escapes from the area. In the

[10] Frederick *Examiner,* June 7, 1854.
[11] Hagerstown *Herald of Freedom and Torchlight,* December 8, 1852, December 21, 1853, October 11, 1854, January 2, March 14, 1855.

fall of 1858, an editor reported, escapes from Washington County had to be counted in the "hundreds." As a consequence, aged widows had been beggared and whole families "plunged to the depths of poverty" from positions of "comparative affluence." Another area editor insisted that, as a result of these escapes, slave property was becoming "increasingly precarious," which, he acknowledged, had diminished the confidence of slaveholders in "slave property."[12] But all was not gloom and doom; other slaveholders in northwest Maryland and northern Virginia did everything they could to reclaim their lost property. As in other areas along the slavery divide, they spent considerable sums, sometimes exceeding the market value of the escaped slave, to reclaim their lost property. This is what prompted William Taylor to go after Samuel Wilson and George Brocks, two of his twenty-four slaves, in Harrisburg in August 1850. Billy, the third fugitive slave, was owned by John E. Page, a fifty-year-old farmer and lawyer and the owner of twenty-seven slaves. The three were arrested on August 17th and charged, not as fugitive slaves, but for stealing a number of horses, a move designed to ease their extradition by circumventing an 1847 state law that banned the use of state prisons to hold slaves awaiting rendition. Six days after their arrest, the three were brought before Judge John L. Pearson on a writ of habeas corpus taken out by unnamed members of the black community. They were represented by two of the city's prominent white lawyers and abolitionists, Charles Rawn and Mordecai McKinney. Rawn, a Free-Soil Democrat, was a leading figure in the defense of fugitive slaves. McKinney was a founding member of the Harrisburg Anti-Slavery Society, the first society of its kind in the state, as well as a member of the Pennsylvania Anti-Slavery Society. The two were hired by William M. Jones, a fifty-nine-year-old black "doctor" and teamster, the owner of property in the city since the 1830s, including a large boardinghouse that was known locally as a "temporary haven for fugitives," and Edward Thompson, a thirty-four-year-old black laborer.[13]

In the hearing before Judge Pearson, witnesses for the owners were their own worst enemies. George H. Isler, Taylor's neighbor, testified that Wilson, Brocks, and Billy had stolen four horses, which were later recovered. This, as far as Isler was concerned, was grounds enough to return the three to Virginia as fugitives from justice. But Taylor had admitted previously that he had offered a reward of $500 for the return of his two slaves as fugitives from labor. Four black witnesses, including William Jones, appeared for the defense, insisting that the three had been in town since June, before they were reputed to have

[12] Hagerstown *Herald of Freedom and Torchlight*, March 19, 1856, October 6, 1858, Frederick *Examiner*, May 30, 1860.
[13] *Pennsylvania Freeman*, August 29, 1850; for Rawn and McKinney see Mealy, *Biography of an Antislavery City*, 51, 132, and Michael Barton's introduction to the website "The Rawn Journals, 1830–1865," www.rawnjournals.com/about; for Jones and Thompson see Mary D. Houts, "Black Harrisburg's Resistance to Slavery," *Pennsylvania Heritage*, 4, No. 1 (December 1977), 12.

stolen the horses. Two local white witnesses, however, recalled seeing a group of unidentified blacks, as many as eight, crossing the bridge into the city in July. The judge dismissed the case against the three on the grounds that they had not stolen the horses for profit but only used them to effect their escape, which he considered a form of trespass and not grounds to return them to Virginia as fugitives from justice. But Pearson did allow that, while he had no jurisdiction in fugitive slave cases, slaveholders had a right, in principle, to reclaim their property as long as it was done peacefully.[14]

Taylor's legal ploy had worked against him, but he had no intention of allowing Pearson's ruling to stymie his objectives. Concerned that Taylor would try to seize the three, a large crowd of African Americans gathered outside the courthouse. The details of what followed are not entirely clear. When Taylor and others tried to retain them as they left the courthouse the three resisted. Members of the crowd, including Joseph Popel, moved to prevent their seizure. Popel was beaten bloody by Taylor's group. Wilson and Brocks were also hurt in the melee, but during the scuffle Billy was hustled away by about twenty blacks, who provided him with a pistol and later got him out of town. On orders of the court, a sheriff's posse arrested Wilson, Brocks, Taylor, and a number of other Virginians. Arrest warrants were also issued for ten African Americans, including Popel, Jones, and Jones's son, David, for rioting, disturbing the peace, attempting a violent rescue of fugitives, and the violent seizure of Billy. Of the ten charged, seven were heads of household. Some, such as Jones, were men of property. Twenty-year-old Henry Bradley, for example, was, according to Mary Houts, a "prosperous" barber. Taylor and ten other Virginians were also charged with violating the 1847 state law that aimed to prevent the kidnapping of blacks and attempts to return fugitive slaves by force of arms. Taylor, in turn, brought charges of assault against the fugitives in an effort to prevent their immediate release.[15]

Before any of the accused could be brought to trial, the Fugitive Slave Law, signed by President Millard Fillmore on September 18th, changed the political climate surrounding the case. Twelve days later, Richard McAllister was appointed commissioner by Robert C. Grier, associate justice of the Supreme Court. A Democrat, McAllister became the most avid enforcer of the law. Soon after he entered office, McAllister appointed a number of policemen to enforce

[14] Harrisburg *Telegraph*, August 28, 1850; Lancaster *Examiner & Herald*, August 28, 1850. The Richmond *Whig*, September 6, 1850, dismissed Pearson's reasoning and decision as "frivolous," resting, as it did, on a "dishonest distinction." An accompanying letter to the editor insisted that the governor of Virginia should demand the fugitives' return but doubted that he would, fearful of being labeled a disunionist.

[15] Harrisburg *Telegraph*, August 28, 1850; Lancaster *Examiner & Herald*, August 28, 1850; Gerald G. Eggert, "The Impact of the Fugitive Slave Law on Harrisburg: A Case Study," *Pennsylvania Magazine of History and Biography*, 109 (October 1985), 540–43; Houts, "Black Harrisburg's Resistance to Slavery," 13; Dauphin County Clerk of Court, Quarter Session Docket Book 9, April 1855, p. 86, Dauphin County Courthouse, Harrisburg, PA.

his rulings. He was the sort of commissioner on whom slaveholders, such as Taylor, depended, and on whom the success of the law rested. Slaveholders seeking the recapture of their slaves anywhere in the area, even in those towns where there were commissioners, beat a path to McAllister's door in search of arrest warrants and the adjudication of their cases.

On the day of McAllister's appointment, Taylor appeared before the new commissioner with the manacled Samuel Wilson and George Brocks. He swore the two were his slaves and that was good enough for McAllister, who ordered them returned. Rawn dismissed the hearing as a farce. There is no report that even the most summary evidence was taken or that Taylor had to produce irrefutable proof that the slaves were his. Aware of what had happened following Pearson's decision, McAllister named Solomon Snyder and Michael Shaeffer to head a posse to return the slaves to Virginia. They, in turn, hired Samuel Kintzer, Thomas Hubbard, Henry Loyer, and seventeen others, a substantial force meant to awe and intimidate any possible opposition from the black community. This would become standard practice throughout the North. At the end of hearings, slaveholders would request that a posse be assembled, fearful that the black community would intervene to prevent the return of slaves. The rendition of Wilson and Brocks, however, did not end court proceedings associated with the case. Taylor and others were scheduled to appear in November to answer the charge of rioting. A jury was never empanelled, yet the defenders were cleared. The trial against the ten African Americans was postponed by Judge Pearson until January 1851. In the end, petitions from the city's leading citizens calling for dismissal or leniency may have persuaded Pearson to drop the case.[16]

About the same time as the case against the ten African Americans was dismissed, there were reports that Billy had been arrested near Danville, Pennsylvania, well north of Harrisburg, and brought before McAllister. As it turned out, the person who appeared before the commissioner was not Billy but David, one of the group who had arrived in Harrisburg with Wilson and the others but had chosen not to remain in the city. The hearing produced one of the more unusual accounts of group escapes. David insisted that he did not realize he was running away when he joined the group. He had gone along in the belief that they were on their way to a wedding "up the country." He soon learned that talk of a wedding was just a way to get him to join the escaping group. Once it became apparent that the group was running away it was too late to turn back. He would have returned long ago, he told McAllister, if only he knew the way home. McAllister was eager to oblige and returned David to

---

[16] Rawn Diary, November 22, 1850, Rawn Collection, MG 062, Diaries, Dauphin County Historical Society, Harrisburg, PA; *Pennsylvania Freeman*, December 12, 1850; Eggert, "The Impact of the Fugitive Slave Law on Harrisburg," 545. One Virginia newspaper estimated that it cost Taylor close to $1,400 to recapture his slaves, a price at least as high as the value of the slaves. *Southern Argus*, December 14, 1850.

his owner, Thomas Briggs of Berryville, Clarke County, under escort, at the expense of the federal government, even though there was no evident threat of resistance from the black community.[17]

Seven other cases followed in quick succession during 1851, a period of rising tension in the North over enforcement of the law. In each case, McAllister ruled in favor of the claimants. The first involved the Franklin family, who had escaped two years earlier. Daniel, the slave of Dr. Robert Franklin of Anne Arundel County, Maryland, and his wife Abby and child Caroline, slaves of Barbara Wailes of Baltimore, were captured in Columbia by the commissioner's constables in April 1851 and taken to Harrisburg. Since their arrival in Columbia, there had been a new addition to the Franklin family. As a result, the case raised the thorny question of whether a ten-month-old freeborn child could be separated from his parents. McAllister set the hearing for 6:45 a.m., partly, one suspects, to preempt opposition from the black community, which had gotten wind of the family's arrival in town. Charles Rawn and Mordecai McKinney requested a delay of one hour, which McAllister summarily rejected. McAllister promptly ruled in favor of the claimant on the evidence of Dr. Franklin's eighteen-year-old son. If the presence of a "suckling child," or the fact that the child was freeborn troubled McAllister, it did not deter him. The law had to be enforced, even if doing so resulted in the separation of a child from his parents.[18]

In early August 1851, Elizabeth O'Neill of Havre de Grace, Maryland, requested a warrant from McAllister for the arrest of her slave William Smith, also known as Bob Sterling. Smith had escaped in the spring of 1845, and O'Neill suspected that he was living in Columbia. Three days later, one of McAllister's constables arrested Smith, who was working on a coal boat, and brought him to Harrisburg. Word of Smith's arrival spread, and a crowd of African Americans gathered outside McAllister's office before the hearing began. Testimony for O'Neill was provided by Matilda Wood, who claimed she had known Smith since he was a child. This was corroborated by a letter from Wesley Levy of Havre de Grace. No opportunity was provided for Smith, or anyone else, to rebut these claims, and he was remanded. Worried that an attempt would be made to free Smith, O'Neill's agents requested protection from McAllister's policemen. Because he could not be held in the city jail, the group was forced to spend the night in a local hotel. A crowd of blacks milled about outside, and during the night someone set fire to the hotel. The fire was

[17] Harrisburg *Union* (n.d.), in Lebanon *Advertiser*, January 29, 1851; Harrisburg *Telegraph*, January 25, 1851; McAllister to John K. Kane, Harrisburg, January 30, 1851, RG 217, Settled Miscellaneous Treasury Accounts, September 6, 1970–September 29, 1894, National Archives, Washington, DC.

[18] Columbia *Spy*, April 26, 1851; Lancaster *Examiner & Herald*, April 30, 1851; Harrisburg *American*, April 23, 1851; *Pennsylvania Freeman*, May 1, 1851; Rawn Diary, April 22, 1851; Eggert, "The Impact of the Fugitive Slave Law on Harrisburg," 546–47.

quickly detected and extinguished before it could cause more than minor damage. The next day, Smith, accompanied by three of the commissioner's policemen, was put on board a train bound for Baltimore, where he was handed over to O'Neill.[19]

The following month, John Stoucher, John Bell, Edward Michael, and Fenton Mercer were arrested in Fishersville, Dauphin County, on suspicion of participating in the bloody events at Christiana, in nearby Lancaster County, a few days earlier, during which one Maryland slaveholder was killed and another badly injured attempting to retake three slaves. The killing, and the escape of those suspected of being responsible, threw the state and, to a more limited extent, the country, into political turmoil. Bell was owned by John L. T. Jones, a twenty-eight-year-old farmer of Montgomery County, Maryland; Stoucher by Mary E. Shreve; Mercer by Esther Trundle, who was described in court proceedings as "a lunatic"; and Michael by Hezekiah W. Trundle, at forty the owner of fourteen slaves. It was clear to Judge Pearson, before whom the four appeared, that the charges were unfounded and a mere pretext to get them to Harrisburg. As a result, he dismissed the charges on the grounds that the warrant for their arrest was issued without a shred of evidence. While Pearson was in the process of writing out his verdict, three of McAllister's policemen arrested the four in Pearson's court. Pearson's threat to have the three arrested was ignored, and the four were taken to the commissioner's office, where, after a speedy hearing, they were remanded. One local newspaper called McAllister's actions a "palpable outrage" and an insult to the court. Pearson, however, never followed up on his threat.[20]

When Rawn and McKinney attempted to act as counsel for the four, the commissioner simply ignored them, or when he deigned to recognize their presence, insulted them. When, for instance, Rawn pointed out that Esther Trundle had been a "lunatic for 20 years" and that there was no evidence that "her late husband had left a will when he died 25 years earlier," McAllister dismissed Rawn's argument as irrelevant. He had the power, he insisted, to conduct hearings as if he were a judge or magistrate. If they chose to appeal his decision, he declared, they, like all other "colored men[,] could have a trial in Maryland." Like many supporters of the law, McAllister regularly employed the fiction that fugitive slaves had a right to a trial in the county from which they escaped. The fact that they were returned to their putative owners, who would do with them as they pleased, and not to state authorities mattered little to the commissioner. The entire proceedings were dismissed by one newspaper as a "ridiculous mockery." McAllister selected a posse of five, headed by the borough

---

[19] Harrisburg *Key Stone*, August 12, 1851; Harrisburg *Whig State Journal*, August 12, 1851; *Pennsylvania Freeman*, August 21, 1851; McAllister to Kane, Harrisburg, October 10, 1851; McAllister to Kane (n.d.), Settled Miscellaneous Treasury Accounts, National Archives.

[20] *Pennsylvania Freeman*, October 2, 1851; Harrisburg *Whig State Journal*, September 30, 1851; Harrisburg *Telegraph*, October 15, 1851.

constable, and including four of his policemen, to escort the fugitives to their owners in Baltimore.[21]

A local reporter accused McAllister of collusion with the slave owners. A day after his ruling, the Harrisburg Telegraph received a letter, ostensibly from the owners, praising McAllister and the five-man posse for the safe return of the slaves. Policemen claimed to have discovered the slaves' whereabouts from a Harrisburg newspaper account. But as the reporter pointed out, the letter could not have been written by the owners and arrived in time to be published by the newspaper so soon after the case was concluded. He wondered how the owners could have heard of the slaves' arrest from newspaper accounts in time to be present in Pearson's court. Pointing the finger at McAllister, the reporter accused him of being the author of the letter. Apparently, a poster offering a reward of $800 had been circulating in Harrisburg prior to the start of the hearings. McAllister's constables had recognized the fugitives from the poster's description but, having no legal grounds to arrest them as fugitive slaves, concocted the claim of their participation in the Christiana shoot-out as a way to hold them. This gave McAllister time to notify the owners. He supported a delay in the habeas corpus hearing before Pearson and telegraphed the owners to come to Harrisburg immediately. The reporter also claimed that the commissioner had accompanied the posse to Baltimore, where the slaves were sold for $3,400 and where he pocketed the $800 reward.[22]

Soon after their capture, questions were raised about the way the four were taken and the grounds on which they were brought to the hearing. McAllister's treatment of the lawyers for the defense, and his refusal to entertain any of their challenges, seemed to go beyond the need to expedite the case. Yet he never addressed the accusations publicly, allowing the charge that he had benefitted directly from the return and sale of the four fugitives slaves to fester. He did offer an explanation of sorts, however, in a letter to the Treasury Department soon after the accusation surfaced. "More fugitives have been remanded by me than any other U. S. Com.," he boasted, and "from the precautions taken" there had been no subversion of the law as, he implied, had occurred elsewhere. "It is much better for the peace and interest of the country," he reasoned by way of an explanation, "that proper force should be employed than by the niggardly parsimony that Fugitives should escape and their claimants and the U.S. officers killed."[23]

[21] Eggert, "The Impact of the Fugitive Slave Law on Harrisburg," 549; McAllister to Kane, Harrisburg, October 1, 1851, McAllister to E. C. Seaman, Harrisburg, October 19, 1851, Settled Miscellaneous Treasury Accounts; see also RG 39, Records of the Bureau of Accounts, Appropriation Ledger for the Treasury and Other Departments, 1807–1945, National Archives, Washington, DC.

[22] See the Harrisburg Telegraph, October 15, 1851, for the report by "YZ" who claimed to have observed the proceedings. Eggert, "The Impact of the Fugitive Slave Law on Harrisburg," 549–50.

[23] McAllister to E. C. Seaman, Harrisburg, October 19, 1851, Settled Miscellaneous Treasury Accounts, National Archives.

The claim of collusion only added to the city's growing disillusion with what many saw as McAllister's apparent enthusiasm for the job and his unrelenting opposition to any challenges to the law. He quickly became the face of the law in southeast Pennsylvania. Even in places where commissioners had been appointed, as they were in Columbia after August 1851, it was to Harrisburg that slaveholders went in search of warrants. His appointed policemen also reached beyond the limits of the city and county to capture suspected fugitive slaves. In early 1851, for example, two of his constables, John Saunders and Solomon Snyder, were charged with kidnapping four suspected fugitives in Lebanon County and taking them to Baltimore two months earlier. McAllister acted as one of their defense counsels. Both were his appointed officers, and had acted with warrants that he had issued, he told the court. In addition, Snyder had been legitimately hired by the owners with an offer of $1,000 to return the four. McAllister did concede that his constables had arrested the wrong men. Handbills circulating in the area mentioned three mulattoes and one black; the four arrested were three blacks and one mulatto. But this was nothing more than an honest mistake, McAllister argued; they had not intentionally taken the wrong men and so should not be indicted for "false imprisonment." He and his constables, he reminded the court, were acting in the best interest of the state. "We do not want to make Pennsylvania," he asserted, "a place of refuge for absconding slaves and free negroes – they are a miserable population – a tax and a pest." Saunders and Snyder were acquitted on the charge of kidnapping but found guilty of assault and battery. The four who were returned to Maryland may have been the wrong four, but they were, the jury agreed without seeing the slightest evidence, fugitive slaves. It was this approach to the enforcement of the law that had prompted the black community of Harrisburg to condemn both the law and McAllister's ruthless enforcement of it not long after Wilson and Brocks were remanded. They dismissed the law as a violation of biblical precepts, vowed to continue to resist its enforcement, established a committee of five to aid fugitives, and, sarcastically, congratulated McAllister on his appointment as "CHIEF KIDNAPPER of the County."[24]

McAllister's problems were compounded by a Treasury Department that seemed incapable, or so McAllister thought, of compensating his constables

[24] Columbia *Spy*, August 2, 1851. McAllister's remit extended well beyond the area around Harrisburg. In December 1851, he issued a warrant for the arrest of William Kelly, a suspected fugitive slave from Carroll County, Maryland. Kelly, who was married with a family, was arrested by Michael Sheaffer in Jersey Shore, Lycoming County, and returned. McAllister also issued warrants for the arrest of six suspects in Wilkes-Barre, more than one hundred miles from Harrisburg. The six managed to evade capture. Harrisburg *Whig State Journal*, December 9, 1851; Harrisburg *American* (n.d.), in Pittsburgh *Gazette*, December 15, 1851; *National Era*, October 31, 1850; McAllister to Kane, Harrisburg, December 10, 1852, RG 217, Entry 347, Settled Miscellaneous Treasury Accounts, National Archives; Lancaster *Examiner & Herald*, April 24, August 30, 1851; *Pennsylvania Freeman*, October 31, 1850, January 23, 1851; Harrisburg *American*, April 21, 1851; Harrisburg *Whig State Journal*, April 30, 1851; Harrisburg *Telegraph*, November 6, 1850; Lebanon *Advertiser*, April 23, 1851.

on time, and when they belatedly did, for the full amount of the expenses they had incurred in returning fugitives to Maryland and Virginia. But those at the Treasury Department who were responsible for the disbursement of funds were not totally at fault. The government was slow to allocate funds to cover the cost of returns and had yet to devise a system of compensation. As a result, Elisha Whittlesey, the first comptroller of the Treasury, was forced to play it by ear. While the issue of compensation went largely unresolved during McAllister's tenure, the commissioner nonetheless continued to remand alleged fugitive slaves. He issued return orders in three cases in November and December 1851. Later, in May 1852, Solomon Snyder, Henry Lyne, and an unidentified constable were at the center of an incident in Columbia that rocked the area. They had gone to the city, south of Harrisburg, with Archibald G. Ridgely, described in some reports as a Baltimore police officer and in others as a member of the independent police firm of John Zell and Ridgely of Baltimore. Such independent police forces – John Pope's in Frederick, Maryland, a prime example – were synonymous with slave-catching firms. Ridgely had obtained a warrant from McAllister for the arrest of William Smith, also known as George Stansbury, and another unnamed fugitive slave who had also settled in Columbia. Ridgley and the others found Smith stacking logs in a lumberyard and arrested him. By then, Smith had been living with his family in Columbia for about eighteen months.

What happened next is unclear. Reports partial to Ridgely and the others say they feared for their lives from the dozen or so black workers in the yard, all of whom were armed with axes and appeared threatening. They surrounded the officers, at which point Ridgely took out his gun in an effort to keep them at bay. At the same time, Smith was forcefully resisting arrest and in the process got Ridgely's thumb in his mouth and was about to bite it off. In the scuffle that followed, and in an attempt to extricate his thumb, Ridgely's gun went off, accidentally killing Smith instantly. A coroner's report, however, painted a different picture. No attempt had been made by his fellow workers to rescue Smith. But Smith did resist, broke free from Ridgely, and was attempting to flee when he was shot. Those who testified at the coroner's inquest reported that Ridgely had shot Smith in the back deliberately in an attempt to stop him from escaping. Later, Ridgely insisted that he offered to give himself up to local police but was advised to leave town immediately because of growing anger among those who had witnessed the shooting. He left, taking back roads around York and Strasburg before catching a train bound for Baltimore.[25]

[25] Richmond *Dispatch*, May 3, 4, 5, 1852; West Chester *Village Record*, May 4, 1852; Lancaster *Examiner & Herald*, May 5, 12, 1852; Harrisburg *Telegraph*, May 5, 1852; Harrisburg *Whig State Journal*, May 6, 13, 1852; Baltimore *Sun*, January 29, 1853; New York *Tribune*, May 4, 8, 1852; *Frederick Douglass' Paper*, May 13, 1852; *National Anti-Slavery Standard*, May 6, 1852; Cleveland *Herald*, May 3, 17, 1852; Cleveland *Democrat*, June 26, 1852; Columbus *Spy* (n.d.), in New York *Tribune*, May 18, 1852; Milt Diggins, *Stealing Freedom along the Mason-Dixon Line. Thomas McCreary, the Notorious Slave Catcher from Maryland* (Baltimore: 2015), 28–29.

Ever since its enactment, opponents of the Fugitive Slave Law had predicted such an outcome. It was inevitable, they insisted, if armed slave catchers were permitted to go into black communities where fugitive slaves had been living, some of them for years, where they had started families, where they had been gainfully employed, and where they had established themselves as members of the community. There had been close calls in other parts of the North, for example when slave catchers from Georgia turned up in Boston in search of William and Ellen Craft. Tensions there were only defused when the slave catchers were persuaded to leave town empty handed and the Crafts left for England. Almost a year later, a handful of former slaves had made a bloody stand at Christiana, a few miles away from Columbus, determined to defend their freedom. Smith's resistance was of a different order, but the result was another incident in which someone had lost his life during an attempt to enforce the law. With the events at Christiana still fresh in everyone's mind, the Maryland House of Delegates called on the governor to appoint a commission of inquiry to look into Smith's death, convinced that what happened did not "constitute the killing, murder, or any other homicide punishable by law." The governor moved swiftly to defuse tensions between the two states by appointing two Marylanders – James M. Buchanan and Otho Scott – as commissioners to investigate the shooting of Smith. The commission visited Harrisburg, where they held meetings with District Attorney John L. Thompson, Richard McAllister, and others. Their first order of business was to show that Smith was a fugitive and not free, as some had claimed. McAllister assisted the commission in the collection of evidence. At the inquest, Solomon Snyder admitted that Ridgely had never shown Smith the arrest warrant because Smith, who throughout the inquiry was described as "very strong," did not give him the chance. McAllister insisted that the search had followed all the necessary and required procedures: Ridgely had a valid power of attorney, he had ample proof that Smith was an escaped slave, and on the basis of this evidence, the commissioner had issued a warrant for the fugitive's arrest. Snyder also testified that he was holding one of Smith's arms when he was shot, implying that Ridgely would not have endangered his partner's life by firing his gun at such close quarters. Finally, it was reported that Ridgely had been offered $400 to return Smith alive, a sum he would have forfeited only if his life was in danger. As a result, the Maryland commissioners concluded that Smith's death was accidental.[26]

In spite of these findings, the issue refused to die. District Attorney Thompson, therefore, felt it necessary to explain his actions publicly. He had visited Columbia on a fact-finding mission, he reported, the day after the shooting, at the end of which he recommended to Governor William Bigler that he

---

[26] *Journal of Proceedings of the House of Delegates of Maryland* (Annapolis: 1852), 827; *Journal of Proceedings of the House of Delegates of Maryland* (Annapolis: 1853), 1–2; Lancaster *Examiner & Herald* (n.d.), in West Chester *Village Record*, June 1, 1852, February 8, 1853; Baltimore *Sun*, January 29, 1853.

request the extradition of Archibald Ridgely. But the governor was out of town at the time and so nothing could be done immediately. The Maryland commissioners arrived prior to Bigler's return and Thompson accompanied them to Columbia, where another hearing concerning Smith's death was held. The additional evidence collected convinced Thompson that Smith's death was accidental, although he continued to believe it could have been prevented. As a result, he recommended that Bigler shelve any extradition request until a Lancaster grand jury concluded its investigation. But if the Pennsylvania authorities were satisfied with the commission's findings, and hoped the delay in requesting the extradition would ease political tensions between Maryland and Pennsylvania, others were not. Ohio congressman Joshua Giddings called for the erection of a monument in honor of Smith, for the nation, he declared, had always honored those who had died in the fight for freedom. Let a "suitable mausoleum," he wrote, be erected for Smith, who "was slain...while defending his inalienable right to freedom against a gang of piratical men stealers who dared pollute the soil of Pennsylvania," protected by the "inhuman and infamous" Fugitive Slave Law. He called for a brief history of Smith's life and the events leading up to his death to be inscribed on the monument so that "the execrations of posterity may rest upon the memory of those who have perverted the powers of government to the base purpose of oppressing, degrading and brutalizing our fellow men." Nothing came of Giddings's suggestion, but the memory of what occurred in the Columbia lumberyard lingered and, as we shall see, would have a direct bearing on the political future of some of those who participated in Smith's arrest.[27]

A few days after Smith's death, Harrisburg was thrown into turmoil over another slave case. It involved a thirty-two-year-old teamster, James Phillips, who was arrested at work. A married man with two children, Phillips was accused of having escaped slavery in 1838 as a teenager. Since then he had established a life for himself in the city. Two Virginians testified that they knew Phillips when he was a slave and, although they had not seen him in fourteen years, could still recognize him because of his strong resemblance to "a certain slave family." One of the witnesses for Augustine G. Hudson, the owner, offered some of the most convoluted (if not the most bizarre) testimony presented at any fugitive slave hearing. He claimed that Phillips was originally the slave of his father, Dennis Hudson, of Culpeper County, Virginia, who had given the slave, "with no bill of sale," to his brother, who, in turn, sold him to Henry T. Fant of Fauquier County, who then hired Phillips out to a Mr. Blackford of Page County. Such breathless testimony, it would seem, should have required a modicum of proof, but Commissioner McAllister demanded none. As ever, he was anxious to expedite the hearing. Neither Rawn nor McKinney, hired to

---

[27] *Pennsylvania Freeman*, May 13, 1852; Lancaster *Examiner & Herald*, March 2, 1853; West Chester *Village Record*, February 8, 1853; Eggert, "The Impact of the Fugitive Slave Law on Harrisburg," 550–51.

defend Phillips, was notified of the start of the hearing and when they did arrive McAllister refused to recognize them. He also ordered witnesses not to answer questions about how they had discovered that Phillips was in Harrisburg. Before either attorney could question witnesses for the claimant, McAllister produced an already filled-out order for Phillips's rendition. Phillips's wife, Mary, who attended the hearing with the couple's children, lost her composure when the verdict was read and her husband was led out in chains.[28]

The case, one reporter observed, had caused a "most intense excitement." The streets were "filled with citizens of both sexes." But there was little chance that those gathered in the streets could prevent Phillip's rendition. Whereas, in the past, fugitives awaiting return had to be housed in hotels at the expense of owners or hurried out of town under heavy guard, now, because of the recent repeal of the section of the 1847 state law banning the use of state prisons to hold fugitive slaves, Phillips could be held securely in the city's jail. The following day, he was put on board a train bound for Richmond, where he was sold to a slave trader for $505. While he waited to be shipped further south, Phillips sent a plaintive letter to his wife from the Richmond slave pen, pleading with her to get his Harrisburg employer to raise the $800 his new master, William A. Branton, a Richmond slave trader, was asking. Phillips's employer, John H. Brant, contributed $300 to a fund that a "group of Harrisburg whites" had started soon after McAllister's decision. Once the group had succeeded in raising the asking price, Charles Rawn was sent to Richmond in July to retrieve Phillips and return him to his family and friends.[29]

Gerald Eggert has argued that the remanding of slaves from Harrisburg came to an abrupt halt following the Phillips case. Richard McAllister, and those associated with him, seemed to have lost all credibility as a result of the eagerness with which they enforced the law. The decision to return Phillips may have been the straw that broke the camel's back. Not only was the evidence presented at the hearing suspect, but Phillips had been for fourteen years a hardworking resident of the city, where he was well known and respected, had raised a family, and had been a productive member of the black community. The speed with which the money was raised to ransom him was testimony to his standing in the city. The case must have also made some people, even those who were not openly opposed to the law, wonder why there was no statute of limitations on the return of fugitives. The problem was undoubtedly larger than the commissioner, but, by his actions, he had placed himself squarely at

[28] *Pennsylvania Freeman*, June 3, 1852.
[29] Harrisburg *Whig State Journal*, May 27, 1852; McAllister to Kane, Harrisburg (n.d.), and June 9, 1852, Kane to McAllister, Philadelphia, July 5, 1852, Settled Miscellaneous Treasury Accounts, National Archives; John Blassingame, *Slave Testimony*, 95–96; Eggert, "The Impact of the Fugitive Slave Law on Harrisburg," 552–53; Gerald G. Eggert, "A Pennsylvanian Visits the Richmond Slave Market," *Pennsylvania Magazine of History and Biography*, Vol. 109, No. 4 (October 1985), 572–76.

the center of the dispute. At the heart of his problems was the black community, which, ever since the case involving Wilson, Brocks, and Billy, had made its presence felt. They did what they could to impede the return of slaves, kept vigil outside McAllister's office during hearings, raised money to hire two of the city's prominent lawyers to defend suspects, and established a committee to hide and pass fugitives through the city. But the killing of Smith in Columbia, and the speed with which all fugitives who came before McAllister were remanded over the course of less than two years, made the commissioner and his officers politically unpalatable. McAllister seemed impervious to any criticism and politically deaf to the controversies swirling around him. Only on one occasion did he extend an olive branch to his critics. In early 1852, John Joseph, a black teenager, traveled to Baltimore to visit relatives. He must not have known it was illegal, under Maryland law, for free blacks to visit the state without a pass. He was caught and bound out to a Mr. Fetherbridge until the age of twenty-one. Joseph's mother hired a lawyer, who tracked her son to Baltimore. When the Maryland commissioners visited Harrisburg to inquire into Smith's death in Columbia, McAllister lobbied them to intercede. Fetherbridge agreed to release Johnson if he was reimbursed the $100 he had paid for the boy. Johnson's mother went door to door in Harrisburg and Lancaster in an effort to raise the required amount. One report suggested that the Maryland commissioners made the payment without using any of the money raised by the boy's mother, bought Johnson a suit of clothes, and returned him to Harrisburg in midsummer 1852. Many hoped his return would ease tensions between the two states over Smith's killing. McAllister must have also calculated that his involvement would take the edge off his reputation for callousness.[30]

Before long, all of the constables who were actively involved with McAllister in these renditions were voted out of office. Henry Lyne – the high constable – as well as the three regular constables – Loyer, Snyder, and James Lewis, all Democrats – had been elected in local elections in 1852. Although city elections were dominated by Democrats, when the four ran for reelection a year later, the results were different. All of them, with the exception of Lewis, had been involved in the series of fugitive slave cases. Lyne, Loyer, and Snyder were voted out of office; Lewis was reelected with 79 percent of the vote. Lyne stood again in three subsequent yearly elections and each time lost by wide margins. Snyder and Loyer declined to face the electorate again. Of the three, Snyder had developed an unenviable reputation. Not only was he involved in slave catching and renditions, he was also involved in kidnapping. He was first tried and then acquitted of kidnapping four African Americans in 1851. Twice over the next few years he would be charged with similar crimes, once in Harrisburg, in early 1855, and in Lancaster four months later. One local observer described

---

[30] Baltimore *Sun*, June 4, 1852; Lancaster *Examiner & Herald*, June 9, 1852; Eggert, "The Impact of the Fugitive Slave Law on Harrisburg," 552.

him as an "inveterate slave hunter" who had "largely escaped penalty of the law on two or three former occasions."[31]

McAllister came under enormous political pressure. Although he did not have to face the electorate, he saw the writing on the wall, resigned his position in March 1853, and left for Kansas soon after. When he ran in the election for delegates to the State Democratic Convention in August 1852, he failed to carry a single city ward. He was reelected as a vestryman of his local Episcopal church by one vote and was told, in no uncertain terms, that he would have to resign his position as commissioner if he hoped to continue to serve his church. A generally supportive Philadelphia editor reluctantly concluded that the commissioner's reputation had been destroyed by his relentless and unwavering application of the law. Far from building confidence in the law, McAllister's "excessive zeal," at least in the eyes of this sympathetic editor, had rendered it odious. Another commentator was fairly clear about the consequences of the commissioner's unpopularity: "No decent man in Harrisburg would accept the place," he predicted.[32]

As it turned out, McAllister was never replaced. In the future, escaping slaves passing through Harrisburg would not have to contend with a commissioner or his constables. In the years after his departure, fugitive slaves who arrived in the city were aided by the Fugitive Aid Society, formed in early 1856 and headed by Joseph Bustill. One historian has called the society a "neighborhood watch" located in Tanner's Alley, the heart of the black community, where fugitives appeared to have blended in relatively easily. Escapees were sent to William Still and the vigilance committee in Philadelphia or, alternatively, by rail through Reading to Elmira, New York. In their first action, Bustill sent Still eight fugitives through Reading. Months later, G. S. Nelson, an African American resident of Reading, passed on small and large boxes (his words to describe children and adults) to Still from Harrisburg. The society continued to operate for the rest of the decade. There were regular reports of the movement of runaways through town. Between September and November 1859, for instance, the society aided eighteen escapees. Daily they came, one report stated, "several at a time, and the aggregate business of the year is counted by hundreds." After their arrival, another reported, they "became invisible. They are as hard to find as the 'Know Nothings.' Nobody 'knows nothing' about their whereabouts." Yet, in spite of the absence of a resident commissioner, the authorities still had the means, although admittedly limited after 1853, to recapture fugitive slaves. Relying on warrants issued by the Philadelphia commissioner, the authorities would arrest Daniel Webster (Dangerfield) in

---

[31] *Pennsylvania Freeman,* March 24, 1853; New York *Tribune,* February 26, 1855; Eggert, "The Impact of the Fugitive Slave Law on Harrisburg," 562–63.

[32] *Anti-Slavery Bugle,* July 22, 1854; *Pennsylvanian,* February 1, 1853; Eggert, "The Impact of the Fugitive Slave Law on Harrisburg," 566–67; Mealy, *Biography of an Antislavery City,* 153–54.

April 1859, and Moses Horner the following March, and transport them to Philadelphia, where their cases were heard.[33]

McAllister's future was also wrapped up in broader political developments surrounding the law and its enforcement in the state. The inability to use state prisons to hold fugitive slaves who were awaiting return had led to a concerted effort to repeal the portions of the 1847 state law prohibiting such use. In early 1851, the effort to rescind Section 6, which dealt with the use of state prisons, failed by a razor-thin margin. The Senate did vote in favor of repeal, sixteen to fourteen, but by its rules a two-thirds vote was needed to take up the matter. To supporters of the Fugitive Slave Law, the 1847 law, which they described, echoing the language of an earlier dispute, as the "nullification act of 1847," amounted to open obstructionism. The failure to repeal Section 6 also had national consequences. "No state of the Union is more sound on the question of slavery than the Keystone," a Washington, DC, editor admitted, and he anticipated that the state would soon "take the lead in revoking the mad scheme of the abolitionist agitators by repealing their abolition law, passed under a state of unprecedented excitement." There was growing pressure on lawmakers, and especially Governor William Johnson, a Whig, to repeal the offending section, which many believed was "essential to the execution of the congressional act on the subject of fugitives." The 1851 Whig State Convention had expressed its support for the federal law by a wide margin. And a Harrisburg editor, partial to President Fillmore, and with an eye on what had transpired in the city, condemned the 1847 law because it endangered fugitives and encouraged mob violence. Repeal would demonstrate the state's commitment to enforcing the federal law. It would also be a "decided benefit to persons wrongly claimed as fugitives, as it will allow of more deliberation being exercised in the hearing than was generally practicable when there was no place provided for their safe keeping." The editor felt no obligation to explain the relationship between speedy hearings, as required by the federal law, and a place to house those who were to be returned. But Johnson would not budge. He opposed the Fugitive Slave Law as unnecessary and rejected the arguments of those who believed it was the last best chance of keeping the country together. In the midst of that year's election campaign for governor, and before the Christiana shootout altered the political landscape, Johnson pocket vetoed an amendment of the 1847 law. Johnson was defeated in that year's gubernatorial election by William Bigler, a Democrat, who, in his inaugural address, promised to sign the amendment repealing Section 6 and to resist opposition to the Fugitive Slave

[33] Mealy, *Biography of an Antislavery City*, 71, 161, 165; Still, *The Underground Railroad*, 24–25; Harrisburg *Telegraph*, October 31, November 14, December 20, 1859, January 20, March 29, July 31, 1860; Pittsburgh *Gazette*, November 24, 1859; Harrisburg *Herald*, June 15, 1854; Charles L. Blockson, *The Underground Railroad in Pennsylvania* (Jacksonville, NC: 1981), 86; for details of the two cases see Harrisburg *Telegraph*, April 2, 4, 1859, and Philadelphia *Public Ledger*, March 27, 1860.

Law, for, he argued, together they "engendered hostile feelings between the different sections of the Union."[34]

Over the next few years, a number of proposals were submitted to the state legislature that aimed to ease the concerns of Southern slaveholders that the state was hostile to their interests. In 1853, a senator proposed to allow masters to transit the state with their property. Two years later, the House Judiciary Committee, in a split vote, passed a similar proposal, the majority arguing that, under the law of nations and the Constitution, slaveholders possessed such a right, and the minority contending that, as a local institution, slavery should not be recognized by the "law of nature, the common law, or the civil law." Competing petitions were also regularly presented to the legislature from groups opposed to the settlement of African Americans in the state and those who rejected such exclusionary proposals. One from Philadelphia and Bucks County in 1857, for example, justified the call for exclusion because of the "trouble, inconvenience and expense on account of runaway *niggers* from other states." Others called for a complete ban on the settlement of Negroes and mulattoes, free or otherwise, in the state.[35]

Although none of these proposals resulted in laws that denied the right of free African Americans to come into the state, political sentiment generally favored the vigorous enforcement of the Fugitive Slave Law. It is this commitment to the law that lay behind the drive to repeal Section 6. The rest of the law was left intact, however, reflecting a widespread concern about the frequent kidnapping of free blacks, which the 1847 law was also meant to address. In the heated debate leading up to the passage of the federal law, opponents had predicted that, because the law denied accused fugitive slaves the right to a trial by jury, it increased the chances that African Americans, who were born free, and so had no need for free papers, would fall victim to kidnappers. Although kidnappings from southeast Pennsylvania were not uncommon before 1850, fears of an increase in their frequency seem to have been borne out by developments in the months after the passage of the law. William Kashatus has counted at least "a dozen kidnappings" in Chester County in the six months after September 1850. There was a pattern to these operations. A group of white men would attack the home of a black family, nab one of the occupants, bundle them into a carriage, and race to the Maryland line to catch a train for Baltimore, where they hoped to – and many times did – sell the person to

---

[34] *Pennsylvania Freeman*, January 30, 1852; Philadelphia *Evening Bulletin*, February 5, 1852; Washington, DC, *Union*, January 16, March 23, June 27, July 24, October 11, 1851; Harrisburg *Whig State Journal*, August 12, 1851; Lancaster *Examiner & Herald*, April 2, 1851; *National Era*, July 3, 1851; W. W. Griest, ed., *Pennsylvania Archives*, Vol. 7, *Papers of the Governors* (Harrisburg: 1902), 491–96, 520.

[35] Harrisburg *Whig State Journal*, January 13, 1853; New York *Tribune*, January 16, 1852, January 31, February 1, 1856; Harrisburg *Semi-Weekly Telegraph*, May 12, 1856; Harrisburg *Telegraph*, February 20, 1857; *Twenty-Second Annual Report of the Philadelphia Female Anti-Slavery Society* (Philadelphia: 1856), 16.

slave traders. Black and white neighbors attempted to foil these activities. They sometimes followed in the hopes of intercepting the kidnappers before they got to Baltimore, or, when that failed, tried to retrieved the kidnapped from slave pens before they were sold further south.[36]

There were organized bands of kidnappers throughout the area. The most notorious was the Gap Gang, centered in the town of Gap, just north of Christiana, which operated mainly in western Chester and southeastern Lancaster counties. On a lecture visit to Gap, in early 1851, Charles C. Burleigh, the abolitionist, reported on the depredations of the gang and the efforts of African Americans to resist its activities. "The colored people," he reported, "were desperately resolved on self-defense against the land pirates, which have been let loose upon them by the recent Slave catching Law." Burleigh had in mind the recent kidnapping of Marsh Chamberlain by six men who stormed his home, bound and gagged him, and raced to the Maryland line. Chamberlain resisted, but was no match for his abductors or their accomplices. Neighbors raised the alarm and a group of armed black men set out in pursuit, but they were too late to prevent the kidnappers from boarding the Baltimore train with their victim. This was the second case of kidnapping in the area in a month.[37] The gang also participated in a wide array of other illegal activities, including horse stealing, counterfeiting, receiving stolen goods, burglary, incendiarism, as well as hunting fugitive slaves. Attempts to break up the gang were largely ineffective. Many were optimistic in 1854 that the "dangerous band of villains" was on the verge of being disbanded when a few of its members were arrested and its leader, the "notorious kidnapper" William Bear, was forced to flee to Maryland, "that refuge of kidnappers." In spite of this success, the gang was still in operation two years later when nine of its members were arrested, among them John Townsend, "a man advanced in years." Clearly, one report had to admit, many of the gang's members were still at large and in business.[38]

The most sensational incident in the area involved the kidnapping of two young sisters, Elizabeth and Rachel Parker, from Chester County in late December 1851. Both girls lived in West Nottingham Township in the southwestern corner of the county, a short distance from the Maryland line. The group of kidnappers was led by Thomas McCreary, thirty, a resident of Elkton,

[36] William C. Kashatus, *Just Over the Line: Chester County and the Underground Railroad* (University Park, PA: 2001), 29–32. See also Carol Wilson, *Freedom at Risk. The Kidnapping of Free Blacks in America, 1780–1865* (Lexington, KY: 1994) for a general discussion of kidnapping.

[37] *Pennsylvania Freeman*, February 20, 23, 1851; Lancaster *Union* (n.d.), in New York *Tribune*, January 24, 1851; Lancaster *Examiner & Herald*, January 22, 1851; *National Anti-Slavery Standard*, January 30, 1851; *Liberator*, January 31, 1851; Lucy Maddox, *The Parker Sisters. A Border Kidnapping* (Philadelphia: 2016), 72–74.

[38] *Pennsylvania Freeman*, April 20, 1854; Lancaster *Examiner & Herald*, June 18, 1856; M. G. Brubaker, "The Underground Railroad," *Lancaster County Historical Journal*, Vol. 15, No. 4 (April 1911), 117. An unnamed black man who was taken from Columbia to Baltimore was very likely a victim of the gang. Fortunately, he was recognized, freed, and sent home. Lancaster *Examiner & Herald*, December 8, 1853.

Maryland, close to the Pennsylvania state line. For some years, he had been the mail carrier between Elkton and Chestnut Level, Pennsylvania. His brother lived near the Parker sisters, and so McCreary was familiar with the area: he knew the sisters were free, knew the neighborhood where they were raised, and knew the persons in whose homes they worked. McCreary also had a history of kidnapping: he was suspected of a kidnapping in Downingtown in 1848 and two in Unionville the following year. His was a simple mode of operation. He would wait outside the home alone until his victim came out, while another accomplice sat in a carriage nearby. One of his known confederates was John Merritt, twenty-one, formerly of Pennsylvania, but in 1851 living near McCreary in Cecil County, Maryland. His victims were taken by carriage across the state line, put on a train to Baltimore, where they were lodged in the slave pen of James Campbell, owner of one of the leading slave trading firms in the city. Campbell's brother, Walter L. Campbell, was owner of a pen in New Orleans, to which slave cargoes from Baltimore were shipped. He also owned a farm, eighty miles from New Orleans, where slaves, who were not sold at the pen, were "acclimated to the Southern Market."[39]

Elizabeth, about ten years old, was kidnapped by McCreary and an unnamed man from the home of Matthew Donnelly, where she was working, taken by wagon to Elkton, Maryland, and from there by train to Baltimore, where she was housed in Campbell's pen. John Merritt was working at Donnelly's at the time and was clearly a party to the kidnapping, as was Donnelly himself. McCreary claimed he was hired by Luther A. Schoolfield, a Baltimore lottery dealer, to reclaim his slaves who had escaped four year earlier. Elizabeth spent two weeks in the Baltimore slave pen before she was shipped off to New Orleans, where she was sold to a woman who owned a large flower garden business and for whom she sold flowers and candy. Apparently, Elizabeth later convinced a city watchman with whom she had a conversation that she was born free and had been kidnapped and sold into slavery. The man took her to a local magistrate, who demanded an explanation of how Elizabeth was acquired. Word of her whereabouts got back to Chester County, where locals raised $1,500 to purchase her freedom and return her to Baltimore. There, new attempts were made to get her to admit she was a slave. Days later, three men from Chester County visited Campbell's pen and won her release.[40]

[39] West Chester *Village Record*, January 13, February 10, 1852, January 18, 1853; Lancaster *Examiner & Herald*, December 31, 1851; Columbia *Spy*, January 3, 1852; *Cecil Whig*, December 27, 1851 (my thanks to Milt Diggins for this reference and information on McCreary). For McCreary's earlier troubles with Pennsylvanians see Upper Marlboro *Planters' Advocate*, December 31, 1852; *Pennsylvania Freeman*, January 22, 1852; Ralph Clayton, *Cash for Blood: the Baltimore to New Orleans Domestic Slave Trade* (Bowie, MD: 2002), 114; Maddox, *The Parker Sisters*, 60–61, 65–67, 106–09, 204.

[40] West Chester *Village Record*, July 20, 1852, February 1, 1853; New York *Tribune*, January 22, 1853; *Pennsylvania Freeman*, January 20, 1853; *National Era*, August 5, 1852; *Liberator*, August 6, 1852; Baltimore *Sun*, January 5, 6, 7, 8, 10, 11, 13, 1853.

One week after Elizabeth was shipped off to New Orleans, McCreary and two unnamed accomplices nabbed Rachel, her older sister, from the home of Joseph C. Miller, a forty-year-old farmer. A visitor later reported that Miller's modest two-story house sat in an isolated section of the township three-quarters of a mile from the nearest neighbor. McCreary followed the familiar route to Baltimore and Campbell's pen, claiming that, like her sister, Rachel had escaped from Schoolfield. Unlike her sister, Rachel did not go quietly. On the way to Baltimore she told anyone who would listen that she was free and being kidnapped. She told the landlord at a tavern where the party stopped as well as several persons at the railroad office. When a man she later described as having "large light colored whiskers" visited her in the slave pen to persuade her to admit she was Schoolfield's slave, she refused; when he threatened to cowhide her and throw her in a dungeon, she defiantly continued to insist she was free, and when, in an attempt to get her to admit she was a runaway, she was told that Elizabeth had confessed, Rachel responded that her sister must have been coerced. That no one on the way to Baltimore was willing to intercede speaks to the ease with which kidnappers, such as McCreary, operated, and the dangers freeborn blacks faced. Yet one can only marvel at young Rachel's determination to resist as best she could.[41]

Unlike Matthew Donnelly, who colluded with McCreary in the abduction of Elizabeth, Joseph Miller and a neighbor followed in an attempt to cut off the kidnappers before they reached the Maryland line, but were unsuccessful. The following day, Miller and a group of seven neighbors – described by one local newspaper as anything but abolitionists – followed McCreary to Baltimore, where they accused him of kidnapping. McCreary and one of his associates were arrested, but after a hearing were released with bail set at $300. Miller and his neighbors may not have given much thought to the possible consequences of their actions. It had been less than three months since Edward Gorsuch, the Maryland slaveholder, was killed by runaway slaves from Maryland at Christiana. Not surprisingly, Miller and the others were threatened with violence in revenge for the death of Gorsuch. Possibly because of these threats, the Pennsylvanians decided to return home soon after. On the way, Miller disappeared from the train. His friends went in search of him and were told that he had stepped off the train either to smoke a cigar or to get some fresh air, as the cars were unusually muggy. They failed to find him. On January 2nd, Miller's body was discovered hanging from a tree. Because there was suspicion of foul play, his body was taken to Baltimore for a postmortem. The coroner's inquest concluded that Miller had committed suicide due to depression, possibly brought on by the fact that he knew Rachel to be a slave and had lied about it. Questions were raised immediately about the hasty inquest and its

⁴¹ West Chester *Village Record*, January 13, February 10, 1852; New York *Tribune*, January 22, 1853; Philadelphia *Evening Bulletin*, January 21, 1852; *National Era*, January 15, 1852.

speculative findings, as well as the way Miller's body was unceremoniously disposed of at the end of the hearing. If he had hung himself, observers in Pennsylvania and elsewhere in the North wanted to know, why were there no bruises on his body? They also questioned why the body was allowed to remain unpreserved for ten days between the time it was discovered and the time of the hearing. Soon after his body was discovered, it was reported, "a hole was dug under the tree where he was found, and coffinless and brutally his corpse so dear to others far away, was thrust into it and covered over." Another sympathetic report confirmed some of the details about the way in which the body was disposed of, saying that it was "thrown into an old box, the cover of which was too narrow by three inches, and buried at a depth of two feet." Weeks later, another postmortem was performed, this time in West Chester, by Drs. J. W. Hutchinson and E. V. Dickey, who concluded that Miller had first been poisoned with arsenic before he was hung. The new findings unleashed a flurry of accusations and counterclaims. A Richmond, Virginia, newspaper dismissed the Pennsylvania findings as "utterly incredible," the conclusion of "a strong Abolitionist prejudice or the pretended opinion of Abolitionist rascals." If it was foul play, the editor wanted to know, why would anyone wait for "the operation of arsenic upon the system" before hanging Miller? All the evidence, another editor insisted, pointed to suicide as the cause of Miller's death. If it was, an abolitionist editor responded, why was Miller's body dry when it was raining heavily during the return trip to Pennsylvania? The only logical conclusion, he maintained, was that the body was buried after the arsenic had taken effect and after the rain had stopped.[42]

Defense witnesses at McCreary's trial insisted that Rachel was in fact Elizabeth Crocus, who, with her mother, June, and sister, Henrietta, had escaped from Schoolfield or had been "taken off by other persons" in April 1847. They could identify Rachel, they explained, because she looked so much like her mother. The mother was described as "a light chestnut color," while Elizabeth Crocus was a "shade darker," and Henrietta "nearly the same color." The fact that Elizabeth Parker was described as being "as deep a black as one can imagine" did not seem to bother those whose case was built on their ability to correctly identify the alleged fugitives by the color of their skin. Contrary to other witnesses for Schoolfield, a Mrs. Martin was convinced that Rachel was not the girl Elizabeth Crocus who had lived with her for some time. But four or five other witnesses, including Schoolfield's mother and son, pointed to her as the daughter of their slave, June, to whom she had a very close resemblance. Both Thomas McCreary and Schoolfield's son, Luther, claimed that they heard of Rachel's whereabouts only after the capture of her sister Elizabeth. In an effort

---

[42] West Chester *Village Record,* January 13, 20, 1852; *Pennsylvania Freeman,* January 8, 22, 29, 1852; Richmond *Dispatch,* January 31, 1852; Hagerstown *Herald & Torchlight,* January 14, 1852. One reasonable explanation is that Miller was strangled before he was hanged. See Diggins, *Stealing Freedom,* 101–14; Maddox, *The Parker Sisters,* 132–37.

to undermine the veracity of witnesses from Pennsylvania, McCreary's attorneys demanded to know if they had ever been members of societies opposed to the Fugitive Slave Law or of any other abolitionist associations. McCreary was acquitted based largely on the testimony of John Merritt, described by some who knew him as a "worthless and abandoned character" who had been tried previously for counterfeiting and who, according to Charles C. Burleigh, had been involved with a gang of depredators – possibly the Gap gang – who "infested the lower part of Chester County, engaged in gambling, passing counterfeit money, and other swindling operations."[43]

During McCreary's trial, supporters of Rachel Parker petitioned the courts for her freedom in an effort to prevent her from being moved or put on a ship to New Orleans. But the petition was also meant to address the difficulty created by the fact that blacks could not testify in Maryland courts in cases involving whites, nor could they come into the state to give evidence. As a result, Rachel was forced to petition for her freedom, which in effect put the onus on her to prove that she was free. Normally, in such situations, a writ of habeas corpus would have been sufficient to win her release. Rev. John M. Dickey, and a number of other Pennsylvanians, visited Schoolfield to plead with him to release Rachel, but were rebuffed as a "set of abolitionists." Schoolfield would not let her leave prison, to which she had been moved from Campbell's pen, fearful she would be spirited away and so deny him the chance to prove that she was his slave. Rejected, Dickey promised to organize a group of "prominent citizens" to push for her release. Finally, the case came to trial in a Baltimore County court in early January 1853, more than a year after the girls had been kidnapped. Dozens of witnesses from Chester County descended on the courthouse, at their own expense; among them were employers, doctors, and lawyers – all of whom claimed that they had known both Rachel's mother, who had lived near Oxford, Pennsylvania, for almost twenty years, and Rachel since she was a baby. The trial lasted eight days. Under the sheer weight of the evidence, Schoolfield finally capitulated and withdrew his claim to the girls. A Baltimore editor thought Schoolfield's decision to abandon his claim "reflected creditably the spirit in which it [had] been actuated." After all, he was only driven by a desire to recover his property. The nature and weight of the testimony convinced the editor that "a mistake in the identity" had been made.[44]

If this was simply a case of mistaken identity then it was an error that had gone terribly wrong. In the end, pluck, luck, and organized resistance paid

---

[43] West Chester *Village Record*, January 13, 20, 27, February 10, 1852, January 25, 1853; Philadelphia *Evening Bulletin*, January 21, 1852; *Pennsylvania Freeman*, January 22, February 12, 1852; *National Era*, January 15, 1852; Lancaster *Examiner & Herald*, January 19, 1853.

[44] West Chester *Village Record*, February 3, 10, April 15, 1852, January 11, 18, 20, 1853; *National Era*, January 15, April 24, 1852; Hagerstown *Herald of Freedom & Torchlight*, January 19, 1853; Baltimore *Sun*, January 13, 1853.

off for the sisters. Rachel's and Elizabeth's refusals to admit they were slaves, Thomas McCreary's reputation as a kidnapper, the speed with which the small community in Nottingham Township rallied to the girls' support, and the attention the case garnered in the local and national abolitionist media finally led to the sisters' freedom. But coming so soon after the furor over the Christiana crisis, and in the midst of the controversy over William Smith's killing at Columbia, the kidnapping of the girls only increased tension between Pennsylvania and Maryland. It also had the potential to embarrass Governor Bigler politically. There had been widespread support in Pennsylvania for a full-scale inquiry into what had happened at Christiana and the federal government had accused those suspected of supporting the actions of the fugitive slaves of treason. Why, many wondered, had Bigler and the press not insisted on an inquiry, or called on the governor of Maryland to extradite McCreary for the kidnapping of two of its citizens and the murder of another? In its condemnation of the majority of the state's press, the *Pennsylvania Freeman* wondered if "their veins [ran] water." Even less was heard from the political leaders of the state. The governor never publicly raised the question of extradition. "There seems to be very little prospect at present," the *Pennsylvania Freeman* editor lamented, "that Pennsylvania will utter even a whimper. Shame!" But within two weeks of the editorial the state legislature authorized the governor to hire a lawyer to defend Rachel. Those opposed to the move attempted to buy time by referring the resolution to a committee for investigation. But the attempted referral was voted down, the majority insisting that the facts of the case were widely known and incontrovertible. As one senator pointed out: "The state of Maryland, upon the death of Gorsuch [at Christiana], one of her citizens[,] had employed the ablest counsel and dispatched the Attorney General of that State" to litigate the treason trial. Pennsylvania owed it to its citizens to act similarly. Under pressure, Bigler finally relented and appointed Thomas S. Bell, a former associate justice of the state supreme court, and the state's attorney general, James Campbell, to defend Rachel.[45]

Once the girls were freed in January 1853, there were calls for a grand jury inquest in Chester County to determine the details of the "naked kidnapping." At the same time, friends and neighbors of the girls offered a $1,000 reward for the arrest and conviction of Miller's murderer. The pressure on Bigler and county authorities seemed to have had the desired effect when, in March, a grand jury in Chester County indicted Thomas McCreary and John Merritt for murder and the governor requested the extradition of McCreary (but not Merritt). The exclusion of Merritt from the extradition request struck some observers as unusual, if not odd. "Gov. [Enoch] Lowe will probably

[45] *Pennsylvania Freeman*, February 5, 1852; West Chester *Village Record*, February 24, April 15, 1852; *National Era*, April 24, 1852.

understand" Governor Bigler's request "in a Pickwickian sense," the editor of the West Chester *Village Record* predicted, "as going through with a mere formality."[46]

In response to Bigler's requisition, Lowe asked for time to consult with the attorneys for Schoolfield and McCreary. As far as he could tell, he told Bigler, there was an agreement between the two teams of attorneys not to bring charges against Schoolfield and McCreary, which he considered tantamount to an agreement between the state of Pennsylvania and the defense attorneys. In the end, Lowe refused to extradite McCreary on the grounds that he had set out to capture the sisters with the clear authority of their master and with the appropriate power of attorney. He had captured them believing they were fugitives based on information received in the area and the "extraordinary likeness which exists" between them and one of Schoolfield's slaves. Given these facts, McCreary should not be considered a criminal because he had not acted with malicious intent. If he were guilty, Lowe reasoned, it was "purely technical." Lowe also worried that, given the level of prejudice against McCreary in Chester County, he could not possibly receive a fair trial there. Finally, Lowe enclosed a letter from James Campbell in which the attorney general of Pennsylvania had agreed with lawyers from Maryland that there would be no further prosecutions. This pledge, Lowe reasoned, reinforced his contention that there was an agreement with the state of Pennsylvania not to pursue the case further.[47]

Bigler rejected Lowe's reasoning. If, he pointed out, McCreary had followed procedures laid down by the law, all subsequent problems could have been avoided. Comity, he insisted, demanded McCreary be handed over, and the fact that the citizens of Chester County were upset, because they knew the girls to be free, did not jeopardize McCreary's chances for a fair trial. There was little doubt that McCreary had carried Rachel away in violation of the law. Bigler was also concerned that Lowe had taken the unusual step of looking into the record to determine the facts of the case. Normally, extradition requests were promptly executed without any examination into the merits of the case. That usually came under the purview of a state requesting the extradition. Finally, Bigler rejected the contention that Attorney General Campbell, in writing to the Maryland lawyers, was acting for the state. He did not appear at the girls' trial in his capacity as the attorney general, but as one of the defense attorneys named by Bigler. His remit, then, was the same as those of Judge Bell, the other lawyer appointed to the defense team. There was simply no connection, Bigler insisted, between the trial of the freeborn Parker girls and the prosecution of McCreary.

---

[46] *Pennsylvanian Freeman*, January 20, March 3, 1853; West Chester *Village Record*, January 25, 1853; Maddox, *The Parker Sisters*, 184–87.

[47] West Chester *Village Record* (n.d.), in *Pennsylvania Freeman*, March 10, 1853. Diggins points to the fact that, for years, McCreary had been defended and protected by successive governors, and supported by slaveholders in Cecil County for his protection and recapture of slave property. Diggins, *Stealing Freedom*, 168–80.

In spite of his vigorous response, Bigler let the matter drop. He may have concluded that Lowe would not budge. But such pragmatism hid a long record of accommodation, if not appeasement, of slaveholding interests among leading Pennsylvania Democrats, including the governor. At the end of the trial, Attorney General Campbell saw fit to issue a gratuitous apology condemning the "foul spirit of abolitionism" and reiterating Pennsylvania's commitment to return fugitive slaves. Bigler himself had come to power riding the wave of revulsion against the Christiana shoot-out and committed to the repeal of the 1847 state law, a law that he had supported as a state senator. Within weeks of his inauguration, Bigler pardoned George Alberti, a notorious Philadelphia slave hunter and kidnapper. Many also wondered why Bigler had not insisted on the extradition of Archibald Ridgely for the killing of William Smith in Columbia, or, for that matter, why he had accepted the findings of the Maryland commissioners sent to investigate Smith's death.[48]

The problem of kidnapping and the rendition of fugitive slaves continued to plague relations between Pennsylvania and Maryland throughout the 1850s. Some of the cases involved current and former officers of the law, such as Solomon Snyder, John Saunders, and Henry Loyer of Harrisburg, who had gained an unenviable record as Richard McAllister's slave-hunting constables. All three, along with Jacob Waltman and Daniel Gillard, were indicted by a Lancaster County grand jury in December 1852, charged with kidnapping Fleming Hawkins, a free black. Hawkins claimed he was made drunk and taken in the direction of Maryland, but managed to escape his captors. Evidently, Bigler called on Lowe to extradite Saunders, who had fled Pennsylvania once the kidnapping was foiled. There is no report of what became of that request.[49] Snyder and Saunders were not deterred and continued their efforts to take Pennsylvania free blacks into Maryland. In February 1855, Snyder, with the aid of two African Americans, James Jackson and David Thompson, attempted to kidnap George Clarke, and eighteen-year-old born and raised in Carlisle, Cumberland County. Jackson and Thompson asked Clarke to help them carry "some things" to a house where there was to be a dance. The house, it turned out, was Snyder's. When Clarke realized where he was, he tried to flee, but was caught. He made enough noise, however, to attract a crowd. Snyder and Jackson were arrested, but Thompson managed to elude capture. Jackson later fled while on bail. Snyder was found guilty and fined $1,000 plus cost and sentenced to six years in prison. He was released three years later.[50]

[48] *Pennsylvania Freeman*, June 30, 1852, January 20, 1853; West Chester *Village Record*, August 8, September 9, 1854. According to Milt Diggins, Lowe and his predecessor, Philip Thomas, had also refused to extradite McCreary for one of two earlier kidnappings. Correspondence with Diggins, July 16, 2010.

[49] Complaint of Fleming Hawkins, Quarter Sessions Docket, 1851 to 1853, Lancaster County Historical Society, Lancaster, PA; Harrisburg *Whig State Journal*, May 19, 1853; Lancaster *Inland* (n.d.), in Pittsburgh *Gazette*, May 25, 1853; *Anti-Slavery Bugle*, June 18, 1853.

[50] Harrisburg *Telegraph & Journal*, March 10, 1855; New York *Tribune*, February 26, 1855; *Liberator*, March 16, 1855; Dauphin County Clerk of Courts, Quarter Session Docket Book 9,

Looking back on his youth spent in Chambersburg, "J. P. M.," writing in 1901, recalled the existence of a kidnapping gang that operated in Franklin and Cumberland counties with close connections to Hagerstown, Maryland. Members of the gang included the town's constable and the owner of a hotel, where victims were held. Their Hagerstown connection was William Treaner, who had been town constable for "20 to 30 years." Treaner was also active in the recovery of fugitive slaves, as was his brother, Henry, who "J. P. M." remembered as the "last Maryland kidnapper who visited Shippensburg." In Adams County to the south, Ferdinand Buckingham, Philip Snyder, and Joseph Tuckey tried to seize Meg Palm in Gettysburg in early 1858. Palm was on her way home after doing the laundry of the Tuckey family. But the kidnappers had picked on the wrong woman. Palm, who is described, by a contemporary, as "a woman of strong muscular power," resisted and drove them off when they tried to bundle her into a wagon. Palm swore out a warrant for their arrest. Buckingham was arrested, but Snyder and Tuckey "decamped for parts unknown," according to one report. The charges against Buckingham were later dropped for insufficient evidence. In 1952, David Schick who grew up in Gettysburg, and for whose family Palm worked, recalled Palm telling him that during the scuffle she bit off Buckingham's – Schick calls him Cunningham – thumb. Years later, when Palm got wind that Buckingham was in town visiting his sister, she went in search of him, promising to shoot him on sight, but he was never found.[51]

The last major case to come to court before the Civil War occurred in Adams County. It was, for all intents and purposes, a fugitive slave case that had all the trappings of a kidnapping. It involved James Butler, his wife, and daughter, slaves of the Warfield family of Frederick County, Maryland. Eliza Warfield had manumitted James by will in 1854. At her death, her heirs discovered that she was deep in debt. In February 1858, the Orphans' Court of Frederick County directed the executor to sell the family for terms; the mother for five years, the daughter not to exceed twenty-eight years. At this point, they escaped into Pennsylvania, settling first in Cumberland and later in Adams County. Emmanuel Myers, a well-known Pennsylvanian slave catcher, was hired to capture the family and return them to Maryland. Backed by accomplices, Myers took them one night in June 1859 and hurried them into Maryland, where they were placed in the Frederick County jail. He had initially approached the commissioner in Carlisle for a warrant but was informed that the office had only been recently vacated. With the financial backing of John Morrison, James Butler's employer, Sheriff McCartney of Cumberland County, who had

---

RG 47, County Records, Dauphin County Quarter Session, Oyer & Terminer Papers, True Bills, April/May 1855, Dauphin County Courthouse, Harrisburg, PA.

[51] The "J. P. M" letter can be found in the UGRR Vertical File, Coyle Free Library, Chambersburg; the Schick letter is located in the Meg Palm Folder, Adams County Historical Society; Smith, *On the Edge of Freedom,* 148–50.

formerly been involved in the capture of fugitive slaves, devised a plan to capture Myers and return him to Pennsylvania for trial. In an effort to avoid prosecution, Myers had earlier moved forty yards across the state line into Maryland. McCartney persuaded the driver of the stagecoach that delivered the mail to slow down as he passed Myers' house and shout out that there were a number of handbills offering rewards for the return of runaways. As Myers stepped out of his house to collect the mail, he, in effect, crossed over into Pennsylvania. McCartney arrested him and brought him to the jail in Carlisle.

Myers was brought to trial in November 1859 in Cumberland County. His defense team included William H. Miller of Carlisle, Bradley T. Johnson of Frederick, Maryland, and Jonathan Meredith, appointed by Maryland's governor, Hicks, on the grounds that Myers was a Maryland resident. They argued that Butler was a slave and that he and his family had escaped. Moreover, they insisted that Myers had been captured by "fraud and deception." The judge instructed the jury that the case turned on three issues: were the three slaves when they were captured; had they been legally manumitted; and were they allowed to go at large while in slavery, that is, live as if they were free, and, if so, was this a recognition of their freedom under Maryland law. Because they were allowed to live as if they were free until the ruling of the Orphans' Court in 1858, the jury concluded that, under Maryland law, they were free. As a result, Myers was found guilty of kidnapping and sentenced to eight years. But in what David Smith has called "another border quid pro quo," Myers was released when he agreed to return the family to Pennsylvania.[52]

As we have seen, kidnapping was not the exclusive preserve of whites; African Americans were sometimes active partners in the capture and removal of free blacks. In late 1852, John Anderson was hired by someone, who was never named, to lure John M'Kinney away from his place of work at an inn in Maytown on the banks of the Susquehanna River. M'Kinney, a free black from Boonsboro, Washington County, Maryland, was taken to Baltimore and placed on a boat bound for New Orleans. The following year, Solomon Fisher – described as a "yeoman" in the indictment – and an accomplice persuaded Thomas Stanton of Lebanon County to help them move wood from a shed owned by Charles M. Stein. When Stanton got there he was seized, tied

[52] Harrisburg *Telegraph*, June 17, 28, 1859; Carlisle *Volunteer* (n.d.), in *Adams Sentinel*, July 4, 1859; New York *Tribune*, June 24, 1859; Carlisle *American* (n.d.), in Pittsburgh *Gazette*, June 20, 1859; Philadelphia *Enquirer* (n.d.), in *National Era*, August 18, 1859; Carlisle *Compiler* (n.d.), in *Adams Sentinel*, June 27, 1859; Pittsburgh *Gazette*, November 29, 1859; Lancaster *Examiner & Herald*, December 7, 1859; Wertz Scrapbook, Vol. 34, Adams County Historical Society; Staunton *Vindicator*, February 3, 1860; "The Trial of Emanuel Myers of Maryland for Kidnapping Certain Fugitive Slaves held at Carlisle, Pennsylvania," in www.memory.loc .gov/rbc/rbcmisc/1st/1st0088/0000/00010000.grf.; Smith, *On the Edge of Freedom*, 152–53; Blockson, *The Underground Railroad of Pennsylvania*, 144–45; Barbara Jeanne Fields, *Slavery and Freedom on the Middle Ground. Maryland During the Nineteenth Century* (New Haven: 1985), 36.

up, placed in a carriage, and taken to Baltimore, where he was lodged in prison. When the sheriff visited, Stanton informed him about what had happened. The sheriff must have threatened the kidnappers, for next evening he visited Stanton in jail and told him to get ready to return home. One of the kidnappers also bought Stanton a train ticket, and gave him "one dollar spending money." Charges were brought against Fisher and his accomplices. Two were sent to prison, but there is no record of what became of the others. In February 1857, Jeremiah Logan was hired by Tom Nathans, an African American, to carry goods to the river in Harrisburg, where he was seized by a group of men, one of whom was John Saunders. Logan managed to fend them off. Saunders and Nathans were arrested. Some of the other men may have left town, however, after the botched attempt. Saunders was subsequently indicted, along with George Westfall and Daniel Gillard (who had been indicted earlier by a Lancaster County grand jury) and Nathans.[53]

African Americans were also sometimes involved in decoying fugitive slaves into the hands of slave catchers. S. S. Rutherford goes so far as to argue that, "in the majority of cases where slaves were captured and returned to their master, they owed their betrayal to men of their own color." Rutherford exaggerated the extent of black collusion in the recapture of runaways, but there is no doubt, as Gerald Eggert has shown, that policemen, such as Harrisburg's Solomon Snyder, paid black spies to "ferret out fugitives in the black community." George Walls, a former agent of the UGRR in Oxford, Lancaster County, was suspected of welcoming fugitives to his home, then later contacting their owners, although some doubt has been raised about his involvement in such activities. Marianne and Paul Russo suggest that tongues may have wagged because of political differences and/or jealousy of Walls' economic success as a farmer and landholder. Perhaps, they suggest, Walls' less prosperous black neighbors "secretly resented, rather than admired, his wealth." But while there is no doubt that here as elsewhere along the slavery divide African Americans did sometimes collude with kidnappers and slave catchers, it is equally clear that without their active opposition to such activities many more would have been sent into slavery. It was largely because of the vigilance of African Americans that the activities of slave catchers and kidnappers were curtailed. They put paid to the activities of George Gross and James Warden in 1855. The two would decoy free blacks to a spot outside Chambersburg, clap them in irons, and drive them to Maryland. Opponents baited a trap for the two with an African American. Both managed to escape punishment, but thought it

53 Lancaster *Examiner & Herald*, December 8, 1852, January 26, 1853; Commonwealth v. John Anderson, January Session, 1853, Commonwealth v. Solomon Fisher, Charles M. Stein, and Joseph Smith, April Session, 1853; "Complaint of Thomas Stanton against Saunders and others" given to the mayor, February 24, 1853, all in Lancaster Historical Society, Lancaster PA; Harrisburg *Telegraph*, February 28, March 2, 1857; RG 47, County Records, Dauphin County Quarter Session, Oyer & Terminer Papers, April 1857, Dauphin County Courthouse.

best to take up permanent residence in Maryland. More significantly, African Americans suspected of aiding slaveholders and kidnappers were usually dealt with harshly. When Bob Steward, a banjo player, was falsely accused of being involved in an attempt to kidnap a black child in Harrisburg, he was cornered at, of all places, a revival meeting, and roughly handled. More typical were the actions of the crowds that gathered outside the Harrisburg courthouse to prevent the return of Wilson, Brocks, and Billy to Virginia in 1850. Joseph Popel, who led the charge, heeded a long-standing community mandate to impede slave catchers. He took his cue, one suspects, from the actions of the thirty African Americans who, a few months earlier, had rescued a family of five who had taken refuge in Tanner's Alley. Although the sheriff called out the militia and shots were fired, the fugitives were never found.[54]

The depredations of kidnapping gangs in Dauphin and adjacent counties were a marked feature of the decade. When, in March 1860, John Brown was kidnapped in Chester County and later found in a slave pen in Baltimore, one local newspaper despaired of the history of numerous raids that had taken place in the county and all along Pennsylvania's southern border. It revisited the history of kidnapping in the area, recalling the attempt, in 1820, on Jack Reed, who killed his assailant, and was later tried for murder but acquitted; the capture from a school in Downingtown in either 1848 or 1849 (possibly by Thomas McCreary) of a girl who was never heard from again; and finally, the five or six African Americans who had disappeared without a trace from the area in the preceding six months. While less frequent, the disappearances from Harrisburg were no less alarming. "There are still men among us," one editor lamented, "who will steal negroes, and...several have been missing of late."[55] Black communities and authorities throughout southeastern Pennsylvania struggled to contain these activities and break up the gangs. The constant threat was just one measure of the vulnerability of black communities in the region. That they fought to protect themselves and sometimes managed to prevent rendition or to retrieve those who had been kidnapped attests to the complex nature of the contest to secure a free space for themselves north of slavery's dividing line. In the months before the outbreak of the Civil War, the state legislature revisited the emasculated 1847 law and enacted a new personal liberty law that imposed heavy fines and lengthy prison sentences on anyone caught taking free blacks south. The law also banned state judges, justices of the peace, or aldermen from involvement in fugitive slave cases.

---

[54] S. S. Rutherford, "The Underground Railroad," *Publications of the Historical Society of Dauphin County* (1928), 7; Eggert, "The Impact of the Fugitive Slave Law on Harrisburg," 563, 566; Marianne H. Russo and Paul A. Russo, *Hensonville, a Community at the Crossroads: the Story of a Nineteenth-Century African-American Village* (Selinsgrove, PA: 2005), 79; Kashatus, *Just Over the Line*, 31; Chambersburg *Repository* (n.d.), in Pittsburgh *Gazette*, September 22, 1855; Harrisburg *Telegraph*, September 3, 5, 1857; www.afrolumens.org/rising_free/fugitives .html.

[55] West Chester *Village Record*, March 17, 1860; Harrisburg *Telegraph*, January 5, 1858.

Anyone convicted of doing so faced a fine of $1,000. In addition, anyone who "violently and tumultuously" seized a fugitive slave in an "unreasonable manner," one that disturbed the "public peace," faced a fine of $1,000 and jail time not exceeding three months.[56]

In spite of the many kidnappings, the area continued to be a magnet for those seeking freedom from states immediately to the south. From the politically tumultuous early years of the decade to the outbreak of the Civil War, there was an unbroken flow of fugitives into southeastern Pennsylvania. They came individually and in large groups. As we have seen, twenty-six men, women, and children, the entire holding, bar one, of Edward Cheney of Funkstown, near Hagerstown, arrived in Lancaster in October 1852, followed by their owner, whom they managed to give the slip. On a cold Christmas eve morning in 1855, Barnaby Grigby, twenty-six, Margaret Elizabeth, his twenty-four-year-old wife, Frank Wanzer, twenty-five, and Emily Foster, Margaret Elizabeth's sister, along with two others, both unnamed, one of whom was from Fauquier County, left Aldie, Loudoun County, Virginia. The Wenzer family traveled by carriage, the two unnamed by horse. They were well armed with double-barreled pistols and dirks. At Cheat River, close to the Frederick-Carroll county line in Maryland, they were accosted by six men who tried to take them into custody. But the six met fierce resistance from the fugitives, including the women, who threatened to shoot if any attempt was made to stop them. The two traveling on horseback were separated from the group during the confrontation and possibly captured. Those in the carriage continued on to Columbia, reaching Philadelphia three weeks after their escape. They were soon sent on to Syracuse by William Still and the vigilance committee, where Frank and Emily were married by Rev. Jermain Loguen before they left for Toronto. Eight months later, Frank returned to Aldie unannounced and brought out his sister Betsy Smith, her husband Vincent, and a friend, Robert Stewart.[57]

With organizations such as the Fugitive Aid Society in Harrisburg and similar vigilance committees in other areas in the region, including the one in Chester County dominated by Quakers, those seeking freedom found support, comfort, and protection. Many remained only long enough to recover from the harrowing trip before moving on further north or east to Philadelphia. Some stayed a while longer, convinced that they were safe where they were until the arrival of their master or slave catchers forced them to move on to more secure places. And yet others took up permanent residence. Security could not always be guaranteed, as Daniel Webster and Moses Horner discovered in 1859. Federal and state officials still had the means to disrupt the lives of those who took refuge in black communities. The level of despair and frustration this must have caused can only be imagined. The message behind

---

[56] Lancaster *Examiner & Herald,* November 28, 1860.
[57] *Pennsylvania Freeman,* November 18, 1852; Journal C, Black Abolitionists Papers, 7: 13603; Still, *The Underground Railroad,* 116–22.

Richard McAllister's decisions was unmistakably clear: those seeking freedom from slavery must be and would be hunted down and returned at all costs. The actions of commissioners such as McAllister, buttressed, as they were, by the full weight of the federal government, had a decided effect on free and enslaved blacks. The dislocations caused by the Fugitive Slave Law and McAllister's decisions, when coupled with frequent expressions of opposition to the presence of blacks in the state, symbolized by the state's promotion of African colonization, sent a clear message to African Americans that they were not wanted in Pennsylvania. Some African Americans, not surprisingly, thought the time had come to turn their back on America for a future elsewhere, whether it was in Liberia, Canada, or the Caribbean.

If the views of editors are a useful barometer of white attitudes toward the effort of African Americans to make a future for themselves in places such as southeast Pennsylvania, free from the taint of slavery, then that future was anything but bright. Even editors who opposed the Fugitive Slave Law, were generally sympathetic to the plight of fugitive slaves, and reported favorably on the activities of the UGRR in the area remained unwaveringly committed to the idea that the interests of African Americans were better served if they left for another country, particularly Liberia, which many argued was set aside as a place where their talents could flourish free from the taint of American racial antipathy. Even when some of these editors were impressed with the ways African Americans had demonstrated their ability to struggle against continued oppression, and build institutions to cater to their needs, they continued to insist on a separation of the races. America, they maintained, was a white's man's country. It was in the context of such ambivalence and antagonism that black communities throughout southeastern Pennsylvania attempted to establish free spaces for themselves, spaces that were created, in part, out of a willingness and commitment to welcome those seeking freedom from slavery and to struggle against a law they considered emblematic of all that was wrong with the United States.

# 8

# Eastern Shore of Maryland and Philadelphia

"I find myself in a Position to address you a few lines and I hope that they may find you in as good health as I am myself in." There is nothing unconventional about this opening salutation, except that it was written by a slave to his master soon after he escaped. It is, however, unusual in other important ways: the author clearly meant to thumb his nose at his master, to demonstrate his capacity for independent action, and to assert his commitment to freedom. But this sort of communication, written so soon after an escape, ran the risk of destroying the best laid plans. That it did not says something about the person who executed what, by any measure, was a masterful plan of escape from slavery in 1853. Written by Henry W. Banks to William M. Buck, a forty-three-year-old slaveholder of Front Royal in the Shenandoah Valley of Virginia, the letter was ostensibly mailed from New York on February 15, 1853. Buck had hired Banks in 1849 from his owner, Edward W. Massey, who lived a short distance from Front Royal. Evidently, Banks had requested the move so he could be near his wife. But he may have had other plans. Less than two years after the transfer, Massey got word that Banks was planning to escape. Massey had him jailed, but Buck intervened and had Banks released, confident that the rumors were baseless. In April 1852, Massey got wind of another planned escape and this time sold Banks to a local slave trader. Again, Buck came to Banks's defense: family connections, he predicted confidently, would keep Banks close to home. To convince Massey that there was nothing to the latest rumor, Buck agreed to post a security of $800 should Banks escape before the expiration of the contract they had renewed every year since 1849. In less than a year, Banks was gone – where to no one knew. Massey was convinced that he had fled with his brother Landon and despaired of ever retaking him. His "smartness," Massey predicted, ensured he would not be captured.

Buck received the letter two days after Banks's escape. In it, Banks spoke of plans to go either to Albany or Buffalo, New York. Curiously, he

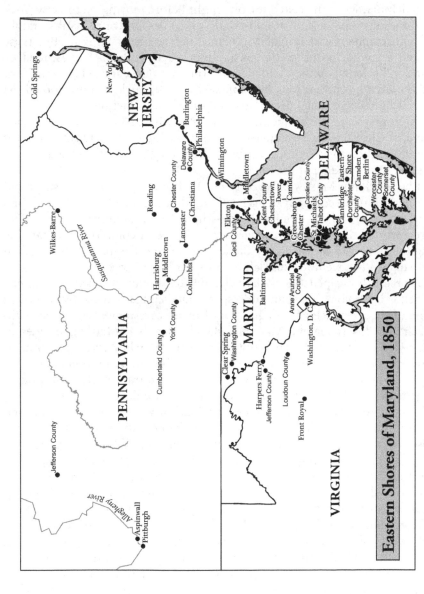

MAP 5. Eastern Shore of Maryland and Philadelphia.

informed Buck of the escape route he had followed. First, he traveled north to Washington County, Maryland, which lay close to the Pennsylvania state line. But rather than cross into free territory at that point, he instead turned southeast to Baltimore, where he spent two days. From there, he headed north to Philadelphia, where he rested for one night before moving on to New York City. If nothing else, the course supposedly taken demonstrated Banks's familiarity with escape routes out of Maryland and northern Virginia. But these details clearly were meant to confuse likely pursuers. If Banks had escaped, as he states in his letter, on the 13th, then he could not have arrived in New York two days later, given the stops he supposedly took. Buck was not fooled: he suspected Banks had gone directly to Philadelphia. In fact, he sent an advertisement announcing the escape to Kinzell and Doyle, slave traders and slave catchers, of Clear Spring, Washington County, hoping they could cut Banks off before he reached free territory. Unfortunately for Buck, both were away on business in Pennsylvania at the time.

Neither Buck nor Massey believed Banks had acted alone. Massey suspected that he had left in the company of his brother. While it is not clear that Banks had worked with his brother – or anyone else – there were a number of escapes from the area around the same time, suggesting a degree of collusion and planning among the slaves. Two weeks after Banks's departure, Thomas Ashby, William Buck's stepbrother, went to Philadelphia in search of George, one of the slaves who had recently escaped. George had also written a number of letters to family and friends back home from an address in Philadelphia that Ashby described as "one of the receptacles for fugitives and their correspondence." Even without such a lead, Virginia and Maryland slaveholders had a fairly good idea of where to look in the black community for escapees. Ashby tracked George to the address from which the letters were written, but arrived too late. He next turned to a policeman with fifteen years' experience tracking fugitives, but it was, he frustratingly observed, like "looking for a needle in a haystack"; there were, simply, too many places to hide and "such a variety of faces" that confused and threw "difficulties in the way." The community had erected its own defenses against such incursions. Ashby next contacted Edward D. Ingraham, the city's commissioner responsible for adjudicating fugitive slave cases, showing several of the letters George had written, but Ingraham had few answers to the riddle of the slave's whereabouts. In the end, Ashby threw up his hands in frustration, suggesting that his brother employ someone who knew both Banks and George and was willing to spend "several weeks" scouring the city.

Following Ashby's advice, Buck contacted Henry H. Kline, a deputy marshal, who almost two years earlier had been a member of the Philadelphia posse that accompanied Edward Gorsuch, a Maryland slaveholder, to Christiana, on his ill-fated attempt to reclaim his slaves. In spite of his experiences at Christiana, Kline had remained active in the business of tracking down fugitive slaves. Buck suggested that Kline hire a policeman from each of the city's wards where African Americans lived to help in the recapture of Banks and George. But Kline was out of town when Buck's letter arrived. When he finally replied in April, he declined to follow Buck's suggestion because, as he observed, many of the city policemen were under the influence of abolitionists and were opposed to hunting down fugitive slaves. He also did not think it wise to write Banks a letter in the hope of ferreting him out because, as he informed Buck, blacks in the city protected fugitives and quickly removed them to safer locations once they got wind of any danger. He would have to be more circumspect. He instead suggested hiring two or three black men he could trust, and who were willing to betray fugitives for a price. He already had a few leads, he wrote Buck, from a "pigeon" who had informed him that Banks was not now in the city but would soon return. The news must have raised Buck's spirits. If it did, they were soon dashed when he received a second letter from Banks, this one posted from a steamer on the Allegheny River near Pittsburgh, saying he had changed his plans and was now on his way to California. Buck shared the letter with Massey, who saw through the ruse; Banks, he responding, was leading them on a merry dance. The letter, Massey believed, was meant to draw Buck's "attention away" from where Banks was hiding. He knew Banks well enough to know that he was not on his way to California. He did concede that Banks may have had the support of someone who knew the preferred routes to California and was feeding him information. Massey was also convinced that Banks would never settle on a farm or small town such as Aspinwall along the Allegheny River, where a brother lived and where he would be most vulnerable. Instead, Massey predicted, Banks would opt for the security and anonymity of a large city, such as Pittsburgh, Philadelphia, or New York. That is where the search should concentrate, he advised. But Ashby's efforts in Philadelphia had drawn a blank, as had Kline's.

Banks, it turned out, was also using stamps in a way designed to throw Buck and Massey off his track: "He has found means," Massey observed, "to have a very imperfect stamp put on his letter." Not only was the stamp imperfect (whatever that means), but the second letter was unusually imprecise about the location from which it was posted: it was headed "steamship" without giving the name of the ship. Massey suggested that Buck contact the postmaster at Front Royal to verify that the stamps used by Banks were legitimate. Massey may have been skeptical about Banks's ultimate destination, but others whom Buck had hired to help him recapture Banks were convinced he was headed to his brother's home in western Pennsylvania. The idea was not too farfetched. If Banks was not heading to Aspinwall, then he may have been trying to make contact with Maria Cooper and her family, recently freed slaves from Front Royal who had settled in Washington County just south of Pittsburgh. In spite of his best efforts, Buck failed to locate Banks. The trail went cold until November 1853 when Buck received a third letter from Banks informing him that he had arrived safely in Hamilton, Ontario.[1]

[1] H. W. Banks to Dear Friend, New York, February 15, 1853, William M. Buck to Dear Sir, Front Royal, February 1, 1854, Buck Family Papers, University of Virginia, Charlottesville (my thanks

While Banks's escape speaks to the fragility of the slave system, it also provides us with an opportunity to explore the nature and consequences of what Henry Bibb, himself a fugitive from Kentucky, called the work of "self emancipation." At first glance it seems odd that Banks would go to such lengths to stay in touch with his former master. There is no doubt that he felt some attachment to the man who had protected him from the dark unknown of the internal slave trade. Banks showed his gratitude by offering, in his final letter, to repay Buck the $800 security he had forfeited as a result of the escape. But neither his attachment to his wife and friends in Front Royal nor the gratitude he felt for Buck's kindness diminished Banks's determination to be free.[2] But determination was no guarantee of success. Both Banks and George had relied on the aid of friends and family, slave and free, in Front Royal. Apparently, someone had gotten word to them that slave catchers were on their heels in Philadelphia. Such communications frustrated Ashby's carefully laid plans to intercept them. Had those letters been intercepted "without being known amongst the negroes, [and] a correspondence kept up, purporting to be from either or all," Ashby had no doubt his mission would have been successful. He was baffled and frustrated by the ease with which letters were exchanged between the fugitives on the run and their friends and family in Front Royal. Both he and Massey wondered if the local postmaster had colluded with the slaves or if he was simply ignoring his responsibilities, under local and state laws, to prevent the transmission of such letters. Massey put it bluntly: the local postmaster should be asked if he thought it wise to "deliver letters to slaves without informing their master." He knew the answer, but that did little to ease his and other slaveholders' concerns.[3]

to Ervin Jordon for copies of these and other letters from the collection); Thomas Ashby to William M. Buck, Philadelphia, February 28, 1853, C. B. Fristoe to Dear Sir, Front Royal, April 13, 1853, H. H. Kline to William M. Buck, Philadelphia, April 22, 1853, E. W. Massey to William Buck, n. p., May 2, 1853, Buck Family Papers, in Kenneth Stampp, ed., "Records of the Ante-Bellum Southern Plantations from the Revolution through the Civil War" (microfilm), series E reel 9; Ellen Eslinger, "Freedom Without Independence: the Story of a Former Slave and Her Family," *Virginia Magazine of History and Biography*, 114, No. 2 (2006), 264–66. On Henry Kline see Thomas P. Slaughter, *Bloody Dawn: The Christiana Riot and Racial Violence in the Antebellum North* (New York: 1991), 52–53, and William Still's letter to *Voice of the Fugitive*, January 1, 1852, in Black Abolitionists Papers Project, BAP (microform), reel 7, 318.

[2] For Bibb see John Blassingame, *Slave Testimony: Two Centuries of Letters, Speeches, Interviews, and Autobiographies* (Baton Rouge: 1977), 50. Harriet Jacobs used a similar ruse. In an effort to lead her owner to think she had escaped to New York City, Jacobs wrote two letters, one to her owner and the other to her grandmother. She had a friend take the letters, which were post-dated New York. The one to her grandmother asked that a reply be sent to Boston and not to New York City, which she visited frequently. Harriet Jacobs, *Incidents in the Life of a Slave Girl* (1861, rpr., New York: 2001), 101–02.

[3] Thomas Ashby to William H. Buck, Philadelphia, February 28, 1853, E. W. Massey to William Buck, n. p., May 2, 1853, Buck Family Papers, in Stampp, ed., "Records of the Ante-Bellum Southern Plantations," series E, reel 9. As an example of the very complex and sophisticated

Banks's letters confirm he had followed one of the well-marked routes of escape from Maryland and Virginia, routes which led to Philadelphia and the relative security of a large and vibrant black community. The enslaved who left the area followed a number of alternative routes to Philadelphia. Those from northern Virginia and central and western Maryland headed north, first into southeastern Pennsylvania and from there, usually by train, to Philadelphia. Those fleeing Baltimore and adjacent counties went overland or by boat up Chesapeake Bay. Escapees from the middle counties on the Eastern Shore sometimes went east through Delaware before heading north. Those from northern counties went directly north into the southern counties of eastern Pennsylvania. Others from the easternmost counties of Virginia used coastal escape routes, traveling sometimes by steamers. It is impossible to determine with any degree of precision exactly how many fugitive slaves from Maryland, Virginia, and Delaware passed through Philadelphia and other sections of eastern Pennsylvania. In the years following the formation of the Philadelphia Vigilance Committee in 1853, William Still, head of its acting committee, estimated the organization aided more than eight hundred fugitives. William Dusinberre suggests Still only recorded 82 percent of those assisted. In either case, the numbers receiving aid from the vigilance committee suggests that Philadelphia and eastern Pennsylvania attracted significant numbers of fugitive slaves.[4]

Although those who arrived at the offices of the vigilance committee came from all the eastern Border States, the majority originated from the Eastern Shore of Maryland. Many of them had acted on their own initiative. But as in other sectors of the upper South, escapees were also aided by free blacks, other slaves who chose to remain in slavery, sympathetic whites, and by outsiders, black and white, committed to the destruction of slavery. The search for Banks points to another feature of escapes that troubled slaveholders – the tendency of slaves to act together. Ashby never said so explicitly, but he did imply that Banks and George had acted in concert and with the aid of others

---

method of communication employed by fugitives and their families, see the case of Sally Thomas, a Nashville, Tennessee, laundress, her free black son, John, living in Florence, Alabama, and her son Henry, a fugitive slave living in Buffalo, New York, in John Hope Franklin and Loren Schweninger, *In Search of the Promised Land: A Slave* Family *in the Old South* (New York: 2006), 47.

[4] On Still's activities see James Oliver Horton, "A Crusade for Freedom. William Still and the Real Underground Railroad," in David W. Blight, ed., *Passages to Freedom. The Underground Railroad in History and Memory* (Washington, DC: 2004), 175–94; Larry Gara, "William Still and the Underground Railroad," *Pennsylvania History*, Vol. 28 (January 1961), 33–44; William Dusinberre, *Civil War Issues in Philadelphia 1856–1865* (Philadelphia: 1965), 53, 62–64. Using Journal "C," the vigilance committee's manuscript record, which covers the years 1853–56 and William Still's book, published in 1872, which includes the years 1857–60, Dusinberre estimates that Still overlooked an additional 153 cases for the period 1853–60. See J. Blaine Hudson's and Pen Bogart's estimates of more than one thousand escapes from the Louisville area during the decade of the 1850s discussed in chapter 5.

in Front Royal. Such cooperation was a common feature of escapes rising to possibly unprecedented levels in parts of Maryland after 1850. If the Fugitive Slave Law was meant to stem the flow of slaves then here, as elsewhere along the border, it had little appreciable effect. The Eastern Shore lost an estimated sixteen slaves in the first two months following the passage of the law. While the numbers of escapes fluctuated, they rose dramatically in the middle years of the decade, later tapering off slightly. Even more disturbing for slaveholders was the frequency of group escapes. Late in 1855, for example, twenty-eight slaves left from near Chestertown, Kent County. Ten left in September, taking with them three horses and two carriages. It is not clear if they were related, but this escape suggests a high level of coordination. Two were owned by Edward Ringgold, two women and two children by a Col. Ricard, two by Joseph Ringgold, one by John S. Constable, and another by Henry A. Porter. The horses and "double carriage" belonging to John Greenwood were found abandoned in Cecil County. Less than a month later, another seven fled, followed six days later by eleven more. The following year, area slaveholders lost another twenty-seven slaves, five from near Cambridge in late September. As many as fifty fled the area around Cambridge in 1857, including a group of five in October, and two groups of eleven and twenty-eight in early November. In the group of eleven were Daniel Stanly, his wife, and six of their seven children. The group of twenty-eight included Aaron Cornish, his wife, and six children; Kit Anthony, his wife, and three children; Joseph Hall, his wife, and child, as well as Joseph's sister. But not all group escapes were uneventful. Earlier, in March 1857, eight heavily armed slaves, six men and two women, led by Henry Predo and Daniel Hughes, a giant of a man, described by William Still as "stout and well-made quite black, and no fool," hired Thomas Otwell, a free black, to pilot them to freedom after their master had threatened to sell them. Their owner had posted a reward of $3,000 for their recapture. This may have persuaded Otwell to betray them. He and a collaborator persuaded the eight that it would be safe to spend the night in the Dover, Delaware, jail run by a sympathetic jailer. But Predo soon grew suspicious that they had been lured into a trap. What followed was a dramatic escape from the prison following an exchange of gunfire. Six of the group were tracked to Camden, but gave their pursuers the slip before heading to Philadelphia. William Still later reported that they were part of the forty-four escapees assisted by the vigilance committee in the first two weeks of November 1857.[5] Slaveholders had some success in foiling escapes, but stampedes like these had become so frequent that one unsympathetic newspaper reported that many slaveholders in the area were seriously considering moving their slaves further south, away from the danger posed by the UGRR.

[5] *Kent News*, September 22, 29, 1855; Pittsburgh *Gazette*, October 2, 1855; Evansville *Courier*, October 3, 1855; Dover *Republican* (n.d.), in West Chester *Village Record*, March 24, 1857; Philadelphia *Public Ledger*, October 16, November 4, 1857; New York *Tribune*, December 16,

As Kate Larson has shown, the UGRR was well in place on the Eastern Shore by 1849, exploiting vital maritime and overland trading networks. The troubling weekly escapes prompted observers to call for the establishment of a telegraphic line on the peninsula as a way to staunch the bleeding. At the center of operations was Harriet Tubman, who had escaped from Dorchester County in 1849 and who, over the next eleven years, would make thirteen trips back to the area to take out family and friends. Pivotal to her success were black communities on the Eastern Shore of Maryland, Chesapeake Bay in Delaware, eastern Pennsylvania, and New York.[6] Tubman's activities are legendary, but there were other examples of former slaves returning to Maryland to aid slaves to escape. In January 1853, Richard Neal was picked up at his workplace in Philadelphia and charged with returning to Maryland in 1849 to entice his family and other slaves to escape. Neal had bought his freedom some time after his marriage to Mathilda, a slave of Isaac Mayo of Anne Arundel County. Mayo, who by 1850 owned fifty-three slaves, gave Neal a small plot of land close by, hoping to persuade him not to encourage Mathilda to flee. Neal, it appears, failed as a farmer and subsequently moved to Philadelphia, where he started soliciting support to buy his wife and four children. Even before he could raise the asking price, Neal persuaded his family to make a bid for freedom. The family was caught in Baltimore and sold into Tennessee. Over the following months, Neal managed to raise $3,000 to purchase their freedom.

Mayo – commodore of the African Squadron stationed on the west coast of Africa, set up to curtail the illegal slave trade – was about to sail for Africa when he persuaded Enoch Louis Lowe, Maryland's governor, to request Neal's extradition from Pennsylvania as a fugitive from justice. The request could not have come at a worse time; relations between the states were strained following the kidnapping of Rachel and Elizabeth Parker. Following a brief hearing, Neal was handed over to John Lamb, a Baltimore policeman acting for Mayo. Fortunately for Neal, the last train had already left for Baltimore. Anxious to get out of town, Lamb headed for Chester to catch a later train. Members of the Abolition Society followed with a writ of habeas corpus, demanding Neal's release, which Lamb ignored, insisting that the writ had no power outside of Philadelphia. When Lamb tried to board the train, there was a violent struggle.

1857; *National Anti-Slavery Standard*, June 27, August 8, 1857; Cleveland *Herald*, November 2, 1857; Jeffrey R. Brackett, *The Negro in Maryland. A Study of the Institution of Slavery* (Baltimore: 1889), 89; James A. McGowan, *Station Master on the Underground Railroad. The Life and Letters of Thomas Garrett* (Jefferson, NC: 2005), 107–09; William H. Williams, *Slavery and Freedom in Delaware 1639–1865* (Wilmington, DE: 1996), 169; William Still, *The Underground Railroad* (1872, rpr., Chicago: 1970), 541–42, 554–55; William Still to Elijah Pennypacker, Philadelphia, November 2, 1857, Pennypacker Papers, Friends Historical Library, Swarthmore College in BAP, Reel 10: 19161. There were an estimated seventeen escapes in 1859 and thirteen in 1860.

6 Kate Clifford Larson, *Bound For the Promised Land. Harriett Tubman, Portrait of an American Hero* (New York: 2004), XVI–XVIII, 86–87.

Within minutes, Neal's supporters arrived with a second writ, this one from a judge of the state supreme court. Lamb was forced to hand over his prisoner to a contingent of the Philadelphia police. Why, one editor wanted to know, had it taken three years after the attempted abductions of his slaves for Mayo to bring charges against Neal, and why the unseemly haste to get Neal out of Pennsylvania? To some observers, the incident looked strangely similar to the kidnapping of the Parker sisters. There was something inexplicable about the entire affair; it was also a violation of Pennsylvania law. Members of the state Senate called on Governor William Bigler to provide them with the documents on which he had based his decision to issue a warrant for Neal's arrest. But the governor refused on the grounds that to do so would set an unacceptable precedent. He had followed the letter of the law: arrest requisitions from one state accompanied by relevant documents had to be executed. The Maryland governor's request, it turned out, was based on the testimony of William Hunter, a slave of Mayo's, who swore that Neal, with the aid of an unnamed black man and a white man, had persuaded his family and the others to escape. According to the request, Neal had escaped the "justice of the State" and taken refuge in Pennsylvania. Bigler could not shake the accusation, however, that he was simply fulfilling an election pledge to enforce the Fugitive Slave Law and repeal the state's 1847 personal liberty law in an effort to mollify the South.[7]

Free blacks were also deeply invested in the operations of the UGRR on the Eastern Shore and assisted Tubman during her forays into the state. One of these was the fifty-five-year-old Rev. Samuel Green, a former slave who had purchased his freedom and who, according to Kate Larson, was a "confidant, friend, and possible relative" of Tubman's. Green had long been suspected of helping slaves escape. Tubman had helped his twenty-five-year-old son, Samuel, to escape to Canada in the summer of 1854. When thirty slaves decamped from Cambridge in one night in 1858, passing directly in front of Green's home, the local authorities decided to move against him, convinced of his involvement in the escapes. They raided his home, where they found a map of Canada, train schedules and escape routes to the North, a letter from his son "detailing the pleasant trip he had, the number of friends he met on the way, with plenty to eat and drink," and telling his father to let two slaves know that it was time to leave. The two slaves, as it turned out, were among the thirty who had passed outside Green's home on their way to freedom. It was also discovered that Green had recently visited his son in Canada. But more damning was the discovery of a copy of Harriet Beecher Stowe's *Uncle Tom's Cabin*. The

---

[7] Philadelphia *Public Ledger,* January 29, February 1, 1853; *Pennsylvanian,* January 27, February 1, 1853; *Pennsylvania Freeman,* February 3, 1853; West Chester *Village Record,* February 1, 1853; Pittsburgh *Gazette,* January 29, 1853; New York *Times,* January 27, 1853; George Edward Reed, ed., *Pennsylvania Archives, Vol VII, Papers of the Governors, 1845–1858* (Harrisburg: 1902), 610–15; Byron A. Lee, *Naval Warrior. The Life of Commodore Isaac Mayo* (Linthicum, MD: 2002), 162, 192.

SAMUEL GREEN, SENTENCED TO THE PENITENTIARY FOR TEN YEARS
FOR HAVING A COPY OF *Uncle Tom's Cabin* IN HIS HOUSE

FIGURE 4. Samuel Green. (William Still, *Underground Railroad*)

authorities were ultimately unable to tie Green directly to the escapes, but they were determined to punish him nonetheless. He was convicted under the terms of an obscure 1841 law that banned free blacks from possessing abolitionist information and literature and sentenced to ten years in the state penitentiary.[8]

According to one editor, this was only the second time someone had been prosecuted under the 1841 law. Although he did not discuss the first, he was troubled by the decision to prosecute Green for owning a copy of the novel. If Stowe's novel was to be considered an incendiary publication under the terms of the law, a "number of our most respectable citizens," he reasoned, were liable to the same fate as Green. What would supporters of Green's prosecution make of subscriptions to the New York *Tribune*, which some consider inflammatory? The editor of the *Tribune* seized on the question to point out that whites did not fall under the law's purview; it was, in fact, enacted precisely to

---

[8] Philadelphia Vigilance Committee, Journal "C" in BAP, reel 7: 13424; Still, *The Underground Railroad*, 251–55; Larson, *Bound for the Promised Land*, 106, 140–43; Jean M. Humez, *Harriet Tubman. The Line and the Life Stories* (Madison, WI: 2003), 225; Easton *Gazette*, August 28, 1858; Richard Albert Blondo, "Samuel Green: A Black Life in Antebellum Maryland," (MA thesis, University of Maryland, 1998), 15–17.

limit free blacks' access to abolitionist literature. But other local editors were unperturbed by this use of the law or of Green's prosecution. "A more righteous verdict," a Cambridge editor declared, "was never rendered in a trial of any court." In the past, few slaves had fled the area because nowhere in the entire South, he insisted, were slaves better treated; here there existed between master and slave feelings of "mutual confidence" that are generally "found in those communities where the evil influence of abolitionism or its emissaries [did] not make itself felt." For some inexplicable reason things had suddenly changed for the worse. Slaves began to flee "not singly and at long intervals as before, but in gangs collected together from various parts of the county, with a concert of action and celerity of movements that defied all attempts at recapture." Then, in one Saturday night, twenty-seven left, followed by thirteen others soon after, taking with them "even the bedding and all their clothes, etc." One unfortunate master woke one morning to find that he no longer had slaves "to cultivate his land." These escapes continued for a year or more, completely destroying "confidence between master and slave." Given these conditions, Green was rightly charged under the law banning free blacks from possessing abolitionist handbills, pamphlets, newspapers, pictorial representations, or other papers of an "inflammatory character." The editor did concede that prosecuting Green for owning a copy of *Uncle Tom's Cabin* was a convenient way to bring him to account for his known participation in the UGRR. As he reasoned, Green would "never have been arrested upon that charge but for his well ascertained agency in the escape of our slaves." He admitted that only after the state attorney had examined the case closely, and found that "sufficient local evidence could not be had" to convict Green "for aiding slaves to escape," was it decided to test the applicability of the 1841 law to such works as Stowe's. The blame, therefore, should rest squarely where it belonged: until Green was "wrought upon by such publications, and by the more direct appeals of abolitionist emissaries, [he] had lived quietly and contentedly in the community in which he was born, and had the respect and confidence of all who knew him." The governor ignored an appeal for clemency from 114 ministers of the New York Black River Conference of the Methodist Episcopal Church, the denomination to which Green belonged. Green would languish in jail until finally pardoned in May 1862, on the condition that he leave the state within sixty days.[9]

As in other Border States, the power of the courts was reinforced by rough justice meted out to those suspected of aiding fugitive slaves. Late one night in the summer of 1858, a group of white men knocked at the home of James Bowers near Chestertown, Kent County, and asked if he could help them fix

9 Elkton *Democrat*, May 23, 1857, in New York *Tribune*, June 3, 1857; Cambridge *Eagle* (n.d.), in Easton *Gazette*, August 28, 1858; Larson, *Bound for the Promised Land*, 151, 349; Rev. J. Mayland M'Carter, *Border Methodism and Border Slavery* (Philadelphia: 1858), 72–71 (my thanks to Frances Bristol of the Methodist Archives, Drew University, New Jersey for this reference).

a broken-down carriage. Bowers was attacked as he stepped outdoors. His shouts brought his wife, seven months pregnant, to his aid, but she was left injured as the gang made preparations to hang Bowers. But others in the group protested; instead, Bowers was stripped, tarred, and feathered and threatened with his life if he did not leave the state immediately. Bowers was known for his antislavery opinions and for the fact that he subscribed to the New York *Tribune,* although he had made it known to anyone who would listen that he would never persuade or help a slave to flee. Yet many were unpersuaded. Five years earlier, Bowers was charged with providing a slave with a pass, but was freed for a lack of evidence. He again came under suspicion following the upsurge of escapes from the area in 1858 in which, as we have seen, horses and carriages were commandeered. To one observer, these escapes had all the telltale signs of a well-coordinated and executed plan devised by those experienced in the "business of planning and assisting escapes." But without hard evidence to support such claims, the courts were likely to dismiss, as they had done in the past, any charges brought against Bowers. Communities that came under attack by subversives such as Bowers, therefore, had no alternative but to expel the culprits. Hours after Bowers was punished and forced to flee, the mob visited the home of a Mr. Butler, searching for Harriett Tillison, a frequent visitor to the area from Cecil County, who they also suspected of being involved in the abduction of slaves. "Dwarfish... [and] scarcely weighing fifty pounds," the fifty-year-old Tillison, who plied her trade as a conjurer and fortune-teller, was dragged from the home and the "upper portion of her person" tarred and feathered before she was thrown in jail for preaching and circulating incendiary literature.[10]

In the wake of these incidents, Kent County slaveholders called a meeting to discuss ways to protect their property. The depth of the crisis could be measured by the cast of county gentry who attended. They included Judge Ezekiel Chambers, who presided; and his neighbor, US Senator James A. Pearce; James B. Ricaud, a member of the US House of Representatives; George B. Westcott, a local bank president; and physician T. C. Kennard. Chambers decried the tarring and feathering, but insisted that something had to be done to curtail the number of escapes. They would not fold their arms and submit to be "gradually stripped" of their property by the "secret machinations of those who operated in the dark and in communion with blacks, who could not legally testify against them." Measures had to be taken to protect their property. As in other parts of the upper South that suffered similar losses, Chambers called on the state legislature to adopt laws that permitted blacks to testify against whites in such cases. Were these provisions not adopted, there would be a gradual

[10] Chestertown *News,* June 26, 1858; New York *Tribune,* June 30, 1858; New York *Herald,* June 30, 1858; Larson, *Bound for the Promised Land,* 150; Barbara Jeanne Fields, *Slavery and Freedom on the Middle Ground. Maryland During the Nineteenth Century* (New Haven: 1985), 63–64.

"lessening," as he put it, in the number of slaves, and the "corrupting" of those who remained. James Pearce defended the actions of the mob. They were sober, he insisted, did not harm Bowers' wife, and only acted against a person who habitually proclaimed hostility to slavery and whom they suspected of assisting slaves to escape. James Ricaud recalled a recent conversation with a friend who reported meeting a couple of fugitive slaves from Kent County on their way through Pennsylvania who reported that they had been "furnished" at five miles intervals with "a place of refreshment and refuge." Clearly, slaveholders in Kent County, under siege from both internal and external enemies of slavery, had to respond. The meeting pledged not to deal with anyone who did not openly express opposition to tampering with slaves and called for the expulsion of those suspected of interfering with their property. The tenor of the resolutions, Barbara Fields observes, had "little in common with the spirit of patience, moderation, and compromise in which Maryland politicians customarily took public pride."[11]

But Bowers was up to the fight. He returned to the area in October, ostensibly to reclaim a house taken from him and to visit his sister. This "foolhardy" venture, as one editor put it, was met by a mob – estimated to be as large as three hundred – determined to punish Bowers for violating the earlier order not to return. In an effort to defuse the situation, James Ricaud offered to head a group that would drive Bowers to Middletown, Delaware, and put him on a train to Philadelphia with a warning that he was never to return. Those in the escorting party, according to one newspaper, were among "the first men of the community – men of intelligence" who, after suffering losses for many years from agents of the UGRR, had met in convention and decided to "execute summary vengeance upon any trespasser." But not all agreed with the decision to expel Bowers. There were reports of fights between pro- and anti-Bowers groups "culminating in Knock-downs, black eyes and bloody noses, in every direction," a reprise, according to an observer sympathetic to Bowers, of running fights that had occurred, over a two-week period, following his earlier tarring and feathering. As far as a Chicago editor was concerned, it appeared that, finally, "white mechanics and laboring men" had begun "to assert their manhood, and rights, and to denounce the system, which [was] a daily reproach to them as men, and which [was] depriving them and their children of the means of a comfortable existence."

Here was another undeniable sign that the Slave Power's hegemony was being further undermined from within, this time by the yeomen of Kent County. Another Northern editor was not so sanguine, but was nonetheless struck by James Ricaud's report of the levels of support for those fleeing Maryland slavery. It represented, he calculated, a slow retreat of slavery throughout the upper South brought on by five major developments: the pressure of a more

[11] Baltimore *American,* July 19, 1858, in New York *Herald,* July 20, 1858; Louisville *Journal,* July 22, 1858; Baltimore *Sun,* July 20, 1858; Fields, *Slavery and Freedom on the Middle Ground,* 66.

productive Northern free white labor force; the climate, which was only marginally conducive to successful plantation cultivation; the soil of the region, which had been made relatively unproductive by overuse; the activity of the UGRR; and the growth of local antislavery sentiment. For these reasons, slavery had become increasingly precarious, as demonstrated by the rising number of escapes, the high rewards offered by slaveholders, and by the "long continuance of such ads in their local newspapers." He predicted that slaveholders would have to remove what slaves did remain to the more productive soil of the cotton states. That eventuality, and the "natural prejudice against free niggers" in the Border States, would result in the ultimate expulsion of the free black population, affording a more secure "barrier for the protection of the cotton states." These developments were a guarantee, the editor suggested, against disunion. In the meantime, as this process worked its wonders, it was the responsibility of the Northern states to faithfully enforce the provisions of the constitution and the Fugitive Slave Law, and to "discountenance these underground railroads and all their agents." Where the Chicago editor saw the undermining of the Slave Power, his New York counterpart envisaged the erection of a bulwark protecting slavery where it was most productive, and in so doing ensuring the survival of the Union as it was: half slave and half free.[12]

One other case added to the sense of crisis on the Eastern Shore. Hugh Hazlett, a thirty-one-year-old white man who had lived in the area for about three years, was caught north of Greensboro in Caroline County with a group of seven slaves from Dorchester County on their way to Delaware and Philadelphia. Hazlett and the seven were betrayed by Jesse Perry, a free black. An angry crowd gathered on the wharf as Hazlett and the slaves were boarding a steamer for the return to Cambridge. Concerned Hazlett may be lynched, the sheriff ordered the captain of the steamer to head to another location. Hazlett was sentenced to forty-four years, six months, and nine days by a Dorchester County court. In the context of all that had gone before, the unusually lengthy and oddly exact sentence suggests that local authorities were determined to make an example of Hazlett, one that sent a clear message to anyone involved in "tampering" with slaves.[13]

The dramatic, large-scale escapes from Kent, Dorchester, and Talbot counties were preceded by an equally troubling, if more limited, number of escapes from other sectors of the Eastern Shore. In less than two years in the early 1850s, nine slaves from the small community of Berlin, Worcester County, fled,

[12] Baltimore *Clipper,* October 20, 1858, in New York *Tribune,* October 22, 1858, and in Easton *Gazette,* October 23, 1858; *Adams Sentinel,* October 25, 1858; *Montgomery Sentinel,* October 22, 1858; Fields, *Slavery and Freedom on the Middle Ground,* 66; Wilmington *Republican,* July 8, 1858, in Nashville *Patriot,* July 23, 1858; Chicago *Democrat,* November 12, 1858; New York *Herald,* July 23, 1858.

[13] Easton *Star,* August 10, 1858; Secretary of State Pardon Records, 1845–1865, Governor (Proceedings), 1861–69, and Governor (Miscellaneous Papers), 1856–1865, all in Maryland State Archives, Annapolis; Larson, *Bound for the Promised Land,* 150.

among them Sarah Aires, who left just before Christmas 1853, and her husband Peter Johnson, who, in a coordinated effort, followed ten months later. Such losses were relatively insignificant in an area with a slave population estimated at three thousand in 1850. Nonetheless, the apparent coordination of the escapes troubled slaveholders, who saw them as a prelude to wider slave disturbances. Their fears were not misplaced. Over the next few months, four from the area successfully reached the Philadelphia Vigilance Committee. An equal number were caught short of their goal. As a result, two slaveholders, Curtis Jacobs and his father-in-law, William Howard, decided, in June 1856, to put some distance between their slaves and those who would persuade them to leave, an approach that would be followed more systematically by slaveholders during the Civil War. The two transferred thirty-eight "head of negroes," as Jacobs put it, to Prairie Bluffs, Wilcox County, Alabama, where they were hired out to local slaveholders at a handsome profit of $1,030. Their decision was prompted, Jacobs reasoned, by a number of troubling developments on their farms. Hardy, one of their slaves, had escaped in June 1855; six months later, Joshua left, but was retaken. A number of women, including Sally and Julia, had murdered their children. Others had taken "teas and dregs" to induce abortions. Several men and women, including Obed, Leah, and Charlotte, he discovered, had "united together" to poison him and his family. Other plans of escape were coordinated with slaves on adjoining farms. Jacobs responded by rallying a number of neighboring slaveholders to join an impromptu organization to recapture those who fled. He traveled to Philadelphia to purchase cuffs and ankle locks. The following January, he reported intercepting letters from "paid abolitionists" mailed from Cold Springs, New York, and from Canada West, informing his slaves that wagons and mules had been procured to take them out, rather auspiciously, on July 4th.

Jacobs spoke for other slaveholders on the Eastern Shore, even those who were reluctant to adopt his proposed solution, when he called for united action in the face of continued loss of property and the growing danger of slave revolts. The villains of the piece, as far as Jacobs was concerned, were the growing number of free blacks in the state, who by their very presence set a bad example to the slaves, and whites from outside who participated in and financed the activities of the UGRR. Much of the money to finance these schemes, he believed, was supplied by British abolitionists to Jacobs's nemesis, Thomas Garrett, the Wilmington, Delaware, abolitionist and possibly the pivotal player in the UGRR on the Delmar peninsula. Garrett did receive a regular stream of small donations from such British organizations as the Edinburgh Ladies Emancipation Society. Jacobs estimated that Garrett had amassed a war chest of $158,750, most of it from Britain. This seems very unlikely. If his past actions were a reliable indicator, much of the money to finance Garrett's activities came out of his own pocket. As far as Jacobs was concerned, these activities had pulled together an alliance of considerable reach, one that threatened the future of slavery in the state. "The large number of free negroes around us," he confided to his diary, "and I am sorry to say so but it is true, that we have also in our white population many who put them up to this plot, together with several regular abolitionists who have been travelling amongst us under the pretence [*sic*] of other business." The federal government had proved itself singularly ineffective in protecting slave property. It was now time for the state to act, for "state sovereignty" was their only security. They were also under attack from "Greeley's agents" (named for the editor of the New York *Tribune*), who were paid $150 for every male slave brought out and $100 for every female. Abolitionists, he concluded, had at their disposal $197,912 for these operations.[14]

These were grossly inflated numbers far surpassing the accumulated means of abolitionist societies. Jacobs offered no evidence to support his claims for the financing of UGRR operations in the state. His claims of outside inter-ference and internal subversion, however, rang true with many. His call for a convention to discuss ways to secure the "property of slaveholders" in what he called "this exposed portion of Maryland" echoed those of others. The ear-lier meeting in Kent County, following the loss of slaves and the expulsion of Bowers, had set a standard of possible responses to continued depredations. A number of local conventions were held in 1858, all pointing to an area-wide slaveholders convention set for Baltimore the following year. The Worcester County meeting, which met in Snow Hill in September 1858, expressed commonly held concerns and suggested a number of possible solutions. The meeting quickly came under the influence of Jacobs, the owner, at that point, of almost fifty slaves, most of them inherited from his father-in-law. Most of the other participants owned considerably fewer slaves. A series of resolutions were adopted that called on the state legislature to pressure the federal gov-ernment to enforce the Fugitive Slave Law or, alternatively, indemnify slave-holders for the full value of slaves lost. They also called for the appointment of paid agents to recapture fugitives. Rewards of $100 for whites and $50 for blacks were recommended fines for those caught "tampering" with slaves. They recommended slaveholders discontinue the practice of "allowing slaves corn patches," allowing them to leave without passes, and permitting them to find their own homes. The police should be empowered to break up "woods meetings and all unlawful gatherings of slaves and free negroes." Finally, post-masters should be given the power to open and read all mail addressed to free blacks and slaves. Jacobs was named to head a delegation of twelve to

---

[14] Philadelphia Vigilance Committee, Journal "C" in BAP, reel 7: 13460–61, 13473–74, 13531 and 13579; Still, *The Underground Railroad*, 319, 354; Baltimore *Sun*, August 19, 1853; Curtis Jacobs Diary, Maryland Historical Society, Baltimore; McGowan, *Station Master on the Underground Railroad*, 151, 166, 171, 181; Easton *Gazette*, September 9, 1858. Sally and Julia were part of the group taken to Alabama. Of the thirty-eight taken to Alabama, eleven had died by 1859 and three were reported missing. Much to Jacobs's discomfort, escapes continued in Alabama untouched by the machinations of free blacks and white abolitionists.

the Cambridge convention, which met three weeks later and attracted additional representative from Talbot, Caroline, Dorchester, and Somerset counties. If the loss of slaves had been the impetus for these meetings, the Cambridge gathering devoted most of its time to ways to control the free black population, a pet project of Jacobs's, a development that surprised many of those in attendance. Nonetheless, the convention declared the presence of free blacks a detriment to slave societies. Consequently, ways had to be found to return free blacks to slavery, or, alternatively, laws adopted that expelled them from the state. Their "vast numbers...vicious habits...refusal to labor...incapacity for self government" were enough reasons to enact such laws. They demanded that the Baltimore convention address the state legislature on the adoption of laws to better regulate the Negro population.[15]

A few cautioned that, if these recommendations were followed, the Baltimore convention ran the risk of making a bad situation considerably worse. "Conservative," who claimed to be a slaveholder, thought the meeting unnecessary, as did slaveholders in other parts of the state who refused to attend. Existing laws on free blacks, he insisted, were stringent enough. Any further tightening of restrictions would be inhumane. He rejected the notion that free blacks were "responsible for the absconding of slaves." Marriage between free blacks and slaves was to be encouraged, for it reduced the likelihood that slaves would abscond and abandon their families. Proponents also needed to be careful not to alienate non-slaveholders, many of whom relied on the labor of free blacks. He cautioned the convention to tread carefully, fearful their actions would interrupt "the harmony and good feeling that exists between" slaveholders and non-slaveholders to the detriment of those who owned slaves. The Baltimore convention elected Ezekiel Chambers president. He and others tried to set the tone of the meeting by calling for a dispassionate discussion of the issues, for, as George W. Hughes of Anne Arundel County acknowledged, they "stood on a volcano." Jacobs was appointed to the business committee. Clearly, his was a minority position. The committee voted against the expulsion of free blacks and for the tightening of existing laws. Free blacks, they conceded, were an "evil," but one which had to be endured, for they furnished an important and irreplaceable supply of labor in both agricultural areas and cities.[16]

There were those, admittedly not sympathetic to the plight of slaveholders, who considered delegates to the conventions a collection of "desperate half-mad slaveholders." But the expulsion of free blacks had for years been a pet

---

[15] Easton *Gazette*, August 28, September 9, 25, October 30, November 13, 1858; Easton *Star*, November 9, 1858 (my thanks to Kate Larson for this reference); Baltimore *Sun*, November 6, 8, 1858; Cleveland *Herald*, September 24, 1858; Fields, *Slavery and Freedom on the Middle Ground*, 67–68.
[16] Baltimore *Sun*, June 10, 1859; Baltimore *American*, June 9, 10, 1859; *National Era*, June 16, 1859; New York *Tribune*, June 14, 1859.

project of Jacobs. His had long been a strident voice for more stringent controls on the state's free black population. As chair of the Committee on the Free Black Population, set up by the state constitutional convention of 1851, Jacobs had declared that the free black population was fast becoming intractable and menacing. His committee speculated on the size of the free black population, how many had been colonized in Liberia since 1831, and made a number of recommendations to address the problem of their rising numbers. Concerned that they would outstrip the white population in a "few years," the committee recommended that no free black be allowed to purchase real estate after the adoption of the constitution, that there be no future emancipation unless the free person left the state within thirty days, and that no free black be allowed to settle in the state in the future.[17]

Labeled the slaveholders' "salon" by the New York *Tribune,* the business committee under Jacobs's leadership insisted that the link between the growth of the free black population and the instability of the slave system was indisputable. The situation in Worcester County drove the point home. In 1790, there was one free black for every forty-three whites; by 1850, the ratio stood at 1 to 3.5. Not only was the number of free blacks, as a percentage of the white population, higher in Maryland than in any other state, in Jacobs's home county the percentage was even higher. Nothing came of Jacobs's committee recommendations in 1851. They were allowed to languish until the upsurge of escapes from the Eastern Shore, beginning in 1855, breathed new life into them. But expulsion, many continued to insist, was a step too far; it would seriously threaten the livelihood of those who depended on hired labor, especially the "poor man" who was almost "entirely dependent on day or month hands to work his crops, and who, if the free negro were deposed of, as proposed, would be without assistance." Enforced removal would result in a rise in the cost of labor, as those free blacks "worth having" would abandon the state, leaving behind "the worthless...the maimed and aged." Many farms in the state were worked exclusively by free blacks; they also performed nearly all of the services in the homes of non-slaveholders. More significantly, they performed most of the "heavy, disagreeable, but *indispensable,* duties of 'laborers.'" They were, simply, a critical element in the state's "system of political economy." Although Jacobs was one of the driving forces at the convention, the committee on resolutions made a point of rejecting calls for a blanket removal as both "impolitic and inexpedient," and reiterated what Jacobs saw as a timeworn policy of strengthening the law of 1831 that promoted the piecemeal removal of free blacks to Liberia. Jacobs immediately opposed the committee's recommendations and issued a minority report which declared the free black population "positively injurious to the best interest of the State." He dismissed

---

[17] *Debates and Proceedings of the Maryland Reform Convention to Revise the State Constitution,* Vol. 2 (Annapolis: 1851), 220–23. By the end of the decade, a number of Southern states, including Tennessee and Arkansas, would adopt laws calling for the expulsion of free blacks.

colonization as a "great humbug," and a "fruitless enterprise." He had no doubt that he would be ultimately vindicated. Free blacks had shown no inclination to go to Africa and much preferred staying in Maryland. As his 1851 committee report had shown, only 1,001 had moved to Liberia since 1831, a paltry return on the state's expenditure of $298,000. If they were refusing to leave the state, what, then, was to be done with this menace in slavery's midst? The state, he insisted, had the power to do with its free black population as it wished. It could decide to either expel them or give them the option of choosing a master and returning to slavery. Borrowing a page from George Fitzhugh, he declared, "I would have all negroes...be slaves in order that all whites may be free."[18]

Following John Brown's attack on the federal arsenal at Harpers Ferry in October 1859, Democrats swept that year's state elections, winning control of both houses of the legislature. A beneficiary of the Democratic landslide, Jacobs was once again named chair of the Committee on the Free Black Population, all but one of whose members were substantial slaveholders. Even more significant, five of the committee's seven members came from southern Maryland and the lower Eastern Shore. Early in 1860, the committee issued a series of bills reflecting Jacobs's concerns. With an eye on the Rev. Green case, it revised and strengthened clauses dealing with "incendiary documents" to include abolitionist books, handbills, and newspapers that tended to create discontent among Negroes or induced them to abscond. Any free black convicted of breaking the law was to be sold into slavery for life. Any postmaster who knowingly distributed such documents was liable to imprisonment for ten to twenty years. Letters addressed to free blacks were to be opened by a justice of the peace in the presence of the postmaster. No longer were there to be manumissions by "verbal order, last will or testament." With the exception of those Baltimore black churches conducted by white ministers, all black churches were to be sold and the proceeds made available for the "benefit of white congregations." Free blacks were not allowed to enter the state. With the exception of those traveling to Virginia or Washington, DC, on a business assignment for their white employers, those who left the state were not allowed to return on pain of being sold into slavery. Free blacks were not permitted to keep dogs

---

[18] Easton *Gazette*, December 11, 1858; Baltimore *Sun*, June 9, 10, 1859; New York *Tribune*, June 14, 1859; Curtis W. Jacobs, *The Free Negro Question* (Baltimore: 1859), 5–6, 14–15, and *Speech of Col. Curtis W. Jacobs on the Free Colored Population of Maryland Delivered in the House of Delegates, on the 17th of February, 1860* (Annapolis: 1860), 10. On Fitzhugh's argument see George Fitzhugh, *Cannibals All! Or Slaves Without Masters* (1856, rpr., Cambridge, MA: 1973). One year earlier, a memorial to the state house worried that free blacks were a "Trojan horse" in their midst, an ungrateful people who had spurned the good work done for them by slaveholders who freed them and set them up for the future. They were a people incapable of using the boon of freedom for their advancement so that, once freed, they retreated into poverty and indolence. The memorial's recommendations echoed those of Jacobs, who may have been a signatory. *Journal of Proceedings of the House of Delegates* (Annapolis: 1858), 444–54.

or firearms. That the bill was rejected says something about divisions among slaveholders over the best course to follow. One western Maryland editor dismissed Jacobs's recommendation as a "batch of the most absurd nonsense – the grossest unconstitutionality – and the most barbarous inhumanity that ever emanated from the mind of a cracked-brained mono maniac." There were, opponents reasoned, when they were not openly belittling Jacobs, more than enough laws on the books to control the free black population. But behind the questioning of Jacobs's sanity was a genuine fear that, should such laws be implemented, free blacks would abandon the state, and, in doing so, ruin its economy. On the eve of the new census, free blacks outnumbered slaves and had risen to 19 percent of the total population. But even if this rise validated Jacobs's worst fears, Barbara Fields has argued that labor shortages on the Eastern Shore, if not elsewhere in the state, were the result less of poor distribution of labor and more the result of a "mal-distribution of landownership" that gave free blacks some bargaining leverage. It was this leverage, what she calls the "irreducible difficulty," that riled the likes of Jacobs.[19]

The steady increase in slave escapes and the support they received from free blacks and whites – in other words, the activities of the local arm of the UGRR – coupled with the perceptible decline of slavery in sections of the state such as the Eastern Shore, put enormous pressure on slaveholders to devise adequate responses. As the Baltimore convention put it, Maryland was being "despoiled of her property, and her rights...trampled upon with impunity." Jacobs suggested a solution, one part personal, the other systemic. He chose to send his slaves to Alabama to get them out of harm's way while leading the charge against free blacks. His recommended solution may have been rejected, but slaveholders found other ways to defend their interests; they simply became more vigilant, using the courts, enhancing policing systems, and employing the mob to curtail the activities of local and outside opponents. Some thought actions such as the sentencing of Rev. Samuel Green and the series of conventions less a sign of strength and more a reflection of deep uncertainty and weakness. "The citadel" of slavery, the Philadelphia Ladies Anti-Slavery Society pronounced, was "in imminent danger"; as a result, "every outpost" had to be "vigilantly defended." But Eastern Shore slaveholders did have some successes if the number of escapes after 1857 is a reliable indicator. There were fewer between 1858 and 1860, although Harriett Tubman continued her activities, bringing out her last group in December 1860. The ten who left in August 1858 decided to return following a shoot-out with slave catchers. The seven who escaped from Talbot County, a few days later, armed to the teeth, were retaken in Delaware. They claimed to have been deceived into thinking they were attending a camp meeting. If true, observers wondered why there was the

---

[19] Frederick *Herald*, February 7, 1860; Easton *Gazette*, February 2, November 10, 1860; Baltimore *Sun*, February 10, 13, 14, 1860; Fields, *Slavery and Freedom on the Middle Ground*, 69–73, 76–79.

FIGURE 5. William Still. (William Still, *Underground Railroad*)

need for guns. Nonetheless, the situation on the Eastern Shore remained tense throughout. In late 1859, it was rumored that a letter was found on a street in St. Michaels, Talbot County, laying out a planned slave uprising in southern Worcester County near the Virginia state line. Although the letter was a hoax, a meeting was held to organize protection and to select an investigative delegation that was to be sent to Virginia.[20]

If the activities of Henry Banks and George are any indication, there were fugitive slaves from the area who did not make contact with the vigilance committee once they got to Philadelphia. If fugitive slave advertisements in Baltimore, Norfolk, and Richmond newspapers are reliable indicators, then there were scores of escapees whose owners suspected they were heading for Philadelphia but who do not appear in the records of the committee. The driving force of the vigilance committee was its acting committee, made up of three blacks – William Still; Nathaniel W. Dupree, a tailor; and Jacob C. White Sr., a barber – and one white, Passmore Williamson, a conveyancer. Still,

---

[20] *National Era*, June 30, 1859; Annapolis *Gazette*, June 23, 1859; Still, *The Underground Railroad*, 554–55; Annapolis *Republican* (n.d.), in New York *Journal of Commerce*, September 2, 1858; New Albany *Ledger*, September 4, 1858; West Chester *Village Record*, September 11, 1858; Easton *Gazette*, December 3, 1859; Baltimore *Sun*, December 1, 1859; Fields, *Slavery and Freedom on the Middle Ground*, 85; *Report of the Twenty-Fourth and Twenty-Fifth Years of the Philadelphia Ladies Anti-Slavery Society* (Philadelphia: 1859), 12.

sometimes with the aid of other members of the acting committee, interviewed and recorded the history of every escapee who passed through its offices on North Fifth Street. While they worked closely with supporters in Harrisburg, Reading, and elsewhere in the state, there is no evidence that the acting committee went in search of fugitives to help. The one major exception occurred dramatically in July 1855, when a young boy brought a note to the office of the vigilance committee informing Still that a slave woman and her two children were being held at a local hotel by their owner and were about to leave for New York City. The woman was twenty-five-year-old Jane Johnson, along with her sons, Daniel and Isaiah, ages seven and eleven, who were owned by John Hill Wheeler of North Carolina. Wheeler was on his way from Washington, DC, to New York City to catch a boat bound for Nicaragua to resume his duties as US resident minister. Still hurried to Williamson's office with the news but was told he would have to act alone, as Williamson was about to leave for an important meeting in Harrisburg. By the time Still got to the hotel the four had already left for the boat. On his way to the wharf, he met Williamson, who had decided to delay his trip to Harrisburg. Together, they boarded the boat and approached the group, who were sitting on the upper deck. They asked Wheeler if they could talk to his "servant." When he protested, they broached the question directly to Johnson, who made it known that she wished to be free. Wheeler resisted, but could do nothing to prevent the removal of Johnson and her children from the boat. In fact, a group of African American onlookers intervened to stop Wheeler from barring their removal. Still hailed a carriage and took the three from the wharf, first to a "temporary resting place," then to his home before they were sent off to New York City. Williamson returned to his office and soon after left for Harrisburg.[21]

Wheeler clearly miscalculated when he thought he could safely pass through a Free State with his slaves. His father-in-law, Thomas Sully, the famous portrait artist, had warned him against bringing Johnson and her children to Philadelphia. Any slaveholder, especially one in Wheeler's position, must have known that Pennsylvania law did not protect a slaveholder who voluntarily brought a slave into the state. Locking the three in his hotel room, and prohibiting them from making contact with any black person, suggests that Wheeler was aware that he ran the risk of losing his slaves. Johnson later made it clear that she had every intention of trying to escape, either in Philadelphia or New York City. Wheeler, however, was determined to regain his property. He swore out a writ of habeas corpus with District Court Judge

[21] New York *Tribune* (n.d.), in *Liberator*, August 10, 1855; Philadelphia *Public Ledger*, July 21, 18, 1855; Still, *The Underground Railroad*, 74–79; Nat Brandt and Yanna Kroyt Brandt, *In the Shadow of the Civil War. Passmore Williamson and the Rescue of Jane Johnson* (Columbia, SC: 2007), 15–17; Stanley W. Campbell, *The Slave Catchers. Enforcement of the Fugitive Slave Law* (New York: 1968), 142–44; Phil Lapsansky, "The Liberation of Jane Johnson," www.librarycompany.org/janejohnson/index.htm.

JANE JOHNSON

FIGURE 6. Jane Johnson. (William Still, *Underground Railroad*)

John K. Kane. The judge was likely to look favorably on Wheeler's plea; he had long made his anti-abolitionist views known, particularly after the shoot-out at Christiana in September 1851. Kane was also an avid supporter of the Fugitive Slave Law, and, at the time, was locked in a running dispute with Williamson, who he thought was pursuing a vendetta against local police-men who had shot and wounded, but failed to apprehend, a fugitive slave in Wilkes-Barre, Pennsylvania. Kane ruled in favor of Wheeler and ordered Williamson to produce the three fugitives. Williamson responded that he could not, as they were not in his possession, nor did he know where they were, as he had left for Harrisburg immediately after the incident. US District Attorney James Van Dyke insisted that Williamson be held in contempt for his evasive response and perjured testimony. The judge agreed to hear arguments on both counts. He rejected Williamson's response as "evasive and false." Williamson, he declared, was "the spokesman and first actor" on the boat. Of all the par-ties to the act of violence, "he was the only white man, the only citizen, the only individual having recognized political rights, the only person whose social training" equipped him to "interpret either his own duties or the rights of oth-ers under the constitution of the land." Unlike blacks, whites, Kane seemed to suggest, should know better. More significantly, Kane declared that he knew of

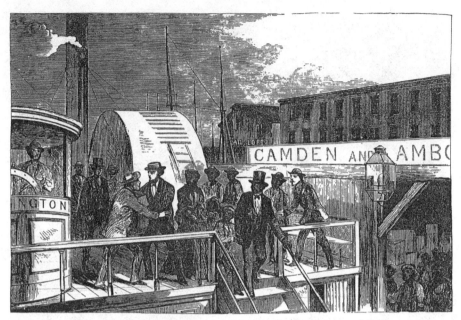

RESCUE OF JANE JOHNSON AND HER CHILDREN

FIGURE 7. Rescue of Jane Johnson and Her Children. (William Still, *Underground Railroad*)

no "statute of Pennsylvania which affects to divest the rights of property of a citizen of North Carolina, acquired and asserted under the laws of that State, because he has found it needful or convenient to pass through the territory of Pennsylvania." Even if there were such a statute, it had not been "recognized as valid in a court of the United States." The right of a slaveholder to pass through Pennsylvania with his slaves unmolested, he concluded, "has always seemed to me too clear for argument." Although he was willing to ignore the perjury charge, Kane found Passmore Williamson in contempt and ordered him to go to Moyamensing prison.[22] What followed, over the next three months, was a contest of wills between Williamson, who refused to acknowledge the contempt charge, and Kane, who refused to permit Williamson's release unless he first apologized to the court for his inadequate response to the habeas corpus writ. During those three months, Williamson's imprisonment would become an antislavery cause célèbre.

[22] Philadelphia *Public Ledger,* July 21, 28, 1855; New York *Tribune,* July 23, August 28, 1855; Washington, DC, *Union,* July 29, 1855; Brandt and Brandt, *In the Shadow of the Civil War,* 59, 61, 73; Still, *The Underground Railroad,* 79. There were those who refused to be involved in the public condemnation of Kane, who believed he was wrong to find Williamson in contempt. See Nicholas B. Wainwright, ed., *A Philadelphia Perspective. The Diary of Sidney George Fisher Covering the Years 1834–1871* (Philadelphia: 1967), 250.

PASSMORE WILLIAMSON,

IN MOYAMENSING PRISON FOR ALLEDGED CONTEMPT OF COURT.

FIGURE 8. Passmore Williamson. (Courtesy of the Chester County Historical Society)

Wheeler also swore out a complaint against six African Americans –
William Still, John Ballard, William Curtis, James Martin, James S. Braddock,
and Isaiah Moore – for assisting in the abduction of his slaves. The complaint
was first heard by Alderman James B. Freeman, who set bail at prohibitive

levels. The six appeared at the Court of Quarter Sessions a couple of weeks later, charged with riot and unlawful assembly, breach of the peace, and assault and battery for "forcing servants" away from Wheeler against the "will and entreaties of the servants" and their master. Wheeler testified that Still tried to persuade Johnson that she was free. She replied that she did want to be free but did not want to leave her master, at which point the three were seized and forcibly taken off the boat. Wheeler claimed that he tried to intervene but was restrained by Ballard and Curtis, who threatened to "cut his throat." One witness for the prosecution claimed that there were about fifteen African Americans on the wharf. These men, the defense maintained, did not come there in concert, but were there to do their jobs as porters. There was no evidence of rioting. Just as the first defense witness had completed his testimony, Jane Johnson made a dramatic appearance flanked by Lucretia Mott, Sarah Pugh, Mary Grew, Rebecca Plumly, and Sarah McKim, members of the Female Anti-Slavery Society. According to Still, it was J. Miller McKim, his coworker at the vigilance committee, who had orchestrated Johnson's appearance. But the authorities had gotten wind of the plans and were prepared to arrest Johnson once she left the court. The abolitionist checkmated this move, however, by persuading the city police to protect Johnson. Her testimony, partly a story of her life and partly an account of events on the boat and the wharf, was decisive. "I went very willingly to the carriages," she told the court. "I was very glad to go." The six accused were acquitted of rioting. Ballard and Curtis, however, were found guilty of assault and battery, and fined $10 each and sentenced to one week in prison.[23]

Not unexpectedly, the rescue of Jane Johnson and her two sons, the imprisonment of Passmore Williamson, and the trial of William Still and the others drew the attention of the public across the North for its potential impact on matters of comity as well as federal and state laws. "The recent robbery and outrage committed on a citizen of North Carolina in the city of Philadelphia," a correspondent wrote the New York *Herald,* is "one of the most audacious violations of state comity and obligations of hospitality, honesty and humanity that ever was perpetrated in any State or community of civilized people." The slaves were "pleased" to be traveling with their master. He was not sure which was worse, the taking of the slaves or the manhandling of Wheeler by "two colored ruffians." By taking the three away from Wheeler, "these human kidnappers [had] by their acts torn [them] forever asunder" from their family. Others, including the editor of the New York *Tribune,* condemned Kane for converting

---

[23] Philadelphia *Public Ledger,* August 10, 30, 31, September 1, 4, 10, 1855; *National Era,* September 6, 1855; New York *Tribune,* August 9, 1855; [J. Miller McKim] *Narrative of Facts in the Case of Passmore Williamson* (Philadelphia: 1855), 14–16 in BAP, reel 9: 16486; Still, *The Underground Railroad,* 81–84; Brandt and Brandt, *In the Shadow of the Civil War,* 122–25; Ira V. Brown, *Mary Grew. Abolitionist and Feminist (1813–1896)* (Selinsgrove, PA: 1991), 58–59.

the writ of habeas corpus, something normally used to procure freedom, into an "instrument of slave catching" and as a way to punish abolitionists.[24]

With the completion of the case against William Still and the others, abolitionists could give their undivided attention to freeing Passmore Williamson. His cell became something of a shrine. Supporters visited almost daily, providing Williamson with as many creature comforts as were permitted. Thomas Curtis' portrait of Williamson "confined [to his cell] by Judge Kane" sold for fifty cents a copy. James W. C. Pennington's New York church sent him a letter of support. A delegation from the National Convention of Colored Americans, meeting in Philadelphia, visited and praised Williamson, Still, and the others for rescuing Jane Johnson and her sons. He also received letters of support from the Progressive Friends of Chester County. Writing from on board a ship on Lake Superior, Charles Sumner denounced Kane's decision to imprison Williamson as an "unmitigated outrage" perpetrated "through the perversion of the great writ of habeas corpus." Like all those who upheld the wrong of slavery, Sumner declared, Kane had lost the ability to reason.[25]

Neither Kane nor Williamson would budge. Kane refuse to consider lifting the contempt citation until Williamson provided what he considered a reasonable set of explanations about Johnson's location and why he could not produce her. Williamson continued to insist he neither had possession of her nor did he know where she was. During the first month of his incarceration, Williamson took his case to the state supreme court, arguing, in effect, that the district court had no jurisdiction over fugitive slave cases except to issue warrants, and so Kane had no authority to issue a writ of habeas corpus calling on Williamson to produce the three slaves. Consequently, Kane had no power to declare someone in contempt. In fact, the case should never have come under the jurisdiction of Kane and the district court. As Williamson's lawyers rightly argued, this should have been a case for the circuit court. The five-member supreme court rejected Williamson's appeal, insisting that it did not have the power to interfere with the decision of a federal court. Writing for the majority, Chief Justice Jeremiah S. Black, who despised abolitionists, declared that all courts had the power to issue writs of habeas corpus; the district court was no exception. Williamson held the key to his future; he could, if he wished, "amend his return and make a true statement." If he did not, and so chose to remain in prison, it was either because "he [liked] the quarters, or the notoriety he [had] acquired in consequence." Justice John C. Knox dissented, insisting that the supreme court was legally obligated to determine if Kane's court had jurisdiction over the Johnson case. Knox also declared that slaves were free the

[24] New York *Herald*, July 24, 1855; New York *Tribune*, July 27, 1855.

[25] *Ohio State Journal*, October 25, 1855; *Frederick Douglass' Paper*, August 24, 1855; New York *Tribune*, August 10, 14, 25, 1855; Philadelphia *Public Ledger*, October 18, 1855; William C. Nell to Passmore Williamson, Boston, December 3, 1855, Passmore Williamson Scrapbook, West Chester College, BAP, Reel 9:17356.

moment they were brought into the state: "When Col. Wheeler and his servants crossed the border of Pennsylvania, Jane Johnson and her sons became as free as he."[26]

As far as Williamson was concerned, the supreme court's rejection of his appeal closed off all other legal options. Neither could he expect anything from Kane "without dishonorable submission." Because he had done nothing wrong, he saw no need for a "degrading capitulation" to Kane. It is not clear if Williamson approved of the petition by twenty lawyers asking Kane if he would consider purging Williamson of contempt. James Van Dyke, the US district attorney, responded that the petition did not meet the necessary standards to warrant the removal of the contempt charge. The petitioners argued that Williamson did not mean to offer any "personal indignity to the court," nor was "his conduct in Court...any other than correct and proper." Kane agreed to read the petition before ruling on the appeal. Van Dyke continued to insist that Williamson had to first purge himself of contempt before he could be "reinstated before the Court." The following day, Kane ruled that the petition failed to demonstrate that Williamson wished to "purge himself of the contempt." Williamson's lawyers continued to argue that it did, citing English and US legal precedents. Kane refused to budge. Some local editors who had been sympathetic to Williamson thought the time had come for him to concede the point. He had been evasive all along, refusing to concede his role in the rescue even after boasting to Wheeler that he would take full responsibility for removing the three slaves. If this were not a case involving slavery, the editor observed, most would have come to the reasonable conclusion that Williamson was in the wrong. Williamson was being poorly advised and manipulated by politicians. In early November, his lawyers submitted a revised petition expressing a willingness to answer any questions submitted by the court. They pointed out that Williamson had not heard of the writ to produce the slaves until after his return from Harrisburg, at which time the three were out of his hands. He did not know where they were and so could not answer the writ. Van Dyke finally accepted a subsequent amendment which read: "I did not seek [to obey] because I verily believed that it was entirely impossible for me to produce the said person agreeably to the command of the Court."[27]

---

26 Philadelphia *Public Ledger,* September 10, 1855; Washington, DC, *Union,* September 11, 1855; *National Era,* September 13, 20, 27, 1855; Brandt and Brandt, *In the Shadow of the Civil War,* 108–10; Paul Finkelman, *An Imperfect Union. Slavery, Federalism, and Comity* (Chapel Hill, NC: 1981), 142–43; Ralph Lowell Eckert, "Antislavery Martyrdom: The Ordeal of Passmore Williamson," *Pennsylvania Magazine of History and Biography,* Vol. 100, No. 4 (October 1976), 528.
27 Philadelphia *Public Ledger,* October 13, 27, 29, 30, November 1, 5, 1855; Washington, DC, *Union,* October 17, 1855; *National Era,* October 18, 1855; Brandt and Brandt, *In the Shadow of Civil War,* 134–42; Sidney George Fisher claimed that he had offered a draft of the new appeal to Kane, which McKim took to Williamson, who refused to sign it. Fisher thought

With this admission, Kane agreed to release Williamson from contempt. But observers were hard put to see exactly what had changed in Williamson's most recent response. The law had been wrested, one editor observed, "to purposes of injustice and tyranny." Kane had declared Williamson guilty of contempt because he said Jane Johnson and her children were not in his custody and so he "could not produce them." After being imprisoned for three months, he was allowed to amend his original answer to say he did not produce them because "it was impossible to do so." Such criticism was nothing new, one Democratic editor responded. Kane, a "high-tone jurist," who had been a credit to his profession, had been vilified by the "know-nothing, Whig and abolitionist press for his [initial] decision." Only the Democratic press had "steadily and eloquently rallied to his support." In fact, the opposition press had called for Kane's impeachment. The New York *Tribune* was convinced that Kane, like other Northern judges, would not have been "elevated to the bench" had he been opposed to slavery. This was the same judge who at the Christiana treason trials had transformed a "fugitive slave riot" into an act of war, and who argued that those who had held meetings to denounce the Fugitive Slave Law had acted treasonably. Even if he believed Williamson had provided a false return, it was nothing more than a misdemeanor that did not rise to the level of contempt punishable at the pleasure of a judge without trial.[28]

Williamson's release from prison did not end the tussle with Kane; he promptly swore out a writ against the judge in an effort to test the legality of his imprisonment. He also claimed damages against Kane of $50,000. Kane was served with a writ while on a visit to nearby Delaware County, a county that the judge's supporters dismissed as a "snug little Abolitionist County." Only in a place like that was Williamson likely to find a sympathetic judge. Kane immediately applied for a change of venue. He and his supporters also tried to persuade the legislature to move the case to Philadelphia, where all of the parties to the case lived. More disturbingly, his supporters pointed out, the Delaware judge was "prejudiced." The legislature, they insisted, should not "tolerate such miserable vindictiveness." But efforts to sway legislators failed. The case continued for more than two years, at considerable cost to Kane, who, in spite of regular appeals to the national government, headed by a Democratic president from Pennsylvania, failed to produce the desired results. Kane's death in February 1858 would finally put an end to the lawsuit and a case that had roiled the city and state for almost three years.[29]

Williamson made "the mistake of thinking Judge Kane should concede to him the position now." Wainwright, *A Philadelphia Perspective*, 251.

[28] New York *Tribune*, November 5, August 28, 29, 1855; Washington, DC, *Union*, August 11, 1855.

[29] *Pennsylvanian* (n.d.), in Washington, DC, *Union*, November 10, 1855; New York *Tribune*, February 5, 13, 1856; Philadelphia *Sun* (n.d.), in New York *Tribune*, February 5, 1856; Brandt and Brandt, *In the Shadow of the Civil War*, 144–50; The case of Jane Johnson and her children has been recaptured in the novel by Lorene Cary, *The Price of a Child* (New York: 1995).

If the vigilance committee could act decisively, as it did in the case of Jane Johnson and her sons, it could do little once a suspected fugitive slave fell into the hands of city authorities. The Anti-Slavery Society, its parent organization, the venerable Abolition Society, formed almost sixty years earlier – of which Passmore Williamson was a member – and the Philadelphia Female Anti-Slavery Society provided valuable legal resources and support, which buttressed the activities of the black community. They ensured that lawyers were on hand to defend fugitive slaves at hearings before commissioners. Prominent female abolitionists, such as Lucretia Mott, were regularly on hand to lend moral support to the accused, especially women, sitting alongside them at hearings as she and others did during Jane Johnson's court appearance. And the black community never failed to appear, filling hearing rooms and gathering in the streets outside. Word of the capture of fugitives, even those that occurred outside the city, spread quickly throughout the community. News of the capture of a fugitive in Lancaster, for instance, where there was no sitting commissioner, was telegraphed to one of the antislavery societies in Philadelphia, who ensured that attorneys were on hand to represent the accused, as was the black community, to show its support. Philadelphia's opponents of the Fugitive Slave Law had ample opportunities to test their organizational and political skills during the decade. There were an estimated twenty-one hearings in the city in the ten years following the passage of the law. Not all the fugitives were captured in the city; two were taken in Columbia in 1851. At the end of the decade, two cases originated in Harrisburg. In these cases, slaveholders procured warrants of arrest from Philadelphia's commissioner, who ordered city policemen to make the arrest and bring the fugitive to the city for a hearing. There were nine hearings between October 1850 and October 1851, most of them discussed in Chapter 2: one in 1852, five in 1853, two in 1857, one in 1859, and three in 1860. Thirteen of those heard by a commissioner or judge resulted in judgments in favor of owners, three fugitives were freed, one ransomed, and one rescued. The peak in the first year of the law's operation should come as no surprise, as considerable effort was made to ensure its enforcement and in so doing assert its political legitimacy. The pace of arrest in subsequent years is harder to explain. Without proffering possible explanations, the 1855 and 1859 annual reports of the Philadelphia Female Society observed that while the numbers of cases fell off dramatically after 1855, the number of fugitive slaves passing through the city continued to rise.[30]

---

The Wheelers of North Carolina and Jane, a fugitive slave, play major roles in the first known novel written by an African American slave, one that remained unpublished until 2002. Hannah Crafts, *The Bondwoman's Narrative*, ed., Henry Louis Gates (New York: 2014).

[30] *Twenty-First Annual Report of the Philadelphia Female Anti-Slavery Society* (Philadelphia: 1855), 15; *Report of the Twenty-Fourth and Twenty-Fifth Years of the Philadelphia Female Anti-Slavery Society* (Philadelphia: 1859), 17.

The legal machinery of enforcement was built around Commissioner Edward D. Ingraham, with the support of District Court Judge John Kane and Supreme Court Justice Robert C. Grier. It is not clear when Ingraham was named to the position. It appears that he had been a traditional commissioner long before 1850 and was reassigned to hear fugitive slave cases in the weeks after the adoption of the law. In fact, Grier heard the first case in Philadelphia in October 1850, which involved Henry Garnett, twenty-five, who was claimed by Thomas P. Jones of Cecil County, Maryland. Concerned that the machinery of the law had yet to be set in place, and worried about the levels of opposition it had already generated, Grier took on the case, met with Jones, and advised him to have all his documents in order. Anticipating that he would also be confronted by a battery of skilled lawyers for Garnett, including William S. Pierce, described by William Still as "one of the oldest, ablest, and most faithful lawyers of the slave of the Philadelphia bar," and, interestingly, Robert P. Kane, one of Judge Kane's sons, Grier also advised Jones to hire a competent attorney. Jones apparently did neither. When David Paul Brown, the lead counsel for Garnett, and for almost thirty years the old Abolition Society's counsel, pointed out that Jones's documents did not meet the standards set by the Fugitive Slave Law, and that his only witness, his son, was an interested party and should not be allowed to testify on his father's behalf, Grier angrily refused Jones's attorney's request for a postponement. He had done all he could to prepare Jones for the hearing: he had taken his deposition, issued a warrant secretly, warned him to hire good counsel, and be ready with proof. Grier, therefore, had no alternative but to rule that the evidence presented by the claimant was insufficient to return Garnett.

Frustrated, Grier directed his anger at opponents of the law: he denounced those who organized public opposition to it, and particularly those who advised African Americans to resist its enforcement. Those who did, he warned, were acting treasonously and in rebellion against the government. According to one observer, Grier's courtroom was packed on the day of the hearing and the "vast crowd" in the streets outside were "wild with delight" on hearing that Garnett had been released. As the crowd rushed across the square, officers tried to rearrest Garnett. He resisted and the crowd came to his assistance. Robert Purvis, one of the city's leading African American citizens, addressed an impromptu meeting and thanked David Paul Brown for his work in winning Garnett's freedom. One Maryland newspaper took a different view of the proceedings; the crowd's "exultation," it reported, bordered on a riot. They disobeyed the mayor's call to disperse and clashed with officers. During this clash, one policeman had a finger "nearly bitten off by a colored man." Garnett's supporters planned to call a meeting at which, the newspaper anticipated, "incendiary resolutions" against the Fugitive Slave Law would be adopted. The meeting at the Brick Street Wesley Church, chaired by William T. Catto, denounced the law and pledged, as their sacred duty, one they owed to themselves, their wives, their children, and to their "common nature, as well as to the panting fugitive from oppression, to resist...at any cost and at all hazards," for the law was "anti-Republican, anti-Christian [and] anti-human."[31]

Although the results were not always what opponents of the law hoped for, the Garnett case set a pattern of legal and political challenges that made every hearing a test of the government's ability to enforce its will. Garnett's freedom was followed two months later by the return of Adam Gibson to Cecil County, which, as we saw in an earlier chapter, turned out to be an embarrassment to both Edward Ingraham in his first hearing as commissioner and to the government. In spite of clear evidence that Gibson was not the fugitive sought, Ingraham returned the suspect after the briefest of hearings, only to have the Maryland slaveholder to whom Gibson was handed over decline to accept him. Gibson, the slaveholder informed the Philadelphia police delivering him, was not his slave. Supporters of the law in Congress rallied around Ingraham, insisting that his was an honest mistake, one that was quickly rectified by an honest slaveholder. Local commentators were less understanding: wicked statutes, one abolitionist editor observed, required "wicked men to enforce [them]." Condemnation of Ingraham, long an opponent of Whig politicians' attempts to dismantle the law, the very same people responsible for the passage of the 1847 state law that banned the use of state prisons to hold suspected fugitives, was inexcusable. He might have granted the delay requested by David Paul Brown, he might even have "quailed before the fierce anger of the colored agitators around him," but he was not to be intimidated. Instead, he realized that the future of the Union rested upon the "faithful fulfillment of the provisions of the Law under which the whole fabric" of the political union depended. If he erred, he did so from a "high love of the Union," which could not be said of those "advocates of disunion, and the confederates of a party the success of which must be the overthrow of our social, as well as our political institutions." The country was under assault, according to this line of reasoning, and only the actions of men such as Ingraham stood in the way of its destruction. The law, moreover, was the glue, the "one link of the chain" – to mix metaphors – of the Union "which once severed, dissolution would be demanded by the voice of a united South." Fugitive slave cases – and Gibson's was no exception – had to be resolved promptly. It was better that a wrong decision be rectified and the Union saved than for the demands of the Constitution to be subverted. One editor even speculated that Gibson might have allowed himself to be martyred to justify the position taken by those opposed to the law and, by extension, the Union.[32]

---

[31] *Pennsylvania Freeman*, October 19, 24, 31, 1850; Philadelphia *Public Ledger*, October 19, 1850; West Chester *Village Record*, October 22, 1850; Gettysburg *Republican Compiler*, November 4, 1850; *Anti-Slavery Bugle*, June 25, 1853; Still, *The Underground Railroad*, 53; Milt Diggins, *Stealing Freedom along the Mason-Dixon Line. Thomas McCreary, the Notorious Slave Catcher from Maryland* (Baltimore: 2015), 61–64.
[32] *Pennsylvania Freeman*, December 12, 1850, January 2, 1851; Philadelphia *Public Ledger*, December 23, 1850; *Pennsylvanian*, December 21, 23, 27, 30, 1850; West Chester *Village*

It appears Ingraham may have been duped by George F. Alberti and a number of his black confederates, including James Frisby Price and his brother George. Alberti and his associates had long been involved in capturing fugitive slaves and kidnapping free blacks. His actions in this case were not unusual. He had visited Elkton, Maryland, and persuaded William S. Knight that he knew the location of his escaped slave. Alberti returned to Philadelphia with a power of attorney from Knight, which he and Frisby Price used to arrest Gibson in a Philadelphia market where he was selling Christmas decorations. At the time of his testimony in the Gibson case, Frisby Price was under indictment for kidnapping. The son of a physician, the sixty-year-old Alberti, with his "gray locks, and jet-black suit and white neck cloth," gave the appearance of a "venerable and even clerical" figure. As a young man, he was accused of robbing graves to provide cadavers for surgical experiments. Alberti had a deep dislike of African Americans, against whom he waged an unrelenting war of terror. No fugitive slave escaped his attention. His spies informed him of any new arrivals. He also prowled about sections of the city where blacks lived, "peeping into houses, and entering them under all sorts of pretexts." He was, this observer later recalled, "the evil genius of the region about Lombard Street." Slavery, Alberti later told an interviewer, was justified by the bible; nowhere did it condemn slavery. God's law had made the children of Ham slaves forever. As a result, slaveholders had as much right to reclaim their runaway slaves as they did their horses. He was simply facilitating the return of lost property to their rightful owners. He was reputed to have returned thirty-four fugitive slaves in the six years prior to Gibson's arrest. Alberti was, one unsympathetic observer recalled, "one of the most inhuman, desperate and at the same time sagacious characters, that has ever disgraced the ancient city of Penn."[33]

In January 1851, weeks after Gibson was returned to his family in New Jersey, Alberti and Frisby Price were charged with kidnapping thirteen-month-old Joel Henry Thompson and taking him into slavery in Maryland. Price had visited Joel's parents, William and Catherine Thompson, in Burlington, New Jersey, where they lived, and persuaded them to visit his family in Philadelphia and to bring the child so his wife could see him. During the visit, Price took Catherine to visit Alberti, who knocked her insensible and took her and Joel to Elkton, Maryland, and handed them over to James Mitchell, a thirty-one-year-old farmer. Thomas Richardson, whom Alberti had hired to drive Joel and his mother to Maryland, testified that Catherine was not kidnapped, but had

*Record*, December 31, 1850; Lancaster *Examiner & Herald*, January 11, 1851; New York *Herald*, December 27, 1850; New York *Tribune*, January 1, 1851; Washington, DC, *Union*, January 10, 1851; Diggins, *Stealing Freedom*, 64–66.

[33] Anonymous, *Life of the Notorious Kidnapper George F. Alberti by a Member of the Philadelphia Bar* (Philadelphia: 1851), 7, 9, 12, 16–17, 23, 25; *National Anti-Slavery Standard*, February 19, 1859; Pittsburgh *Gazette*, July 27, 1853. One editor, opposed to the law, said of the Ingraham-Alberti relationship, "one beats the bush, the other catches the bird." Albany *Evening Journal*, July 26, 1853.

been arrested for stealing her master's jewelry. She had also admitted that she was Mitchell's slave. Evidently, Price was to be paid $75 and Alberti $1,000, half the profits from Catherine's sale. According to Richardson, Alberti had taken Joel along out of "pure feelings of humanity," not wanting to separate the boy from his mother. One incredulous reporter could not resist pointing to the irony of such an explanation: "It is the first time that George F. Alberti has been suspected of being troubled with any such feelings." It took the jury five minutes to return a verdict of guilty against the two. Price was sentenced to ten years in Eastern State Penitentiary and fined $700; Alberti was sentenced to ten years and fined $1,000. In sentencing Alberti, Judge Parsons scolded him, wondering why "an old man, whose worldly race was nearly run" would involve himself in such a despicable crime.[34]

Peter A. Browne, Alberti's defense counsel, insisted that there was a terrible miscarriage of justice. All of the evidence pointed to the fact that Catherine, twenty-eight, was, in fact, Betsy Galloway, Mitchell's slave, who had run away in 1845 with Peregrine Berry, now known as William Thompson, who was born free in Cecil County. At the time of the escape, she was married to Moses Wright, with whom she had two children. William was married to Maria Brooks. Mitchell did provide Alberti with a power of attorney, which he used to arrest Catherine. A rendition hearing was held before Alderman William Allen of Philadelphia County, who ruled in favor of Mitchell. At the time of Catherine's capture, Joel was ill and "still at her breast." Alberti did suggest that she leave Joel behind and he would ensure that he was returned to his father, but she refused. The court rejected all of these "facts" in coming to its verdict. The imposition of a ten-year sentence on a man in his sixties was tantamount, Browne concluded, to a death sentence.[35]

The case had immediate and wider repercussions. In February 1851, Pennsylvania's governor, William F. Johnson, requested the extradition of James Mitchell. In response, Maryland's governor, Enoch Louis Lowe, consulted Attorney General Robert Brent; could a citizen of the state, he asked, be claimed as a fugitive of justice if he were not "personally present in the state" when the crime was committed, and, more significantly, which state's law was applicable, the one from which the slave mother fled, or the one in which the offspring was born? Brent advised that the criminal must have committed the crime in, and then fled from, the state making the demand. The question of which state's law applied was irrelevant, for the US Constitution was clear: fugitives from labor had to be returned and no law in Pennsylvania could impede that right. Any law or act of Pennsylvania, such as its 1847 law that impaired "the right to the *incident or natural increase* of the fugitive property"

[34] Harrisburg *Telegraph*, March 3, 26, 1851; Philadelphia *Spirit of the Times* (n.d.), in *Pennsylvania Freeman*, January 9, 1851.
[35] Peter A. Browne, *A Review of the Trial, Conviction, and Sentence of George F. Alberti for Kidnapping* (Philadelphia: 1851), 2–4, 6, 24.

was "*null and void* as if it sought to deny the right to the property itself." Mitchell, therefore, could not be considered a fugitive from justice, nor could it possibly be a crime in Pennsylvania, under the Constitution, for "a master to recapture his runaway female slave with the offspring she may have born, while a fugitive from service." Brent had earlier visited the Court of Quarter Sessions during the hearing, according to a Baltimore newspapers, to explore possible grounds of appeal, including whether the child of a slave mother inherited the status of the mother regardless of where it was born. Armed with Brent's reasoning, Lowe rejected Johnson's request. He also got Mitchell to provide a series of affidavits from "competent witnesses" to testify that he had never crossed into Pennsylvania and that Catherine and Joel were handed over to him in Maryland. The Maryland Reform Convention, which was meeting in Baltimore at the time, established a committee to investigate the case against Alberti and Price and to determine if their conviction could be appealed to the Supreme Court by the state of Maryland.[36]

The dispute over Alberti's prosecution was a prelude to running disagreements between the two states over cases relating to fugitive slaves, including both the killing of William Gorsuch, the Maryland slaveholder, by fugitive slaves he was tracking in Christiana in September 1851, and that of William Smith in Columbia by Archibald G. Ridgely, a Baltimore policemen, the following May. The Christiana shoot-out reshaped Pennsylvania's political landscape, leading to the defeat of Johnson, a Whig, and the election of William Bigler, a Democrat. With an eye on improving relations with Maryland, Bigler had promised that, if elected, he would enforce the Fugitive Slave Law and pardon Alberti, who, he believed, had been harshly treated. Not even the kidnapping of the Parker sisters in December 1851, and the murder in Maryland of Joseph Miller who went in search of Rachel, deterred Bigler from fulfilling his pledge to pardon Alberti and Price. Weeks after the pardon, the Maryland legislature adopted a vote of thanks to Bigler for his decisions.[37]

Alberti promptly resumed his activities following his release. He was once again at the center of a contentious case in the summer of 1853, this one involving the capture and return of George Smith, also known as William Fisher. At the time of his capture, the twenty-five-year-old Smith was married and living near Salem, New Jersey, where he owned a house and farmed four acres. He was only suspected of being a fugitive following his arrest in May for his involvement in a brawl between groups of blacks and whites in a

---

[36] "Report of the Committee on the Fugitive Slave Case," in *Journal of the Proceedings of the Senate of Maryland* (Annapolis: 1852), 7–20; Baltimore *Sun*, July 16, 1851.

[37] *Pennsylvania Freeman*, February 5, 1852; Harrisburg *Whig State Journal*, February 5, April 15, 1852. Alberti rejected the argument that he had been pardoned in an effort to mollify the South and that Maryland slaveholders had promised to show their gratitude by compensating him. He told an interviewer many years later that the compensation never materialized, even after many visits to Annapolis to meet with legislators. *National Anti-Slavery Standard*, February 19, 1859.

Moyamensing grog shop, during which one white was injured. While he was in prison, Jacob C. Howard, a lumber merchant of Cecil County, Maryland, claimed that Smith was his slave who had escaped in 1847. As he had done on other occasions, Alberti had visited Howard and informed him of Smith's whereabouts. In an effort to prevent his return, Littleton Hubert, a prominent member of a black masonic lodge to which it appears Smith belonged, swore out a writ of habeas corpus in criminal court. Smith was released and left for New Jersey. But for some inexplicable reason he returned to Philadelphia, where he was arrested on a warrant issued by Commissioner Ingraham. At his hearing, witnesses for the claimant swore that they had known Smith since he was a boy and were fairly certain about the date of his escape. Two witnesses also claimed that Smith had lost the first joint of his right little finger, the sort of identification mark that was critical at hearings. But its significance might have been undermined when, under cross examination, one of the witnesses admitted that Alberti had pointed out the injury to him. Howard also testified that he had bought Smith as a boy in 1827 or 1828 for $75. Counsel for Smith argued that he had been detained illegally on suspicion of violating bail following the riot. Ingraham, citing a precedent established by Judge John K. Kane, ruled that it did not matter what means were used to get Smith to the hearing. An owner, he declared, "may use any deception to get his slave into his possession." Ingraham ruled in favor of Howard and ordered US Marshal Francis Wynkoop to return Smith to Maryland.

What followed was a clash of courts. A writ of habeas corpus was sworn out against Wynkoop immediately after Ingraham's ruling, ordering him to produce Smith so he could stand trial in state court for his involvement in the "riot." John W. Ashmead, US attorney for the eastern district of Pennsylvania and Wynkoop's defense counsel, requested an hour's delay so he could prepare a response to the writ. William Pierce agreed, but only if Smith was brought before the court immediately, as Wynkoop had earlier tried to avoid a writ, arguing that the state prison was not secure, an argument that struck Pierce as nothing if not perverse. "After years of clamor for the use of the prison to commit fugitive slaves for custody, and the repeal of the law of Pennsylvania prohibiting the use of it for that purpose, the US was afraid to use it, and detained the prisoner in their own custody." Pierce worried that Wynkoop would use the hour's delay to take Smith south. When Wynkoop delayed answering the writ, he was threatened with contempt. Jacob Howard was also dragged into court for not responding to a writ against him. Wynkoop insisted that he had no authority to hand over the prisoner, as he was holding him on the order of Ingraham, a federal official. If he did, Ashmead claimed, he would be liable to a charge of $1,000 under the Fugitive Slave Law. David Paul Brown countered that the court was not trying to take Smith away from Wynkoop, only to have him tried for violation of state law. Ashmead then called for a further delay to show that the state court had no jurisdiction in fugitive slave cases. But the court ruled that Smith had to be produced. Wynkoop, however, refused and

was arrested by the sheriff. Facing contempt, Wynkoop, in one of those curious turns of history, followed Kane's advice and explained to the court that he
was not acting contemptuously but was only trying to do his duty under the
Constitution. He also provided Ingraham's removal order, at which point the
judge removed the contempt charge.

At a subsequent habeas corpus hearing at the Court of Quarter Sessions,
William Pierce argued that the state had the first claim on George Smith, as
charges of rioting had been leveled against him prior to the hearing before
the commissioner. The court ruled that, because Littleton Hubert had not
used a "bail-piece," it therefore had no authority to adjudicate the writ. Pierce
promptly moved to apply for a bailpiece. While the clerk was drawing it up,
Francis Wynkoop removed Smith, placed him in a cab and drove him, "at a
rapid rate," in the direction of the train station. Hubert and "a posse of friends"
followed. They failed to find Smith at the train station; Wynkoop had instead
taken a "private carriage" to Paoli, northwest of Philadelphia, "beyond the
jurisdiction of the opposing parties," to catch the midnight train to Baltimore.
Supporters of Smith did not give up easily; they placed guards on the train
lines to Baltimore in a futile attempt to prevent Smith's return. The marshal's
actions to deny Smith the right to habeas corpus confirmed what opponents of
the law had predicted; if not explicitly guaranteed, habeas corpus, a bedrock of
jurisprudence, could be evaded. Wynkoop's eagerness to send a carriage to the
prison to fetch Smith, his subsequent escape from the courthouse with his "victim" before a bailpiece could be issued, "the celerity and secrecy with which
[Smith] was hurried away," one editor observed, looked more like "the haste of
an accomplice, than the dignified action of an officer of the law awaiting legal
investigation."[38]

Here, as elsewhere throughout the Free States, the return of fugitives such
as Smith confirmed the supremacy of federal over state laws. Nevertheless,
opponents of the Fugitive Slave Law continued to challenge its primacy. Timing
mattered, they argued. Smith was first charged with a crime against the state of
Pennsylvania and, consequently, that should take precedent. The same applied to
capital crimes such as Margaret Garner's murder of her daughter in Cincinnati
in January 1856. But in this instance, the fact that Alberti was up to his old
tricks of traveling to Maryland to inform slaveholders of the whereabouts of
their former slaves, prompted opponents to revisit unresolved issues associated
with the earlier case of Adam Gibson. In August 1853, David P. Brown applied
for a bench warrant against Alberti, Price, and all those involved in carrying
Gibson to Maryland. It is not clear if there was a trial or what became of the
indictment. One thing is clear: abolitionists were determined to put a halt to
Alberti's activities once and for all. They may have only partially achieved their

---

[38] Philadelphia *Register* (n.d.), in *Pennsylvania Freeman*, July 28, 1853, and August 4, 1853;
    Philadelphia *Public Ledger*, July 25, 26, 27, 28, 1853; Baltimore *Sun*, July 25, 26, 27, 1853;
    Richmond *Dispatch*, July 30, 1853; *National Anti-Slavery Standard*, August 11, 1853.

goal, as little more was heard from Alberti after 1853, although in a later interview he claimed, with some pride, to have returned "easy a hundred" fugitive slaves in a career spanning forty years.[39]

When Alberti was arrested and sentenced for his involvement in the return of Catherine and Joel Thompson, Samuel Halzell, described as the "leading official slave-catcher," stepped in to fill the void. He took into custody Helen Dellam, forty years old, and her son, Dick, who was ten. The arrest of the pair had an eerie similarity to the Thompson case; Helen Dellam was pregnant at the time of her arrest. The pair – along with Dick's father, a free black – had escaped with five or six other members of the same family in 1849 from Baltimore County, Maryland, and settled in Columbia. Helen and her son were claimed by John Purdue, who, according to the 1850 slave schedules, owned two slaves. The pair was arrested in Columbia under a warrant issued by Ingraham. Evidently, others in the escaping group had gotten wind of the Philadelphia posse's arrival and left. At the time, Helen's husband was away working on a canal boat. Before Ingraham could hear the case, a writ of habeas corpus was sworn out before Judge Kane. Passmore Williamson and James Miller McKim were in attendance, as one reporter observed, "to superintend examination of the case." Kane again had to face his son Robert, a member of the team of lawyers for the Dellams, including the ever-present David Paul Brown. A "large number of ladies," including Lucretia Mott, were also present. Lawyers for Dellam moved to have the warrants squashed as insufficient; descriptions were vague, they argued, and no evidence was provided showing the two were fugitive slaves. Kane rejected their objections, in the process setting the bar of evidence alarmingly low. All that was needed in such warrants, he ruled, was the sort of description a "father would require to recover possession of his child." He insisted that he would have heard the case even if the warrant were blank, as long as the master was present to claim the slaves. Brown objected to the affidavits from Baltimore County as falling short of what was required under section six of the Fugitive Slave Law. While Kane conceded that the Maryland certificate did not include a detailed description of the slaves, he refused to reject it. Purdue's father-in-law testified that he had given Helen, whom he had raised as a child, and whose mother and father he owned, to the claimant as a wedding gift. Two black witnesses for the defense, Charles Clark and Henry Bundy, recalled that they first met Helen in Columbia

39 Philadelphia *Public Ledger*, August 1, 1853. The *Ledger* seems confused about whether Alberti and the others were being charged with their involvement in the Gibson or the Joel Thompson case. The *Pennsylvania Freeman*, August 18, 1853, reports that the charges were in connection with the Gibson case. *National Anti-Slavery Standard*, February 19, 1859. Age did not diminish Alberti's enthusiasm for his work. In December 1860, he was involved in the attempted kidnapping of Petry Simmons from "Timbuctoo," a black settlement in New Jersey. He and a party of eleven confederates were forced to withdraw in the face of an angry crowd of African Americans. New York *Tribune*, December 12, 1860.

in 1848, prior to the time of her reputed escape. Another African American, Elizabeth Gael, testified that she first met Helen in 1847, when they were both members of the Wesleyan Methodist church. A white baker, Godfrey Keeble, was also a witness for the defense. Kane was unimpressed; why, he wondered, was neither the white person for whom Helen worked, nor the pastor of the church she attended, called as witnesses. As he would do in the Jane Johnson case two years later, Kane was adamant that the evidence of white witnesses for the claimant carried more weight in his court. Helen and Dick were remanded. As in the Franklin case in Harrisburg, Kane's decision, according to one editor, raised the question of whether a child conceived in freedom came under "a law for the return of fugitive slaves." Were Helen convicted of a capital crime, her sentence would have been suspended until after the birth of her child. "The blossom and the bough," the editor concluded, were to wither together. The abolitionist press published the names of the "Columbus Catchpoles," those involved in the capture of Helen and Dick, in an effort to make them social pariahs and so dissuade others from following their example.[40]

Kane, however, could not ignore the power and persuasiveness of black testimony during the case of Euphemia Williams, the mother of six children, all born in Pennsylvania, which he heard less than a month later. He would later claim that his ruling in favor of the accused demonstrated his evenhandedness and dispassion. The case for the claimant was admittedly complicated by the fact that none of his witnesses had seen Williams since her reputed escape from Worcester County, Maryland, in 1829. A group of "white ladies," the majority of whom "appeared to belong to the Society of Friends," occupied one side of the courtroom every day of the trial while Williams' "colored female friends" and her children sat close by. The defense set out to prove that the witnesses for the claimant were mistaken and their evidence contradictory. Moreover, they brought black witnesses to show that Williams had been living free in Chester County and Philadelphia as early as 1825. The shoemaker, Henry G. Cornish, testified that he first met Williams in Chester County in 1825, where her first two children were born, died, and were buried. Henry's younger brother insisted that he knew her when he was a young lad. Deborah Ann Boyer had known her since 1826. Sarah Gurley met Williams in Chester County in 1824, when they worked in the same house as domestics. The fact

[40] Philadelphia *Evening Bulletin*, March 8, 10, 11, 13, 1851; *Pennsylvania Freeman*, March 13, 20, 1851; Columbia *Spy*, March 8, 1851; Lancaster *Examiner & Herald*, March 12, 1851. Two months before the arrest of the Dellams, Stephen Bennett was taken in Columbia and carried to Philadelphia, where he was remanded following a failed attempt to have Kane issue a writ of habeas corpus. The black women of "Tow Hill," Columbia's black community, had threatened to prevent Bennett's arrest. Those who knew him described him as an "industrious citizen" who, over three years, had managed to save $400. Philadelphia *Evening Bulletin*, January 24, 25, 1851; *Pennsylvanian*, January 25, 1851; Philadelphia *Public Ledger*, January 25, 1851; Columbia *Spy*, January 15, 1851; Lancaster *Examiner & Herald*, January 29, 1851; *Pennsylvania Freeman*, January 30, 1851.

that claimants failed to point out an obvious scar on her forehead helped to seal the case in favor of Williams. In freeing Williams, Kane admitted that it was difficult to identify a person after twenty-four years. More importantly, he was impressed by the "intelligence" of the defense witnesses, whose evidence, he ruled, was "conclusive."[41]

Black witnesses, and the support of the black community, also played a critical role in the release of Daniel Webster, also known as Daniel Dangerfield, in 1859. Webster, who was living with his family in Harrisburg, was arrested at the local market under a warrant issued by the Philadelphia commissioner J. Cooke Longstreth. Webster was accused of escaping from Loudoun County, Virginia, five years earlier. His arrest was the most recent in a series of misfortunes; both of his children had died recently, the last one a week before his arrest. Word of Webster's arrest was telegraphed to Philadelphia by the Harrisburg Friends of the Fugitive Association. An unnamed member of the House of Representatives immediately began the search for witnesses to testify on Webster's behalf. Witnesses for the claimant, Elizabeth Simpson, testified that they became aware of Webster's whereabouts from rumors making the rounds in Loudoun County. Simpson's son-in-law and a constable visited Harrisburg on a scouting expedition the month prior to his arrest, when they identified, but did not approach, him on a city street. Five African American witnesses traveled from Harrisburg, including sixty-six-year-old "Dr." William Jones, who had long played an active role in the black community's resistance to enforcement of the law. All claimed to have known Webster a year before Simpson testified that he had escaped. Jones recalled that Webster had worked on a house he was building in 1853. Scores of Philadelphia supporters arrived early for the hearing, occupying all the seats available in the cramped commissioner's office, which, according to one report, measured a mere twelve by eighteen feet. They included Lucretia Mott, her husband James and their grandson, Mary Grew, the men and women of black Philadelphia's most recognizable families, the Purvis-Fortens, Passmore Williamson, J. Miller McKim, and a number of unidentified black women. The US district attorney, James Van Dyke, tried to have the room cleared, arguing that the hearing could not proceed in such a setting, but William Pierce protested against the "Star Chamber practice of excluding the public" from a court of justice. A large crowd of Webster's supporters, gathered in the streets surrounding the hearing room, threatened to storm the commissioner's office in support of those inside. Some in the crowd were arrested for disorderly conduct, which, as one observer reported, only "aggravated public feelings." The cramped quarters of the hearing room, and the unrelenting protests of counsels for Webster against conditions in the room, finally forced Longstreth to transfer proceedings to a larger courtroom nearby. The crowd followed and again a number of arrests were made. Those who

---

[41] Philadelphia *Evening Bulletin*, February 6, 8, 1851; New York *Tribune*, February 11, 1851; *Pennsylvania Freeman*, February 13, 1851.

came to testify in support of Webster were initially locked out of the court-room, but following protests by Webster's attorney, were admitted. Black and white supporters who could not gain admittance milled about outside, super-vised by a contingent of three hundred policemen.

The hearing lasted until five o'clock the following morning, yet most of the crowd outside remained on their watch even though the night was bitterly cold. All but two of the women sat through the entire proceedings. In his sum-mation, Benjamin H. Brewster argued for the claimant that, once the "details of ownership and flight" were established, when the fugitive fled was immate-rial. It was sufficient that all the witnesses from Loudoun knew Webster, knew he was a slave, and knew he escaped. That they were all from the same county where Webster was enslaved was "all for the better." He concluded by posing what could be called the Judge Kane query: Why were no white men called to corroborate the evidence given by the black witnesses who testified on behalf of Webster? As they had done in the Euphemia Williams case, defense counsels successfully raised the issue of identity as a way of testing the reliability of the warrant under which Webster was arrested by demanding he be measured to determine his height. The measurement, however, proved inconclusive. When Longstreth ruled in favor of Webster, the crowd, in and outside the courtroom, was surprised but jubilant. His decision turned on differences between the claim that Webster had escaped in November 1854 and those by black wit-nesses, especially the elderly Jones, who produced a work book to show that Webster had helped build his home in March 1853.[42]

The decision to release Webster came as a surprise to even the most diehard abolitionists and a black community weary from successive defeats. Following the release of Euphemia Williams in February 1851, ten suspected fugitives had been remanded. As McKim later admitted, at the start of the Webster hear-ing, they had little hope for a successful resolution: "The most we expected to do was to make a good fight; to protract the issue; to turn the case to general account, and build up public opinion against the recurrence of a similar exi-gency." Local abolitionists knew little about Longstreth and wondered why a man of "old Quaker stock," and the son of a prominent judge, would have accepted an appointment as commissioner, and why he would agree to issue a warrant for Webster's arrest. The situation looked bleak when Longstreth subsequently met with the agent for the claimant to inform him that the arrest warrant was incorrectly drawn up and to give him an opportunity to return to Virginia to amend the form. Up to that point, all signs pointed to an unhappy outcome. But the commissioner also demonstrated an evenhandedness that surprised onlookers; he allowed two continuances so lawyers could consult with Webster and to allow witnesses to arrive from Harrisburg. He did this,

---

[42] Harrisburg *Telegraph*, April 2, 4, 6, 7, 1859; Philadelphia *Evening Bulletin*, April 5, 6, 7, 1859; Philadelphia *Public Ledger*, April 5, 6, 1859; New York *Times*, April 9, 1859; [J. Miller McKim], *The Arrest, Trial, and Release of Daniel Webster, Fugitive Slave* (Philadelphia: 1859), 3–4.

Longstreth explained, not because appeals were "made to his feelings, but because he recognized the right under the law, of the respondent to have the opportunity to have his case heard." This was an interpretation of the law's mandate that few other commissioners were willing to assert. Yet evenhandedness was no guarantee of a successful outcome. Some observers believed that Longstreth may have been influenced by the sheer size of the crowds, what one observer called the "cloud of spectators," as well as the number of "respectable" people, of both sexes, who crowded his courtroom. Young Charlotte L. Forten thought the commissioner was swayed by the "pressure of public sentiment – which was, strange to say, almost universally on the right side," and which was too overwhelming for him to resist. But she also thought Longstreth had come under enormous pressure from his Quaker family, especially his wife, who declared that they would "discard him if he sent the man into slavery." McKim was less understanding, even if he was elated by the outcome. "How any man with a heart in his bosom," he observed, and "especially how a man born and bred as John Cooke Longstreth has been, can accept such an odious office, can perform its hideous functions, can sit in judgement on an innocent man's right to liberty, is almost past comprehension." But, in the end, he had to admit that the commissioner conducted the hearing with "dignity, with ability," if with "almost cruel impartiality." It is difficult to determine why Longstreth ruled the way he did. It was his first case since his appointment in 1855. It would be his last. Given his ruling, one could not imagine that, in the future, slaveholders would beat a path to his office in search of arrest warrants.[43]

News of Webster's release was greeted by a spontaneous street celebration. In a move reminiscent of the celebration following the Euphemia Williams verdict, the cheering crowd attached a brace of horses to a chaise and drove Webster through the streets in what one reporter described as "the very delirium of joy and triumph." The "extraordinary commotion," according to another observer, did offend some sensibilities, but the joy was, he had to admit, understandable. That evening, Webster's defense counsels were serenaded by blacks and young members of the Anti-Slavery Society accompanied by a brass band. Back in Harrisburg, almost the entire black population marched through town, "keeping time with martial music," to the train station to welcome Webster home. But he never appeared. Supporters in Philadelphia, fearing an appeal of the commissioner's decision, had taken the precaution of sending him and his wife to Rev. Jermain Loguen in Syracuse, who made sure they got safely to Canada.[44]

---

[43] [McKim], *The Arrest, Trial, and Release of Daniel Webster*, 7–8, 17–18, 28; Ray Allen Billington, ed., *The Journal of Charlotte L. Forten* (New York: 1953), 111; Philadelphia *Evening Bulletin*, April 5, 7, 1859; Philadelphia *Public Ledger*, April 5, 1859.

[44] Philadelphia *Evening Bulletin*, April 7, 1859; Harrisburg *Telegraph*, April 7, 1859; New York *Times*, April 30, 1859. Webster wrote McKim soon after they got to Canada, asking him to "send some money" to tide him over until he could find a job. Daniel Webster to McKim, Canada, May 1, 1859. Anti-Slavery Collection, Cornell University in BAP Reel 11: 20505.

Questions about the legality of Webster's seizure and removal to Philadelphia were raised in the state House. Some argued that the case should have been heard in Harrisburg. But ever since the resignation of Richard McAllister, the unpopular slave commissioner, six years earlier, federal authorities had been unable to find a replacement. Still, that did not mollify opponents of the law or even those supporters who wondered about the political wisdom of transporting suspected fugitives in manacles to another city for trial. The case roiled the political waters in other ways as well. The Philadelphia meeting to celebrate Webster's release attracted both opponents and supporters of the Fugitive Slave Law, all of them determined to make their views known. One local newspaper reported that the meeting was the work of "ultra-abolitionists" and attended by "plenty of negroes...carrying a very high head since the late decision in favor of the alleged slave Webster." A number of Democrats, supporters of the law, were also in attendance, as were a "number of Southern medical students" enrolled in the city's medical schools. Interestingly, many of these same students would abandon their training and return home following Lincoln's election in 1860. The meeting was frequently disrupted by shouts and catcalls, so much so that speakers could not be heard. But even in this tense situation there were moments of levity. The proceedings were interrupted, particularly at moments of high tension, by someone in the audience imitating a rooster. At one juncture, a group described as "Democratic roughs" advanced on the stage in an attempt to silence speakers and capture the meeting. The police had to be called out before order could be restored and the meeting could continue. It was the first time in living memory, McKim recalled, that a "pro-slavery mob" was "put down by the authorities in this city." Things were looking up; the "day of Pennsylvania's redemption," McKim wrote an associate optimistically, "draweth nigh."[45]

The release of Webster also seemed to have reenergized those in Harrisburg who had profited from their involvement in the business of returning suspected slaves in ways that had not been seen since the days of Commissioner McAllister. There were reports of the presence of slave catchers from Virginia and Maryland and their connection to a kidnapping gang centered in adjoining York and Cumberland counties, a gang that had gone to ground temporarily following the successful prosecution of some of its leaders three years earlier. Apparently, half a dozen fugitives who had been living in town and were employed at local hotels now thought it best to leave for Canada. One editor pleaded with the city to rid itself of these "mercenary dealers in human flesh and blood...the meanest specimens of humanity extant." He also intimated

[45] Harrisburg *Telegraph*, April 2, 1859; Philadelphia *Evening Bulletin*, April 9, 1859; Billington, ed., *The Journal of Charlotte L. Forten*, 112; [McKim], *The Arrest, Trial, and Release of Daniel Webster*, 30–31. McKim quoted in Eric Foner, *Gateway to Freedom. The Hidden History of the Underground Railroad* (New York: 2015), 218.

that the black community was on the verge of taking matters into their own hands and giving these slave catchers a "warm reception."[46]

Supporters of Webster in Philadelphia were a little more sanguine. They saw the release as the dawn of a new era, reflecting a profound change in the city's attitude toward the law. McKim saw the verdict as the "harbinger of better things to come," the result of twenty-five years of *"steady presentation to this community of anti-slavery truths"* (italics in the original). His colleague, Mary Grew, agreed; it was proof of a "great change wrought in popular feeling; in which change we saw the result of twenty-five years of earnest effort to impress upon the heart of this community anti-slavery doctrines and sentiments."[47] Their elation and consequent overreach was understandable, but it would come a cropper within one year when the city's new commissioner, someone without Longstreth's qualms or religious and family connections, chose to return a suspected fugitive slave. The case of Moses Horner was eerily similar to Webster's. Horner was arrested on a farm three miles outside Harrisburg under a warrant issued by the Philadelphia commissioner. He had escaped eight months earlier from near Harpers Ferry, where he had been hired out by the claimant, Charles Butler of Jefferson County, Virginia – today part of West Virginia. Worried about a possible rescue, Deputy Marshal Jenkins, who had arrested Webster, avoided passing through Harrisburg by walking the eight miles to Middletown, where they caught the train to Philadelphia. Alerted by Harrisburg colleagues, Philadelphia abolitionists planned to meet the train in Philadelphia, but Jenkins once again eluded them. Horner was brought before Commissioner John Cadwalader, a stalwart Democrat, whose brother was reputed to own slaves. The claimant was represented by Benjamin H. Brewster, a rising star in the Democratic Party, Horner by a group with relatively little experience. Cadwalader allowed the defense a three-hour postponement to get witnesses from Harrisburg. When the hearing resumed, however, only Catherine Jones was on hand to testify. She claimed to have first met Horner over the 1858 Christmas holidays, when he visited her parents' home. It is not clear if Catherine was related to the father and son who testified on Webster's behalf. Two witnesses for the claimant testified that they lived near Butler and had known Horner for more than fifteen years. Both added that Horner was pigeon-toed. A third witness, who was born in Jefferson County, but now resided in Philadelphia, claimed that Horner was once owned by his grandfather and that, as kids, they were playmates. Horner's lawyers called for a dismissal on grounds that Butler could not identify any "distinctive marks, nor was there a full description in the certificate" of arrest. But no member of the defense team could challenge the one critical identification alluded to by Butler's witnesses – namely, that Horner was pigeon-toed. Even before Brewster could sum up, Cadwalader decided that Butler's witnesses had provided ample evidence to show that Horner was a slave and that he had escaped in August 1859. Immediately, Lucretia Mott, who was in her customary place at the hearing, approached the bench and berated the commissioner for a ruling she considered precipitous and unfounded.[48]

Before the marshal could remove Horner, he was served with a writ of habeas corpus issued by Joseph Allison, a Republican and a judge of common pleas. As in the George Smith case in 1853, as well as many others across the North, the marshal refused to comply. As an officer of the federal government, he maintained, he had no "right to submit to the order of any court when he is in discharge of a duty imposed upon him by a court acting under the government." A state court had no authority to interfere with a marshal executing a "process issued out of the U.S. Circuit Court." As the marshal left the hearing with the prisoner, a crowd of African Americans, who were gathered outside the building, rushed the carriage in which Horner was being transported to prison to await his final rendition. Twice during the tussle they seized the horses but were beaten back by the police. They did manage to break the shaft of the carriage, which immobilized it. The marshal soon found a new carriage, however, and Horner was taken away. Ten African Americans were arrested and jailed for their involvement in the attack on the posse – St. Clair and John Bailey, Basil and David Hall, Richard Williams, Albert M. Green, Jerry and Joshua Buck, John Johnson and John Hart – with bail set between $600 and $800. Henry Knockson was later added to the list of the accused. If those arrested are any indication, the protest seemed, in part, to have been a family affair.[49]

Taking a page out of the abolitionists' playbook, friends of "law and order and the constitutional rights of the citizens" organized what one speaker called a "spontaneous demonstration," a march of "many thousands," to Benjamin Brewster's home accompanied by the Pennsylvania Cornet Band. In a speech to the crowd, Brewster attacked those who encouraged wild insurrections by openly supporting violations of the law. The Fugitive Slave Law, which "authorizes the extradition of fugitives from service or labor, be they white or be they black men" was meant as a "constitutional means to a constitutional end," to protect citizens in their rights and property. Men will no longer suffer the constant loss of property and have their names defiled, their political rights denied, without resisting. "We stand in the breach," he told the crowd, for if the law cannot be enforced in Pennsylvania "our Union is a rope of sand." The "institution of domestic servitude is a great political necessity – social, commercial necessity [and] a political right – socially and morally right." It is, he concluded, the "law of God as well as the law of men." Brewster's was a standard defense

---

[48] Philadelphia *Public Ledger,* March 27, 28, 1860; Harrisburg *Telegraph,* March 28, 29, 1860.
[49] Philadelphia *Public Ledger,* March 29, 30, April 4, 1860; Harrisburg *Telegraph,* March 29, 1860.

of the law. He, like many others, saw it as the glue that kept the Union together, a glue that had been growing increasingly brittle especially after John Brown's raid on Harpers Ferry the previous October. But even those partial to such views must have wondered where, in the Fugitive Slave Law, the issue of white "fugitives from service or labor" was addressed.[50]

One of those arrested for resisting the removal of Horner, writing under the pseudonym "Veritas," explained that their action was prompted by their exclusion from the hearing room, which whites were permitted to enter freely. The crowd outside, therefore, had to rely on information from those leaving the room. These reports were conflicting and, consequently, bred frustration among those locked out. This is why, he insisted, they tried to block the carriage taking Horner away, to provide themselves time to determine exactly how Cadwalader had ruled. A meeting of African Americans at the Philadelphia Institute named a committee of five, including John C. Bowers of the vigilance committee, to raise money to meet bail for those in prison and to cover the cost of their trial. They quickly raised enough to meet bail for each of the ten. Alfred Green appealed for support to cover the cost of the upcoming trials. But whatever unity there was soon after the arrest of the ten evaporated in the weeks before their trial. The source of the rift is unclear. Apparently, there was a misunderstanding about what was promised during the meeting at which the committee of five was selected. William Still, some believed, had promised that the Anti-Slavery Society would provide lawyers for the defense as they had done in every fugitive slave case to date. As a result, the committee of five suspended its money-raising efforts. Still evidently reneged on his promise when it was rumored that the committee had raised much more money than was needed. Still later claimed he had made no such promise. Short of funds, Alfred Green traveled to New York City in an attempt to raise the $200 needed to "secure counsel" but only managed to attract a paltry $53.50 from a number of black congregations. Four weeks later, he reported that his efforts had shown some progress, but had still fallen short by about $25. Their efforts in Philadelphia were equally frustrating; a half-dozen meetings, many poorly attended, collected only $100. But they did manage to pull together a purse large enough to hire lawyers who had shown their mettle in many of the fugitive cases in the city, including William S. Pierce and David Paul Brown, who had largely retired from the fray. Some were troubled by the choice of Brown, since his son of the same name had not only accepted an appointment as a commissioner, but in 1857 had issued a warrant of arrest and later ordered the return of Michael Brown to Baltimore.[51]

[50] Philadelphia *Public Ledger,* March 31, 1860. Although a rising star in the Democratic Party, Brewster would join the Republican Party at the outbreak of the war. He was appointed attorney general in 1881.

[51] *Weekly Anglo-African,* April 14, May 19, 26, June 2, 16, 30, 1860. On the Michael Brown case see Philadelphia *Public Ledger,* January 17, 19, 1857; Baltimore *Sun,* January 17, 1857.

Jerry Buck was the first to come to trial in district court in early June. He was found guilty, with bail set at $1,000. Testifying on behalf of Buck, Robert Purvis confirmed that the problem outside the courthouse was due entirely to the fact that blacks had been excluded from the hearing room, a decision that bred rumors which could not be verified and, consequently, frustrated many in the crowd. Alfred Green was up next. He, too, was found guilty, with bail set at the same level as Buck's. Henry Knockson was found not guilty. Unlike his brother Basil, David Hall was found not guilty. Both St. Clair Bailey and Richard Williams were declared guilty. There are no reports of the trials of the other four; the authorities may have decided to drop charges against them. Two sympathy meetings were called and additional funds raised to cover bail. Frances Ellen Watkins, the African American poet, called for support of the men who, as she mused, threw "themselves across the track of the general government" and, as a result, were in danger of being "crushed by the monstrous Juggernaut of organized villainy, the Fugitive Slave Law." They were all brave men whose "ears were quicker than ours; they heard the death-knell of freedom sound in the ears of the doomed and fated brother, and to them they were clarion sounds, rousing their souls to deeds of noble daring – trumpet tones, inciting them to brave and lofty actions." Those found guilty were sentenced to thirty days in prison and fined $25 each. Weeks later, Alfred Green wrote from what he called his "summer retreat," Eastern State Penitentiary (also known as the Cherry Hill prison), of his loneliness and isolation. He had not heard a human voice except that of the warden, whom he saw through the slat in his cell door three times a day. The dispute over the promised support from William Still and the Anti-Slavery Society still rankled. Green was scathing in his condemnation of some members of the society. He dismissed J. Miller McKim as one of those who "profess philanthropy," but who was "either wickedly selfish, or desperately hypocritical." He and his fellow prisoners wanted nothing more to do with McKim and other members of the society.[52]

The pressure and anxiety caused by disappointments such as the return of Horner, especially coming so soon after the exuberance and elation following the release of Webster, not surprisingly bred frustration among and antagonism between allies who had shown, over the years, a remarkable sustained opposition to the Fugitive Slave Law by delaying, where they could not prevent, the return of suspected fugitives. When David Paul Brown Jr. returned Michael Brown in the summer of 1857, the Philadelphia Female Anti-Slavery Society denounced abolitionist colleagues – and by extension, members of the black community who "acknowledge in the slave a brother man" – for standing by in the courtroom mingling "their tears with his," speaking "parting words of

---

[52] *Weekly Anglo-African*, June 9, 16, 23, July 14, 1860; Biddle and Dubin, *Testing Freedom*, 241–44; Margaret Hope Bacon, "'One Great Bundle of Humanity': Frances Watkins Harper (1825–1911)," *Pennsylvania Magazine of History and Biography*, Vol. 113, No.1 (January 1989), 30.

sympathy," and organizing a few meetings to protest the decision at which the "outrage on human rights" was discussed, but, in the end, doing nothing to forestall the fugitive's return. All of this inaction was to be expected in a city and state that remained indifferent so long as its commerce and politics were not disturbed. Two years later, however, they would exult in the "enthusiastic outbreaks of popular opposition to the execution" of the Fugitive Slave Law following Webster's release. These conflicting responses were understandable, for successes were few in commissioners' courts. For every Henry Garnett, Euphemia Williams, and Daniel Webster freed, there were depressingly many more returned. Compared to other areas of the North, those who struggled against the law in Philadelphia showed little inclination to ransom accused fugitives. The only slave ransomed before 1860 was Stephen Bennett in January 1851 and, in this instance, it was the people of Columbia, and especially the residents of "Tow Hill," the black section of town, who raised the $700 needed to buy his freedom. The payment of ransoms was anathema to many in both the men's and ladies' antislavery societies in Philadelphia. The leaders of the African American community seemed to have adopted a similar policy, one that departed from the more pragmatic approaches followed in other communities.[53]

Some of this frustration and disappointment was eased by the knowledge that fugitive slaves continued to escape in what Maryland and Virginia slaveholders considered depressingly large numbers and that threatened to undermine the pillars of an institution on which the area's economy rested. The expeditions of Harriett Tubman and the other outsiders who brought out or assisted slaves to escape, the actions of free blacks who facilitated escapes, and the slaves who organized their own escapes without the aid of others, all represented a direct economic and political threat to the system. Those who reached William Still and the vigilance committee were guaranteed safe passage to places further north and to Canada. In the seven years of its operations, the committee experienced only two losses. With its network of agents and safe houses, the vigilance committee laid down a zone of security that the authorities failed to penetrate, much less disrupt. Their operations were buttressed by the black community and white supporters who were able to protect fugitive slaves such as Henry Banks and George and defy the efforts of slave catchers to retake them. And on every occasion, they gathered outside hearing rooms and courthouses to demonstrate their solidary with those who were caught. White abolitionists, especially the members of the Female Anti-Slavery Society, never failed to pack hearings in acts of solidarity. Lawyers such as David Paul Brown volunteered their services to defend the accused even when the law insisted that hearings had to be expedited. They deftly used the writ of habeas corpus to

[53] *Twenty-Third Annual Report of the Philadelphia Female Anti-Slavery Society* (Philadelphia: 1857), 4; *Report of the Twenty-Fourth and Twenty-Fifth Years of the Philadelphia Female Anti-Slavery Society* (Philadelphia: 1859), 8–9; Philadelphia *Evening Bulletin*, January 25, 30, 1851.

delay hearings. As one editor observed, Philadelphia abolitionists had "become experts in setting the fugitive slave law at defiance. Let a runaway be arrested, and while he is in the hands of the U. S. marshal they will procure a writ of *habeas corpus*, in an attempt to bring him before the State courts upon some trumped up charge – in every instance sustained by the most shameless and shameful perjury – of petty larceny or assault and battery."[54] Together, those who fled slavery and those who sheltered them demonstrated that those who put their faith in the law to stop the flow of fugitive slaves were sadly mistaken.

[54] Washington, DC, *Union*, November 4, 1853.

# 9

# New York

Throughout the lengthy and acrimonious debate over the Fugitive Slave Law, opponents in and out of Congress warned that, without guaranteed legal rights, such as habeas corpus and trial by jury, there would be social and political dislocations and even violence. In September 1851, just one year after the law came into effect, these dire warnings were fulfilled in the black rural community in the small Pennsylvania village of Christiana, an area, one observer later recalled, which had become a focal point of opposition to the law. Over the years, the black community had formed a "mutual protection" organization to defend themselves, especially those fugitive slaves who had made a home there, against intrusion by kidnappers and slave catchers from across the state line in Maryland. Before "we can have peace," they vowed, "we must have trouble." Its leader was William Parker, who, as a young man of nineteen, had escaped with his brother from Maryland in 1839. As Parker later recalled, every two or three weeks the alarm was sounded warning of a possible intrusion. They had some successes repelling these incursions, but there were also painful losses. One night early in the fall, the alarm was raised again. A party headed by Edward Gorsuch, members of his family, and a small posse led by a deputy marshal from Philadelphia had arrived in search of Gorsuch's former slaves. One hundred and fifty blacks and a small number of white farmers responded to the alarm. Rather than withdraw, Gorsuch insisted on storming the small farmhouse where Parker and his family had barricaded themselves. Shots were exchanged, at the end of which Gorsuch lay dead and his son and nephew seriously wounded.

What followed was an escape that had all the hallmarks of a fugitive's flight to freedom. Parker, his brother-in-law, Alexander Pinkney, and Abraham Johnson left Christiana almost immediately, following a route familiar to any operative of the UGRR. They headed east first to Penningtonville, then to Parkersburg and Downington in Chester County. From there, they traveled

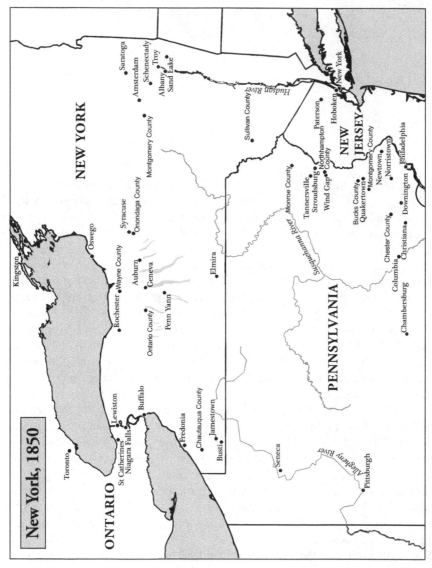

New York, 1850

**ONTARIO**

Toronto

St Catherines
Niagara Falls
Lewiston
Buffalo

Kingston

Oswego

Rochester ● Wayne County

**NEW YORK**

Saratoga
Amsterdam
Schenectady
Albany ● Troy
Sand Lake

New York

Montgomery County

Sullivan County

Hudson River

Syracuse
Onondaga County

Auburn
Geneva

Ontario County
Penn Yann

Elmira

Fredonia
Chautauqua County
Jamestown
Busti

Seneca

Monroe County
Tannersville
Stroudsburg
Wind Gap ● Northhampton
County

Paterson
Hoboken

**NEW
JERSEY**

Montgomery County
Newtown
Norristown

Bucks County
Quakertown

Chester County
Columbia
Chambersburg

Christiana
Downington ● Philadelphia

**PENNSYLVANIA**

Susquehanna River

Allegheny River

Pittsburgh

MAP 6. New York.

358

northeast to Norristown in Montgomery County, where they were aided by William Lewis, a black operative on the UGRR. Lewis took them by wagon north to Quakertown in Bucks County. Their next stops were Wind Gap in Northampton County and Tannersville, north of Stroudsburg in Monroe County, "one of the chief stations on the freedom route to Canada." From there they crossed into Sullivan County, New York, where they boarded a train bound for Rochester. The three covered the roughly five-hundred mile journey by foot, wagon, and train in roughly forty-eight hours, arriving, as so many other fugitive slaves who came to Rochester, at Frederick Douglass' home on Alexander Street. Parker later recalled that he had known Douglass as a slave in Maryland. But there was little time to reminisce; word of Gorsuch's death and their escape was, by the time of their arrival, national news. Had they been tailed, Douglass worried his home would become a bloody battle site. He and Julia Griffiths, his English coworker, thought of driving them to Lewiston, but abandoned that idea as too risky. Instead, Griffiths purchased tickets for the three on the next ferry leaving for Kingston, Canada. That night, Douglass drove them in his "Democratic carriage" (a wagon with three seats) to the terminus and anxiously waited until the ferry left. As the gangplank was lifted, Parker handed Douglass the revolver that "fell from the hand of Gorsuch when he died," a token of gratitude, Douglass recalled, and "a memento of the battle for liberty at Christiana."[1]

The experience of the three was not unique. Many others who escaped slavery in Maryland, Virginia, or Delaware and had settled in Pennsylvania – some, like Parker, for close to a decade – were later compelled to pick up stakes and head for the safety of Canada when word arrived that their master or his heirs had discovered their whereabouts. One of three former slaves who arrived in Rochester in October 1853, for example, had been living in Philadelphia twenty-two years when his "claimant" came after him. In the wake of the new Fugitive Slave Law, this unnamed fugitive from slavery became convinced his safety was not assured anywhere in the United States. Unlike this unnamed contemporary, Parker, Abraham, and Johnson had killed a slaveholder in the process of reclaiming his property, a right guaranteed by federal law. They also faced a government committed to enforcing the new law. No wonder Douglass thought it best to get them to Canada as quickly as possible. As a rule, fugitives

[1] On the shoot-out and escape from Christiana see Thomas P. Slaughter, *Bloody Dawn, The Christiana Riot and Racial Violence in Antebellum America* (New York: 1991), 77–79; William Parker, "The Freedman's Story," *Atlantic Monthly*, XVII (February 1866), http://docsouth .unc.edu/neh/parker1/parker.html; in tracing the escape route I relied on Charles Blockson, *The Underground Railroad in Pennsylvania* (Quantico, VA: 1981), 94–95, 133–35; Frederick Douglass, *The Life and Times of Frederick Douglass* (1892, rpr., New York: 1962), 280–81. Julia Griffiths to Gerrit Smith, Rochester, September 24, 1851, Gerrit Smith Papers, Syracuse University. My thanks to David Blight for sharing chapter 3, "By the Rivers of Babylon," in his forthcoming biography of Frederick Douglass and to Leigh Fought for a copy of the Griffiths letter.

who arrived in Rochester and other cities and towns in upstate New York were welcomed by organized vigilance committees, clothed, fed, and found employment, or, if they wished, sent on to Canada. These committees – with the exception of those in Albany and Elmira, which had been in existence before 1850 – were organized in the months following passage of the law: Syracuse's in October 1850, and Rochester's, a year later, were fairly typical. Syracuse's was integrated; others, including the smaller organization in Troy, were dominated by African Americans. But whatever their composition, the driving force, the persons who took on the principal responsibility of protecting and ensuring safe passage to Canada, were invariably black: Rev. Jermain Loguen in Syracuse, John W. Jones in Elmira, Stephen Myers in Albany, and Douglass in Rochester. Their homes were the hubs of local activity. Loguen's, at 293 E. Genesee Street, was such a safe haven that, by the end of the decade, he could invite the public to visit his home at a time when, it was widely known, he was sheltering twenty fugitives. All of these cities and towns stood at vital junctions in the network of lines along which fugitives traveled. Rochester, for instance, connected Baltimore, Wilmington, Delaware, Philadelphia, New York City, and St. Catherines, Canada.[2]

It is next to impossible to determine exactly how many escaping slaves these organizations assisted. One of the major organizations of the national movement was the Philadelphia Vigilance Committee, whose acting committee, headed by William Still, might have assisted close to one thousand. Many of these were sent on to sympathizers in New York City, who transshipped them to places further north, including Syracuse, Albany, Boston, and New Bedford, Massachusetts. Some were also sent directly to Elmira from Philadelphia. An untold number who crossed into Canada through Buffalo seemed to have originated in Kentucky and arrived via Pittsburgh. But as we have seen, some fugitives bypassed Still and his colleagues, choosing instead to make their own way. They undoubtedly made up a portion of those assisted by organizations in the northern tier of the state.

The numbers aided locally were substantial at times. In Albany, for instance, the local organization was headed by Stephen Myers, who had worked as a steward on a Hudson River steamboat before retiring full-time to UGRR work. Over a ten-year period, he created a "vast network of co-conspirators"

---

[2] See, for example, *Frederick Douglass' Paper*, October 23, 1851; Rochester *Union*, October 15, 1853; Syracuse *Journal*, January 12, 1859; Angela Murphy, "'It Outlaws Me, and I Outlaw It,' Resistance to the Fugitive Slave Law in Syracuse, New York," *Afro-Americans in New York Life and History*, 28 (January 2004), 58–61; see also Angela F. Murphy, *The Jerry Rescue: The Fugitive Slave Law, Northern Rights, and the American Sectional Crisis* (New York: 2016); Tom Calarco, *The Underground Railroad in the Adirondacks Region* (Jefferson, NC: 2004), 188; Abner C. Wright, "Underground Railroad Activities in Elmira," *Chemung Historical Journal*, 14 (September 1968), 1755–56; Tendai Mutunhu, "John W. Jones Underground Railroad Station-Master," *Negro History Bulletin*, 41, No. 2 (March-April 1978), 814; Scott Christianson, *Freeing Charles. The Struggle to Free a Slave on the Eve of the Civil War* (Urbana, IL: 2010), 91.

to finance his operations. In 1857, Myers assisted 287 fugitives to safety. The following year, a local newspaper reported that two hundred were aided in the "present season." Jermain Loguen reported assisting 187 in the twelve-month period beginning January 1856. Within a year, the Fugitive Aid Society, which Loguen and others, including Unitarian minister Rev. Samuel J. May, had formed in February 1856, disbanded, choosing instead to leave operations almost exclusively in the hands of Loguen, who issued regular annual reports of fugitives passing through the city. Even the small Troy Vigilance Committee reported assisting fifty-five for the year ending September 1857, a number that dropped only slightly the following year. These figures are significant in the aggregate, but they undoubtedly masked some duplication. William Still's reports, for instance, point to a significant increase in the number passing through Philadelphia in 1857. Some of these likely made up a portion of those who passed through Albany and elsewhere in upstate New York. But these figures only tell part of the story. As Stephen Myers reported in early 1858, his committee assisted thirty-six "through passengers" during the first twenty-three days of February. These did not include the "usual amount of way travel," as he put it – those who decided to settle in New York rather than go on to Canada. Some of these are undoubtedly lost to history. But as one sympathetic editor concluded, rather prematurely, the battle over slavery and the law was almost won when fugitives felt secure enough to remain in New York.[3]

Years later, Dr. William Henry Johnson, the flamboyant black barber from Albany, recalled that, "the escutcheon of the great Empire State" was never tarnished by "the return of a single fugitive slave."[4] One has to assume that he was referring to the record of the northern and western counties and not to the entire state. Even so, his memory was only slightly flawed; of the seven cases brought before commissioners in the area during the decade, one did result in a rendition. The profile of those cases speaks to the level of resistance and to the vigilance of those who opposed the law. Of the seven cases, three occurred in 1851 as the government made a concerted attempt to enforce the new law and so demonstrate its commitment to the Compromise. Two were heard in 1853, one the following year, and the final one in early 1860, not long after John Brown's attack on Harpers Ferry. This is not to suggest that fugitives who settled in the area always felt secure and confident that they would be protected by their new neighbors. When an unnamed fugitive from Tennessee who had been living in Oswego got word that slave catchers were in town, he left for

[3] Calarco, *The Underground Railroad in the Adirondack Region*, 161–62; Albany *Journal*, December 28, 1857; Troy *Times*, November 26, 1858; Louisville *Journal*, March 14, 1859, reported a speech by a New York assemblyman who estimated that 176 had passed through Albany in the six months after June 1858; Christianson, *Freeing Charles*, 67; Syracuse *Standard*, January 1, 1856, April 16, September 30, 1857; Syracuse *Journal*, May 12, 1859; Troy *Arena* (n.d.), in Pittsburgh *Gazette*, November 2, 1859, and Sandusky *Commercial Register*, November 5, 1859; Chicago *Tribune*, March 6, 1858.

[4] William Henry Johnson, *Autobiography of Dr. William Henry Johnson* (New York: 1970), 191.

Lewiston. The best way to cross into Canada at that point was by ferry, but, concerned that the catchers would get there before the ferry sailed, he came up with an ingenious, if dangerous, scheme: he simply used a gate to float across the lake. Fortunately, he was picked up by a steamer twelve miles from Niagara and taken to safety.[5]

As we have seen in Chapter 2, the case of Daniel Davis – the twenty-four-year-old escapee from Louisville, Kentucky – posed a disturbing challenge to efforts to enforce the law in the area. One year after his escape in August 1850, Davis, a chef on a Lake Erie steamer, was clubbed senseless by Benjamin S. Rust, agent of the Louisville merchant George T. Moore, as he climbed out of a hatch. Bleeding from his wounds, and slipping in and out of consciousness, Davis was brought before Commissioner Henry K. Smith, a Democrat, former mayor of Buffalo, and a member of the New York City Union Safety Committee formed in the fall of 1850 to ensure the enforcement of all aspects of the Compromise. Davis was defended by John Talcott and Seth Hawley, both Whigs and participants in a local anti-Fugitive Slave Law meeting the previous October. The scene was set for the sort of political clash that worried proponents of the law. Talcott immediately called for a dismissal on the grounds that, in permitting Davis to work on an Ohio River steamer that frequently stopped in Cincinnati, Moore, in effect, had freed his slave by allowing him to go into free territory. Determined to follow the dictates of the law, the commissioner brushed aside this and all the other defense lawyers' challenges, and on the testimony of one witness – Moore's sixteen-year-old-son – remanded Davis into the custody of his owner. While Davis was awaiting his return, supporters swore out two writs of habeas corpus. The first was rejected by Judge Alfred Conkling, sitting in Auburn, as inadequate, but he granted the second. After a brief hearing, Conkling made a startling ruling – one that, if accepted as a legitimate precedent, would have scuttled the law in its infancy. As written, he ruled, the law could not be enforced retroactively; it could be applied only to those who escaped after its enactment. Davis left the courtroom and immediately headed for Canada.

But the case also had wider political resonance. Smith's ruling was met with open resistance. The speed with which the decision was made, one opponent remarked, was "indecent." Even more alarming was the publication of a letter ostensibly written by Davis while in jail and addressed to the "Colored People of Buffalo." Black people of Kentucky, it declared, were "about as well off as you are." He decided to return because life was better in Louisville than in Buffalo, and because Moore had always treated him well. It was wrong of him to run away. He had simply followed bad advice. On his return, he planned to tell "Kentucky boys" to stay where they were. Finally, he thanked blacks and white abolitionists for all they had done for him but asked them to cease further activities on his behalf. The letter was a rather heavy-handed and politically naive attempt to influence public opinion. Not only was it signed "X," a clear indication that Davis could not write and was, therefore, not its author, but there was not a shred of evidence that Davis was involved in its composition. By leaving immediately for Canada following his release, Davis's actions spoke louder that any suspect letter could; it was, an abolitionist editor observed, a demonstration of "his estimation of slavery and his attachment to his old master." But the letter may also have been an attempt to take the steam out of the black community's demonstrated determination to prevent Davis's return. As he was being taken to jail following Smith's decision, badly cut and bloody, a "large and excited crowd" seized the horses by the bits and threatened violence, even though he was escorted by a "large body of police." Conkling's decision also may have gone a long way to ease the community's restlessness. As soon as the hearing was completed, supporters of Davis brought assault and battery charges against Benjamin Rust. The prosecution was led by H. S. Love, a Whig, who had also participated in the October 1850 meeting that condemned the law, and was the lead counsel at the hearing before Conkling. In his defense, Rust claimed he was compelled to use force because Davis and his coworkers on the boat threatened to resist. In the end, Rust pled guilty and was fined a paltry $50.[6]

Within a couple of months, Commissioner Smith would have another chance to make amends for his failure to return Davis. Harrison Williams and six others had escaped from Hardy County, Virginia – today a part of West Virginia – in the winter of 1850–51. Williams' owner, Dr. Nathaniel P. Parran, along with a number of neighborhood slaveholders, followed and caught up with the group in Philadelphia, but their effort to return the fugitives was stymied by the black community. The group headed to Busti, a small village in Chautauqua County, in far western New York, whose small black community and white supporters had established an enviable record of protecting fugitive slaves. Among its residents were William Storum and his wife Catherine, daughter of Jermain Loguen, himself a fugitive from slavery in Tennessee and a leader of the vigilance committee in Syracuse. The six found work among area farmers. Williams worked for Storum. Among Storum's other employees was Lewis Clarke, who, like his brother Milton, had escaped from slavery in Kentucky a few years earlier and had married into the community. In August, two of the escapees returned to Hardy County in an attempt to bring

---

[6] Buffalo *Courier*, August 18, 19, 29, 30, 1851; Buffalo *Express*, August 21, 30, 1851; New York *Tribune*, August 18, 19, 1851; *Frederick Douglass' Paper*, September 4, 1851; New York *Herald*, August 24, 1851; Chicago *Democrat*, August 21, 22, September 5, 1851; *National Era*, August 28, 1851; *Liberator*, September 12, 1851; *Pennsylvania Freeman*, August 21, 28, September 4, 1851; *National Anti-Slavery Standard*, August 28, 1851. See also Chris Densmore, "The Underground Railroad: Facts, Folklore and Fiction," a lecture given at the Community Historical Fair, North Collins Historical Society, June 5, 1999. My thanks to Densmore for a copy of the lecture.

out their wives. They were caught and, under interrogation, divulged the location of Williams and the others. Parran and a neighbor who owned one of the fugitives still in Busti hired a slave catcher and headed for Buffalo. There, Commissioner Smith issued them arrest warrants and ordered Deputy Marshal George B. Gates to assist in the recapture of the fugitives. The others got wind of the slave catchers' arrival and slipped away, but not Williams, who was captured in a barn, handcuffed to two policemen, placed in a carriage under heavy guard, and driven towards Jamestown. An armed group of thirty residents of the village, headed by Lewis Clarke, followed. They made an unsuccessful attempt to procure a writ of habeas corpus in Jamestown. At Fredonia, near Lake Erie, the group lost contact with the slave catchers. They wired friends in Buffalo, however, to be on the lookout for the party. A large crowd met the boat in Buffalo and followed as Williams was transferred to jail. As he had done during Davis's hearing, Smith rejected all attempts by defense counsel to dismiss Parran's claims. After the briefest of hearings, during which only one witness for the claimant was called, Smith ruled in favor of the slaveholder. On his return, Williams was sold to a Georgia slaveholder.[7]

Not long after Williams' return, residents of Busti held a public meeting and pledged armed resistance to any future attempts to capture fugitives. Lewis Clarke, who one observer reported was always well armed, announced that he had once considered either buying his freedom or settling in Canada, but, in the end, decided to make his activities in the village public at the risk of being recaptured. Not only had he married into the community but he had buried his wife in Busti. Because of these attachments, he was committed to defending all those who came to the village seeking freedom. Four years later, John Harness of Hardy County got word that his former slave, who had fled nine years earlier, was living in Jamestown, a few miles north of Busti. At the time, the fugitive was serving a six-month jail sentence in a Buffalo jail. When Harness arrived in Buffalo, he found, to his surprise, that none of the city's lawyers would agree to prepare an affidavit for his slave's arrest. Even Henry K. Smith, who had now gone into private practice, refused to get involved, according to one report, because of the "excited state of the popular mind on the subject." Smith's successor as commissioner also refused to help Harness, who, as a result, was forced to return home empty handed.[8] The price of Williams' return was a general revulsion against the law, even among those who had earlier worked to enforce it.

---

7 New York *Tribune*, October 2, 1851; Buffalo *Express*, October 2, 3, 4, 1851; Ohio *Star* (n.d.), in *Frederick Douglass' Paper*, November 6, 1851; William S. Bailey, "The Underground Railroad in Southern Chautauqua County," *New York History*, XVI, No. 1 (January 1935), 56–58; Lewis and Milton Clarke *Narratives of the Sufferings of Lewis and Milton Clark* (Boston: 1846); John Blassingame, *Slave Testimony. Two Centuries of Letters, Speeches, Interviews and Autobiographies* (Baton Rouge: 1977), 151–64.
8 Romney *Intelligencer* (n.d.), in *Pennsylvania Freeman*, December 8, 1855. The same article is reprinted in Buffalo *Express*, September 6, 1855, and *National Era*, September 20, 1855.

There were a couple of other cases involving fugitive slaves who were incarcerated in upstate prisons and whose former owners attempted to recapture them on their release. In both instances, employees at the prison had made contact with owners hoping to be compensated for their information. The actions of vigilance committees and community pressure, however, prevented the return of either. Two days before James Snowden was due to be released from Sing Sing prison in May 1852, Rev. James W. C. Pennington, a member of the American and Foreign Anti-Slavery Society and the New York State Vigilance Committee, visited Albany and persuaded Governor Washington Hunt to release Snowden, who, he argued, had been incorrectly convicted of larceny. But Snowden was a fugitive who had escaped from Dr. Allen Thomas of Howard County, Maryland, in 1849. Following his escape, Snowden found employment on a boat out of Providence, Rhode Island, which visited New York City regularly. During one of these trips, while the steamer was anchored in New York harbor, Snowden stole a skiff and went ashore. The ship captain had him arrested for theft. Before the trial could begin, Thomas arrived to claim his property. John Jay, the leading defense counsel in many of the city's fugitive slave cases, convinced the court that state law took precedent and that Snowden, therefore, should be tried for the theft of the skiff. On the advice of Jay, Snowden pleaded guilty and was sentenced to two years in prison. Days before his release, Thomas's son procured an arrest warrant from New York City's commissioner, George W. Morton. But by the time he and two deputy marshals arrived in Albany, Snowden had been released and handed over to Pennington, who took him immediately to Canada. In his defense, Governor Hunt claimed that a letter from Dr. Thomas laying out his claims for Snowden had arrived after he had granted the pardon and the prisoner was released.[9]

It is clear in Snowden's case that members of the vigilance committee, aware of his impending release, had worked to prevent his master reclaiming him. The timing of his release to Pennington also suggests that the governor, in spite of his public explanation, might have been a party to the escape. The situation was equally confusing two years later on the eve of the release of twenty-year-old George Washington from the state prison in Auburn, where he had been serving a ten-year-and-one-month sentence for burglary and larceny committed in Wayne County. Later, Washington's Sabbath school-teacher, who described him as "three-quarters white" and a mere youth, claimed that he had been wrongfully convicted. This had so depressed the prisoner that he attempted to commit suicide on more than one occasion.

[9] New York *Herald*, May 15, 18, 1852; *Voice of the Fugitive*, June 17, 1852; New York *Tribune*, May 17, 25, 1852; New York *Times*, May 25, 1852; *Anti-Slavery Bugle*, May 29, 1852; *National Era*, June 10, 1852; *Frederick Douglass' Paper*, June 10, 1852; Eric Foner, *Gateway to Freedom. The Hidden History of the Underground Railroad* (New York: 2015), 138; R. J. M. Blackett, *Beating Against the Barriers. Biographical Essays in Afro-American Nineteenth-Century History* (Baton Rouge: 1986), 57.

Evidently, William Ashley, a turnkey or "under keeper" at the prison, had also befriended Washington and from him learned that he was a fugitive slave from South Carolina. Ashley got in touch with Washington's owner and kept him informed of the release date. On the eve of his release, Ashley and the owner, a Mr. Jones, appeared to claim Washington with a warrant that turned out to be flawed. Ashley hurried back to Wayne County in the hope of amending the arrest warrant. But opponents had gotten wind of their plans. They held meetings with the prison warden, and the marshal and his deputy, at which they protested against Washington's release to the slaveholder. Anticipating trouble, officials appealed unsuccessfully for aid from local military companies. Washington's supporters also brought in large crowds from Syracuse and surrounding towns, which gathered outside the prison gates on the morning of his release in the midst of a fearsome snowstorm. As Washington left the prison, he was surrounded by "several hundred," amid "loud acclamations from a large collection of his colored friends," and taken to safety. An ad hoc committee was then formed to visit Ashley at a local hotel, but as one observer gleefully reported, he was nowhere to be found.[10]

This sort of community resistance to the law was earlier on display in Syracuse when, as one sympathetic observer remarked, if exaggerating only slightly, the city prevented the return of Jerry Henry to slavery. Jerry, as he was commonly known, was arrested on the same day Daniel Davis was in Buffalo, as he worked at his bench at the cooperage owned by Frederic Morrell. The forty-year-old Jerry had escaped from near Hannibal, Missouri, in 1843 and had been living in Syracuse for about two years. Weeks before, John McReynolds, who had bought Jerry in absentia eight years after his escape, became aware of the fugitive's whereabouts and set in motion plans to retake him. James Lear, McReynold's agent, swore out an arrest warrant with Commissioner Joseph Sabine. The commissioner had served in the office prior to passage of the Fugitive Slave Law and was deeply troubled by his new responsibilities. He had reluctantly agreed to accept the new appointment under pressure from family and friends, who reasoned he could bring a balanced and sympathetic approach to fugitive hearings. Nevertheless, Sabine took his duties seriously and insisted that, before he would issue an arrest warrant, Lear had to show undeniable proof that Jerry was McReynold's slave. In fact, Lear was compelled to return to Hannibal to procure the evidence, which delayed Jerry's arrest. The delay proved unfortunate for the slaveholder. On the day Jerry was taken into custody by Marshal Henry Allen, the city was teaming with visitors attending the Onondaga County Agricultural Fair, and, more critically to the outcome of the case, the Liberty Party's convention. Within minutes of Jerry's arrest, most

[10] New York *Tribune*, April 4, 1854; Albany *Journal*, March 27, 1854; Judith Wellman, et al., *Uncovering the Freedom Trail in Auburn and Cayuga County, New York* (Fulton, NY: 2005), 59–67.

of the city's church bells tolled a prearranged warning that a fugitive slave had been taken. The Liberty Party immediately suspended its proceedings so members could attend the hearing. They flooded the commissioner's office. Gerrit Smith, leader of the party and a major figure in the abolitionist movement, volunteered to act as Jerry's counsel. Lear testified that he had known Jerry since 1820, but before he could proceed further, the crowd started hissing, forcing Sabine to call an adjournment. Within minutes of the resumption, the shackled Jerry threw himself across the commissioner's desk, scattering papers. A crowd of blacks and whites then hoisted Jerry over their heads to the door, but he fell down a flight of stairs and was injured. Pulling himself together, he tried to reach a carriage, but was recaptured and taken to the police station, where the hearing later continued. The hearing had not gotten far when it was again interrupted, this time by stones thrown through the windows. Worried, some recommended calling out the militia, but opponents of the law persuaded its leaders not to act, a decision that, in the end, would help the rescuers. While the hearing was in progress, about two dozen abolitionists, including Rev. Samuel J. May, Gerrit Smith, and Rev. Samuel Ringgold Ward and Jermain Loguen, both fugitive slaves, met to plan a rescue. As Loguen told a crowd of African Americans, if white men would not fight "let fugitives and black men smite down Marshals and Commissioners – anybody who holds Jerry – and rescue him or perish."

During the day of the hearing, Donald Yacavone writes, the city was in a "state of near anarchy," with crowds roaming the streets. By dusk, an estimated crowd of three thousand milled about outside the police station. Following a prearranged signal, part of the crowd stormed the building, bludgeoning the police on guard and shattering windows. Angela Murphy writes, the "rescuers smashed the windows, chipped and pried out castings and removed bricks from the building in order to gain entry." They also procured a ram to batter in the door leading to the room where Jerry was being held. The marshal appeared at the entrance with his gun drawn. Someone clubbed him and the rescuers removed Jerry, who was taken to a safe place outside the city. He remained there five days before he was sent to Canada.

Under pressure from President Fillmore, who insisted that those involved in the rescue be prosecuted for violating the law, warrants for the arrest of twenty blacks and four whites were issued by Judge Alfred Conkling in mid-October. May estimated that the grand jury would bring charges against him, twelve other whites, and twelve blacks, nine of whom, including Loguen, Samuel Ringgold Ward, and Rev. James Baker, all fugitive slaves, had already fled to Canada to avoid capture. Unlike his counterparts in Christiana, Conkling tried to defuse a potential political crisis by making it clear on the first day of the trial that no one would be tried for treason, in spite of the efforts of US Attorney James R. Lawrence to build such a case against May and the others. Enoch Reed, an African American, was the first to be brought to trial in January

1852. Although the government used questionable tactics in an effort to win a conviction, the case quickly unraveled. Because it had never been established through a hearing that Jerry was the property of McReynolds, Reed could not be charged with violating the Fugitive Slave Law. Instead, he was charged and convicted of resisting a federal officer, a comparatively minor violation. The other cases against the rescuers were postponed first to June, then to October 1852, and again to January 1853. After two years and expenditures of an estimated $50,000, the government had nothing to show for its efforts to punish those who had broken the law. There were hung juries and indefinite postponements before the hearings were finally brought to an end in mid-1853, although, as Angela Murphy points out, the government did not officially drop the charges until January 1861.

Supporters of Jerry found some ingenious ways to express their opposition to the law and to the government for its insistence on prosecuting those involved in the rescue. Some were pure political theater. A group of Syracuse women, for instance, sent US Attorney Lawrence thirty pieces of silver. More significantly, Samuel J. May organized the first "Jerry Celebration" in October 1853, on the anniversary of the rescue. Every year for the rest of the decade, the anniversary brought together abolitionists and black leaders from across the North to celebrate what they considered a successful defiance of a hated law and confirm Loguen's declaration at the city's first public meeting following the adoption of the law that Syracuse was a "free city." May insisted that the citizens of the city and county had not violated the law. What they had done was "set at naught an unrighteous, cruel edict; they trampled on tyranny." Earlier, John Thomas, a white newspaperman who worked with Frederick Douglass on his newspaper, had predicted that the rescuers would not be found guilty because the government would be unable to find jurors willing to "perjure their souls." The law would be resisted because "it is itself to the last degree lawless." The first celebration brought together many of the leading lights in the abolitionist movement, including Frederick Douglass, William Lloyd Garrison, Gerrit Smith, Lucy Stone, and Lucretia Mott, all of whom praised the rescue as an expression of popular resistance to a morally indefensible law. Initially, Loguen, Ward, and the other blacks who fled to Canada must have questioned whether the city was in fact as free as they had boasted. In a letter to Governor Washington Hunt from Canada, Loguen compared his exile to that of the Hungarian Lajos Kossuth fleeing Austrian tyranny. It was, he told Hunt, his "misfortune," not his "fault," to have been born in the South. Contrary to the Declaration of Independence's assertion that all men were created equal, he was, as it were, born "unconstitutionally." He was willing, nonetheless, to return if the governor guaranteed that he would only be prosecuted for his involvement in the rescue and not as a fugitive from slavery. It was a pledge no governor could give. Ward would never return to the United States, spending the rest of his life first in Canada, then England, before settling permanently in Jamaica. But Loguen returned in the spring of 1852 to resume his duties as the driving force in the city's UGRR, sobered, one suspects, but still convinced that the city would protect him from recapture.[11]

Following the Jerry Henry and Daniel Davis cases, "J. T." (John Thomas) wrote Frederick Douglass that he was convinced, because of community opposition to the law, that fugitive slaves were now "perfectly safe at every point between Buffalo and Albany."[12] Surprisingly, for someone as deeply invested in the abolitionist movement and resistance to the law as Thomas was, he chose to ignore the return of Harrison Williams. But over the span of the decade, his observation largely held true, even as late as the spring of 1860, when the country seemed to be spinning out of control. Five months after John Brown's attack on Harpers Ferry, thirty-eight-year-old Charles Nalle was picked up on his way to a bakery in Troy. Nalle and two other slaves, Jim Banks and Percy Clexton, had escaped from Culpepper County, Virginia, in October 1858. According to William Still, who recorded the arrival of the three in Philadelphia, Nalle left because his master would not allow him to live with his wife and children and refused to hire him out so he could be near his family. Nalle settled briefly in Sand Lake, New York, before moving to Troy, where he found employment as a coachman for Uri Gilbert, the city's leading industrialist and a prominent Republican. While at Sand Lake, Nalle was befriended by a down-on-his-luck lawyer, Horatio F. Averill, who learned from Nalle that he had escaped from Blucher W. Hansbrough. Averill made contact with Hansbrough and offered to act as his lawyer. Following receipt of the news, Hansbrough sent Henry J. Wale, an experienced slave catcher, and William L. Parr, a bounty hunter, to return Nalle. An arrest warrant was issued by Commissioner Miles Beach, a twenty-seven-year-old Democrat. Wale and Parr were accompanied by Deputy Marshal John W. Holmes, also a Democrat. As in the earlier cases in Buffalo, Beach rushed through the hearing and ruled in favor of the slaveholder even before Nalle's counsel, Martin I. Townsend, had arrived. It was rumored that

---

[11] My account of the rescue draws heavily on Donald Yacovone, *Samuel Joseph May and the Dilemmas of the Liberal Persuasion 1797–1871* (Philadelphia: 1991), 143–51, Angela F. Murphy, *The Jerry Rescue*, especially chapter 10 but also pp. 1, 5, 17, 27–28, 118, 140–41, and J. W. Loguen, *The Rev. J. W. Loguen as a Slave and as a Freeman. A Narrative of Real Life* (1859, rpr., New York: 1968), 398–424; New York *Tribune*, October 4, 1851, January 28, February 3, 1853; *Carson League*, August 10, 1851. My thanks to Angela Murphy for a copy. *Liberator*, May 14, 1852; *Frederick Douglass' Paper*, January 8, 1852; *Speech of Rev. Samuel J. May to the Convention of the Citizens of Onondaga County, in Syracuse on the 14th of October, 1851* (Syracuse: 1851), 18; Milton C. Sernett, *North Star Country. Upstate New York and the Crusade for African American Freedom* (Syracuse: 2002), 136–45; Samuel Ringgold Ward, *Autobiography of a Fugitive Negro* (1855, rpr., New York: 1970), 84–90. Contemporary reports said that local opponents of the law also sent President Fillmore the shackles used to hold Jerry, but in the 1890s, Lucy Watkins, a black woman who was involved in the rescue, recalled that Jerry was brought to her house, where the manacles were removed and buried in her garden. The shackles now form part of a permanent exhibit at the Onondaga Historical Association.

[12] *Frederick Douglass' Paper*, August 1, 1852.

Beach had drawn up the rendition papers even before the hearing began, a claim the commissioner would later deny. Townsend immediately applied for a writ of habeas corpus from Judge George Gould of the state supreme court.

A crowd had gathered outside his office even before Beach issued his ruling. They were addressed by William Henry, an African American grocer with whom Nalle boarded and a leading figure in the local vigilance committee. The crowd also lined the stairs leading up to Beach's office. Among them was an "elderly woman" who no one seemed to know. Unsure of her identity, one local newspaper dubbed her Moll Pitcher, after the aged eighteenth-century Massachusetts clairvoyant. Later, without naming her, another newspaper provided details of her life that made it clear that she was Harriet Tubman. She happened to be passing through town from her home in Auburn to attend antislavery meetings in Boston and to visit family. Tubman had donned the disguise of an old woman, shrinking herself "into the posture of an ancient grandmother," Scott Christianson writes, so she could make her way unmolested and past the police cordon up the stairs, where she positioned herself at a window so she could signal the growing crowd below. Things were at a stalemate for some time. The police dared not move Nalle out of the commissioner's office nor could the crowd reach the fugitive. At one point the heavily shackled prisoner attempted to jump through a window but was restrained by the police.

When Townsend appeared with the writ of habeas corpus at Beach's office, those holding Nalle had no alternative but to brave the crowd on the stairs in order to respond to the writ. As Nalle was being taken out of the building, surrounded by police officers headed by Deputy Marshal Holmes, the old lady gave the signal. When the group reached the sidewalk they were engulfed by a crowd of blacks and whites estimated to be as large as two thousand, composed, as one observer recorded, of some "resolute colored men." The police successfully resisted the initial rescue attempt. A few streets away, the crowd once again surged around the officers. Some in the crowd suggested that it was in Nalle's best interest to go before Judge Gould, who, they argued, would be sympathetic to the plight of the fugitive. Others, including the old lady, adamantly rejected the suggestion and "urged the rescuers on." One observer reported that "[t]wenty times the prisoner was taken from the officers, and twenty times they recovered him." Black women, including the old lady, were in the thick of the fray. She fought "like a demon," losing all "her gearing save a dilapidated outskirt." As the crowd and police fought, two men managed to get Nalle away and took him to the river, where he was put in a skiff and ferried to West Troy. But the police of the sister city were up to the challenge; soon after the boat landed, Nalle was arrested and taken to the office of Justice Daniel C. Stewart. About three hundred men and women, including the old woman, commandeered the ferry and crossed into West Troy. They stormed the building where Nalle was being held. The police fired on the crowd, forcing them to retreat, but they quickly regrouped and tried to enter the office. One of the attackers was felled by a blow. His body blocked the door providing an opening through which the crowd surged. In the melee outside Gould's office, the old lady held Nalle "tightly around his arm and wouldn't let go, regardless of what was done to him or her....[P]olicemen's clubs rained down on her head and grip but she never for a moment released her hold." Nalle was rescued and hurried away, placed in a wagon accompanied by two armed black men, Hank York and Andrew Parker. He was driven from West Troy six miles toward Schenectady, where his handcuffs were removed. He was later taken to Amsterdam, Montgomery County, and from there moved ten miles into the country.[13]

Even before Judge Gould issued the writ of habeas corpus, offers were made to ransom Nalle. Freeing Nalle should have put paid to any plans to pay Blucher Harbrough for his former slaves. Such payments, especially after the fugitive had been freed, were rare and largely frowned upon. Why, opponents asked, should a former master be paid when a fugitive had successfully eluded recapture? But Nalle's supporters were convinced that the best outcome would be his return to Troy, where a job with Uri Gilbert awaited him, and where he could be reunited with his wife Kitty and their five children, who since his escape from Maryland, had been living in Columbia, Pennsylvania. The decision not to send Nalle to Canada suggests that the negotiations were close to completion. Days after the rescue, Harbrough agreed to accept an offer of $650. Nalle and his family were reunited in Troy, but the government could not ignore the fact that the law had been openly defied. As in other cases, a grand jury was empaneled to decide what charges to bring against those who had participated in the rescue. But identifying those involved was easier said than done. The rescue, insisted one unnamed Democrat, who contributed to the fund to ransom Nalle and who had observed the event, was the work of folks of all political persuasions, including, as he put it, the "Democratic Irishman." The authorities took their time mulling over the charges. The first arrest, that of John M. Van Buskirk, was not made until mid-July. But the charge brought against him seemed trivial given the seriousness of the crime. Evidently, in the midst of the melee, Van Buskirk had shouted out an offer to pay anyone who would rescue Nalle $250. Van Buskirk's trial was adjourned twice before the charges were eventually dropped. John T. Perry was also charged with resisting authority. There were reports that other names were on the prosecutor's list, some of them leading figures in the Republican Party, a clear indication that the authorities were conscious of the political nature of the rescue. But nothing came of any of these charges, largely because, by this time, the country's gaze was focused on larger national political developments.[14]

---

[13] Troy *Times*, April 27, 30, May 23, 26, 30, 1860; Troy *Whig*, April 28, May 1, 2, 1860; Albany *Journal*, April 28, 1860. My account draws heavily on Scott Christianson, *Freeing Charles*, 96–122; William Still, *The Underground Railroad* (1872, rpr., Chicago: 1970), 509.

[14] Troy *Times*, May 1, 7, 26, July 18, 26, 28, August 23, 1860; Troy *Whig*, April 28, 1860; Albany *Journal*, August 24, 1860; Christianson, *Freeing Charles*, 120–22.

Upstate New York could look back from the vantage point of 1860 and say with some justification, as John Thomas had done earlier in the decade, that fugitive slaves were guaranteed both safe passage if they wished to go on to Canada, and a sanctuary from slave catchers if they chose to settle in the area. But this was also an area that, by 1853, had come to be associated with the most infamous case of kidnapping in the period. For twelve years, Solomon Northup, a man born free, had languished on Louisiana plantations until he got word to friends of his whereabouts. Northup had been lured away from Saratoga by two men with the promise of a job, first in New York City and then Washington, DC, where he was drugged and sold to a slave catcher. Even after Northup's rescue, the fear of kidnapping remained palpable. In early 1854, for instance, young Alexander B. Brookenborough left Buffalo to visit his grandmother in Washington, DC. His father, Alexander S. Brookenborough, a tailor and a prominent figure in the city's black community, grew worried when his son had not returned two weeks after leaving the capital. The father had taken the precaution of supplying young Alexander with a pass, signed by the mayor of Buffalo, stating that he was the son of free parents. It is not clear what became of Alexander, but the fact that his father felt it necessary to make his son's apparent disappearance public speaks to the widespread fear of kidnapping even among those who were well-known figures in their community.[15]

Four years later, the small town of Geneva – known as a refuge for escaping slaves, a place where prior to the passage of the Fugitive Slave Law, two-thirds of the black community was composed of fugitive slaves – was devastated by the news that two young black men, Daniel Prue (or Price) and John Hite, had been kidnapped. Prue was born in Seneca; Hite, nineteen, was the son of a freedman. Both were lured away with the promise of jobs at a hotel in Columbus, Ohio, owned by the uncle of Napoleon Bonaparte Van Tuyl. Twenty-one, and the son of a wealthy family of "irreproachable character" from Penn Yan, New York, Van Tuyl had only recently moved to Geneva, where he worked as a dry goods clerk. On the train from Cleveland to Columbus, Van Tuyl struck up a conversation with three Kentucky slaveholders – B. W. Jenkins, Henry Giltner, and George W. Metcalf, who were on their way home after failing to track down fugitive slaves who had escaped from Warsaw. Van Tuyl introduced himself as Paul Lensington, returning to Tennessee with two fugitive slaves. The Kentuckians promised to help Van Tuyl get the two across the river. Prue

[15] Solomon Northup, *Twelve Years a Slave* (1853, rpr., Baton Rouge: 1968); Buffalo *Express*, March 21, 1854. For the elder Brookenborough's activities dating back to the early 1840s see *Colored American*, February 30, 1841. The 1850 census lists Alexander's mother, forty-year-old Margaret, as born in Scotland. In fact, the same census provides no racial designation for the elder Brookenborough, which suggests that the census taker considered him white. The 1860 census designates him as "colored," the following, ten years later, simply as "white."

overheard their conversation and left the train as it pulled out of the next station, in spite of Van Tuyl's efforts to prevent him. At the next train stop, Van Tuyl and Jenkins caught the first train going north in an unsuccessful effort to find Prue. Giltner and Metcalf continued with Hite to Cincinnati, where they crossed over to Covington, Kentucky, and then to Carrollton, where Van Tuyl sold Hite to Jenkins for $500. Jenkins promptly resold him to Lorenzo Graves for a profit of $250. Worried that Hite would try to escape, Graves took him to Warsaw and then to a jail in Louisville, where he was to be held until resold to slave traders.

Van Tuyl returned home through Canada, but was arrested at Niagara Falls. His whereabouts became known when he mailed a gift box to a young women to whom he was engaged. An irate crowd, many of them black, greeted Van Tuyl on his return, but the presence of a large police force prevented any violence. Van Tuyl's father and another prominent merchant of Penn Yan posted bail. Within days of his release, Van Tuyl disappeared. Under pressure from prominent residents of Geneva, the governor of New York selected two agents – Judge Calvin Walker of Ontario County and Robert Hay of Geneva, Hite's employer – to go in search of Hite and Prue. The two retraced the route traveled by Van Tuyl, Prue, and Hite, going first to Columbus, where they found Prue, then to Cincinnati and Warsaw. There they interviewed Lorenzo Graves, who agreed to release Hite on the condition that the agents also interview Jenkins and Metcalf in Carrollton so they could prove they were not involved in a kidnapping but had simply agreed to help Van Tuyl get the alleged fugitive slave to Kentucky. Following the interview in Carrollton, Graves accompanied Walker and Hay to Louisville, where he handed Hite over to the agents. Graves also accompanied them back to Cincinnati and provided Hite, Walker and Hay reported, with gifts for his mother.

Months later, while Jenkins was in New Orleans on business, he recognized Van Tuyl in the lobby of a hotel, in spite of Van Tuyl's heavy disguise. Van Tuyl was registered at the hotel as Edwin Reed. Jenkins made a citizen's arrest and handed Van Tuyl over to the police. Jenkins also procured an extradition request from the governor of Kentucky, under which Van Tuyl was ordered back to Carrollton, Kentucky, to face charges of obtaining money under false pretenses and selling a free black into slavery. On the way to Carrollton, Van Tuyl attempted to jump ship at Memphis but was foiled. Van Tuyl was returned to New York, where he was held in jail in Canandaigua to await trial in April. It is not clear what happened next, but in July it was reported that he was out on bail set at $5,000. Two months later, Van Tuyl disappeared from his parents' home in Penn Yan. A reward of $100 was offered for his recapture. The story disappeared from local newspapers until it was announced that the case would be reopened in January 1859. The trial ended in a hung jury, with ten voting for conviction and two against. At his retrial, Van Tuyl's defense called on expert witnesses to prove that their client was insane. The jury was unconvinced and Van Tuyl was sentenced to two years in the state prison at Auburn. He died soon after his release in the early months of the Civil War. Prue and Hite, one local historian recalled, were both killed in battle during the Civil War.[16]

There were four similar cases of possible kidnapping in the area at the time of Van Tuyl's trial. Two of them, one involving Henry Dixon of Rochester and the other Charles Grandy of Auburn, took the most unexpected twists and turns. In early 1857, Frederick Douglass received a letter from a Mr. Chamberlain of Summit County, Ohio, informing him that Reed, a fugitive Chamberlain had assisted, mentioned that Grandy was being held as a slave by Henry Hill of Haysville, Louisiana. This was evidently confirmed by another informant who knew Grandy in Rochester. An agent was dispatched to Louisiana, but could find no trace of Grandy on Hill's plantation along the Mississippi River. Grandy's kidnapping, many concluded, must have been a hoax concocted by Reed. Grandy, it turned out, had never been kidnapped, but was living freely in Peoria, Illinois. How Reed came to know Grandy well enough to provide Chamberlain with a description or information about where he lived was never explained.[17]

The case of Henry Dixon was even more bizarre. A well-known barber in Rochester, Dixon had left the city several years before and settled in Washington, DC, where he drove a hack. Sometime later, he decided to return to Rochester. On his way home, he was arrested on a train between Washington and Baltimore and sent to a slave pen. Another report claimed Dixon had committed what it vaguely called "some misconduct," for which he was tried, found guilty, and was sold into slavery "under order of the Court." Dixon was later sold to James Dean of Macon, Georgia. Like Solomon Northup, Dixon managed to get a letter to a friend back home. The governor of New York promptly sent an agent to Georgia in an effort to win Dixon's release. By the time of the agent's arrival, however, Dean had sold Dixon and refused to divulge his whereabouts until he was paid $700. In an effort to raise what many saw as an extortionate ransom, Douglass gave a public lecture in Rochester charging fifteen cents admission. Many eagerly subscribed to the Dixon Fund, part of which was used to send Samuel D. Proctor, as the state's agent, to Georgia. When Proctor did make contact with Dixon, a Macon newspaper reported, he "resolutely refused to be free – to leave his master – to leave Georgia and go to New York." Dean, Dixon evidently told Proctor, had been kind to him, was a "friend and protector." A local editor saw a political opening and exploited it for all it was

---

[16] Geneva *Courier*, November 25, December 2, 9, 16, 23, 1857, February 24, April 7, July 14, September 29, December 1, 1858; Cincinnati *Gazette*, November 23, December 4, 5, 7, 10, 14, 1857, February 16, March 12, 17, 22, 30, 1858; New York *Tribune*, December 12, 1857; Louisville *Journal*, February 15, 1857, March 31, 1858; Columbus *Journal* (n.d.), in Albany *Journal*, December 7, 1857; Albany *Journal*, January 4, 1858; Charles F. Milliken, *A History of Ontario County, New York and Its People*, Vol. I (New York: 1911), 198–200. For the composition of the black community in Geneva see Bryan Prince, *A Shadow on the Household. One Enslaved Family's Incredible Struggle for Freedom* (Toronto: 2009), 52–53.

[17] Albany *Journal*, January 31, March 31, 1857.

worth. "Will the [New York] *Independent,* the [New York] *Tribune,* Henry Ward Beecher, [George B.] Cheever, the Rochester Knockers and Abolitionists, Uncle Tom, Aunt Beecher Stowe and Little Topsey," it asked gleefully, "give us their views upon this subject?" Judge Ashley Simpson, the driving force behind the Dixon Fund, rejected the conclusion that Dixon had refused their proffered support, insisting instead that a "spurious Henry Dixon [had been] palmed off on them." But such a hoax seemed farfetched, even to some supporters of the effort to return Dixon. Proctor clearly had met Dixon during his visit to Macon and left convinced he was a *"good for nothing character ... a loose, lying fellow* whose representations could not be relied upon." It was a strange ending to an even stranger event. Periodically during the decade, Southern apologists would chortle over infrequent decisions by escapees to return to their masters, but the Dixon denouement was, to put it mildly, deeply disquieting. The editor of the Albany *Journal* reached for a psychological explanation for Dixon's behavior: he had no doubt that Dixon had "become a lunatic, probably from grief under the infliction of slavery." His counterpart at the New York *Tribune* took a different tack, but thought the incident might help to resolve a growing political impasse over fugitive slaves: it provided an opportunity, he suggested, for both the North and South to agree that anytime someone escaped to their section they would not be pursued. A Democratic editor rejected both suggestions as "unreasonable" and a typical Republican overreaction, a replay, if on a less politically dangerous level, of their responses to the troubles in the Kansas Territory.[18]

Regardless of the outcome of the Dixon case, the fear of kidnapping had long haunted free black residents of Northern states. It was a problem that antislavery advocates, dating back to the founding of the early movement at the end of the eighteenth century, had fought to prevent by pressuring state and national governments to enact laws criminalizing such activity, and resisting, wherever possible, the capture of free blacks. As we have seen, those living on the margins between free and slave states were particularly vulnerable. But so, too, were those such as Daniel Prue and John Hite, who resided in more secure places far removed from slave territory. Those born free, such as Solomon Northup, were potentially even more vulnerable, for, unlike those born into slavery and later freed, they had no way to prove their status. By refusing to include legal guarantees, the authors of the Fugitive Slave Law, in effect, had voted to increase the vulnerability of freeborn black people wherever they

---

[18] Albany *Journal,* December 8, 17, 1856; Rochester *Union and Advertiser,* June 2, 23, 24, 26, July 24, August 10, 1857; Rochester *Democrat,* June 4, 1857; Georgia *Telegraph,* June 16, 1857; New York *Tribune,* July 28, 1857. The Rochester Ladies Anti-Slavery Society (RLASS) contributed $90 to the fund to reclaim Dixon. It is not clear if this sum was in addition to the fund or if the society was acting as a repository of all the monies collected. See Account Book for 1857 in RLASS Papers, Clements Library, University of Michigan, http://quod.lib.umich.edu/c/clementsmss/umich-wel-M-2084roc?byte=63002 51;focusrgn=contentslist;subview=standard;view=reslist My thanks to Leigh Fought for sharing this information with me.

lived. This was particularly so in port cities such as New York, where slavery and merchant capitalism converged, where the ships that carried Southern cotton to the world were constructed and where city bankers and merchants financed and conducted that trade. It was, Eric Foner writes, an "epidemic of kidnapping" that, in part, led to the formation of the city's first vigilance committee in 1835, headed by David Ruggles.[19]

It is impossible to determine how many free blacks were kidnapped from the city in the ten years between the passage of the Fugitive Slave Law and the outbreak of the Civil War. But the city's vigilance committees were kept busy trying to curtail the activities of kidnappers. Three cases, which occurred late in the decade, were fairly typical. In March 1858, James P. Finley, described as a Canadian citizen who had been in the country three months, and his wife Anna Brainard, persuaded the parents of Sarah Harrison, fourteen, to allow them to take her to Newark, where she would be employed as a servant. Instead, they took her to Washington, DC, where they attempted to sell her for $600. But the young Harrison "made so much trouble," as one newspaper reported, that Finley and Brainard abandoned their plans and fled to Maryland, where they were later arrested. Nine months later, Jeremiah Simpson, eighteen, was persuaded to sign on as a seaman on a ship bound for Liverpool, England. His mother grew suspicious and complained to the mayor, who sent city policemen to investigate. What they found was a crew made up entirely of black boys. The only whites on board were the ship's mates. More troubling was the fact that none of the boys on the ship, which was on its way to Mobile, Alabama, had free papers. The sergeant of the harbor police reported that ships frequently sailed from New York to Southern ports with black crews, none of whom returned. Simpson, and one assumes the others, were released and provided with free papers. Two years later, fourteen-year-old William Percival, whose father was a black soldier in the British army stationed in Trinidad, had grown tired of school and decided to sign on the ship *Napoleon*, captained by D. D. Sirmond of South Carolina, which sailed from Port-of-Spain to New York. On the way, they called at Hampton Roads, Petersburg, and Norfolk, Virginia. Once the ship had completed its business in New York, Sirmond announced that they would return to Trinidad after making a stop in Charleston. The six-man crew, all of whom were black, refused to go, fearing that they would

---

[19] Foner, *Gateway to Freedom*, 62. For a detailed account of Ruggles's life and work see Graham Russell Goa Hodge, *David Ruggles. A Radical Black Abolitionist and the Underground Railroad in New York City* (Chapel Hill, NC: 2010). See the case of Sarah Jane Giddings, née Young, who was born free in New York City. She was kidnapped at age twelve and taken to Texas. Ten years later, her master brought her with him on a summer's visit to Niagara Falls. Sarah Jane took the opportunity to escape into Canada, where she found work at the Clifton House Hotel. Her master visited her at the hotel in an unsuccessful attempt to persuade her to return with him to Texas. Chicago *Tribune*, September 15, 1859. For a general history of kidnapping see Carol Wilson, *Freedom at Risk. The Kidnapping of Free Blacks in America, 1780–1865* (Lexington, KY: 1994).

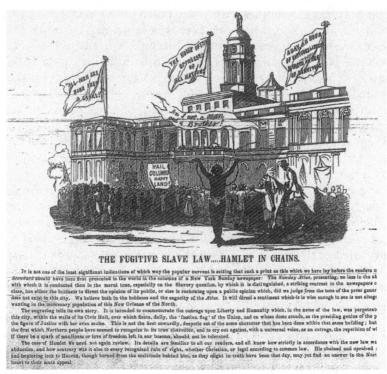

FIGURE 9. The Fugitive Slave Law…Hamlet in Chains. (*National Anti-Slavery Standard*, October 17, 1851)

be sold into slavery. They all left the ship. Percival went to live with Thomas Lewis, who kept a boardinghouse for black sailors, where Sirmond had him arrested as a runaway. Lewis went in search of Percival and found him at another boardinghouse. Following an interview, the police became convinced that Sirmond planned to sell Percival into slavery. Percival, who claimed he was anxious to return to his parents, was handed over to the British consul.[20]

It is not clear why these cases clustered the way they did at the end of the decade. The same is true of the pattern that emerges of fugitive slave cases that were brought to hearings during the decade. The first case adjudicated under the law, that of James Hamlet in September 1850, days after President Fillmore put his signature to the act, occurred in New York City. Of the eleven cases that came to hearing during the decade, eight occurred between September

---

[20] New York *Herald*, March 25, 1858; New York *Tribune*, March 26, December 9, 1858, December 10, 1860. There were also the cases of Samuel Johnson, sixteen, who was born in Luanda, and of Isaac Moore, fourteen, who was confined to the hold for four days on a ship bound for the South before he managed to escape. New York *Herald*, June 18, 19, 1858; New York *Tribune*, August 9, 10, 1858.

1850 and May 1854. No other cases were heard until December 1857. A lull then followed until 1860, when one case was heard in May and another in December. One of the eleven cases was not technically a fugitive slave case. As in the case of Jane Johnson and her two children in Philadelphia, it involved the decision of a slaveholder to travel through a Free State with his slaves. It, too, resulted in the freeing of the slaves. Of the cases heard, five resulted in renditions, three were returned and later ransomed, one was freed, and one was released to the custody of a parent. In addition, one case, which originated in Poughkeepsie, was adjudicated in New York City and resulted in the fugitive's rendition and ransom. As in other areas, the city's commissioners generally were favorably disposed to the claims of slaveholders.

The speed with which Commissioner Alexander Gardiner remanded the twenty-five-year-old James Hamlet surprised even the most ardent supporters of the Fugitive Slave Law. Hamlet was claimed by Mary Brown of Baltimore, who had known of his whereabouts for some time, but had decided to postpone any attempt to reclaim him until the law was passed. The decision was made on the testimony of two members of the claimant's family even before Hamlet's lawyers had arrived. There were no more than eighteen people at the hearing, including court officials, police officers, and reporters. No members of the black community were present. In fact, Rev. Charles B. Ray, the black Congregationalist minister and leading figure in the vigilance committee, arrived as Hamlet was being led out. Although he anticipated that the decision would cause commotion throughout the city among blacks and "abolitionist fanatics," one editor, who lamented the need for the law, nonetheless commended the promptness with which the decision was made. The action of the commissioner, he thought, sent a clear message to "southern citizens" that the law would be executed. If nothing else, it was also an unequivocal warning to African Americans who would consider resisting its enforcement. Hamlet was returned under guard to Baltimore. Even before his departure, offers were made to purchase Hamlet's freedom, mainly by members of the recently formed Union Safety Committee. The committee, made up of leading merchants and bankers involved in the Southern trade, pledged to support the law and all other aspects of the Compromise. The editor of the *Journal of Commerce* launched his "own fund raising campaign." The collective effort quickly raised the $800 required, and John H. Woodgate, a city merchant, traveled to Baltimore to reclaim Hamlet.

A large open-air meeting of African Americans in early October welcomed Hamlet home to his family and friends. They, nonetheless, tried to distance themselves from the means used to procure his freedom. It was a triumph, William P. Powell, a proprietor of a boardinghouse for black seamen, argued, not of the "universal genius of emancipation, but the universal genius of the almighty dollar." It was, Charles B. Ray agreed, a "triumph of gold" and not a moral victory. There had long been and would continue to be deep divisions among antislavery allies about the merits and value of ransoming slaves, especially those who had already made their escape. The general opposition to such ransoms ran up against the support, in this case, of Hamlet, a decision that exposed the raw edges of those divisions. A lengthy editorial in the *Journal of Commerce* poured scorn on those who found such purchases morally and politically unpalatable: How many abolitionists – and by extension African Americans – the editor wondered, had contributed to the fund to ransom Hamlet? He did admit that the first contributor to the fund was Isaac Hollenbeck, an African American who worked on the Troy and Erie railroad. But as a supporter of abolitionism, Hollenbeck was, the editor remarked, the exception to the rule. While abolitionists were generally averse to purchasing the freedom of slaves, those such as the editor and other members of the committee had contributed, over the last five months, $3,900 to such purchases on the understanding that the emancipated would go to Liberia, the African colony set up by the American Colonization Society thirty years earlier. How then, he wondered, could those who acted in support of colonization be dismissed as proslavery? Abolitionists, on the other hand, were willing to throw good money after bad causes, such as the release from prison of William Chaplin, who had been caught aiding slaves to escape, knowing full well that Chaplin had no intention of returning South for his trial. Had that money gone into colonization efforts, many slaves would now be free. The time will come, the editor predicted, when "'things will be called by their right names.'" James Gordon Bennett at the New York *Herald* agreed: if blacks and abolitionists would commit to giving as much as they could, the estimated fifteen thousand fugitives slaves now in the North could be redeemed for the relatively paltry sum of $7.5 million. Doing so would redeem slaves "without robbing the owners of their legal rights."

In Hamlet's case, the alternative would have required a rescue attempt, something both editors feared would further sour the present political climate. Black New Yorkers were faced with a dilemma. While all at the open-air meeting rejoiced at Hamlet's return, they were deeply troubled by the decision, largely led by supporters of the law, to purchase Hamlet's freedom. At meetings before and after Hamlet's return, they had made their views of the law and those who enforced it abundantly clear. Robert Hamilton – who, with his brother, Thomas, would later become the owners of the *Weekly Anglo-African* – promised to strike dead anyone who laid hands on a "brother to throw him into bondage." George Downing, the proprietor of a popular café, vowed to live up to his responsibility as a father and husband to protect his children and wife: any "man – and fiend in human shape" who dared to cross the threshold of "his castle" would be sent to hell before he could accomplish his mission. And John H. Jacobs, a former North Carolina slave and the brother of Harriet Jacobs, called on his listeners to arm themselves: "If you have not swords...sell your garments and buy one." Follow-up meetings in Brooklyn and Williamsburg passed similar resolutions. It was exactly the sort of "commotion" the *Herald* had warned against. While blacks continued to protest against and resist enforcement of the law, the decision about the method of Hamlet's freedom was taken out of their hands by those who thought they saw a better way forward – one that recognized the rights of slaveholders, the freedom of slaves, and, most importantly of all, the prosperity of the Union as they knew it.[21]

Two months after Hamlet's return, Henry Long was arrested at the hotel where he worked. Long was claimed by John T. Smith of Russell County, Virginia, who had hired him out to William W. Parker, a Richmond doctor, from whom he escaped in December 1848. As far as Parker was concerned, Long had proved intransigent, insisting that he control to whom he should be hired. When Parker refused to accede to Long's demands, the slave declined to hand over the portion of the hire due to Parker. Why Parker would want to reclaim so troublesome a slave was never addressed. On this occasion, opponents of the law were out in force. Long was represented by Charles Whitehead, Joseph L. White, and John Jay. Lewis Tappan, the city's leading abolitionist, and Charles B. Ray were on hand for the hearing, as were a small group of blacks who gathered on the streets outside Commissioner Charles M. Hall's room. Whitehead persuaded the commissioner to grant a delay until the following day so witnesses could be summoned. When the hearing resumed, much of the time was taken up with a motion by defense counsel to move to a larger room so more could attend. Henry M. Western, Parker's lawyer, opposed moving, for it only encouraged what he called the "mawkish curiosity of the public." The commissioner rejected Whitehead's request. What followed established a pattern that would be replayed at subsequent hearings, here and elsewhere, throughout the decade. Defense lawyers called for a dismissal, claiming there was no legal evidence that Long was "held to labor in Virginia" or that John T. Smith ever owned him. Lawyers for the claimant countered by trying to introduce testimony that Long had admitted he was a slave in Richmond, a claim that was inadmissible, Jay argued, because slaves were not permitted to testify in Virginia courts. At this point, the defense produced a writ of habeas corpus returnable to Judge Betts of the state superior court. Western objected, but the commissioner ruled that he had no choice but to obey the writ and postpone the hearing.

At the habeas corpus hearing, Long's lawyers tried to undermine the principal legal foundation of the Fugitive Slave Law by questioning whether Commissioner Hall had been properly appointed. Under the law, they argued,

---

[21] New York *Tribune*, September 28, 30, October 1, 2, 14, 1850; New York *Herald*, September 28, October 1, 2, 6, 1850; Baltimore *Sun*, September 30, October 3, 8, 1850; *Journal of Commerce*, October 1, 4, 7, 1850; *National Anti-Slavery Standard*, October 10, 1850; Foner, *Gateway to Freedom*, 127; Don Papson and Tom Calarco, *Secrets of the Underground Railroad in New York City. Sydney Howard Gay, Louis Napoleon and the Record of the Fugitives* (Jefferson, NC: 2015), 75–77. For Chaplin see Mary Key Ricks, *Escape of the Pearl. The Heroic Bid for Freedom on the Underground Railroad* (New York: 2007) and Stanley Herrold, *Subversives: Anti-Slavery Community in Washington, D. C., 1828–1865* (Baton Rouge: 2003).

all commissioners had to be appointed by a court. Charles Hall, they pointed out, had not; he had simply moved over from his previous position as a clerk of court. In the midst of the dispute, someone from the marshal's office produced a certificate, the seal of which was still wet, showing that Hall had been appointed by a court. As it turned out, the case would be resolved by a higher court. As in the Hamlet case, the Union Safety Committee stepped in and hired George Wood for the claimant. Long's supporters countered by putting out an appeal for funds to defend him. They also brought in witnesses who claimed they had known Long before the date of his reputed escape. A "large body of colored people," among them a "number of females," were present inside and outside the court, even though it was a bitterly cold day. The authorities mustered a police force of two hundred to keep order. Betts, who was ill, was replaced by Judge Judson of the District Court of Connecticut, who put an end to the delays that had lasted almost three weeks by ruling in favor of the claimant.

As they had done at the end of Hamlet's case, "Union men" quickly raised $600 to ransom Long but the offer was rejected by his owner. Ransoms, he and others argued, only encouraged "further escape of slaves from the South." Following Long's return, William Parker published an announcement praising the Union Safety Committee for its support, which he calculated exceeded $500. They were also willing, he pointed out, to cover his cost, which amounted to an additional $300. The recently formed "Central Southern Rights Association" in Richmond worried that the sort of resistance to the law shown in Long's and Hamlet's cases would deter slave owners from pursuing fugitives in the future. While acknowledging the support of the Union Safety Committee, it doubted such assistance could aid in the recapture, according to its estimates, of the twenty thousand fugitives then living in the North. The association also called for a boycott of Northern newspapers and periodicals that described slavery as a sin. Parker and others thought they should make an example of Long, whose continued defiance surprised many. On their way south, the posse found a dirk knife on Long. When asked by a Richmond newspaperman if he was glad to be back in Virginia, Long replied: "Well, I often thought I would like to come back sometime, but I meant to come independently." Long was sold to David Clapton of Georgia for $750. Later, it was reported, he was jailed in Decatur, accused of stealing $65 and "making insurrectionary speeches to the negroes." Long seemed to have lived up to his reputation. One Rochester editor thought there was a lesson here for all slaveholders: "The return of half a dozen chaps [such as Long] might cool the ardor of our Southern friends in chasing runaways."[22]

[22] New York *Tribune*, December 24, 25, 28, 1850, January 1, 3, 9, 15, 31, 1851; New York *Herald*, January 9, 14, 1851; *National Anti-Slavery Standard*, January 2, 23, 1851; New York *Evening Post* (n.d.), in *Liberator*, January 31, 1851; Richmond *Whig* (n.d.), in *Liberator*, January 24, 1851; New York *Independent*, January 23, 1851; Atlanta *Intelligencer*, August 2, 1851, and

The arrest of Horace Preston in April 1852 showed a remarkable level of collusion between the owner, city police officers, and the lawyer for the claimant. The twenty-six-year-old Preston had escaped in March 1847 and settled in Williamsburg, where he married and started a family. He was arrested by Officer James Martin on the trumped-up charge of stealing a watch and money. Once in custody, the larceny charge was replaced by what the editor of the *Tribune* called another sort of theft, that of Preston's freedom. Soon after taking him into custody, Martin sent word to William Reese, Preston's Baltimore master. Richard Busteed, a young Irish-born lawyer and an acquaintance of Reese, swore out an arrest warrant before Commissioner George Morton and agreed to act as the owner's counsel. Preston was held in secret, so much so that his lawyer, E. D. Culver, had difficulty finding him. John Jay later joined Culver in Preston's defense. Reese's son testified that he had known Preston for thirteen years and that they had lived in the same house in Baltimore. Under cross examination he admitted that Martin had contacted his father and they had agreed to a fee for Martin's assistance in capturing Preston. Jay requested a subpoena so Martin could be forced to testify about the grounds on which he had arrested Preston. Although the subpoena was granted, the marshal refused to serve it. When Jay insisted Morton enforce the order, the commissioner refused, claiming he had no power to order the presence of witnesses; he was there solely, he responded, to determine if "the testimony is sufficient to satisfy him."

On the second day of the hearing, Jay took the unusual step of calling Busteed to the stand because he had admitted drawing up the affidavit that led to Preston's arrest. Busteed admitted that he knew Reese and that they had visited one another's homes. It was on one of these visits that he came to know Reese owned Preston. Busteed also admitted that he knew Reese had many relatives in New York City. As the exchanges between the two grew increasingly testy, Busteed refused to answer any more of Jay's questions. Jay demanded that Morton compel Busteed to answer his questions because they were pertinent to the case and because Busteed had perjured himself in the affidavit. Without warning, Busteed rose from his chair, walked over to Jay, and punched him in the face. Stunned, Commissioner Morton suspended the proceedings and promptly left the room. Moments later, Judge Betts, who had been temporarily involved in Henry Long's case, entered the room, took Morton's place on the bench and threatened to jail both counsels. Both Jay and Busteed requested Betts take over the case, as Morton had admitted that he was powerless to force witnesses to answer questions. Betts declined on the grounds that, since the Long decision, his case load had been assumed by Judson. Commissioner Morton later resumed his position, but the testy exchanges continued. Busteed did apologize for striking Jay and Jay in turn conceded that he may have been

Atlanta *Republican* (n.d.), both in Boston *Herald*, August 6, 1851; Rochester *Democrat*, August 8, 1851; Foner, *Gateway to Freedom*, 130–32.

a trifle overzealous in his questioning. But Busteed continued to give evasive answers to Jay's questions. While he admitted that Reese had visited him at home, he could not recall the nature of any of their conversations, nor would he say how he came to know Preston was Reese's slave because, he responded, the question was "asked from bad motives." No one, Busteed declared, but "dishonest, corrupt persons would suppose that [he] made the affidavit from improper motives."

As a result of the apparent but unproven collusion between Reese, Busteed, and Martin, Jay called on Morton to strike the affidavit and dismiss the case. He also pointed to the requirement of Section 6 of the Fugitive Slave Law, which required proof that the accused was owned by the claimant. The only such proof, Jay pointed out, was contained in the faulty affidavit. There was no evidence that Preston or his mother was ever a slave. There claimed to be a bill of sale, Jay observed, but it was never produced. In response, Busteed employed an unusual analogy: as a "man having the accent of an Irishman was held to be an Irishman," so, too, the presumption was that a black man in a slave state was a slave. In both cases the burden of proof, he reasoned, was on the individual to prove he was not who everyone logically assumed he was. Given the large free black population in Maryland, the analogy seemed ill-advised and inappropriate. How, Jay wondered, was such proof to be obtained if, under the law, the accused was not permitted to testify? Morton ruled in favor of the slave owner because, he explained, the defense had provided no witnesses. Consequently, he had no alternative but to base his decision on the testimony of Reese's son and Busteed's affidavit. Preston was taken from the hearing room flanked by US Marshal Henry F. Tallmadge, his two sons, both deputy marshals, and two other deputies and placed in a covered wagon. Crowds of blacks and whites rushed around saying their goodbyes. An elderly black woman shouted at Preston: "God'll punish 'em."

These were, the *Tribune* was forced to admit, the most "extraordinary proceedings." How, it wondered, could a case where "liberty was concerned" be decided "without hearing the testimony in favor of liberty"? But the editor surely knew that the law was enacted not to prove the "liberty" of the accused, only the "rights" of the claimant. Commissioner Morton's decision, however, did not bring closure to the case. In a letter to the *Tribune,* Busteed claimed that he only heard of Preston's arrest after it had occurred and had not contacted Reese to let him know where to find his slave. The editor responded with a scathing editorial that poured scorn on Busteed's explanation. When, in 1849, Busteed was nominated for alderman by the Free-Soil Party, he came out firmly in opposition to the extension of slavery, expressed support for the Wilmot Proviso, openly condemned slavery, and pointed out that his father, who owned slaves on the island of St. Lucia, had freed them before the 1833 law abolishing slavery in the West Indies. Busteed, it seemed, had betrayed his own antislavery credentials as well as those of his father. The editor also called on the mayor and the chief of police to conduct an inquiry into Martin's arrest

of Preston, especially when it became known, days later, that Martin happened
to be in Baltimore the day of Preston's arrival and had collected $50 for his
part in the fugitive's arrest. He called on all those opposed to the notion that
"kidnapping was essential to the preservation of the Union" to meet to express
their abhorrence of the decision. His opponent at the *Herald* dismissed these
calls as the product of the fevered brain of the editor of a "Fourier abolition organ." Should any of these suggestions be followed, the *Herald* warned,
"friends of law and order and the good faith of the South [must] counteract
this incendiary experiment." Tensions were defused within days of Preston's
return when Reese offered to sell him for $1,500. Busteed claimed that it was
he who had suggested and arranged the purchase and the return of Preston
to New York City. Among those contributing were Erasmus Culver, Preston's
wife, and Richard S. Emmet, who had joined Preston's defense team when
Culver was called away on another case.[23]

The ransom of two returnees and the failure to buy a third in less than two
years troubled some Southern observers. The editor of the Mobile *Tribune*
spoke for many opposed to what was considered an unnecessary and dangerous concession: allowing the purchase of fugitives once they were caught and
returned. The "moral effects" of such purchases were damaging and sprang
from a "motive which down here [was] not considered sound or estimable,"
for it induced "observing men to believe that there [was] great friendship for
Southern institutions in New York." There was, the editor observed, general
opposition in other Free States to any form of restitution for slave owners,
including the payment of ransoms. New York City, on the other hand, had
adopted this approach simply "for a mercantile purpose." The unintended consequence of such purchases, however, was a growing revulsion in the North to
the Fugitive Slave Law, not reconciliation between the sections. Contributors
to these funds proceeded from the "presumption that both Slavery and the law
[were] evil." But, because returning escaped slaves was the law, such payments
were the price opponents were reluctantly willing to pay, the editor concluded,
as a way to evade and nullify the law. The Virginia Central Southern Rights
Association, as we have seen, concurred wholeheartedly with this assessment
and, at least in the case of Henry Long, demanded that he be sold out of state
as an example to other slaves, as a way to protect the slave population from
the inculcation of false notions of freedom and liberty, and as a clear message
to opponents that slaveholders would no longer collude in the destruction of
the system by accepting what many considered bribes. Many opponents of the
law were also averse to such payments, but for diametrically different reasons.
Horace Greeley at the New York *Tribune*, who reprinted the Mobile editor's

---

[23] New York *Tribune*, April 1, 2, 3, 5, 6, 7, 12, May 25, 1852; New York *Herald*, April 2, 3, 9,
    1852; Baltimore *Sun*, April 5, 1852; Rochester *American*, April 4, 1852; *National Anti-Slavery
    Standard*, April 15, 1852; Foner, *Gateway to Freedom*, 133–34.

reactions, dismissed ransoms as "sin offerings" for those whom slaveholders helped to "consign to perpetual bondage."[24]

That is precisely the dilemma abolitionists of all stripes faced when confronted with the reality of a fugitive's imminent return to slavery. Defeated by a law they considered unjust, ransoming the returnee was sometimes the only alternative option. If the owner was partial or anxious to accept such ransoms, the chances of gaining the fugitive's freedom were greatly enhanced. When, on the other hand, owners such as Long's, who wished to make an example of an intransigent slave, closed the door on negotiations, such purchases failed. Where they thought it unavoidable, abolitionists in New York City and elsewhere continued to pursue this line. When, in 1854, Rev. J. W. C. Pennington's brother Stephen Pembroke and his two nephews, Robert and Jacob, who had escaped from Maryland, were retaken in New York City, the black community and their white supporters rallied around a distraught Pennington and raised almost $1,400 to ransom Stephen. But the owner of Robert and Jacob would not consider a similar offer and sold the brothers to a North Carolina lumber merchant soon after their return to Baltimore.

The following summer, Ann Maria Weems, a young Maryland slave, arrived in New York City dressed as a boy. Charles Ray recalled entering his home to find "sitting on the sofa at my house, a little boy about ten years old in appearance, and looking rather feminine. I knew at once who it was, that it was Ann Maria." For some time, a coalition linking Washington, DC, Philadelphia, and New York City abolitionists had been working with John Weems, Ann Maria's father, to purchase his wife and seven children from different Maryland slaveholders. Their efforts were complicated by the plans of some of the slaveholders to sell members of the family further south. On a tour of the North, John Weems had contacted Ray asking for his assistance in raising the necessary funds. Ray, in turn, made contact with Rev. Henry Highland Garnet, who was then in England, asking Garnet to appeal to British abolitionists for support. Garnet and his family had taken along with them Stella Weems, Ann Maria's older sister, who had escaped earlier and had been living with the Garnets in upstate New York. Garnet, who, in 1849, had been invited by proponents of the Free Produce Association to help revive the movement in Britain, was about to leave to head up the United Presbyterian Church of Scotland's missionary station in Sterling, Jamaica. Before leaving, Garnet appealed to his contacts Henry and Anna Richardson of Newcastle, leading proponents of the movement. In the end, the Weems Fund would raise more than $5,000 towards the purchase of family members. But those who supported John Weems's effort had balked at the asking price for the young Ann Maria, and instead devised a plan of escape. Dressed as a boy, the fifteen-year-old met an agent of the UGRR at the gates of the White House. They traveled by carriage, she as the driver, to

---

[24] New York *Tribune*, May 6, 1852.

the outskirts of the city. They later went on to Philadelphia, where they were assisted by William Still, who sent them on to New York City. Those such as Jacob Bigelow in Washington, DC, William Still in Philadelphia, and Charles Ray and Lewis Tappan in New York City, driving forces in what slaveholders considered a movement to entice their slaves to escape, were willing to entertain simultaneously absconding and purchasing slaves. Anna Richardson spoke for many about what she considered the "principle" that motivated such purchases. Although they all abhorred giving money to "bad men for the freedom of the bodies and souls of our fellow-creatures," she wrote Charles Ray as the negotiations to purchase the Weems came to a head, "this feeling has been overpowered by the stronger necessity of doing as we would be done by, under similar circumstances." It was, she insisted, at "least as Christian an act to give money to set people free from bondage, as it is to give it to the same slave-holders for the purchase of slave-grown produce."[25]

Many balked at Anna Richardson's reasoning. Such purchases – or ransoms – they argued, did not rise to the level of a "principle." Neither did they support the free produce movement, which they considered marginal to the larger political struggle against slavery. But such differences were usually muted when it came to helping fugitive slaves reach safety or when there seemed to be no other available option. Although not a typical fugitive slave case, the contentious dispute over the Lemmon slaves would last almost the entire decade. Jonathan Lemmon, his family, and eight slaves arrived in New York City from Norfolk, Virginia, in November 1852 on their way to Texas, where the Lemmons planned to resettle. Soon after the ship docked, its clerk went on shore to hire carriages to transfer the group to the ship bound for their new home. Instead, they were taken to a house where they spent the night, by which time the ship that was to carry them to Texas had sailed. It is not clear why the clerk took this detour rather than going directly to the ship. One city newspaper suggested that the carriage drivers had acted in concert with abolitionists, who bribed them to take the group to the house rather than the dock. It seems likely that the detour was taken under the guidance of Louis Napoleon, a freedman and a close associate of Sydney Howard Gay, a leading figure in the UGRR and editor of the *National Anti-Slavery Standard,* whose office was a major stop for fugitives who arrived in the city. The ship's black steward very likely was the one who informed Napoleon and others of the slaves' arrival. Napoleon, who could not write, swore out a writ of habeas corpus. The eight – Emeline, twenty-three; her two brothers, Lewis and Edward; her daughter, two-year-old Amanda; and Nancy, twenty; and her children,

[25] On the Pembroke family see Blackett, *Beating Against the Barriers*, 57–59; Florence T. Ray, *Sketch of the Life of Charles B. Ray* (New York: 1887), 41–45. My thanks to Eric Foner for a copy of the Ray memorial. For the Weems escape see Stanley Harrold, *Subversives. Antislavery Community in Washington, DC, 1828–1865* (Baton Rouge: 2003), 203–24; Bryan Prince, *A Shadow on the Household* (Toronto: 2009) is a history of the family.

two-year-old Ann; and her seven-year-old twins, Lewis and Edward – were brought before Superior Court Judge Elijah Paine. E. D. Culver and John Jay, assisted by Chester Arthur, the future president of the United States, appeared for the slaves. They argued that the eight were free and had been kidnapped with the intention of selling them into slavery. Culver called for their discharge on the grounds that they were brought into the state in contravention of an 1841 state law that repealed an earlier law allowing slave holders in transit through the state to keep their slaves for up to nine months. Jonathan Lemmon claimed that the eight were owned by his wife, Juliet, who was on her way to Texas to settle permanently. His counsel insisted that the family had a constitutional right to pass through the state for, under the principle of comity, the laws of one state had to be respected in all other states. Jay reached back to the eighteenth-century ruling in the Somerset case to show that the issue had been long settled as a common-law principle in Anglo-American jurisprudence; once brought into a Free State voluntarily, a slave could not be forced to return to slavery. The large number of black men and women who packed the courtroom was delighted with Judge Paine's decision to free the eight based on the 1841 state law. It was the first opportunity, Paul Finkleman writes, that a New York court had to interpret the twenty-year-old law. The New York State Vigilance Committee organized a public celebration at Pennington's church. The group left soon after for the black settlement in Buxton, Canada, accompanied by Richard Johnson, Nancy's brother, who had earlier escaped and settled in Cleveland, Ohio.

Opponents were quick to denounce Paine's decision. The 1841 state law, one insisted, conflicted with the "federal compact," violated the spirit of the Constitution, and was "at war with the object and interest of the federal Union." If it were true, a Richmond editor agreed, that "the inhabitants of one State had not the right to pass with their property through the territory of another, without forfeiting it, then the Union no longer exists." The work of the separation of the states, James Gordon Bennett at the *Herald* declared, had effectively begun. One New York City newspaper predicted that the ruling would be successfully appealed and another called for the repeal of the 1841 law. Virginia Governor John Johnson, in a note to the legislature, maintained that the ruling conflicted with previous decisions, was unprecedented, and violated the "rights and interests" of Virginia's citizens. If it were sustained it would put paid to the principle of comity. Horace Greeley at the *Tribune* did not mince his words in response to Johnson; the case was simple and easily understood. No one but "a natural born fool (or someone made so by being educated to the profession of the law) [could] fail to see the perfect justice and propriety of Judge Paine's decision." The following year, the Virginia legislature provided funds to appeal Paine's decision in the hope of establishing the "legal right to transport slaves through free states."

Soon after the eight were discharged, there were calls for the indemnification of the Lemmons for the loss of their property worth an estimated $5,000.

Why, the editor of the *Tribune* asked, should the slaveholder be indemnified? It was the slaves who had long suffered grave personal losses. In an interview, Nancy had responded emphatically that she had been mistreated and her husband sold away from her three years earlier. Lemmon dismissed these claims as totally unfounded; neither he nor his wife had ever sold a slave. The editor was willing to grant Lemmon the benefit of the doubt, but then asked him to explain the absence of the "husbands and fathers of your late slave women and children." The question was meant to reiterate an old abolitionist criticism of the slave system, in which slaveholders had the power to (and frequently did) separate slave families. Such criticisms aimed to pull the moral rug from under the appeal for indemnification. In fact, Greeley initiated a counter appeal in an effort to raise $1,000 to aid the eight. In spite of the opposition, the indemnification appeal raised $5,240, mainly from city merchants. While not directly criticizing the fund, the editor of the *Times* wondered if the merchants would consider a comparable fund to aid the city's poor in the upcoming winter. Not surprisingly, the *Tribune* was deeply skeptical of the merits of the indemnification fund; there was, he thought, no difference between paying to indemnify Lemmon and participating in a slave sale. Given existing market prices and the cost the Lemmons incurred getting from Virginia to New York City, he calculated that, by the indemnity, the slaveholders had made a handsome profit of $1,800. An Albany editor even suggested that Lemmon may have come to New York on what he called "speculation," anticipating that his slaves would be taken and that he would be generously compensated. The editor also wondered why Lemmon had not gone on to Texas as he had planned but instead pocketed the money and returned to Richmond.[26]

Within weeks of Paine's decision, Democrats in the New York Assembly submitted resolutions calling for repeal of the 1841 law and recognizing the right of slaveholders to transit the state with their property on the grounds that such rights were the foundations of the principle of comity that demanded "full faith and credit be given by each of the public laws, local laws and municipal regulations of its sister States." Nothing came of these attempts to repeal the law. In fact, by the end of the decade, as Paine's decision moved slowly through appeal courts, the state would adopt a more stringent personal liberty law that, by further limiting a slaveholder's right to reclaim his slave, helped to curtail

---

[26] New York *Tribune*, November 8, 9, 10, 15, 19, 20, 22, 23, December 1, 24, 1852, January 25, 1853; New York *Times*, November 10, 11, 15, 22, December 19, 24, 1852; *National Era*, November 25, 1852; Washington, DC, *Union* (n.d.), in *Liberator*, December 3, 1852; Albany *Journal*, November 23, 24, December 1, 1852; *Journal of Commerce* (n.d.), in *Liberator*, December 3, 1852, and in Rochester *Democrat*, November 17, December 25, 1852; New York *Herald* (n.d.), in Rochester *Democrat*, November 17, 1852; Foner, *Gateway to Freedom*, 140–42; Papson and Calarco, *Secret Lives of the Underground Railroad in New York City*, 83, 86–87; Paul Finkelman, *An Imperfect Union, Slavery, Federalism, and Comity* (Chapel Hill, NC: 1981), 297–99; Paul Finkelman, "The Protection of Black Rights in Seward's New York," *Civil War History*, XXXIV, No. 3 (1988), 212.

the effectiveness of the Fugitive Slave Law. The Virginia Assembly's appeal against the Lemmon decision was finally heard by the New York Supreme Court in October 1857, only days after the ruling in the Dred Scott case, in which the Supreme Court of the United States effectively declared that blacks were not, nor could they ever be, citizens. The state supreme court upheld Paine's decision with one dissent. Comity, it asserted, "does not require any state to expand any greater privilege to the citizens of another state than it grants to its own. As this state does not allow its own citizens to bring a slave here, *in transitu,* and to hold him as a slave for any portion of time, it cannot be expected to allow the citizens of another state to do so." The Supreme Court's ruling was upheld by the state's highest court, the New York Court of Appeals, in 1860 in a 5-3 decision.[27]

Although not legally a fugitive slave case, the emancipation of the Lemmon slaves by Judge Paine in November 1852 was followed by four years of relative calm, during which few cases were considered by the courts or commissioners. In May 1853, Rose Cooper of New Orleans, described by abolitionists as a prostitute, traveled to Cincinnati with twelve-year-old Jane Trainer, the daughter of Emma, a slave of Cooper's, and Charles Trainer, a free black carpenter whose efforts to buy his daughter had been rejected by Cooper. Evidently, Cooper was on her way to settle in California. Charles Trainer followed the two to Cincinnati. Soon after his arrival, Cooper left for New York City. Friends in Cincinnati wired Lewis Tappan, alerting him to Cooper's arrival. Charles Trainer followed. Under instructions from Tappan, Jacob R. Gibbs, a former Maryland slave who had purchased his freedom and who for years had aided slaves' escapes from Baltimore before moving to New York City, located Cooper and the girl. Tappan and Louis Napoleon swore out an affidavit with the police, who arrested Cooper. Before the case could be heard, Charles Trainer was beaten by unknown assailants. As a result, he thought it best to leave the city for the relative safety of Buffalo. He told Tappan, who was also threatened, that he would not return unless he could be guaranteed protection. The first case ended disappointingly; Judge Duer ruled that he had no authority to adjudicate the case. E. D. Culver, however, persuaded Judge Seward Barculo of Brooklyn to take up the case. At the hearing, Cooper claimed that Jane was the "illegitimate" child of one of her slaves, that she became free once she arrived in Cincinnati, and she was traveling voluntarily with her to California. Barculo ruled in favor of the father on the grounds that Charles and his wife had constituted what in New York would be considered a "common-law marriage," that, following the Lemmon ruling, Cooper had no claim to the slave once

[27] Oswego *Journal,* January 12, 1853; Rochester *Democrat,* January 8, 1853; *Journal of the Assembly of the State of New York at their Seventy-Sixth Session,* Vols. I & II (Albany, NY: 1853), 46; the Supreme Court decision is quoted in Finkelman, *An Imperfect Union,* 302; Foner, *Gateway to Freedom,* 141–42; William A. Link, *Roots of Secession. Slavery and Politics in Antebellum Virginia* (Chapel Hill, NC: 2003), 108–09.

she brought her to New York, that as a young child Jane did not have enough powers of discretion to decide where she should go, and, finally, that a house of "ill fame" was no place to raise a child. The rights of slave parents, Barculo seemed to be saying, were superior to the claims of slaveholders, an assertion that flew in the face of legal precedent. Soon after Jane's release, Rev. J. W. C. Pennington headed a list of subscribers, including Lewis Tappan and E. D. Culver, who raised $700 to purchase Jane's mother. Emma was reunited with her child and husband at a public meeting in Pennington's church six months later. A collection was also taken up to aid the family. Tappan spoke for many in the audience who believed, like Anna Richardson did, that such purchases followed the principles of a new golden rule: what slaveholders separated, abolitionists reunited.[28]

In spite of such successes, Pennington would come to know, if he did not know already, that the city remained a dangerous place for fugitives. The capture and return of his brother Stephen and his two nephews six months after the reunion of the Trainers was a devastating blow. Pennington took it personally; the joy of seeing his brothers after seventeen years had led him to drop his guard. Many were forgiving, but not William Still in Philadelphia, who recognized that such lapses endangered the effective operations of the UGRR. In the following months, Still shied away from sending his charges to New York City, choosing instead what he considered safer locations. Still's decision may, in part, help to explain why, in early 1855, Pennington felt it necessary to issue a report on conditions facing blacks in the city following the capture of the Pembrokes. He was still smarting under the criticism about the lapse in security. He wrote the New York *Tribune* about a recent incident in which two African Americans working on a pilot boat were approached on the wharf by two men in plain clothes who claimed to be police officers and who demanded that the two black men accompany them to the police station. The black men had their wits about them and refused unless they were shown a warrant. Subsequently, two policemen in uniform made a similar request. On this occasion, the two men went along, accompanied by two friends. Remembering the way his family was bundled off to a secret location, Pennington reminded his readers that arrests for serious crimes had to be accompanied by a warrant. "It is certainly not safe in these times," he warned, for "a colored man to be led into a place surrounded by so many grates and bars without the protection of a legal warrant."[29]

[28] New York *Tribune*, May 10, 11, 31, June 14, 1853, January 10, 1854; New York *Herald*, May 11, 14, 19, 1853; New York *Times*, June 10, 1853; *National Anti-Slavery Standard*, May 28, June 18, 1853; *Frederick Douglass' Paper*, August 5, 1853; *Journal of Commerce* (n.d.), in Rochester *American*, May 12, 1853; American and Foreign Anti-Slavery Society, *Annual Report* (New York: 1853), 197–207; *Fugitive Slave Law and Its Victims* (New York: 1861), 25–26; Foner, *Gateway to Freedom*, 138–39; Papson and Calarco, *Secret Lives of the Underground Railroad in New York City*, 132.
[29] New York *Tribune*, March 6, 1855.

Pennington's account suggests that he and members of the vigilance committees had learned a lesson from the failure to protect the Pembrokes. Not only were there no other fugitives taken between the summer of 1854 and December 1857, but there were frequent reports of a regular flow of fugitives through the city. Husbands, the observer reported, were usually followed by their wives soon after. Someone familiar with the operations of the vigilance committees spoke of weekly arrivals averaging eight in late 1855. They were supported by a number of vigilance committees. The earliest, the New York State Vigilance Committee, was established in 1848, the successor to David Ruggles's committee, formed thirteen years earlier. It was closely associated with the American and Foreign Anti-Slavery Society, which was formed in the wake of the split in the American Anti-Slavery Society in 1840 over the issue of the proper role of women in the organization and abolitionists' participation in electoral politics. It was led by Lewis Tappan and drew the support of a number of prominent African Americans, including Charles Ray and Pennington. The Committee of Thirteen was established by African Americans in 1850 specifically to aid James Hamlet. A number of its members, including Dr. James McCune Smith, George Downing, and Philip A. Bell, were veterans of the 1835 committee. Two smaller committees were formed in Brooklyn and Williamsburg. These were joined by another committee headed by Sydney Howard Gay. For two years, beginning in 1855, Gay, like William Still in Philadelphia, kept an account of those he assisted, the *Record of Fugitives.* Gay worked closely with Louis Napoleon, whom he employed as a porter in the *Standard's* office. Together these organizations protected escapees passing through the city and got them safely to areas further north and to Canada. The authorities did manage, on a number of occasions, to disrupt the work of the committees by capturing and returning escapees. As we have seen, when they did, the committees reverted to legal challenges and when those failed, to ransoming the slaves. But the lull in returning fugitives in a city under the control of the Democratic Party, a staunch defender of the Fugitive Slave Law, coincided with the two years during which Gay kept the *Record.* It also reflected the tightening of the committees' operations, and more importantly, a greater level of cooperation between the various vigilance committees in spite of their continued ideological differences. When, in May 1860, Allan Graff and Josiah Hoy, two fugitives from Frederick, Maryland, who were sent on by William Still, were retaken and returned because of a breakdown in communications between the committees in the two cities, William H. Leonard, a black printer at the *Standard,* could claim with confidence that it was "the first case in over six years I have been actively engaged in the business I have failed to receive and safely dispose of and I sincerely hope it may be the last."[30]

[30] New York *Tribune,* March 17, 27, December 30, 1851, January 9, 1852, November 30, 1855; for a history of the vigilance committees see Foner, *Gateway to Freedom,* 98–99, 166, and Papson and Calarco, *Secret Lives of the Underground Railroad in New York City,* 77–78, 81.

The *Record of Fugitives* is made up of two books covering the period from January 1855 to November 1856. It contains 226 entries, 135 of them sent on by William Still. Nearly half of those who made contact with Gay came from Maryland and Delaware. There were fifty-six from Virginia and nineteen from North Carolina. Three from Kentucky and two each from South Carolina and Georgia also made it to Gay's office. Gay interviewed each arrival, recording the reasons for their leaving, details of their flight, the names of their owners, those who assisted them, and how much he spent to send them on to another location further north.[31] Among other things, the *Record* provides interesting additional details on those who escaped from the central region and Eastern Shore of Maryland, some of which were discussed in the previous two chapters. In the three months between October and December 1855, for example, twenty, most of them traveling in groups, made contact with Gay. Sam Turner and Wesley James, with seven others, including two women, traveled first to Wilmington, Delaware, then on to New York City via Newtown, Pennsylvania, the first week of October. Three weeks later Harriet Shepherd, her five children, ages three to seventeen, accompanied by her brother, John Bright, his wife, and two other men, left in a carriage drawn by two horses. They headed for Wilmington, Delaware, where they made contact with Thomas Garrett, the driving force in the UGRR in that city. Garrett persuaded the group to abandon the carriage and horses, anticipating slave catchers would follow the carriage. Garrett sent them to Chester County, Pennsylvania. The group finally made their way to Still in Philadelphia, who forwarded them to Gay. John T. Jones and Washington Bradley had planned to escape together, but in the end left separately, going to Garrett in Wilmington, then to Gay, who recorded their arrival in early December. The longest of Gay's entries records the arrival of Harriet Tubman in May 1856 with a group of four valued at $6,000. The vast majority of those Gay received were forwarded to Jermain Loguen in Syracuse. Others were sent to Albany, Boston, and New Bedford.[32]

Beyond the 226 aided by Gay, it is next to impossible to determine with any certainty how many fugitives passed through New York City in the two years during which Gay recorded their arrivals. As in the case of Philadelphia and other major hubs of the UGRR, the evidence suggests that not all slaves made contact with the vigilance committees. In addition, there are no comparable

On the Gaff and Hoy case see New York *Herald*, May 2, 1860; New York *Tribune*, May 2, 1860; the Leonard quote is in Foner, *Gateway to Freedom*, 213.

[31] The breakdown relies on Foner, *Gateway to Freedom*, 194–95, and Papson and Calarco, *Secret Lives of the Underground Railroad in New York City*.

[32] Record of Fugitives, Box 75, Sydney Howard Gay Papers, Columbia University, http://exhibitions.cul.columbia.edu/exhibits/show/fugitives/records_fugitives/transcription. Foner had these records transcribed and placed on the web. Papson and Calarco, *Secret Lives of the Underground Railroad in New York City*, 140–43, 178–80, and Appendix I.

figures for the city's other vigilance committees. Papson and Calarco estimate collectively that they aided five hundred each year or five thousand over the period of the fifties. Foner, on the other hand, is a little less precise, estimating that "over 1,000 fugitives passed through" the city during the decade. When we factor in the numbers who passed through Philadelphia and were sent on to New York City and other locations it becomes even more difficult to calculate the actual flow of fugitive slaves from the eastern slave states. As we have seen, supporters in upstate New York frequently published figures of the numbers they assisted to either settle among them or to go on to Canada. Whether it was Jermain Loguen in Syracuse or Stephen Myers in Albany, it seems likely that their estimates included some of those accounted for in crucial way stations such as Philadelphia and New York City. When, in March 1855, Frederick Douglass reported that the New York State Vigilance Committee had aided somewhere between three hundred and four hundred fugitives to reach Canada during the previous year, it is not clear how many of those were already accounted for by other stations along the way. What mattered, at least to slaveholders in Maryland and elsewhere, was not so much the aggregate number of escapes, although that was undoubtedly important, but the regularity of and unexplained peaks in escapes, and the fact that, over the years, they increasingly came to involve groups of the discontented. Group escapes also suggested a level of planning and coordination that raised the levels of anxiety among slaveholders, who in Maryland, Missouri, Kentucky, and other locations that experienced such loses, organized public meetings to pressure state governments to intercede. But they also went a step further by organizing associations to protect their interests, and by prosecuting those – whites, free blacks, and slaves – who they suspected were involved in plots to undermine the system.[33]

Their worst fears were confirmed on October 16, 1859, when John Brown, at the head of a group of nineteen, including fourteen whites and five blacks, invaded the town of Harpers Ferry and took control of the armory, arsenal, and other federal buildings. Three residents of the town were killed during the raid. Brown took about fifty slaves, issued an emancipation proclamation and armed anyone who seemed willing to join the cause. Brown and his men held out for thirty hours until the arrival of Col. Robert E. Lee, at the head of a company of United States troops who quickly retook the town. Three of the invaders were killed and Brown was seriously wounded. Fearing that he would die from his wounds and become a martyr, Brown was hurried off to Charlestown ten miles away, tried as he laid wounded on a cot, convicted, and executed on December 2, 1859.

Over the years, Brown had gathered around him a group of supporters, including such prominent figures as Gerrit Smith, Joshua Giddings, Samuel

[33] Papson and Calarco, *Secret Lives of the Underground Railroad in New York City,* 102; Foner, *Gateway to Freedom,* 150.

G. Howe, and Frederick Douglass, all of whom came under suspicion for aiding and abetting the attack. Douglass had first met Brown in 1847 in Springfield, Massachusetts, where Brown then lived. They did not agree on the best means to confront slavery. Brown insisted that neither moral suasion nor political involvement, the two principal approaches adopted by abolitionists, would bring about an end to slavery. What was needed, he told Douglass, was a direct assault on slavery. He planned to set up camp with an armed force of about twenty-five men in the Allegheny Mountains and, following the methods employed by maroon slaves in Jamaica or Surinam, run off "the slaves in large numbers, retain the brave and strong ones in the mountains, and send the weak and timid North by the underground railroad." Such an approach was necessary, Brown insisted, because slaveholders "would never be induced to give up their slaves until they felt a big stick about their heads." Douglass failed to convince Brown about the shortcomings of his plans but left deeply impressed with his commitment to the destruction of slavery.

Over the years, the two kept in regular contact. During the crisis over the Kansas Territory, when Brown came east to raise money and buy arms and supplies to confront slaveholders in the disputed territory, he spent nights at Douglass' home in Rochester, where they continued to debate the merits of his plan. On the verge of putting his plans into operation, Brown summoned Douglass to a meeting in Chambersburg, Pennsylvania, in August 1859 in a last-ditch attempt to get him to join in the attack. Douglass brought along Shields Green, a fugitive from Charleston, South Carolina, who had been living with him in Rochester since his escape. Green had met Brown during one of his visits to Rochester and committed himself to the cause. It was at the meeting at the stone quarry in Chambersburg that Douglass first learned of Brown's new plan to seize the town, occupy the federal armory, and hold prominent citizens hostage. Brown would not be moved in spite of Douglass' warnings that the plan of attack was doomed to fail. As they parted, Brown pleaded with Douglass to join him. He had a special role for Douglass, he told his old friend. "When I strike the bees will begin to swarm," Brown predicted, "and I shall want you to help hive them."

Following the failed attack, there was what Douglass called a "scream for vengeance." Anyone remotely associated with Brown had to be hunted down and brought to trial. A carpetbag full of letters was found on Brown, implicating Douglass and others in the attack. Word of the attack reached Douglass while he was lecturing in Philadelphia. The telegraph and newspapers announced that all those associated with the attack were to be arrested. Douglass slipped out of Philadelphia with the aid of friends and headed first for New York City, then Hoboken, New Jersey, which he left at night in a "private conveyance" for Paterson. He boarded a train at Paterson bound for Rochester. But even in the city he had called home for many years, a city from which no fugitive slave had been taken, Douglass was vulnerable. Although he had taken the precaution to get his son Lewis to secure all the papers in his desk, by the time he arrived in Rochester it was clear that Governor Henry Wise of Virginia had contacted President James Buchanan seeking Douglass' arrest for "murder, robbery, and inciting servile insurrection." In was rumored that several United States marshals were on their way to Rochester. Douglass must have recalled the night eight years earlier when he and Julia Griffiths had helped William Parker and his two companions evade federal officers following the shoot-out at Christiana by hurrying them to Canada. He followed a similar route, he said, to keep "out of the way of those gentlemanly United States marshals." He sailed from Montreal to England, where he remained until the death of his youngest child persuaded him to throw caution to the wind and return the following spring.

Before leaving Canada, Douglass wrote a letter to a Rochester newspaper in which he rejected claims by one of Brown's men that he had endorsed and encouraged Brown to attack Harpers Ferry. In fact, he had done all in his power to dissuade Brown from the course of action he had long contemplated. Although he knew of Brown's plans and was convinced they were ill advised, he would not stoop to be a critic or an informer. "If anybody is disposed to think less of me" because he opposed Brown's plans, Douglass later recalled, "or because I may have had a knowledge of what was about to occur, and did not assume the base and detestable character of an informer, he is a man whose good or bad opinion of me may be equally repugnant and despicable." Of one thing he was sure, the right hand of the "old hero" had shaken the foundations of the country to its core. His ghost, he predicted will "haunt the bedchambers of all the born and unborn slaveholders of Virginia through all their generations, filling them with alarm and consternation." It was an association of which he was proud. As Jermain Loguen had done when he fled to Canada following the Jerry rescue, Douglass declared his willingness to return to face an "impartial jury" but, as he said, he had "quite insuperable objections to being caught by the hounds of Mr. Buchanan, and 'bagged' by Gov. Wise." Like William Parker, the former fugitive from labor had been transformed by another major political event involving slavery into a fugitive from justice. The editor of the New York *Herald* relished the irony: "Having some experiences in his early life of the pleasures of Southern society," Douglass had "no desire to trust himself again even on the borders of the Potomac." In a final ironic twist, Douglass' return to Rochester coincided with the opening of an inquiry by the United States Senate into events at Harpers Ferry, headed by James Mason, the author of the Fugitive Slave Law.[34]

---

[34] Tony Horwitz, *Midnight Rising. John Brown and the Raid that Sparked the Civil War* (New York: 2011), 114–15; Douglass, *Life and Times of Frederick Douglass*, 270–75, 302–13; the *Herald* quotation taken from Benjamin Quarles, *Frederick Douglass* (1948, rpr., New York: 1968), 183.

# Massachusetts

Not long after their arrival in Pennsylvania, during the 1848 Christmas holidays, William and Ellen Craft were advised to move to the safer environs of Boston. They had only recently escaped slavery from Macon, Georgia. Ellen was owned by Eliza, to whom she was given as a child by her father at the time of her wedding to Robert Collins in 1837. In one of those ironies of slavery, Eliza's father, it was generally believed, was also the father of Ellen. Collins, a "Whig Unionist," was a leading figure in the rapidly growing city's economy and politics. He and Elam Alexander had won the contract to build a thirty-mile stretch of railroad from Macon to Oconee in 1840. Three years later, the line was extending, linking Macon to the Atlantic coast at Savannah. At the time of his death in 1861, Collins owned 102 slaves valued at $438,000; his landholdings included 1,200 acres in Macon, 5,390 acres "in joint account" in other parts of the state, and 23,343 acres in "Pine and Swamp land." In comparison, William's owner, Ira H. Taylor, was listed in the census as a farmer of few means.

Although they were living as husband and wife since 1846, William and Ellen took the conscious decision not to have children while they were enslaved. Over the next two years, William later recalled, they "prayed and toiled" until an ingenious plan of escape materialized. On the day of their escape, Ellen, visibly white, was dressed as a slave master traveling to Philadelphia for treatment for a rheumatic complaint; William accompanied her as a valet. Since Ellen could not write, her right arm was placed in a sling to dissuade officials from asking her to sign documents acknowledging ownership of her slave, as was required by law. William also wrapped a poultice on her face, hoping to limit conversations with strangers. Silence, they calculated, increased their chances of success. In yet another irony, they traveled on the first leg of their escape to Savannah on the line built by Robert Collins. From Savannah the pair took a series of boats, trains, and coaches, first to Charleston, then Wilmington, North

Carolina, Richmond, Washington, DC, and Baltimore before crossing into Pennsylvania. They covered the thousand miles from Macon to Philadelphia in just four days. Their dramatic escape became an instant sensation among abolitionists. The trip, one abolitionist editor enthused, was "as difficult...as Bonaparte's journey from Egypt through a coast and sea studded with the British fleet." Another insisted that their plan of escape "displayed a degree of ingenuity which could not have been acquired under the ordinary circumstances of life." Such ingenuity, he implied, could only have been born out of a debilitating oppression. When coupled with Henry Brown's equally dramatic escape from Richmond, Virginia, in a box sent to the office of the Anti-Slavery Society in Philadelphia, a few months earlier, it appeared that the enslaved, by their actions, had caught the revolutionary spirit of 1848.[1]

Boston and the Bay State, from which no slave had been returned under the old Fugitive Slave Law, was considered a safe space for fugitives from slavery. The capital city was home to a vibrant black community and to the modern abolitionist movement. It was also the refuge for scores of fugitives. But the "Cradle of Liberty" was also the home of the politically powerful Cotton Whigs, cotton and textile barons, many of them members of the Boston Associates, who dominated the political and economic life of the city and much of the state. Deeply invested in the cotton economy, the city's merchants, as well as textile manufacturers in such cities as Lowell, were ardent supporters of the Compromise of 1850 and had endorsed Daniel Webster's insistence that the Fugitive Slave Law was constitutional and had to be enforced if the Union was to be preserved. Ever since his March 7th speech in the Senate in support of Henry Clay's Compromise proposals, Webster had endured a series of vitriolic denunciations from political opponents, especially abolitionists, who considered his views a betrayal of cherished antislavery traditions. He became, as James Brewer Stewart has argued, a "compelling rhetorical symbol of the South's corrupting power." A special place in hell, Wendell Phillips predicted, had been reserved for Webster: "If, in the lowest deep, there be a lower deep for profligate statesmen, let all former apostates stand aside and leave it vacant. Hell, from beneath, is moved for thee at thy coming." Supporters of the law had arranged the firing of canons on Boston Common to celebrate President Fillmore's endorsement of the law. As Wendell Phillips saw it, Boston was "wholly choked with cotton dust." Henry Highland Garnet agreed: if Boston was the cradle of liberty, he told a British audience, it had rocked the cradle

[1] William Still, *The Underground Railroad* (1872, rpr., Chicago: 1970) 384; J. C. Butler, *Historical Record of Macon and Central Georgia* (Macon: 1879), 115, 158, 161, 179; Census of 1860, Bibbs County, Georgia; Bibbs County, Record Book R, Georgia Department of Archives and History, Atlanta: William Craft, *Running a Thousand Miles for Freedom* (1861, rpr., Baton Rouge: 1992), 8; John E. Talmadge, "Georgia Tests the Fugitive Slave Law, *Georgia Historical Quarterly*, 49, No. 1 (March 1965), 58; *Anti-Slavery Bugle*, July 14, 1849; Barbara McCaskill, *Love, Liberation, and Escaping Slavery. William and Ellen Craft in Cultural Memory* (Athens, GA: 2015)

so hard "it had killed the baby." At the height of the controversy over the Fugitive Slave Law, Samuel Ringgold Ward observed, the city was controlled by "cottonocrats, casteocrats and slaveocrats." Neologisms aside, Ward spoke for many African Americans and abolitionists in the city who could take little comfort from the fact that many, in both the North and South, anticipated that the city would stand foursquare against the law, that fugitives, in their midst, would never be taken.[2]

Soon after the Crafts had settled in Boston, William Wells Brown, himself a fugitive from slavery, invited William to join him on the abolitionist lecture circuit. A seasoned lecturer, Brown anticipated that he would speak on the nature of slavery, and William would follow with the story of their escape. In early January 1849, Brown wrote of their plan to organize meetings in a number of New England cities, including Norwich, Worcester, Pawtucket, New Bedford, Boston, Kingston, Abington, and Northborough. They were later joined by Henry "Box" Brown at the annual meeting of the Massachusetts Anti-Slavery Society, which pledged to protect them from recapture. An entire session of the meeting was devoted to the Crafts' escape and it closed with a ringing statement from Wendell Phillips: "We would look in vain through the most trying times of our Revolutionary history," he thundered, "for an incident of courage and noble daring to equal that of the escape of William and Ellen Craft; and future historians and poets would tell the story of one of the most thrilling in the nation's annals."[3]

Such public defiance of the law undoubtedly lifted the spirits of abolitionists, but it also caused deep anxiety among those who worried that such displays put the Crafts at risk of possible recapture. It also foreclosed the possibility that other slaves could successfully emulate the daring of the Crafts and Box Brown. Simply put, such public displays, they reasoned, put slaveholders on heightened alert. This concern may explain why the Crafts promptly disappeared from center stage at abolitionist meetings. For the next eighteen months they settled into the city's relatively small but vibrant black community, which, at the time of their arrival, supported four churches and a host of benevolent and social clubs. William established himself as a cabinetmaker, Ellen as a seamstress. It was a community with a tradition of unified action against slave catchers and a commitment to protect the estimated four hundred fugitives who made the city their home. Six years earlier, the community, with the aid of white supporters, had fought to prevent the extradition of George Latimer, and when that failed, quickly raised the funds needed to redeem him. They also simultaneously fought to overcome discrimination, particularly the

[2] Phillips quoted in Kathryn Grover, *The Fugitive's Gibraltar. Escaping Slaves and Abolitionism in New Bedford, Massachusetts* (Amherst, MA: 2001), 281; James Brewer Stewart, *Wendell Phillips. Liberty's Hero* (Baton Rouge: 1986), 146, 166; *Anti-Slavery Reporter*, August 1, 1851; *Impartial Citizen*, October 5, 1850.
[3] *Liberator*, January 12, February 2, 1849.

segregation of city schools. Throughout the 1850s, they petitioned the legislature to remove the word "white" from the state's militia law. When that failed, they created their own militia companies.[4]

As in other black communities throughout the North, the passage of the Fugitive Slave law threatened to dislocate the lives of blacks in Boston. Dozens left for Canada or other safer locations in the state in the days after the law was adopted. Some black churches, it was reported, saw a drop in membership, although the exact size of these losses is unclear. The example of the small Fugitive Slave Church may be illustrative. Construction, which began in 1849, had to be suspended when a majority of the congregation left for Canada. There was not only a loss of jobs, but, as one observer put it, "an uncertain and melancholy future" for those who chose to stay.[5] Opponents organized a series of meetings to protest against the law and to rally the community. The first, called on September 30th, elected Lewis Hayden, a fugitive slave from Kentucky and a leading figure in the city, chairman. Resolutions pledged mutual defense against the law. William was elected to a committee to organize a second meeting at which a "League of Freedom" to protect the community and resist enforcement of the law was announced. Its success, proponents realized, was only possible if fugitives chose to stay and fight. "The liability of ourselves and families becoming" victims of the law "at the caprice of Southern manstealers," they declared, "imperatively demands an expression whether we will tamely submit to chains and slavery, or whether we will, at all and every hazard, *live* and *die* freemen." Ten days later, 3,500 blacks and whites attended a meeting at Faneuil Hall at which it was decided to form a vigilance committee to coordinate opposition to the law and aid fugitive slaves. Initially, the committee was made up of fifty members, a number that would swell to more than two hundred within a year. Its size, as we shall see, sometimes militated against effective action. The committee was headed by Timothy Gilbert, a piano manufacturer. Theodore Parker chaired its executive committee, and Francis Jackson, president of the Massachusetts Anti-Slavery Society, acted as treasurer. Parker wielded extraordinary influence: five of the eight members of the Executive Committee were connected to his church. Eight blacks, including Lewis Hayden, were members of the general committee. Some of the best legal minds in the state gave their support, including Charles Sumner, Samuel

4 James Oliver Horton and Lois E. Horton, *Black Bostonians. Family Life and Community Struggle in the Antebellum North* (New York: 1979), 106; George A. Lavesque, "Inherent Reformers – Inherent Orthodoxy: Black Baptists in Boston, 1800–1873," *Journal of Negro History*, LX (October 1975), 492, 510; Stephen Kantrowitz, *More Than Freedom. Fighting for Black Citizenship in a White Republic, 1829–1889* (New York: 2012), 200–04; *Directory of the City of Boston, 1850–1851* (Boston: 1850).
5 Benjamin Quarles, *Black Abolitionists* (New York: 1969), 199–200; Wilbur H. Siebert, *The Underground Railroad in Massachusetts* (Worcester, MA: 1936), 40–41; John Weiss, ed., *Life and Correspondence of Theodore Parker*, 2 Vols. (London: 1863), II, 92.

Sewall, Richard H. Dana, and Charles C. Loring. Boston seemed well prepared to combat any attempt to enforce the law.[6]

Weeks later, newspaper headlines screamed "excitement" with word that two slave catchers from Georgia were in town searching for the Crafts. Willis Hughes, Macon's jailor, and John Knight, a laborer with whom William had worked at a cabinetmaking shop, were commissioned by Robert Collins to secure the return of the Crafts. Not long after their arrival, Knight visited William at his shop, feigning delight at seeing him, and with news of Ellen's family, who, he reported, were anxious to see them back in Macon. Knight also asked William to take him on a tour of the city. When William declined, Knight invited them to his hotel. One wonders why he did; he could not possibly have expected the ploy to work. The visit put William and his supporters on high alert. At the same time, Hughes was undertaking a series of equally fruitless visits to commissioners and magistrates in an effort to find someone who would issue a warrant for the Crafts' arrest. As he later reported, he was given the runaround; some claimed not to know the workings of the law, others insisted that their offices were not mandated to issue such warrants, and yet others worried that they did not have the man power to execute an arrest in the black community. According to Hughes, Judge Levi Woodbury of the US Circuit Court informed him on October 22nd that he was not "the proper person to issue" an arrest warrant and recommended that the slave catcher contact the US district attorney, George Lunt. The district attorney, however, declined to act. He had taken on a similar case some time before, he informed Hughes, and it had turned out to be a very "unpleasant business," creating a "great deal of excitement," a mistake he had no intention of repeating. Hughes next made contact with Benjamin F. Hallett, one of the local commissioners, who responded that Hughes did not need a warrant. All Hughes had to do, Hallett observed, was arrest the Crafts and bring them before the commissioner. Hughes was stunned by Hallett's response; after all, he was a commissioner and should have known the law. Finally, Hallett insisted Hughes make out his charges in legal form before he would consider the request for a warrant. With the aid of local contacts, Hughes hired attorney Seth J. Thomas, a friend of Daniel Webster, who met with Judge Peleg Sprague of the US District Court of Massachusetts. But Sprague was no more forthcoming. Finally, Hughes turned to another commissioner, George Curtis, who suggested Hughes return after the city's six commissioners had an opportunity to discuss the case with Woodbury and Sprague.

---

[6] Others who attended the Faneuil Hall meeting put the number in attendance at closer to six thousand. Gary Collison, *Shadrach Minkins. From Fugitive Slave to Citizen* (Cambridge, MA: 1997), 81; *Liberator*, October 4, 11, 1850; Siebert, *Underground Railroad in Massachusetts*, 39–40; New York *Tribune* (n.d.), in *Anti-Slavery Bugle*, November 16, 1850; Harold Schwartz, "Fugitive Slave Days in Boston," *New England Quarterly*, XXVII (June 1954), 192; Gary Collison, "The Boston Vigilance Committee. A Reconsideration," *Historical Journal of Massachusetts*, 12 (June 1984), 104–05, 111; Dean Grodzins, "'Slave Law' versus 'Lynch Law' in Boston. Benjamin Robbins Curtis, Theodore Parker, and the Fugitive Slave Crisis, 1850–1855," *Massachusetts Historical Review*, 12 (2010), 4.

The meeting seemed to have broken the logjam; it was agreed that one of the judges would hear the case the following day. Hughes reasserted his claim for a warrant and one was finally issued, by which time, Hughes complained, it was known "all over Boston that the warrant was issued, and who for, and who applied for it." But his troubles were not yet over: even with a legally issued warrant, the marshal doubted that he could arrest William at his home, or even if he was still there. He informed Hughes that he had sent someone to investigate and to report on William's whereabouts. When it was established that William had moved to a secure location, the marshal refused to act, claiming he did not have a large enough police force at his disposal.[7]

The eight days it had taken Hughes to procure the warrant gave the Crafts, and their supporters, ample time to devise an appropriate response. Soon after Knight's visit, Ellen was moved to Brookline, to the relative safety of the home of Dr. Henry Bowditch, a member of the vigilance committee. A week later, she was moved again, this time to Theodore Parker's. William, meanwhile, armed and barricaded himself in his shop while friends stood guard outside. "No man could approach within 100 yards of Craft's shop," one reporter observed, "without being seen by a hundred eyes, and a signal would call a powerful body at a moment's warning." Concerned that the law would, in the end, work against them, Frederick Douglass suggested the Crafts leave town. William emphatically refused; he was tired of running. More importantly, he and Ellen had become recognized symbols of resistance to an immoral law. To leave would be a disservice to the countless fugitives who had decided to stand their ground. As tension mounted, and it became apparent that the authorities were determined to test their defenses, William moved to Lewis Hayden's, where it was made public that kegs of gunpowder were placed in the basement in anticipation of an arrest attempt. Black homes on Belknap and Cambridge streets, the main thoroughfares of the black community, were fortified and their occupants well armed with guns, swords, and knives. According to one observer, the "colored community" was "really roused in this matter" and had made their homes "like barricades."[8]

---

[7] For Hughes's account of the troubles he encountered see Boston *Post*, December 2, 1850; Georgia *Telegraph*, November 26, 1850; Georgia *Journal & Messenger*, November 13, 1850; *Liberator*, December 6, 1850; Baltimore *Sun*, November 20, 1850; *National Era*, November 7, 1850; Collison, *Shadrach Minkins*, 94.

[8] Nina Moore Tiffany, "Stories of the Fugitive Slaves, I: The Escape of William and Ellen Craft," *New England Magazine*, 7, No. 1 (March 1890), 528; *Anti-Slavery Bugle*, November 16, 23, 1850; *Pennsylvania Freeman*, November 28, 1850; *Anti-Slavery Standard*, November 7, 1850; Vincent Y. Bowditch, *Life and Correspondence of Henry Ingersoll Bowditch*, 2 Vols. (Boston: 1902), I, 205–06. George Thompson, on a visit to Hayden, recalled: "There were windows barricaded and doors double locked." Hayden "sat around a table covered with loaded weapons...his young son and a band of brave colored men armed to the teeth and ready for the impending death struggle with the U. S. marshal and his armed posse." Quoted in Stanley J. Robboy and Anita W. Robboy, "Lewis Hayden: From Fugitive Slave to Citizen," *New England Quarterly*, XLVI (December 1973), 601.

FIGURE 10. Lewis Hayden. (Courtesy of the Ohio Historical Society)

The marshal knew of what he spoke. But Hughes's inability to procure a warrant and have it executed was the least of his problems. He also had to face a barrage of potential legal challenges from a subcommittee of the vigilance committee, which aimed to question the powers vested in commissioners under the Fugitive Slave Law, and whether the law encroached on state jurisdiction. Should these moves fail to produce the desired effect, the committee intended to have William arrested for violating the state's anti-fornication laws on the grounds that his slave marriage was not legal. It was finally agreed to hold these plans in reserve and to employ instead other forms of legal intimidation. The legal subcommittee initiated a series of legal and physical harassments aimed at forcing Hughes and Knight to leave Boston. The vigilance committee also appealed directly to the public, posting handbills throughout the city that described the slave catchers. Hughes and Knight were met by hostile crowds wherever they went: they were greeted by shouts of "slave-hunters, slave-hunters! There go the slave-hunters!" When Hughes accused the Crafts of being slaves, the legal subcommittee had them arrested for slander. Bail was set at an exorbitant $10,000, which the slave catchers were only able to meet with the aid of local supporters led by Seth Thomas. The following morning they were again arrested, this time for the attempted kidnapping of William, with bail again set at $10,000. There was another arrest that same afternoon, this time for the attempted kidnapping of Ellen, with bail set at the same amount. Hughes later reported, in utter disbelief, that they were issued a total of five arrest warrants in the space of a few days. But their problems were not over. After their third release on bond, a large and angry crowd of African Americans charged the coach that they had hired to take them to their hotel. Realizing the danger he faced, the coachman whipped his horses into a gallop in an effort to elude the crowd, but they followed. He drove across the bridge leading to Cambridge, calculating that the need to pay a toll would deter his pursuers, but someone paid the toll and the crowd followed. Hundreds were in the chase, shouting abuse at the slave catchers. Fearing for his life, the coachman abandoned his passengers to the mob in West Cambridge. The hunters were the hunted, and although they were not harmed, Hughes and Knight thought it best to abandon their mission. But before they could leave, they had to endure yet another encounter, this one in their hotel room with Theodore Parker, backed up by a large boisterous crowd of African Americans outside. Parker's message to the slave catchers was a simple one: if they did not leave town immediately, he could no longer guarantee their safety. Hughes and Knight took the next train to New York City. Hughes later insisted that, under the advice of their attorney, they had agree to leave even before Parker arrived at their hotel with his "piece of friendly advice," as Hughes sarcastically put it.[9]

---

[9] *Anti-Slavery Standard*, November 7, 1850; *Constitutionalist* (n.d.), in *Liberator*, December 6, 1850; Tiffany, "Stories of Fugitive Slaves," 529; Weiss, ed., *Theodore Parker*, II, 529, I, 91;

The black community and local abolitionists were understandably elated; together they had struck the first major blow against the Fugitive Slave Law. "Not since the days of '76," the *Liberator* enthused, reflecting the mood of the black community, had there been such "a popular demonstration on the side of human freedom in this region. The humane and patriotic contagion has infected all classes. Scarcely any other subject has been talked about in the streets, or in the social circles." George Thompson, the British abolitionist, on an antislavery tour of New England, told a packed audience at Faneuil Hall, "I see that the South demands of Massachusetts that the noble Craft and his equally noble companion should be given up, and I see that this demand is in derision of the established law of nations. Gentlemen, there is something on earth greater than arbitrary and despotic power. The lightning has its power, the whirlwind has its power; but there is something among men more capable of shaking despotic power than lightning, whirlwind and earthquake – that is the threatened indignation of the whole civilized world." Others saw things differently. In no other city or state of the Union, local observer "Plymouth Rock" lamented, was to be found such an assortment of "hot-headed, crack-brained fellows as there are at present in the Puritan City." At their head was William Lloyd Garrison, backed by a "large force of dark ones at the west part of the city." On a recent visit to Southac Street, "one colored volunteer" had showed him "two revolvers, an old musket, and other implements of war, and stated that some hundreds of like instruments could be found about the west end." It is not clear what worried "Plymouth Rock" more – the abolitionists, the guns, or the "dark ones."[10]

But the "British meddler," or "mad Englishman" and his supporters, opponents chortled, did not have things all their own way in Boston. Thousands packed a meeting at Faneuil Hall organized by supporters to welcome Thompson. Edmund Quincy, Wendell Phillips, William Henry Channing, Theodore Parker, Abbey Kelly, Frederick Douglass, and the "entire tribe of Garrison fanatics," according to one opponent, were in attendance. None were allowed to speak. Opponents in the hall kept up a constant din. They cheered for Webster, Henry Clay, and anyone else they could think of, including Jenny Lind. Fights occurred, during which "hats were smashed, and ivory-headed canes flew briskly." Parker was hissed off the stage, as was Douglass, after which the crowd sang Yankee Doodle and cheered for the Union. Several African Americans were assaulted.

Robboy and Robboy, "Lewis Hayden," 601; New York *Tribune* (n.d.), in *Anti-Slavery Bugle*, November 16, 1850. Daniel J. Coburn, the deputy sheriff, later wrote that it was Seth Thomas who raised the money to meet their bail. Boston *Herald,* December 6, 1850; Washington, DC *Union,* December 11, 1850. See also Hughes's letter published in the Georgia *Telegraph,* November 26, 1850, and elsewhere for an account of the meeting with Parker. Henry Steele Commager, *Theodore Parker. Yankee Crusader* (Boston: 1947), 214–15.

[10] *Liberator,* December 1, 1850; *Anti-Slavery Bugle,* December 7, 1850; the letter from "Plymouth Rock" in Washington, DC, *Union,* November 11, 1850.

Opponents of the meeting even fought among themselves while the police took no action to prevent the disruption. Quincy later complained to the mayor about the police's inaction, but the marshal claimed that the crowd was too large to be effectively controlled. With the memory of the failure to retake the Crafts still fresh, anti-abolitionists took comfort in this demonstration of the city's opposition to those who would defy the law. The principal figures involved in the meeting came in for particular ridicule and vitriol. Quincy, for instance, was dismissed as an "abolitionist popinjay," a label that paled in comparison to the description of Douglass, that "black scab on the face of humanity." Days later, the black church on Belknap Street provided Thompson with a welcoming audience in a relatively secure venue. This time there was a heavy police presence and no whites were allowed to enter the church except by special invitation. Following the meetings, Quincy brought charges against Marshal Francis Tukey for not intervening to stop the disruption at Faneuil Hall. In his defense before the Board of Aldermen, Tukey insisted that the "spirit of lawlessness" seen at the meeting had been "engendered and fostered" by the very people who had leveled the charges against him. It was part of the same spirit of recklessness, he responded, that had prompted a "portion of the citizens" to arm themselves to resist "the enforcement of certain obnoxious laws," a clear reference to the Crafts' case. As we have seen in Chapter 1, the pro-Union meeting organized by George T. Curtis and other Webster support-ers at Faneuil Hall, on November 26th, was seen as the ultimate expression of opposition to those who were bent on destroying the Union. Webster did not attend, but he made every effort to capitalize on the meeting, recommending the printing of fifty thousand copies of the proceedings and their distribution in both the North and the South. As he told a friend: "Nothing can do half so much good." The disruption of the Thompson meeting, Tukey's testimony, together with the pro-Union meeting, demonstrated that Boston was politically contested ground, one on which opponents of the law did not have it all their own way, in spite of the failure to retake the Crafts.[11]

Rhetorical flourishes such as Thompson's were also freighted with wider political significance. How was the government going to respond to the fact that the Fugitive Slave Law, for many the centerpiece of the Compromise, had been openly defied at the most conspicuous center of abolitionist activity? Would others in the North emulate such popular forms of resistance to the law in an effort to abrogate the Compromise and destroy the Union? The Compromise, as its proponents had insisted from its inception, rested on the North's willing-ness and commitment to enforce the Fugitive Slave Law. The retreat of Hughes and Knight, as well as declarations of resistance to the law from many other locations in the fall of 1850, threatened to destroy the political glue that held the Union together. In addition, Robert Collins raised the political stakes by

[11] Boston *Herald*, November 13, 14, 15, 16, 19, December 12, 1850; Boston *Post*, November 16, 19, December 28, 1850; Collison, *Shadrach Minkins*, 102–03.

publicly demanding to know how the president planned to respond to such an open flaunting of the law. Why, he asked, had federal and state officials thrown so many impediments in the way of his agents? Daniel Webster did not help matters. He castigated the district attorney, George Lunt, whom he despised, as a man of little "talent," "fitness," or "disposition" for the job. He had declined to assist Hughes. Without providing any evidence, Webster also suspected that it was Lunt who had made public the slave catchers' presence in town. On the other hand, Charles Devens, the US marshal, might have been "well disposed," but he, too, was not "entirely efficient." The *"general weight"* of federal officials in the area, Webster concluded, was "against the Government, and against the execution of the Fugitive Slave Law." In light of such an assessment of his officers' shortcomings, Collins's questions helped to put the president on the defensive. Rather than address Collins's pointed questions, Fillmore demanded that the slaveholder provide "satisfactory evidence of official delinquency, or forcible resistance," rather than rumors and "newspaper statements." Officials, he responded, had not been derelict in their duty. If Collins could provide evidence to the contrary, Fillmore pledged to use all available means at his disposal to bring them to heel. At the same time, he called for a lowering of the heated political rhetoric surrounding the law and giving its implementation time to take its "usual course." Every effort, he hoped, would be made "to cultivate a fraternal feeling. We should be one people," he pleaded, "of one interest and one sentiment, knowing no local division; and tolerating no sectional injustice." The Union, he implied, was at a political crossroads, and would only be preserved by a "strict observance of the Constitution and impartial administration of laws."[12]

Much of the blame for the failure to retake the Crafts fell on Marshal Charles Devens. He had not acted promptly, critics other than Webster agreed, to ensure the rendition of the Crafts, nor had he kept the president informed of developments. Others suspected that the law had been "purposely evaded by Boston authorities." Whatever the cause of the failure, an example had to be made of those responsible for the debacle. Devens' removal would send a clear message that the law would never again be "prostrated before a mob." Commissioner George T. Curtis, however, came to Devens' defense. Because he lacked adequate power to execute the warrant, the course he took, in a period of uncertainty about how the law should operate, Curtis suggested, prevented a potentially calamitous social and political upheaval. Fillmore commissioned Attorney General J. J. Crittenden to look into the complaints of "neglect and dereliction of duty" made against Devens. There was no cause for censure or removal, Crittenden reported, although he was struck by the lack of what he called "activity and energy" by Devens and his deputies. A "more commendable

[12] Boston *Post*, November 21, 1850; Georgia *Citizen*, November 14, 1850; New York *Tribune*, November 20, 1850; Charles M. Wiltse and Michael J. Birkner, *The Papers of Daniel Webster. Correspondence, Vol. 7, 1850–1852* (Hanover, NH: 1986), 177–88.

activity and energy might have been exerted," by the marshal and his men, he observed, but all the evidence pointed to the fact that they had worked closely and in consultation with Hughes.[13]

In this instance, the Crafts may have benefitted from the fact that the law, less than a month old, had not been fully operationalized. Hughes's report of his experiences may have been self-serving, but there is little doubt that those in Boston responsible for enforcing the law were, at this stage, unsure of how it was to be implemented. While many of the city's six commissioners were committed to its enforcement, one (Charles Sumner, and possibly others) had made his opposition known. That may explain why Hughes took his request for arrest warrants to those who, he was advised, were sympathetic to the law. Equally significant is the fact that Devens knew the city in which he lived and the difficulty he would face from the black community should he attempt to retake the Crafts. An unnamed Southerner who was visiting friends at the time of the crisis rejected the idea that the city was in a "state of nullification," as some believed; it was, he believed, simply unprepared. Hughes's mission had "overawed a great many who wanted to avoid a riot and bloodshed." But the city had learned from the experience; were there another case, the results, he predicted, would be different. Many had come to the realization that the "resistance by the negroes" was clearly "subversive of law and order."[14]

There was also political fallout in Georgia from the failure to retake the Crafts. Hughes's lengthy explanation of the resistance he and Knight encountered was meant to mollify a public at home that had long been skeptical of the law's efficacy and the North's willingness to enforce it. Knight also published his own explanation, which, in its details and conclusions, reinforced much of what Hughes had said. Their explanations did little to satisfy the skeptics. The Democratic press "crowed" over the failure to take the Crafts. It had predicted such an outcome all along; the law, it insisted, would never be enforced. One Whig editorialist did all he could to quiet what he saw as secessionist attempts to use the case to demonstrate that there was no commitment in the North to the enforcement of the law. All the evidence, he argued, showed that Hughes and Knight were surprisingly overwhelmed. But the actions of the mob, he pointed out, had created a backlash and generated greater support for the law. Those who were hoping that the upcoming Georgia convention would come out in favor of opposition to the Compromise should, he warned, pay attention to the signs of change already evident in Boston. "Justice" was less sanguine; Hughes, he wrote his local newspaper, was "making disunion capital," pandering to the fire-eaters in the hope that they would carry the upcoming elections. Why, he wondered, had Hughes spent time in New York City rather than going directly to Boston? The delay meant word of his mission got to Boston before

[13] Washington, DC, *Union*, November 27, December 7, 13, 1850; New York *Herald*, December 19, 1850.
[14] Georgia *Citizen*, November 23, 1850.

he did. He also criticized Hughes for not taking a witness with him, someone who could testify that the Crafts were slaves and that they had escaped from Collins and Taylor. He also had failed to take a warrant with him from Bibbs County, as the law required. Without it, Boston commissioners were understandably skeptical of his claims and worried about possible prosecution if the claim was unfounded. Finally, had Hughes stayed in Boston, and not succumbed to the mob, he would have forced Fillmore to call out the military. Hughes responded with a lengthy reiteration of his actions. In it he included testimonials to his probity from leading citizens of Macon, including Robert Collins and Ira H. Taylor, who assured Hughes that they were convinced that he had done all he could to reclaim the Crafts. As to "Justice's" claim of political calculation, Hughes responded that, like Collins, who would top the polls in the upcoming elections as a Whig candidate, he was opposed to disunion.[15]

In spite of the failure to retake the Crafts, signs pointed to the fact that the Southern visitor's optimism was well founded. In the days after the departure of Hughes and Knight, Boston was alive with rumors that the president had plans to deploy roughly seven hundred troops to enforce the law. It was also becoming increasingly apparent that Robert Collins would make another attempt to retake the Crafts, if only to save face following the ignominious retreat of his agents. The Crafts' dramatic escape two years earlier had brought them such fame and renown that their recapture, many calculated and hoped, would send a clear message of the country's determination to enforce the law and the Constitution. The timing of Hughes's and Knight's mission suggests that Collins had bided his time until the passage of the law cleared the way for the Crafts' recapture. Their defiance and the support they won in the city laid down a political marker and challenge to authority that neither Collins nor the federal government could ignore. Successful resistance increased the possibility that, should Collins try to retake the Crafts, he would have the full backing of the federal government. Boston, it quickly became evident, was no longer safe for the Crafts. On the advice of friends, they left for England in early November. For the next three weeks they followed a tortuous course, in many ways reminiscent of their escape from Georgia, one which took them to Portland, Maine, Saint John, New Brunswick, and Windsor and Halifax, Nova Scotia. Two weeks later, they caught the steamer for England, another terminus on the Underground Railroad.[16]

---

[15] Georgia *Citizen,* November 23, 1850; Georgia *Journal & Messenger,* December 4, 1850, January 27, 1851; Georgia *Telegraph,* December 10, 1850; Talmadge, "Georgia Tests the Fugitive Slave Law," 62.

[16] *Liberator,* November 29, 1850; Craft, *Running a Thousand Miles,* 46–53. Before their departure, they were married by Theodore Parker, who handed William a copy of the bible and a sword, one to nourish his soul, the other to defend his wife and himself. Weiss, ed., *Theodore Parker,* I, 99; Wiltes and Birkner, eds., *The Papers of Daniel Webster. Correspondence,* Vol. 7, 189–90.

The organization of the resistance to Hughes and Knight provided a model, an unnamed member of the vigilance committee suggested, that should be adopted to counter any future activity of "kidnappers." If it were followed, no fugitive would be returned from New England, not even from Marshfield, the home of Daniel Webster. The proposal rested on the coordinated activities of vigilance committees and black communities. Once it was known that slave catchers were in town, the vigilance committee should appoint a subcommittee to organize resistance. They should post handbills throughout town listing the names and descriptions of the slave catchers. Hotelkeepers and landlords should be pressured to deny them accommodation, as they would "pickpockets, gamblers, or horse-stealers"; if they did not, members of the coalition should take up lodgings in the same establishment so they could monitor the activities of suspected slave catchers. The doors of the hotel should be watched at all hours. The slave catchers should be followed into every "shop, office, or place of public business" they entered. If they entered a private residence, he recommended, "wait outside, watching all the avenues, and [be] ready to renew the attendance" when they left. This sort of vigilance and intimidation, he knew, had proven successful in the case of the Crafts. Boston, he intimated, had not only set a standard of resistance in the case of the Crafts, it was also prepared for any future attempt to reclaim fugitive slaves.[17]

In less than two weeks following the publication of the recommended plan of action, the streets of Boston were plastered with posters warning of the presence of a slave catcher: "He is a *thin, tall* fellow, rather *lean* and *lanky,* and about *six feet long.* His hair is *reddish* or *dirty brown,* like *weather-beaten tan* in color; is *long, straight,* and *lank, thin* on the top of the head, and *parted on the side.* His face is *rather short* for a man so long, rather *square shaped;* an uncommonly *hard, bad face,* and *ugly,* not only in form and feature, but expression, – *a face which seems made for a slave hunter,* or by his business."[18] The description of John Caphart of Norfolk, Virginia, contained all the hallmarks of suspected slave catchers that were standard in all such posters: gaunt, lank, ruddy faced, and always ugly. Caphart was in town in search of Shadrach Minkins, who had escaped nine months earlier from John De Bree, of Norfolk, a purser in the US Navy. Minkins was arrested on February 15, 1851, at the coffeehouse where he worked by the assistant deputy marshal and taken before Commissioner George T. Curtis. A large crowd of blacks, many of them women, quickly gathered outside the courthouse. Lawyers from the vigilance committee, including Richard H. Dana and Charles G. Davis, visited the prisoner, as did Elizur Wright, editor of the *Commonwealth.* As Wright and Davis were leaving the courtroom, a group of blacks – some estimated as many as twenty – barged past them, seized Minkins, "at broad noon-day," from under

[17] *Liberator,* January 31, 1851.
[18] Quoted in Collison, *Shadrach Minkins,* 111.

the noses of federal officers and hustled him down the steps, as Dana recalled, with "his clothes half torn off." They hurried Minkins through the square, followed by a growing crowd of African Americans, to the Fourth Ward, home to most blacks in the city, where he was hidden in the attic of Mrs. Elizabeth Riley, a neighbor of Lewis Hayden. He was taken across the river, first to Cambridge, then Leominster, and later sent on his way to Montreal, Canada, through New Hampshire and Vermont.[19]

The first fugitive slave to be taken in Boston since the passage of the Fugitive Slave Law had been rescued from federal officers from a courthouse, which, although built by the state, was considered federal property. As far as opponents of the law were concerned, Boston had lived up to its reputation. But this second failure, in a matter of months, to execute the law in Boston, brought about by a "degraded portion of the population" who violated "the sanctuary of justice," proponents of the law declared, was an outrage that must not be tolerated. As far as James Gordon Bennett at the New York *Herald* was concerned, such actions were to be expected in a city that tolerated "disorganizers" such as William Lloyd Garrison, Wendell Phillips, and their "coadjutors of mischief." This stigma would not be erased until all those involved were punished, especially the "vagabonds who broke into the court room and rescued" Minkins. "If it is necessary to shed blood and take life, in vindicating the law," he concluded, "let it be done, even if a thousand be sacrificed." His contemporary at the Washington, DC, *Union* concurred: the abolitionists of Boston have "to render a fearful account of their nefarious proceedings. Here are the laws violated – their sanctity profaned; a measure which was intended to cement the Union itself is ground into the dust and ashes by an ignorant and infuriated rabble of blacks whom these abolitionists have misled, excited, and prompted to the most outrageous violence and rebellion." Although both editors were convinced that blacks could not have acted on their own initiative, they were, nevertheless, deeply concerned about the alliance with abolitionists in the cradle of abolitionism.[20]

In the Senate, Henry Clay, realizing that the Compromise, which he had done so much to fashion, was threatened by what had transpired in Boston, demanded to know how the "majesty of the government" could be under assault from a "people who possess no part…in our political system," and wondered if the president needed additional powers to deal with this and other

---

[19] Ibid., 3, 126, 130–33, 159; Charles Francis Adams, *Richard Henry Dana. A Biography*, 2 Vols. (Boston: 1890), I, 182; Austin Bearse, *Reminiscences of Fugitive-Slave Law Days in Boston* (Boston: 1880), 3, 17; Boston *Herald*, February 15, 1851. Years later, Robert Morris, the black lawyer, recalled "the noble conduct of a colored woman who assisted in the rescue of Shadrach." Unfortunately, he gave no details, but Stephen Kantrowitz and Collison suspect it was the fifty-nine-year-old Mrs. Riley. Philip S. Foner & George Walker, eds., *Proceedings of the Black State Conventions, 1840–1865*, 2 Vols. (Philadelphia: 1980), II, 101; Kantrowitz, *More than Freedom*, 191.

[20] New York *Herald*, February 17, 1851; Washington, DC, *Union*, February 19, 1851.

expected future challenges. For the next week, the Senate focused its attention almost exclusively on Clay's resolution, pushing aside all other business.
In response, Fillmore admitted that, what he curiously called the "flagitious
proceeding," a "high handed contempt" of authority, and a surprise attack,
should have been anticipated. Had it been, he had no doubt that the people
of Boston would have risen to the defense of the law. After pointing out limits
imposed on him by the Constitution, Fillmore pledged, in the future, to use all
the powers at his disposal to ensure the proper execution of the law. Clay saw
the hand of George Thompson, the foreign agitator, that "vile disturber of the
public peace," at work. It defied logic, he mused, to think that an assault of
this nature was exclusively the work of a score of blacks. The responsibility lay
elsewhere, among the abolitionists, who for years had been promoting violence
against slaveholders and anyone pursuing fugitive slaves. Those who attacked
the courtroom and freed Minkins were the "catspaws of those who had not the
courage to show their own faces." George Badger of North Carolina saw the
telltale signs of a wider conspiracy to destroy the country. State laws, abolitionists preaching hatred, foreign agitators spreading their vile messages, constant
public condemnation of the law, every "species of obstruction by pettifogging
lawyers, false charges brought forward, false arrests made for the purpose of
deterring those gentlemen who are in pursuit of slaves who had escaped from
them," and using as foot soldiers a "collection of free negroes, members of a
degraded race...having the effrontery to come forward in the public view, in a
great city, and by violence overpower and insult officers of the law and rescue
the prisoner," were acts of "alarming importance" that warranted the heavy
hand of the government. Others, such as Stephen Douglas and J. Macpherson
Berrien, also thought that white men were the instigators of this "insane crusade." Clay's and Badger's views, as well as Fillmore's pledge, struck some,
especially senators from New England, as a blind and unnecessary overreaction. John Hale of New Hampshire, for instance, dismissed Fillmore's letter to
the Senate as "labored," and his pledge to use force, if necessary, ridiculous.
Why, he wanted to know, would the president call on the might of the military
to defend the "great republic against a handful of negroes?" The reaction was
"entirely misplaced, misconceived, ill-judged, impolitic, improper, injudicious,
and weak." If the events in Boston did not rise to the level of an insurrection,
as no one argued they did, why then did the president require additional powers? The authorities in Boston, Hale maintained, were handling the situation
appropriately.[21]

Hale may have been aware that the Board of Aldermen had requested
the mayor to use the full weight of the city police to prevent future rescues.

---

[21] *Appendix to the Congressional Globe, Second Session, Thirty-First Congress* (Washington,
DC: 1851), 292–93, 299–301, 351; Collison, *Shadrach Minkins*, 141–47, 194–95; Washington,
DC, *Union*, February 22, 1851; *Liberator*, February 21, 1851; Boston *Post*, February 18, 1851;
Springfield *Republican*, February 24, 1851; Baltimore *Sun*, February 24, 1851.

Others called for more immediate action. Stunned by the rescue and the second denial of the law, Daniel Webster insisted that George Curtis send him all the details. In response, Curtis blamed the rescue on the "gross negligence" of the city marshal. He dared to articulate a view of such events that others had only hinted at: opponents, he had no doubt, were committing treason, "levying war" against the nation, a view that would grow more salient in the months ahead. By September, those who were suspected of involvement in the shoot-out at the small farm in Christiana, Pennsylvania, during which a slave master was killed, would be tried unsuccessfully with levying war against the country. Webster insisted that all those involved in Minkins's rescue should be brought to trial. Convictions would demonstrate Boston's commitment to the Compromise. They would also, as Gary Collison has argued, have boosted Webster's chances of gaining the White House. In the days after Minkins was taken from the courtroom, ten men, white and black, were arrested and accused of involvement in the rescue. They included Elizur Wright, Charles Davis, John Foye, a black truckman, three black clothing merchants – John Scott, Thomas Paul Smith, and John P. Coburn – Lewis Hayden, Robert Morris, and Joseph K. Hayes, a white member of the vigilance committee. The accused were defended by John P. Hale, the New Hampshire senator, and Richard H. Dana. District Attorney George Lunt led the prosecution. Scott, the first to be brought to trial, was promptly released. So was Hayden, in spite of considerable eyewitness evidence of his involvement. Robert Morris's case was suspended until the November term of the court. At the renewed trial, Peleg Sprague, of the District Court of Massachusetts, was joined by Benjamin R. Curtis, recently named to the Supreme Court of the United States by President Fillmore, and the brother of George T. Curtis, the sitting commissioner at the Minkins's hearing. Throughout the hearing, defense counsels spent much of their time flaying the constitutionality of the Fugitive Slave Law, or, as Dana did, insisting that there was no proof that Minkins was a slave or was descended from a slave woman as required by Virginia law. The jury ruled in favor of Morris. Elizur Wright's case was heard in June 1852 and resulted in a hung jury. He was retried in November and, in one of those curious twists of history, was acquitted the very week of Webster's death.[22]

The fact that the mayor of the city had publicly declared his commitment to use the full weight of the police in future cases caused deep concern in the black and abolitionist communities. But there were also troubling signs from other quarters: a number of merchants and editors predicted that there would be collateral damage to the city's economy. The dry goods trade had already been negatively affected, they pointed out, as were the "dealers in brogans and boots and shoes." Boston's loss would be New York City's gain, as there city

---

[22] Gary Collison, "'This Flagitious Offense': Daniel Webster and the Shadrach Rescue Cases, 1851–1852," *New England Quarterly*, 68 (December 1995), 610, 615, 617–24; Collison, *Shadrach Minkins*, 146–47, 193–94; *Liberator*, June 20, 1851.

authorities had acted promptly to return both James Hamlet and Henry Long to slavery without encountering similar opposition. Many in the black community anticipated having to pay a price for such damages to the city's economy and political image. As a consequence, hundreds of fugitives – as many as four hundred, some have estimated – fled the city for Canada in the wake of the rescue. The successful rescue had also bred a sense of increased vulnerability in the black community.[23]

The day Minkins crossed into Canada, Gary Collison writes, Thomas Sims climbed on board the *M & J. C Gilmore,* docked in Savannah, and hid in its forecastle. The twenty-three-year-old Sims was owned by James Potter, a substantial Chatham County rice planter, owner of 199 slaves, including Sims' mother and sister. Sims also left behind a wife and several children.[24] Fearing being sold into slavery, Sims, who claimed he was a free man, had fled to Savannah in late February, where he boarded the *Gilmore* as it was about to leave for Boston. He was discovered as the ship neared Massachusetts and locked in a cabin by the captain. He managed to escape, stole one of the ship's boats and rowed unnoticed into Boston harbor. He subsequently found odd jobs in the black community. His whereabouts were discovered, however, when he tried to make contact with his wife. Here was another opportunity for the forces of law and order to prove their commitment to the Fugitive Slave Law. The city, state, and federal government were fully prepared to prevent a repeat of the Minkins debacle. On April 3rd, Sims was approached by a "strong posse of officers" in Hanover Street. He resisted and managed to stab Officer Asa O. Butman in the groin before he could be subdued. He was rushed off to the courthouse, where a large crowd quickly gathered. The authorities took no chances. The prisoner was taken to the third floor of the courthouse, with police officers stationed at every door. In an act of political symbolism, "stout chains" were placed around the perimeter of the courthouse under orders of City Marshal Francis Tukey. Anyone entering – and that included state supreme court justices – had to bend their backs under the chains. Two companies of infantry were put on alert by the mayor and it was rumored that 258 men were on standby at the nearby Charlestown Navy Yard. At night a "strong detachment" of the "Brighton Artillery" was deployed in the square outside the courthouse to disperse the crowds. Police, estimated to be as many as five hundred, patrolled the area. With the chains and heavy guards, the courthouse was transformed, as it were, into a "baracoon."[25]

[23] Boston *Post,* February 18, 1851; Collison, "'This Flagitious Offense,'" 613; Kantrowitz, *More than Freedom,* 193.

[24] Collison, *Shadrach Minkins,* 190; Boston *Herald,* April 4, 1851; Savannah *Republican,* April 10, 1851.

[25] Boston *Herald,* April 4, 5, 10, 1850; Boston *Post,* April 7, 1850; Savannah *Republican,* April 10, 1850; Savannah *News,* April 9, 1851; Leonard Levy, "Sims' Case: the Fugitive Slave Law in Boston," *Journal of Negro History,* 35 (January 1950), 45–47; Bowditch, *Life and Correspondence of Henry Ingersoll Bowditch,* I, 217.

**Likeness of Thomas Sims, the alledged Fugitive Slave.**

FIGURE 11. Likeness of Thomas Sims. (*Boston Herald*, April 7, 1851)

The vigilance committee met to rally support for Sims, but could find little common ground. Garrisonian "nonresistants" eschewed violence, while others insisted on working within the law. Black members – including Lewis Hayden and Leonard Grimes, minister to the small church made up largely of fugitive slaves, many of whom had left for Canada in late 1850 – were eager to act. Such indecision, in the face of this new threat, drove Thomas Wentworth Higginson to distraction. The radical cleric, and a member of the vigilance committee from Worcester, demanded that his colleagues devise a plan to rescue Sims. "There is neither organization, resolution, plan nor popular sentiment," he fumed; "the negroes are cowed and the abolitionists irresolute and hopeless, with nothing better to do on Saturday than to send off circulars to clergymen." But the committee did move quickly to organize a public meeting. They applied to use Faneuil Hall but were denied by the mayor because it was being used to billet a militia company. They then applied to use the lawn outside the State House, but that, too, was denied. Denied the use of both venues, they called an open-air meeting on Boston Common, which was attended by a crowd estimated at one thousand. The meeting was continued at Tremont Temple, at which Wendell Phillips suggested that it would be far better if all the railroads in the state, and its entire shipping fleet, were destroyed, than a slave be taken from Boston: "Block the locomotives...tear up the rails," he shouted.

Nathaniel Colver, minister at the temple, and a member of the vigilance committee, recalled a conversation he had had recently with a black woman on Belknap Street. If she ran into one of the slave catchers, he wryly suggested to her, hug him as tightly as possible. Although neither meeting agreed on a specific course of action to rescue Sims, there were those who were fearful the situation could spin out of control. The best way out of the crisis, one editor offered, was to ransom Sims and all other fugitive slaves. It was the only way to ensure that the "integrity of our laws [are] maintained, and the sympathies of our people quieted." Those who made such purchases, in effect, would wash "their hands of all participation in treason." Using a strange analogy, the editor reasoned, the farmer would never "burn down his barn in order to destroy the rat which has committed depredation upon his property."[26]

Twenty-five police were present at Sims' hearing before Commissioner Curtis. Seth Thomas, who had advised Hughes and Knight, appeared for the claimant, James Potter; Charles G. Loring and Robert Rantoul, Webster's successor as senator, represented Sims. Potter made sure he had a fair representation of witnesses on hand who knew Sims in Georgia. Edward Barney, a bricklayer, who had lived in Savannah for sixteen months, testified that Sims worked with him building slave houses for Potter. John Bell, a seaman on the *Gilmore*, claimed to have seen Sims on the wharf in Savannah and later on the ship after he was captured. John Bacon, granted a power of attorney by Potter, claimed to have known Sims for fifteen years. Cephas J. Ames of Barnstable, Massachusetts, testified that he had caught the stowaway and "wrung his nose." The captain of the *Gilmore* confirmed that Sims was brought to his cabin after he was taken. A Mr. Dyton, a slave catcher, admitted that he was offered $350 to capture Sims. Not only had Potter scrupulously prepared the documents required by the law for the capture of fugitive slaves, he also had marshaled an impressive array of witnesses.[27]

Curtis, however, decided to adjourn the hearings so Sims' counsels could apply for a writ of habeas corpus. Samuel Sewall first approached State Supreme Court Justice Lemuel Shaw the morning of the hearing. Shaw at first declined, but after consultation with other members of the court, decided to entertain the application. Commentators in Savannah were convinced that this was part of a practiced delaying tactic and predicted that the result would be "little justice and *no negro*." Sims' supporters returned with a second application for a writ of habeas corpus. At this hearing, Robert Rantoul questioned the legality of the warrant under which Sims was being held. He also insisted, as others had done during the debate in Congress prior to the adoption of the law, that Congress had no power to legislate on fugitive slaves. He called

---

[26] Higginson quoted in Kantrowitz, *More than Freedom*, 193–94, and Albert J. von Frank, *The Trials of Anthony Burns. Freedom and Slavery in Emerson's Boston* (Cambridge, MA: 1998), 28; Boston *Herald*, April 5, 7, 1851.

[27] Boston *Herald*, April 5, 1851; Savannah *News*, April 7, 1851.

for prompt action, worried that Curtis could decide to return Sims and so preempt the supreme court's decision. The court also rejected this petition. Such writs could only be granted, they ruled, if someone's liberty was being unconstitutionally violated. This was not so in this case. Neither the 1793 law nor the 1850 update, Shaw ruled, was unconstitutional. Shaw then applied the well-established, but historically suspect, argument that the Constitution would not have been ratified without a clause requiring the return of fugitive slaves. Before the thirteen states could agree to unite, he observed, it was necessary to arrive at such an agreement. Consequently, the clause in question "must...be construed as a treaty entered into on the highest considerations of reciprocal benefit, and to secure peace." The creation and continued peace of the Union was only assured by such "reasons of high policy." To free Sims, the court concluded, would be to bring "the State into controversy with the Federal government."[28]

On the same day as Shaw's ruling, Samuel Sewall also called on Curtis to delay the hearing further so he could gather evidence to confirm Sims' claim that he was a free man, but Curtis declined. Frustrated, Sims' legal team turned to other options: they took out a writ of personal replevin against Marshal Devens, ordering him to produce Sims in court and to submit to a jury trial to prove his right to hold the suspected fugitive. Devens simply refused to honor the writ. Sims' lawyers then drew up a suit against their client, accusing him of stabbing Asa Butman. Civil processes, they argued, must yield to criminal ones. But these claims were rejected, as were other writs, which were filed in quick succession. On April 11th, Curtis ruled in favor of Potter and ordered Sims' return to Georgia.[29]

As Sims' legal team struggled to influence state courts, Hayden, Higginson, and Grimes came up with a rescue plan. A Minkins-type rescue was impossible, as Sims was being held under tight security. But Grimes did manage to arrange a meeting with Sims the day after the Tremont Temple meeting at which the plot was hatched. Sims agreed to the plan of escape. He would jump from the third floor onto mattresses that were placed on the ground. The mattresses were stored in the law offices of William Bowditch, brother of Henry, across Court Square. But Devens got wind of the plan and arranged to have iron bars placed on the windows of the room in which Sims was being held. The plot was foiled. The authorities, nevertheless, remained vigilant. Police stationed outside the courthouse stopped, questioned, and searched African Americans suspected of carrying weapons. At three o'clock in the morning, on April 12th, nearly one hundred policemen mustered outside the courthouse. Sims was brought out at half past nine, surrounded by a large complement of police and

[28] Boston *Herald*, April 7, 1851; Boston *Post*, April 8, 1851. Shaw's ruling quoted in Levy, "Sims' Case," 55–57.

[29] For George Curtis' lengthy ruling, much of which was devoted to a discussion of constitutional issues, see Boston *Courier*, April 12, 1851.

city watch – estimated at three hundred – and marched off down State Street toward Long Wharf followed by a crowd of about two hundred sympathizers. He was placed on the brig *Acorn,* which was to return him to Savannah under guard by six of Devens' officers. Supporters tried to board a vessel moored nearby but were driven back. In his prayer at the wharf as the *Acorn* slipped away, Henry Bowditch expressed what he called the "lofty hope" that the "last slave [had] been carried from Massachusetts." On their return home, Bowditch and others stopped at the spot where Crispus Attucks, the first martyr of the Revolution, had fallen to pay tribute to their city and state's honored history now defiled. The city that had played such a major role in the Revolution, and had once been occupied by foreign troops, now found itself under armed occupation by its own government. Sims arrived in Savannah on the 19th and was placed in jail, where he was flogged. James Potter refused all offers from Massachusetts abolitionists to ransom Sims. He would only consent to part with his recalcitrant slave to someone who pledged to keep him in slavery.[30]

Supporters of the law had finally recorded a victory in the very heart of abolitionism, although some skeptics wondered at what price. One Augusta, Georgia, newspaper put it simply: "Massachusetts owes the South the fugitive slaves within her limits; efforts have been made to get several of them back. We lost the two Crafts and Shadrach, and recovered Simms. A faithful execution of the law, indeed! When costs have been subtracted, we should like to know how much has been gained." A colleague in Savannah arrived at a similar conclusion: the recovery of "fugitives under this much vaunted Fugitive Slave Law" proved to be rather "uncertain and very expensive business." Others were a bit more sanguine about the larger political significance of Sims' return. The abolitionists, another Georgia editor reasoned, had "been allowed full swing in the exercise of all their legal quibbles and their legal ingenuity, and they have been beaten in them all." The citizens of Boston were to be praised for their actions, for they had "vindicated the majesty of the constitution and laws," according to a Baltimore editor, an achievement all the more commendable because it was done in the "face of faction and the most reckless fanaticism." The return of Sims, he declared, was one of the "grandest exhibitions of the conservative energy of republican institutions." The New York *Herald* spoke for many Northern supporters of the law: the return of Sims had finally settled the issue of whether Boston could continue to defy the law, a sentiment endorsed by a colleague in Boston who believed the city had finally been "redeemed from the odious epithets" regularly thrown at it for its abolitionist activities. Yet the

[30] Kantrowitz, *More than Freedom,* 196–97; Bowditch, *Life and Correspondence of Henry Ingersoll Bowditch,* I, 224; Boston *Herald,* April 12, 1851; Savannah *News,* April 21, 1851; *National Era,* July 31, 1851. Levy writes that Sims escaped during the Civil War and returned to Boston. In 1877, he became an employee of US Attorney General Charles Devens, the very person who had refused to accede to a writ to release him days before his return to Georgia. Levy, "Sims' Case," 70–72, 74.

*Herald* conceded that Sims' return would do little to quell abolitionist agitation in Boston or elsewhere.[31]

Supporters of the law in Boston celebrated what they saw as a major political victory. Daniel Webster, who had tried unsuccessfully to manage the two previous fugitive slave cases, was the featured speaker at a meeting in Bowdoin Square attended by a crowd estimated at ten thousand. The past convulsions of the political world, he declared in victory, have been finally "quieted" by the outcome of the Sims case. Petty "sectional quarrels and minor differences" were now but "dust in the balance." Were he in command of one thousand voices, they would cry out in unison: "Union! Now and forever." The size and enthusiasm of the meeting was ample proof that the city had rallied to the cause of law and order and, personally, was ample compensation for the "storm of abuse with which [he] has been assailed by the disunionists and fanatics of the city and State."[32]

Webster spoke for many. Just a month before, the rescue of Minkins had cast a pall of gloom over Senator James Mason, the chief architect of the law. Things seemed not to be going the way he and others had hoped. Taking into account the result of cases since the passage of the law, Henry Clay, however, had cause to be optimistic: under "circumstances really of great embarrassment, doubt and difficulty," he told colleagues, fugitives had been returned from New York City, Harrisburg, Pennsylvania, Philadelphia, and New Albany, Indiana, since the law's inception. His one regret was that Boston had twice failed to follow the lead of other cities. But all things considered, these results were a "beautiful exhibition of the moral power of the law." Mason saw things differently: if not a dead letter, the law had "not answered the ends for which it was designed." The only true measure of success, he had long maintained, was enforcement that was done with "alacrity, diligence, zeal, and good faith." That was not achieved in any of the cases Clay had referenced. Moreover, the price extracted for the capture and return of fugitive slaves was unacceptably steep. The efforts of William Taylor, his Clarke County, Virginia, neighbor to secure and return his two slaves, Samuel Wilson and George Brocks, from Harrisburg, Pennsylvania, soon after the law was adopted, was a case in point. Taylor barely recovered his losses, clearing a mere $50 from the sale of the two slaves following their return. If this were an effective execution of the law, it was one, Mason lamented, in which the claimant got "his property at the cost of the whole of it." Mason could have added that the Sims return had cost the federal and state governments an estimated $20,000 over the course of ten days. Senator Solon Borland, an Arkansas Democrat and, at best, a lukewarm

---

[31] Augusta *Republican,* quoted in Bearse, *Reminiscences of Fugitive–Slave Days,* 30; Savannah *Republican,* April 14, 21, 22, 1851; Savannah *Georgian* (n.d.), in Boston *Herald,* April 26, 1851; Savannah *News,* April 17, 1851; Baltimore *Sun,* April 14, 1851; New York *Herald,* April 13, 1851; Philadelphia *Bulletin,* April 7, 1851.

[32] Boston *Herald,* April 18, 22, 1850.

supporter of the law, was even more skeptical about its effectiveness. How can the capture and return of five or six out of an estimated fifteen thousand escapees be considered anything but an abject failure? Even when fugitives were returned, owners had to endure long "delays, difficulties, annoyances, expenses and in some instances personal dangers." The law, he concluded, was "an empty promise and a delusive hope." Mississippi's Jefferson Davis, who from the beginning of the debate over the Compromise had dismissed the law as, among other things, a violation of state's rights, reiterated the point he had made earlier: the law would never be effective, for there was no "sentiment in the northern States" in favor of its enforcement. Here and there, perhaps, "a fugitive may be recovered, but it is seldom that he can be found; seldom, indeed, that the process can be executed against him." He conceded that they may be taken from "commercial communities," such as New York City (and, in this instant, Boston), cities with direct trading ties to the South, but never from "rural settlements."[33]

One year after Sims' return, the vigilance committee called a daylong public meeting at the Melodeon to commemorate the anniversary of the first rendition from the city, or as Theodore Parker wrote in an ode composed for the occasion, to wipe away the city's "public shame." There were days of "great crimes," dark days of loss and grief, Parker told the large audience, that should be remembered, as were the days of victory. April 12, 1851, the occasion of a great crime, was such a day. What was written in tears should not be erased from the pages of history. In losing Sims they had suffered a great defeat. More tellingly for the people of Boston, Sims came to them a fugitive, and, by failing to protect him, they "made him a slave." He asked for liberty, but the "Boston churches of commerce, in the name of their trinity, the golden eagle, the silver dollar and the copper cent…baptized him a slave." This was a permanent blot on the state's reputation. Had this occurred a hundred years ago, "the people would have fasted one day and then looked to their aims. They would have trusted to God one day, and the next have seen to it that their powder was dry." The day of Sims' return must rank, therefore, as one of the darkest days in the state's history. Wendell Phillips called for the anniversary of the great defeat to be treated as a "Fast day." There was a time when fugitive slaves could have expected to be protected in the state, but that day had passed. Sims was the "first man that the City of Boston ever openly bound and fettered, and sent back to bondage." But abolitionists must never concede: they must continue to trample the law under their feet. Although he declared his reticence to use fugitive slaves to make an abolitionist point, he nonetheless believed that if slave catchers and slaveholders were stabbed or shot on the streets of Boston by escapees, the state would be forced to step in and try them in state

[33] *Appendix, Congressional Globe, Second Session, Thirty-First Congress* (Washington, DC: 1851), 293–94, 297–98, 306–07; *Congressional Globe, Second Session, Thirty-First Congress* (Washington, DC: 1851), 398.

court, and, in so doing, lay down a challenge to the federal law. Lawyers for
the Crafts and Sims had laid out plans to force their cases into state courts,
but Phillips seemed to be suggesting the open use of violence. When he speculated that, if Curtis was shot on "the bench of the Commissioner," such an act
"might have had a beneficial effect," there were protests from the floor. Phillips
had overstepped the mark. It is not clear how committed Phillips was to this
call for violence or how far he was willing to go to challenge the Garrisonian
commitment to nonviolence. James Brewer Stewart insists Phillipps was deeply
ambivalent. As he contemplated such calls to violence, Stewart writes, Phillips
"did so only by assuring himself at the same time that his actions helped his
cause to progress peacefully."[34]

Phillips's frustration at the failure to rescue Sims stemmed, in part, from the
vigilance committee's inability to act decisively. The debate among its members,
while Sims lay shackled in the courthouse, frustrated those who believed the
time for debate had long passed. There was, as Thomas Wentworth Higginson,
Lewis Hayden, and Leonard Grimes believed, too much talk and too little action
among abolitionists when confronted by such a direct challenge. The coalition
of city, state, and federal forces that came together to ensure enforcement of the
law, and the support they received from the business community and political
opponents following the successful rescue of Shadrach Minkins, should not
have surprised opponents of the law, but it evidently did. Once the daring and
ingenious plan to rescue Sims was thwarted, those calling for direct action were
left with few options. The subsequent plan to rescue Sims from the boat taking
him to Georgia was never likely to work, even if the authorities had not taken
precautions to prevent such an eventuality. But Phillips could have taken some
comfort in the fact that, in the space of five months since the passage of the
Fugitive Slave Law, the black community and their abolitionist supporters had
managed to prevent the recapture of three of the four fugitives sought. William
and Ellen Craft were safe in England and Shadrach Minkins in Canada.

Since its formation, the vigilance committee – or at least its executive
committee – had successfully aided fugitive slaves to reach Canada or to settle
in other areas considered safe, a pattern that would continue throughout the
decade. In its first two years of operation, the committee aided 174 fugitives,
helping most of them get to Canada but also a fair number to other parts of
the state, including Hopedale, Westminster, and Worcester. This number should
have raised the spirits of Phillips. The records of the committee are not always
clear about the origins of those they assisted, or whether fugitives came to them
directly. Many of those they received came through the vigilance committees
of Philadelphia and New York City. Most of its resources were expended in
boarding and lodging and getting fugitives out of the city. The $10 paid to

34 Weiss, *Life and Correspondence of Theodore Parker*, II, 108–09; Commager, *Theodore Parker*,
197; *Liberator*, April 9, 23, 1852; Boston *Herald*, April 12, 13, 1852; Stewart, *Wendell
Phillips*, 158.

Lewis Hayden in December 1851 for boarding James Hall and Thomas Pew for two weeks was fairly typical. But the committee also devoted its time and resources to aiding fugitives who, like Sims, had stowed away from Southern seaports. They allocated funds for Austin Bearse, a seaman and member of the committee, to build a yacht to be used in rescues. There is no evidence that it was ever used, but Bearse did use his other boat, the *Moby Dick*, to rescue fugitives. It was manned by a crew of whites and blacks who quickly gained a reputation for the rescue of fugitives from ships anchored in the harbor. When, in July 1853, Amos Hopkins, the captain of the brig *Florence*, carrying lumber from Wilmington, North Carolina, discovered Pompey Williams, a fugitive, on board, he hurried ashore to consult with the US district attorney. While Hopkins was away, Bearse and his crew pulled the *Moby Dick* alongside the brig and removed Williams.[35]

In the months and years after Sims' return, Boston reasserted its reputation as a safe place for fugitives. Bearse recalled taking Harriet Beecher Stowe to Lewis Hayden's home in 1853, where she met thirteen escapees. By the end of the year, William J. Watkins, Southern-born, and a relative newcomer to the city, asserted with some authority: "No more fugitives will be carried from Boston."[36] The calm was shattered, however, on May 25, 1854, with the arrest of Anthony Burns by a posse led by Asa Butman, who had arrested Sims. Burns was placed in irons and taken before Commissioner Edward Greely Loring. The twenty-three-year-old Burns, born in a small rural settlement in Stafford County, Virginia, had been sent to Richmond by his owner, Charles F. Suttle, where he was hired out by William Brent, a city merchant. Burns found work on the city wharves loading and unloading ships. He escaped in late March by secreting himself on a ship sailing for Boston. It is clear that he was assisted by one of the black crewmen, who supplied him with food and water throughout the journey. When the ship dropped anchor in Boston harbor, Burns slipped away. He found odd jobs in the black community and joined Leonard Grimes' small church. Grimes got word of the arrest to the vigilance committee and headed directly to the courthouse, where he found Burns under heavy guard. US Marshal Watson Freeman was surprised and angered that the arrest was already public but did allow Grimes to meet with Burns. Richard Dana later recalled that he happened to be passing the courthouse when he heard a fugitive

---

[35] "Vigilance Committee's Treasurer's Account Book, Siebert Collection," Harvard University in Black Abolitionists Papers (BAP) 6: 10948; "List of Fugitive Slaves Aided by the Vigilance Committee since the passage of the Fugitive Slave Bill, 1850," Massachusetts Anti-Slavery Society Collection, New York Historical Society, in BAP, 6: 10367; *Liberator*, July 29, 1853; Boston *Herald*, July 20, 21, 1853; Boston *Post*, July 21, 1853; Pittsburgh *Gazette*, July 28, 1853; Kantrowitz, *More than Freedom*, 197–98; Bearse, *Reminiscences*, 34. Bearse narrates the number of times he used his yacht to rescue fugitives from New England vessels trading in the South. He also suggested that a contact in the South informed Phillips of fugitives who were heading to Massachusetts by boat.

[36] Bearse, *Reminiscences*, 8; Watkins quoted in Kantrowitz, *More than Freedom*, 205.

was being held inside. He entered and saw what he described as a "piteous object, rather weak in mind and body, with a large scar on his cheek, which looked like a brand, a broken hand from which a large piece of bone projects, and another scar on his other hand." Burns cut a dejected, distracted figure, surrounded by a "large corps of officers." As far as Dana was concerned, Burns had already reconciled himself to being returned.[37]

Seth Thomas, who had worked with the claimants in both the Crafts and Sims cases, joined Edward G. Parker as Suttle's counsels; Dana appeared for Burns. Following William Brent's testimony that Burns had worked for him and that he had expressed a desire to return, Dana called for a delay on the grounds that he could not adequately defend someone in Burns' state of mind; he had to be given an opportunity to determine if Burns did not wish to put up a defense. Wendell Phillips, who had also met with Burns, was convinced the fugitive had no intention of returning. Loring agreed to a delay, convinced that the evidence against Burns was such that his return was inevitable, but aware, also, that the suspect should be afforded the time to marshal a defense. The day after Loring agreed to the postponement, the mayor called out the city's entire military force of 1,800. These were supplemented by three companies of regulars who filled the "streets and squares" outside the courthouse, reminding Theodore Parker that, once again, the people's court had been turned into a "slave pen."[38]

The vigilance committee promptly called a meeting, but again, as in the crisis over the arrest of Sims, was immobilized by differences over what course of action it should take. It had become, at least as far as Higginson was concerned, a committee of "mere talk and discussion," a sort of "disorderly convention" during which each member had his own plan. There were Garrisonians opposed to any form of violence, political abolitionists and Free-Soilers who were "full of indignation" but no action. Even Lewis Hayden, he recalled, doubted that many blacks would join, as most of those who had participated in Shadrach's rescue had left Boston. It was the first time in three years that they had met, and Henry Bowditch recalled that "each man wanted to talk, and no man entirely trusted his neighbor or himself apparently." But they did agree to call a public meeting at Faneuil Hall. Higginson brought two hundred men from Worcester to Boston, to do what, according to Bowditch, the committee would not or could not do. The packed hall heard Phillips declare that the start of the hearing the following day "begins a contest between Massachusetts and Virginia." He called on the people of Boston to make sure that the Sims debacle was not repeated. He recommended that they start by blocking every entrance to the courthouse. If Burns were returned, Theodore Parker mocked, they should all

[37] Charles Emery Stevens, *Anthony Burns. A History* (Williamstown, MA: 1856), 151, 169; Adams, *Richard Henry Dana*, I, 265; von Frank, *The Trials of Anthony Burns*, 1.
[38] Boston *Herald*, May 25, 29, 1854; Boston *Post*, May 29, 1854; *Liberator*, June 2, 1854; Adams, *Richard Henry Dana*, I, 276.

be considered citizens of Virginia. Higginson and one of his Worcester allies, Martin Stowell, might have had a hand in what transpired next. It had all the hallmarks of the October 1851 Jerry rescue in Syracuse. Evidently, Stowell was in Syracuse at the time, and, apparently, was involved in the rescue. On cue, someone in the balcony disrupted a speaker to announce that eight hundred African Americans were gathered outside the courthouse and were about to rescue Burns. The meeting was abandoned and the crowd hurried to the court square, where the rescuers, according to one report, were armed with axes, guns, and stones bought by Higginson, at a discount, from a nearby hardware store. Higginson and Stowell had also procured a large wooden beam, which they planned to use to gain entrance to the heavily guarded courthouse. Using the beam as a battering ram, Higginson and a handful of blacks forced their way into the building through a door on the west side of the building. They were met on the first floor by fifty to sixty of Marshal Freeman's police. In the melee that followed, the defenders prevented the intruders from reaching Burns on an upper floor. Additional contingents of police soon arrived, followed by divisions of militia. Order was soon restored and nine people were arrested, including four blacks and Stowell.[39]

During the melee, a shot rang out and James Batchelder, a thirty-five-year-old officer who had come to the assistance of his colleagues, fell dead with a wound to the groin. Batchelder was the first person to die while enforcing the law. John C. Cluer, a Scots and former Chartist, was arrested for killing Batchelder, as was Nelson Hopewell, an African American, for being an accessory to murder. Many laid the blame for the death of Batchelder at the door of Phillips and Parker: their treasonous speeches at the Faneuil Hall meeting had influenced "ignorant blacks and infuriated whites to bathe their hands in blood." A Rochester observer was convinced that the "abolitionist population" of Boston was in a state of open rebellion. "They are constantly in the commission of acts of treason against the US Government," he declared, and "have adopted a course essentially revolutionary." Others thought the blame for what happened laid elsewhere. A Washington, DC, editorialist charged Senator Charles Sumner and his "abolitionist gang." He had circulated letters throughout New England whipping up hatred of slavery and declaring that no more fugitives would be taken from Massachusetts. He was, the editor believed, "the monkey flourishing a burning fire-brand above a magazine of powder." Remove him from office, he recommended, and all treasonous activities will cease. A colleague in New York City laid the blame instead on

[39] Boston *Herald*, May 27, June 6, 1854; *Liberator*, June 2, 1854. On Stowell see von Frank, *The Trials of Anthony Burns*, 23–26, the Faneuil Hall meeting, 61–66, and the assault on the courthouse 62–70; Tilden G. Edelstein, *Strange Enthusiasm. A Life of Thomas Wentworth Higginson* (New Haven: 1968), 157–59; Thomas Wentworth Higginson, *Cheerful Yesterdays* (1898, rpr., New York: 1968), 140, 145. On the Jerry rescue see Angela F. Murphy, *The Jerry Rescue: the Fugitive Slave Law, Northern Rights, and the American Sectional Crisis* (New York: 2016).

that state's senior senator, William Seward. But Frederick Douglass dismissed such views as the simpering of proslavery advocates. When a working "truckman," such as Batchelder, abandoned his "useful employment" and took up the "revolting business of a Kidnapper, and undertook to play the bloodhound on the track of a crimeless brother Burns, he labeled himself the common enemy of mankind, and his slaughter was as innocent, in the sight of God, as would be the slaughter of a ravenous wolf in the act of throttling an infant." Because of his actions, Batchelder "forfeited his right to live." Douglass saw the death as not only necessary, but also as a "warning to others liable to pursue a like course."[40]

The next morning, two thousand gathered outside the courthouse. They were greeted by the entire city police force. The militia was also put on standby and one hundred US marines were stationed on the "upper part" of the courthouse. The mayor pleaded for calm, calling on the crowd to disperse. Parker's church was packed to overflowing to hear his views on the crisis. If Boston had peacefully resisted the return of Sims, he told his listeners, there would have been such a general outpouring of opposition to slavery and the Fugitive Slave Law that Congress would not have dared to agree to the recently adopted Kansas-Nebraska Act. Piloted through Congress by Stephen Douglas, the act left it up to the residents of a territory to decide if they wished to enter the Union as a free or a slave state. In enshrining the principle of "popular sovereignty," it abrogated the Compromise of 1820, which, many believed, had permanently set the limits of slave territory. If, one editor reasoned, proponents of the act maintained that no law could impinge on the rights of citizens to express their sovereignty, a right that, they believed, the Missouri Compromise evidently violated, on what constitutional grounds did Congress have the power to make rights for the states? "If the principle of popular sovereignty overrides an express provision of the constitution with respect to the territories, while they are in a state of acknowledged tutelage to the general government," the editor wondered, "why should not the same principle override a less express provision in its application to a sovereign state?" The editor spoke for many: if the principle of states' rights applied in this case, why did it not inform the Fugitive Slave Law? There was a massive outpouring of opposition to the act throughout the Free States. Meetings denounced it as yet another concession to the Slave Power. Not so in Boston, which remained eerily silent. Whigs, the dominant political force in the city, who had eagerly rushed to support the Fugitive Slave Law, now adamantly refused to call a meeting. To add to the crisis, the Richmond slave catchers seeking Burns arrived just as the furor over the legislation was at its zenith.

---

[40] Boston *Herald*, May 27, 29, 1854; Rochester *American*, May 31, June 2, 3, 1854; Washington, DC, *Evening Star*, June 1, 1854; New York *Herald*, May 30, 1854; von Frank, *The Trials of Anthony Burns*, 137. There is some evidence pointing to Lewis Hayden as the person who shot Batchelder. See Kantrowitz, *More than Freedom*, 207–08.

The North acceded to every demand from the "Southern task-master," Parker told his listeners; they were granted all they asked for. In everything involving their interests, slaveholders were deeply earnest; in comparison, he scolded, Northern lovers of liberty were not.[41]

Every road leading to the courthouse was under heavy guard on the morning of Burns' hearing. Inside, half of the hearing room was occupied by special police. Even one of the counsels for the claimant was armed. William Brent was the first to testify. He had known Burns to be Suttle's slave for about twelve years and had agreed to hire him in 1851. He could identify Burns by the scars on his cheek and the cut across his right hand. Richard Dana, for Burns, countered with eight black witnesses who all testified that they had first met Burns prior to the date he was supposed to have escaped from Richmond. It was a defense that had proven successful in other fugitive slave hearings. William Jones claimed that he had hired Burns to clean windows in early March. James F. Whittmere recalled seeing Burns cleaning windows and noticed, at the time, a "mark upon his cheek," and also realized that "something was the matter with his right hand." Stephen Maddox confirmed that Burns had cleaned his shop window. The others all acknowledged that they had seen Burns in the company of Jones cleaning windows in early March. In a lengthy summation lasting over four hours, Dana built a case for Burns' release around a number of legal principles, as well as, more prosaically, the issue of identity and the claim that Burns was not in Richmond at the time it was claimed that he had escaped. Seth Thomas responded with a novel claim: if Burns is "returned to Virginia, and is still held in slavery it is not because he has lost any rights, but because, by the laws of Virginia, he never had any rights." Burns had no rights in Richmond, consequently, no rights could be "taken from him by any acts of ours." Thomas's arguments seemed to anticipate those that would be laid down by the US Supreme Court in the Dred Scott case three years later: blacks had no rights in either Boston or Richmond, or for that matter, anywhere else.[42]

There were rumors that a "large amount of money" had been raised for a rescue. The night before Loring was to issue his ruling, Marshal Freeman mustered 140 armed assistants at the courthouse. They were reinforced by the addition of 145 US troops. Few were surprised by Loring's ruling in favor of Suttle. He may have granted a one-day delay at the start of the hearing, but as far as Philipps and others were concerned, it was a convenient way to immunize himself against criticism for a decision he had already contemplated making. In ordering the return of Burns, Loring rejected the testimony of those witnesses who claimed to have met Burns weeks before it was reputed that he

---

[41] Boston *Herald*, May 27, 29, June 5, 1854; Springfield *Republican*, June 14, 1854. On the political maneuvering around the passage of the act see William W. Freehling, *The Road to Disunion. Secessionists at Bay, 1776–1854* (New York: 1990), 558–59.

[42] Boston *Herald*, May, 29, 30, 31, June 1, 1854.

had escaped, and instead accepted, as both persuasive and more convincing, Brent's testimony and familiarity with Burns.[43]

Grimes and others tried to console a disconsolate Burns, who feared he would be sold to the Deep South on his return to Suttle.[44] The streets around Court House Square were closed by the police on the morning of Burns' return. Convinced that there would be a rescue attempt, Marshal Freeman wrote the mayor and President Franklin Pierce that local forces needed to be strengthened. Benjamin Hallett sent a similar warning. The president replied, ordering that no expenses should be spared to enforce the law. A company of US artillery brought up a couple of canons and went through the motions of loading them. The Boston Brigade was put under arms. An additional nineteen companies of artillery and regiments and two of cavalry were deployed, totaling an estimated 1,500. Businesses were temporarily closed on roads leading to the wharf. Some lawyers along the route draped their windows in black as an act of protest. Flags on public buildings were at half-mast or flown upside down. The authorities felt much more secure than they had during the return of Sims. The military did not muster at three o'clock in the morning; in this instance, Burns was brought out in broad daylight in front of "the assembled merchant princes of State Street," Henry Bowditch recalled, "with a right royal cortege of two companies of United States troops, and canon loaded with grape, and all the military of Suffolk County." Burns was marched down the major streets of Boston flanked by the military, as onlookers – estimated to be as many as fifty thousand – lined the sidewalks and watched anxiously from windows. People jeered and spat at soldiers from upstairs windows. Cayenne pepper and a bottle of acid were thrown at the troops. A cavalryman's horse was stabbed and had to be put down. A hackman tried to drive his carriage through the lines, killing, in the process, another horse. As if to thumb their noses at the protesting crowd, a section of militia broke into a rendition of "Carry Me Back to Old Virginny." Burns was put on board a cutter to be taken to the *Morris,* which lay at anchor some distance out to sea.[45]

Burns' return was greeted with some satisfaction by Virginians. One Norfolk newspaper announced the arrival of the "ungrateful runaway slave from a comfortable home where he was well treated." The deputies who escorted Burns were feted by the city before he was put on a boat to Richmond. A public meeting in Hampton rejoiced at the "late triumphant vindication of the Constitution and the laws." Enforcing the Fugitive Slave Law, particularly in Boston, was an "example of patriotic conduct." The meeting expressed thanks

---

[43] Boston *Post,* June 8, 1854; Boston *Herald,* June 2, 1854.

[44] Boston *Herald,* May 29, July 7, 1854; Boston *Chronicle* (n.d.), in Boston *Herald,* May 30, 1854; Boston *Post,* July 8, 1854; von Frank, *The Trials of Anthony Burns,* 80–81, 204–05.

[45] Von Frank, *The Trials of Anthony Burns,* 213–19; Bowditch, *Life and Correspondence of Henry Ingersoll Bowditch,* I, 263–64; Stevens, *Anthony Burns,* 269–74; Stewart, *Wendell Phillips,* 172; Edelstein, *Strange Enthusiasm,* 161.

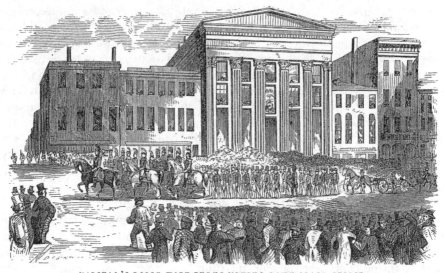

MARSHAL'S POSSE WITH BURNS MOVING DOWN STATE STREET.

FIGURE 12. Marshal's Posse with Burns Moving Down State Street. (Charles Emery Stevens, *Anthony Burns. A History*)

to the mayor of Boston for his prompt action in suppressing "mob violence," and praised the president for providing the ship in which Burns was returned. Such actions demonstrated "the endurance of the Union and its blessings," and were evidence of the existence of a "law-abiding spirit in the land." The meeting also set up a committee to raise funds to aid the Batchelder family and called on other Southern communities to do the same.[46]

Even before the hearing had concluded, an offer was made to ransom Burns. Some had hoped word of a possible ransom would ease growing tensions in the city. Edward Parker, one of Suttle's lawyers, claimed that he had initiated the scheme and had consulted with Leonard Grimes, who agreed to raise the needed $1,200. But Suttle reneged on the agreement before the money was collected, insisting that no exchange was possible until the supremacy of the law "can be maintained." Burns' ransom would have to wait until after his return to Richmond. In June, Suttle offered to sell Burns for $1,500, the additional $400 reflecting the cost of he had incurred in recapturing Burns. But when nothing came of the offer, Burns was sold at auction to David McDaniel, a Rocky Mount, North Carolina, cotton planter, for $905. Burns managed to get word to Richard Dana and other supporters in Massachusetts that his new owner was willing to accept $1,300. Almost $700 was raised by Grimes; the balance by Charles Barry, a member of the Pine Street Anti-Slavery Society and cashier

---

[46] *Southern Argus*, June 12, 15, 1854.

at a Boston bank. Grimes met McDaniel in February 1855 in Baltimore, where the exchange took place. In early March, Burns was officially welcomed back to the North at a public meeting held in the Presbyterian Church in New York City, headed by J. W. C. Pennington. He informed his listeners of his decision to escape, his capture in Boston on the pretext of stealing, and his return and sale to Grimes. Days later, a crowd in excess of one thousand welcomed him back to Boston. Burns later enrolled at Oberlin College to study for the ministry.[47]

The capture and rendition of Burns, coming as it did in the midst of the heated debate over the Kansas-Nebraska Act, had a profound impact on city and state politics. The annual meeting of the New England Anti-Slavery Society, a Garrisonian organization that eschewed violence, was in session during the Burns hearing. Henry C. Wright called for continued resistance to the Fugitive Slave Law and denounced the state for allowing fugitives to be returned. Others demanded that every effort should be made to prevent returns in the future. Stephen S. Foster and others proposed the formation of secret societies to repel slave catchers and protect the good name of Massachusetts. "If we can find the pathway where the devil treads," one delegate declared, "it is right for us to dig pit-falls for him to tumble into." The call for open defiance and the prospect of violence prompted Garrison to express his continued opposition to taking up arms or, for that matter, the formation of secret societies. He acknowledged that the Slave Power had carried the day in the case of Burns. The Mason-Dixon Line had, in effect, been redrawn to include Massachusetts. Yet he pleaded: "Let everything that is done by us come before Israel and the people." In the wake of the rendition, however, the people, and that included many abolitionists, seemed ripe, as Henry Bowditch observed, for revolution. Although many continued to eschew violence, they nevertheless endorsed the formation of the "Anti-Man-Hunting League," whose sole purpose was to kidnap the kidnappers and so prevent the return of fugitives. It is not clear how much the league accomplished, but branches were quickly established throughout the state. Many, who at the time of Sims' return had "enrolled themselves as special policemen," Richard Dana recalled, now committed themselves to the protection of fugitives. Cotton Whig Amos Lawrence spoke for many: "We went to bed one night old fashioned, conservative, Compromise Union Whigs, and waked up stark mad Abolitionists."[48]

[47] Von Frank, *The Trials of Anthony Burns*, 233–34, 288–90; New York *Tribune*, March 3, 1855; Boston *Herald*, March 8, 1855. Burns was not totally rid of slavery. While at Oberlin, he wrote to his former church in Union, Fauquier County, for a letter of dismission, which was refused because he had run away, defying both "the laws of God and man." Albany *Journal*, February 11, 1856; New York *Tribune*, February 15, 1856; Ashtabula *Sentinel*, February 28, 1856; Earl M. Maltz, *Fugitive Slave on Trial. The Anthony Burns Case and Abolitionist Outrage* (Lawrence, KA: 2010), 62–63.

[48] Boston *Herald*, May 30, 31, 1854; Bowditch, *Life and Correspondence of Henry Ingersoll Bowditch*, I, 273–74. Lawrence quoted in von Frank, *The Trials of Anthony Burns*, 207, 216; Kantrowitz, *More than Freedom*, 212; Adams, *Richard Henry Dana*, 269.

Two days after Burns' return, Higginson, still bearing the scar on his chin from his encounter with the police inside the courthouse during the abortive rescue attempt, took to his pulpit in Worcester to assess conditions in the country. The nation, he declared, was "intoxicated and depraved," dominated, as it was, by a slaveholding oligarchy. With the exception of the right to petition, antislavery forces had won only one victory in twenty years, and even in that instance, it was no more than the recovery of lost ground, during what he described as an "anti-slavery spasm." Massachusetts, and, by extension, all other Northern states, consistently conceded ground to proslavery forces. South Carolina, in comparison, never flinched, never retreated an inch in its demands. As a result, free territory had shrunk measurably over the years. Now, it was to be found only in a handful of cities – Syracuse, Wilkesbarre, Milwaukee, and Chicago – where, recently, the law had been resisted and slave catchers repulsed. The law, he predicted, would not be repealed in his lifetime by politicians in Washington. It could only be vanquished by the people "upon the soil of Massachusetts." The community, in other words, would determine the law's constitutionality. The ineffectiveness of the vigilance committee in both the Sims and Burns cases still rankled. As he later observed, these "personally admirable" men were not "fitted…to undertake any positive action in the direction of the forcible resistance to authorities." In spite of his gloomy assessment, Higginson saw signs that the tide had turned, that "a revolution had begun." The failure to rescue Burns had galvanized the otherwise reticent to act. To confirm Amos Lawrence's observation, traditional Whigs and Democrats had grown so averse to the law and its effects that they were rapidly becoming Free-Soilers and even disunionists. Massachusetts needed to stand its political ground. No longer should it hide or send fugitives to Canada; it should, instead, openly and defiantly "show them" at public meetings and dare the authorities to retake them. Massachusetts, not Canada, had to be made the terminus of the UGRR: "*Here O Richmond! And give ear O Carolina! henceforth Worcester is Canada to the Slave!*"[49]

A few months later, Worcester was to demonstrate that Higginson's was no idle boast. In the late fall, the city's vigilance committee was informed that Deputy Marshal Asa Butman, who had arrested Sims and Burns, was in town and registered at the American House. It was rumored that he was there to arrest a fugitive slave. The vigilance committee printed and posted handbills announcing his presence. A crowd quickly gathered outside the hotel, chanting and calling on Butman to come out. They rang the doorbell constantly during the night. When Butman finally responded, he came to the hotel door brandishing a pistol and threatening to use it. The threat backfired; at three o'clock in the morning, he was arrested on a warrant for carrying a weapon and taken to the local jail. The next morning, the police court was packed with angry

---

[49] *Liberator,* June 16, 1854; Edelstein, *Strange Enthusiasm,* 162–63.

onlookers. During a temporary adjournment, half a dozen African Americans managed to gain access to the room where Butman was held. The city marshal had to rescue him from a beating. Some in the crowd outside the courthouse called for Butman to be lynched, others that he be tarred and feathered. A young lawyer, George F. Hoar, tried unsuccessfully to quiet the crowd by appealing for law and order. Even in Charleston, South Carolina, he reasoned, crowds would not threaten such violence. Hoar knew better: his father and sister were run out of Charleston by a mob almost twenty years earlier while on a mission to gain the release of black Massachusetts seamen taken into custody under that state's Negro Seamen Act. Hoar promised Butman safe passage if he would agree to leave town, but the crowd was not to be appeased. In what some saw as a poetic twist of history, Higginson, Martin Stowell, Stephen Foster, and others now offered to act as a guard to protect Butman on his way to the train station. A crowd of nearly six hundred followed. Eggs and stones were thrown, and according to one report, a "powerful negro" managed to get close enough to Butman to strike him so hard that the marshal's legs buckled. By the time they reached the station, the crowd had grown to one thousand. Unfortunately for Butman, the train had left already. Higginson and the others were forced to hide Butman in a privy for his own safety. Foster again informed the crowd that Butman had promised to leave and never return to Worcester. When another attempt was made to move Butman by carriage, the crowd rushed in and again assaulted him. Fortunately for the marshal, he did manage to escape further harm, protected by abolitionists who, as one report noted wryly, "periled their own lives to shield a kidnapper." Butman's treatment was a testament to the black community's and abolitionists' vigilance, and a confirmation, if one was needed, that Worcester, and, by extension, Massachusetts, were indeed free soil.[50]

Another sign that the tide had turned in favor of fugitives following Burns' rendition was the massive petition to Congress, endorsed by what one local newspaper described as "the most prominent merchants in the city," calling for the repeal of the Fugitive Slave Law. Many of the 2,900 signatories, it was reported, were former supporters of the law whose positions had been altered by their revulsion against the treatment of Burns. The petition provided opponents of the law in Congress with another opportunity to revisit the debate over its constitutionality. The "gag" agreed to by both parties in Congress in 1851 was simply not sustainable in the face of such events. The silence had been

[50] New York *Tribune*, October 30, 1854, *National Era*, November 9, 1854; Worcester *Spy*, October 31, 1854; Edelstein, *Strange Enthusiasm*, 167–71; Higginson, *Cheerful Yesterdays*, 162–65; George F. Hoar, *Autobiography of Seventy Years*, 2 Vols. (New York: 1903), I, 24–25, 184–85. On the Negro Seamen's Acts see Michael A. Schoeppner, "Status Across Borders: Roger Taney, Black British Subjects, and a Diplomatic Antecedent to the Dred Scott Decision," *Journal of American History*, 100, No. 1 (June 2013) and Horton and Horton, *Family Life and Community Struggle*, 107.

previously broken, as we have seen, following the rescue of Shadrach Minkins. On this occasion, Charles Sumner led the charge against the law. He had long opposed the law, he told colleagues, and had worked to render it "practically inoperative" in the hope that Congress would see the necessity to repeal it. He had no doubt that the law was unconstitutional. Those who opposed its passage had made it abundantly clear why it did not pass constitutional muster. Yet the law was adopted and enforced. Much like the Stamp Acts, almost a century earlier, enforcement of the unpopular Fugitive Slave Law had generated so much opposition that it had been effectively annulled in many parts of the country. Like vice, the law had "so hideous a mien, that 'to be hated it needs only to be seen.'" James Jones of Tennessee rejected Sumner's arguments and the memorial, which, he declared, was "surcharged with treason and with blood." How many of the signees, those with "treason in their hearts, and with knives in their hands," he wondered, had been actively resisting the law since its inception? Jones predicted that the country would be torn apart if the law were repealed, for the South would not permit such an invasion of its rights, nor would it allow its property to be stolen. When Southerners went to Massachusetts to reclaim their property, instead of finding cooperation, they were met by "heartless, odious hypocrites in the pulpit, preaching sedition and treason." Northerners wanted "our negroes," they wanted "our property," they wanted to "dishonor us…to disgrace us"; they wished to instigate a servile war during which "our wives and daughters" would be "degraded and dishonored."

Andrew P. Butler of South Carolina made it clear that he had little time for the law. But if Sumner wanted to appeal to history, surely he could not ignore the fact that the country had been formed by a confederation of slave states, each of which had established an obligation, under the Constitution, to return slaves who fled their owners. The "independence of America, to maintain republican liberty, was won by the arms and treasure, by the patriotism and *good faith* of slaveholding communities." At times, the debate degenerated into a pointless squabble over which section of the country contributed more to the success of the Revolution. But differences over the historical foundations of the country aside, Butler wanted to know, if they agreed to the repeal of the law, would Massachusetts return all absconding slaves as they were obligated to do under the Constitution? Sumner evaded the question by insisting he, personally, would never send back a slave. The law was unconstitutional, for it failed, among other things, to guarantee the suspect's right to habeas corpus. That claim brought James Mason to his feet. He thought he had laid to rest such misconceptions during congressional debates over the law in 1850. Yet it continued to be a major line of defense in fugitive slave cases. There was nothing in the law, he reiterated, that denied this foundational principle. In fact, it had no application in such cases. The writ was meant to inquire into the legality of a detention. If it was proven that a fugitive was "held to service, or labor, and did escape, whether justly so held or no, under the Constitution," he was to "be returned whence he escaped." The proof established the "legality of the arrest and detention," and was "an answer to the writ of habeas corpus." In so doing, the Fugitive Slave Law did "not depart from the policy regulating the administration of all penal law." Similarly, a person who was arrested as a "fugitive from justice" was granted a writ of habeas corpus not to determine if he committed the offence in the place from which he escaped, but only to determine if he was properly charged, and if he could be held until a trial, at which point, if proof was provided, he had to be remanded without inquiring whether the charge was true or false. It was an argument that carried little weight with opponents in 1850; it carried even less now. But, at least on this occasion, Mason seemed to have dropped the legal fiction that, like the fugitive from justice, the escaped slave could appeal his status on his return to his master.

Sumner was "mad enough," Mason concluded, to admit that he did not recognize the constitutional right of slaveholders to reclaim their lost slaves. But, he insisted, Charles Suttle was not a "slave hunter," as Sumner claimed; he had gone to Massachusetts to reclaim his property under protection of the Constitution. Unlike Andrew Butler, Mason believed that the law had "done its office" in the case of Burns, and, that in spite of mobs "roused and inflamed to the very verge of treason." Mason, Sumner responded, was entitled to his opinion; after all, he was the author of "that enormity; [f]rom his brains came forth the soulless monster." Mason may have resisted the urge to claim that all opposition to the law was treasonous, but bandying about the word had become so much a feature of political disputes over the law that no one could have missed Mason's and Butler's message: Sumner's declared refusal to return fugitives was nothing short of an act of treason. One editor even insisted that Sumner had "raised the arm of rebellion." Views such as Sumner's, Senator John Pettit of Indiana observed, were grounds enough for expulsion from the Senate. The opposition, however, could not muster the votes to remove Sumner. In the weeks after the conclusion of the debate, Sumner and other senators from the North continued to submit petitions calling for the law's repeal.[51]

Following Burns' return, abolitionists, led by Wendell Phillips, set their sights on removing Edward G. Loring from office. The effort became something like a crusade. The commissioner, Parker told a packed audience at the Music Hall, had "prejudged the case." In a private meeting with Phillips on the first morning of the hearing, according to Parker, Loring had made it clear that he thought the case was clear cut and, as such, hoped that Phillips would not interfere with the proceedings. Phillips later recalled Loring telling him: "I don't think you

[51] Boston *Herald*, May 30, 1854; *Defence of Massachusetts. Speeches of Hon. Charles Sumner, on the Memorial for the Repeal of the Fugitive Slave Bill* (Washington, DC: 1854), 4–6, 8, 10, 13, 15; *Congressional Globe, Thirty-Third Congress* (Washington, DC: 1854), 28, 33, 282, 1472, 1515–18; *Appendix, Congressional Globe, Thirty-Third Congress* (Washington, DC: 1854), 1037; David Donald, *Charles Sumner and the Coming of the Civil War* (New York: 1974), 262–64; *Southern Argus*, June 3, 1854. Another petition, on a scroll measuring two hundred feet, was sent to Congress by a meeting of New England clergy protesting the arrest of Burns.

are justified in placing any obstacle to this man being sent back, as he probably will be." "When a bad man does a bad deed, nobody is astonished," Parker concluded, "but when a good man is guilty of wrong doing, it destroys confidence in human nature." Such expressions of disappointment were not grounds enough to have a commissioner dismissed. But Loring was also a state probate judge as well as a lecturer at Harvard University's law school. Even before he had made the decision to return Burns, John Gorham Palfrey, leader of the state's Free-Soil Party, had warned Loring about the possible ramifications of a decision in favor of Suttle. Loring had one of two choices: he could resign both his position at Harvard and his judgeship, or resign as commissioner. To hold on to all three positions would make him vulnerable to recall should he decide to return Burns. Loring thought otherwise.[52]

The fall elections of 1854 provided a political opening to move against Loring. Democrats had lost political ground lately as a result of their sponsorship of the Kansas-Nebraska Act. So had the Whigs, who remained divided, and whose refusal to support a public demonstration against the act had alienated many in the party. Free-Soilers, in the process of transitioning into the newly formed Republican Party, had yet to find any traction with the electorate. In the midst of this political uncertainty, the Know-Nothing Party swept to victory, winning majorities in both houses as well as the governor's mansion, on a platform based largely on opposition to continued Irish immigration. But many in the party were known opponents of the law, as was its candidate for governor, Henry J. Gardner, who nonetheless hedged his bets by insisting that the law had to be enforced until such time as it was repealed.[53]

In February 1855, the Joint Standing Committee on Federal Relations opened an inquiry into whether Loring's actions warranted removal. Loring refused to attend, insisting that nothing he had done justified either his removal or his withdrawal. Robert Morris, the African American lawyer, was the first to testify, emphasizing that Burns' hearing was hurried and, although he had acted as the fugitive's unofficial counsel, he was not given an opportunity to consult with his client. Although others testified, it was Phillips who led the charge. Loring, he maintained, had "sinned against the high characteristics of a Judge." He did not call for his impeachment, but his removal "by address," by either the legislature or governor, for violating the "expressed will of the Commonwealth" as contained in the 1843 law, which barred all citizens of the state from assisting in the return of fugitive slaves. Based on his private conversation with the commissioner on the first day of the hearing, Phillips had no doubt that Loring had prejudged the case. Loring, he pointed out, was named a probate judge in 1847, years after the 1843 law denied a state judge

---

[52] Boston *Herald*, June 5, 1854, February 21, March 1, 1855; von Frank, *The Trials of Anthony Burns*, 120–21; *Liberator*, February 23, March 2, 1855.

[53] Tyler Anbinder, *Nativism and Slavery. The Northern Know Nothings and the Politics of the 1850s* (New York: 1992), 89–92, 155.

the right to participate in the return of fugitives. That law "thundered forth its command, that no officer shall hold the broad seal of the State in one hand, and reach forth the other for a slave-catcher's fee." Phillips rejected the argument that Loring had acted not as a state judge, but as a federal commissioner. Acting as a commissioner, Loring had "defied the well-known, settled, religious convictions of the State, *officially* made known to him." Clothed in the "ermine of Massachusetts," Loring should not have involved himself in the return of the hapless fugitive. Richard Hildreth, lawyer, journalist, historian, and member of the vigilance committee, supported the call for Loring's removal. Even if one conceded that the Fugitive Slave Law was constitutional, Loring, he argued, should be removed for "having ventured to act at all; thereby setting himself in opposition not merely to the letter of a Massachusetts statute, but to the moral sentiment of her people." There was a clear conflict between Massachusetts and the United States as to "their several powers and rights in relation to fugitives from labor." Until this was settled by the "repeal of the obnoxious act," it was inconceivable that Loring could be both a state judge and a commissioner.[54]

Richard Dana, who had defended Sims and Burns, surprised his colleagues with a spirited defense of Loring and opposition to his removal. The commissioner's conduct, throughout the hearing, Dana recalled, had been "mild, humane and eminently favorable towards giving Burns every chance for making a defence." Removal was an extraordinary decision that should not be lightly taken. Only once in the history of the country had a judge been removed. No one had demonstrated that Loring was unqualified for the position. Qualifications were being set aside in favor of "fealty to party," which, if successful, would do irreparable damage to the antislavery cause. Would they be having this discussion, he wondered rhetorically, if Loring had ruled in favor of Burns? The commissioner had given Burns every opportunity to defend himself, even when the fugitive made it clear that he had reconciled himself to his return. A defense, Burns worried, would make things difficult for him when he was returned. Loring permitted time for the defense to consult with its client, even when lawyers for the claimant had demanded a speedy hearing. Loring was "considerate and humane." Although he believed Loring's decision to return Burns was wrong, as was his decision to act as a commissioner while he held the position of a judge of Massachusetts, Dana opposed removal.[55]

In spite of Dana's plea, the majority of the standing committee recommended Loring's removal. A lengthy minority report, which expressed opposition to the federal law, nevertheless insisted that Loring was neither responsible for its passage, nor was there any evidence that the commissioner had been derelict in his duties. The House voted 207 to 111 in favor of Loring's removal; the Senate

---

[54] *Liberator*, February 23, March 2, 23, 1855; Boston *Herald*, February 21, March 1, 1855.
[55] Adams, *Richard Henry Dana*, 341–43; *Liberator*, March 9, 1855; Boston *Herald*, March 7, 1855.

later concurred.[56] The call for Loring's dismissal produced a spirited debate far from Boston. According to one abolitionist editor, his removal was a statement against the Fugitive Slave Law and the commissioner's voluntary decision to administer it. Loring was "not bound to accept the appointment" as commissioner, given that already occupied an "important post" at the Harvard Law School, and "the honorable office of State Judge." It was a point that Phillips had driven home during testimony before the joint committee: others, such as the commissioner in Chicago, had resigned, or refused to accept the position rather than send men, as one editor put it, "to endless misery." The law was popularly seen as abhorrent, "subversive of the principles and rules of procedure of the Common Law, incompatible with State Sovereignty, inhuman, anti-democratic, utterly revolting to the instincts, education, habits and institutions of the Free States." A Free-Soil colleague in Indiana concurred. He took the opportunity to condemn the law as well as those who believed the North should act as the bloodhounds of slaveholders, and surrender the "Free States as the hunting ground for the South," with judges, such as Loring, acting as the "Lord Jeffries of the Bloody Assizes." Comparing the decisions of commissioners to the draconian rulings of the seventeenth-century British judge had become, by 1854, a recognized metaphor of condemnation among abolitionists. Those who opposed removal believed hounding Loring out of office was part of a wider abolitionist conspiracy. A man of considerable standing, the judge had done nothing more than follow precedence and the judgment of superior courts on the law's legality. Since his decision, Loring had become the "shining mark for the arrows of fanaticism." Something had gone terribly wrong, James Gordon Bennett, editor of the New York *Herald* observed, when a legislature combined the passage of a personal liberty law in 1855 with one that called for the integration of the city's schools. "Now the blood of the Winthrops, the Otises, the Lymans, the Endicotts and the Eliots," he worried, like only Bennet could, "is in a fair way to be amalgamated with the Sambos, the Catos and the Pompeys."[57]

Although some anticipated that Gardner would go along with the legislature, the governor rejected the call for Loring's removal on the grounds that he had broken no laws nor had he committed any crimes. If there was an official misdemeanor, the Constitution provided for impeachment, not removal by two legislative branches. Furthermore, to remove the judge would undermine the independence of the judiciary. In spite of the existence of the 1843 law, Gardner insisted that there was no state law in place, at the time, prohibiting a state judge acting to return a fugitive slave. Gardner and the legislature would

[56] *Liberator*, March 16, April 13, 20, 1855; Boston *Herald*, March 12, 1855.
[57] *National Era*, May 10, 1855; *Indiana Journal*, May 4, 15, 1855; Dedham *Gazette* (n.d.), in *Liberator*, March 9, 1855; New York *Herald*, February 19, 1855; Washington, DC, *Union*, March 22, April 29, 1855; Worcester *Spy* (n.d.), in *Liberator*, February 16, 1855; New York *Herald*, April 20, 28, 1855; Cleveland *Herald*, May 16, 1855.

cross swords again when, soon after his rejection of the call to remove Loring, he vetoed the personal liberty law passed in April 1855, which, among other stipulations, required that detained fugitives be guaranteed a hearing before a jury, banned state jails from holding fugitive slaves, and guaranteed the rights of habeas corpus. The law, Gardner responded, was simply unconstitutional. The legislature overrode the veto, but the law was never operationalized. Its existence, however, like similar laws in other states, was a symbol of Northern resistance to the Fugitive Slave Law, so much so that, by the end of the decade, as the country stood on the brink of secession, Southerners could claim, with some justification, that the personal liberty laws had been responsible for the country's political malaise.[58]

In spite of Gardner's refusal to remove Loring, opponents of the commissioner could take some comfort from the decision of the board of overseers at Harvard to remove him from his post at the law school. John Gorham Palfrey's warning aside, many had questioned Loring's qualifications for the position at the time of his appointment. As one commentator put it, the appointment had been made as a favor to a small group of influential men. It appears he was later denied a promotion because of his support of the Fugitive Slave Law. The denial was evidently kept a secret so "the College might continue to enroll the many Southern students on whose fees it largely depended."[59] The call to remove Loring as a judge, which never totally subsided, would resurface, once again, two years later, in the weeks after the US Supreme Court issued its decision in the Dred Scott case. A meeting of African Americans at the Joy Street Church on February 12th, spoke for many who were stunned by the court's decision that blacks were not (and could never be) citizens: the ruling was, the meeting observed, a "high-handed act of judicial usurpation, constituting one of a long series of acts on the part of a slaveholding oligarchy to uproot all the safeguards of Northern freedom." They planned to memorialize the state legislature to declare "the tyrannical decision" nonbinding on Free States. In such a political climate, Loring, once again, became an easy target for opponents of the Fugitive Slave Law. When Gardner first rejected the call for removal, the *Liberator* recalled, he suggested that the legislature could pass a law banning state officers from holding two positions. That is exactly what the 1855 Personal Liberty Law did: no person, it declared, could hold office under the Fugitive Slave Law, and, at the same time, "hold any office of honor, trust, or emolument, under the laws of the Commonwealth." Gardner, however, had refused to endorse the law, rejecting it as unconstitutional. Months later, he again rejected the renewed call for Loring's removal on the grounds that a person could only be removed by address if it could be shown that he was incapacitated. No one had proven Loring unfit. If, on the other hand, the judge

---

[58] *National Era*, May 17, 1855; *Liberator*, May 18, 25, 1855; Boston *Herald*, May 11, 1855; Maltz, *Fugitive Slave on Trial*, 130–35.
[59] New York *Tribune*, February 1, 1855; von Frank, *The Trials of Anthony Burns*, 16–17, 120–21.

had broken state laws, he should be impeached and given a hearing. The 1855 Personal Liberty Law, Gardner reiterated, was unconstitutional and so had no bearing on the issue. Even if it were constitutional, he concluded, it could not be applied retroactively in Loring's case.[60]

Gardner's defeat by Nathanial Banks, and by what one editor called a coalition of antislavery fusionists, in the elections of November 1857, provided another opening for Loring's opponents, who immediately petitioned the legislature for his removal. Some estimates put the initial number of signees to the petition at ten thousand, rising to almost fifty thousand before the legislature met to consider the appeal. Speaking for the petitioners, William Lloyd Garrison insisted that removal was necessary if the state wished to maintain its honor and sovereignty and the "imperiled cause of liberty throughout the land." Twice, he reminded his readers, the legislature had voted for removal, and twice Gardner had declined to act. This, and previous calls for removal, he observed, were not the work of a small group of abolitionist extremists, but a demonstration of the will of the people of Massachusetts. Others thought differently. One local editor put the number of petitioners at only six thousand, a mere fraction of the one million citizens of the state. Another in New York City observed that, ever since the return of Burns, Loring had become "a fair mark for the shafts of fanaticism" whose dreams he haunted at night. According to Caleb Cushing, the former attorney general in the government of Franklin Pierce, and now the Democratic member from Newburyport in the State House, a proposal before both houses of the legislature, in February 1858, to consolidation the probate and insolvent courts was a thinly disguised and heavy-handed scheme to get rid of Loring. The House, he feared, had been intimidated by the "menaces and insults" of the Massachusetts Anti-Slavery Society, which, to date, had been granted all it had asked of the legislature except Loring's removal.[61]

Loring again declined an invitation to appear before the standing committee. Like Gardner, he insisted that the 1855 law was unconstitutional, a position, he pointed out, that was confirmed by the state's attorney general. Since its passage, other committees of the legislature had twice come to the same

---

[60] *Liberator,* March 6, 27, April 24, 1857, February 26, 1858; Boston *Herald,* March 3, 25, July 8, 1857. On the reach and limits of the personal liberty laws after the Burns decision see Thomas D. Morris, *Free Men All. The Public Liberty Laws of the North, 1780–1861* (Baltimore: 1974), 168.

[61] *Liberator,* November 13, December 25, 1857, February 19, March 5, 12, 1858; Boston *Herald,* December 10, 1857, March 3, 1858; Boston *Bee* (n.d.), in *Liberator,* March 12, 1858; Boston *Post,* in *Liberator,* March 26, 1858; New York *Journal of Commerce,* March 12, 1858; New York *Times,* February 19, 1858; Maltz, *Fugitive Slave on Trial,* 147–48. Cushing's dislike of abolitionists and his support of the Fugitive Slave Law was well known. See Don E. Fehrenbacher, *The Slave Holding Republic. An Account of the United States Government's Relations to Slavery* (New York: 2001), 236 and Claude M. Fuess, *The Life of Caleb Cushing,* 2 Vols. (New York: 1923), II, 144–45.

conclusion. The legislature, moreover, had no power to address the question of the incompatibility of judicial offices. If the section of the Constitution on incompatibility was unconstitutional, then he had violated the Constitution and so should be impeached not removed. Caleb Cushing tried unsuccessfully to forestall the hearing by recommending that the case be referred to a committee to investigate whether Loring was guilty of violations of the law. Those promoting removal, he observed, were no more than the representatives of the "monomaniacs of negro idolatry." In again recommending removal, the joint special committee ruled that it mattered little if the 1855 law was deemed unconstitutional, the state law of 1843, it pointed out, barred the holding of both federal and state offices. Both houses of the legislature concurred with the special committee's findings, as did Governor Banks. Loring's removal was almost four years in the making. In a speech to the House following the governor's decision, John A. Andrew, who two years later would be elected governor, justified the removal as the culmination of a "consistent, determined... struggle to defend the rights and honor of Massachusetts – the rights and honor of one of the sovereign States of this confederacy." The *Liberator* exulted in the removal's larger political meaning: the power of proslavery advocates, it boasted, was "gone forever."[62]

Both Garrison and Cushing, it seems, had arrived at a similar conclusion: Loring's removal represented an important victory for the black community, and abolitionists more generally, in a heated political struggle that had its origin in the passage of the Fugitive Slave Law. It was, moreover, according to Garrison, a testament to the "unextinguishable disgust of the people of Massachusetts with the Fugitive Slave Law and especially with the miserable spirit of doughface subserviency which led Judge Loring to consent to act as one of its executioners." He took the opportunity to revisit the unresolved question of the constitutionality of both commissioners and the duties they performed as a way to justify Loring's removal. But what seemed to matter most to Garrison was Loring's apparent greed: he was not satisfied with being a state probate judge and a law professor, he had to add the "incompatible business of a slave-catcher." That was grounds enough to warrant removal. To have done otherwise would have been to hand a political victory to the "partisans of the law." Even among those who believed that Loring may have acted as the law required, they nevertheless were convinced that he was "false to Liberty, and false to Massachusetts." One anonymous author, who arrived at similar conclusions, nonetheless expressed grave doubt about a system that,

---

[62] Boston *Herald*, March 19, 29, 1858; *Liberator*, March 12, 26, 1858; New York *Times*, March 25, 1858. Weeks after his ouster, President James Buchanan named Loring to the court of claims in Washington, DC, a post he held until retirement in 1877. Von Frank, *The Trials of Anthony Burns*, 321. The editor of the New York *Tribune* had predicted such an outcome, the reward and consolation of doughfaces: "A good fat Federal appointment." New York *Tribune*, March 24, 1858.

since 1850, had elected politicians who were committed to enforcement of the law and who allowed commissioners to act as they did, to now punish Loring for fulfilling the duties of the office. It was patently absurd, not to say wicked, to require Loring "to do an act," and then punish him "by law for doing it."[63]

With the removal of Loring, Boston had symbolically reasserted its claim to being both the capital of abolitionism and the major center of resistance to the Fugitive Slave Law. In the face of overwhelming odds, the black community and its abolitionist supporters had managed to hold the government at bay. They had lost Sims and, until he was ransomed, Burns, and had managed to protect the Crafts and Shadrach Minkins from being returned. Many of those involved were indicted, fewer were brought to trial, and none, even those involved in the attempt to rescue Burns, or the death of Batchelder, were convicted for resisting enforcement of the law. More significantly, no fugitives would be retaken from the city after 1854; an impressive record, made even more so by the fact that other parts of the state also successfully managed to protect the regular flow of fugitives into the state. The one exception seemed to have been Columbus Jones, who escaped from Pensacola, Florida, in April 1859, by stowing away on a ship heading for Massachusetts. With his food and water running short, Jones gave himself up to the captain. When the ship docked at Hyannis, Jones was transferred to a ship heading for Norfolk, Virginia. The captain and other officers who took part in Jones's return were subsequently tried for kidnapping, but ultimately freed.[64]

The Boston Vigilance Committee recorded aiding 163 fugitives in the four years after Burns' return, a not unimpressive number. Some were housed temporarily by Lewis Hayden and other members of the black community. Others found work until they moved on. The work of the committee extended beyond providing temporary board and lodging. In August 1858, for instance, they managed to raise $100 to provide Johnson Walker with an artificial leg. Walker's leg was crushed by a train at a railroad station in Wilmington, Delaware, during his escape from Maryland. Half of the money was raised by subscription; the balance was donated by the Palmer Company, which had recently perfected a new artificial limb. By 1859, the committee reported expending roughly $6,000 aiding fugitive slaves to safety. There were no recorded fugitive slave

---

[63] *Liberator,* April 2, 1858; New York *Tribune,* March 24, 1858; Springfield *Republican,* February 20, 24, 26, 27, 1855. A placard of unknown origin, which appeared soon after Banks's decision, called on "white men of Massachusetts" to resist being "trampled on by enemies of your race" by the "fanatical lovers of the black man." *Liberator,* March 26, 1858.

[64] *National Era,* June 9, 1859; New York *Herald,* November 18, 1859; Springfield *Republican,* September 23, November 21, 1859; *Southern Argus,* May 16, November 26, 1859; Norfolk and Portsmouth *Herald,* November 28, 1859. Stanley Campbell mentions the rescue, in January 1855, of John Anderson from officials in Boston but I have not been able to verify the incident. Stanley W. Campbell, *The Slave Catchers. Enforcement of the Fugitive Slave Law, 1850–1860* (New York: 1968), 202. For accounts of fugitives, long resident in the city, fleeing ahead of slave catchers see Boston *Herald,* July 19, 1854, October 10, 1855.

hearings in other parts of the state. Thomas Wentworth Higginson's was no idle boast: Worcester was as safe as Canada. So too, one should add, was New Bedford, a major port city and the whaling capital of the world, which, since the arrival of a young Frederick Douglass, in 1838, had been considered "the fugitive's Gibraltar." Whenever there were rumors of slave catchers in Boston, the black community sprang into action to protect fugitive slaves. When, in mid-1860, William Lloyd Garrison turned up at a public meeting with two Kentucky fugitive slaves in tow, Wendell Phillips could boast, with some justification and pride, that Boston, and by extension, Massachusetts, had been transformed into a zone of freedom.[65]

[65] "List of Fugitive Slaves Aided by the Vigilance Committee since the Passage of the Fugitive Slave Bill"; "Vigilance Committee, Treasurer's Account Book"; *Liberator,* June 8, 1860; Boston *Herald,* March 19, April 21, 1857, June 1, 1860. For New Bedford see Grover, *Fugitive's Gibraltar.*

# Conclusion

If there was a place in the Free States where fugitive slaves could feel secure, it was the area along the shores of Lake Erie known as the Western Reserve. Elisha Whittlesey, a longtime resident of Cleveland, and a Treasury Department official in the Fillmore administration, recalled that the area's residents not only openly violated the law, they also employed agents to go south to aid and encourage slaves to run away. He knew it as the "most rabid antislavery district" in the North. In early 1861, one local editor looked back with some pride at the fact that no escapee had been returned from Cleveland in almost nineteen years. But the editor had gotten ahead of himself. If, in the past, the city had remained steadfastly committed to the protection of fugitive slaves, times had now changed. The victory of the Republican Party in the presidential and congressional elections of 1860, on a platform to limit slavery to its existing territory, had altered the national political landscape. These results were met by a chorus of counterclaims from Southern states demanding guaranteed constitutional protection for slavery and slave property. There were also voices calling on Southern states to withdraw from the Union. South Carolina took the first step on December 20, 1860. Within a month, three other states would join the movement to leave the Union.[1]

In the midst of this crisis, John Goshorn and his son William, two slaveholders from western Virginia, arrived in Cleveland in search of Sarah Lucy Bagby, a twenty-eight-year-old slave who had escaped in October 1860. In Cleveland, Bagby was taken under the care of William E. Ambush, president of the Fugitive Aid Society, a black organization. Ambush found her a job, first, at the home of A. G. Riddle, the Republican congressman-elect, and, later, at

---

[1] Elisha Whittlesey to E. M. Whittlesey, Washington, DC, October 12, 1850, Container 50, Elisha Whittlesey Papers, Western Reserve Historical Society, Cleveland, Ohio; John E. Vacha, "The Case of Sara Lucy Bagby. A Late Gesture," *Ohio History*, 76, No. 4 (Autumn 1967), 223.

L. A. Benton's, where she was captured in mid-January by the Goshorns, assisted by two deputy US marshals, who took her to the city jail to await a hearing. Word of her capture spread quickly. The authorities were taken by surprise at the speed with which a large crowd of African Americans gathered in the courtyard between the jail and the courthouse where the hearing was to be held. Before the hearing could begin, a writ of habeas corpus was sworn out claiming that Bagby was being held in a city prison contrary to state law. Bagby was defended by Rufus P. Spalding, a lead attorney in the defense of those accused in the Oberlin-Wellington rescue case, A. G. Riddle and C. W. Palmer. In granting Spalding's request that the case be held over for a couple days, Probate Court Judge D. A. Tilden hoped to persuade the crowd gathered outside his court to disperse and not attempt a rescue. But the judge was also concerned about the case's potential impact on the already deepening political crisis facing the country. In spite of its reputation, he almost pleaded, "Cleveland was not disloyal to the Union." There was a heavy police presence on the morning of the habeas corpus hearing. There were also reports that the Cleveland Grays, a militia company, were being held in readiness at the Armory. Tilden dispensed with the habeas corpus claim, promptly ruling that Bagby was being held illegally in the city jail. But rather than release her, the judge transferred Bagby to Commissioner Bushnell C. White's court, where Goshorn's claim could be adjudicated under the terms of the Fugitive Slave Law. The black crowd outside the courthouse grew increasingly agitated following Tilden's decision. There were reports that a group of armed outsiders were seen coming into town the morning of the hearing. Eight were arrested, including four from Oberlin, among them John Wall, brother of one of the accused in the Oberlin-Wellington rescue. Two women were also arrested, including Eveline Souse, who was accused of throwing powdered pepper in the face of police.

At the hearing, Spalding again requested a continuance so Bagby's claim that she was free, because she had once been taken into Pennsylvania by Goshorn's daughter, could be investigated. In granting the stay, White was determined to show the South that Cleveland, in spite of its long and cherished abolitionist traditions, could hold an impartial hearing in a fugitive slave case. The facts, not passion, would determine the outcome of the case, he declared. Bagby's claims, the investigators reported, were baseless; there was no evidence that she had ever been taken into Pennsylvania. White promptly ruled in favor of the Goshorns. The sense of relief that greeted the report that Bagby would be returned was palpable among those in the city concerned about the worsening political situation. Although he was no radical in his opposition to the Fugitive Slave Law, one could not imagine Spalding expressing views such as the following during the trials of the Oberlin-Wellington rescuers: "We are this day offering to the majesty of the law," he observed in the wake of White's decision, "a homage that taken with it a surrender of the finest feelings of our nature; the vanquishing of many of our strictest resolutions, the mortification of a freeman's pride, and, I almost said, the contravention of a Christian's duty to his God! While we do this, in the city of Cleveland, in the Connecticut Western Reserve, and permit this poor piece of humanity to be taken, PRACTICALLY, through our streets, upon our railways, back to the land of bondage, will not the frantic South stay its parricidal arms? Will not our compromising legislation cry 'Hold, enough!' " The Goshorns' lawyer concurred: the decision showed that "the Northern people will execute the law and be faithful to the Union." Indeed, the South had been looking for such signs for some time. Cleveland had been tested in an hour of crisis and was not found wanting. The case, one editor agreed, was a "test question" in an area Southerners considered "the hot-bed of Abolitionism." If, by their actions, the people of Cleveland proclaimed "to the country and the world that they can set aside their feeling and their sympathies, that they will submit to the power of the Federal laws, even though those laws be totally repugnant and unjust; that they have a calm judgment which outbalances the impulses of the moment, and brings the latter in subjugation to the former," the decision should have a positive effect at this moment of crisis. Although the law was "unjust, oppressive, infamous and unconstitutional," he continued, the city's "law-abiding" citizens, nevertheless, had shelved their reputation and submitted to it in the interest of keeping the country together. Nothing would have given more aid and comfort to seceding traitors than a rescue in Cleveland. The time will soon come, he seemed to promise his readers, without offering any concrete evidence, when the reins of power will be transferred to those who abhorred the law and who had the will to change it. An opposing editor thought the return had a contrary and even larger symbolic significance: Cleveland, he declared, had changed its political spots and should no longer be considered a "Congo City."[2]

Bagby had been sacrificed on the altar of appeasement by those who admittedly abhorred the law and the system it represented, in the hope of keeping the Union together at the precise moment it was falling apart. Cleveland had done its part by submitting to what one local editor called the "infliction" of the law. It will continue to do so, he observed, until this one-sided law was repealed, but only if the South was compelled to obey all laws, and leading "southern traitors be tried and hung according to law, as promptly as were the citizens of Oberlin punished for being engaged in the Wellington Rescue Case." It was a strange sort of comity at a time when several states had already seceded, and at a time when no Southern politician worth his salt would have entertained such reciprocity. More to the point was John Goshorn's response to the decision. He was grateful to the citizens of Cleveland for the way he was treated. Admitting that his mission was an "unpleasant one," he nevertheless hoped Commissioner White's decision would help to ease the nation's

---

[2] Cleveland *Herald*, January 19, 21, 25, 28, February 12, 1861; Cleveland *Leader*, January 21, 22, 24, 25, February 1, 14, 1861; Ashtabula *Sentinel*, January 21, 30, 1861; Wheeling *Intelligencer*, January 23, 25, 26, 1861. The case is covered extensively in Vacha, "The Case of Sara Lucy Bagby."

troubles. The South, he insisted, had long been looking for such signs of conciliation. If the slaves were bent on destroying the Union, Goshorn believed he – and, one assumes, Northerners such as Commissioner White – had a duty to do what they could to preserve it. Southerners had rightly charged the North with encouraging slaves to abandon their owners. Hopefully, the return of Bagby would usher in a new era of cooperation and understanding. Days after Bagby's return, the Wheeling city council praised the Cleveland authorities for their demonstrated "goodwill" toward Virginia and their "fidelity to the Constitution which binds the States together."[3]

Leading voices in Cleveland and Wheeling may have considered Bagby's return a gesture of reconciliation, a demonstration of the North's willingness to obey the law and the Constitution. Such concessions did little, however, to appease those who believed, as Goshorn did, that what mattered most was not only a slaveholder's right to reclaim his lost property, but also his freedom to take his slaves wherever he wished unimpeded. The future of the country, he insisted, would only be assured if he, and other slaveholders "could come among you with the same girl as my servant, and enjoy your hospitality as I have now." Cleveland's black community and abolitionists, however, overwhelmingly rejected reconciliation on these terms. The crowds gathered outside the courthouse had kept up a vigil during both hearings and showed little sign of acceding to the demands of Spalding and the others that the law be allowed to take its course. They were committed to preventing Bagby's return. William Ambush came to the commissioner's hearing armed. Before the hearing began, he and William Goshorn got into a heated argument. Pistols were drawn, but cooler heads ultimately prevailed. Once Commissioner White made his decision, the authorities employed a heavy guard to escort Bagby to Wheeling. The train on which she was traveling had to be diverted in order to foil an anticipated rescue. The black community also floated the idea of purchasing Bagby's freedom, but nothing came of the suggestion. The failure to win her freedom, however, affected the black community negatively. Not only did a number of fugitive slaves who had made the city home leave for Canada, but, for a while, the community seemed to turn on itself, opening an inquiry into who may have betrayed Bagby's whereabouts to Goshorn. Ambush was compelled to testify on his role in the case and was only exonerated when he convinced members of the Fugitive Aid Society that he had done everything he could to protect Bagby.[4]

The willingness to return Bagby from a city with such impeccable abolitionist credentials troubled those who had struggled against the law since its passage. In broad daylight, a slave had been returned from what Joshua Giddings

---

[3] Cleveland *Leader*, January 22, 1861; Cleveland *Herald*, January 23, 1861; Wheeling *Intelligencer*, January 26, 1861; *Liberator*, March 15, 1861.

[4] John Malvin, *Autobiography of John Malvin. A Narrative* (Cleveland: 1879) 37–39; Cleveland *Herald*, January 21, 1861.

called the "citadel of freedom." Those who witnessed it and did nothing to prevent it consented to Bagby's "moral death." More troubling, "persons of her own complexion were told they must not interfere to save this helpless, this friendless woman." He was sure this would not have happened in Africa, but in Cleveland – civilized Cleveland, he implied – "barbarism was protected by their public men." If the "Ft Sumter of abolition," as the *Liberator* designated Cleveland, could fall so easily, the future did indeed look bleak.[5] Stopping and then reversing secession, Southerners insisted, required two principal concessions on the part of Northerners: a constitutional guarantee securing slavery in perpetuity and the muzzling of abolitionist activity, particularly its interference with slave property. Bagby's return seemed to acknowledge those demands.

As Bagby was leaving Wheeling in October 1860, William Yancey, the Alabama fire-eater and an early advocate of Southern independence, arrived in Boston on the second leg of his tour of the North, a tour that would also take him to such abolitionist strongholds as Rochester and Syracuse, New York. In famed Faneuil Hall, Yancey reiterated his defense of slavery and laid out his plans for a future America in which slavery would be secure. The audience was largely sympathetic. Although pointed questions were lobbed at him from the floor, no attempt was made to silence the proponent of slavery in the "cradle of abolitionism." Yancey ended his lecture with three cheers for the Union and the Constitution and offered a eulogy for Daniel Webster, a move guaranteed to win the approval of many of his listeners.[6] The situation was completely different weeks later when a coalition of black and white supporters of John Brown met at Tremont Temple to remember the martyr of Harpers Ferry. Before J. Sella Martin, a fugitive slave and minister at the Joy St. church, could call the meeting to order, opponents started a hubbub in an effort to disrupt the proceedings and to gain control of the meeting. They succeeded in electing an alternative slate of officers headed by Richard Fry, a broker and former candidate for Congress and a supporter of the Constitutional Union Party, whose platform in the recent elections advocated strict adherence to the Constitution. The disrupters were, as one observer put it, lackeys of "Cotton and State Street Mammon-worshippers," supported by the "pitiable tools of the Slave Power; armed and equipped with poor rum and North Street bully-ism." Brown was dismissed by the insurgents as a madman. Whenever any of the meeting organizers attempted to speak they were threatened with violence. Frederick Douglass did manage to get the floor but could not be heard above the din created by Fry's supporters. A number of running skirmishes broke out in the hall, which a group of policemen could not, or would not, quell. When

---

[5] The *Liberator* and Giddings' quote in Vacha, "The Case of Sara Lucy Bagby," 229, 231.
[6] Eric H. Walther, *William Yancey and the Coming of the Civil War* (Chapel Hill, NC: 2006), 265–66. There were African Americans in the audience, but they did nothing to disrupt Yancey's lecture. Instead, they met the following day at J. Sella Martin's Joy St. Church to hear an analysis of the lecture by William Wells Brown. *Liberator,* October 26, 1860.

Douglass was attacked and defended himself, the police finally moved in under orders from the mayor, closing the hall and threatening to read the riot act. That night, Martin reconvened the meeting at his church under a heavy police presence. Thousands milled about outside, threatening those entering and leaving the church. Inside, Martin took all possible precautions against a repetition of the earlier disturbances. The meeting was addressed by Wendell Phillips, Parker Pillsbury, H. Ford Douglas, and John Brown Jr., who called on African Americans to arm themselves. The events of the day brought back memories of the disruption of George Thompson's meeting following the failure of Georgia slave catchers to retake William and Ellen Craft. Although the police presence prevented attacks on the church, they could do little to protect those leaving the meeting. A number of blacks were assaulted, and property owned by African Americans on Cambridge Street was damaged.[7]

Anti-abolitionist mobs were in full flight. Over the next few weeks, abolitionists would have to face the sort of unrelenting and violent opposition that was a feature of the 1830s. Attacks were launched against meetings in Buffalo, Rochester, Syracuse, Utica, Rome, and Albany, New York, cities that had provided safe havens for fugitives throughout the decade. In Albany, they were able to meet only because the mayor sat on the platform with a revolver on his lap and made it clear that anyone who attempted to disrupt the meeting would be arrested by his police, who were scattered throughout the hall. But sensing trouble, the mayor persuaded the organizers not to continue the meeting for a second day as was customary. In Buffalo, the police ignored the orders of the Republican mayor to prevent disruption. In Utica, organizers were denied the hall they had rented. Such meetings, one Rochester editor argued, "wound the sensibilities of their fellow-citizens, and injure the reputation of our city by contributing to the fire which is consuming the nation." He dismissed the organizers as traitors who had avowed "their preference for the government of Great Britain." Taking refuge behind the skirt of free speech, they assailed the country, which they "have longed ceased to have an interest other than to facilitate its overthrow." Attendees at the Syracuse meeting were greeted with rotten eggs. The meeting was taken over and resolutions passed condemning abolitionists for creating the crisis and accusing supporters of the Underground Railroad of deliberately undermining the Constitution. Opponents plastered the town with placards condemning abolitionists and insisting that the concerns of the South had to be addressed. Images of Susan B. Anthony and Samuel J. May, the

---

[7] Boston *Herald*, December 3, 4, 1860; Boston *Atlas and Bee*, December 4, 1860; *Douglass Monthly*, January 1861; *Liberator*, December 14, 1860; Edith Ellen Ware, *Political Opinion in Massachusetts During the Civil War and Reconstruction* (New York: 1916); James M. McPherson, *Struggle for Equality: Abolitionists and the Negro in the Civil War and Reconstruction* (Princeton: 1964), 41–44; Stephen Kantrowitz, *More than Freedom. Fighting for Black Citizenship in a White Republic, 1829–1889* (New York: 2012), 268–70; R. J. M. Blackett, *Beating Against the Barriers. Biographical Essays in Nineteenth-Century Afro-American History* (Baton Rouge: 1986), 197–99.

meeting's organizers, were publicly burned, but only after the mob suggested that there were improper sexual relations between the two. One local editor, no apologist for abolitionists, was utterly dismayed by the turn of events: free speech, he responded, had been laid "prostrate before the proscriptive interposition of the infatuated bigoted and intolerant votaries of mock conservatism." But one Virginia editor saw things differently. He headed his report of the Syracuse meeting: "Another Abolitionist Stronghold Broken Up."[8]

Following the John Brown anniversary meeting, an editor located the source of the problem in the city and state's lax approach to the dangers posed by abolitionists who were allowed to influence public opinion unopposed for so long that, by the election of 1860, more than one hundred thousand had voted for the abolitionist Lincoln. They had carried the day. Now they were rubbing salt in the wounds of the country by organizing a meeting to memorialize a madman and traitor, a meeting organized by Negroes aided and abetted by the "Englishman" James Redpath, the author of a laudable biography of John Brown, who was "reputed to be an *emissary* to stir up disturbance here, under pay of British abolitionists."[9] It was an old canard. But for those looking back over thirty years, it appeared that the international alliance of African Americans and British and American abolitionists had proven their power by electing Lincoln. Tensions between the sections also had the potential to disrupt trading relations and to stifle the economies of some Northern cities. Even before the elections of 1860, the balance sheet of some prominent New York City merchants had begun to reflect the uncertainties of the time. Initially, the majority of the city's merchants upheld the right of peaceful secession. Early in the New Year, they dispatched two delegations to Washington, DC, in an effort to end the crisis, insisting that all "necessary concessions" should be made to ensure the survival of the Union. From Pittsfield, Massachusetts, came an ominous prediction: "The doors of every mill will be closed" in ninety days if something was not done to stem the tide of secession. In the wake of the Harpers Ferry raid, the editor of the New York *Herald* had predicted such a trade war, with damaging consequences for the economies of many Northern cities. In order to protect its interests, the South, out of necessity, would have to establish "native factories," he anticipated, and, if that failed to curtail the influence of abolitionists, would necessarily have to resort to "gunpowder, the rifle, the bayonet and cannon." Such retaliation was understandable and inevitable. There were unmistakable signs that the South was preparing to retaliate against Northern economic interests. Every dollar expended in the North,

[8] Syracuse *Journal*, January 29, 30, 31, February 1, 4, 1861; Rochester *Union and Advertiser*, January 14, 21, 1861; Donald Yacavone, *Samuel Joseph May and the Dilemmas of the Liberal Persuasion, 1797–1871* (Philadelphia: 1991), 170–71; Kathleen Barry, *Susan B. Anthony. A Biography of a Singular Feminist* (New York: 1988), 147–48; Richmond *Dispatch*, February 1, 1861.

[9] Boston *Courier*, December 4, 1860, in *Liberator*, December 28, 1860.

one Richmond editor maintained, gave aid and comfort to "wretches who are thirsting for Southern blood."[10]

Although not as large as those held in late 1850, Union meetings, both in 1859 following Harpers Ferry, and those a year later as the crisis worsened, offered a set of solutions to address the country's political problems. As the crisis deepened, Kentucky senator John J. Crittenden took the lead with a set of proposals that collectively came to be known as the Crittenden Compromise. Unlike his mentor Henry Clay's compromise in 1850, Crittenden's offered little to opponents of slavery. In fact, his was a way to guarantee slavery's survival. But in an effort to appease those who despised the 1854 Kansas-Nebraska Act, which effectively destroyed the hard-won results of the Missouri Compromise of 1820, with its prohibition of slavery north of the 36-30 line, Crittenden proposed returning to the 1820 agreement but extending the line to the Pacific Ocean, as many in the South had been demanding for a decade and more. Slavery would be permanently protected south of the line. The inhabitants of states wishing to join the Union would determine whether they entered as a slave or free state. The federal government would compensate slaveholders fully when resistance prevented the return of fugitive slaves, a frequent demand of slaveholders. All personal liberty laws would be repealed. The slave trade would be permanently banned. No future amendments could empower Congress to interfere with slavery, nor could Congress banish slavery from federal territories. Not only did Crittenden's recommendations preserve and secure slavery, they also anticipated a future when slavery would expand beyond the limits of the United States.

Crittenden's proposals were at the center of all the Union meetings held in late 1860 and early 1861. Philadelphia's was fairly representative. "Concessions before Secession" read one bunting at the meeting in Independence Square, attended by an estimated crowd of fifty thousand, the majority of whom milled about unable to hear what any of the speakers had to say. Philadelphia, a supportive editor reasoned, had "assembled to do the Union reverence." The South had understandably been alarmed by the results of the recent presidential election. There were two options available to the North to address these concerns: they must commit the Free States to recognize the rights of all, to live in peace with their neighbors by not interfering with the "domestic institutions"

[10] Philip S. Foner, *Business and Slavery. The New York Merchants and the Irrepressible Conflict* (1941, rpr., New York: 1968), 232, 248–49; Ware, *Public Opinion in Massachusetts,* 49; New York *Herald,* January 19, February 2, 1860; Richmond *Dispatch,* December 1, 1859. The "Central Southern Rights Association," which was formed following the passage of the Fugitive Slave Law, advocated boycotts against those Northern cities that, by their actions, undermined slavery. It was reactivated in the weeks after the attack on Harpers Ferry. Richmond *Enquirer,* November 30, 1859. William Link sees a growing sense of alarm and foreboding in Virginia in the second half of the decade. Harpers Ferry and the election of Abraham Lincoln brought this into sharp relief. William A. Link, *Roots of Secession. Slavery and Politics in Antebellum Virginia* (Chapel Hill, NC: 2003), 191, 209, 215–17, 229.

of the South; and Northern state governments must repeal all legislation of an "unconstitutional character," that is, all personal liberty laws. Addressing these concerns would necessitate no "humiliating concessions" from non-slaveholding states, he assured his readers. Mayor Alexander Henry cleared away all potential impediments by pressuring the organizers of an antislavery lecture by George W. Curtis to cancel the event. As he told the organizers, if he had the power he would not permit the lecture at this critical moment. The organizers bowed to the pressure but moved the lecture to West Chester, twenty miles away.[11]

The survival of the Union, the meeting declared, depended on the implementation of all constitutional requirements. That meant that all personal liberty laws, which, over the years, had been enacted by eleven Northern states as a means of protecting their black residents from kidnappings, had to be repealed. These laws were nothing more than a thinly disguised attempt to subvert the Fugitive Slave Law. The meeting also expressed support for the 1857 Supreme Court decision in the Dred Scott case, which had ruled, among other things, that slavery could not be excluded from any portion of the Union. Continued denunciation of slavery had to cease, for it violated the spirit of brotherhood. Finally, the meeting appealed to South Carolina and all the states that had seceded or were considering leaving the Union, to reconsider their decision so as to give the country time to negotiate their way out of the impasse. In the words of Mayor Henry, who chaired the meeting, the Union had to be preserved at all costs and doing so required Northern states and abolitionists to stop meddling in the affairs of their neighbors. Joseph R. Ingersoll, a Constitutional Unionist, supported the call for a national convention to address outstanding issues, and the repeal of personal liberty laws, which, he believed, interfered with the right of slaveholders to recover their property. In so doing, the North would show their determination to eschew interference with the rights of slaveholders. Ingersoll was followed by the Pennsylvania Supreme Court judge, George Woodward, a Democrat, who believed that slavery was divinely inspired. Put simply, the Republican Party, he insisted, aimed to destroy slavery. It should come as no surprise, then, that the South could not stand idly by as its economy and society were assailed. The party also promoted the passage of personal liberty laws, which, like the Underground Railroad, violated the original "bargain" on which the country was established. If slavery was not a sin, he asked, what right do abolitionists have "to cheat tender consciences into hostility to an institution on which our Union is founded in part?" The rights of slaveholders must be reasserted and upheld. Doing so would require constitutional guarantees that protected their property from the "spoliation of religious bigotry and persecution." The country should not sacrifice its "sacred inheritance" to Negro freedom. Charles Lox, the city solicitor, insisted that the

---

[11] Philadelphia *Public Ledger*, December 12, 13, 1860; Philadelphia *Dispatch*, December 15, 1860; William Dusenberre, *Civil War Issues in Philadelphia, 1856–1865* (Philadelphia: 1965), 103.

Fugitive Slave Law had to be enforced, although he conceded that a few of its provisions should be modified in the interest of peace. All in all, it was a total capitulation to Southern demands. A month later, a banner at a meeting organized by the Democratic Party and attended by four thousand declared: "No Civil War; Justice to the South; Equal Rights in the Territories." The meeting was addressed by an "imposing group of socially prominent Philadelphians," among them Benjamin Brewster, counsel for the claimant in the 1859 Daniel Webster fugitive slave case. When a white apprentice fled Maryland, Brewster reminded his audience, abolitionists did not come to his aid "because he wasn't a nigger. Curl his hair into wool, blacken his face, and make him stink a little," the speaker continued, and "he would be the object of dearest interest – a nigger." The meeting called for peaceful separation before war, insisted that state laws should comport with the dictates of the Constitution, and demanded that slaveholders be permitted to sojourn in Free States with their property. Its call for a convention to determine if Pennsylvania should side with the South was greeted with warm applause. An outdoor meeting of workingmen held in a driving snow storm two weeks later rejected war and called for amendments to the Constitution that would ensure the Union's survival and the repeal of all laws "obnoxious to the citizens of any portion of the Union."[12]

To some Southerners, these Union meetings, as well as those held earlier in Philadelphia, New York, and Boston in the wake of Harpers Ferry, which brought together the "best men," the "intelligent and virtuous," of the cities, represented the emergence – a belated one, to be sure – of reliable "conservative" elements who recognized the danger to the nation and were willing to address the concerns of the South. Unfortunately, a Richmond editor observed, they were outstripped by a "reeking mass of ignorance and barbarism." Flowery speeches in praise of the things that bound the country together were fine, but the times now demanded action and that involved enforcing legal and constitutional guarantees, and repealing those laws that did not. But all of the Philadelphia meetings were one sided; none came up with proposals that addressed the interests of both sides in the dispute. As the country drifted closer to war, subsequent meetings in Philadelphia would attempt to recalibrate some of their recommendations. For instance, the decision of Maj. Robert Anderson, head of Union forces in Charleston, to move his troops to a more secure position at Ft. Sumter, a decision that was greeted with threats of war from South Carolina, halted the drift of these meetings, William Dusenberre argues,

---

[12] New York *Times*, December 12, 1860; Philadelphia *Dispatch*, December 12, 1860; Philadelphia *Public Ledger*, December 12, 1860, January 16, 17, 21, 28, 1861; *Speech of Hon. George W. Woodward Delivered at the Great Union Meeting in Independence Square, Philadelphia, December 13th, 1860* (Philadelphia: 1863); Dusenberre, *Civil War Issues in Philadelphia*, 106–09. Brewster would later switch his allegiance to the Republican Party and serve as attorney general from 1881–85; for an earlier Union meeting in Rochester, New York, see the Rochester *Union and Advertiser*, January 19, 1860.

away from openly accepting secession toward a less complacent approach to Southern demands. But many considered these changes futile and doomed to failure, as useless and quixotic, the *Liberator* observed, as attempting to cover "Vesuvius with a sheet of straw paper."[13]

Underlying all these proposals to ease tensions was an acknowledgement that the rights of the South to its property in slaves had to be constitutionally guaranteed and protected. With that came an attendant right: slaveholders must be able to move freely about the country with their property as the Supreme Court had ruled in Dred Scott. That was only possible if the Fugitive Slave Law was enforced and personal liberty laws, which many believed were meant to impede the enforcement of the federal law, were repealed. It was, one Philadelphia editor believed, simply a matter of "fairness and constitutional equity." But achieving fairness was easier said than done. No one seemed to know what would be considered a fair and honorable compromise of the fugitive slave question, one that could command the assent of both free and slave states. How could one balance what the editor described as the harsh federal law against "running off slaves from the Southern states" and the need of Northern states to protect their black residents from kidnapping? These were issues that had bedeviled the country at the time of the passage of the first fugitive slave law in 1793. It was resolved by simply ignoring the vulnerability of free blacks to kidnapping; states, supporters of the 1793 law argued, had ample means to protect their black residents. The issue would reemerge on occasion over the years, most recently during the debate over the 1850 law, and always it was side stepped. The result was an alarming number of kidnappings, as we have seen.[14] Some Free States took matters into their own hands and adopted personal liberty laws as one way to address the problem. But in the context of the continuing crisis over the rising number of escaping slaves, these laws came to be seen in the South as a thinly disguised effort to impede efforts to retake fugitive slaves. Slaveholders had grounds to complain. A clause in Pennsylvania's 1847 law, for instance, denied the use of state prisons to hold suspected fugitive slaves and impeded the workings of the Fugitive Slave Law in the years between 1850 and 1852 when that section of the law was repealed. Similar laws in ten other Northern states were of more recent vintage, including Massachusetts', enacted in response to the return of Anthony Burns. Six

---

[13] Dusenberre, *Civil War Issues in Philadelphia*, 106; *Liberator*, quoted in Ware, *Public Opinion in Massachusetts During the Civil War and Reconstruction*, 50; Richmond *Dispatch*, December 10, 1859. For an example of meetings held in smaller communities, with few commercial connections to the South, see the one held in Patoka Township, DuBois County, Indiana, in February 1861, which adopted strikingly similar resolutions to those of Philadelphia, including a call for the enforcement of the Fugitive Slave Law and the repeal of personal liberty laws. Jasper *Courier*, February 27, 1861, quoted in Richard F. Nation and Stephen Towne, eds., *Indiana's War. The Civil War in Documents* (Athens, OH: 2009), 40–41.

[14] Ira Berlin, *Slaves Without Masters. The Free Negro in the Antebellum South* (New York: 1974), 99, 160–61.

New England states, plus Ohio, Michigan, and Wisconsin, adopted similar laws between 1854 and 1858. Vermont's was passed in December 1850, soon after the failure to recapture William and Ellen Craft from Boston, and generated strong reaction from the South, including from the "Central Southern Rights Association of Virginia," which considered it a nullification of the Fugitive Slave Law.[15]

Here was the crux of the problem according to one Philadelphia editor: "It may not be in morals the same thing to conceal a man with his own consent to secure his liberty, as it is by force and fraud to carry him off to reduce him to slavery, but so far as, by force and fraud, a master is deprived by our citizens, after identification of his legal title, to the services of the fugitive he is entitled by every principle of the Constitution, to demand from each and every one assisting" some form of constitutional recompense for the injuries suffered. In spite of identifying the problem, the editor had little to offer by way of a solution. A contemporary also put his finger on the problem: it was remarkably easy to aid and protect fugitives, he pointed out, without directly and openly confronting the law.[16] Months earlier, the New York *Times* had floated a trial balloon: compensate slaveholders for the loss of their slaves. Enforcing the Fugitive Slave Law, the editor admitted, was "the most embarrassing duty" imposed on the federal government. The South demanded enforcement, and while Northern governments agreed that the law should be enforced, its people were reluctant to become involved. This was the source of the bitterness between the two sections. On the one hand, slaveholders saw the denial of their property as a violation of their constitutional rights. On the other, attempts to retake a slave nerved "the heart of brave and sturdy yeomanry to resist the law." Only "the baser sort" in the North volunteered to participate in the return of fugitive slaves, while "respectable people" remained passive and refused to get involved. Administrations – Whig and Democrat – that enforced this "obnoxious statute" invariably suffered politically. There was a need to find common ground – one that would save slaveholders from serious loss and, at the same time, acknowledge the "moral sentiment" of those who opposed rendition. This balance could be attained if fugitives were not returned and slaveholders were compensated for the value of slaves lost. It was the only way to heal the "chafing and irritating wound." A similar plan had been raised during the debate over the Fugitive Slave Law in 1850, but had been rejected. The agreement could be framed in such a way as not to encourage owners to be less vigilant, and the compensation should be set at such a level as not to make slaveholders

[15] On the personal liberty laws see Thomas D. Morris, *Free Men All. The Personal Liberty Laws of the North, 1780–1861* (Baltimore: 1974), 168; Don E. Fehrenbacher, *The Slaveholding Republic. An Account of the United States Government's Relations to Slavery* (New York: 2001), 238; "Central Southern Rights Association of Virginia," Record Book, 1850–60, Virginia Historical Society, Richmond, Virginia.

[16] Philadelphia *Public Ledger*, January 14, 1861; Springfield *Republican*, December 1, 1860.

indifferent to their losses. The cost of such a plan, the *Times* estimated, would be a paltry $1 million annually, compared to the much larger sums expended on reclaiming fugitives. It was a proposal that both recognized the "claim to property on the one hand [and the] conscience and humanity on the other." The plan, not surprisingly, generated heated exchanges about both its constitutionality and practicality. One Baltimore editor, for example, while partial to the idea, argued that Northern states, and not the federal government, should foot the bill. After all, it is there that the constitutional infractions occurred. To expect the federal government to cover the cost would, in effect, be to burden those who had lost slaves with part of the bill of compensation. This was more than a matter of dollars and cents. Compared to the total value of slave property, such losses were relatively insignificant and were even considered by some slaveholders to be part of the price of doing business. What rankled were those Northern state laws that thumbed their noses at the "Constitutional rights of the South." If these loses were so insignificant, the *Times* editor wondered, why the hue and cry from slaveholders? From the "current declamations," he observed, one was inclined to think that slaveholders were "irretrievably ruined" by the North's refusal to surrender fugitives. If the South continued to treat the issue as a "matter of feeling," they must also grant the legitimacy of Northern feelings that rebelled against returning runaways to their masters. The problem could only be solved, he reiterated, if it were seen as a matter of dollars and cents and not feelings, for it was much easier to "legislate for property than for feelings." Compensation, the editor recalled, had earlier been supported by Charles Sumner, who described it fittingly as "spanning the chasm which separates the North and South, by a bridge of gold." Pushed to justify such outlays by the federal government, the editor later retreated a little with an altered proposal: compensation should be limited to two-thirds the value of the slave lost. The adjusted sum, he calculated, was more than adequate to cover the cost slaveholders incurred traveling to hearings in the North, bringing along witnesses, and hiring lawyers. It was even more generous given the fact that the majority of fugitives managed to eluded capture and so never had to face a hearing.[17]

Although limited, the *Times'* adjusted compensation proposal drew on a longstanding, but relatively marginal, antislavery proposal of compensate emancipation that had never attracted much support. But if few in the South were likely to entertain the idea, they overwhelmingly rejected the editor's insistence that compensation be coupled with a determined effort to address the issue of the kidnapping of free blacks. Once again, the editor returned to a proposal that had been floated and rejected at the time of the debate over the Fugitive Slave Law: ensuring that the accused was guaranteed a hearing before a jury. Some Border State representatives were willing, in 1850, to entertain

[17] New York *Times*, November 14, 17, 22, 1860.

the idea only if trials were held not where the fugitive was captured, but in the place from which he was reputed to have escaped. But even that alternative failed to gain traction. The law as it now stood, the editor reiterated, was a "disgrace to the legislation of the country" in that it omitted "this guarantee for the identity of the negro claimed as a slave" by not closing the gap "through which a regiment of kidnappers" had passed. It was also the only way, he surmised, to encourage the repeal of personal liberty laws, which, in his view, were the direct result of the "offensive and outrageous provisions" of the Fugitive Slave Law. As he had done earlier, William Seward proposed an amendment to the law that would permit jury trials for accused fugitives. Stephen Douglas countered that these trials should only occur in the state from which the slave had escaped. Weeks later, the House agreed to Douglas' proposal only if the suspected fugitive claimed that he was free. But the Senate never acted. The debate had come full circle since 1850. As then, the suggestion failed to address one of the law's major and intractable failings.[18]

Both partial compensation and minor proposals to reform the law only tinkered at the edges of the problem facing the nation. The editor nevertheless took comfort in the fact that proposals for compensation, or indemnity, were also frequently floated by Southern congressmen and senators as a way to address the problem of the loss of slaves. As far as James Mason, author of the Fugitive Slave Law, was concerned, indemnity would at least be an acknowledgement of the federal government's "inefficiency or inaction." It was a point he had made during the debate leading up to the 1850 law. Again, things had come full circle without showing any appreciable progress toward a resolution. In his final message to Congress, President James Buchanan attempted to address what he considered the major problems besetting the country. The crisis, he insisted, was the result of the "long-standing and intemperate interference of Northern people with the question of slavery in the Southern States." Efforts to exclude slavery from federal territories and the effort to defeat the "execution of the fugitive-slave law" had disrupted the political equilibrium that had kept the country together since its inception. The present dislocation would not have occurred had there not been a constant drumbeat against slavery in the North, one that also produced a maligned "influence on the slaves and inspired them with vague notions of freedom," and, at the same time, produced a sense of siege in the South. Secession could only be prevented if the South were left alone to "manage their domestic institution in their own way." He saw no reason to dissolve the Union. In evidence, he pointed to the fact that the federal government had never enacted a law denying slavery's legitimacy. Moreover, the Supreme Court had ruled recently that slavery was constitutionally recognized,

---

[18] New York *Times,* November 22, December 10, 1860; Cleveland *Herald,* January 31, 1861; Syracuse *Journal,* January 9, March 4, 1861. The Fugitive Slave Law remained on the books through most of the Civil War, with some embarrassing results for the Lincoln administration. It was not repealed until June 1864.

which meant that slaveholders had the right to take their property with them wherever they went in the Union. The only assaults on slavery were those state laws meant "to defeat execution of the fugitive-slave law," which he considered "null and void" because they were violations of the Constitution. Since 1850, all courts, federal and state, had ruled the Fugitive Slave Law constitutional. Opposition to the law had admittedly caused some inconvenience to masters, but the record showed that it had been generally enforced. Buchanan offered two possible ways out of the crisis: repeal all personal liberty laws and convene a constitutional convention to address outstanding issues. The latter, he suggested, would recognize the right of property in slaves where they now existed or may exist in the future; slavery would be protected in federal territories until such time as they entered the Union, when the citizens would decide whether the state would be free or not; the Fugitive Slave Law would be validated; and all personal liberty laws would be repealed. Buchanan's proposals were not only one sided, they were stunningly naïve. As David Donald put it, these were "proposals of surrender" to the demands of the fire-eaters.[19]

Armed and contemplating leaving the Union, the Virginia legislature nonetheless called for a national convention as a last-ditch attempt to resolve the crisis. As one of the Maine representatives to the convention put it, armed to the teeth, and preparing for war, Virginia was proposing "to step between the Government and the States." The tone of the Virginia resolutions – or more accurately, its demands – attempted to dictate the basis of any potential settlement. Among other things, slavery was to be protected in the territories, and the right of slaveholders to transit Free States guaranteed. Given these preconditions, the convention – which met in Washington, DC, on February 4, 1861, the same day seceding states convened in Montgomery, Alabama, to form the Confederacy – was doomed to failure. Speaking for many in the North, one editor was willing to concede the South's right to retain the privileges it now enjoyed under the Constitution, but, he flatly declared, it could "have no more." Twenty-one of thirty-four states sent delegations to the convention. Every Northern state, with the exception of Michigan, Wisconsin, and Minnesota, were in attendance; those states that had already seceded, not surprisingly, were not. The proceedings opened inauspiciously. James Seddon of Virginia insisted that the convention address only those issues raised by his state's call for the conference. This was necessary, in part, because the Republican Party and its supporters had plans in place to establish a "cordon of free states" around the

---

[19] Julius W. Muller, ed., *Presidential Messages and State Papers*, 10 Vols. (New York: 1917), V, 1810–17; David M. Donald, *The Impending Crisis, 1848–1861* (New York: 1976), 519–20. Buchanan overlooked the fact that the Wisconsin Supreme Court had ruled, following the rescue of Joshua Glover, that the law was unconstitutional, a ruling that was overturned by the Supreme Court in 1859. But he was right that a number of state and federal courts ruled it constitutional. See H. Robert Baker, *The Rescue of Joshua Glover. A Fugitive Slave, the Constitution and the Coming of the Civil War* (Athens, OH: 2006) for a discussion of the case.

South so as to extinguish slavery forever. Virginia and other slave states had a right to guard against this eventuality; as an equal partner, it should be guaranteed all existing constitutional protections. Slaves were as honorable a form of property as any other. Virginia was also duty bound to protect the African race, which it had raised under the influence of a "Christian civilization" from its "native barbarism" and elevated to "a standing and position which they could never have otherwise secured." As a result, they were far in advance of their counterparts in Haiti and Jamaica. Leave the "colored people where they are," he demanded, and do not "interfere with a neighboring state." None of these problems would have arisen had Northern states controlled the activities of abolitionists operating under the prompting of the British. The failure to do so had its fullest expression in John Brown's attack on Harpers Ferry. Without these guarantees, Seddon concluded, the Union was "unsafe for the people of the South." If the Union could not be preserved without these guarantees, George Boutwell of Massachusetts countered, then it ought not to be. The North would never consent to separation, peaceful or otherwise. If the course being pursued by some Southern states was not reversed, the Union would have no alternative but to march its armies south, even to the Gulf of Mexico.[20]

Nothing came of the convention. Delegates had arrived carrying irreconcilable proposals, which periodically threatened to scuttle the proceedings; when they left, three weeks later, they had nothing to show for their efforts. They agreed to seven amendments to the Constitution almost identical to those proposed by Crittenden, which, even before the convention had convened, had been almost universally rejected as unattainable. These were presented to Congress three days before the end of the session at a time when many Southern delegates had already abandoned their seats.[21] Even before the delegates had arrived in Washington, DC, states that had already seceded sent out dozens of commissioners in an effort to persuade other states to join the cause. Their messages were almost identical: slavery had been under assault for twenty-five years, resulting in the election of an antislavery president under whose rule their property would be appropriated and blacks elevated to a position of social and political equality. More importantly, the decision to leave the Union was justified by the North's failure to adhere to the terms of the Fugitive Slave Law and by its adoption of personal liberty laws. In explaining their decision to leave, South Carolina pointed, among other reasons, to the "thousands of...slaves" who were encouraged to leave "their homes." Those who did not, they observed, had been "incited by emissaries, books and pictures to servile

[20] L. E. Chittenden, *A Report of the Debates and Proceedings of the Conference Convention* (1864, rpr., New York: 1971), 49–52, 94–97, 100, 146; Foner, *Business and Slavery*, 267–68; Potter, *The Impending Crisis*, 507; Syracuse *Journal*, January 25, 1861.
[21] Potter, *The Impending Crisis*, 547; Foner, *Business and Slavery*, 270–71; Mark Tooley, *The Peace that Almost Was. The Forgotten Story of the 1861 Washington Peace Conference and the Final Attempt to Avert the Civil War* (New York: 2015), 235–40.

insurrection." As William l. Harrick, the Georgia commissioner, put it, the citizens of the South had been "deprived of their property, and for attempting to seek the redress promised" by law, had sometimes even "lost their liberty and their lives." The right of return was guaranteed by the Constitution and the Fugitive Slave Law, yet both had been continually "nullified," and the solemn pledge of the Compromise of 1850 "faithlessly disregarded."[22]

Although neither South Carolina nor any other Deep South state had suffered much from the operations of the Underground Railroad, the perceived failure to enforce the Fugitive Slave Law had come, by 1860, to symbolize the North's inability or reluctance to implement an agreement that many in 1850 saw as the last best chance to preserve the Union. What became known as the "Georgia Platform" had articulated the political expectation of the law in 1850: upon "the faithful execution of the Fugitive Slave Bill by the proper authorities," it made clear, "depends the preservation of our much loved Union." Clearly, that promise had not been fulfilled. Slaves continued to escape in record numbers, aided and encouraged, many thought, by an increasingly active band of emissaries, black and white, who went into the South to "entice" slaves to escape. Years earlier, a Missourian pointed out, opponents would cross the Mississippi River from Quincy, Illinois, to encourage slaves to leave their masters. They were, she observed, as "thick as maggots on a dead horse."[23] The records of Border State courts show that these claims of Northern interference were merited. Escapees were also aided by other slaves who chose to remain behind, as well as by Southern free blacks and whites. Even more troubling was the fact that the law seemed to have had little effect on either the numbers who escaped, or the frequency and size of these escapes. While escapes were many times foiled, they continued, rising at times to unprecedented numbers. Those seeking freedom slipped away singly, as family units, or as groups of coworkers. Kentucky slaveholders lamented what they saw as a new development in the 1850s: the rising number who escaped in family units. The observation applied equally all along the divide between slavery and freedom. Slaves devised ingenious ways to leave. They had themselves crated and sent by rail and steamboat, they commandeered carriages and stole horses, white associates bought them train tickets, or they simply walked away. They acquired free passes. Meant originally as a device to control their movement, these passes were transformed by the enslaved into passports of freedom. Some even planned ahead, arranging with family members and friends who had left earlier for jobs in their new homes. In the North they were aided by an increasingly sophisticated Underground Railroad system. When, under the law, slaveholders attempted to reclaim their property, they ran into sustained opposition

[22] The work of these commissioners is covered by Charles B. Dew, *Apostles of Disunion. Southern Secession Commissioners and the Causes of the Civil War* (Charlottesville, VA: 2001), 11–19, 86.

[23] Quoted in Joseph Yannielli, "George Thompson among the Africans. Empathy, Authority, and Insanity in the Age of Abolition," *Journal of American History*, 96, No. 1 (March 2010), 984.

from black communities and their white supporters. There is no doubt that commissioners such as Harrisburg, Pennsylvania's Richard McAllister stuck to their task and ensured the return of fugitives, but others approached their duties reluctantly, and yet others were intimidated by the rage of omnipresent black crowds who made their presence felt at hearings. Lawyers for the defense, who offered their services pro bono, continually challenged the law's constitutionality. The situation was made even more difficult for slaveholders, because the government never managed to staff the office of commissioner adequately; large swaths of the North, particularly sparsely populated areas, were never represented. Fugitives were sometimes seized from under the noses of the authorities and taken to freedom. These barriers to the return of fugitives were symbolized, in the eyes of Southerners, by the existence of the personal liberty laws. They may have been "useless irritants," as one Northern editor acknowledged, but they did make renditions more expensive and annoying. In the first two years of the law's operation, fugitives remanded from Harrisburg had to be held in insecure hotels rather than city prisons.[24]

Putting as positive a spin as he could on the record of the law's operation, President Buchanan observed that, in "contested cases," it had been successfully executed. He had to admit, however, such successes were marred by the fact that they were achieved only at "great loss and inconvenience to the master and with considerable expense to the Government."[25] The New York *Times'* compensation proposal was based, in part, on the unproven calculation that only one in ten fugitives were ever reclaimed. Assuming the figure was accurate, it was a paltry return on the amount of energy and resources expended both by slaveholders and the government. But there is no evidence that the rate of return was that high. In addition, returns involved the expenditure of considerable resources by both the government and the slaveholder. The return of Thomas Sims from Boston, for instance, cost the federal and state governments an estimated $20,000; Anthony Burns more than twice that amount. Neither of these figures included the cost slaveholders incurred getting to the site of hearings, the prices charged by slave catchers and agents or the per diem and other expenses of witnesses. One estimate put the estimated cost incurred in excess of "$50,000 for a single slave," clearly an inflated number, but one that captured the potential expenses involved in the effort to return fugitives. Success came at both an economic and political price. The *Times'* estimation raises another intriguing question: Were slaveholders as successful in reclaiming their slaves as Buchanan believed? While it is true, as Stanley Campbell has shown, that in the majority of cases heard fugitives were returned, he says little about the numbers who successfully evaded capture. Even when they were caught, they

[24] For the "Georgia Platform" see Morris, *Free Men All,* 147; Springfield *Republican,* November 17, December 1, 25, 1860. Rhode Island repealed its law in January 1861, the only state to do so. Syracuse *Journal,* January 25, 1861.
[25] Muller, *Presidential Messages,* 1814.

not infrequently defied the law, either because the black community marshaled sufficient evidence to persuade commissioners, as it did in the case of Daniel Webster in Philadelphia in late 1859, or because the evidence presented by the claimant was considered inadequate. When coupled with dramatic rescues such as Jerry's in Syracuse, Shadrach Minkins's in Boston, and Joshua Glover's from the courthouse in Milwaukee, or the failure to recapture William and Ellen Craft in Boston, all of which received wide coverage, it is not surprising that Southerners considered the law ineffective.[26] James Mason had suggested what he considered the true measure of effectiveness: expeditious implementation in Northern communities that believed in the law's legitimacy. Neither was the case. Even in hearings that were speedily conducted and resulted in returns, as was the case in Harrisburg from 1850 to 1852, claimants and commissioners were regularly challenged by black communities and their supportive teams of lawyers in ways that sometimes slowed, and other times threatened to overwhelm, the process. Such resistance many times pushed the system to overreact and to employ increasingly draconian methods, with the result that the law quickly lost whatever claims Mason thought it should have to community support. Holding hearings early in the morning so as to limit community presence, ringing the Boston courthouse with chains during the Thomas Sims case, hurrying suspects out of town, taking others out in broad daylight under heavy guard at the cost of thousands of dollars to the federal government, while it demonstrated the power of the federal government and its willingness to use all means at its disposal to return fugitive slaves, such heavy handedness alienated many. The Harrisburg commissioner did all that the law required, returning every fugitive who came before him. But in his zealous execution of the law he alienated the community in which he lived and worked and, as a result, was pressured to abandon his post. Following his departure, the government could find no one willing to take his place. There were no other recorded hearings in the city in the years after his departure. The methods by which Anthony Burns was returned from Boston in 1854 so alienated many in the city that some who had earlier pledged to assist the government following the rescue of Minkins, three years earlier, announced their determination to resist future returns. No fugitive was returned from Boston after 1854.[27]

The *Times'* calculations were inaccurate; many more fugitives escaped the clutches of the law than were apprehended and returned. The law was an inadequate mechanism to address the problem. That inadequacy undermined the political calculus at the heart of the law – namely, that its execution would demonstrate the North's commitment to the constitutional guarantees stretching back to the founding of the country and, in doing so, ensure the maintenance of the Union. As the political agreement unraveled in 1860, not even the decision to return Lucy Bagby from Cleveland, a hotbed of abolitionism, could

[26] New York *Times*, November 17, 1860.
[27] On Glover's rescue see Baker, *The Rescue of Joshua Glover.*

stem the tide of disunion. If ever there was a demonstration of the North's commitment to the execution of the law it was surely Bagby's return. By the end of 1860, however, such renditions were of little political consequence. They could do little to compensate for the losses slaveholders had incurred since 1850. It could do even less to convince Southerners that the law was anything but an unmitigated failure. In their quest for freedom, the enslaved had contributed to the political debate about the future of slavery as well as the future of the country. With few resources other than a concerted and united opposition to the law's implementation, black communities throughout the North, backed by abolitionist supporters, did their part to undermine the law's legitimacy. Together, they managed to undermine the law and bring the country to a moment of reckoning. As John Goshorn was forced to concede, the enslaved cared little about saving the Union.

There was, however, a price to pay for this success. The law disrupted and, in some instances, shattered, the lives fugitives had made for themselves in the North. By their "industry and economy," Frederick Douglass recalled, "[they had] saved money and bought little homes for themselves and their children." The law forced them to uproot their settled lives and flee for safety "from an enemy's land – a doomed city – and take up a dismal march to a new abode, empty-handed, among strangers." Free blacks also felt an increased vulnerability. In 1853, young Moses Anderson wrote the Rochester Ladies Anti-Slavery Society from his home in Greencastle, Pennsylvania, as he put it "so near the lines of the slave state" from which there were weekly escapes. He enclosed one dollar to support the society's annual antislavery bazaar. But he was motivated by other more personal considerations: he was planning a tour of western New York and Michigan, he announced, to see if he could "suit [himself] any better than I can here." Life for a young black man, close to a slave state, was dangerously unpredictable. It might be marginally better further north, he hoped, but even there, he must have realized, free blacks had to be constantly vigilant. The search for freedom and equality was a constant struggle.[28]

[28] Frederick Douglass, *The Life and Times of Frederick Douglass* (1892, rpr., New York: 1962), 279–80; Moses Anderson to Maria G. Porter, Greencastle, December 12, 1853, Folder 1:4, Rochester Anti-Slavery Society Papers. My thanks to Leigh Fought for a copy of the letter.

# Bibliography

## Archives

Abraham Lincoln Library, Springfield, IL.
  Lincoln Legal Papers.
Chicago Historical Society, Chicago, IL.
  Zebina Eastman Papers.
Dauphin County Courthouse, Harrisburg, PA.
  Dauphin County Clerk of Court, Quarter Session Docket Book 9.
  Quarter Session, Oyer & Terminer Papers.
Dauphin County Historical Society, Harrisburg, PA.
  Charles Rawn Diary, Rawn Collect ion.
Filson Historical Society, Louisville, KY.
  Bullitt Papers.
  James Rudd Papers.
Indiana Historical Society, Indianapolis, IN.
  Valentine Nicholson Transcripts.
Indiana State Archives, Indianapolis, IN.
  State Board of Colonization, Gov. Joseph A. Wright Papers.
Kentucky State Library and Archives, Frankfort, KY.
  Mason County Circuit Court of Justice, Case Files.
  Register of Prisoners, 1855–1861.
Library of Congress, Washington, DC.
  American Colonization Society Papers. (microfilm)
Maryland Historical Society, Baltimore, MD.
  Curtis Jacobs Papers.
  Maryland Colonization Society Papers.
Maryland State Archives, Annapolis, MD.
  Frederick County Circuit Court, Minutes 1860.
  Secretary of State Pardon Records, 1845–1865.
  Governor (Miscellaneous Papers), 1856–1865.
  Governor (Proceedings), 1861–1869.

Missouri Historical Society, St. Louis, MO.
  Case Family Papers.
Missouri State Library and Archives, Jefferson City, MO.
  Missouri State Register of Inmates Received, Office of the Secretary of State Pardon
    Papers, 1837–1909.
  Records of Governor Sterling Price, 1853–1857.
National Archives, Washington, DC.
  Records of the Bureau of Accounts, Appropriation Ledger for the Treasury and Other
    Departments, 1807–1945.
  Settled Miscellaneous Treasury Accounts, September 6, 1790–September 29, 1894.
Pennsylvania Historical Society, Philadelphia, PA.
  Pennsylvania Anti-Slavery Society Papers.
University of Virginia, Charlottesville, VA.
  Buck Family Papers.
Virginia Historical Society, Richmond, VA.
  John Letcher Papers.
  Minute Book, Central Southern Rights Association of Virginia, 1850–1860.
  Minutes of the Virginia Branch of the American Colonization Society, November 4,
    1823–February 5, 1859.
Virginia State Library and Archives, Richmond, VA.
  Executive Papers, January–February 1851, Governor Floyd.
Western Reserve Historical Society, Cleveland, OH.
  Elisha Whittlesey Papers.
Black Abolitionists Papers, Chadwyck microfilm.
Kenneth Stampp, ed. Records of the Ante-Bellum Southern Plantations from the
    Revolution through the Civil War, University Publications of America microfilm.

## Books

Adams, Charles F., *Richard Henry Dana. A Biography*. 2 Vols. Houghton Mifflin, 1890.
Anbinder, Tyler, *Nativism and Slavery. The Northern Know Nothings and the Politics of
    the 1850s*. Oxford University Press, 1992.
Anderson, William J., *Life and Narrative of William J. Anderson. Twenty Four Years a
    Slave; Sold Eight Times! In Jail Sixty Times!! Whipped Three Hundred Times!!! Or
    the Dark Days of American Slavery Revealed*. Daily Tribune Book, 1857
Anderson, William W., *Jamaica and the Americas*. Stanford and Swords, 1851.
  *A Description of the History of the Island of Jamaica*. George Henderson, 1851.
Anonymous, *Life of the Notorious Kidnapper George F. Alberti by a Member of the
    Philadelphia Bar*. n.p., 1851.
Baker, H. Robert, *The Rescue of Joshua Glover. A Fugitive Slave, the Constitution and
    the Coming of the Civil War*. Ohio University Press, 2006.
Barry, Kathleen, *Susan B. Anthony. A Biography of a Singular Feminist*. New York
    University Press, 1988.
Bearse, Austin, *Reminiscences of Fugitive-Slave Days in Boston*. Warren Richardson,
    1880.
Berlin, Ira, *Slaves Without Masters. The Free Negro in the Antebellum South*.
    Pantheon, 1974.

Biddle, Daniel R. & Dubin, Murray, *Tasting Freedom. Octavius Catto and the Battle for Equality in Civil War America*. Temple University Press, 2010.

Bigelow, John, *Jamaica in 1850 or, the Effects of Sixteen Years of Freedom on a Slave Colony*. 1851, rpr., University of Illinois Press, 2006.

Billington, Ray A., ed., *The Journal of Charlotte L. Forten: A Free Negro*. Norton, 1953.

Bingham, Darrell, *We Ask Only a Fair Trial. A History of the Black Community of Evansville, Indiana*. Indiana University Press, 1987.

On Jordan's Banks. Emancipation and Its Aftermath in the Ohio River Valley. Kentucky University Press, 2006.

Blackett, R. J. M., *Beating Against the Barriers. Biographical Essays in Nineteenth-Century Afro-American History*. Louisiana State University Press, 1986.

*Making Freedom. The Underground Railroad and the Politics of Slavery*. University of North Carolina Press, 2013.

Blassingame, John, *Slave Testimony: Two Centuries of Letters, Speeches, Interviews, and Autobiographies*. Louisiana State University Press, 1977.

ed., *Frederick Douglass Papers, Series 1, Vol. 2, 1847–54*. Yale University Press, 1982.

Blockson, Charles, *The Underground Railroad in Pennsylvania*. Flame International, 1981.

Blue, Frederick J., *Salmon P. Chase. A Life in Politics*. Kent State University Press, 1987.

*No Taint of Compromise. Crusaders in Antislavery Politics*. Louisiana State University Press, 2005.

Bogger, Tommy, *Free Blacks in Norfolk, Virginia, 1790–1860: The Darker Side of Freedom*. University of Virginia Press, 1997.

Bordewich, Fergus M., *Bound for Canaan. The Underground Railroad and the War for the Soul of America*. Amistad, 2005.

*America's Great Debate. Henry Clay, Stephen A. Douglas and the Compromise that Saved the Union*. Simon & Schuster, 2012.

Bowditch, Vincent Y., *Life and Correspondence of Henry Ingersoll Bowditch*. 2 Vols. Houghton Mifflin, 1902.

Brackett, Jeffrey R., *The Negro in Maryland. A Study of the Institution of Slavery*. Johns Hopkins University Press, 1889.

Brandt, Nat, *The Town that Started the Civil War*. Syracuse University Press, 1990.

Brandt, Nat & Kroyt, Brandt Y., *In the Shadow of the Civil War. Passmore Williamson and the Rescue of Jane Johnson*. University of South Carolina Press, 2007.

Brown, Hallie Q., *Tales My Father Told and Other Stories*. Eckerle Printing Co., n.d.

Browne, Peter A., *A review of the Trial, Conviction, and Sentence of George A. Alberti for Kidnapping*. n.p., 1851.

Bruce, H. C., *The New Man. Twenty-nine Years a Slave, Twenty-nine Years a Free Man*. 1895, rpr., Negro University Press, 1969.

Buchanan, Thomas C., *Black Life on the Mississippi. Slaves, Free Blacks, and the Western Steamboat World*. University of North Carolina Press, 2004.

Burin, Eric, *Slavery and the Peculiar Solution. A History of the American Colonization Society*. University of Florida Press, 2005.

Butler, M. B., *My Story of the Civil War and the Underground Railroad*. United Brethren, 1914.

Calarco, Tom, *The Underground Railroad in the Adirondack Region*. McFarland, 2004.

Campbell, James M., *Slavery on Trial. Race, Class, and Criminal Justice in Antebellum Richmond, Virginia*. University of Florida Press, 2007.

Campbell, Penelope, *Maryland in Africa. The Maryland State Colonization Society 1831–1857*. University of Illinois Press, 1971.

Campbell, Stanley W., *The Slave Catchers. Enforcement of the Fugitive Slave Law, 1850–1860*. University of North Carolina Press, 1968.

Carmony, Don, *Indiana 1816–1850. The Pioneer Era*. Indiana Historical Society, 1998.

Cecelski, David S., *Waterman's Song. Slavery and Freedom in Maritime North Carolina*. University of North Carolina Press, 2001.

Cheek, William & Cheek, Aimee L., *John Mercer Langston and the Fight for Black Freedom, 1829–1865*. University of Illinois Press, 1989.

Christianson, Scott, *Freeing Charles. The Struggle to Free a Slave on the Eve of the Civil War*. University of Illinois Press, 2010.

Clamorgan, Cyprian, *The Colored Aristocracy of St. Louis*. (Edited with an Introduction by Julie Winch) University of Missouri Press, 1999.

Clavin, Matthew J., *Aiming for Pensacola. Fugitive Slaves on the Atlantic and Southern Frontiers*. Harvard University Press, 2015.

Clayton, Ralph, *Cash for Blood: the Baltimore to New Orleans Domestic Slave Trade*. Heritage Books, 2002.

Cochrane, William C., *Western Reserve and the Fugitive Slave Law: A Prelude to the Civil War*. De Capo Press, 1972.

Cockrum, William M., *History of the Underground Railroad As It Was Conducted by the Anti-Slavery League*. 1915, rpr., Heritage Books, 1991.

Coffin, Levi, *Reminiscence of Levi Coffin*. Arno Press, 1968.

Cohen, Anthony, *The Underground Railroad in Montgomery County, Maryland. A History and Driving Guide*. Montgomery Co. Historical Society, 1997.

Coleman, Chapman, *The Life of John J. Crittenden with Selections from His Correspondence and Speeches*. 2 Vols. J. P. Lippincott, 1871.

Coleman, John F., *The Disruption of the Pennsylvania Democracy 1848–1860*. The Pennsylvania Historical and Museum Commission, 1975.

Coleman, J. Winston, Jr., *Slavery Times in Kentucky*. Johnson Reprint Co., 1970.

Collison, Gary, *Shadrach Milkins. From Fugitive Slave to Citizen*. Harvard University Press, 1997.

Commager, Henry S., *Theodore Parker: Yankee Crusader*. Beacon Press, 1960.

Conway, Moncure D., *Autobiography. Memories and Experiences*. 2 Vols. Houghton Mifflin, 1904.

Cooper, William J., Jr., *The South and the Politics of Slavery 1828–1856*. Louisiana State University Press: 1978.

Cover, Robert M., *Justice Accused: Antislavery and the Judicial Process*. Yale University Press, 1975.

Craft, William, *Running a Thousand Miles for Freedom. The Escape of William and Ellen Craft*. William Tweedie, 1861.

Curtis, Benjamin R., ed., *A Memoir of Benjamin Robbins Curtis LL.D*. 2 Vols. Little Brown, 1879.

Davis, David B., *The Problem of Slavery in the Age of Emancipation*. Knopf, 2014.

Delany, Martin R., *The Condition, Elevation, Emigration and Destiny of the Colored People of the United States*. 1852, rpr., Ayer Co., 1988.

Dew, Charles B., *Apostles of Disunion. Southern Secession Commissioners and the Causes of the Civil War.* University of Virginia Press, 2001.

Deyle, Steven, *Carry Me Back. The Domestic Slave Trade In American Life.* Oxford University Press, 2005.

Diggins, Milt, *Stealing Freedom along the Mason-Dixon Line. Thomas McCreary, the Notorious Slave Catcher from Maryland.* Maryland Historical Society, 2015.

Donald, David, *The Impending Crisis, 1848–1861.* Harper & Row, 1976.

Douglass, Frederick, *The Life and Times of Frederick Douglass.* 1892, rpr., Collier Books, 1962.

Drew, Benjamin, *North Side View of Slavery. The Refuge of the Narrative of Fugitive Slaves in Canada Related by Themselves.* 1856, rpr., Negro University Press, 1968.

Dusinberre, William, *Civil War Issues in Philadelphia 1856–1865.* University of Pennsylvania Press, 1965.

Essah, Patience, *A House Divided. Slavery and Emancipation in Delaware 1638–1865.* University of Virginia. Press, 1996.

Edelstein, Tilden G., *Strange Enthusiasm: A Life of Thomas Wentworth Higginson.* Yale University Press, 1968.

Etcheson, Nicole, *The Emerging Midwest. Upland Southerners and the Political Culture of the Old Northwest, 1787–1861.* Indiana University Press, 1996.

*A Generation at War: the Civil War Era in a Northern Community.* University Press of Kansas, 2011.

Fairbank, Rev. Calvin, *Rev. Calvin Fairbank During Slavery Times: How He "Fought The Good Fight" To Prepare "The Way."* Negro Universities Press, 1969.

Faulkner, Carol, *Lucretia Mott's Heresy. Abolition and Women's Rights in Nineteenth-Century America.* University of Pennsylvania Press, 2011.

Fehrenbacher, Don E., *The Slaveholding Republic, An Account of the United States Government's Relations to Slavery.* Oxford University Press, 2001.

Fields, Barbara J., *Slavery and Freedom on the Middle Ground. Maryland During the Nineteenth Century.* Yale University Press, 1985.

Finkelman, Paul, *An Imperfect Union. Slavery, Federalism, and Comity.* University of North Carolina Press, 1981.

*Millard Fillmore.* Times Books, 2011.

Fladeland, Betty, *James Gillespie Birney: Slaveholder to Abolitionist.* Cornell University Press, 1955.

Foner, Eric, *Gateway to Freedom. The Hidden History of the Underground Railroad.* W. W. Norton, 2014.

Foner, Philip S., *Business and Slavery. The New York Merchants and the Irresistible Conflict.* North Carolina University Press, 1941.

*Essays in Afro-American History.* Temple University Press, 1978.

Foner, Philip S. & Walker, George E., eds., *Proceedings of the Black State Conventions, 1840–1865.* 2 Vols. Temple University Press, 1979.

Frazier, Harriet C., *Runaway and Freed Missouri Slaves and Those Who Helped Them.* McFarland, 2004.

Franklin, John H. & Schweninger, Loren, *Runaway Slaves. Rebels on the Plantation.* Oxford University Press, 1999.

*In Search of the Promised Land. A Slave Family in the Old South.* Oxford University Press, 2006.

Freehling, William W., *The Road to Disunion. Secessionists at Bay, 1776–1854.* Oxford University Press, 1990.

Frost, Karolyn S., *I've Got a Home in Glory Land. A Lost Tale of the Underground Railroad.* Farrar, Straus & Giroux, 2007.

Gara, Larry, *The Liberty Line: The Legend of the Underground Railroad.* University of Kentucky Press, 1961.

Gibson, W. H., Sr., *History of the United Brothers of Friendship and Sisters of the Mysterious Ten in Two Parts: A Negro Order.* Bradley and Gilbert, 1897.

Goldman, Mark, *High Hopes. The Rise and Decline of Buffalo, New York.* SUNY Press, 1983.

Griffler, Keith P., *Front Line of Freedom. African Americans and the Forging of the Underground Railroad in the Ohio Valley.* University of Kentucky Press, 2004.

Grover, Kathryn, *The Fugitive's Gibraltar: Escaping Slaves and Abolitionism in New Bedford, Massachusetts.* University of Massachusetts Press, 2001.

Gura Philip F., *American Transcendentalism. A History.* Hill & Wang, 2007.

Guy, Anita A., *Maryland's Persistent Pursuit to End Slavery, 1850–1864.* Garland, 1997.

Guyatt, Nicholas, *Bind Us Apart. How Enlightenment Americans Invented Racial Separation.* Basic Books, 2016.

Hagedorn, Ann, *Beyond the River. The Untold Story of the Heroes of the Underground Railroad.* Simon & Schuster, 2002.

Hamm, Thomas D., *God's Government Begun. The Society for Universal Inquiry and Reform, 1842–1846.* Indiana University Press, 1995.

Harrison, Benjamin S., *Fortune Favors the Brave. The Life of Horace Bell, Pioneer Californian.* Ward Ritchie Press, 1953.

Harrison, Lowell H., *The Antislavery Movement in Kentucky.* University of Kentucky Press, 1978.

Harrold, Stanley, *Border Wars. Fighting Against Slavery before the Civil War.* University of North Carolina Press, 2010.

 *Subversives. Antislavery Community in Washington D.C., 1828–1865.* Louisiana State University Press, 2003.

Haviland, Laura S., *A Woman's Life Work: Including Thirty Years of Service on the Underground Railroad and In the War.* S. B. Shaw, 1881.

Henson, Josiah, *The Life of Josiah Henson, Formerly a Slave, Now an Inhabitant of Canada as Narrated by Himself,* in Taylor, Yuval, *I was Born a Slave. An Anthology of Classic Slave Narratives, Vol. 1, 1772–1849.* Lawrence Hill Books, 1999.

Hensel, W. U., *The Christiana Riot and the Treason Trials of 1851: An Historical Sketch.* New Era Printing, 1911.

Hesslink, George K., *Black Neighbors: Negroes in a Northern Rural Community.* Bobbs-Merrill, 1968.

Heuman, Gad, *Between Black and White. Race, Politics, and the Free Coloreds in Jamaica, 1792–1865.* Greenwood, 1981.

Higginson, Thomas W., *Cheerful Yesterdays.* 1898, rpr., Arno Press, 1968.

Hinton, Richard, *John Brown and His Men.* Funk & Wagnalls, 1894.

Hise, Daniel H., *Selections from the Diary of Daniel Howell Hise: 1813–1878.* Weingart, 1967.

Hoar, George F., *Autobiography of Seventy Years.* 2 Vols. Charles Scribner, 1903.

Hodge, Graham Russell Goa, *David Ruggles. A Radical Black Abolitionist and the Underground Railroad in New York City*. University of North Carolina Press, 2010.

Holt, Michael F., *The Rise and Fall of the American Whig Party. Jacksonian Politics and the Onset of the Civil War*. Oxford University Press, 1999.

Horton, James O. & Horton, Lois E., *Black Bostonian's Family Life and Community Struggle in the Antebellum North*. Holmes & Meier, 1979.

Horwitz, Tony, *Midnight Rising. John Brown and the Raid that Sparked the Civil War*. Henry Holt, 2011.

Howard, Victor B., *The Evangelical War against Slavery and Caste: The Life and Times of John G. Fee*. Associated University Press, 1996.

Hudson, J. Blaine, *Fugitive Slaves and the Underground Railroad in the Kentucky Borderland*. McFarland, 2002.

Hudson, James L., *Stephen A. Douglas and the Dilemma of Democratic Equality*. Rowan & Littlefield, 2007.

Humez, Jean M., *Harriet Tubman. The Line and the Life Stories*. University of Wisconsin Press, 2003.

Hunter, Carol M., *To Set the Captives Free: Reverend Jermain Wesley Loguen and the Struggle for Freedom in Central New York 1835–1872*. Garland, 1993.

Hurt, R. Douglas, *Agriculture and Slavery in Missouri's Little Dixie*. University of Missouri Press, 1992.

Jacobs, Curtis W., *The Free Negro Question*. John W. Woods, 1859.

  *Speech of Col. Curtis W. Jacobs on the Free Colored Population of Maryland Delivered in the House of Delegates on the 17th of February, 1860*. Elihu S. Riley, 1860.

Jacobs, Harriet A., *Incidents in the Life of a Slave Girl*. Harvard University Press, 1861.

Jennings, Thelma, *The Nashville Convention: Southern Movement for Unity, 1848–1851*. Memphis State University Press, 1980.

Kantrowitz, Stephen, *More than Freedom. Fighting for Black Citizenship in a White Republic, 1829–1889*. Penguin, 2012.

Kashatus, William C., *Just Over the Line: Chester County and the Underground Railroad*. Penn State University Press, 2001.

Katz, Jonathan, *Resistance at Christiana. The Fugitive Slave Rebellion, Christiana, Pennsylvania, September 11, 1851. A Documentary Account*. Thomas Y. Crowell, 1974.

Langston, John, *From the Virginia Plantation to the National Capitol*. 1884, rpr., Arno Press, 1969.

LaRoche, Cheryl J., *The Geography of Resistance. Free Black Communities and the Underground Railroad*. University of Illinois Press, 2014.

Larson, Kate C., *Bound for the Promised Land: Harriet Tubman, Portrait of an American Hero*. Ballantine Books, 2004.

Link, William A., *Roots of Secession. Slavery and Politics in Antebellum Virginia*. University of North Carolina Press, 2003.

Lipin, Lawrence M., *Producers, Proletarians, and Politicians. Workers and Party Politics in Evansville and New Albany, Indiana, 1850–87*. University of Illinois Press, 1994.

Loguen, J. W., *The Reverend J. W. Loguen as a Slave and as a Freeman: A Narrative of a Real Life*. 1859, rpr., Syracuse University Press, 1968.

Lubet, Steven, *Fugitive Justice. Runaways, Rescuers, and Slavery on Trial*. Harvard University Press, 2010.

Lucas, Marion B., *A History of Blacks in Kentucky, Volume 1: From Slavery to Segregation, 1760–1891*. Kentucky Historical Society, 1992.

Mabee, Carleton, *Black Freedom. The Nonviolent Abolitionists from 1830 through the Civil War*. Macmillan, 1970.

Maddox, Lucy, *The Parker Sisters. A Border Kidnapping*. Temple University Press, 2016.

Madison, James H., *Hoosiers. A New History of Indiana*. Indiana University Press, 2014.

Maltz, Earl M., *Fugitive Slave on Trial. The Anthony Burns Case and Abolitionist Outrage*. University of Kansas Press, 2010.

Mann, Charles W., *The Chicago Common Council and the Fugitive Slave Law of 1850*. Chicago Historical Society, 1903.

May, Samuel J., *Some Recollections of Our Antislavery Conflict*. Arno Press, 1968.

McDougall, Marion G., *Fugitive Slaves, 1619–1865*. Ginn & Co., 1891.

McGowan, James A., *Station Master on the Underground Railroad. The Life and Letters of Thomas Garrett*. McFarland & Co., 2005.

McCaskill, Barbara, *Liberation, and Escaping Slavery. William and Ellen Craft in Cultural Memory*. University of Georgia Press, 2015.

McKim, J. Miller, *The Arrest, Trial, and Release of Daniel Webster, Fugitive Slave*. n.p., 1859.

McPherson, James M., *Ordeal by Fire. The Civil War and Reconstruction*. McGraw Hill, 1982.

Mealy, Todd, *Biography of an Antislavery City: Antislavery Advocates, Abolitionists, and Underground Railroad Activities in Harrisburg, Pa.* Publish America, 2007.

Middleton, Stephen, *The Black Laws. Race and the Legal Process in Early Ohio*. Ohio University Press, 2005.

Miller, Floyd J., *The Search for a Black Nationality. Black Colonization and Emigration, 1787–1863*. University of Illinois Press, 1975.

Mingus, Scott, *The Ground Swallowed Them Up. Slavery and the Underground Railroad in York County, Pa.* York County Historical Center, 2016.

Mitchell, Rev. W. M., *The Under-Ground Railroad*. Tweedie, 1860.

Morris, J. Brent, *Oberlin. Hotbed of Abolitionism. College, Community, and the Fight for Freedom and Equality in Antebellum America*. University of North Carolina Press, 2014.

Morris, Thomas D., *Free Men All. The Personal Liberty Laws of the North, 1780–1861*. Johns Hopkins University Press, 1974.

Moses, Wilson, ed., *Liberian Dreams. Back-to-Africa Narratives of the 1850s*. Penn State University Press, 1998.

Murphy, Angela F., *The Jerry Rescue: The Fugitive Slave Law, Northern Rights, and the American Sectional Crisis*. Oxford University Press, 2016.

Nevins, Allan, *Ordeal of the Union. Fruits of Manifest Destiny, 1847–1852*. Scribner, 1947.

Nivens, John, et al., *The Salmon P. Chase Papers, Vol. 1, Journals, 1829–1872*. Kent State University Press, 1993.

Northup, Solomon, *Twelve Years a Slave*. 1853, rpr., Louisiana State University Press, 1968.

Papson, Don & Calarco, Tom, *Secrets of the Underground Railroad in New York City. Sydney Howard Gay, Louis Napoleon and the Record of the Fugitives*. McFarland, 2015.

Pease, Jane H. & Pease, William H., *They Who Would Be Free: Blacks' Search for Freedom, 1830–1861*. Atheneum, 1974.

Peskin, Alan, ed., *North into Freedom: The Autobiography of John Malvin, Free Negro, 1795–1880*. Western Reserve University, 1966.

Peters, Pamela R., *The Underground Railroad in Floyd County, Indiana*. McFarland & Company, 2001.

Philadelphia Female Anti-Slavery Society. *Twenty-First Annual Report*. 1855. *Twenty-Third Annual Report*. 1857. *Report of the Twenty-Fourth and Twenty-Fifth Years*. 1859.

Phillips, Christopher, *Freedom's Port. The African American Community of Baltimore, 1790–1860*. University of Illinois Press, 1997.

Pierce, Edward L., *Memoir and Letters of Charles Sumner*. 3 Vols. 1894, rpr., Mnemosyne, 1969.

Potter, David, *The Impending Crisis, 1848–1861*. Harper & Row, 1976.

Prince, Bryan, *A Shadow on the Household. One Enslaved Family's Incredible Struggle for Freedom*. McClelland & Stewart, 2009.

Pybus, Cassandra, *Epic Journey of Freedom. Runaway Slaves of the American Revolution and Their Global Quest for Liberty*. Beacon Press, 2006.

Quarles, Benjamin, *Frederick Douglass*. 1948, rpr., Prentice Hall, 1968. *Black Abolitionists*. Oxford University Press, 1969.

Ray, Florence T., *Sketch of the Life of Charles B. Ray*. J. J. Little, 1887.

Rayback, Robert J., *Millard Fillmore. Biography of a President*. Buffalo Historical Society, 1959.

Reed, Christopher R., *Black Chicago's First Century. Volume 1, 1833–1900*. University of Missouri Press, 2005.

Renehan, Edward J., Jr., *The Secret Six: The True Tale of the Men Who Conspired with John Brown*. Crown Publishers, 1995.

Reinyon, Randolph P., *Delia Webster and the Under-Ground Railroad*. University of Kentucky Press, 1996.

Ricks, Mary K., *Escape of the Pearl. The Heroic Bid for Freedom on the Underground Railroad*. William Morrow, 2007.

Riddleberger, Patrick W., *George Washington Julian, Radical Reformer*. Indiana Historical Bureau, 1966.

Robbins, Coy D., *Reclaiming African Heritage at Salem, Indiana*. Heritage Books, 1995.

Robertson, Stacey, *Hearts Beating for Liberty: Women Abolitionists in the Old Northwest*. University of North Carolina Press, 2010.

Ross, Alexander M., *Recollections and Experiences of An Abolitionist, from 1855 to 1865*. 1875, rpr., Metro Books, 1972.

Ruggles, Jeffrey, *The Unboxing of Henry Brown*. The Library of Virginia, 2003.

Salafia, Matthew, *Slavery's Borderland. Freedom and Bondage along the Ohio River*. University of Pennsylvania Press, 2013.

Sanborn, F. B., ed., *The Life and Letters of John Brown*. 1885.

Schwarz, Philip J., *Slave Laws in Virginia*. University of Georgia Press, 1996.

Sernett, Milton C., *North Star Country: Upstate New York and the Crusade for African American Freedom*. Syracuse University Press, 2002.

Sharfstein, Daniel J., *The Invisible Line: Three American Families and the Secret Journey from Black to White*. Penguin, 2011.

Shapiro, Samuel, *Richard Henry Dana, Jr., 1815–1882*. Michigan State University Press, 1961.

Siebert, Wilbur H., *The Underground Railroad From Slavery to Freedom*. 1898, rpr., Dover Publications, 1968.

  *The Underground Railroad in Massachusetts*. American Antiquarian Society, 1936.

  *Vermont's Anti-Slavery and Underground Railroad*. Spahr & Glenn, 1937.

  *The Mysteries of Ohio's Underground Railroads*. Long's College Book Co., 1951.

Slaughter, Thomas P., *Bloody Dawn: The Christiana Riot and Racial Violence in the Antebellum North*. Oxford University Press, 1991.

Smedly, R. C., M.D., *History of the Underground Railroad in Chester and Neighboring Counties of Pennsylvania*. Arno Press, 1969.

Smith, David W., *On the Edge of Freedom. The Fugitive Slave Issue in South Central Pennsylvania, 1820–1870*. Fordham University Press, 2013.

Sprague, Stuart S., ed., *The Autobiography of John P. Parker, Former Slave and Conductor of the Underground Railroad*. Norton, 1996.

Staudenraus, P. J., *The American Colonization Movement 1816–1865*. Octagon, 1980.

Sterling, Dorothy, *The Making of an Afro-American. Martin Roberson Delany, 1812–1885*. DeCapo, 1971.

Stewart, James B., *Wendell Phillips. Liberty's Hero*. Louisiana State University Press, 1986.

Still, William, *The Underground Railroad*. 1872, rpr., Johnson Publishing, 1970.

Strother, Horatio T., *The Underground Railroad in Connecticut*. Wesleyan University Press, 1962.

Stuckey, Sterling, *The Ideological Origins of Black Nationalism*. Beacon Press, 1972.

Switala, William J., *Underground Railroad in Delaware, Maryland, and West Virginia*. Stackpole Books, 2004.

Taylor, Henry L., Jr., ed., *Race and the City: Work, Community, and Protest in Cincinnati, 1820–1970*. University of Illinois Press, 1993.

Taylor, Nikki M., *Frontiers of Freedom: Cincinnati's Black Community, 1802–1868*. Ohio University Press, 2005.

  *America's First Black Socialist. The Radical Life of Peter H. Clark*. University of Kentucky Press, 2013.

  *Driven Toward Madness. The Fugitive Slave Margaret Garner and the Tragedy on the Ohio*. Ohio University Press, 2016.

Thornbrough, Emma L., *The Negro in Indiana. A Study of a Minority*. Indiana Historical Bureau, 1957.

Thornbrough, Gayle, et al., eds., *The Diary of Calvin Fletcher*. Indiana Historical Society, 1977.

Tregillis, Helen F., *River Roads to Freedom. Fugitive Slave Notices and Sheriff Notices Found in Illinois Sources*. Heritage Books, 1988.

Trotter, Joe W., Jr., *River Jordan: African American Urban Life in the Ohio Valley*. University of Kentucky Press, 1998.

Turner, Glennette T., *The Underground Railroad in Illinois*. Newman Educational Publishing, 2001.

Tyler-McGraw, Marie, *An African Republic. Black and White Virginians in the Making of Liberia*. University of North Carolina Press, 2007.

Tyler-McGraw, Marie & Kimball, Gregg D., *In Bondage and Freedom. Antebellum Black Life in Richmond, Virginia.* Valentine Museum, 1998.

Ullman, Victor, *Martin R. Delany. The Beginnings of Black Nationalism.* Beacon Press, 1971.

Vincent, Stephen A., *Southern Seed, Northern Soil. African-American Farm Communities in the Midwest, 1765–1900.* Indiana University Press, 1999.

Von Frank, Albert J., *The Trials of Anthony Burns. Freedom and Slavery in Emerson's Boston.* Harvard University Press, 1998.

Walther, Eric H., *The Fire-Eaters.* Louisiana State University Press, 1992.

    *William Lowndes Yancey and the Coming of the Civil War.* University of North Carolina Press, 2006.

Waugh, John C., *On the Brink of Civil War. The Compromise of 1850 and How It Changed the Course of American History.* Scholarly Resources Books, 2003.

Webster, Daniel, *The Writings and Speeches of Daniel Webster.* 18 Vols. Little Brown, 1903.

Weisenburger, Steven, *Modern Medea. A Family Story of Slavery and Child-Murder from the Old South.* Hill & Wang, 1998.

Weiss, John, *Life and Correspondence of Theodore Parker.* 2 Vols. D. Appleton, 1863.

Wellman, Judith, et al., *Uncovering the Freedom Trail in Auburn and Cayuga County, New York.* Historical New York Research Associates, 2005.

Whitman, T. Stephen, *Challenging Slavery in the Chesapeake. Black and White Resistance to Human Bondage, 1775–1865.* Maryland Historical Society, 2007.

Williams, William H., *Slavery and Freedom in Delaware 1639–1865.* Scholarly Books, 1996.

Wilson, Clyde N. & Cook, Shirley B., *The Papers of John C. Calhoun*, 28 Vols. South Carolina University Press, 2001.

Wilson, Carol, *Freedom at Risk: The Kidnapping of Free Blacks in America, 1780–1865*, University of Kentucky Press, 1994.

Wiltse, Charles M., & Birkner, Michael J., eds., *The Papers of Daniel Webster.* University Press of New England, 1988.

Yacavone, Donald, *Samuel Joseph May and the Dilemmas of the Liberal Persuasion, 1797–1871.* Temple University Press, 1991.

## Articles & Chapters

"A Typical Colonization Convention." *Journal of Negro History* 1, no. 3 (July 1916): 318–38.

Anthrop, Mary E. "The Road Less Travelled. Hoosier African Americans and Liberia." *Traces of Indiana and Midwestern History* 19, no.1 (Winter 2007): 12–21.

Atherton, Lewis E. "Daniel Howell Hise, Abolitionist and Reformer." *The Mississippi Historical Review* XXVI, no.3 (December 1939): 343–58.

Bacon, Margaret H. "'One Great Bundle of Humanity': Frances Watkins Harper (1825–1911)." *Pennsylvania Magazine of History and Biography* 113, no. 1 (January 1989): 21–43.

Bailey, William S. "The Underground Railroad in Southern Chautauqua County." *New York History* XVI, no.1 (January 1935): 53–63.

Bartlett, Irving H. "Abolitionists, Fugitives, and Imposters in Boston, 1846–1847." *The New England Quarterly* 55, no. 1 (March 1982): 97–109.

Beeler, Dale. "The Election of 1852 in Indiana." *Indiana Magazine of History* XI, no.4 (December 1915) 301–23 (Continued XII, no. 1 (March 1916): 34–52.

Bellamy, Donnie D. "Free Blacks in Antebellum Missouri, 1820–1860." *Missouri Historical Review* LXVII, no.2 (January 1973): 198–226.

"The Persistency of Colonization in Missouri." *Missouri Historical Review* LXXII, no.1 (October 1977): 1–24.

Borome, Joseph A. "The Vigilant Committee of Philadelphia." *Pennsylvania Magazine of History and Biography* 92 (July 1968): 320–51.

Brinder Jr., Elwood L. "The Fugitive Slaves of Maryland." *Maryland Historical Magazine* 66, no.1 (Spring 1971): 33–50.

Brown, Ira V. "Miller McKim and Pennsylvania Abolitionism." *Pennsylvania History* 30 (January 1963): 56–72.

Brubaker, M. G. "The Underground Railroad." *Lancaster County Historical Journal* 15, no.4 (April 1911): 95–119.

Bruns, Roger & Fraley, William. "'Old Gunny': Abolitionist in a Slave City." *Maryland Historical Magazine* 100, no.3 (Fall 2005): 315–25.

Campbell, Penelope. "Some Notes on Frederick Country's Participation in the Maryland Colonization Scheme." *Maryland Historical Magazine* 66, no.1 (Spring 1971): 51–59.

Cecelski, David S. "The Shores of Freedom: The Maritime Underground Railroad in North Carolina, 1800–1861," *North Carolina Historical Review* 71, no.2 (April 1994): 175–206.

Christy, Sarah R. "Fugitive Slaves in Indiana County." *Western Pennsylvania Historical Magazine* 18, no.4 (December 1935): 278–88.

Clark, T. D. "The Slave Trade Between Kentucky and the Cotton Kingdom." *Mississippi Valley Historical Review* 21, no.3 (December 1934): 331–42.

Coleman, J. Winston Jr. "Delia Webster and Calvin Fairbank Underground Railroad Agents." *Felson Club Historical Quarterly* 17, no.3 (July 1943): 129–42.

Collison, Gary. "The Boston Vigilance Committee: A Reconsideration." *Historical Journal of Massachusetts* 12 (June 1984): 104–16.

"'This Flagitious Offense': Daniel Webster and the Shadrach Rescue, 1851–1852." *New England Quarterly* 68, no.4 (December 1995): 609–25.

Cooley, Vera. "Illinois and the Underground Railroad to Canada." *Transactions of the Illinois State Historical Society For the Year 1917*, 76–98.

Cord, Xenia E. "Black Rural Settlements in Indiana before 1860," in Gibbs, Wilma L., ed., *Indiana's African American Heritage. Essays from Black History News and Notes*. Indiana Historical Society,1993, 99–110.

Crenshaw, Gwen J. "Brother John Freeman's Homecoming Celebration: The Black Reaction to the Freeman Case and the Fugitive Slave Law of 1850." *Black History News and Notes* 91 (February 2003): 5–8.

Davis, David B. "Reconsidering the Colonization Movement: Leonard Bacon and the Problem of Evil." *Intellectual Historical Newsletter* 14 (1992): 151–78.

Debian, Marty. "One More River to Cross. The Crosswhites' Escape from Slavery" in Frost, Karolyn S. & Tucker, Veta S., eds., *A Fluid Frontier. Slavery, Resistance, and the Underground Railroad in the Detroit Borderland* Wayne State University Press, 2016, 119–214.

Demos, John. "The Antislavery Movement and the Problem of Violent 'Means.'" *The New England Quarterly* 37 (December 1964): 501–26.

Eckert, Ralph L. "Antislavery Martyrdom: The Ordeal of Passmore Williamson." *Pennsylvania Magazine of History and Biography* 100, no. 4 (October 1976): 521–38.

Eggert, Gerald G. "The Impact of the Fugitive Slave Law on Harrisburg: A Case Study." *Pennsylvania Magazine of History and Biography* 109 (October 1985): 537–69.

"A Pennsylvanian Visits the Richmond Slave Market." *Pennsylvania Magazine of History and Biography* 109, no. 4 (October 1985): 572–76.

"'Two Steps Forward, A Step-and-a-Half Back': Harrisburg's African American Community in the Nineteenth Century." *Pennsylvania History* 58, no. 1 (January 1991): 1–36.

Eslinger, Ellen. "The Brief Career of Rufus W. Bailey, American Colonization Society Agent in Virginia." *Journal of Southern History* LXXI, no. 1 (February 2005): 39–74.

"Freedom Without Independence: The Story of a Former Slave and Her Family." *Virginia Magazine of History and Biography* 114 (2006): 262–91.

Feller, Dan. "A Brother in Arms: Benjamin Tappan and the Antislavery Democracy." *Journal of American History* 88, no. 1 (June 2001): 48–74.

Fellman, Michael. "Theodore Parker and the Abolitionist Role in the 1850s." *Journal of American History* LXI, no. 3 (December 1974): 666–84.

Finkelman, Paul. "The Protection of Black Rights in Seward's New York." *Civil War History* XXXIV, no. 3 (September 1988): 211–34.

"The Treason Trial of Caster Hanway," in Belknap, Michael R., ed., *American Political Trials*. Greenwood, 1994, 77–95.

Finkenbine, Roy. "A Community Militant and Organized. The Colored Vigilance Committee of Detroit," in Frost, Karolyn S. & Tucker, Veta S., eds., *A Fluid Frontier. Slavery, Resistance, and the Underground Railroad in the Detroit Borderland.* Wayne State University Press, 2016, 154–64.

"A Beacon of Liberty on the Great Lakes. Race, Slavery, and the Law in Antebellum Michigan," in Finkelman, Paul & Hershock, Martin J., eds., *The History of Michigan Law*. Athens, 2006, 83–106.

Gara, Larry. "William Still, and the Underground Railroad." *Pennsylvania History* 28, no. 1 (January 1961): 33–44.

"The Fugitive Slave Law: A Double Paradox." *Civil War History* 10, no. 3 (September 1964): 229–40.

"The Fugitive Slave Law in the Eastern Ohio Valley." *Ohio History* 72, no. 2 (April 1963): 116–28.

Garb, Margaret. "The Political Education of John Jones: Black Politics in a Northern City, 1845–1879." *The Journal of the Historical Society* VIII, no. 1 (March 2008): 29–60.

Gliozzo, Charles A. "John Jones. A Study of a Black Chicagoan." *Illinois Historical Journal* 80 (Autumn 1987): 177–88.

Grodzins, Dean. "'Slave Law' versus 'Lynch Law' in Boston. Benjamin Robbins Curtis, Theodore Parker, and the Fugitive Slave Crisis, 1850–1855." *Massachusetts Historical Review* 12 (2010): 1–33.

Grossman, Lawrence. "In His Vein Coursed No Bootlicking Blood: The Career of Peter H. Clark." *Ohio History* 86, no. 2 (Spring 1977): 79–95.

Guelzo, Allen C. "Houses Divided: Lincoln, Douglas, and the Political Landscape of 1858." *Journal of American History* 94, no. 2 (September 2007): 391–417.

Guyatt, Nicholas. "'Outskirts of Our Happiness': Race and the Lure of Colonization in the Early Republic." *Journal of American History* 95, no.4 (March 2009): 986–1011.

Harris Jr., Robert L. "H. Ford Douglas: Afro-American Antislavery Emigrationist." *Journal of Negro History* 62, no.3 (July 1977): 217–34.

Harrison, Theresa A. "George Thompson and the 1851 Anti-Abolition Riot." *Historical Journal of Western Massachusetts* 5, no.1 (1976): 36–44.

Harrold, Stanley. "Freeing the Weems Family: A New Look at the Underground Railroad." *Civil War History* XLII, no.4 (December 1996): 289–306.

Hepburn, Sharon A. Roger. "Following the North Star: Canada as a Haven for Nineteenth-Century American Blacks." *Michigan Historical Review* 25, no.2 (Fall 1999): 91–126.

Horton, James O. "A Crusade for Freedom. William Still and the Real Underground Railroad," in Blight, David W., ed., *Passages to Freedom. The Underground Railroad in History and Memory*. Smithsonian, 2004, 175–94.

Hossack, John. Speech at Sentencing, "Historical Notes." *Journal of the Illinois State Historical Society* XLI, no.1 (March 1948): 67–74.

Houts, Mary D. "Black Harrisburg's Resistance to Slavery." *Pennsylvania Heritage* IV, no.1 (December 1977): 9–13.

Hudson, J. Blaine. "Crossing the 'Dark Line': Fugitive Slaves and the Underground Railroad in Louisville and North-Central Kentucky." *Filson Historical Quarterly* 75 (2001): 33–83.

Humphreys, Huge C. "Agitate! Agitate! Agitate!: The Great Fugitive Slave Law Convention and its Rare Deguereotype." *Madison County Heritage* 19 (1994): 3–64.

Huston, James. "Southerners vs. Secession: The Arguments of the Constitutional Unionists in 1850–51." *Civil War History* XLVI, no.4 (December 2000): 281–99.

Irons, Charles F. "And All These Things Shall be Added Onto to You. The First African Baptist Church, Richmond, 1841–1865." *Virginia Cavalcade* 47 (Winter 1998): 26–35.

Johnson, Allen J. "The Constitutionality of the Fugitive Slave Acts." *Yale Law Journal* 31 (1921–22): 161–82.

Jones, James P. "The Illinois Negro Law of 1853. Racism in a Free State." *Illinois Quarterly* 40, no.2 (Winter 1977): 5–22.

Kaplan, Sidney, "The Moby Dick in the Service of the Underground Railroad." *Phylon* 12, no.2 (1951): 173–76.

Karst, Frederick A. "A Rural Black Settlement in St. Joseph County, Indiana, before 1900." *Indiana Magazine of History* LXXIV, no.3 (September 1978): 252–67.

Keller, Ralph A. "Methodist Newspapers and the Fugitive Slave Law: A New Perspective for the Slavery Crisis in the North." *Church History* 43, no.3 (September 1974): 319–39.

Kelley, Sean. "'Mexico in His Head': Slavery and the Texas-Mexico Border, 1810–1860." *Journal of Social History* 37, no.3 (Spring 2004): 709–23.

Kellow, Margaret M. R. "Conflicting Imperative: Black and White American Abolitionists Debate Slave Redemption," in Appiah, Kwame A. & Bunzl, Martin, eds., *Buying Freedom: the Ethics and Economics of Slave Redemption*. Princeton University Press, 2007, 200–10.

Kenny, Gale L. "Manliness and Manifest Destiny: Jamaica and African American Emigration in the 1850s." *Journal of the Civil War Era* 2, no.2 (June 2012): 151–78.

Kotlowski, Dean. "The Jordan Is a Hard Road to Travel: Hoosier Responses to Fugitive Slave Cases, 1850–1860." *International Social Science Review*. 79, no.3–4 (2003): 71–88.

Kneebone, John T. "A Breakdown on the Captain B. and the Capture of Keziah, 1858." *Virginia Cavalcade* 48, no.2 (Spring 1999): 74–83.

Landon, Fred. "The Negro Migration to Canada after the Passing of the Fugitive Slave Act." *Journal of Negro History* V, no.1 (January 1920): 22–36.

Levy, Leonard W. "Memoranda and Documents. The 'Abolition Riot': Boston's First Slave Rescue. *The New England Quarterly* 25 (March 1952): 85–92.

"Sims' Case: The Fugitive Slave Law in Boston in 1851." *Journal of Negro History* 35, no.1 (January 1950): 39–74.

Lindquist, Charles. "The Origins and Development of the United States Commissioner System." *American Journal of Legal History* 14, no.1 (January 1970): 1–16.

Link, William A. "The Jordon Hatcher Case: Politics and 'A Sprit of Insubordination' in Antebellum Virginia." *Journal of Southern History* LVIX, no.4 (November 1998): 615–48.

Lumpkin, Katherine D. "The General Plan Was Freedom: A Negro Secret Order of the Underground Railroad." *Phylon* 28, no.1 (1st Quarter 1967): 63–77.

Staughton, Lynd. "The Abolitionist Critique of the United States Constitution," in Duberman, Martin, ed., *The Antislavery Vanguard. New Essays on the Abolitionists*. Princeton University Press, 1965, 209–39.

Madison, James H. "Race, Law, and the Burdens of Indiana's History," in Bodenhamer, David J. & Shepherd, Randall T., eds., *The History of Indiana Law*. Ohio University Press, 2006, 37–59.

Mahoney, Olivia. "Black Abolitionists." *Chicago History* 20, nos.1&2 (Spring & Summer 1991): 22–37.

McGraw, Marie T. "Richmond Free Blacks and African Colonization, 1816–1832." *Journal of American Studies* 21, no.2 (1987): 207–24.

McKivegan, John R. "Prisoner of Conscience: George Gordon and the Fugitive Slave Law." *Journal of Presbyterian History* 60, no.4 (Winter 1982): 336–54.

Merkel, Benjamin G. "The Underground Railroad and the Missouri Borders, 1840–1860." *Missouri Historical Review* XXVII, no.3 (April 1943): 271–85.

Middleton, Stephen. "The Fugitive Slave Crisis in Cincinnati, 1850–1860: Resistance, Enforcement, and Black Refugees." *Journal of Negro History* 72 (Winter/Spring 1987): 20–32.

Money, Charles. "The Fugitive Slave Law of 1850 in Indiana." *Indiana Magazine of History* XVII (June 1921) 159–98 and (September 1921): 257–97.

Moore, N. Webster. "John Berry Meachum (1789–1854): St. Louis Pioneer, Black Abolitionist, Educator, and Preacher." *Bulletin of the Missouri Historical Society* 19 (January 1973): 96–103.

Muelder, Hermann R. "Galesburg: Hot-Bed of Abolitionism." *Journal of the Illinois State Historical Society* XXXV, no.3 (September 1942): 216–35.

Murphy, Angela. "'It Outlaws Me, and I Outlaw it,' Resistance to the Fugitive Slave Law in Syracuse, New York." *Afro Americans in New York Life and History* 28, no.1 (January 2004): 43–72.

Mutunhu, Tendai. "John W. Jones: Underground Railroad Station-Master." *Negro History Bulletin* 41, no.2 (March-April 1978): 814–18.

"Tompkins County, an Underground Railroad Transit in New York." *Afro-Americans in New York Life and History* 3 (July 1979): 15–33.

Nash, Roderick W. "William Parker and the Christiana Riot." *Journal of Negro History* XLVI, no.1 (January 1961): 24–31.

"The Christiana Riot: An Evaluation of Its National Significance." *Journal of the Lancaster County Historical Society* 65 (Spring 1961): 65–91.

Newman, Richard S. "'Lucky to be Born in Pennsylvania': Free Soil, Fugitive Slaves and the Making of Pennsylvania's Anti-Slavery Borderland." *Slavery & Abolition* 32, no.3 (September 2011): 413–30.

Oakes, James. "The Political Significance of Slave Resistance." *History Workshop* 22 (Autumn 1986): 89–107.

O'Brien, John T. "Factory, Church, and Community: Blacks in Antebellum Richmond." *Journal of Southern History* XLIV, no.4 (November 1978): 509–36.

Owens, Robert M. "Law and Disorder North of the Ohio. Runaways and the Patriarchy of Print Culture, 1793–1815." *Indiana Magazine of History* 103, no.3 (September 2007): 265–89.

Parker, William. "The Freedman's Story in Two Parts." *Atlantic Monthly* XVII (1866): 152–295.

Phillips, Christopher. "'The Dear Name of Home': Resistance to Colonization in Antebellum Baltimore." *Maryland Historical Magazine* 91, no.2 (Summer 1996): 181–202.

Plagg, Eric W. "'Let the Constitution Perish': Prigg v. Pennsylvania, Joseph Story, and the Flawed Doctrine of Historical Necessity." *Slavery & Abolition* 25, no.3 (December 2004): 76–101.

Porter, Dorothy. "David Ruggles, An Apostle of Human Rights." *Journal of Negro History* XXVIII, no.1 (January 1943): 23–50.

Prince, Benjamin F. "The Rescue Case of 1857." *Ohio Archeological and Historical Society Publication* XVI (1907): 292–308.

Prude, Jonathan. "To Look Upon the 'Lower Sort': Runaway Ads and the Appearance of Unfree Laborers in America, 1750–1800." *Journal of American History* 78, no.1 (June 1991): 124–59.

Reed, Christopher. "African American Life in Antebellum Chicago, 1833–1860." *Journal of the Indiana State Historical Society* 94, no.4 (Winter 2001–2002): 356–82.

Reid, Patricia. "Margaret Morgan's Story: A Threshold between Slavery and Freedom, 1820–1842." *Slavery & Abolition* 33, no.3 (September 2012): 359–80.

Richardson, Jean. "Buffalo's Antebellum African American Community and the Fugitive Slave Law of 1850." *Afro-Americans in New York Life and History* 27, no.2 (July 2001): 29–46.

Roach, Monique P. "The Rescue of William 'Jerry' Henry: Antislavery and Racism in the Burned-over District." *New York History* 82 (Spring 2001): 135–54.

Robboy, Stanley J. & Anita, W. "Lewis Hayden: From Fugitive Slave to Statesman," *The New England Quarterly* XLVI, no.4 (December 1973): 591–613.

Rutherford, S. S. "The Underground Railroad." *Publications of the Historical Society of Dauphin County* (1928): 3–8.

Ryan, John H. "A Chapter from the History of the Underground Railroad in Illinois." *Journal of the Illinois State Historical Society* 8, no.1 (April 1915): 23–30.

Ryland, Robert. "Reminiscences of the First African Baptist Church, Richmond, VA." *American Baptist Memorial* XIV (November 1855): 321–27.

Savage, W. Sherman. "The Contest over Slavery between Illinois and Missouri." *Journal of Negro History* XXVII, no.3 (July 1943): 311–25.

Schweninger, Loren. "A Fugitive Negro in the Promised Land: James Rapier in Canada, 1856–1864." *Ontario History* LXVII (June 1975): 91–104.

Schoeppner, Michael A. "Status across Borders: Roger Taney, Black British Subjects, and a Diplomatic Antecedent to the Dred Scott Decision." *Journal of American History* 100, no.1 (June 2013): 46–67.

Schuelke, Freida. "Activities of the Underground Railroad in Oswego County." *The Publication of the Oswego Historical Society* (1940): 1–14.

Schwartz, Harold. "Fugitive Slave Days in Boston." *New England Quarterly* XXVII, no.2 (June 1984): 191–212.

Sernett, Milton C. "'On Freedom's Trail': Researching the Underground Railroad in New York State." *Afro-Americans in New York Life and History* 25, no.1 (January 2001): 7–32.

"A Citizen of No Mean City; Jermain W. Loguen and the Antislavery Reputation of Syracuse." *Syracuse University Library Associates Courier* XXII, no.2 (Fall 1987): 33–55.

Sloane, Rush R. "The Underground Railroad of the Firelands." *The Firelands Pioneer* V (July 1888): 28–59.

Slotten, Martha C. "The McCormick Slave Riot of 1847." *Cumberland County History* 17, no.1 (Summer 2000): 14–35.

Smith, Eric L. "Rescuing African American Kidnapping Victims in Philadelphia as Documented in the Joseph Wilson Papers at the Historical Society of Pennsylvania." *Pennsylvania Magazine of History and Biography* CXXIX, no.3 (July 2005): 317–45.

Sokolow, Jayme A. "The Jerry McHenry Rescue and the Growth of the Northern Anti-Slavery Sentiment during the 1850s." *Journal of American Studies* 16 (1982): 427–43.

Strange, Douglas C. "From Treason to Antislavery Patriotism: Unitarian Conservatives and the Fugitive Slave Law." *Harvard Library Bulletin* 25, no.4 (October 1977): 466–88.

Talmadge, John E. "Georgia Tests the Fugitive Slave Law." *Georgia Historical Quarterly* 49, no.1 (March 1965): 57–64.

Taylor, Henry L. "Spatial Organization and the Residential Experience: Black Cincinnati in 1850." *Social Science History* 10, no.1 (Spring 1986): 45–69.

Taylor, Henry L. & Dula, Vicky. "The Black Residential Experience and Community Formation in Antebellum Cincinnati," in Taylor, Henry L., ed., *Race and the City. Work, Community, and Protest in Cincinnati, 1820–1970.* University of Illinois Press, 1993, 96–125.

Theriault, Sean M. & Weingast, Barry R. "Agenda Manipulation, Strategic Voting, and Legislative Details in the Compromise of 1850," in Brady, David W. & McCubbins, Mathew D., eds., *Party, Process, and Political Change in Congress. New Perspectives on the History of Congress.* Stanford University Press, 2002, 343–91.

Tiffany, Nina M. "Stories of the Fugitive Slaves, I: The Escape of William and Ellen Craft." *New England Magazine* 7, no.5 (January 1890): 524–41.

Thornbrough, Emma L. "Indiana and Fugitive Slave Legislation." *Indiana Magazine of History* L, no.3 (September 1954): 201–28.

Toplin, Robert B. "Peter Still vs. The Peculiar Institution." *Civil War History* 13, no.4 (December 1967): 340–49.

Troutman, Paul. "Grapevine in the Slave Market. African American Geopolitical Literacy and the 1841 Creole Revolt," in Johnson, Walter, ed., *The Chattel Principle. Internal Slave Trades in the Americas.* Yale University Press, 2004, 203–33.

Turner, Wallace B. "Kentucky Slavery in the Last Ante Bellum Decade." *Register of the Kentucky Historical Society* 58, no.4 (October 1960): 291–307.

Vacha, John E. "The Case of Sara Lucy Bagby." *Ohio History* 76, no.4 (1967): 222–31.

Van Bolt, Roger H. "The Hoosiers and the 'Eternal Agitation,' 1848–1850," *Indiana Magazine of History* XLVIII, no.4 (December 1952): 331–68.

"Indiana in Political Transition, 1851–1853." *Indiana Magazine of History* XLIX, no.2 (June 1953): 131–60.

Van Tassel, David D. "Gentlemen of Property and Standing: Compromise Sentiment in Boston in 1850." *New England Quarterly* 23 (September 1950): 307–19.

Von Frank, Albert J. "John Brown, James Redpath, and the Idea of Revolution," *Civil War History* LII, no.2 (June 2006): 142–60.

Waldstreicher, David. "Reading the Runaways: Self-Fashioning, Print Culture, and Confidence in Slavery in the Eighteenth-Century Mid-Atlantic." *William and Mary Quarterly* LVI, no.2 (April 1999): 243–72.

Warnes, Kathy. "Across the Lakes to Liberty: The Liquid Underground Railroad." *Quarterly Journal of the Great Lakes Historical Society* 56, no.4 (Winter 2000): 284–93.

Watts, Ralph M. "History of the Underground Railroad in Mechanicsburg." *Ohio Archeological and Historical Society Publication* XLIII (1934): 233–51.

Wayne, M. "The Black Population of Canada West on the Eve of the Civil War," *Social History* 28 (1995): 465–85.

Wellman, Judith. "This Side of the Border: Fugitives from Slavery in Three Central New York Communities." *New York History* 79, no.4 (October 1998): 359–92.

Wellman, Judith. "Larry Gara's *Liberty Line* in Oswego County, New York, 1838–1854: A New Look at the Legend." *Afro-Americans in New York Life and History* 25, no.1 (January 2001): 33–54.

Williams-Meyer, A. J. "The Underground Railroad in the Hudson River Valley: A Succinct Historical Composite." *Afro-Americans in New York Life and History* 27, no.1 (January 2003): 55–65.

Williams, Irene. "The Operation of the Fugitive Slave Law in Western Pennsylvania, from 1850–1860." *Western Pennsylvania Historical Magazine* 4, no.3 (July 1924): 150–60.

Wilson, Major L. "Of Time and the Union: Webster and His Critics in the Crisis of 1850." *Civil War History* 14, no.4 (December 1968): 293–306.

Winch, Julie. "Philadelphia and the Other Underground Railroad." *The Pennsylvania Magazine of History and Biography* 111, no.1 (January 1987): 3–25.

Wish, Harvey. "The Slave Insurrection Panic of 1856." *Journal of Southern History* 5, no.2 (May 1939): 206–22.

Yannelli, Joseph. "George Thompson among the Africans. Empathy, Authority, and Insanity in the Age of Abolition." *Journal of American History* 96, no.4 (March 2010): 979–1000.

## Unpublished Manuscripts

Beckert, Sven. "The Making of the New York City's Bourgeoisie, 1850–1886." Unpublished dissertation, Columbia University, 1995.

Bennett, Charles R. "All Things to All People: The American Colonization Society in Kentucky, 1829–1860." Unpublished dissertation, University of Kentucky, 1980.

Blakemore, Jacqueline Y. "African Americans and Race Relations in Gallatin County, Illinois, from the Eighteenth Century to 1870." Unpublished dissertation, Northern Illinois University, 1996.

Blondo, Richard A. "Samuel Green: A Black Life in Antebellum Maryland." Unpublished thesis, University of Maryland, 1988.

Bogart, Pen. "Making Their Way to Freedom: Runaway Slave Advertisements from Louisville Newspapers, 1788–1860." 1999.

"Soul Drivers, Professional, and Good Citizens: Antebellum Perspectives on Kentucky Slave Traders." 2002.

Boyd, Tim. "Resistance in the Queen City; the Fugitive Slave Law in Buffalo." Paper prepared for a seminar, Vanderbilt University, 2002.

Brown, Maxine F. "The Role of Free Blacks in Indiana's Underground Railroad. The Case of Floyd, Harrison and Washington Counties." Report prepared for the Indiana Department of Natural Resources, 2001.

Crane,Jr., John M. "Slavery on the Edge of Freedom: The Lower Ohio Valley in the Antebellum and Civil War Era." Unpublished dissertation, Vanderbilt University, 2009.

Cord, Xenia E. "Free Black Rural Communities in Indiana. A Selected Annotated Bibliography." Typescript, Indiana Historical Society, n.d.

Densmore, Chris. "The Underground Railroad: Facts, Folklore and Fiction." Typescript, 1999.

Finger, Joel L. "Virginia Fugitives of the 1850's." Unpublished thesis, University of Virginia,1969.

Furnish, Mark A. "A Rosetta Stone on Slavery's Doorstep: Eleutherian College and the Lost Antislavery History of Jefferson County, Indiana." Unpublished dissertation, Purdue University, 2014.

Gamble, Douglas A. "The Western Antislavery Society: Garrisonian Abolitionism in Ohio." Unpublished thesis, Ohio State University, 1970.

Gifford, II, Ronald M. "George Thompson and Atlantic Anti-Slavery, 1831–1865." Unpublished dissertation, Indiana University, 1999.

Glasman, Paula. "Zebina Eastman: Chicago Abolitionist." Unpublished thesis, University of Chicago, 1968.

Goliber, Thomas J. "Cuyahoga Blacks: A Social and Demographic Study, 1850–1880." Unpublished thesis, Kent State University, 1972.

Henry, Raquel I. "The Colonization Movement in Indiana, 1826–1864: A Struggle to Remove the African American." Unpublished dissertation, Indiana University, 2008.

Hickok, Charles T. "The Negro in Ohio, 1802–1870." Unpublished dissertation, Western Reserve University, 1896.

Innis, Darleen. "Poke Patch Station." Typescript, Lawrence County Public Library, n.d.

McElvey, Kay. "Early Black Dorchester 1776–1870: A History of the Struggle of African Americans in Dorchester County, Maryland, to be Free to Make Their Own Choices." Unpublished dissertation, University of Maryland, 1990.

Miller, Caroline R. "Slavery in Mason County, Kentucky: A Century of Records, 1788–1882, 2 Vols." Typescript, Maysville, Kentucky, National Underground Railroad Museum, 1999.

Miller, Caroline R. "African American records, Bracken County, Kentucky, 1797–1919, 2 Vols." Bracken County Historical Society, 1999.

Oblinger, Carl D. "New Freedoms, Old Miseries: The Emergence and Disruption of Black Communities in Southeastern Pennsylvania, 1780–1860." Unpublished dissertation, Lehigh University, 1988.

Osborn, Elizabeth R. "The Influence of Culture and Gender on the Creation of Law in Antebellum Indiana, and Kentucky." Unpublished dissertation, Indiana University, 2004.

Peck, Graham A. "Politics and Ideology in a Free Society: Illinois from Statehood to Civil War." Unpublished dissertation, Northwestern University, 2001.

Peters, Pamela R. "Gateway to Freedom. New Albany, Floyd County, Indiana."

Pico, Fernando. "Running Away and Finding Concealment: Runaway Slaves in Nineteenth-Century Puerto Rico." 2008.

Prisloo, Oleta. "The Case of 'The Dyed-in-the-Wool Abolitionists' in Mark Twain County, Missouri: An Examination of a Slaveholding Community's Response to Radical Abolitionism in the 1830s and 1840s." Unpublished dissertation, University of Missouri-Columbia, 2003.

Pritchard, James M. "Into the Fiery Furness. Anti-Slavery Prisoners in the Kentucky State Penitentiary, 1844–1870."

Rankin, Adam L. "Autobiography of Rev. Adam Lowry Rankin." Typescript, Rankin Papers, Stanford University. Copy in the Ripley Public Library.

Regan-Dinius, Jeannie. "Federal Court Cases: Holdings at the National Archives, Chicago." Typescript in author's possession.

Rives, Nancy J. "'Nurseries of Mischief': Origins and Operations of the Underground Railroad in Richmond, Virginia, 1848–1860." Unpublished thesis, Virginia Commonwealth University, 1998.

Scott, Herbert H. "The Pioneer People of Poke Patch." Typescript, Lawrence County Public Library, n.d.

Scott III, Julius S. "The Common Wind: Currents Of Afro-American Communication in the Era of the Haitian Revolution." Unpublished dissertation, Duke University, 1986.

Singleton Jr., Paul L. "The Keziah Affair of 1858 and its Impact upon Underground Railroad Activities in Eastern Virginia." Unpublished thesis, Virginia State University, 1983.

Stafford, Hanford D. "Slavery in a Border City: Louisville, 1790–1860." Unpublished dissertation, University of Kentucky, 1982.

Saulman, Earl O. "Blacks in Harrison County, Indiana. A History." Typescript copy in the Corydon Public Library, n.d.

Willey, Larry G. "The Reverend John Rankin: Early Ohio Antislavery Leader." Unpublished dissertation, University of Iowa, 1976.

Wolfe, H. Scott. "The Fate of Jerimiah Boyd. A Tale of Kidnapping and Murder in Old Galena." Blog post, 2004.

## Government Publications

*Answers of the Agent on the Indiana Colonization Society to the Resolution of Inquiry on the Subject of African Colonization Passed by the House of Representatives of the General Assembly of the State of Indiana, on the 3rd of February, 1852.* Indianapolis, 1852.

*Debate and Proceedings of the Maryland Reform Convention to Revise the State Constitution.* 2 Vols. Annapolis, 1851.

*Journal of the House of Representatives during the Thirty-Eight Session of the General Assembly of the State of Indiana.* Indianapolis, 1855.

*Journal of the House of Representatives of the State of Indiana during the Thirty-Ninth Session of the General Assembly.* Indianapolis, 1857.

*Journal of the House of Representatives of the State of Vermont, October Session, 1850.* Burlington, 1851.

*Journal of the Proceedings of the House of Delegates of Maryland.* Annapolis, 1852.

*Journal of the Proceedings of the House of Delegates of Maryland.* Annapolis, 1853.

*Journal of the Proceedings of the House of Delegates of Maryland.* Annapolis, 1858.

*Journal of the Senate of the Commonwealth of Virginia Begun and Held in the Capitol, in the City of Richmond on Monday the Second Day of December in the Year One Thousand Eight Hundred and Fifty.* Richmond, 1850.

*Journal of the Senate of the State of Vermont, October Session, 1850.* Burlington, 1850.

*Proceedings of the Constitutional Meeting at Faneuil Hall, November 26th, 1850.* Boston, 1850.

*Proceedings of the Great Union Meeting Held in the Large Saloon of the Chinese Museum, Philadelphia, on the 21st of November 1850.* Philadelphia, 1850.

*Report of the Debates and Proceedings of the Convention for the Revision of the Constitution of the State of Indiana, 1850.* Indianapolis, 1850.

*Report of the Debates and Proceedings of the Convention for the Revision of the Constitution of the State of Ohio, 1850–51.* 2 Vols. S. Medary Printers, 1851.

*Report of the Rev. John McKay Colored Agent of the State Board of Colonization on Liberia.* Indianapolis, 1854.

*Report of the Secretary of the State Board of Colonization of the State of Indiana to the Governor for 1853.* Indianapolis, 1853.

*Report of the Secretary of the State Board of Colonization of the State of Indiana.* Indianapolis, 1859.

*Speech of the Hon. Robert J. Brent, Attorney-General of Maryland, in the Case of the United States v. Castner Hanway, for Treason.* Philadelphia, n.d.

# Index

Abby, 282
Abolition Society, 55, 315, 337–38
abolitionism, xiii, xiv, 7n5, 14–15, 20, 22,
    25–26, 33, 57, 59, 64, 66, 68, 70, 82,
    85–86, 88, 102, 114, 127, 143, 149–51,
    155, 166–67, 175, 192, 203, 238n22,
    258, 260, 272, 292, 297–99, 301,
    317–18, 323, 326, 346, 379, 388, 398,
    405, 410–11, 417–20, 423, 435, 439,
    442, 444–45, 447
abolitionist activities, xiii, 7, 38, 248, 417
abolitionist movement, xii, 71, 73, 244,
    367–69, 397
abolitionists, xi, xiv, 4–6, 9, 11, 15, 22, 24–25,
    27–28, 32–35, 40, 44, 46, 48–49, 52,
    58, 66–68, 73, 77, 79, 82, 85, 88–89,
    89n1, 96–97, 106, 114, 118–19, 129,
    131–34, 137, 142, 142n10, 145–46,
    149–50, 153, 157, 160, 179, 184, 195,
    204, 208, 212, 217, 221, 227, 229,
    232–33, 237–38, 242, 246–48, 253n41,
    253–54, 258, 261, 277–78, 294, 296,
    298, 311, 322–23, 323n14, 334, 337,
    344, 348, 350–52, 354–55, 362,
    367–68, 375, 378–80, 385–86, 389,
    391, 394, 397–98, 404, 410–12, 414,
    417, 419–20, 422, 428, 430, 432, 435,
    437–38, 444, 446–47, 449, 456, 460
Adams, Benjamin J., 190
Affleck, Mary, 190
Africa, xii, 30, 88, 91–93, 95, 97, 104,
    106–07, 112–13, 120–21, 121n53,
    123, 127, 130, 132–34, 185, 277, 315,
    326, 445

African Americans, xiv, 6, 14–15, 18, 20,
    28, 32, 56, 87, 95, 98, 109, 111, 116,
    120–21, 124, 127, 131–32, 137, 152,
    155–58, 163–66, 172, 176, 186–87,
    200, 204–07, 210–11, 214, 218, 221,
    231, 238–40, 242, 250, 262–63, 265,
    269, 280–82, 290, 293–94, 301,
    303–05, 307, 310, 332, 338, 340,
    345n39, 352–53, 360, 367, 378,
    390–91, 398, 403–04, 410, 416, 423,
    430, 436, 442, 445n6, 445–47
African Methodist Episcopal Church, 74n53,
    95, 111–12, 166, 229
African Squadron station, 315
Aires, Sarah, 322
Akin, George, 191, 205
Alabama, 37–38, 57, 93, 323n14,
    327, 445
    Florence, 313n3
    Mobile, 26, 376
    Montgomery, 455
    Wetumpka, 212
    Wilcox County
        Prairie Bluffs, 322
Alberti, George F., 55, 301, 340n33, 342n37,
    340–45, 345n39
Alexander, Charlotte, 177
Alexander, Elam, 396
Alexander, William. See Lewis
Alfred, 187, 215
Alfred, Henry, 267
Allegheny Mountains, 3, 48, 394
Allegheny River, 311
Allen, Alderman William, 341

Allen, Henry, 366
Allen, Richard, 95
Allison, Joseph, 352
Amanda, 190, 235, *See* Lemmons family
Ambush, William E., 237, 441, 444
American Anti-Slavery Society, 4, 79, 391
American Colonization Society, 94–101, 106,
    112, 116–17, 120, 120n52, 122–24,
    127–32, 379
American and Foreign Anti-Slavery Society,
    365, 391
American Missionary Association, 254
American Mysteries Secret Underground
    Railroad Society, 18n23
American Revolution, 50n14, 68, 98, 246,
    312n1, 417, 431
Ames, Cephas J., 415
*Amistad*, 254
Anderson, David, 240
Anderson, Elijah, 75, 188, 203–04
Anderson, George, 172
Anderson, James, 168
Anderson, John, 303, 439n64
Anderson, Maj. Robert, 450
Anderson, Moses, 460
Anderson, Washington, 168–69
Anderson, William, 203–04
Anderson, William Wemyss, 99–102, 106
Andrew, John A., 438
Anthony, Kit, 314
Anthony, Susan B., 446
Anti-Man-Hunting League, 428
Anti-Slavery Society, 164, 176, 337, 349,
    353–54, 397
Anti-Slavery Society of Chicago, 164
Arkansas, 207, 251, 325n17, 418
    Fort Smith, 207
Armistead, Rosetta, 247–48, 252,
    265, 268
Armstrong, Charles Q., 182–83
Armstrong, James, 180, 180n1, 182, 186,
    188–89, 192, 197
Arthur, Chester, 387
Ashburn, Mr., 183
Ashby, Thomas, 310–13
Ashcon, Thomas, 51
Ashley, William, 366
Ashmead, John W., 343
Atchison, David, 5, 77
Attucks, Crispus, 417
Averill, Horatio F., 369
Avery, Charles, 19–20

Backus, Franklin, 258
Bacon, John G., 257, 415
Badger, George, 10, 52–53, 411
Bagby, Sara Lucy, 264–65, 268, 441–45,
    459–60
Bailey, Gamaliel, 33, 253n41
Bailey, John, 352
Bailey, St. Clair, 352, 354
Bain, George C., 130
Baker, Mr., 178
Baker, Rev. James, 367
Ball, Samuel, 112, 132
Ballard, John, 332–33
Ballenger, Jeremish S., 239
Banks, Henry W., 50, 50n14, 308, 310–13,
    328, 355, 437–38
Banks, Jim, 369
Banks, Landon, 308
Baptiste, George, 188
Barber, Isaac, 231
Barculo, Judge Seward, 389–90
Bard, Moses, 180, 186–89, 192
Barney, Edward, 415
Barry, 146
Barry, Charles, 427
Bartlett, Ruben, 147
Batchelder, James, 423–24, 424n40, 427, 439
Bates, Edward, 132
Beach, Miles, 369–70
Bear, William, 294
Bearse, Austin, 421
Beecher, Rev. Henry Ward, 100, 211, 375
Beeler, Christopher, 180
Belden, U.S. Attorney George, 258, 261
Bell, Charles, 201–02
Bell, David, 201–02
Bell, Horace, 201–02
Bell, James, 130, 141
Bell, John, 201, 283, 415
Bell, Mary Ann, 201
Bell, Montgomery, 130, 141, 141n7
Bell, Philip A., 119, 391
Bell, Thomas S., 299–300
Ben, 189, 189n13
Benjamin, 30, 215, 272
Bennett, James Gordon, 28, 379, 387,
    410, 435
Bennett, Stephen, 28, 73, 346n40, 355
Benton, L. A., 264, 442
Benton, Thomas, 13
Berea College, 231
Berjona, Elizabeth, 98

Berkley, 177
Bermuda, 191
Bernard, 137, 139
Berrien, J. Macpherson, 411
Berry, Peregrine. *See* Thompson, William
Bethell, T. F., 220
Betts, Judge, 380–82
Bibb, Edmond, 250
Bibb, Henry, 32, 312
Bigelow, Jacob, 386
Bigelow, John, 99–100
Bigler, Governor William, 287–88, 292,
    299–301, 316, 342
Billy, 3–4, 65, 69, 235, 269, 271, 279–81,
    290, 305
Birney, James G., 246
Bishop, 48
black communities, xi, xii, xiii, xiv, 8, 19–20,
    32–33, 42, 44, 54, 55n20, 55–56,
    59, 64–67, 69–70, 72, 74n53, 74–75,
    81, 84, 110, 112, 114, 116–19, 128,
    143n11, 152, 158–59, 161–64, 166,
    168–71, 171n57, 178, 186–87, 219,
    222, 224, 235, 244, 246–48, 264, 269,
    279, 281–82, 285, 287, 289–91,
    304–05, 307, 310, 313, 315, 337,
    346n40, 346–48, 354–55, 357, 363,
    372, 378, 385, 397–400, 404, 407,
    409, 412–13, 420–21, 430, 438–39,
    444, 458–60
  involvement in kidnapping, 303–05
  protection of fugitives, xiv, 171–72, 179,
    183, 188, 224, 235–39, 274, 304–06,
    311, 351, 357, 360, 363, 369–70,
    398–99, 401, 440
  resisting the Fugitive Slave Law of
    1850, 161–65
  support in fugitive slave trials, 346–49
  support of fugitives, 355
Black, Chief Justice Jeremiah S., 334
Blackenbaker, Elizabeth Ann, 235
Blackenbaker, Jasper, 235
Blackford, Mr., 288
Blackwell, Henry, 238, 266
Blackwell, Lucy Stone, 232
Blanchard, J. P., 246–47
Bliss, George, 258
Bloody Island, 168
Bodman, Charles, 239
Bogy, Lewis, 137
Bolding, John, 62, 69, 71–72
Bond, Benjamin, 152

Border States, xii, 5–6, 31, 74, 149, 151, 220,
    236, 313, 318, 321, 453, 457
Borland, Senator Solon, 418
Boston Associates, 397
Boulton, Peter, 178
Boulton, Rice, 178
Boutwell, George, 456
Bowditch, Henry, 401, 416–17, 422,
    426, 428
Bowditch, William, 416
Bowe, Nathaniel F., 38
Bowers, James, 318–20, 323
Bowers, John C., 353
Boyd, Jerry, 177–78
Boyd, Mary, 177–78
Boyd, Rebecca, 241
Boyer, Deborah Ann, 346
Boynton, Shakespeare, 257–58
Braddock, James S., 332
Bradford, J. T., 226n4
Bradley, C. P., 167
Bradley, Henry, 280
Bradley, Washington, 392
Brainard, Anna, 376
Brandon, Girard, 241
Brant, John H., 289
Branton, William A., 289
Breckenridge, Isaac, 143
Brent, Robert J., 83, 341–42
Brent, William, 421–22, 425–26
Brewster, Benjamin H., 348, 351–52, 353n50,
    450, 450n12
Briggs, Thomas, 282
Bright, Jesse, 58, 213
Bright, John, 392
British and Foreign Anti-Slavery
    Society, 100
Broadhus family, 253, 255
Broadhus, Angeline, 252
Broadhus, Irvin, 252, 265
Brocks, George, 3–4, 53, 64, 70,
    269, 271, 279–81, 285, 290,
    305, 418
Brooke, Dr. Abraham, 266
Brookenborough, Alexander B., 372
Brookenborough, Alexander S., 372
Brooks, Maria, 341
Brown Jr., John, 446
Brown, David Paul, 55, 74, 338–39, 343–45,
    353, 355
Brown, George, 239
Brown, Henry, 4, 24, 397–98

Brown, John, 15, 17–18, 54, 179, 258,
    326, 353, 361, 369, 393–95, 445,
    447, 456
  raid
    implications of, 393–95
Brown, John (free black), 305
Brown, John P., 105
Brown, Jr., David Paul, 354
Brown, Mary, 71, 378
Brown, Michael, 353–54
Brown, Mrs., 198
Brown, Thomas, 198–201, 203–04
Brown, William Wells, 71, 398, 445n6
Browne, Peter A., 341
Bryan, John, 51
Bryan, Joseph, 93
Bryant, Eli, 199–200
Buchanan, George, 166
Buchanan, James M., 287
Buchanan, John, 166
Buchanan, President James, 163, 256, 395,
    438n62, 454–55, 458
Buck, Jerry, 352, 354
Buck, Joshua, 352
Buck, William M., 308, 310–12
Buckingham, Ferdinand, 302
Bucknell, Judge, 206
Buckner, Dick, 190–92, 201
Buckner, Obadiah, 205–06, 219
Bulah, Rev., 45–46
Bullitt, Dr. Henry, 204
Bundy, Henry, 345
Burgoyne, Judge John, 249
Burleigh, Charles C., 294, 298
Burns, Anthony, 58, 421–30, 432–34, 437,
    439, 451, 458–59
  aftermath of trial, 426–28
Burns, Henry and Family, 243, 244n29, 423
Burris, Jim, 130
Burrows, Judah, 143
Bush, Marshal, 65
Bushnell, Simeon, 257–59, 262
Busteed, Richard, 382–84
Bustill, Joseph C., 273, 291
Butler, Andrew P., 77–78, 352, 431–32
Butler, Charles, 351–52
Butler, James, 302–03
Butler, Mr., 319
Butler, Mrs. Pierce, 187
Butler, Senator Arthur, 5
Butman, Officer Asa O., 413, 416,
    421, 429–30

Cadwalader, John, 351–53
Caldwell, Abraham, 122–23
Calhoun, John C., 7n5, 7–8, 14, 39
California, 8, 13, 201, 311, 389
Calvert, John, 164
Cambridge Maryland African Colonization
    Society, 115, 127, 133
Camden, Peter, 161
Campbell, Harvey C., 173
Campbell, James, 179, 295–96, 298–301
Campbell, John, 224
Campbell, Walter L., 295
Canada, xiii, xiv, 4n1, 19, 21, 22n32, 42,
    49n12, 45–50, 64–65, 67, 71, 74, 81,
    85, 102, 106, 106n30, 115, 127–28,
    139, 147, 163–64, 167, 170, 172–73,
    178–79, 183, 185–87, 191, 194, 198,
    201, 203, 210, 213–16, 222, 224,
    226–27, 230, 234–36, 245, 249, 257,
    263–64, 268, 273, 275–76, 278, 307,
    316, 349n44, 349–50, 355, 359–65,
    367–68, 371–73, 376n19, 391, 393,
    395, 399, 413–14, 420, 429, 440, 444
  Buxton, 45, 387
  Chatham, 187, 190, 193, 278
  Kingston, 359
  Lewiston, 359, 362
  Malden, 212, 226, 228
  Montreal, 47, 275, 395, 410
  Niagara, 362
  Nova Scotia, 46
    Halifax, 408
    Windsor, 408
  Ontario, 47
    Hamilton, 311
    London, 182
    Windsor, 178, 216
  St Catherines, 360
  Toronto, 101–02, 306
Canada West, 234, 322
Canton, Edgar, 160–61
Cantwell, Robert, 272
Caphart, John, 409
Caribbean, 307
Carmichael, Deputy Marshal Jesse D., 219
Caroline, 282
Carpenter, Commissioner Sam S., 60, 245–46,
    246n31
Carter, George Washington, 186, 191
Carter, James, 209
Carter, John, 105n29
Carter, Mrs., 199

Carter, Nathan, 141
Carter, William, 225
Cash, John, 148
Cass, Lewis, 11, 25, 28, 34, 38
Cassa, 272
Cassday, John, 199
Caton, John, 173–74, 177
Catron, Edgar, 178–79
Catto, Octavius V., 56
Catto, William T., 338
Celia, 191
Central Southern Rights Association, 381, 448n10, 452
Chamberlain, Marsh, 294
Chamberlain, Mr., 374
Chamberlin, E. W., 173–74
Chambers, Francis T., 250
Chambers, Judge Ezekiel, 319, 324
Channing, William Henry, 404
Chaplin, William, 379
Chardon Fugitive Guards, 17
Charles, 147, 201, 204
Charlotte, 272, 322
Chase, Salmon, 9, 9n8, 22, 34, 39, 51–52, 75, 247, 251
Chavers, Alfred, 158
Chavers, Amanda, 179, *See* Kitchell, Amanda
Cheat River, 306
Cheever, George B., 375
Chelson, Benjamin, 242
Cheney, Edward, 306
Cheney, Elias, 272
Chesapeake Bay, 269, 313, 315
Chester, Thomas Morris, 112–14, 125–26, 133
Chicago Mutual Protection Society, 84
Chouteau family, 157
Christy, W. T., 148
Churchill, Deputy Marshal B. P., 255–56
Cilla, 249, 251
Cincinnati and Cleveland Railroad, 203
Circuit Court, 52, 189–91, 193, 195, 197, 204, 206, 211, 334, 352, 400
Civil War, xi, xv, 42, 99n18, 129, 140, 162, 172, 214, 241–42, 245, 248, 302, 305–06, 322, 374, 376, 450, 454n18
Clapton, David, 381
Clark, Charles, 345
Clark, Peter H., 246, 263
Clarke, George, 301
Clarke, Lewis, 363–64
Clarke, Milton, 363

Clay, Henry, 7–8, 10, 13–14, 24–25, 27, 34, 38, 41, 68–70, 78–79, 85, 92–94, 96–98, 101, 134, 198, 397, 404, 410–11, 418, 448
Clements, Frederick, 159–60, 162, 179
Clements, Miriam, 146
Clements, Samuel, 146
Clexton, Percy, 369
Cluer, John C., 423
Cobb, Howell, 28
Coburn, John, 218
Coburn, John P., 412
Cocke, Mrs., 184
Coe, Deacon W. V., 176
Coffin, Levi, 229, 254
Coleman, Paul, 232
Colfax, Schuyler, 104
Collins, Robert, 396, 400, 405–06, 408
colonization, 89n1, 88–98, 102, 104, 106–19, 120n52, 120–27, 129, 131, 134, 307, 326, 379
  constitutionality, 93
  debate over, 89–93, 96, 126–27
  Ebony Line, 93–94, 97
  failure of, 131–34
  justifications for leaving the United States, 114
  meetings in opposition to, 95
  opposition to, 94–97, 102, 117, 123–25
  resistance to, 127–31
  solution for stability, 93
  supporters of, 89, 91–92, 94–96, 98–99, 101, 110, 114, 116–17, 119, 121, 123–26, 131–34
  ventures, 114–18
Colver, Nathaniel, 415
commerce, 26
commissioners, xiv, 7–8, 10–13, 20, 36, 51n16, 51–54, 60n27, 56–64, 67, 69–70, 73–74, 85, 153, 158–59, 161–62, 165–66, 172–73, 179, 185, 209, 211, 213, 218, 220, 228, 236, 244, 246, 250, 253, 257, 264, 267–68, 274, 280–91, 301–02, 307, 310, 337–39, 343, 347–53, 355, 361–62, 364, 366–67, 370, 378, 380–82, 389, 400, 403, 407–09, 412, 432–35, 438, 444, 456–59
  role of, 52–59
Committee of Thirteen, 118–19, 121n53, 123, 391

Compromise of 1850, 7–8, 13–14, 22–23,
    25–29, 32, 32n54, 34–35, 37, 40, 50,
    67–68, 75–76, 78, 89, 102, 361–62,
    378, 397, 405, 407, 410, 412, 419,
    424, 457
Confederacy, 455
Congress, xi, 7n5, 7–8, 10–13, 20–21, 25, 29,
    33, 35, 40–41, 44, 52, 56, 63, 69,
    75–80, 86, 91, 93, 95, 116, 159, 162,
    164, 169, 175, 213, 247, 269, 339, 357,
    415, 424, 430, 445, 448, 454, 456
Conkling, Judge Alfred, 362–63, 367
Connecticut, 173, 381
    Hartford, 113
    Norwich, 398
Connelly, William, 252–55, 267–68
Constable, John S., 314
Constitution, xi, 6, 9–10, 12, 21–22, 28,
    30–31, 36, 39, 50, 75, 83, 85, 103, 159,
    215, 248, 260, 293, 406, 426, 431, 444,
    450, 452, 456
Constitutional Union Party, 445
Cook, unknown first name, 242
Cooper, James, 11, 56, 78–79, 83
Cooper, Maria, 311
Cooper, Rose, 389
Cope, F. George, 193–94
Copeland, John, 258
Corbella, 148
Corneau, Stephen A., 159–60, 172
Cornish, Aaron, 314
Cornish, Henry G., 346
Cornish, Samuel, 96, 100, 117, 122–23
Corwin, Thomas, 253–54
Cotes, James, 209
Coulter, James H., 247
Craft, Ellen, 396, 398, 400–01, 403
Craft, William, 19, 396, 398–401, 403
Craft, William and Ellen, 3–4, 21, 24, 30, 33,
    59, 66–67, 69, 77, 287, 396, 398,
    400–01, 403–09, 417, 420, 422, 439,
    446, 452, 459
Crane, Joseph H., 22
Crisler, Jonas, 235
Crittenden Compromise, 448
Crittenden, John J., 12–13, 13n13, 22, 31, 86,
    406, 448, 456
Crocus, Elizabeth. *See* Parker, Rachel
Crocus, Henrietta, 297
Crocus, June, 297
Crosswhite, Adam, 4n1
Crosswhite, Sarah, 4n1

Culver, E. D., 382, 384, 387, 389–90
Cumberland River, 139
Cummings, Velonious H., 210
Cunningham, James, 191–92, 302
Curtis, Benjamin R., 30, 412
Curtis, George T., 29, 59–60, 67, 400, 405–06,
    409, 412, 415–16, 420
Curtis, George W., 449
Curtis, Thomas, 334
Curtis, William, 332–33
Curtly, Anna and J., 172
Cushing, Caleb, 213, 437n61, 437–38
Cyrus, 129

Dallas, George Mifflin, 31
Daly, Richard, 188
Dana, Richard H., 400, 409–10, 412, 421–22,
    425, 427–28, 434
Dangerfield, Daniel. *See* Webster
    (Dangerfield), Daniel
Daniel, 282
Daniel, Jerry, 57, 71
Dartmouth College, 113
David, 281
Davis, Charles G., 409, 412
Davis, Daniel, 49, 60–61, 362–64, 366, 369
Davis, Gideon, 130
Davis, Jefferson, 10, 13, 93–94, 419
Davis, Levi, 158
Davis, Samuel, 257
Davis, William H., 232
Dayton, William, 10, 22, 51–52
De Bree, John, 409
De Wolf, Calvin, 170–72
Dean, James, 374
Declaration of Independence, 98, 175, 368
Deep South, 141, 426, 457
defense associations, 149
Delany, Martin, 32, 102, 117, 124–25, 191
Delaware, xiii, 94, 313, 315, 321, 327,
    359, 392
    Dover, 314
    Middletown, 320
    Wilmington, 269, 322, 360, 392, 439
Dellam, Dick, 345–46
Dellam, Helen, 345–46
Democrats, 11, 20, 22–23, 26–27, 29, 31,
    34–36, 57–58, 99, 156, 159–60,
    163–64, 167, 173, 213, 247, 250, 258,
    262–63, 280, 290, 292, 301, 326, 342,
    350–51, 353n50, 362, 369, 371, 388,
    391, 418, 429, 433, 449–50, 452

Dennison, Rev. Henry M., 229, 238, 247–48, 265
Deputie, Charles, 114, 124, 128
Devens, Marshal Charles, 406–07, 416–17
DeWolf, Calvin, 165
Dickey, Dr. E. V., 297
Dickey, Rev. John M., 298
Dickinson, Daniel, 28, 34
Dickinson, George, 160
Dickson, U.S. Marshal, 159
Ditcher, John, 224
Ditto, Dr. C. H., 201
Dixon, Archibald, 198, 375
Dixon, Henry, 374–75
Dixon, William, 232
Donelson, Alexander, 128
Donelson, Andrew Jackson, 39
Donnelly, Matthew, 295–96
Douglas, H. Ford, 170, 446
Douglas, Stephen A., 13, 23, 163–64, 167, 170, 170n56, 173, 176, 411, 424, 454
Douglass, Anna, xiii
Douglass, Frederick, xiii, 20, 24, 44, 48, 57, 59, 66, 71, 79, 81, 91, 97, 99, 101, 121, 151, 170n56, 191–92, 195, 359–60, 368–69, 374, 393–95, 401, 404–05, 424, 440, 445–46, 460
Douglass, Lewis, 394
Downing, George, 72, 117–18, 121n53, 121–23, 379, 391
Downs, Solomon, 28
Doy, Dr. John, 177
Drayden, James, 177–78
Dred Scott Case, 218, 261, 263, 389, 425, 436, 449, 451
Drew, Benjamin, 215
Drummond, Judge, 174
Dryden, US Marshal Manuel, 245
Duer, Judge, 389
Dupree, Nathaniel W., 328
Dyton, Mr., 415

Eastern State Penitentiary, 341, 354
Edda, 183
Edinburgh Ladies Emancipation Society, 322
Edmonds, Thomas, 206
Edmund, 137
Edward, 180, 186, *See* Lemmons family
Elbert, 272
Ellen, 149
Ellington, Rev. Pleasant, 211–13
Ellis, Mary, 144

emancipation, 23, 29, 71, 88, 89n1, 99–100, 107, 128, 134, 150, 170, 325, 378, 389, 393, 453
Emeline. *See* Lemmons family
Emmet, Richard S., 384
England, 21, 38, 60, 67, 74–75, 98, 98n18, 130, 191, 287, 368, 385, 395, 408, 420
    Liverpool, 376
    London, 24–25
Erdman, Charles, 168
Erie Canal, 48
Ernst, Sarah Otis, 237
escape advertisements, 50, 74, 140–42, 154–55, 182, 233, 271, 328
Esther, 149
Evans, John P., 207
Evans, Robert E., 210
Evansville and Central Railroad, 207
Ewing, Andrew, 39

Fairbank, Calvin, 192, 194–96, 199–200, 204, 231
Fairchild, James, 257
Fairfield, John, 229
Fant, Henry T., 288
Farrell, Charles, 144
Fayette, 161
Fee, John G., 231
Fellows, John H., 166
Female Anti-Slavery Society, 333, 355
Ferguson, Rev. William B., 247
Fetherbridge, Mr., 290
Fiery, Henry, 272–73
Fillmore, Cyrus, 216–17
Fillmore, President Millard, 12, 15, 21, 27, 34, 41, 46, 48, 66–67, 76–77, 82, 86, 88, 94, 253, 280, 292, 367, 369n11, 377, 397, 406, 408, 411–12, 441
Findley, William, 108, 113–14
Finley, James P., 376
Fisher, Solomon, 303–04
Fisher, William. *See* Smith, George
Fitch, James, 258
Fletcher, Calvin, 214
Florida, 37–38, 78
    Pensacola, 439
Floyd, Governor John B., 11, 37, 89
Foote, Henry, 28, 34
Forten, Charlotte L., 349
Foster, Emily, 306
Foster, Stephen, 153
Foster, Stephen S., 428, 430

Foster, William, 103
Fowler, Mr., 62
Fox, D. M., 154
Fox, Jerry, 258
Foye, John, 412
Franklin family, 282
Franklin, Daniel, 49
Franklin, Dr. Robert, 282
free blacks, xii, xiv, 5, 8, 40, 42, 46, 50, 76, 80,
        84, 88–89, 92–94, 96–97, 100, 102–03,
        107, 111, 115–16, 120–21, 126,
        131–34, 143, 145, 148–51, 154–55,
        161, 177, 183, 190–91, 205, 216, 224,
        226, 230, 232, 237, 242, 276–77,
        277n9, 290, 303–04, 313, 316–18,
        323n14, 325n17, 326n18, 322–27,
        355, 393, 457, 460
    kidnap of, 155, 177–78, 201, 209–10, 239–
        44, 290, 293–303, 305–06, 316, 340–
        41, 372–77, 376n19, 387, 451, 453
    prosecution of, 277–78
    re-enslavement of, 209
    wrongful identification as fugitives, 211–14
Free Produce Association, 385
Free Soil movement, 214
Free Soil Party, 75, 99, 105, 191, 383, 422,
        429, 433, 435
Free States, xi, xiii, 3–8, 13, 15, 20, 37, 50, 57,
        79, 88, 104, 120, 127, 130–31, 134,
        139, 150–51, 158, 160, 187, 195, 209,
        215, 218–19, 221, 226, 231, 244, 261,
        264–65, 275, 329, 344, 378, 384, 387,
        424, 435–36, 441, 448, 450–51, 455
Freeman, James B., 332
Freeman, John, 211–15
Freeman, Marshal Watson, 421, 423, 425–26
Frees, L. C. P., 165
Frost, D. M., 168–69
Fry, Richard, 445
Fugitive Aid Society, 237, 264, 291, 306, 361,
        441, 444
Fugitive Slave Law of 1793, xi, 6–7, 9, 12, 34,
        52, 397, 451
Fugitive Slave Law of 1850, xi, xii, 11, 13, 23,
        25, 27–29, 31–32, 34, 36–39, 45, 58,
        61, 75, 78, 82–84, 88, 92–95, 97–98,
        103, 106, 111–12, 115, 118–20, 128,
        150–51, 153, 155n30, 155–56, 159,
        161–62, 170, 174–75, 177, 179, 186,
        195, 201, 207–10, 213–15, 220, 228,
        234, 237, 252, 256, 258, 263–65,
        267–69, 275, 280, 288, 293, 298, 307,
        314, 336, 338–39, 343, 345, 353–55,
        359, 366, 372, 375–76, 380, 383–84,
        395, 397–98, 403–06, 417, 424, 432,
        435–36, 438, 442–43, 451n13, 451–52,
        454n18, 454–55, 457
    adoption of, 244
    Anti-Fugitive Slave Law meetings,
        14–15, 25
    attempt to repeal, 94
    battle over, 361
    calls to repeal, 430
    challenges to, 61
    circumvention of, 4
    commitment to, 413
    Congressional opposition of, xi
    constitutionality of, 13n13, 20, 40, 60, 68,
        72, 74, 78, 163, 214, 246–47, 250,
        261, 268, 412, 429–30, 434, 438, 453,
        455, 458
    critics of, 45, 58
    debate over, 8–11, 40, 44, 77–79,
        357, 452–53
    debates on meaning and significance of,
        34–38, 75–76
    debates over significance of, 254
    defense of, 352
    defiance of, xi, 4–5, 14–15, 23, 30, 48, 74,
        79, 86, 368, 371, 398, 459
    effectiveness of, 40–41, 69, 389, 419
    efficacy of, 44, 49, 407
    efficiency of, 220
    enforcement of, xi, 22, 40, 51, 54, 60, 66,
        68, 79–80, 97, 115, 150, 165, 178–79,
        184, 205, 254, 266, 292–93, 316, 321,
        323, 342, 359, 361–62, 405, 407, 423,
        426, 431, 450, 452
    failure of, 456, 459
    free state reaction to, xiii
    hearings of, xiii, 7, 12, 83, 86, 89, 167
    impact of, 50
    implementation of, 64
    ineffectiveness of, 74, 459
    interference with, 5
    interpretation of, 59–64
    issue of trials by jury, 7, 10–12, 20,
        23, 27, 36, 55, 175, 293, 357,
        416, 454
    legitimacy of, xi, 159
    limitations of, 407
    meetings in support of, 26–27
    need to obey, 31
    operation of, xii

opponents of, 41, 56, 58, 75, 79, 94, 239,
 243, 247–48, 252, 287, 337, 344, 350,
 357, 380, 384, 399, 410, 433, 436
opposition to, xiv–xv, 20, 31, 44, 66–67, 72,
 97, 102, 163, 169, 292, 338–39, 354,
 369, 399, 424, 431, 442, 455
passage of, xi, xii, 13–14, 42, 99,
 170, 203, 399, 408, 410, 418, 420,
 438, 448n10
political consequences of, 26
political debates over, 430–32
political implications of, 410–11
political meanings of, 59
political rhetoric of, 406
political significance of, 59
politics of, xi
protests about, 40
question of treason, 80
resistance to, 15, 19–20, 38, 48, 65–67,
 72–75, 78–80, 162–63, 176, 208, 262,
 338, 347, 352, 361, 364, 366, 368,
 380, 399–403, 405, 408–09, 428, 436,
 439, 459
state interference with, 35
submission to Senate, 6–7
subversion of, xiv, 4, 192, 236, 449
supporters of, 22, 32, 52, 55–56, 68, 79,
 118, 123, 167, 292, 330, 339, 350, 362,
 378, 391, 417–18, 424
trials of, 258
undermining of, xiv, 248
violation of, 153, 367–68, 441
violent responses to, 33–34, 47, 201
fugitive slaves, xiv, 4n1, 9n8, 4–12, 14–15,
 19–22, 22n32, 24, 24n36, 29–32,
 37n60, 35–39, 41–46, 48–50,
 55n20, 55–57, 59–67, 69, 71–75, 77,
 79–80, 84–86, 97, 101, 106, 115–16,
 118–19, 128, 140–41, 147–49, 151n21,
 151–55, 155n30, 158n35, 157–59,
 161n39, 161–65, 167–68, 170–77,
 183, 185, 186n7, 186–87, 191, 198,
 200, 205–08, 210–13, 215–18, 220–21,
 225, 227–30, 232, 234–37, 239–40,
 242–46, 249–50, 252–53, 258, 263–69,
 271, 275n6, 274–76, 278–79, 280n14,
 285n24, 283–87, 289, 291–94, 297,
 299–304, 306–07, 310–13, 313n3,
 320, 328, 330, 336–43, 345–46, 348,
 350–52, 355–57, 359–61, 363–75,
 379, 381, 384–86, 390–91, 393–95,
 397–99, 401, 409–11, 413–17, 419–23,

 428–36, 439–41, 444–46, 448, 451–52,
 454, 458–60
aid in escape attempts, 142–49, 152–53,
 156–57, 161, 164, 166, 182, 188, 190,
 192–94, 197–205, 224, 228–31, 236,
 276, 290–92, 315, 318–19, 399, 457
resulting in prison sentences, 231–32
attempts to reclaim, 5–6, 44, 47, 74, 153,
 157–59, 166–67, 174
violence in, 153–54
violence of, 153
attempts to return, 280
cases of, xiv, 14, 35, 38, 53, 55, 58, 61–63,
 65, 67–68, 70, 73, 146–48, 165–76,
 179–84, 188–97, 207–08, 211–20, 238,
 244–65, 279–84, 286–90, 302–03, 305,
 310, 334, 337–39, 342–46, 351–54,
 361–66, 369–71, 377–84, 386–91,
 396–97, 409–10, 413–18,
 421–26, 431, 439, 441–45, 450
the Jerry rescue, 366–69
political implications of, 341–42, 350
efforts to reclaim, xi, xii, 142
escapes as political statements of, 140
escapes of, xi, xiv, 3–4, 7, 47, 50–51, 57,
 61–62, 88, 137–40, 142, 144–45, 167,
 182, 184–86, 189, 196, 200, 205,
 220–28, 232–36, 272–74, 277–78,
 308–19, 321, 325, 327, 357, 360,
 457, 459
slaveholders' responses to, 319–27
evasion of recapture, 47
experiences in Canada, 186–88
flight after the passage of the Fugitive Slave
 Law, 44, 46, 50
motivations to escape, xiii–xiv, 182
political dispute over, 222
politics of escape, xii–xiii
prevented escapes, 145
recapture of, xi, xii, xiii, xiv, 6–7, 14, 25,
 30, 34–37, 41, 45–49, 53–54, 69n46,
 70n47, 72, 75, 79, 83–84, 92–93,
 139, 141, 145, 149–50, 152–54, 159,
 162, 169, 179–80, 185, 196–97, 205,
 207, 226, 235–36, 240, 252–53, 265,
 272, 274–76, 281, 281n16, 284, 291,
 300n47, 304, 310–11, 314, 318,
 322–23, 337, 340, 342, 364–65, 369,
 371, 373, 381, 398, 408, 420, 452
renditions of, 7, 9, 11–12, 40–41, 49, 59, 65,
 69–70, 76, 88, 93, 151, 153, 179, 215,
 243, 246–47, 249, 264, 266, 279, 281,

fugitive slaves (*cont.*)
  289–90, 301, 305, 341, 352, 361, 370,
    378, 406, 419, 428, 430, 452, 458, 460
  rescue of, xii, 40–41, 64, 85, 177, 213, 219,
    238, 242, 367, 371
  resistance of, 154, 306
  return of, xii, 10, 40, 155, 206, 219, 344,
    355, 384–85, 418–19, 434, 458
  stampedes, 50, 140, 145, 184–85, 314
  struggle for freedom, xi, 47, 139
  vulnerability after passage of Fugitive Slave
    Law, 44–48
  white community reaction to
    escapes, 149–52
Fuller, Thomas, 115, 133
Furness, Mr., 155n30

Gael, Elizabeth, 346
Gaines, Archibald K., 249, 251
Gallagher, Martin, 147n16
Galloway, Betsy. *See* Thompson, Catherine
Gantz, Charles, 170–71
Gap Gang, 294, 298
Gardiner, Alexander, 378
Gardner, Gov. Henry J., 433, 435–37
Garlick, Charles, 49n12
Garner family, 250–51
Garner, Margaret, 65n36, 249, 251–52, 267, 344
Garner, Mary, 249
Garner, Simon, 248
Garnet, Henry Highland, 24, 191, 385, 397
Garnett, Henry, 65–66, 338–39, 355
Garrett, Thomas, 322, 392
Garrison, William Lloyd, 24, 194, 368, 404,
    410, 428, 437–38, 440
Gates, George B., 364
Gavitt, John, 186, 198, 200, 206
Gay, Sydney Howard, 386, 391–92
Gayley, Sarah, 61–62
Gena, Thomas, 258
George, 310, 312–13
Georgia, xiii, 21, 28, 38, 45, 59, 66, 147, 211,
    213, 264, 287, 364, 381, 392, 400,
    407–08, 415–16, 420, 446, 457
  Augusta, 417
  Chatham County, 68, 413
  Decatur, 381
  Macon, 3, 200, 374–75, 396–97, 400, 408
  Monroe, 212
  Oconee, 396
  Savannah, 53, 68, 396, 413, 415, 417
  Walton County, 212

Gerard, James W., 27
Gholson, John M., 154
Gibbs, Jacob R., 389
Gibson, Adam, 54–56, 339–40, 344, 345n39
Gibson, Charles M., 227–28
Gibson, O. L., 103–04
Giddings, Joshua, 21–22, 34, 241, 262, 288,
    393, 444
Giddings, Sarah Jane, 376n19
Gilbert, John, 241
Gilbert, Timothy, 399
Gilbert, Uri, 369, 371
Gilchrist, William, 193
Gillard, Daniel, 301, 304
Giltner, Henry, 372–73
Givens, George, 57, 185
Glover, Joshua, 455n19, 459
Gooden, John, 178
Gordon, J. H., 141
Gorsuch William, 342
Gorsuch, Edward, 50, 50n14, 81–82, 84,
    84n72, 166, 296, 299, 310, 357, 359
Goshorn, Isabella, 264
Goshorn, John, 264, 441–44, 460
Goshorn, William, 264, 441, 444
Gould, Judge George, 370–71
Graff, Allan, 391
Graham, R. A., 229
Grandy, Charles, 374
Grant, William, 166
Graves, Lorenzo, 373
Gray, Jim, 172–74, 176–77, 179
Grayson, Eliza, 171–72
Great Britain, 23–24, 24n37, 71, 194n19, 275,
    322, 385, 446
  Newcastle, 385
Greeley, Horace, 97, 120n52, 118–21, 323,
    384, 387–88
  views on colonization, 118–21
Green, Albert M., 352
Green, Alfred, 353–54
Green, Frank, 239
Green, Harriet Ann, 277
Green, Peter, 3–5
Green, Rev. Samuel, 4, 28, 316–18, 326–27
Green, Samuel, 316
Green, Shields, 394
Green, William, 15
Greenwood, John, 314
Grew, Mary, 333, 347, 351
Grier, Robert C., 53, 65–66, 280, 338
Griffiths, Julia, 359, 395

Grigby, Barnaby, 306
Grigby, Margaret Elizabeth, 306
Grimes, Leonard, 414, 416, 420–21, 426–28
Griswold, Seneca O., 258
Grooms, William, 154, 154n29
Gross, Dr., 190
Gross, George, 304
Grove, Jacob H., 273–74
Guba, Miles, 148
Gulf of Mexico, 456
Gurley, Sarah, 346
Guttridge, Hiram, 255–56
Gyser, John, 235

habeas corpus, 8, 11–13, 13n13, 20, 23, 27,
    36, 37n60, 59, 61, 68, 70, 76, 148,
    167, 173, 211, 219–20, 238–39, 243,
    246–47, 249, 255, 257, 261, 264, 267,
    279, 284, 298, 315, 329, 334, 343–45,
    346n40, 352, 355, 357, 362, 364,
    370–71, 380, 386, 415, 431, 436, 442
Haiti, 127, 456
Hale, John, 53, 78–79, 94, 411–12
Hall, Basil, 352, 354
Hall, Charles M., 380–81
Hall, David, 352, 354
Hall, James, 421
Hall, Joe, 30n52, 130
Hall, Joseph, 314
Hallett, Benjamin F., 400, 426
Halzell, Samuel, 345
Hamilton, Robert, 148, 379
Hamilton, Thomas, 379
Hamlet, James, 70–72, 118, 377–81,
    391, 413
Hansbrough, Blucher W., 369, 371
Hanway, Castner, 82–84
Harding, William, 191–92
Hardy, 322
Hardy, James A., 126–27, 133
Harness, John, 364
Harper, Andrew, 128–29
Harper, Emerine, 128, 131
Harrick, William L., 457
Harris, Catherine, 48
Harris, Chapman, 188, 203n29
Harris, George, 133
Harris, Mahala, 192
Harris, Phillip, 133–34, 143–44
Harris, William, 48
Harrison, John O., 182
Harrison, Joseph H., 130n69

Harrison, Sarah, 376
Hart, John, 352
Hartman, George, 263
Hartwell, John, 258
Harvard University, 433
Hastings, Orlando, 59
Haviland, Laura, 195
Hawkins, Fleming, 301
Hawkins, L., 226n4
Hawkins, Rev. H. H., 234
Hawley, Seth, 362
Hay, Robert, 373
Hayden, Harriet, 194, 198
Hayden, Jo, 194, 198
Hayden, Lewis, 19, 194, 198, 399, 401, 410,
    412, 414, 416, 420–22, 424n40, 439
Hayes, Joseph K., 412
Hayes, Rutherford B., 245, 247
Hazlett, Hugh, 321
Hedgebeth, Thomas, 215
Henderson, A.J., 198
Henderson, Shadrach, 180, 186, 188–89, 192
Henry, 137, 168, 184, 190, 313n3
Henry, Jerry, 366–69
Henry, John, 200
Henry, Mayor Alexander, 449
Henry, William, 85, 370
Henshaw, David, 30
Hensley, Isaac, 242
Henson, Josiah, 222
Herndon, Elliot, 159
Herndon, William H., 159–61
Hicks, Gov., 303
Hicks, N. M., 207
Higginson, Thomas Wentworth, 414, 416,
    420, 422–23, 429–30, 440
Hildreth, Richard, 434
Hill, Henry, 374
Hitchcock, S. E., 227
Hite, John, 372–75
Hoar, George F., 430
Hollenbeck, Isaac, 379
Holly, James Theodore, 112
Holmes, John W., 369–70
Hope, Thomas M., 158
Hopewell, Nelson, 423
Hopkins, Amos, 421
Horner, Moses, 292, 306, 351–54
Hossack, John, 157, 173–76
Howard, C. M., 158
Howard, Jacob C., 343
Howard, Magdalena, 277

Howard, William, 322
Howe, Samuel G., 394
Hoy, Josiah, 391
Hoyne, Thomas, 167
Hubbard, Thomas, 281
Hubert, Littleton, 343–44
Hudson River, 360
Hudson, Augustine G., 288
Hudson, Dennis, 288
Hughes, Daniel, 314
Hughes, George W., 324
Hughes, Willis, 400–01, 403, 405–09, 415
Hughlett, Samuel, 178
Hunt, Washington, 123, 365, 368
Hunter, William, 316
Huntington, Judge E. M., 216–17
Hurst, Moses. *See* Bard, Moses
Hutchinson, Dr. J. W., 297
Hyde, Russell, 255–56
Hyde, Udney, 255
Hyller, Elisha, 197

Illinois, xiii, 13, 30, 37, 42, 70n47, 103,
    104n26, 104–05, 111, 132, 139, 141n7,
    143, 148, 151, 154, 156, 158, 162,
    177–78, 186
  Alexander County, 154
  Alton, 42, 112, 139, 147–48, 152, 156–58,
    158n35, 161n39, 170, 179
  Atlanta, 159
  Belleville, 26, 31
  Black Law, 154–56, 170
  Bloomington, 145
  Bridgeport, 164
  Cairo, 146, 148, 153, 162, 171n57
  Chicago, 14, 18, 23, 42, 48, 62, 64, 70,
    74n53, 139–40, 143–45, 148, 154–57,
    161–71, 171n57, 174, 176–79, 217,
    320–21, 429, 435
  Clinton County, 152
  Delhi, 139
  Edwardsville, 144
  Egypt district, 43, 151–53, 156–58, 162–63,
    165, 172, 177, 179
  Galena, 177–78
  Gallatin County, 152
  Jacksonville, 132
  Jonesboro, 172–73
  Miller Grove, 152
  Naples, 218
  Ottawa, 156, 161, 172–74, 177–78
  Peoria, 374
  Perry County, 172

Pike County, 151n21
Pope County, 152
Quincy, xiii, 140, 146, 150, 155n30,
    155–57, 161, 254, 457
Randolph County, 137
Rocky Fork, 42, 139
Sandoval, 146
Shawneetown, 141, 152, 160
Sparta, 137, 152–54
Springfield, xiii, 35, 44, 132, 158, 160–62,
    167, 172–73, 218
St. Clair County, 148
Union County, 172
Upper Alton, 139
Warren County
  Monmouth, 170
Indiana, xiii, 30, 37, 42, 50, 75–76, 93–94,
    103, 105, 107–08, 110n36, 110–11,
    113, 119–20, 120n52, 122, 131,
    155–56, 169, 180, 182, 184–86, 195,
    200–01, 205–07, 209–10, 213, 215,
    217–18, 220, 222, 245, 432, 435
  Aurora, 222
  Brownstown, 201
  Charlestown, 183, 195
  Clarke County, 103, 206
  colonization efforts, 106–11
  Columbus, 209
  Corydon, 109, 201
  Covington, 108
  Crawfordsville, 185
  DeKalb County, 103
  Delaware County, 103
  DuBois County
    Patoka Township, 451n13
  Edinburgh, 210
  Elkhart County, 105
  Evansville, 185–86, 198–200, 206–07, 233
  Floyd County, 184
  Fort Wayne, 105
  Gibson County, 199, 206, 209–10
    Lyles Station, 206
    Princeton, 186, 199
  Gosport, 210
  Grant County, 104
  Greensburg, 209
  Hamilton County, 209
  Harrison County, 201
  Indianapolis, 51, 102, 104, 107, 110,
    183, 195, 198–99, 205, 207,
    211–16, 218–19
  Jeffersonville, 49, 183, 188, 191–92,
    194–95, 200, 205, 209, 233

Knightstown, 183
Knox County, 104
Lafayette, 108
LaGrange County, 105
    South Milford, 215
Lawrenceburg, 75–76, 188, 222, 234
Madison, 51, 106, 183, 188, 194,
    197, 203, 205–06, 211, 213, 215,
    220, 233
Marion County, 103–04, 214
Mauckport, 201
Monroe County, 103
Morgan County
    Martinsville, 210
Negro Exclusion Law, 102–06, 186
New Albany, 49, 106–07, 180, 182, 184,
    186, 188, 190–92, 197, 201–02, 205,
    207–09, 418
New Harmony, 186
Newcastle, 26
Orland, 215, 217
Pike County
    Petersburg, 198
Putnam County, 104
Randolph County, 104
Richmond, 22, 215
Ripley County
    Napoleon, 215
Rush County, 102, 104, 213–14
Seymour, 205
South Bend, 4n1, 104
State Board of Colonization, 107–08
Steuben County, 103, 105, 216–17
Terre Haute, 111
Union County, 104
Vanderburgh County, 206
Vernon, 208
Vincennes, 48, 57–58, 164, 185–86, 186n7,
    207, 239
Washington County
    New Philadelphia, 49, 209
    Salem, 180, 195, 205
Wayne County, 102
Ingersoll, Joseph R., 449
Ingraham, Edward D., 54–56, 63–64,
    74, 81, 310, 338–40, 340n33,
    343–45
Iowa, 54, 111, 140, 147n16, 178
    Drakesville, 76n56
    Dubuque, 26
    Fort Des Moines, 177
    Independence, 178
    Keokuk, 145

Ireland
    Cork, 24
    Londonderry, 107
Irvine, John, 227
Isaac, 137, 207
Isler, George H., 279

Jack, Mr., 184
Jackson, 141
Jackson Mary. *See* Amanda
Jackson, Andrew, 128
Jackson, Francis, 399
Jackson, James, 301
Jacobs, Curtis, 322–27
Jacobs, Harriet, 44, 312n2, 379
Jacobs, John H., 379
Jacobs, Joseph, 177–78
Jamaica, 29, 99–101, 106, 152n24, 368,
    394, 456
    Kingston, 99
    Sterling, 385
Jamaican Hamic Association, 100
James, Wesley, 392
Jane, 141, 149
Janis, Antoine, 137
Jay, John, 365, 380, 382–83, 387
Jay, William, 33, 52
Jeffersonville and Indianapolis Railroad
    Company, 205
Jeffersonville Railroad Company, 190
Jenifer, Benjamin, 115, 121, 126, 133
Jenkins, B. W., 372–73
Jenkins, Marshall, 351, 373
Jenks, Chancellor L., 172
Jennings, Anderson, 257–58, 260–61
Jennings, C. M., 212
Jerry, 85–86, 116, 141, 459, *See* Henry,
    William
Jerry Rescue, 395, 423
Jesse, 147
Jeter, William, 191
Jim, 172n58, 183, 191, 205, 215
Joe, 183
John, 30, 166, 193, 235, 313n3
Johnson, 130, 158, 165, 290
Johnson, Abraham, 357, 359
Johnson, Anna, 15
Johnson, Bradley T., 303
Johnson, Daniel, 329
Johnson, Dr. William Henry, 361
Johnson, Gabe, 224
Johnson, Gov. John, 387
Johnson, Gov. William F., 341–42

Johnson, Henry, 15
Johnson, Isiah, 329
Johnson, Jane, 329, 336n29, 333–37,
    346, 378
Johnson, John, 148n17, 352
Johnson, Mahala, 130
Johnson, Matthew, 262
Johnson, Moses, 62, 70, 74n53,
    165–66, 179
Johnson, Peter, 322
Johnson, Reuben, 183
Johnson, Richard, 387
Johnson, Samuel, 377n20
Johnson, Samuel E., 59
Johnson, William, 36, 77, 170, 292
Joint Standing Committee on Federal
    Relations, 433
Jolliffe, John, 244–46, 249–50, 268
Jones, Catherine, 351
Jones, Columbus, 439
Jones, David, 280
Jones, Dudley C., 190
Jones, Elias, 122–23
Jones, Elisha G., 116
Jones, James, 431
Jones, James A., 127
Jones, John, 170
Jones, John B., 172
Jones, John L. T., 283
Jones, John T., 392
Jones, John W., 360
Jones, Mr., 366
Jones, Thomas Price, 65, 338
Jones, William, 425
Jones, William M., 279–80, 347–48
Joseph, 137, 139
Joseph, John, 290
Joshua, 322
Julia, 322
Julian, George W., 214, 218–20

Kane, John K., 60n27, 83–84, 330–31,
    331n22, 335n27, 333–36, 336n27,
    338, 346n40, 343–48
Kane, Robert P., 338, 345
Kane, Thomas, 60n27
Kansas, 54, 141, 146, 147n16, 150, 177–78,
    291, 375, 394
  Topeka, 214
Kansas-Nebraska Act, 14, 163, 171, 424, 428,
    433, 448
Kansas Territory, 139, 141

Keeble, Godfrey, 346
Kelley, Abby, 57, 404
Kelly, William, 285n24
Kennard, T. C., 319
Kennedy, William, 129–30
Kennett, L. M., 158
Kentucky, xiii, 3, 4n1, 4–5, 7, 19, 32, 42, 48,
    50, 57, 75, 103, 127, 139, 152, 154,
    159, 164, 177, 186–87, 194–95,
    198–99, 202–03, 203n29, 207, 209,
    211–12, 215, 217, 219–20, 222,
    226–28, 231–35, 240–41, 251–53, 264,
    268, 312, 360, 362–63, 372–73,
    392–93, 399, 440, 448, 457
  Bedford, 204
  Boone County, 184, 204, 222, 226,
    233–35, 249
    Burlington, 235
  Bourbon County, 230, 234
  Bracken County, 204, 222, 231, 233
    Minerva, 204, 226–28, 232, 236
  Bracken County Circuit Court, 230
  Campbell County, 222, 233
  Carroll County, 184, 188
  Carrollton, 185, 203, 373
  Caseyville, 207–08
  Covington, 200, 222, 233–34, 236–38,
    241–42, 249–50, 252, 263, 267, 373
  Daviess County, 185, 198, 208, 222
  Dearborn County
    Aurora, 184
  Dover, 178, 224–25
  Estill County, 242
  Fleming County, 226, 245, 255
  Florence, 241
  Floyd County, 202
  Frankfort, 199, 218, 241
  Grant County, 233–35
  Greenup County, 222, 263
  Hamlet, 180
  Harrison County, 202
    Cynthiana, 229
  Henderson, 204
  Henderson County, 185, 186n7, 198, 200,
    204, 207
  Hopkins County, 185, 198
  Jefferson County, 50, 204
    Madison, 105n29, 184
  Jeffersonville, 265
  Jessamine County, 230n10
  Kenton County, 222, 233
  Lawrenceburg, 184

Lewis County, 70, 222
Lexington, 51, 141, 146, 194, 198,
    230n10, 240–43
Louisville, 49, 51, 61, 106, 141, 180,
    182–84, 187–93, 195–97, 203n29,
    200–06, 208–10, 218–19, 221, 233,
    241, 247, 265, 362, 373
Mason County, 204, 222, 225, 228, 230–32,
    242–43, 250, 257
Maysville, 194, 222, 224, 226, 229, 232,
    239, 242
Meade County
    Brandenburg, 201–02
Meade County Rangers, 202
Morganfield, 199
Newport, 234, 240–41
Oldham County, 197
Pendleton, 204
Pendleton County, 233
Portland, 184
Richmond, 252
Scott County, 236
Shelby County, 191
Trimble County, 184–85, 194, 197–98,
    204, 215
Union County, 57, 173, 185, 198, 200, 233
Warsaw, 372–73
Washington County, 245
Kentucky Legion, 202
Kentucky River, 230n10
Ketcham, John L., 211–13
Kilgore, David, 103
King, Claudius B., 173–74
Kintzer, Samuel, 281
Kinzell and Doyle, 310
Kitchell, Amanda, 158–59
Kite, Joseph, 249
Kline, Henry H., 81, 84, 310–11
Knight, John, 400–01, 403, 405, 407–09, 415
Knight, William S., 340
Knights of the Golden Circle, 236
Knights of Liberty, 143, 145
Knockson, Henry, 352, 354
Know-Nothing Party, 433
Knox, Justice John C., 334
Kossuth, Lajos, 24, 368

Lake Erie, 18, 21, 51, 222, 226, 236, 362,
    364, 441
Lamb, John, 315–16
Landon, Dan H., 37
Langston, Charles, 174, 257–58, 260–63, 268

Langston, John Mercer, 19, 262–63
Larned, E. C., 165
Latimer, George, 398
Latimer, Jake, 45
Laville, Harrison, 191
Law, John, 58
Lawrence, Amos, 428–29
Lawrence, James R., 367–68
Lawson, Nelson, 148
Leah, 322
Lear, James, 366–67
Leath, J. T., 158
Leavitt, Judge Humphrey H., 228, 254,
    256, 265
Lee, 235
Lee, Col. Robert E., 393
Lee, Z. Collins, 83
Lemmon, Jonathan, 386–89
Lemmon, Juliet, 387
Lemmons family, 386–88
Lemon, Joseph, 144
Lensington, Paul. *See* Van Tuyl, Napoleon
    Bonaparte
Leonard, 189
Leonard, William H., 391
Lerned, E. C., 62
Levy, Wesley, 282
Lewis, 235, 245, 268, *See* Lemmons family
Lewis, James, 290
Lewis, Thomas, 377
Lewis, William, 190–92, 359
Liberia, xiv, 55, 88–89, 93–96, 98, 100,
    102–04, 106–17, 122n56, 121–30,
    130n69, 132–34, 307, 325, 379
    Monrovia, 89, 108, 110, 115, 125, 132
Liberian Agricultural and Emigration
    Association, 115–18, 122–23
Liberian Enterprise Company, 114–15,
    124, 128
Liberty Association, 18, 163
Liberty Party, 85, 100, 366
Licking River, 233, 236
Lighter, Levi L., 154
Lincoln, Abraham, 132, 159, 176, 350, 447,
    448n10, 454n18
Lind, Jenny, 404
Lindsey, 207
Linton, J. A., 213
Little Dixie, 139
Little, Grafton, 277
Livers, Frederick, 157
Logan, Alfred, 240

Logan, Jeremiah, 304
Loguen, Jermain, 19–20, 32, 45, 71, 79n61,
    306, 349, 360–61, 363, 367–68,
    392–93, 395
Long, Henry, 70–71, 77, 158, 380–82,
    384–85, 413
Long, John C., 187, 187n10
Longstreth, J. Cooke, 347–49, 351
Loring, Charles C., 400
Loring, Charles G., 415
Loring, Commissioner Edward G., 58,
    421–22, 425, 438n62, 432–39
    removal from office, 432–39
Lott, John B., 227
Louisiana, 28, 209, 372
    Haysville, 374
    New Orleans, 177, 231, 233, 295–96, 298,
        303, 373, 389
Love, H. S., 363
Lowe, Gov. Enoch Louis, 82, 299–301,
    301n48, 315, 341–42
Lowe, Jacob, 257, 261
Lower Ohio Valley, 185, 188, 198, 204
Lox, Charles, 449
Loyer, Henry, 281, 290, 301
Lucas, Sarah Ann, 190
Lucy. *See* Bagby, Sara Lucy
Lunt, US District Attorney George, 400,
    406, 412
Luther, 130n69, 183
Luther, John, 130
Lyle family, 206
Lyman, Ansel, 258
Lyne, Henry, 286, 290
Lynn, Walter, 230
Lyton, John E., 256

M'Kinney, John, 303
Maddox, Stephen, 425
Madison, 105n29, 161
Maine, 77, 126, 146, 455
    Bath, 26
    Portland, 14, 18, 95n11, 408
Manierre, George, 62, 165, 167, 176
Manson, Deputy Marshal William L.,
    244, 267
manumission, 88, 128, 237, 239, 241, 302–03
Markham, Thomas, 159
Mars, James, 15
Marsh, Dr. Madison M., 215–16
Marshall, Alexander, 158, 213, 243, 245
Marshall, Thomas and family, 243, 244n29

marshals, xiii, 7, 20, 36, 51, 55, 57, 65, 67,
    81, 244, 249–51, 256–57, 264, 310,
    352, 356–57, 364–67, 369–70, 381–83,
    395, 401, 403, 405, 407, 409, 412, 422,
    429–30, 442
Martha, 49, 149
Martin, J. Sella, 445n6, 445–46
Martin, James, 332
Martin, Mrs., 297
Martin, Officer James, 382–84
Martin, Samuel S., 165–66
Mary, 108, 154n29, 183, 190
Mary Jane, 197
Maryland, 3–5, 9, 37, 42, 44, 50, 55–56, 61,
    80, 82, 92n6, 122, 130n69, 132–33,
    166, 222, 248, 269, 272–73, 275, 279,
    282–83, 285–86, 288, 290, 293–94,
    296, 298–301, 304, 310, 313–15, 320,
    323, 325–26, 338–42, 342n37, 344,
    350, 355, 357, 359, 371, 376, 383, 385,
    389, 392–93, 439, 450
    Anne Arundel County, 80, 282, 315, 324
    Baltimore, 39, 71, 73, 82–83, 115, 126,
        128, 130n69, 132n74, 132–33, 179,
        208, 269, 274–75, 277, 282–86, 290,
        294n38, 293–96, 303–05, 310, 313,
        315, 323–24, 326–28, 342, 344, 353,
        360, 374, 378, 382, 384–85, 389, 397,
        417, 428, 453
    Baltimore County, 81, 298, 345
    Bush Creek, 277
    Cambridge, 122, 314, 316, 321, 324
    Camden, 314
    Caroline County, 324
        Greensboro, 321
    Carroll County, 271, 276, 285n24, 306
    Cecil County, 65, 295, 300n47, 314, 319,
        338–39, 341, 343
        Elkton, 272
    Committee on the Free Black
        Population, 325–26
    Derr Island, 277
    Dorchester County, 315, 321, 324
    Eastern Shore, xii, 15, 51, 313–16, 321–22,
        325–28, 392
        Elkton, 294–95, 340
    Frederick, 51, 271, 276–77, 286, 303, 391
    Frederick County, 271, 273n5, 275n6,
        275–76, 302, 306
        Libertytown, 273n5
    Funkstown, 276, 306
    Hagerstown, 271, 273, 276, 278, 302, 306

Havre de Grace, 282
Howard County, 365
Kent County, 127, 319–21, 323
    Chestertown, 51, 314, 318
Miles River Neck, 51
Montgomery County, 283
Sharpsburg, 273–74
Smithsburg, 271
Snow Hill, 323
Somerset County, 324
Talbot County, 321, 324, 327
    St Michaels, 328
Washington County, 271, 275, 279, 310
    Boonsboro, 271, 303
    Clear Spring, 310
Worcester County, 323, 325, 328, 346
    Berlin, xii, 321
    Worcester, 61, 422–23, 430
Maryland Reform Convention, 342
Mason, Deputy Marshal, 263
Mason-Dixon Line, 428
Mason, George W., 208–09
Mason, Senator James, 7n5, 5–14, 24, 31,
    51–52, 56, 69–70, 93, 395, 418,
    431–32, 454, 459
Massachusetts, xiii, 11, 19, 21, 25, 27, 30, 37,
    40, 44, 101, 121, 146, 150, 160, 187,
    370, 400, 404, 412–13, 417, 422–23,
    427–32, 434, 437–40, 451, 456
    Abington, 398
    Barnstable, 415
    Boston, 14, 18–21, 24–26, 28–29, 32,
        41–46, 51n16, 53, 58–59, 66, 68–69,
        71, 147, 162, 170, 217, 287, 312n2,
        360, 370, 392, 396–401, 403–14,
        417–19, 421–28, 435, 439n64,
        439–40, 445, 450, 452, 458–59
        Boston Common, 397, 414
        Bowdoin Square, 418
        Faneuil Hall, 20, 66, 399, 404–05, 414,
            422–23, 445
        League of Freedom, 19, 399
        Melodeon, 419
        Pine Street Anti-Slavery Society, 427
        Tremont Temple, 414, 416, 445
    Brookline, 401
    Cambridge, 403, 410
    Charlestown Navy Yard, 413
    Hopedale, 420
    Hyannis, 439
    Kingston, 398
    Leominster, 410
    New Bedford, xiii, 42–43, 46, 360, 392,
        398, 440
    Newburyport, 28n46, 437
    Northborough, 398
    Pittsfield, 447
    Springfield, 15, 18, 25, 95, 394
    West Cambridge, 403
    Westminster, 420
    Worcester, 398, 420, 429, 440
Massachusetts Anti-Slavery Society,
    398–99, 437
Massey, Edward W., 308, 310–12
Massey, Theodore, 148
Mather, J. G., 190
Matthews, Stanley, 253n41, 253–54
May, Edward, 103
May, Rev. Samuel J., 28, 85, 361, 367–68, 446
Mayo, Isaac, 315–16
McAllister, Richard, 53–54, 57, 59, 64,
    64n35, 74, 285n24, 280–92, 301, 307,
    350, 458
McCartney, Sheriff, 302–03
McCarty, Mary, 190n14
McCauley, Henry, 278
McClernard, John A., 159
McCreary, Thomas, 294–300, 300n47,
    301n48, 305
McCullon, Malcolm, 158–59
McDaniel, David, 427–28
McDowell, Dr. James, 230
McElroy, Hiram, 159–60
McKay, John, 110n36, 109–11
McKim, J. Miller, 333, 335n27, 345, 349n44,
    347–51, 354
McKim, Sarah, 333
McKinney, Mordecai, 279, 282–83, 288
McLain, William, 128–29
McLean, Dr. Elijah, 129
McLean, John, 246–47
McQuery, George Washington, 238, 245–47
McReynolds, John, 366, 368
Meachum, John Berry, 143
Meachum, John Berry and Mary, 143–46
Meachum, Mary, 143–44
Meeker, George Washington, 165
Mercer, Fenton, 283
Mercer, John, 261
Meredith, Jonathan, 303
Merritt, John, 295, 298–99
Messler, Henry and Mary, 190n14
Metcalf, George W., 372–73
Mexican War, 80, 108, 134

Mexico, 7, 25, 38, 113
Michael, Edward, 283
Michigan, 11, 25, 28, 42, 77, 168, 174, 186, 215, 452, 455, 460
  Detroit, 18, 34, 42, 47, 49, 65, 72, 77, 147–48, 164, 183, 188, 197, 203, 227, 234–35, 245
  Kinderhook, 215
  Marshall, 4n1
  Michigan City, 197
Middleton, Reuben, 178
Mihardo, Aaron, 71
Milburn, Thomas E., 156
Miles, Julett, 231–32
Miller, Dr., 247
Miller, Henry, 246
Miller, Joseph C., 247, 296–97, 299, 342
Miller, Rev. Armistead, 131
Miller, William H., 303
Milliken, James P., 75–76, 76n56
Mills, Thornton, 110
Minkins, Shadrach, 41, 59, 67, 69, 74, 83, 409–13, 416–18, 420, 422, 431, 439, 459
Minnesota, 455
Mississippi, 10, 28, 37–38, 93, 157, 237, 241, 419
  Jackson, 39
  Natchez, 241
  Vicksburg, 76n56, 241
Mississippi River, 137, 140–41, 145, 149, 156, 166, 168, 178, 218, 254, 457
Missouri, xii, 5, 13, 42, 48, 57, 62–63, 70n47, 77, 132, 137, 140–42, 145, 147, 150–51, 153–54, 157–58, 160, 162, 164–65, 169, 173, 175, 177–79, 211, 229, 237, 393
  Alexandra, 139
  Audrain County, 147
  Benton, 26
  Boone County, 150, 234
  Booneville, 142, 147
  Buchanan County, 178
  Caldwell County, 178
  Callaway County, 139
  Cape Girardeau, 31, 142, 149, 173
  Cass County, 147n16
  Charleston, 139
  Chester, 154
  Franklin County, 129
  Hannibal, 139–40, 149, 151n21, 240, 366
  Jackson County, 139

Jefferson City, xiii
Johnson County
  Solon, 178
Kansas City, 139, 165
Kirksville, 76n56
Knox County, 157
La Grange, 140
Lafayette, 62
Lafayette County, 139, 165
Lexington, 142, 146, 150
Livingston County
  Chillicothe, 151
Madison County, 154
  Fredericksburg, 154
Marion County, 139, 149
Nashville, 153–54
New Madrid County, 153
Palmyra, 139–40, 149–50
Pettis County, 147n16
Platte County, 139, 212
  Weston, 151
Ralls County, 149, 151n21
Ray County, 139
Saline County, 139
Shelbyville, 160
St. Joseph, 177–78
St. Louis, 26, 31, 50, 112, 128–29, 132, 137, 139–49, 152, 157–58, 160–61, 161n39, 163–64, 166–70, 177, 179, 209, 238, 240
  State Circuit Court, 146
Ste Genevieve, xii, xiii, 137, 139, 152
Missouri Colonization Society, 92n6, 128
Missouri Compromise, 6, 8, 14, 424, 448
Missouri River, 139, 142, 151
Missouri State Penitentiary, 146
Mitchee, Stephen, 132
Mitchell, 48, 120n52, 164
Mitchell, Alexander, 272
Mitchell, James, 107–11, 131, 249, 340–42
Mitchell, Richard P., 257, 261
Mitchum, 208–09
M'Kinney, John, 303
Monocacy River, 277
Moore, Dick, 184
Moore, George T., 362
Moore, Isaac, 377n20
Moore, Isaiah, 332
Moore, Jane, 242
Moore, John, 57–58, 185, 189, 189n13
Morehead, Charles, 251
Morehead, Henry, 182

Morehead, Mary, 182
Morgan, James, 276
Morrell, Frederic, 366
Morris, Robert, 410n19, 412, 433
Morrison, A.F., 104
Morrison, John, 302
Morton, George, 365, 382–83
Moses, 239
Moss, Francis, 147, 149
Mott, James, 347
Mott, Lucretia, 73, 333, 337, 345, 347, 352, 368
Mottley, W., 192–93
Myers, Emmanuel, 302–03
Myers, Stephen, 360–61, 393

Nalle, Charles, 369–71
Nalle, Kitty, 371
Nancy, 130n69, 148, *See* Lemmons family
Napoleon, Louis, 386, 389, 391
Nat, 141
Nathans, Tom, 304
National Convention of Colored Americans, 334
nativism, 30
Neal, Mathilda, 315
Neal, Richard, 315–16
Nebraska, 171
  Nebraska City, 171
Negro Conventions, 45
Nelson, G.S., 291
Nelson, John, 240
Nelson, Samuel, 52, 78
Nesbit, William, 124–26, 133
New Brunswick
  Saint John, 408
New England, 21, 25, 38, 101, 398, 404, 409, 411, 421n35, 423, 428, 432n51, 452
New England Anti-Slavery Society, 428
New Hampshire, 28, 37, 53, 78, 410–12
  Manchester, 26, 31
New Jersey, 10, 51, 94–95, 122n56, 274, 340, 345n39
  Burlington, 340
  Hoboken, 394
  Newark, 376
  Paterson, 394
  Salem, 342
New Mexico, 8
New York, xiii, 10, 27–28, 33, 43, 45, 52, 55, 65, 67, 77, 94, 98–99, 113, 115, 117, 123, 125, 197, 208–09, 308, 311, 315,

321, 334, 360–61, 372–74, 384, 388, 390, 460
Albany, 21n30, 48, 123, 206, 308, 360–61, 365, 369, 388, 392–93, 446
Auburn, 362, 365, 370, 373–74
Brooklyn, 112, 379, 389, 391
Buffalo, 14, 18, 35, 42, 45, 47–49, 60, 70, 100–02, 308, 313n3, 360, 362, 364, 366, 369, 372, 389, 446
Canandaigua, 373
Castle Garden, 26–27, 29
Chautauqua County
  Busti, 63, 363–64
Cold Springs, 322
Court of Appeals, 389
Elliottsville, 31
Elmira, 18, 274, 291, 360
Fredonia, 364
Geneva, 26, 372–73
Jamestown, 364
Kings County, 59
Lockport, 18
Montgomery County
  Amsterdam, 371
New York City, xiii, 14, 18, 21, 24n37, 26, 28–29, 39, 42, 44, 70–71, 95, 97, 100, 115, 117, 121, 123, 158, 242, 274, 275n6, 310, 312n2, 329, 353, 360, 365, 372, 376n19, 376–78, 382, 384–90, 392–94, 403, 407, 412, 418–19, 423, 428, 437, 447, 450
Niagara Falls, 373, 376n19
Onondaga County
  Jordon, 46
Ontario County, 373
Oswego County, 215
  Oswego, 215, 361
Penn Yan, 372–73
Poughkeepsie, 62, 72, 378
Rochester, xiii, 14, 21n30, 33, 35, 42, 47–48, 59, 76, 81, 359–60, 374–75, 381, 394–95, 423, 445–46, 450n12
Rochester Ladies Anti-Slavery Society, 460
Rome, 446
Sand Lake, 369
Saratoga, 45, 372
Schenectady, 371
Seneca, 258, 372
Sullivan County, 359
Syracuse, 14, 18–20, 32, 42, 45, 47, 57, 79–80, 82–83, 85–86, 96, 116–17, 306, 349, 360, 366, 368, 392–93, 423, 429, 445–47, 459

New York (*cont.*)
  Tarrytown, 26
  Troy, 100, 360, 369, 371
  Utica, 26, 446
  Wayne County, 365–66
  West Troy, 370–71
  Williamsburg, 379, 382, 391
New York State Colonization Society,
    115–17, 122–23
Newhall, Commissioner, 252–53, 255, 267
Newland, Joseph, 197
Nicaragua, 201, 329
Nicholas, Judge, 184
North Carolina, xiii, 10, 37, 42, 44, 52, 115,
    170, 215, 266, 275, 329, 331, 333, 379,
    385, 392, 411
  Edenton, 38
  Rocky Mount, 427
  Wilmington, 396, 421
northerners, 13, 35, 248, 444–45
Northup, Solomon, 209, 372, 374–75
Noyes, Charles, 168–69
Nuckolls, Stephen Friel, 171–72

O'Neill, Elizabeth, 282–83
Obed, 322
Oberlin College, 19, 194, 428
Oberlin-Wellington rescue, 264, 442
O'Fallon, John, 139
Ohio, xiii, 9, 9n8, 28, 34, 46, 51, 75, 77, 103,
    105, 122, 129, 131, 190, 203, 215, 231,
    235, 237, 241–42, 244–45, 247–53,
    256, 258, 260, 262, 265, 267, 288, 452
  Aberdeen, 229
  Adams County, 70
  Akron, 242, 265
  Ashtabula County, 236
    Ashtabula, 21, 49n12, 57, 186
  Auglaize County, 112
  Bellefontaine, 234
  Brown County, 225, 230, 240
    Ripley, 42
  Carlisle, 229
  Centralia, 243
  Champaign County, 255
  Chardon, 17
  Chillicothe, 3, 187, 237, 242
  Cincinnati, 26, 33, 42, 51, 60, 65n36, 106,
    132, 147, 162, 177, 186, 188–89, 195,
    198, 204–05, 222, 226, 229, 230n10,
    233–37, 239–53, 255–57, 263, 266–68,
    344, 362, 373, 389

  Anti-Slavery Sewing Circle, 237, 238n22
  Life Guard, 237–38
  Circleville, 237
  Clark County, 256
  Clermont County, 225
  Cleveland, xi, 14, 21, 32, 47, 59, 86, 237,
    258, 262–64, 372, 387, 441–45, 459
    Colored Ladies Benevolent Sewing
    Society, 237
    Committee of Nine, 237
  Columbus, 14, 18, 42, 227–29, 236, 239,
    245, 247–48, 255, 257, 262–63, 267,
    287, 372–73
  Cuyahoga County, 261
  Dayton, 22, 234, 246
  Fayette County, 266
  Felicity, 231
  Gallia County, 224
  Greene County, 256
  Hudson, 265
  Huron, 227
  Ironton, 222, 224, 232, 237, 263
  Lawrence County, 224
  Lawrenceburg, 75, 203
  Lima, 265
  Lorain County, 261–62
  Lumberton, 256
  Massillon, 26
  Mechanicsburg, 255–56
  Mt Vernon, 240
  Murrow County
    Mt Gilead, 267
  Oberlin, 18n23, 194, 217, 231, 237,
    257–58, 260–61, 263–64, 442–43
  Painesville, 22, 237
  Poke Patch, 224
  Portsmouth, 242
  Preble County, 229
  Ripley, 48, 194, 215, 222, 224–25, 229,
    232–33, 240
  Salem, 266
  Sandusky, 18n23, 188, 203, 226–28,
    235–36, 243–45, 249
  Sardinia, 57, 224, 242
  Springfield, 256
  Summit County, 374
  Toledo, 23n34, 183
  Troy, 245
  Urbana, 255
  Vermillion, 57
  Wellington, 174, 216, 257–59, 261, 263
  Western Reserve, 21, 441

Westport, 187
Williamsfield, 57
Wilmington, 57, 226
Windsor, 22
Xenia, 242
Zanesville, 18n23, 84n72
Ohio Colored American League, 262
Ohio Constitutional Convention, 112
Ohio River, 49–50, 75, 106, 128, 152, 160,
    180, 184, 191, 207, 213, 218, 222,
    233–34, 243, 255, 264, 362
Ohio State Anti-Slavery Society, 263
Oneida Institute, 113
O'Neill, Elizabeth, 282
O'Neill, John H., 256
Order of Twelve, 224
Oregon, 111
Orr, John, 240
Otwell, Thomas, 314
Overstreet, Claiborne, 191

Page, Col., 31
Page, John E., 279
Paine, Judge Elijah, 387–89
Palfrey, John Gorham, 433, 436
Palm, Meg, 302
Palmer, C. W., 264, 442
Parker, Andrew, 371
Parker, Edward G., 422, 427
Parker, Elizabeth, 294–97, 299, 315
Parker, James A., 148
Parker, John, 224–25, 227, 229
Parker, Judge, 247
Parker, Pamela, 144
Parker, Rachel, 294, 296–300, 315, 342
Parker, Renols, 48
Parker, Theodore, 20, 30, 44, 160, 399, 401,
    403–04, 419, 422–25, 432–33
Parker, William, 80–81, 84, 357, 359, 395
Parker, William W., 380–81
Parkier, Pamela, 144
Parr, William L., 369
Parran, Dr. Nathaniel P., 363–64
Parsons, Judge, 341
Patillo, Leroy, 212
Patterson, Rev. D. H., 126
Payne, Daniel M., 215, 217
Payne, Wellington, 215–16
Pearce, Sen. James A., 56, 319–20
Pearson, Judge John L., 280n14,
    279–81, 283–84
Peck, Henry, 258

Peck, Henry E., 33
Pelham, Robert, 147
Pembroke family, 274, 390–91
Pembroke, Jacob, 273, 275, 385
Pembroke, James, 271, 273
Pembroke, Robert, 273, 275, 385
Pembroke, Stephen, 273–75, 385, 390
Pendery, Commissioner John L., 247–51
Pennington, Rev. J. W. C., xiii, 71, 100,
    123, 273–74, 334, 365, 385, 387,
    390–91, 428
Pennsylvania, 3, 5, 11, 19, 31, 35, 40, 56, 59,
    77–78, 79n61, 82, 85, 90, 94–95, 112,
    114, 121, 130n69, 132, 146, 147n16,
    151, 248, 271–72, 275, 278, 285, 288,
    293, 295, 297–303, 305–07, 310–11,
    313, 315, 320, 329, 335–36, 341–42,
    344, 346, 350, 359, 396–97, 442, 451
Adams County, 272, 302
Allegheny City, 19
Aspinwall, 311
Beaver, 264
Bedford, 3, 48
Bucks County, 293
    Quakertown, 359
Chambersburg, 269, 272, 278, 302,
    304, 394
Chester County, 293–95, 298–300, 305–06,
    346, 357, 392
    Progressive Friends of Chester
    County, 334
    West Nottingham Township, 294
Chestnut Level, 295
Christiana, 36, 50, 67, 80–81, 83–86,
    116–17, 166, 249, 269, 283–84, 287,
    292, 294, 296, 299, 301, 310, 330, 336,
    342, 357, 359, 367, 395, 412
    riot at, 80–85
Columbia, 49, 73, 269, 282, 285–87, 290,
    299, 337, 342, 345, 355, 371
Cumberland County, 302–03, 350
    Carlisle, 269, 301–03
Danville, 281
Dauphin County, 53, 305
    Fishersville, 283
Delaware County, 336
Downingtown, 295, 305, 357
Erie, 46
Franklin County, 269, 302
Gap, 294
Gettysburg, 269, 272, 302
Greencastle, 460

Pennsylvania (*cont.*)
  Harrisburg, 3, 42, 53–54, 57, 59, 64–65,
    69–70, 74, 112, 126, 269, 271–73,
    276, 279, 285n24, 281–92, 301,
    304–06, 329–30, 335, 337, 346–51,
    418, 458–59
  Harrisburg Anti-Slavery Society, 279
  Harrisburg Friends of the Fugitive
    Association, 347
  Hollidaysburg, 114, 124, 128, 131
  Johnstown, 112
  Juniata County, 170
  Lancaster County, 49, 283, 294, 301, 304
    Lancaster, 269, 272, 288, 290, 306, 337
    Oxford, 298, 304
  Lebanon County, 285, 303
    Lebanon, 70n47
  Lycoming County
    Jersey Shore, 285n24
  Maytown, 303
  Meadville, 42
  Mercersburg, 269
  Middletown, 51, 320, 351
  Monroe County
    Stroudsburg, 359
    Tannersville, 359
  Montgomery County
    Norristown, 359
  Newtown, 392
  Northampton County
    Wind Gap, 359
  Nottingham Township, 299
  Paoli, 344
  Parkersburg, 357
  Penningtonville, 357
  Philadelphia, 3–4, 14, 18, 26, 31, 40, 42, 44,
    48, 54–55, 55n20, 57, 60n27, 63, 65,
    70, 73–74, 81–85, 95, 114, 128, 193,
    208, 246, 269, 271–74, 291–93, 301,
    306, 310–16, 320–22, 328–29,
    333–34, 336–40, 346n40, 343–47,
    349–51, 353, 355–57, 359–61, 363,
    369, 378, 385–86, 390–94, 396–97,
    418, 448, 451n13, 450–52, 459
    Independence Hall, 83
  Philadelphia County, 341
  Pittsburgh, 14, 18–19, 21n30, 32, 42–43,
    46, 48, 59, 72, 127–28, 170, 191, 264,
    311, 360
  Reading, 291, 329
  Sadsbury Monthly Meeting of Friends, 84
  Shewsbury, 3

Shippensburg, 275, 302
Strasburg, 286
Uniontown, 71
Unionville, 295
Washington County, 311
  Centerville, 48
West Chester, 269, 297, 449
Wilkes Barre, 285n24, 330, 429
York County, 350
  York, 42, 79n61, 269, 276, 286
Pennsylvania Anti-Slavery Society, 279
Pennsylvania Colonization Society, 114
Pepper, James, 226n4
Percival, William, 376–77
Perkins, Doctor, 230–32
Perry, Jesse, 321
Perry, John T., 371
Personal Liberty laws, xiv, 6, 40, 150, 305,
  316, 388, 435–37, 448–49, 451,
  451n13, 454–56, 458
Peter, 190n14, 272
Peter, Dr. Thomas E., 38
Pettit, John, 432
Pew, Thomas, 421
Philadelphia Female Anti-Slavery Society,
  337, 354
Philadelphia Institute, 55, 73, 353
  Committee of Five, 353
Philadelphia Ladies Anti-Slavery Society, 327
Philanthropic Society, 18
Phillips, James, 288–89, 432
Phillips, Mary, 289
Phillips, Richard, 173–74
Phillips, Wendell, 20, 24, 397–98, 404, 410,
  414, 419–20, 422–23, 425, 432–35,
  440, 446
Phillis, 147
Pierce, President Franklin, 213, 426, 437
Pierce, William S., 338, 343–44, 347, 353
Pillsbury, Parker, 446
Pinkerton, Allen, 170–71
Pinkney, Alexander, 357
Pinkney, Frederick Thomas, 277
Pinney, J. B., 115–17, 125
Pistor, William, 232
Plumb, Ralph, 258
Plumly, Rebecca, 333
Plummer, Robert, 130n69
Police Court, 183, 189–91, 193, 205, 429
Polk, President James K., 8
Pollard, B. E., 190n14
Poole, Mrs. M. E., 273n5

Pope, John H., 275–76, 286
Popel, Joseph, 280, 305
popular sovereignty, 424
Porter, Henry A., 314
Portman, John, 229
Post, Alfred C., 62
Potter, James, 68, 413, 415–17
Powell, Edward, 98
Powell, William P., 24n37, 97–99, 117, 378
Pratt, Governor Thomas, 5, 9–10
Predo, Henry, 314
Preston, Horace, 382–84
Preston, William Reese, 382–84
Price, George, 340
Price, James Frisby, 340–42, 344
Price, John, 257–61, 341
*Prigg v. Pennsylvania*, 6, 9
Proctor, Samuel D., 374–75
Prue, Daniel, 372–75
Pugh, Sarah, 333
Pullman, Mr., 230n10
Pullum & Griffin, 241
Purdue, John, 345
Purnell, T. J., 61
Purvis, Robert, 338, 354
Purvis-Fortens family, 347
Putnam, Lewis H., 115–19, 122n56, 121–23

Quakers, 42, 73, 84, 105, 244, 269,
    306, 348–49
Quick, Warren P., 210
Quincy, Edmund, 404–05

Rachel, 193
Ralls, William, 151n21, 240
Ralph, 189
Ramsey, Henry, 230
Ramsey, Isaac, 230
Randall, Josiah, 31
Rankin, Blackstone, 230
Rankin, John, 224
Rantoul, Robert, 415
Rariden, James, 102
Rawlins, Jesse, 276
Rawn, Charles, 279, 281–83, 288–89
Ray, Charles, 385–86, 391
Ray, J. Wesley, 191
Ray, Rev. Charles B., 378, 380
Rea, Commissioner John H., 218–19
Rea, Wright, 206
Read, Daniel, 103
Reed, 374

Reed, Edwin. *See* Van Tuyl, Napoleon
    Bonaparte
Reed, Enoch, 86, 367–68
Reed, Jack, 305
Reese, John J., 146
Remond, Charles Lennox, 20
Republican Central Committee, 176
Republican Party, 162, 176, 191, 203, 221,
    258, 262, 264, 353n50, 371, 375, 433,
    441, 446, 449, 450n12, 455
Republicans, 159, 173, 176, 184, 256, 258,
    261, 263–64, 352, 369, 441
Rhett, Robert Barnwell, 14, 39
Rhode Island, 93–94, 458n24
    Pawtucket, 398
    Providence, 365
Ricard, Col., 314
Ricaud, James B., 319–20
Rice, John, 267–68
Rice, Oliver, 227
Richardson, Anna, 386, 390
Richardson, Henry and Anna, 385
Richardson, Mary, 276
Richardson, Rachel, 276
Richardson, Thomas, 340
Riddle, Albert Gallatin, 258, 264, 441–42
Riddle, William, 182
Ridgely, Archibald G., 286–88, 301, 342
Riley, Mrs. Elizabeth, 410
Ringgold, Edward, 314
Ringgold, Joseph, 314
Ritchie, Dr. Samuel W., 214
River, Mississippi, 374
Robards, Lewis E., 243
Roberts, J. J., 122
Roberts, Mortimer W., 215
Robinson, Andrew L., 58
Robinson, Hiram H., 211, 213, 217, 247,
    250–51, 267
Robinson, Mrs. J. J., 266
Robinson, U.S. Marshal John Larne, 211–15,
    217, 219
Robinson, US Marshal H. H., 247, 267
Rochester Ladies Anti-Slavery Society,
    375n18
Rogers, Warren B., 230–31
Roots, Benajah G., 173
Rose, 49, 65
Rosette, John H., 159
Ross, Rev., 31
Rouse, Charles, 49, 209
Rouse, Martha, 209

Rowe, Elizabeth and John, 147
Rudd, James, 180, 180n1, 196–97, 204, 221
Ruggles, David, xiii, 376, 391
Russell, John, 231
Russwurm, John, 96
Rust, Benjamin S., 362–63
Rust, Frank, 241

Sabine, Joseph, 57, 366–67
Salem, Abbey Kelley, 266
Sally, 322
Sam, 183, 211–12, 249
Sarah, 235
Saunders, John, 285, 301, 304
Savage, Benjamin, 143–44, 146
Sawyer, William, 111
Says, John, 131
Schoolfield, Luther A., 295–98, 300
Scoble, John, 100
Scott, A. H., 200
Scott, Governor, 169
Scott, Henry, 168–69
Scott, John, 412
Scott, Otho, 287
Scott, W. A., 139
Seaton, Henry, 263
secession, 38–39, 41, 82, 85, 156, 436, 441,
    445, 447, 451, 454
Seddon, James, 455–56
self emancipation, 312
Senate, 6–7, 13, 23, 25, 27, 31, 76n56, 76–77,
    92–94, 96, 198, 292, 395, 397, 410,
    432, 434, 454
Seth, 32
Sewall, Samuel, 400, 415–16
Seward, William H., 10, 13, 34, 77, 118,
    424, 454
Shadrach, 235–36
Shaeffer, Michael, 281
Shaw, John, 276
Shaw, Justice Lemuel, 415–16
Shaw, Zachariah, 276
Sheaffer, Michael, 285n24
Shepherd, Harriet, 392
Sherwood, Mr., 153
Shotwell, Alfred L., 194, 196
Shreve, Mary E., 283
Shumate, Rev. W.D., 128, 131
Sierra Leone, 254
Simons, Mr., 116
Simpson, Elizabeth, 347
Simpson, Jeremiah, 376

Simpson, Joshua McCarter, 18n23
Simpson, Judge Ashley, 375
Sims, Thomas, 60, 68–69, 413–22, 424, 426,
    428–29, 434, 439, 458–59
  public reaction to return of, 417–20
Sing Sing prison, 365
Sirmond, D. D., 376–77
Skewes, William, 137
slave catchers, xiii, 3, 9, 18, 21–22, 32–33,
    44–46, 48–49, 59, 66–67, 72, 79, 83,
    154, 164–67, 172, 177, 180, 183, 216,
    227–28, 236, 238, 248, 260, 269,
    271–72, 274–75, 275n6, 287, 302, 304,
    306, 310, 312, 327, 350, 357, 361, 364,
    369, 372, 392, 400, 403, 406, 409, 415,
    419, 424, 428–29, 440, 458
slave interests, xi, 191
Slave Power, 320, 424, 428
Slave States, xiii, 6, 15, 35, 37, 139, 152, 157,
    185, 210, 221, 231, 375, 393, 431,
    451, 456
slave system, xi, 68, 76, 88, 101, 134, 144–45,
    150, 229, 312, 325, 388, 448
slaveholders, xii, xiii, xiv, 4, 6–10, 12, 23, 29,
    35–36, 40–41, 44–45, 47, 50, 52–57,
    59–61, 63–67, 71, 74n53, 74–76,
    79–80, 82, 84, 88–89, 89n1, 101, 116,
    119, 129, 131, 134, 140–42, 149,
    151–54, 157, 158n35, 158–59, 161,
    163, 165–66, 169–71, 175, 178–79,
    182, 184–85, 187, 194, 196–98, 204,
    207, 209, 211–12, 215, 220, 224–29,
    231–32, 234–39, 241, 244, 246, 250,
    252, 254–55, 257, 265, 267, 271–73,
    275–81, 283, 285, 293, 296, 300n47,
    305, 308, 310, 312–14, 319, 326n18,
    321–27, 329, 331, 337, 339–40, 342,
    342n37, 344, 349, 355, 359, 363–64,
    366, 369, 372, 378, 380–81, 384–85,
    388, 390, 393–95, 398, 406, 411, 425,
    432, 435, 444, 448–49, 451–52, 455,
    457–58, 460
slavery, xi, xii, xiii, xiv, xv, 4, 6, 8, 10–11,
    19, 21–23, 26–27, 28n46, 28–30, 32,
    34–36, 38–41, 43, 45, 52, 55, 62, 64,
    66, 71, 75–78, 80, 86, 89n1, 88–90, 92,
    95, 97, 99–100, 102, 104, 107, 113–14,
    118, 124, 127, 129, 133–34, 139, 142,
    149, 151–52, 155, 157, 159–60, 162,
    164, 167, 171, 175, 177, 179, 182,
    185–88, 200, 202, 204–05, 207–10,
    214, 219, 221–22, 225, 228, 230–31,

234, 236, 241, 244–45, 247–48,
250–52, 257–58, 269, 271–72, 276–77,
277n9, 279, 288, 292–93, 295, 303–05,
307–08, 313, 320, 322, 324, 326–27,
331, 334–36, 340, 349, 356, 359, 361,
363, 366, 370, 373–74, 377, 381, 383,
385–86, 394–99, 413, 417, 423, 425,
429, 434, 438, 441, 445, 448n10,
448–49, 452, 454–57, 460
  debate over future of, 87
slaves, xi, xiv, 4, 42, 95, 107, 128, 130–31,
151, 175, 180, 182, 188, 197, 200, 239,
277, 307, 313, 396–97, 457, 460
Sloane, Rush R., 227–28, 254
Smallwood, 207
Smith, Betsy, 306
Smith, Charles W., 168
Smith, Crawford E., 62, 165
Smith, David, 271, 273–74
Smith, George, 342–44, 352
Smith, Gerrit, 367–68, 393
Smith, Henry K., 60–61, 362–64
Smith, James McCune, 96, 118–23, 391
Smith, John T., 380
Smith, Jonathan, 137
Smith, S.P., 173–74
Smith, Thomas Paul, 412
Smith, Vincent, 306
Smith, William, 148, 271, 282–83, 286–88,
299, 301, 342
Snider, Lewis, 273
Snider, Thomas, 154
Snowden, James, 365
Snyder, Philip, 302
Snyder, Solomon, 281, 285–87, 290, 301,
304
Society of Friends, 22, 346
Society for Universal Inquiry and
Reform, 266
Sophia, 148
Souse, Eveline, 442
South Carolina, 5, 7n5, 19, 36–38, 48, 62, 72,
77, 121, 247, 253, 264, 366, 376, 392,
429, 431, 441, 449–50, 456–57
  Charleston, 43, 376, 394, 396, 430, 450
  Negro Seamen Act, 430
southern interests, 8
Southern Rights Association, 37–38, 41
southerners, xiv, 3, 12–13, 27–28, 39, 71, 86,
164, 214, 237, 255, 265–66, 431, 436,
443, 445, 450, 458–60
Spalding, Rufus P., 258, 262, 264, 442, 444

Sparrow, Cornelius, 71
Spaulding, Bishop, 189
Spencer, Henry Ward, 147n16
Sprague, Judge Peleg, 400, 412
Spratt, William, 146
Springs, Rev. Dr., 29
St Lucia, 383
St Paul River, 108, 122
Stallo, John Bernhard, 253–54
Stames, Frances, 144–45
Stanly, Daniel, 314
Stansbury, George. *See* William Smith
Stanton, Frederick, 94
Stanton, Thomas, 303–04
State Convention of the Free People of Color
of Maryland, 126
Steele, James, 199
Stein, Charles M., 303
Stephens. *See* Mitchum
Stephens, Foley, 232
Stephenson, Georgina, 190
Stephenson, Thomas B., 226n4
Sterling, Bob. *See* Smith, William
Stetson, Charles, 59
Stevens, William, 51
Steward, Bob, 305
Stewart, Charles E., 237
Stewart, Justice Daniel C., 370
Stewart, Robert, 306
Stewart, William, 240–41
Still, William, 273–74, 291, 306, 313n4,
313–14, 328–29, 332–34, 338, 353–55,
360–61, 369, 386, 390–92
Stone, Lucy, 249, 368
Storum, Catherine, 363
Storum, William, 363
Story, Justice Joseph, 6
Stoucher, John, 283
Stout, Dr. Joseph, 173–74, 176
Stout, James, 173–74
Stowe, Harriet Beecher, 133, 316–18, 375, 421
Stowell, Martin, 423, 430
Straight, Mrs., 238n22
Sullivan, Commissioner Squire, 211
Sully, Thomas, 329
Sumner, Charles, 11, 51n16, 334, 399, 407,
423, 431–32, 453
Supreme Court, 6, 12, 30, 35, 52–53, 65, 78,
218–19, 239, 246, 253, 261, 280, 342,
389, 412, 425, 436, 449, 451, 454
Surinam, 394
Susan, 235

Susquehanna River, 269, 303
Suttle, Charles F., 421–22, 425–27, 432–33
Swan, Chief Justice Joseph, 261

Talcott, John, 362
Tallmadge, Marshal Henry F., 383
Tamar, 194, 196
Tappan, Lewis, 380, 386, 389–91
Tate, Henry, 271
Tate, John, 271
Tate, Rachael, 271
Taylor, Benjamin, 272
Taylor, Charles, 255
Taylor, Edward, 255, 272
Taylor, George, 166
Taylor, Ira H., 396, 408
Taylor, Joseph, 225
Taylor, Mary, 272
Taylor, Owen, 272–73
Taylor, William, 279–81, 418
Taylor, William H., 132
Tennessee, 13, 19, 57, 65, 94, 127, 129–30,
    139, 141, 152, 177, 315, 325n17, 361,
    363, 372, 431
  Dickson County, 130
  Maury County, 129
  Memphis, 147, 158, 177, 238, 266, 373
  Nashville, 38–39, 45, 49–50, 141, 248,
    313n3
  Shelby County, 158
Territorial Court, 52
Terry, Eli, 209
Texas, 8, 209, 241, 376n19, 386, 388
Theodore, 137, 139
Thomas, 161
Thomas, Dan, 276
Thomas, Dr. Allen, 365
Thomas, Henry, 45, 49
Thomas, John, 21, 368–69, 372
Thomas, Philip, 301n48
Thomas, Sally, 45, 313n3
Thomas, Seth J., 400, 403, 404n9, 415,
    422, 425
Thompson, Catherine, 340–42, 345
Thompson, David, 301
Thompson, Edward, 279
Thompson, George, 24–25, 25n38, 26n43, 30,
    67, 254, 404–05, 411, 446
Thompson, James T., 191, 205
Thompson, Joel Henry, 340–42, 345, 345n39
Thompson, John L., 254, 287–88
Thompson, Samuel, 170–71

Thompson, William, 340–41
Tilden, Judge D. A., 264, 442
Tilghman, Frisby, 271
Tillison, Harriett, 319
Tom, 187, 215–16, 249
Tompkins, Peter and Harriet, 110n36
Townsend, John, 294
Townsend, Martin I., 369–70
Trainer, Charles, 389
Trainer, Emma, 389–90
Trainer, Jane, 389–90
Tramell, Dennis, 207–08
Treaner, Henry, 302
Treaner, William, 302
Treat, Justice, 167
Trinidad, 127, 376
  Port-of-Spain, 376
Trundle, Esther, 283
Trundle, Hezekiah W., 283
Tubman, Harriet, 315–16, 327, 355, 370, 392
Tucker, Nathaniel Beverley, 38–39
Tuckey, Joseph, 302
Tukey, Marshal Francis, 405, 413
Turner, Edward, 157
Turner, Sam, 392
Turner, William, 166–69
Turney, Hopkins, 13–14
Turnverein and Arbiter Verein, 254
Tyler, John, 247, 267

*Uncle Tom's Cabin*, 233, 236, 316, 318
Underground Railroad, xiii, 22, 42, 48, 60n27,
    75, 142, 145, 149, 157, 161, 163, 172,
    178, 185, 189, 191, 193–95, 198, 200,
    203, 206, 215, 220–21, 227, 229, 233,
    235, 237, 245, 253–55, 304, 307,
    314–16, 318, 320–23, 327, 357,
    359–60, 369, 385–86, 390, 392, 408,
    429, 446, 449, 457
Underwood, Joseph, 10–12
Union Association, 143, 145
Union meetings, 29–32, 39
Union Party, 27, 29
Union Safety Committee, 27–29, 70–71, 362,
    378, 381
United League of the Gileadites, 15
United Presbyterian Church of Scotland, 385
United States, 6–7, 24, 30–31, 56, 60, 67, 82,
    93, 98–99, 99n18, 101, 107, 113, 122,
    125, 133–34, 168, 174, 218, 245, 256,
    307, 331, 359, 368, 387, 389, 393, 395,
    412, 426, 434, 448

Upper South, 4, 50, 313, 319–20
Utah, 8

Vallandigham, Clement L., 22
Vallandingham, Austin W., 218–20
Valle lead mines, 137
Valle, Amadee, 137
Valle, Noree, 137
Van Buskirk, John M., 371
Van Dyke, James, 330, 335, 347
Van Slyke, Lewis G., 247
Van Tuyl, Napoleon Bonaparte, 372–74
Vaughn, Dr. Robert, 187
Vermont, 36–37, 40, 46, 194, 255, 410, 452
  Burlington, 112
Vigilance Committees, xiii, 15–20, 151, 170,
    237, 238n22, 274, 306, 360, 365, 370,
    378, 391–93, 409
  Boston, 21, 66–68, 71, 77, 147, 399, 401,
    403, 409, 412, 414–15, 419–22, 429,
    434, 439
  New Madrid, Missouri, 150
  New York City, xiii, 376, 420
  New York State, 365, 387, 391, 393
  Philadelphia, 273, 291, 306, 313–14, 322,
    328–29, 333, 337, 353, 355, 360, 420
  aid in escape attempts, 328–36
  Syracuse, New York, 19–20, 363
  Troy, New York, 361
  Worcester, Massachusetts, 414, 429
  work of, 390–93
Vinson, Henry, 200
Violet, 184
Virginia, xiii, 5, 11, 37–38, 45–46, 48, 49n12,
    51, 53, 64, 75, 89, 93, 122, 132, 177,
    229, 233, 237, 241, 244, 247, 257,
    264, 268, 273, 279, 280n14, 280–81,
    281n16, 286, 305, 310, 313, 326, 328,
    348, 350, 355, 359, 381, 387–89, 392,
    395, 412, 422, 425, 441, 444, 447,
    448n10, 452, 455
  Cabell County, 222, 267
  Charlestown, 393
  Clarke County, 3, 64–65, 269, 271, 418
    Berryville, 282
  Culpeper County, 288, 369
  Fauquier County, 271, 288, 306
  Frederick County, 271
  Front Royal, 50, 308, 311–12, 314
  Giles County
    Newport, 3
  Hampton, 426

  Hampton Roads, 376
  Hardy County, 63, 363–64
  Harpers Ferry, 15, 173, 258, 278, 326, 351,
    353, 361, 369, 393, 395, 445, 447–48,
    448n10, 450, 456
  Jefferson County, 351
  Loudoun County, 271, 347–48
    Aldie, 306
    Leesburg, 271
  Lynchburg, 3–4
  New Market, 26
  Norfolk, 4–5, 50, 67, 71, 328, 376, 386,
    409, 426, 439
  Page County, 288
  Petersburg, 198, 198n23, 376
  Prince George County, 37
  Richmond, 3, 70, 192, 248, 264, 289, 297,
    328, 380–81, 387–88, 397, 421,
    424–27, 448, 450
  Russell County, 380
  Select Committee of the Virginia General
    Assembly, 6
  Shenandoah Valley, 3, 42, 269, 308
  Stafford County, 421
  Washington County, 42
  Wheeling, 238, 264, 444–45
Virginia Central Southern Rights
  Association, 384

Wabash River, 57, 108, 164, 185
Wade, Ben, 21, 34
Waggoner, James, 240–41
Waggoner, Peter, 240
Wagoner, Henry Oscar, 169–70
Wailes, Barbara, 282
Wale, Henry J., 369
Walker, John H., 126, 133
Walker, Johnson, 439
Walker, Judge Calvin, 373
Walker, William, 201
Wall, John, 264, 442
Wall, O. S. B., 258, 264
Wallace, Judge William J., 218–19
Walls, George, 304
Waltman, Jacob, 301
Walton, Isam, 157
Wanzer family, 306
Wanzer, Frank, 306
Ward, Marshal John, 198, 200
Ward, Samuel Ringgold, 27, 32–33,
    367–68, 398
Ward, Zebulon, 241

Warden, James, 304
Warfield family, 302
Warfield, Eliza, 302
Warner, Henry, 277
Warren, Mr., 238
Washington DC, xiii, 5n2, 8, 13, 30, 33,
    64–65, 89, 112, 208, 251, 256, 276,
    326, 329, 372, 374, 376, 385, 397, 410,
    423, 429, 438n62, 447, 455–56
Washington, Augustus, 113–14
Washington, George, 365–66
Washington, Reade, 59
Waterhouse, Benjamin, 215–17
Waterhouse, John, 215
Watkins, Frances Ellen, 354
Watkins, John, 238–39, 242
Watkins, Lucy, 369n11
Watkins, William J., 421
Watson, D. C., 267
Watson, John, 258
Watts, Mrs., 190
Way, E. B., 139
Weatheringill, Mr., 154
Weaver, Michael, 240–41
Webster (Dangerfield), Daniel, 291, 306,
    349n44, 347–51, 354–55, 450
Webster, Daniel, 24, 27n46, 28n46, 28n48,
    27–31, 34, 38, 67, 69, 80, 82–83,
    85–86, 397, 400, 404–06, 409, 412,
    415, 418, 445, 459
Webster, Delia, 194–95, 197–98
Webster, Samuel, 108
Weems, Ann Maria, 385
Weems, John, 385
Weems, Stella, 385
Weigley, Wellington, 178
Weiner, Lewis F., 227–28
Weir, George, 47–48
Wesley, 235
West Indies, 29, 102, 127, 383
    emancipation in, 29
West, John, 218–20
West, Major, 139
West, Robert, 27
Westcott, George B., 319
Western Anti-Slavery Society, 163, 237, 265
Western, Henry M., 380
Westfall, George, 304
Wetherley, John C., 193
Wheeler, John Hill, 329–30, 332–33, 335
Whigs, 11, 20, 26–28, 31, 34–36, 39–40, 56,
    58, 76–77, 88, 152, 155, 248, 253, 292,

    336, 339, 342, 362–63, 396–97,
    407–08, 424, 428–29, 433, 452
White Sr., Jacob C., 328
White, Adam, 132
White, Addison, 255–56
White, Commissioner Bushnell C., 442–44
White, Daniel, 255
White, Joseph L., 380
White, Rev. David, 151
Whitehead, Charles, 380
Whitehead, Martha Ann, 71
Whittlesey, Elisha, 21, 28n49, 65, 88–90, 92,
    98, 134, 251, 286, 441
Whittmere, James F., 425
Wickliffe, R., 184
Wilder, Jo, 177–78
William, 137
William, Samuel, 126
Williams, Euphemia, 61–62, 70, 73–74, 83,
    346–49, 355
Williams, George, 61, 114, 230
Williams, Harrison, 61, 63, 70, 363–64, 369
Williams, Isaac, 240
Williams, Peter, 95
Williams, Pompey, 421
Williams, Richard, 352, 354
Williams, Samuel, 81, 83–84, 112, 114,
    121, 218
Williamson, Charles, 127
Williamson, Passmore, 328–31, 331n22,
    335n27, 336n27, 333–37, 345, 347
Willson, Judge Hiram, 258–61
Wilmot Proviso, 8, 383
Wilmot, David, 8
Wilson, Elijah, 210
Wilson, Joseph, 231
Wilson, Samuel, 3–4, 53, 64, 70, 269, 271,
    279–81, 285, 290, 305, 418
Windsor, Lofton, 147
Winthrop, Robert, 11
Wisconsin, 42, 111, 145, 150, 452, 455,
    455n19
    Kenosha, 18
    Milwaukee, 429
Wise, Gov. Henry, 395
Withers, C. A., 252
Wood, George, 70, 381
Wood, Henrietta, 241–42, 244
Wood, Matilda, 282
Woodbury, Judge Levi, 400
Woodgate, John H., 378
Woods River, 152

Woods, Susan, 232
Woodward, Judge George, 449
Worthington, Gad, 237
Worthington, James, 242
Wright, Elizur, 409, 412
Wright, Henry C., 32, 428
Wright, Joseph, 109
Wright, Moses, 341
Wright, Oswell, 201–02
Wynkoop, U.S. Marshal Francis, 343–44

Yancey, William Lowndes, 39, 445,
    445n6
York, Hank, 371
Young, Mr., 191
Yulee, David, 78

Zell, John, 286
Zimmerman, Joshua, 235
Zollicoffer, Felix, 39
Zuille, John L., 119